T0297677

Advanced Topics in Types and Programming Languages

Advanced Topics in Types and Programming Languages

Benjamin C. Pierce, editor

The MIT Press
Cambridge, Massachusetts
London, England

This book was set in Lucida Bright by the editor and authors using the LaTeX document preparation system.

Library of Congress Cataloging-in-Publication Data

Advanced Topics in Types and programming languages / Benjamin C. Pierce, editor
p. cm.
Includes bibliographical references and index.
ISBN 978-0-262-16228-9 (hardcover), 978-0-262-55267-7 (paperback)
1. Programming languages (Electronic computers). I. Pierce, Benjamin C.
QA76.7.A36 2005
005.13—dc22

200457123

Contents

Preface

Overview

Work in type systems for programming languages now touches many parts of computer science, from language design and implementation to software engineering, network security, databases, and analysis of concurrent and distributed systems. The aim of this book, together with its predecessor, *Types and Programming Languages* (Pierce [2002]—henceforth *TAPL*) is to offer a comprehensive and accessible introduction to the area's central ideas, results, and techniques. The intended audience includes graduate students and researchers from other parts of computer science who want get up to speed in the area as a whole, as well as current researchers in programming languages who need comprehensible introductions to particular topics. Unlike *TAPL*, the present volume is conceived not as a unified text, but as a collection of more or less separate articles, authored by experts on their particular topics.

Required Background

Most of the material should be accessible to readers with a solid grasp of the basic notations and techniques of operational semantics and type systems—roughly, the first half of *TAPL*. Some chapters depend on more advanced topics from the second half of *TAPL* or earlier chapters of the present volume; these dependencies are indicated at the beginning of each chapter. Interchapter dependencies have been kept to a minimum to facilitate reading in any order.

Topics

Precise Type Analyses The first three chapters consider ways of extending simple type systems to give them a better grip on the run time behavior of programs. The first, **Substructural Type Systems,** by David Walker, surveys type systems based on analogies with "substructural" logics such as linear logic, in which one or more of the structural rules of conventional logics—which allow dropping, duplicating, and permuting assumptions—are omitted or allowed only under controlled circumstances. In substructural type systems, the type of a value is not only a description of its "shape," but also a capability for using it a certain number of times; this refinement plays a key role in advanced type systems being developed for a range of purposes, including static resource management and analyzing deadlocks and livelocks in concurrent systems. The chapter on **Dependent Types**, by David Aspinall and Martin Hofmann, describes a yet more powerful class of type systems, in which the behavior of computations on particular run-time values (not just generic "shapes") may be described at the type level. Dependent type systems blur the distinction between types and arbitrary correctness assertions, and between typechecking and theorem proving. The power of full dependent types has proved difficult to reconcile with language design desiderata such as automatic typechecking and the "phase distinction" between compile time and run time in compiled languages. Nevertheless, ideas of dependent typing have played a fruitful role in language design and theory over the years, offering a common conceptual foundation for numerous forms of "indexed" type systems. **Effect Types and Region-Based Memory Management**, by Fritz Henglein, Henning Makholm, and Henning Niss, introduces yet another idea for extending the reach of type systems: in addition to describing the shape of an expression's result (a static abstraction of the possible values that the expression may yield when evaluated), its type can also list a set of possible "effects," abstracting the possible computational effects (mutations to the store, input and output, etc.) that its evaluation may engender. Perhaps the most sophisticated application of this idea has been in memory management systems based on static "region inference," in which the effects manipulated by the typechecker track the program's ability to read and write in particular regions of the heap. For example, the ML Kit Compiler used a region analysis internally to implement the full Standard ML language without a garbage collector.

Types for Low-Level Languages The next part of the book addresses another research thrust that has generated considerable excitement over the past decade: the idea of adapting type system technologies originally developed for high-level languages to low-level languages such as assembly code and virtual machine bytecode. **Typed Assembly Language**, by Greg Morrisett, presents a low-level language with a type system based on the parametric polymorphism of System F and discusses how to construct a type-preserving compiler from a high-level language, through a series of *typed intermediate languages*, down to this typed assembly code. **Proof-Carrying Code**, by George Necula, presents a more general formulation in a logical setting with close ties to the dependent types described in Aspinall and Hofmann's chapter. The strength of this presentation is that it offers a natural transition from conventional type safety properties, such as memory safety, to more general security properties. A driving application area for both approaches is enforcing security guarantees when dealing with untrusted mobile code.

Types and Reasoning about Programs One attraction of rich type systems is that they support powerful methods of reasoning about programs—not only by compilers, but also by humans. One of the most useful, the technique of *logical relations*, is introduced in the chapter **Logical Relations and a Case Study in Equivalence Checking**, by Karl Crary. The extended example—proving the correctness of an algorithm for deciding a type-sensitive behavioral equivalence relation on terms in the simply typed lambda-calculus with a `Unit` type—foreshadows ideas developed further in Christopher Stone's chapter on type definitions. **Typed Operational Reasoning**, by Andrew Pitts, develops a more general theory of typed reasoning about program equivalence. Here the examples focus on proving representation independence properties for abstract data types in the setting of a rich language combining the universal and existential polymorphism of System F with records and recursive function definitions.

Types for Programming in the Large One of the most important projects in language *design* over the past decade and more has been the use of type-theory as a framework for the design of sophisticated *module systems*—languages for assembling large software systems from modular components. One highly developed line of work is embodied in the module systems found in modern ML dialects. **Design Considerations for ML-Style Module Systems**, by Robert Harper and Benjamin C. Pierce, offers an informal guided tour of the principal features of this class of module systems—a "big picture" introduction to a large but highly technical body of papers in the research literature. **Type Definitions**, by Christopher A. Stone, addresses the most critical and technically challenging feature of the type systems on which ML-style module systems are founded: *singleton kinds*, which allow type definitions to be internalized rather than being treated as meta-level abbreviations.

Type Inference The ML family of languages—including Standard ML, Objective Caml, and Moscow ML, as well as more distant relatives such as Haskell—

has for decades been a showcase for advances in typed language design and compiler implementation, and for the advantages of software construction in richly typed languages. One of the main reasons for the success of these languages is the combination of power and convenience offered by their *type inference* (or *type reconstruction*) algorithms. Basic ML type inference has been described in many places, but descriptions of the more advanced techniques used in production compilers for full-blown languages have until now been widely dispersed in the literature, when they were available at all. In **The Essence of ML Type Inference**, François Pottier and Didier Rémy offer a comprehensive, unified survey of the area.

Exercises

Most chapters include numerous exercises. The estimated difficulty of each exercise is indicated using the following scale:

★	Quick check	30 seconds to 5 minutes
★★	Easy	≤ 1 hour
★★★	Moderate	≤ 3 hours
★★★★	Challenging	> 3 hours

Exercises marked ★ are intended as real-time checks of important concepts. Readers are strongly encouraged to pause for each one of these before moving on to the material that follows. Some of the most important exercises are labeled RECOMMENDED.

Solutions to most of the exercises are provided in Appendix A. To save readers searching for solutions to exercises for which solutions are not available, these are marked ↛.

Electronic Resources

Additional materials associated with this book can be found at:

```
http://www.cis.upenn.edu/~bcpierce/attapl
```

Resources available on this site will include errata for the text, pointers to supplemental material contributed by readers, and implementations associated with various chapters.

Acknowledgments

Many friends and colleagues have helped to improve the chapters as they developed. We are grateful to Amal Ahmed, Lauri Alanko, Jonathan Aldrich,

Derek Dreyer, Matthias Felleisen, Robby Findler, Kathleen Fisher, Nadji Gauthier, Michael Hicks, Steffen Jost, Xavier Leroy, William Lovas, Kenneth MacKenzie, Yitzhak Mandelbaum, Martin Müller, Simon Peyton Jones, Norman Ramsey, Yann Régis-Gianas, Fermin Reig, Don Sannella, Alan Schmitt, Peter Sewell, Vincent Simonet, Eijiro Sumii, David Swasey, Joe Vanderwaart, Yanling Wang, Keith Wansbrough, Geoffrey Washburn, Stephanie Weirich, Dinghao Wu, and Karen Zee for helping to make this a much better book than we could have done alone. Stephanie Weirich deserves a particularly warm round of thanks for numerous and incisive comments on the whole manuscript. Nate Foster's assistance with copy editing, typesetting, and indexing contributed enormously to the book's final shape.

The work described in many chapters was supported in part by grants from the National Science Foundation. The opinions, findings, conclusions, or recommendations expressed in these chapters are those of the author(s) and do not necessarily reflect the views of the NSF.

PART I

Precise Type Analyses

1 *Substructural Type Systems*

David Walker

Advanced type systems make it possible to restrict access to data structures and to limit the use of newly-defined operations. Oftentimes, this sort of access control is achieved through the definition of new abstract types under control of a particular module. For example, consider the following simplified file system interface.

```
type file

val open   : string → file option
val read   : file → string * file
val append : file * string → file
val write  : file * string → file
val close  : file → unit
```

By declaring that the type `file` is abstract, the implementer of the module can maintain strict control over the representation of files. A client has no way to accidentally (or maliciously) alter any of the file's representation invariants. Consequently, the implementer may assume that the invariants that he or she establishes upon opening a file hold before any `read`, `append`, `write` or `close`.

While abstract types are a powerful means of controlling the structure of data, they are not sufficient to limit the *ordering* and *number of uses* of functions in an interface. Try as we might, there is no (static) way to prevent a file from being read after it has been closed. Likewise, we cannot stop a client from closing a file twice or forgetting to close a file.

This chapter introduces *substructural* type systems, which augment standard type abstraction mechanisms with the ability to control the number and order of uses of a data structure or operation. Substructural type systems are particularly useful for constraining interfaces that provide access to system resources such as files, locks and memory. Each of these resources undergoes a series of changes of state throughout its lifetime. Files, as we have seen, may be open or closed; locks may be held or not; and memory may be allocated or deallocated. Substructural type systems provide sound static mechanisms for keeping track of just these sorts of state changes and preventing operations on objects in an invalid state.

The bulk of this chapter will focus on applications of substructural type systems to the control of memory resources. Memory is a pervasive resource that must be managed carefully in any programming system so it makes an excellent target of study. However, the general principles that we establish can be applied to other sorts of resources as well.

1.1 Structural Properties

Most of the type systems in this book allow *unrestricted* use of variables in the type checking context. For instance, each variable may be used once, twice, three times, or not at all. A precise analysis of the properties of such variables will suggest a whole new collection of type systems.

To begin our exploration, we will analyze the simply-typed lambda calculus, which is reviewed in Figure 1-1. In this discussion, we are going to be particularly careful when it comes to the form of the type-checking context Γ. We will consider such contexts to be simple lists of variable-type pairs. The "," operator appends a pair to the end of the list. We also write (Γ_1, Γ_2) for the list that results from appending Γ_2 onto the end of Γ_1. As usual, we allow a given variable to appear at most once in a context and to maintain this invariant, we implicitly alpha-convert bound variables before entering them into the context.

We are now in position to consider three basic *structural* properties satisfied by our simply-typed lambda calculus. The first property, *exchange*, indicates that the order in which we write down variables in the context is irrelevant. A corollary of exchange is that if we can type check a term with the context Γ, then we can type check that term with any permutation of the variables in Γ. The second property, *weakening*, indicates that adding extra, unneeded assumptions to the context, does not prevent a term from type checking. Finally, the third property, *contraction*, states that if we can type check a term using two identical assumptions ($x_2{:}T_1$ and $x_3{:}T_1$) then we can check the same term using a single assumption.

1.1.1 LEMMA [EXCHANGE]: If $\Gamma_1, x_1{:}T_1, x_2{:}T_2, \Gamma_2 \vdash t : T$ then $\Gamma_1, x_2{:}T_2, x_1{:}T_1, \Gamma_2 \vdash t : T$ □

1.1.2 LEMMA [WEAKENING]: If $\Gamma_1, \Gamma_2 \vdash t : T$ then $\Gamma_1, x_1{:}T_1, \Gamma_2 \vdash t : T$ □

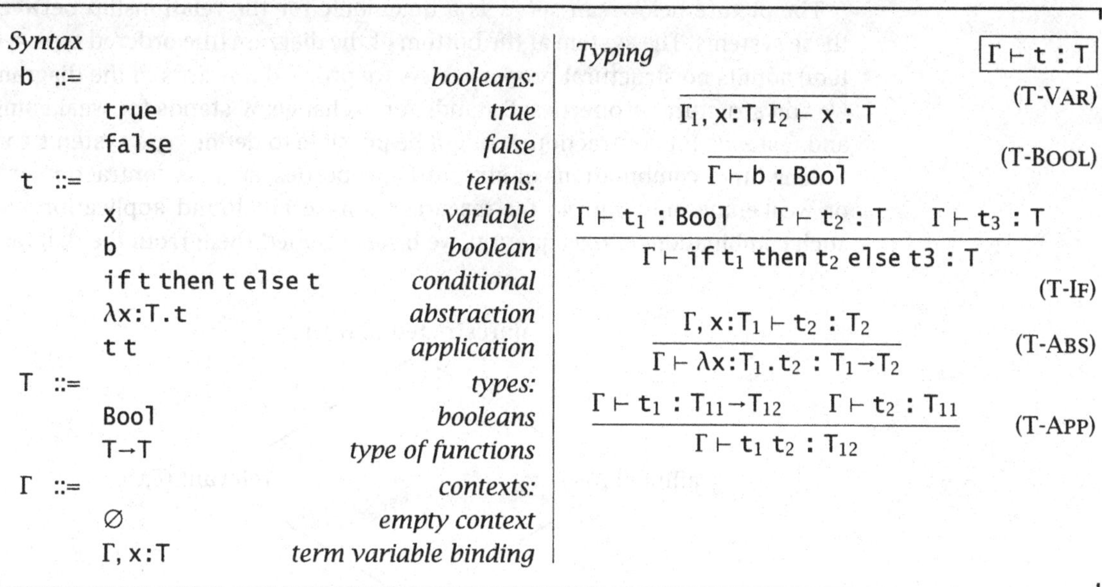

Figure 1-1: Simply-typed lambda calculus with booleans

1.1.3 LEMMA [CONTRACTION]: If $\Gamma_1, \mathtt{x}_2{:}\mathtt{T}_1, \mathtt{x}_3{:}\mathtt{T}_1, \Gamma_2 \vdash \mathtt{t} : \mathtt{T}_2$ then $\Gamma_1, \mathtt{x}_1{:}\mathtt{T}_1, \Gamma_2 \vdash [\mathtt{x}_2 \mapsto \mathtt{x}_1][\mathtt{x}_3 \mapsto \mathtt{x}_1]\mathtt{t} : \mathtt{T}_2$ □

1.1.4 EXERCISE [RECOMMENDED, ★]: Prove that exchange, weakening and contraction lemmas hold for the simply-typed lambda calculus. □

A *substructural type system* is any type system that is designed so that one or more of the structural properties do not hold. Different substructural type systems arise when different properties are withheld.

- *Linear* type systems ensure that every variable is used exactly once by allowing exchange but not weakening or contraction.
- *Affine* type systems ensure that every variable is used at most once by allowing exchange and weakening, but not contraction.
- *Relevant* type systems ensure that every variable is used at least once by allowing exchange and contraction, but not weakening.
- *Ordered* type systems ensure that every variable is used exactly once and in the order in which it is introduced. Ordered type systems do not allow any of the structural properties.

The picture below can serve as a mnemonic for the relationship between these systems. The system at the bottom of the diagram (the ordered type system) admits no structural properties. As we proceed upwards in the diagram, we add structural properties: E stands for exchange; W stands for weakening; and C stands for contraction. It might be possible to define type systems containing other combinations of structural properties, such as contraction only or weakening only, but so far researchers have not found applications for such combinations. Consequently, we have excluded them from the diagram.

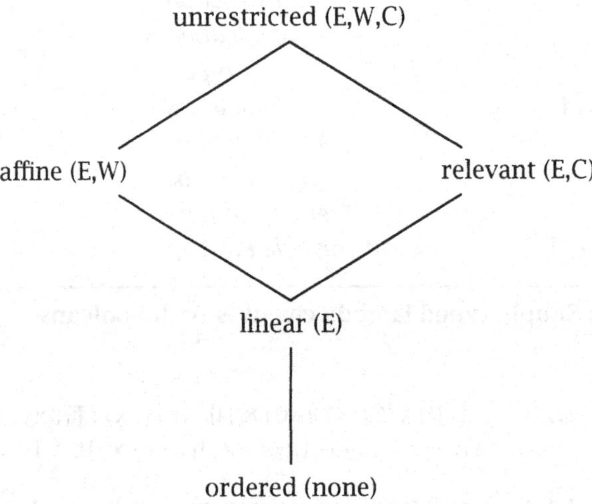

The diagram can be realized as a relation between the systems. We say system q_1 is more restrictive than system q_2 and write $q_1 \sqsubseteq q_2$ when system q_1 exhibits fewer structural rules than system q_2. Figure 1-2 specifies the relation, which we will find useful in the coming sections of this chapter.

1.2 A Linear Type System

In order to safely deallocate data, we need to know that the data we deallocate is never used in the future. Unfortunately, we cannot, in general, deduce whether data will be used after execution passes a certain program point: The problem is clearly undecidable. However, there are a number of sound, but useful approximate solutions. One such solution may be implemented using a *linear type system.* Linear type systems ensure that objects are used exactly once, so it is completely obvious that after the use of an object, it may be safely deallocated.

q ::=		*system:*
	ord	*ordered*
	lin	*linear*
	rel	*relevant*
	aff	*affine*
	un	*unrestricted*

$$\text{ord} \sqsubseteq \text{lin} \qquad \text{(Q-OrdLin)}$$

$$\text{lin} \sqsubseteq \text{rel} \qquad \text{(Q-LinRel)}$$

$$\text{lin} \sqsubseteq \text{aff} \qquad \text{(Q-LinAff)}$$

$$\text{rel} \sqsubseteq \text{un} \qquad \text{(Q-RelUn)}$$

$$\text{aff} \sqsubseteq \text{un} \qquad \text{(Q-AffUn)}$$

$$q \sqsubseteq q \qquad \text{(Q-Reflex)}$$

$$\frac{q_1 \sqsubseteq q_2 \qquad q_2 \sqsubseteq q_3}{q_1 \sqsubseteq q_3} \qquad \text{(Q-Trans)}$$

Figure 1-2: A relation between substructural type systems

Syntax

Figure 1-3 presents the syntax of our linear language, which is an extension of the simply-typed lambda calculus. The main addition to be aware of, at this point, are the type qualifiers q that annotate the introduction forms for all data structures. The linear qualifier (lin) indicates that the data structure in question will be *used* (i.e., appear in the appropriate elimination form) exactly once in the program. Operationally, we deallocate these linear values immediately after they are used. The unrestricted qualifier (un) indicates that the data structure behaves as in the standard simply-typed lambda calculus. In other words, unrestricted data can be used as many times as desired and its memory resources will be automatically recycled by some extra-linguistic mechanism (a conventional garbage collector).

Apart from the qualifiers, the only slightly unusual syntactic form is the elimination form for pairs. The term split t_1 as x,y in t_2 projects the first and second components from the pair t_1 and calls them x and y in t_2. This split operation allows us to extract two components while only counting a single use of a pair. Extracting two components using the more conventional projections $\pi_1\ t_1$ and $\pi_2\ t_1$ requires two uses of the pair t_1. (It is also possible, but a bit tricky, to provide the conventional projections.)

To avoid dealing with an unnecessarily heavy syntax, we adopt a couple abbreviations in our examples in this section. First, we omit all unrestricted qualifiers and only annotate programs with the linear ones. Second, we freely use n-ary tuples (triples, quadruples, unit, etc.) in addition to pairs and also allow multi-argument functions. The latter may be defined as single-argument functions that take linear pairs (triples, etc) as arguments and immediately split them upon entry to the function body. Third, we often use ML-style type

Syntax

q ::=		*qualifiers:*
	lin	*linear*
	un	*unrestricted*
b ::=		*booleans:*
	true	*true*
	false	*false*
t ::=		*terms:*
	x	*variable*
	q b	*boolean*
	if t then t else t	*conditional*
	q <t,t>	*pair*
	split t as x,y in t	*split*
	q λx:T.t	*abstraction*
	t t	*application*
P ::=		*pretypes:*
	Bool	*booleans*
	T*T	*pairs*
	T→T	*functions*
T ::=		*types:*
	q P	*qualified pretype*
Γ ::=		*contexts:*
	∅	*empty context*
	Γ, x:T	*term variable binding*

Figure 1-3: Linear lambda calculus: Syntax

declarations, value declarations and let expressions where convenient; they all have the obvious meanings.

Typing

To ensure that linear objects are used exactly once, our type system maintains two important invariants.

1. Linear variables are used exactly once along every control-flow path.
2. Unrestricted data structures may not contain linear data structures. More generally, data structures with less restrictive type may not contain data structures with more restrictive type.

To understand why these invariants are useful, consider what could happen if either invariant is broken. When considering the first invariant, assume we have constructed a function `free` that uses its argument and then deallocates it. Now, if we allow a linear variable (say `x`) to appear twice, a programmer might write `<free x,free x>`, or, slightly more deviously,

```
(λz.λy.<free z,free y>) x x.
```

In either case, the program ends up attempting to use and then free `x` after it has already been deallocated, causing the program to crash.

Now consider the second invariant and suppose we allow a linear data structure (call it `x`) to appear inside an unrestricted pair (`un <x,3>`). We can

Context Split $\boxed{\Gamma = \Gamma_1 \circ \Gamma_2}$

$$\varnothing = \varnothing \circ \varnothing \quad \text{(M-EMPTY)}$$

$$\frac{\Gamma = \Gamma_1 \circ \Gamma_2}{\Gamma, \mathtt{x}:\mathtt{un}\ \mathsf{P} = (\Gamma_1, \mathtt{x}:\mathtt{un}\ \mathsf{P}) \circ (\Gamma_2, \mathtt{x}:\mathtt{un}\ \mathsf{P})} \quad \text{(M-UN)}$$

$$\frac{\Gamma = \Gamma_1 \circ \Gamma_2}{\Gamma, \mathtt{x}:\mathtt{lin}\ \mathsf{P} = (\Gamma_1, \mathtt{x}:\mathtt{lin}\ \mathsf{P}) \circ \Gamma_2} \quad \text{(M-LIN1)}$$

$$\frac{\Gamma = \Gamma_1 \circ \Gamma_2}{\Gamma, \mathtt{x}:\mathtt{lin}\ \mathsf{P} = \Gamma_1 \circ (\Gamma_2, \mathtt{x}:\mathtt{lin}\ \mathsf{P})} \quad \text{(M-LIN2)}$$

Figure 1-4: Linear lambda calculus: Context splitting

get exactly the same effect as above by using the unrestricted data structure multiple times:

```
let z = un <x,3> in
split z as x1,_ in
split z as x2,_ in
<free x1,free x2>
```

Fortunately, our type system ensures that none of these situations can occur.

We maintain the first invariant through careful context management. When type checking terms with two or more subterms, we pass all of the unrestricted variables in the context to each subterm. However, we split the linear variables between the different subterms to ensure each variable is used exactly once. Figure 1-4 defines a relation, $\Gamma = \Gamma_1 \circ \Gamma_2$, which describes how to split a single context in a rule conclusion (Γ) into two contexts (Γ_1 and Γ_2) that will be used to type different subterms in a rule premise.

To check the second invariant, we define the predicate $\mathtt{q}(\mathsf{T})$ (and its extension to contexts $\mathtt{q}(\Gamma)$) to express the types T that can appear in a q-qualified data structure. These containment rules state that linear data structures can hold objects with linear or unrestricted type, but unrestricted data structures can only hold objects with unrestricted type.

- $\mathtt{q}(\mathsf{T})$ if and only if $\mathsf{T} = \mathtt{q}'\ \mathsf{P}$ and $\mathtt{q} \sqsubseteq \mathtt{q}'$
- $\mathtt{q}(\Gamma)$ if and only if $(\mathtt{x}:\mathsf{T}) \in \Gamma$ implies $\mathtt{q}(\mathsf{T})$

Recall, we have already defined $\mathtt{q} \sqsubseteq \mathtt{q}'$ such that it is reflexive, transitive and $\mathtt{lin} \sqsubseteq \mathtt{un}$.

Now that we have defined the rules for containment and context splitting, we are ready for the typing rules proper, which appear in Figure 1-5. Keep in mind that these rules are constructed anticipating a call-by-value operational semantics.

It is often the case when designing a type system that the rules for the base cases, variables and constants, are hardly worth mentioning. However,

Typing $\boxed{\Gamma \vdash \mathtt{t} : \mathtt{T}}$

$$\frac{\mathtt{un}\ (\Gamma_1, \Gamma_2)}{\Gamma_1, \mathtt{x}{:}\mathtt{T}, \Gamma_2 \vdash \mathtt{x} : \mathtt{T}} \quad \text{(T-VAR)}$$

$$\frac{\mathtt{un}\ (\Gamma)}{\Gamma \vdash \mathtt{q}\ \mathtt{b} : \mathtt{q}\ \mathtt{Bool}} \quad \text{(T-BOOL)}$$

$$\frac{\Gamma_1 \vdash \mathtt{t}_1 : \mathtt{q}\ \mathtt{Bool} \qquad \Gamma_2 \vdash \mathtt{t}_2 : \mathtt{T} \qquad \Gamma_2 \vdash \mathtt{t}_3 : \mathtt{T}}{\Gamma_1 \circ \Gamma_2 \vdash \mathtt{if}\ \mathtt{t}_1\ \mathtt{then}\ \mathtt{t}_2\ \mathtt{else}\ \mathtt{t}_3 : \mathtt{T}} \quad \text{(T-IF)}$$

$$\frac{\Gamma_1 \vdash \mathtt{t}_1 : \mathtt{T}_1 \qquad \Gamma_2 \vdash \mathtt{t}_2 : \mathtt{T}_2 \qquad \mathtt{q}(\mathtt{T}_1) \qquad \mathtt{q}(\mathtt{T}_2)}{\Gamma_1 \circ \Gamma_2 \vdash \mathtt{q}\ \mathtt{<t_1,t_2>} : \mathtt{q}\ (\mathtt{T}_1 {*} \mathtt{T}_2)} \quad \text{(T-PAIR)}$$

$$\frac{\Gamma_1 \vdash \mathtt{t}_1 : \mathtt{q}\ (\mathtt{T}_1 {*} \mathtt{T}_2) \qquad \Gamma_2, \mathtt{x}{:}\mathtt{T}_1, \mathtt{y}{:}\mathtt{T}_2 \vdash \mathtt{t}_2 : \mathtt{T}}{\Gamma_1 \circ \Gamma_2 \vdash \mathtt{split}\ \mathtt{t}_1\ \mathtt{as}\ \mathtt{x,y}\ \mathtt{in}\ \mathtt{t}_2 : \mathtt{T}} \quad \text{(T-SPLIT)}$$

$$\frac{\mathtt{q}(\Gamma) \qquad \Gamma, \mathtt{x}{:}\mathtt{T}_1 \vdash \mathtt{t}_2 : \mathtt{T}_2}{\Gamma \vdash \mathtt{q}\ \lambda \mathtt{x}{:}\mathtt{T}_1.\mathtt{t}_2 : \mathtt{q}\ \mathtt{T}_1 \to \mathtt{T}_2} \quad \text{(T-ABS)}$$

$$\frac{\Gamma_1 \vdash \mathtt{t}_1 : \mathtt{q}\ \mathtt{T}_{11} \to \mathtt{T}_{12} \qquad \Gamma_2 \vdash \mathtt{t}_2 : \mathtt{T}_{11}}{\Gamma_1 \circ \Gamma_2 \vdash \mathtt{t}_1\ \mathtt{t}_2 : \mathtt{T}_{12}} \quad \text{(T-APP)}$$

Figure 1-5: Linear lambda calculus: Typing

in substructural type systems these cases have a special role in defining the nature of the type system, and subtle changes can make all the difference. In our linear system, the base cases must ensure that no linear variable is discarded without being used. To enforce this invariant in rule (T-VAR), we explicitly check that Γ_1 and Γ_2 contain no linear variables using the condition un (Γ_1, Γ_2). We make a similar check in rule (T-BOOL). Notice also that rule (T-VAR) is written carefully to allow the variable x to appear anywhere in the context, rather than just at the beginning or at the end.

1.2.1 EXERCISE [★]: What is the effect of rewriting the variable rule as follows?

$$\frac{\mathtt{un}\ (\Gamma)}{\Gamma, \mathtt{x}{:}\mathtt{T} \vdash \mathtt{x} : \mathtt{T}} \quad \text{(T-BROKENVAR)}$$

The inductive cases of the typing relation take care to use context splitting to partition linear variables between various subterms. For instance, rule (T-IF) splits the incoming context into two parts, one of which is used to check subterm $\mathtt{t}_1$ and the other which is used to check both $\mathtt{t}_2$ and $\mathtt{t}_3$. As a result, a particular linear variable will occur once in $\mathtt{t}_2$ and once in $\mathtt{t}_3$. However, the linear object bound to the variable in question will be used (and hence deallocated) exactly once at run time since only one of $\mathtt{t}_2$ or $\mathtt{t}_3$ will be executed.

The rules for creation of pairs and functions make use of the containment rules. In each case, the data structure's qualifier q is used in the premise of the typing rule to limit the sorts of objects it may contain. For example, in the rule (T-ABS), if the qualifier q is un then the variables in Γ, which will inhabit the function closure, must satisfy un (Γ). In other words, they must all have unrestricted type. If we omitted this constraint, we could write the following badly behaved functions. (For clarity, we have retained the unrestricted qualifiers in this example rather than omitting them.)

```
type T = un (un bool → lin bool)

val discard =
  lin λx:lin bool.
    (lin λf:T.lin true) (un λy:un bool.x)

val duplicate =
  lin λx:lin bool.
    (lin λf:T.lin <f (un true),f (un true)>)) (un λy:un bool.x)
```

The first function discards a linear argument x without using it and the second duplicates a linear argument and returns two copies of it in a pair. Hence, in the first case, we fail to deallocate x and in the second case, a subsequent function may project both elements of the pair and use x twice, which would result in a memory error as x would be deallocated immediately after the first use. Fortunately, the containment constraint disallows the linear variable x from appearing in the unrestricted function (λy:bool. x).

Now that we have defined our type system, we should verify our intended structural properties: exchange for all variables, and weakening and contraction for unrestricted variables.

1.2.2 LEMMA [EXCHANGE]: If $\Gamma_1, \mathtt{x}_1{:}\mathtt{T}_1, \mathtt{x}_2{:}\mathtt{T}_2, \Gamma_2 \vdash \mathtt{t} : \mathtt{T}$ then $\Gamma_1, \mathtt{x}_2{:}\mathtt{T}_2, \mathtt{x}_1{:}\mathtt{T}_1, \Gamma_2 \vdash \mathtt{t} : \mathtt{T}$. □

1.2.3 LEMMA [UNRESTRICTED WEAKENING]: If $\Gamma \vdash \mathtt{t} : \mathtt{T}$ then $\Gamma, \mathtt{x}_1{:}\mathtt{un}\ \mathtt{P}_1 \vdash \mathtt{t} : \mathtt{T}$. □

1.2.4 LEMMA [UNRESTRICTED CONTRACTION]: If $\Gamma, \mathtt{x}_2{:}\mathtt{un}\ \mathtt{P}_1, \mathtt{x}_3{:}\mathtt{un}\ \mathtt{P}_1 \vdash \mathtt{t} : \mathtt{T}_3$ then $\Gamma, \mathtt{x}_1{:}\mathtt{un}\ \mathtt{P}_1 \vdash [\mathtt{x}_2 \mapsto \mathtt{x}_1][\mathtt{x}_3 \mapsto \mathtt{x}_1]\mathtt{t} : \mathtt{T}_3$. □

Proof: The proofs of all three lemmas follow by induction on the structure of the appropriate typing derivation. □

Algorithmic Linear Type Checking

The inference rules provided in the previous subsection give a clear, concise specification of the linearly-typed programs. However, these rules are also highly non-deterministic and cannot be implemented directly. The primary difficulty is that to implement the non-deterministic splitting operation,

Algorithmic Typing $\boxed{\Gamma_{in} \vdash \texttt{t} : \texttt{T};\Gamma_{out}}$

$$\Gamma_1, \texttt{x:un P}, \Gamma_2 \vdash \texttt{x} : \texttt{un P};\Gamma_1, \texttt{x:un P}, \Gamma_2 \quad \text{(A-UVAR)}$$

$$\Gamma_1, \texttt{x:lin P}, \Gamma_2 \vdash \texttt{x} : \texttt{lin P};\Gamma_1, \Gamma_2 \quad \text{(A-LVAR)}$$

$$\Gamma \vdash \texttt{q b} : \texttt{q Bool};\Gamma \quad \text{(A-BOOL)}$$

$$\frac{\Gamma_1 \vdash \texttt{t}_1 : \texttt{q Bool};\Gamma_2 \qquad \Gamma_2 \vdash \texttt{t}_2 : \texttt{T};\Gamma_3 \qquad \Gamma_2 \vdash \texttt{t}_3 : \texttt{T};\Gamma_3}{\Gamma_1 \vdash \texttt{if t}_1 \texttt{ then t}_2 \texttt{ else t}_3 : \texttt{T};\Gamma_3} \quad \text{(A-IF)}$$

$$\frac{\Gamma_1 \vdash \texttt{t}_1 : \texttt{T}_1;\Gamma_2 \qquad \Gamma_2 \vdash \texttt{t}_2 : \texttt{T}_2;\Gamma_3 \qquad \texttt{q(T}_1\texttt{)} \qquad \texttt{q(T}_2\texttt{)}}{\Gamma_1 \vdash \texttt{q <t}_1\texttt{,t}_2\texttt{>} : \texttt{q (T}_1\texttt{*T}_2\texttt{)};\Gamma_3} \quad \text{(A-PAIR)}$$

$$\frac{\Gamma_1 \vdash \texttt{t}_1 : \texttt{q (T}_1\texttt{*T}_2\texttt{)};\Gamma_2 \qquad \Gamma_2, \texttt{x:T}_1, \texttt{y:T}_2 \vdash \texttt{t}_2 : \texttt{T};\Gamma_3}{\Gamma_1 \vdash \texttt{split t}_1 \texttt{ as x,y in t}_2 : \texttt{T};\Gamma_3 \div (\texttt{x:T}_1, \texttt{y:T}_2)} \quad \text{(A-SPLIT)}$$

$$\frac{\texttt{q=un} \Rightarrow \Gamma_1 = \Gamma_2 \div (\texttt{x:T}_1) \qquad \Gamma_1, \texttt{x:T}_1 \vdash \texttt{t}_2 : \texttt{T}_2;\Gamma_2}{\Gamma_1 \vdash \texttt{q }\lambda\texttt{x:T}_1\texttt{.t}_2 : \texttt{q T}_1\texttt{→T}_2;\Gamma_2 \div (\texttt{x:T}_1)} \quad \text{(A-ABS)}$$

$$\frac{\Gamma_1 \vdash \texttt{t}_1 : \texttt{q T}_{11}\texttt{→T}_{12};\Gamma_2 \qquad \Gamma_2 \vdash \texttt{t}_2 : \texttt{T}_{11};\Gamma_3}{\Gamma_1 \vdash \texttt{t}_1 \texttt{ t}_2 : \texttt{T}_{12};\Gamma_3} \quad \text{(A-APP)}$$

Figure 1-6: Linear lambda calculus: Algorithmic type checking

$\Gamma = \Gamma_1 \circ \Gamma_2$, we must guess how to split an input context Γ into two parts. Fortunately, it is relatively straightforward to restructure the type checking rules to avoid having to make these guesses. This restructuring leads directly to a practical type checking algorithm.

The central idea is that rather than splitting the context into parts before checking a complex expression composed of several subexpressions, we can pass the entire context as an input to the first subexpression and have it return the unused portion as an output. This output may then be used to check the next subexpression, which may also return some unused portions of the context as an output, and so on. Figure 1-6 makes these ideas concrete. It defines a new algorithmic type checking judgment with the form $\Gamma_{in} \vdash \texttt{t} : \texttt{T};\Gamma_{out}$, where Γ_{in} is the input context, some portion of which will be consumed during type checking of `t`, and Γ_{out} is the output context, which will be synthesized alongside the type `T`.

There are several key changes in our reformulated system. First, the base cases for variables and constants allow any context to pass through the judgment rather than restricting the number of linear variables that appear. In order to ensure that linear variables are used, we move these checks to the rules where variables are introduced. For instance, consider the rule (A-SPLIT). The second premise has the form

$$\Gamma_2, \texttt{x:T}_1, \texttt{y:T}_2 \vdash \texttt{t}_2 : \texttt{T};\Gamma_3$$

If $\texttt{T}_1$ and $\texttt{T}_2$ are linear, then they should be used in $\texttt{t}_2$ and should not appear in Γ_3. Conversely, $\texttt{T}_1$ and $\texttt{T}_2$ are unrestricted, then they will always appear in Γ_3, but we should delete them from the final outgoing context of the rule so that the ordinary scoping rules for the variables are enforced. To handle both the check that linear variables do not appear and the removal of unrestricted variables, we use a special "context difference" operator ($\div$). Using this operator, the final outgoing context of the rule (A-SPLIT) is defined to be $\Gamma_3 \div (\mathtt{x}{:}\mathtt{T}_1, \mathtt{y}{:}\mathtt{T}_2)$. Formally, context difference is defined as follows.

$$\Gamma \div \varnothing = \Gamma$$

$$\frac{\Gamma_1 \div \Gamma_2 = \Gamma_3 \qquad (\mathtt{x}{:}\mathtt{lin}\ \mathtt{P}) \notin \Gamma_3}{\Gamma_1 \div (\Gamma_2, \mathtt{x}{:}\mathtt{lin}\ \mathtt{P}) = \Gamma_3}$$

$$\frac{\Gamma_1 \div \Gamma_2 = \Gamma_3 \qquad \Gamma_3 = \Gamma_4, \mathtt{x}{:}\mathtt{un}\ \mathtt{P}, \Gamma_5}{\Gamma_1 \div (\Gamma_2, \mathtt{x}{:}\mathtt{un}\ \mathtt{P}) = \Gamma_4, \Gamma_5}$$

Notice that this operator is undefined when we attempt to take the difference of two contexts, Γ_1 and Γ_2, that contain bindings for the same linear variable ($\mathtt{x}{:}\mathtt{lin}\ \mathtt{P}$). If the undefined quotient $\Gamma_1 \div \Gamma_2$ were to appear anywhere in a typing rule, the rule itself would not be considered defined and could not be part of a valid typing derivation.

The rule for abstraction (A-ABS) also introduces a variable and hence it also uses context difference to manipulate the output context for the rule. Abstractions must also satisfy the appropriate containment conditions. In other words, rule (A-ABS) must check that unrestricted functions do not contain linear variables. We perform this last check by verifying that when the function qualifier is unrestricted, the input and output contexts from checking the function body are the same. This equivalence check is sufficient because if a linear variable was used in the body of an unrestricted function (and hence captured in the function closure), that linear variable would not show up in the outgoing context.

It is completely straightforward to check that every rule in our algorithmic system is syntax directed and that all our auxiliary functions including context membership tests and context difference are easily computable. Hence, we need only show that our algorithmic system is equivalent to the simpler and more elegant declarative system specified in the previous section. The proof of equivalence can be a broken down into the two standard components: *soundness* and *completeness* of the algorithmic system with respect to the declarative system. However, before we can get to the main results, we will need to show that our algorithmic system satisfies some basic structural properties of its own. In the following lemmas, we use the notation $\mathcal{L}(\Gamma)$ and $\mathcal{U}(\Gamma)$ to refer to the list of linear and unrestricted assumptions in Γ respectively.

1.2.5 Lemma [Algorithmic Monotonicity]: If $\Gamma \vdash \mathtt{t} : \mathtt{T};\Gamma'$ then $\mathcal{U}(\Gamma') = \mathcal{U}(\Gamma)$ and $\mathcal{L}(\Gamma') \subseteq \mathcal{L}(\Gamma)$. □

1.2.6 Lemma [Algorithmic Exchange]: If $\Gamma_1, \mathtt{x}_1{:}\mathtt{T}_1, \mathtt{x}_2{:}\mathtt{T}_2, \Gamma_2 \vdash \mathtt{t} : \mathtt{T};\Gamma_3$ then $\Gamma_1, \mathtt{x}_2{:}\mathtt{T}_2, \mathtt{x}_1{:}\mathtt{T}_1, \Gamma_2 \vdash \mathtt{t} : \mathtt{T};\Gamma_3'$ and Γ_3 is the same as Γ_3' up to transposition of the bindings for x_1 and x_2. □

1.2.7 Lemma [Algorithmic Weakening]: If $\Gamma \vdash \mathtt{t} : \mathtt{T};\Gamma'$ then $\Gamma, \mathtt{x}{:}\mathtt{T}' \vdash \mathtt{t} : \mathtt{T}; \Gamma', \mathtt{x}{:}\mathtt{T}'$. □

1.2.8 Lemma [Algorithmic Linear Strengthening]: If $\Gamma, \mathtt{x}{:}\mathtt{lin\ P} \vdash \mathtt{t} : \mathtt{T}; \Gamma', \mathtt{x}{:}\mathtt{lin\ P}$ then $\Gamma \vdash \mathtt{t} : \mathtt{T};\Gamma'$. □

Each of these lemmas may be proven directly by induction on the initial typing derivation. The algorithmic system also satisfies a contraction lemma, but since it will not be necessary in the proofs of soundness and completeness, we have not stated it here.

1.2.9 Theorem [Algorithmic Soundness]: If $\Gamma_1 \vdash \mathtt{t} : \mathtt{T};\Gamma_2$ and $\mathcal{L}(\Gamma_2) = \varnothing$ then $\Gamma_1 \vdash \mathtt{t} : \mathtt{T}$. □

Proof: As usual, the proof is by induction on the typing derivation. The structural lemmas we have just proven are required to push through the result, but it is mostly straightforward. □

1.2.10 Theorem [Algorithmic Completeness]: If $\Gamma_1 \vdash \mathtt{t} : \mathtt{T}$ then $\Gamma_1 \vdash \mathtt{t} : \mathtt{T};\Gamma_2$ and $\mathcal{L}(\Gamma_2) = \varnothing$. □

Proof: The proof is by induction on the typing derivation. □

Operational Semantics

To make the memory management properties of our language clear, we will evaluate terms in an abstract machine with an explicit store. As indicated in Figure 1-7, stores are a sequence of variable-value pairs. We will implicitly assume that any variable appears at most once on the left-hand side of a pair so the sequence may be treated as a finite partial map.

A value is a pair of a qualifier together with some data (a *prevalue* w). For the sake of symmetry, we will also assume that all values are stored, even base types such as booleans. As a result, both components of any pair will be pointers (variables).

We define the operation of our abstract machine using a context-based, small-step semantics. Figure 1-7 defines the computational contexts E, which

w ::=		*prevalues:*
	b	*boolean*
	<x,y>	*pair*
	λx:T.t	*abstraction*
v ::=		*values:*
	q w	*qualified prevalue*
S ::=		*stores:*
	∅	*empty context*
	S, x ↦ v	*store binding*

E ::=		*evaluation contexts:*
	[]	*context hole*
	if E then t else t	*if context*
	q <E,t>	*fst context*
	q <x,E>	*snd context*
	split E as x,y in t	*split context*
	E t	*fun context*
	x E	*arg context*

Figure 1-7: Linear lambda calculus: Run-time data

are terms with a single hole. Contexts define the order of evaluation of terms—they specify the places in a term where a computation can occur. In our case, evaluation is left-to-right since, for example, there is a context with the form `E t` indicating that we can reduce the term in the function position before reducing the term in the argument position. However, there is no context with the form `t E`. Instead, there is only the more limited context `x E`, indicating that we must reduce the term in the function position to a pointer `x` before proceeding to evaluate the term in the argument position. We use the notation `E[t]` to denote the term composed of the context `E` with its hole plugged by the computation `t`.

The operational semantics, defined in Figure 1-8, is factored into two relations. The first relation, $(S;t) \longrightarrow (S';t')$, picks out a subcomputation to evaluate. The second relation, $(S;t) \longrightarrow_{\beta} (S';t')$, does all the real work. In order to avoid creation of two sets of operational rules, one for linear data, which is deallocated when used, and one for unrestricted data, which is never deallocated, we define an auxiliary function, $S \overset{q}{\sim} x$, to manage the differences.

$$
\begin{array}{lcl}
(S_1, x \mapsto v, S_2) \overset{\mathtt{lin}}{\sim} x & = & S_1, S_2 \\
S \overset{\mathtt{un}}{\sim} x & = & S
\end{array}
$$

Aside from these details, the operational semantics is standard.

Preservation and Progress

In order to prove the standard safety properties for our language, we need to be able to show that programs are well-formed after each step in evaluation. Hence, we will define typing rules for our abstract machine. Since these typing rules are only necessary for the proof of soundness, and have no place in an

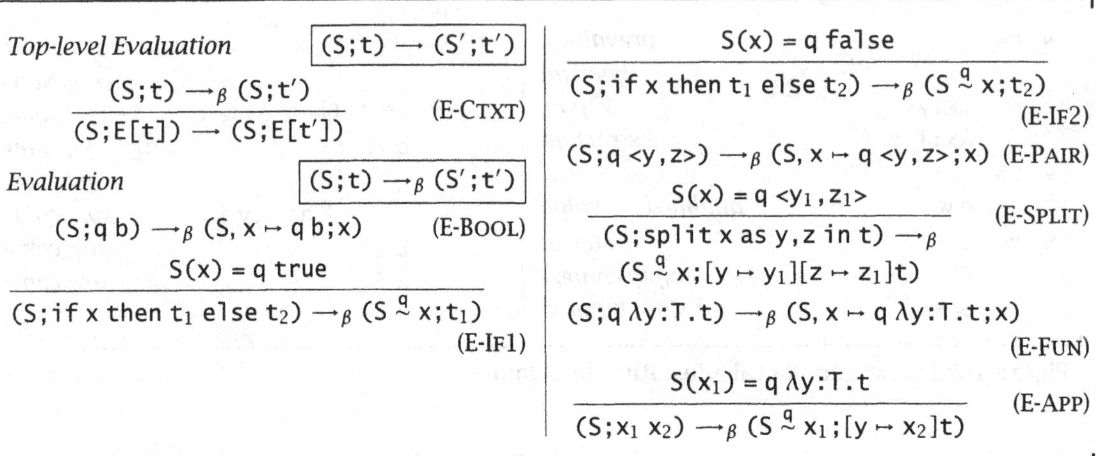

Figure 1-8: Linear lambda calculus: Operational semantics

implementation, we will extend the declarative typing rules rather than the algorithmic typing rules.

Figure 1-9 presents the machine typing rules in terms of two judgments, one for stores and the other for programs. The store typing rules generate a context that describes the available bindings in the store. The program typing rule uses the generated bindings to check the expression that will be executed.

With this new machinery in hand, we are able to prove the standard progress and preservation theorems.

1.2.11 THEOREM [PRESERVATION]: If ⊢ (S;t) and (S;t) ⟶ (S′;t′) then ⊢ (S′;t′). □

1.2.12 THEOREM [PROGRESS]: If ⊢ (S;t) then (S;t) ⟶ (S′;t′) or t is a value. □

1.2.13 EXERCISE [RECOMMENDED, ★]: You will need a substitution lemma to complete the proof of preservation. Is the following the right one?

Conjecture: Let $\Gamma_3 = \Gamma_1 \circ \Gamma_2$. If Γ_1, x:T ⊢ t_1 : T_1 and Γ_2 ⊢ t : T then Γ_3 ⊢ [x ↦ t]t_1 : T_1. □

1.2.14 EXERCISE [★★★, ↛]: Prove progress and preservation using *TAPL*, Chapters 9 and 13, as an approximate guide. □

Store Typing $\boxed{\vdash S : \Gamma}$

$$\vdash \varnothing : \varnothing \qquad \text{(T-EMPTYS)}$$

$$\frac{\vdash S : \Gamma_1 \circ \Gamma_2 \qquad \Gamma_1 \vdash \texttt{lin}\ w : T}{\vdash S, x \mapsto \texttt{lin}\ w : \Gamma_2, x{:}T} \qquad \text{(T-NEXTLINS)}$$

$$\frac{\vdash S : \Gamma_1 \circ \Gamma_2 \qquad \Gamma_1 \vdash \texttt{un}\ w : T}{\vdash S, x \mapsto \texttt{un}\ w : \Gamma_2, x{:}T} \qquad \text{(T-NEXTUNS)}$$

Program Typing $\boxed{\vdash (S;t)}$

$$\frac{\vdash S : \Gamma \qquad \Gamma \vdash t : T}{\vdash (S;t)} \qquad \text{(T-PROG)}$$

Figure 1-9: Linear lambda calculus: Program typing

1.3 Extensions and Variations

Most features found in modern programming languages can be defined to interoperate successfully with linear type systems, although some are trickier than others. In this section, we will consider a variety of practical extensions to our simple linear lambda calculus.

Sums and Recursive Types

Complex data structures, such as the recursive data types found in ML-like languages, pose little problem for linear languages. To demonstrate the central ideas involved, we extend the syntax for the linear lambda calculus with the standard introduction and elimination forms for sums and recursive types. The details are presented in Figure 1-10.

Values with sum type are introduced by injections $\texttt{q inl}_{\texttt{P}}\ \texttt{t}$ or $\texttt{q inr}_{\texttt{P}}\ \texttt{t}$, where P is $T_1{+}T_2$, the resulting pretype of the term. In the first instance, the underlying term t must have type T_1, and in the second instance, the underlying term t must have type T_2. The qualifier q indicates the linearity of the argument in exactly the same way as for pairs. The case expression will execute its first branch if its primary argument is a left injection and its second branch if its primary argument is a right injection. We assume that + binds more tightly that → but less tightly than *.

Recursive types are introduced with a $\texttt{roll}_{\texttt{P}}\ \texttt{t}$ expression, where P is the recursive pretype the expression will assume. Unlike all the other introduction forms, roll expressions are not annotated with a qualifier. Instead, they take on the qualifier of the underlying expression t. The reason for this distinction is that we will treat this introduction form as a typing coercion that has no real operational effect. Unlike functions, pairs or sums, recursive data types have no data of their own and therefore do not need a separate qualifier to control their allocation behavior. To simplify the notational overhead

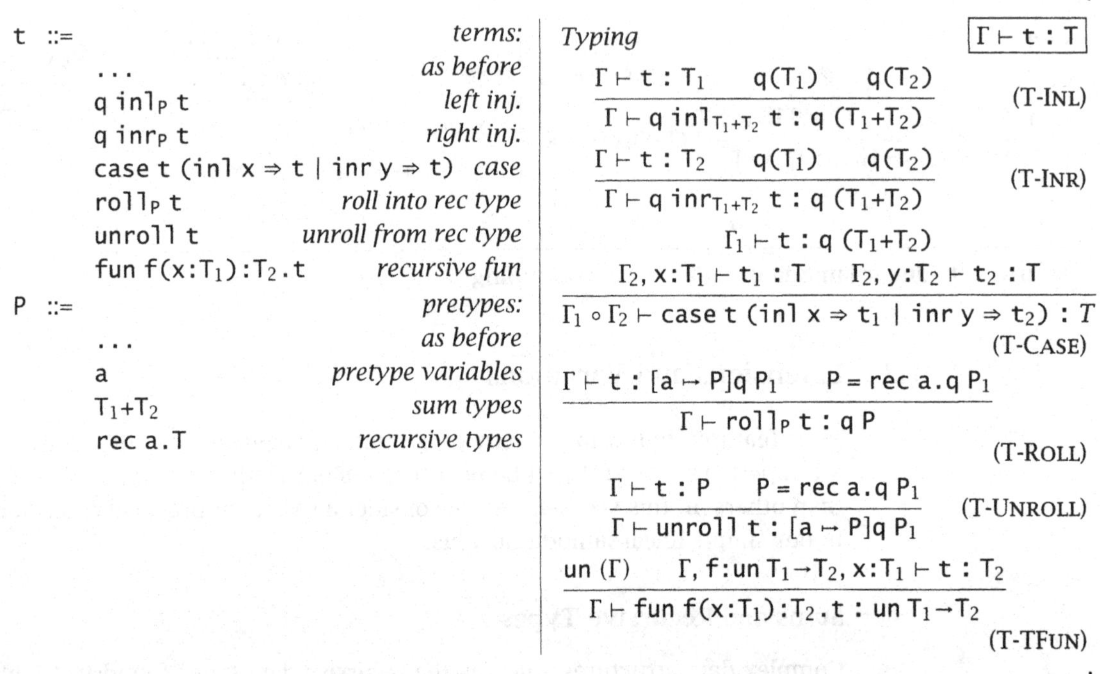

Figure 1-10: Linear lambda calculus: Sums and recursive types

of sums and recursive types, we will normally omit the typing annotations on their introduction forms in our examples.

In order to write computations that process recursive types, we add recursive function declarations to our language as well. Since the free variables in a recursive function closure will be used on each recursive invocation of the function, we cannot allow the closure to contain linear variables. Hence, all recursive functions are unrestricted data structures.

A simple but useful data structure is the linear list of Ts:

```
type T llist = rec a.lin (unit + lin (T * lin a))
```

Here, the entire spine (aside from the terminating value of unit type) is linear while the underlying T objects may be linear or unrestricted. To create a fully unrestricted list, we simply omit the linear qualifiers on the sum and pairs that make up the spine of the list:

```
type T list = rec a.unit + T*a
```

After defining the linear lists, the memory conscious programmer can write many familiar list-processing functions in a minimal amount of space. For example, here is how we map an unrestricted function across a linear list. Remember, multi-argument functions are abbreviations for functions that accept linear pairs as arguments.

```
fun nil(_:unit) : T2 llist =
   roll (lin inl ())

fun cons(hd:T2, tl:T2 llist) : T2 llist =
   roll (lin inr (lin <hd,tl>))

fun map(f:T1→T2, xs:T1 llist) : T2 llist =
  case unroll xs (
    inl _  ⇒ nil()
  | inr xs ⇒
      split xs as hd,tl in
      cons(f hd,map lin <f,tl>))
```

In this implementation of map, we can observe that on each iteration of the loop, it is possible to reuse the space deallocated by `split` or `case` operations for the allocation operations that follow in the body of the function (inside the calls to `nil` and `cons`).

Hence, at first glance, it appears that map will execute with only a constant space overhead. Unfortunately, however, there are some hidden costs as map executes. A typical implementation will store local variables and temporaries on the stack before making a recursive call. In this case, the result of `f hd` will be stored on the stack while map iterates down the list. Consequently, rather than having a constant space overhead, our map implementation will have an O(n) overhead, where n is the length of the list. This is not too bad, but we can do better.

In order to do better, we need to avoid implicit stack allocation of data each time we iterate through the body of a recursive function. Fortunately, many functional programming languages guarantee that if the last operation in a function is itself a function call then the language implementation will deallocate the current stack frame before calling the new function. We name such function calls *tail calls* and we say that any language implementation that guarantees that the current stack frame will be deallocated before a tail call is *tail-call optimizing.*

Assuming that our language is tail-call optimizing, we can now rewrite map so that it executes with only a constant space overhead. The main trick involved is that we will explicitly keep track of both the part of the input list we have yet to process and the ouput list that we have already processed. The output list will wind up in reverse order, so we will reverse it at the end. Both of the loops in the code, mapRev and reverse are *tail-recursive* functions. That is, they end in a tail call and have a space-efficient implementation.

```
fun map(f:T1→T2, input:T1 llist) : T2 llist =
  reverse(mapRev(f,input,nil()),nil())

and mapRev(f:T1→T2,
           input:T1 llist,
           output:T2 llist) : T2 llist =
  case unroll input (
    inl _  ⇒ output
  | inr xs ⇒
      split xs as hd,tl in
      mapRev (f,tl,cons(f hd,output)))

and reverse(input:T2 llist, output:T2 llist)
  case unroll input (
    inl _  ⇒ output
  | inr xs ⇒
      split xs as hd,tl in
      reverse(tl,cons(hd,output)))
```

This *link reversal* algorithm is a well-known way of traversing a list in constant space. It is just one of a class of algorithms developed well before the invention of linear types. A similar algorithm was invented by Deutsch, Schorr, and Waite for traversing trees and graphs in constant space. Such constant space traversals are essential parts of mark-sweep garbage collectors—at garbage collection time there is no extra space for a stack so any traversal of the heap must be done in constant space.

1.3.1 EXERCISE [★★★]: Define a recursive type that describes linear binary trees that hold data of type T in their internal nodes (nothing at the leaves). Write a constant-space function treeMap that produces an identically-shaped tree on output as it was given on input, modulo the action of the function f that is applied to each element of the tree. Feel free to use reasonable extensions to our linear lambda calculus including mutually recursive functions, n-ary tuples and n-ary sums. □

Polymorphism

Parametric polymorphism is a crucial feature of almost any functional language, and our linear lambda calculus is no exception. The main function of polymorphism in our setting is to support two different sorts of code reuse.

1. Reuse of code to perform the same algorithm, but on data with different shapes.

2. Reuse of code to perform the same algorithm, but on data governed by different memory management strategies.

To support the first kind of polymorphism, we will allow quantification over pretypes. To support the second kind of polymorphism, we will allow quantification over qualifiers. A good example of both sorts of polymorphism arises in the definition of a polymorphic map function. In the code below, we use a and b to range over pretype variables as we did in the previous section, and p to range over qualifier variables.

```
type (p1,p2,a) list =
  rec a.p1 (unit + p1 (p2 a * (p1,p2,a) list))

map :
  ∀a,b.
    ∀pa,pb.
      lin ((pa a → pb b)*(lin,pa,a) list)→(lin,pb,b) list
```

The type definition in the first line defines lists in terms of three parameters. The first parameter, p_1, gives the usage pattern (linear or unrestricted) for the spine of the list, while the second parameter gives the usage pattern for the elements of the list. The third parameter is a pretype parameter, which gives the (pre)type of the elements of list. The map function is polymorphic in the argument (a) and result (b) element types of the list. It is also polymorphic (via parameters p_a and p_b) in the way those elements are used. Overall, the function maps lists with linear spines to lists with linear spines.

Developing a system for polymorphic, linear type inference is a challenging research topic, beyond the scope of this book, so we will assume that, unlike in ML, polymorphic functions are introduced explicitly using the syntax Λa.t or Λp.t. Here, a and p are the type parameters to a function with body t. The body does not need to be a value, like in ML, since we will run the polymorphic function every time a pretype or qualifier is passed to the function as an argument. The syntax t′ [P] or t′ [q] applies the function t′ to its pretype or qualifier argument. Figure 1-11 summarizes the syntactic extensions to the language.

Before we get to writing the map function, we will take a look at the polymorphic constructor functions for linear lists. These functions will take a pretype parameter and two qualifier parameters, just like the type definition for lists.

q ::=		*qualifiers:*
	...	*as before*
	p	*polymorphic qualifier*
t ::=		*terms:*
	...	*as before*
	q Λa.t	*pretype abstraction*
	t [P]	*pretype application*
	q Λp.t	*qualifier abstraction*
	t [q]	*qualifier application*
P ::=		*pretypes:*
	...	*as before*
	∀a.T	*pretype polymorphism*
	∀p.T	*qualifier polymorphism*

Figure 1-11: Linear lambda calculus: Polymorphism syntax

```
val nil : ∀a,p2.(lin,p2,a) list =
  Λa,p2.roll (lin inl ())

val list :
  ∀a,p2.lin (p2 a * (lin,p2,a) list)→(lin,p2,a) list =
  Λa,p2.
    λcell : lin (p2 a * (lin,p2,a) list).
      roll (lin inr (lin cell))
```

Now our most polymorphic map function may be written as follows.

```
val map =
  Λa,b. Λpa,pb.
  fun aux(f:(pa a → pb b),
              xs:(lin,pa,a) list)) : (lin,pb,b) list =
    case unroll xs (
      inl _  ⇒ nil [b,pb] ()
    | inr xs ⇒ split xs as hd,tl in
                 cons [b,pb] (pb <f hd,map (lin <f,tl>)>))
```

In order to ensure that our type system remains sound in the presence of pretype polymorphism, we add the obvious typing rules, but change very little else. However, adding qualifier polymorphism, as we have done, is a little more involved. Before arriving at the typing rules themselves, we need to adapt some of our basic definitions to account for abstract qualifiers that may either be linear or unrestricted.

First, we need to ensure that we propagate contexts containing abstract qualifiers safely through the other typing rules in the system. Most importantly, we add additional cases to the context manipulation rules defined in the previous section. We need to ensure that linear hypotheses are not duplicated and therefore we cannot risk duplicating unknown qualifiers, which might turn out to be linear. Figure 1-12 specifies the details.

Context Split $\boxed{\Gamma = \Gamma_1 \circ \Gamma_2}$

$$\frac{\Gamma = \Gamma_1 \circ \Gamma_2}{\Gamma, \mathtt{x{:}p\ P} = (\Gamma_1, \mathtt{x{:}p\ P}) \circ \Gamma_2} \quad \text{(M-ABS1)}$$

$$\frac{\Gamma = \Gamma_1 \circ \Gamma_2}{\Gamma, \mathtt{x{:}p\ P} = \Gamma_1 \circ (\Gamma_2, \mathtt{x{:}p\ P})} \quad \text{(M-ABS2)}$$

Figure 1-12: Linear context manipulation rules

Δ ::=		*type contexts:*
	$\varnothing$	*empty*
	Δ, a	*pretype var.*
	Δ, p	*qualifier var.*

Typing $\boxed{\Delta;\Gamma \vdash \mathtt{t : T}}$

$$\frac{\mathtt{q}(\Gamma) \qquad \Delta, \mathtt{a};\Gamma \vdash \mathtt{t : T}}{\Delta;\Gamma \vdash \mathtt{q\ \Lambda a.t : q\ \forall a.T}} \quad \text{(T-PABS)}$$

$$\frac{\Delta;\Gamma \vdash \mathtt{t : q\ \forall a.T} \qquad FV(\mathtt{P}) \subseteq \Delta}{\Delta;\Gamma \vdash \mathtt{t\ [P] : [a \mapsto P]T}} \quad \text{(T-PAPP)}$$

$$\frac{\mathtt{q}(\Gamma) \qquad \Delta, \mathtt{p};\Gamma \vdash \mathtt{t : T}}{\Delta;\Gamma \vdash \mathtt{q\ \Lambda p.t : q\ \forall p.T}} \quad \text{(T-QABS)}$$

$$\frac{\Delta;\Gamma \vdash \mathtt{t : q_1\ \forall p.T} \qquad FV(\mathtt{q}) \subseteq \Delta}{\Delta;\Gamma \vdash \mathtt{t\ [q] : [p \mapsto q]T}} \quad \text{(T-QAPP)}$$

Figure 1-13: Linear lambda calculus: Polymorphic typing

Second, we need to conservatively extend the relation on type qualifiers $\mathtt{q_1 \sqsubseteq q_2}$ so that it is sound in the presence of qualifier polymorphism. Since the linear qualifier is the least qualifier in the current system, the following rule should hold.

$$\mathtt{lin} \sqsubseteq \mathtt{p} \qquad \text{(Q-LINP)}$$

Likewise, since un is the greatest qualifier in the system, we can be sure the following rule is sound.

$$\mathtt{p} \sqsubseteq \mathtt{un} \qquad \text{(Q-PUN)}$$

Aside from these rules, we will only be able to infer that an abstract qualifier p is related to itself via the general reflexivity rule. Consequently, linear data structures can contain abstract ones; abstract data structures can contain unrestricted data structures; and data structure with qualifier p can contain other data with qualifier p.

In order to define the typing rules for the polymorphic linear lambda calculus proper, we need to change the judgment form to keep track of the type variables that are allowed to appear free in a term. The new judgment uses the type context Δ for this purpose. The typing rules for the introduction and elimination forms for each sort of polymorphism are fairly straightforward now and are presented in Figure 1-13.

The typing rules for the other constructs we have seen are almost unchanged. One relatively minor alteration is that the incoming type context Δ will be propagated through the rules to account for the free type variables. Unlike term variables, type variables can always be used in an unrestricted fashion; it is difficult to understand what it would mean to restrict the use of a type variable to one place in a type or term. Consequently, all parts of Δ are propagated from the conclusion of any rule to all premises. We also need the occasional side condition to check that whenever a programmer writes down a type, its free variables are contained in the current type context Δ. For instance the rules for function abstraction and application will now be written as follows.

$$\frac{\mathtt{q}(\Gamma) \qquad FV(\mathtt{T}_1) \subseteq \Delta \qquad \Delta;\Gamma, \mathtt{x}{:}\mathtt{T}_1 \vdash \mathtt{t}_2 : \mathtt{T}_2}{\Delta;\Gamma \vdash \mathtt{q}\ \lambda\mathtt{x}{:}\mathtt{T}_1.\mathtt{t}_2 : \mathtt{q}\ \mathtt{T}_1{\to}\mathtt{T}_2} \quad \text{(T-ABS)}$$

$$\frac{\Delta;\Gamma_1 \vdash \mathtt{t}_1 : \mathtt{q}\ \mathtt{T}_1{\to}\mathtt{T}_2 \qquad \Delta;\Gamma_2 \vdash \mathtt{t}_2 : \mathtt{T}_1}{\Delta;\Gamma_1 \circ \Gamma_2 \vdash \mathtt{t}_1\ \mathtt{t}_2 : \mathtt{T}_2} \quad \text{(T-APP)}$$

The most important way to test our system for faults is to prove the type substitution lemma. In particular, the proof will demonstrate that we have made safe assumptions about how abstract type qualifiers may be used.

1.3.2 **Lemma [Type Substitution]:**

1. If $\Delta, \mathtt{p};\Gamma \vdash \mathtt{t} : \mathtt{T}$ and $FV(\mathtt{q}) \in \Delta$ then $\Delta; [\mathtt{p} \mapsto \mathtt{q}]\Gamma \vdash [\mathtt{p} \mapsto \mathtt{q}]\mathtt{t} : [\mathtt{p} \mapsto \mathtt{q}]\mathtt{T}$
2. If $\Delta, \mathtt{a};\Gamma \vdash \mathtt{t} : \mathtt{T}$ and $FV(\mathtt{P}) \in \Delta$ then $\Delta; [\mathtt{a} \mapsto \mathtt{P}]\Gamma \vdash [\mathtt{a} \mapsto \mathtt{P}]\mathtt{t} : [\mathtt{a} \mapsto \mathtt{P}]\mathtt{T}$ □

1.3.3 **Exercise [★]:** Sketch the proof of the type substitution lemma. What structural rule(s) do you need to carry out the proof? □

Operationally, we will choose to implement polymorphic instantiation using substitution. As a result, our operational semantics changes very little. We only need to specify the new computational contexts and to add the evaluation rules for polymorphic functions and application as in Figure 1-14.

Arrays

Arrays pose a special problem for linearly typed languages. If we try to provide an operation fetches an element from an array in the usual way, perhaps using an array index expression `a[i]`, we would need to reflect the fact that the $\mathtt{i}^{th}$ element (and only the $\mathtt{i}^{th}$ element) of the array had been "used." However, there is no simple way to reflect this change in the type of an array as the usual form of array types (`array(T)`) provides no mechanism to distinguish between the properties of different elements of the array.

$$
\begin{array}{lll}
E ::= & & \textit{evaluation contexts:} \\
& E\,[P] & \textit{pretype app context} \\
& E\,[q] & \textit{qualifier app context}
\end{array}
$$

$$(S;q\,\Lambda a.t) \longrightarrow_\beta (S, x \mapsto q\,\Lambda a.t;x) \quad \text{(E-PFun)}$$

$$\frac{S(x) = q\,\Lambda a.t}{(S;x\,[P]) \longrightarrow_\beta (S \overset{q}{\sim} x;[a \mapsto P]t)} \quad \text{(E-PApp)}$$

$$(S;q\,\Lambda p.t) \longrightarrow_\beta (S, x \mapsto q\,\Lambda p.t;x) \quad \text{(E-QFun)}$$

$$\frac{S(x) = q\,\Lambda p.t}{(S;x\,[q_1]) \longrightarrow_\beta (S \overset{q}{\sim} x;[p \mapsto q_1]t)} \quad \text{(E-QApp)}$$

Figure 1-14: Linear lambda calculus: Polymorphic operational semantics

We dodged this problem when we constructed our tuple operations by defining a pattern matching construct that simultaneously extracted all of the elements of a tuple. Unfortunately, we cannot follow the same path for arrays because in modern languages like Java and ML, the length of an array (and therefore the size of the pattern) is unknown at compile time.

Another non-solution to the problem is to add a special built-in iterator to process all the elements in an array at once. However, this last prevents programmers from using arrays as efficient, constant-time, random-access data structures; they might as well use lists instead.

One way out of this jam is to design the central array access operations so that, unlike the ordinary "get" and "set" operations, they *preserve* the number of pointers to the array and the number of pointers to each of its elements. We avoid our problem because there is no change to the array data structure that needs to be reflected in the type system. Using this idea, we will be able to allow programmers to define linear arrays that can hold a collection of arbitrarily many linear objects. Moreover, programmers will be able to access any of these linear objects, one at a time, using a convenient, constant-time, random-access mechanism.

So, what are the magic pointer-preserving array access operations? Actually, we need only one: a swap operation with the form `swap (a[i],t)`. The swap replaces the $\mathtt{i}^{th}$ element of the array `a` (call it `t'`) with `t` and returns a (linear) pair containing the new array and `t'`. Notice the number of pointers to `t` and `t'` does not change during the operation. If there was one pointer to `t` (as an argument to `swap`) before the call, then there is one pointer to `t` afterward (from within the array `a`) and vice versa for `t'`. If, in addition, all of the elements of `a` had one pointer to them before the swap, then they will all have one pointer to them after the swap as well. Consequently, we will find it easy to type the swap operation, even when it works over linear arrays of linear objects.

In addition to swap, we provide functions to allocate an array given its list of elements (`array`), to determine array length (`length`) and to deallocate arrays (`free`). The last operation is somewhat unusual in that it takes two arguments `a` and `f`, where `a` is an array of type `lin array(T)` and `f` is a function with type `T→unit` that is run on each element of `T`. The function may be thought of as a finalizer for the elements; it may be used to deallocate any linear components of the array elements, thereby preserving the single pointer property.

Our definition of arrays is compatible with the polymorphic system from the previous subsection, but for simplicity, we formalize it in the context of the simply-typed lambda calculus (see Figure 1-15).

1.3.4 Exercise [Recommended, ★]: The typing rule for array allocation (T-Array) contains the standard containment check to ensure that unrestricted arrays cannot contain linear objects. What kinds of errors can occur if this check is omitted? □

1.3.5 Exercise [★★, ↛]: With the presence of mutable data structures, it is possible to create cycles in the store. How should we modify the store typing rules to take this into account? □

The `swap` and `free` functions are relatively low-level operations. Fortunately, it is easy to build more convenient, higher-level abstractions out of them. For instance, the following code defines some simple functions for manipulating linear matricies of unrestricted integers.

```
type iArray = lin array(int)
type matrix = lin array(iArray)

fun dummy(x:unit):iArray = lin array()

fun freeElem(x:int):unit = ()
fun freeArray(a:iArray):unit = free(a,freeElem)
fun freeMatrix(m:matrix):unit = free(m,freeArray)

fun get(a:matrix,i:int,j:int):lin (matrix * int) =
  split swap(a[i],dummy()) as a,b in
  split swap(b[j],0) as b,k in
  split swap(b[j],k) as b,_ in
  split swap(a[i],b) as a,junk in
  freeArray(junk);
  lin <a,k>
```

P ::=		*pretypes:*
	...	*as before*
	array(T)	*array pretypes*
t ::=		*terms:*
	...	*as before*
	q array(t,...,t)	*array creation*
	swap(t[t],t)	*swap*
	length(t)	*length*
	free(t,t)	*deallocate*
w ::=		*prevalues:*
	...	*as before*
	array[n,x,...,x]	*array*
E ::=		*evaluation contexts:*
	...	*as before*
	q array(v,...,v,E,t,...,t)	*array context*
	swap(E(t),t)	*swap context*
	swap(v(E),t)	*swap context*
	swap(v(v),E)	*swap context*
	length(E)	*length context*
	free(E,t)	*free context*
	free(v,E)	*free context*

Typing $\boxed{\Gamma \vdash \mathtt{t} : \mathtt{T}}$

$$\frac{\mathtt{q(T)} \qquad \Gamma \vdash \mathtt{t}_i : \mathtt{T} \qquad (\text{for } 1 \le i \le n)}{\Gamma \vdash \mathtt{q\ array(t_1,\ldots,t}_n\mathtt{)} : \mathtt{q\ array(T)}} \qquad \text{(T-ARRAY)}$$

$$\frac{\Gamma \vdash \mathtt{t}_1 : \mathtt{q}_1\ \mathtt{array(T_1)} \qquad \Gamma \vdash \mathtt{t}_2 : \mathtt{q}_2\ \mathtt{int} \qquad \Gamma \vdash \mathtt{t}_3 : \mathtt{T}_1}{\Gamma \vdash \mathtt{swap(t_1[t_2],t_3)} : \mathtt{lin}\ (\mathtt{q}_1\ \mathtt{array(T_1)} * \mathtt{T}_1)} \qquad \text{(T-SWAP)}$$

$$\frac{\Gamma \vdash \mathtt{t} : \mathtt{q\ array(T)}}{\Gamma \vdash \mathtt{length(t)} : \mathtt{lin}\ (\mathtt{q\ array(T)} * \mathtt{int})} \qquad \text{(T-LENGTH)}$$

$$\frac{\Gamma \vdash \mathtt{t}_1 : \mathtt{q\ array(T)} \qquad \Gamma \vdash \mathtt{t}_2 : \mathtt{T} \to \mathtt{unit}}{\Gamma \vdash \mathtt{free(t_1,t_2)} : \mathtt{unit}} \qquad \text{(T-FREE)}$$

Evaluation $\boxed{(\mathtt{S;t}) \longrightarrow_\beta (\mathtt{S';t'})}$

$$(\mathtt{S;q\ array(x_0,\ldots,x}_{n-1}\mathtt{)}) \longrightarrow_\beta ((\mathtt{S, x} \mapsto \mathtt{q\ array[n,x_0,\ldots,x}_{n-1}\mathtt{];x}) \qquad \text{(E-ARRAY)}$$

$$\frac{\begin{array}{c}\mathtt{S(x}_i\mathtt{)} = \mathtt{q}_i\ \mathtt{j} \\ \mathtt{S} = \mathtt{S}_1, \mathtt{x}_a \mapsto \mathtt{q\ array[n,\ldots,x}_j\mathtt{,\ldots]}, \mathtt{S}_2 \\ \mathtt{S'} = \mathtt{S}_1, \mathtt{x}_a \mapsto \mathtt{q\ array[n,\ldots,x}_e\mathtt{,\ldots]}, \mathtt{S}_2\end{array}}{(\mathtt{S;\ swap(x}_a\mathtt{[x}_i\mathtt{],x}_e\mathtt{)}) \longrightarrow_\beta (\mathtt{S'} \overset{\mathtt{q}_i}{\sim} \mathtt{x}_i\mathtt{;lin <x}_a\mathtt{,x}_j\mathtt{>})} \qquad \text{(E-SWAP)}$$

$$\frac{\mathtt{S(x)} = \mathtt{q\ array[n,x_0,\ldots,x}_{n-1}\mathtt{]}}{(\mathtt{S;length(x)}) \longrightarrow_\beta (\mathtt{S;lin <x,un\ n>})} \qquad \text{(E-LENGTH)}$$

$$\frac{\mathtt{S(x}_a\mathtt{)} = \mathtt{q\ array[n,x_0,\ldots,x}_{n-1}\mathtt{]}}{(\mathtt{S;free(x}_a\mathtt{,x}_f\mathtt{)}) \longrightarrow_\beta (\mathtt{S} \overset{\mathtt{q}}{\sim} \mathtt{x}_a\mathtt{;App(x}_f\mathtt{,x_0,\ldots,x}_{n-1}\mathtt{)})} \qquad \text{(E-FREE)}$$

where

$$\begin{array}{lcl}\mathtt{App(x}_f\mathtt{,\cdot)} & = & \mathtt{()} \\ \mathtt{App(x}_f\mathtt{,x_0,\ldots)} & = & \mathtt{x}_f\ \mathtt{x_0;App(x}_f\mathtt{,\ldots)}\end{array}$$

Figure 1-15: Linear lambda calculus: Arrays

```
fun set(a:matrix,i:int,j:int,e:int):matrix =
  split swap(a[i],dummy()) as a,b in
  split swap(b[j],e) as b,_ in
  split swap(a[i],b) as a,junk in
  freeArray(junk);
  a
```

1.3.6 EXERCISE [★★, ↛]: Use the functions provided above to write matrix-matrix multiply. Your multiply function should return an integer and deallocate both arrays in the process. Use any standard integer operations necessary. □

In the examples above, we needed some sort of dummy value to swap into an array to replace the value we wanted to extract. For integers and arrays it was easy to come up with one. However, when dealing with polymorphic or abstract types, it may not be possible to conjure up a value of the right type. Consequently, rather than manipulating arrays with type `q array(a)` for some abstract type `a`, we may need to manipulate arrays of options with type `q array(a + unit)`. In this case, when we need to read out a value, we always have another value (`inr ()`) to swap in in its place. Normally such operations are called *destructive reads*; they are a common way to preserve the single pointer property when managing complex structured data.

Reference Counting

Array swaps and destructive reads are dynamic techniques that can help overcome a lack of compile-time knowledge about the number of uses of a particular object. *Reference counting* is another dynamic technique that serves a similar purpose. Rather than restricting the number of pointers to an object to be exactly one, we can allow any number of pointers to the object and keep track of that number dynamically. Only when the last reference is used will the object be deallocated.

There are various ways to integrate reference counts into the current system. Here, we choose the simplest, which is to add a new qualifier `rc` for reference-counted data structures, and operations that allow the programmer to explicitly increment (`inc`) and decrement (`dec`) the counts (see Figure 1-16). More specifically, the increment operation takes a pointer argument, increments the reference count for the object pointed to, and returns two copies of the pointer in a (linear) pair. The decrement operation takes two arguments, a pointer and a function, and works as follows. In the case the object pointed to (call it `x`) has a reference count of 1 before the decrement, the function is executed with `x` as a linear argument. Since the function treats `x`

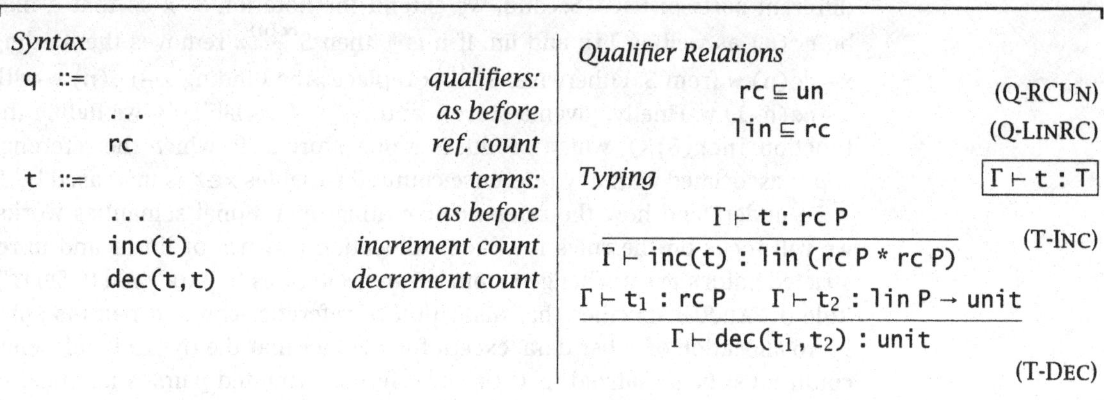

Figure 1-16: Linear lambda calculus: Reference counting syntax and typing

linearly, it will deallocate x before it completes. In the other case, when x has a reference count greater than 1, the reference count is simply decremented and the function is not called; `unit` is returned as the result of the operation.

The main typing invariant in this system is that whenever a reference-counted variable appears in the static type-checking context, there is one dynamic reference count associated with it. Linear typing will ensure the number of references to an object is properly preserved.

The new `rc` qualifier should be treated in the same manner as the linear qualifier when it comes to context splitting. In other words, a reference-counted variable should be placed in exactly one of the left-hand context or the right-hand context (not both). In terms of containment, the `rc` qualifier sits between unrestricted and linear qualifiers: A reference-counted data structure may not be contained in unrestricted data structures and may not contain linear data structures. Figure 1-16 presents the appropriate qualifier relation and typing rules for our reference counting additions.

In order to define the execution behavior of reference-counted data structures, we will define a new sort of stored value with the form `rc(n) w`. The integer `n` is the reference count: it keeps track of the number of times the value is referenced elsewhere in the store or in the program.

The operational semantics for the new commands and reference-counted pairs and functions are summarized in Figure 1-17. Several new bits of notation show up here to handle the relatively complex computation that must go on to increment and decrement reference counts. First, in a slight abuse of notation, we allow `q` to range over static qualifiers `un`, `lin` and `rc` as well as dynamic qualifiers `un`, `lin` and `rc(n)`. Context will disambiguate the two different sorts of uses. Second, we extend the notation $S \overset{q}{\sim} x$ so that q may be rc(n) as well as lin and un. If n is 1 then $S \overset{rc(n)}{\sim} x$ removes the binding x↦rc(n) w from S. Otherwise, $S \overset{rc(n)}{\sim} x$ replaces the binding x↦rc(n) w with x↦rc(n-1) w. Finally, given a store S and a set of variables X, we define the function incr(S;X), which produces a new store S′ in which the reference count associated with any reference-counted variables x∈X is increased by 1.

To understand how the reference counting operational semantics works, we will focus on the rules for pairs. Allocation and use of linear and unrestricted pairs stays unchanged from before as in rules (E-PAIR') and (E-SPLIT'). Rule (E-PAIRRC) specifies that allocation of reference-counted pairs is similar to allocation of other data, except for the fact that the dynamic reference count must be initialized to 1. Use of reference-counted pairs is identical to use of other kinds of pairs when the reference count is 1: We remove the pair from the store via the function $S \overset{rc(n)}{\sim} x$ as shown in rule and substitute the two components of the pair in the body of the term as shown in (E-SPLIT'). When the reference count is greater than 1, rule (E-SPLITRC) shows there are additional complications. More precisely, if one of the components of the pair, say y_1, is reference-counted then y_1's reference count must be increased by 1 since an additional copy of y_1 is substituted through the body of t. We use the incr function to handle the possible increase. In most respects, the operational rules for reference-counted functions follow the same principles as reference-counted pairs. Increment and decrement operations are also relatively straightforward.

In order to state and prove the progress and preservation lemmas for our reference-counting language, we must generalize the type system slightly. In particular, our typing contexts must be able specify the fact that a particular reference should appear exactly n times in the store or current computation. Reference-counted values in the store are described by these contexts and the context-splitting relation is generalized appropriately. Figure 1-18 summarizes the additional typing rules.

1.3.7 **EXERCISE** [★★★, ↛]: State and prove progress and preservation lemmas for the simply-typed linear lambda calculus (functions and pairs) with reference counting. □

1.4 An Ordered Type System

Just as linear type systems provide a foundation for managing memory allocated on the heap, *ordered* type systems provide a foundation for managing memory allocated on the stack. The central idea is that by controlling the

v	::=		*values:*
		$\ldots$	*as before*
		$\mathtt{rc(n)}\ w$	*ref-counted value*
E	::=		*evaluation contexts:*
		$\ldots$	*as before*
		$\mathtt{inc(E)}$	*inc context*
		$\mathtt{dec(E,t)}$	*dec context*
		$\mathtt{dec(x,E)}$	*dec context*

Evaluation $\boxed{(S;t) \longrightarrow_\beta (S';t')}$

$$\frac{(q \in \{\mathtt{un},\mathtt{lin}\})}{(S;q\ \langle y,z\rangle) \longrightarrow_\beta (S, x \mapsto q\ \langle y,z\rangle; x)} \quad \text{(E-PAIR')}$$

$$(S;\mathtt{rc}\ \langle y,z\rangle) \longrightarrow_\beta (S, x \mapsto \mathtt{rc(1)}\ \langle y,z\rangle; x) \quad \text{(E-PAIRRC)}$$

$$\frac{\begin{array}{c} S(x) = q\ \langle y_1,z_1\rangle \\ (q \in \{\mathtt{un},\mathtt{lin},\mathtt{rc(1)}\}) \end{array}}{(S;\mathtt{split}\ x\ \mathtt{as}\ y,z\ \mathtt{in}\ t) \longrightarrow_\beta (S \overset{q}{\sim} x; [y \mapsto y_1][z \mapsto z_1]t)} \quad \text{(E-SPLIT')}$$

$$\frac{\begin{array}{c} S(x) = \mathtt{rc(n)}\ \langle y_1,z_1\rangle \qquad (n > 1) \\ \mathtt{incr}(S;\{y_1,z_1\}) = S' \end{array}}{(S;\mathtt{split}\ x\ \mathtt{as}\ y,z\ \mathtt{in}\ t) \longrightarrow_\beta ((S' \overset{\mathtt{rc(n)}}{\sim} x); [y \mapsto y_1'][z \mapsto z_1']t)} \quad \text{(E-SPLITRC)}$$

$$\frac{(q \in \{\mathtt{un},\mathtt{lin}\})}{(S;q\ \lambda y{:}T.t) \longrightarrow_\beta (S, x \mapsto q\ \lambda y{:}T.t; x)} \quad \text{(E-FUN')}$$

$$(S;\mathtt{rc}\ \lambda y{:}T.t) \longrightarrow_\beta (S, x \mapsto \mathtt{rc(1)}\ \lambda y{:}T.t; x) \quad \text{(E-FUNRC)}$$

$$\frac{\begin{array}{c} S(x_1) = q\ \lambda y{:}T.t \\ (q \in \{\mathtt{un},\mathtt{lin},\mathtt{rc(1)}\}) \end{array}}{(S;x_1\ x_2) \longrightarrow_\beta (S \overset{q}{\sim} x_1; [y \mapsto x_2]t)} \quad \text{(E-APP')}$$

$$\frac{\begin{array}{c} S(x_1) = \mathtt{rc(n)}\ \lambda y{:}T.t \\ (n > 1 \text{ and } X = FV(\lambda y{:}T.t)) \\ \mathtt{incr}(S;X) = S' \end{array}}{(S;x_1\ x_2) \longrightarrow_\beta (S' \overset{\mathtt{rc(n)}}{\sim} x_1; [y \mapsto x_2]t)} \quad \text{(E-APPRC)}$$

$$\frac{\mathtt{incr}(S;\{x\}) = S'}{(S;\mathtt{inc}(x)) \longrightarrow_\beta (S';\mathtt{lin}\ \langle x,x\rangle)} \quad \text{(E-INC)}$$

$$\frac{(S(x) = \mathtt{rc(n)}\ w) \qquad (n > 1)}{(S;\mathtt{dec}(x,x_f)) \longrightarrow_\beta (S \overset{\mathtt{rc(n)}}{\sim} x; \mathtt{un}\ ())} \quad \text{(E-DEC1)}$$

$$\frac{\begin{array}{c} S = S_1, x \mapsto \mathtt{rc(1)}\ w, S_2 \\ S' = S_1, x \mapsto \mathtt{lin}\ w, S_2 \end{array}}{(S;\mathtt{dec}(x,x_f)) \longrightarrow_\beta (S';x_f\ x)} \quad \text{(E-DEC2)}$$

Figure 1-17: Linear lambda calculus: Reference counting operational semantics

exchange property, we are able to guarantee that certain values, those values allocated on the stack, are used in a first-in/last-out order.

To formalize this idea, we organize the store into two parts: a stack, which is a sequence of locations that can be accessed on one end (the "top") and a heap, which is like the store described in previous sections of this chapter. Pairs, functions and other objects introduced with unrestricted or linear qualifiers are allocated on the heap as before. And as before, when a linear pair or function is used, it is deallocated. Also, we allow programmers to allocate simple data structures on the stack. Without the exchange property, an ordered object can only be used when it is at the top of the stack. When this happens, the ordered object is popped off the top of the stack.

Syntax

Γ ::= *typing contexts:*

... *as before*

Γ, `x:rc(n)P` *rc(n) context*

Store Typing

$$\frac{\vdash \texttt{S} : \Gamma_1 \circ \Gamma_2 \qquad \Gamma_1 \vdash \texttt{rc w} : \texttt{rc P}}{\vdash \texttt{S,x} \mapsto \texttt{rc(n) w} : \Gamma_2\texttt{,x:rc(n) P}} \quad \text{(T-NextRCS)}$$

Context Splitting

$$\frac{\Gamma = \Gamma_1 \circ \Gamma_2 \qquad \texttt{n} = \texttt{i} + \texttt{j}}{\Gamma\texttt{, x:rc(n)P} = (\Gamma_1\texttt{, x:rc(i)P}) \circ (\Gamma_2\texttt{, x:rc(j)P})} \quad \text{(M-RC)}$$

(when `i` or `j` is 0, the corresponding binding is removed from the context)

Variable Typing

$$\frac{\texttt{un } (\Gamma_1,\Gamma_2)}{\Gamma_1\texttt{, x:rc(1)P, }\Gamma_2 \vdash \texttt{x : rc P}} \quad \text{(T-RCVar)}$$

Figure 1-18: Linear lambda calculus: Reference counting run-time typing

Syntax

The overall structure and mechanics of the ordered type system are very similar to the linear type system developed in previous sections. Figure 1-19 presents the syntax. One key change from our linear type system is that we have introduced an explicit sequencing operation `let x =` $\texttt{t}_1$ `in` $\texttt{t}_2$ that first evaluates the term $\texttt{t}_1$, binds the result to `x`, and then continues with the evaluation of $\texttt{t}_2$. This sequencing construct gives programmers explicit control over the order of evaluation of terms, which is crucial now that we are introducing data that must be used in a particular order. Terms that normally can contain multiple nested subexpressions such as pair introduction and function application are syntactically restricted so that their primary subterms are variables and the order of evaluation is clear.

The other main addition is a new qualifier `ord` that marks data allocated on the stack. We only allow pairs and values with base type to be stack-allocated; functions are allocated on the unordered heap. Therefore, we declare types `ord` $\texttt{T}_1 \to \texttt{T}_2$ and terms `ord λx:T.t` to be syntactically ill-formed.

Ordered assumptions are tracked in the type checking context Γ like other assumptions. However, they are not subject to the exchange property. Moreover, the order that they appear in Γ mirrors the order that they appear on the stack, with the rightmost position representing the stack's top.

Typing

The first step in the development of the type system is to determine how assumptions will be used. As before, unrestricted assumptions can be used

```
Syntax
q ::=                                  qualifiers:
      ord                              ordered
      lin                              linear
      un                               unrestricted

t ::=                                  terms:
      x                                variable
      q b                              Boolean
      if t then t else t               conditional
      q <x,y>                          pair
      split t as x,y in t              split
      q λx:T.t                         abstraction
      x y                              application
      let x = t in t                   sequencing

P ::=                                  pretypes:
      Bool                             booleans
      T*T                              pairs
      T→T                              functions

T ::=                                  types:
      q P                              qualified pretype

Γ ::=                                  contexts:
      ∅                                empty context
      Γ, x:T                           term variable binding
```

Figure 1-19: Ordered lambda calculus: Syntax

as often as the programmer likes but linear assumptions must be used exactly once along every control flow path. Ordered assumptions must be used exactly once along every control flow path,in the order in which they appear.

As before, the context splitting operator ($\Gamma = \Gamma_1 \circ \Gamma_2$) helps propagate assumptions properly, separating the context Γ into Γ_1 and Γ_2. Some sequence of ordered assumptions taken from the left-hand side of Γ are placed in Γ_1 and the remaining ordered assumptions are placed in Γ_2. Otherwise, the splitting operator works the same as before. In the typing rules, the context Γ_2 is used by the first subexpression to be evaluated (since the top of the stack is at the right) and Γ_1 is used by the second subexpression to be evaluated. Formally, we define the "=" relation in terms of two subsidiary relations: "$=_1$," which places ordered assumptions in Γ_1, and "$=_2$," which places ordered assumptions in Γ_2. See Figure 1-20.

The second step in the development of the type system is to determine the containment rules for ordered data structures. Previously, we saw that if an unrestricted object can contain a linear object, a programmer can write functions that duplicate or discard linear objects, thereby violating the central invariants of the system. A similar situation arises if linear or unrestricted objects can contain stack objects; in either case, the stack object might be used out of order, after it has been popped off the stack. The typing rules use the qualifier relation $q_1 \sqsubseteq q_2$, which specifies that `ord⊑lin⊑un`, to ensure such problems do not arise.

The typing rules for the ordered lambda calculus appear in Figure 1-21. For the most part, the containment rules and context splitting rules encapsulate

Context Split $\boxed{\Gamma = \Gamma_1 \circ \Gamma_2}$

$$\frac{\Gamma =_2 \Gamma_1 \circ \Gamma_2}{\Gamma = \Gamma_1 \circ \Gamma_2} \quad \text{(M-TOP)}$$

$$\varnothing =_1 \varnothing \circ \varnothing \quad \text{(M-EMPTY)}$$

$$\frac{\Gamma =_1 \Gamma_1 \circ \Gamma_2}{\Gamma, \mathtt{x:ord\ P} =_1 (\Gamma_1, \mathtt{x:ord\ P}) \circ \Gamma_2} \quad \text{(M-ORD1)}$$

$$\frac{\Gamma =_2 \Gamma_1 \circ \Gamma_2}{\Gamma, \mathtt{x:ord\ P} =_2 \Gamma_1 \circ (\Gamma_2, \mathtt{x:ord\ P})} \quad \text{(M-ORD2)}$$

$$\frac{\Gamma =_1 \Gamma_1 \circ \Gamma_2}{\Gamma =_2 \Gamma_1 \circ \Gamma_2} \quad \text{(M-1TO2)}$$

$$\frac{\Gamma =_{1,2} \Gamma_1 \circ \Gamma_2}{\Gamma, \mathtt{x:lin\ P} =_{1,2} (\Gamma_1, \mathtt{x:lin\ P}) \circ \Gamma_2} \quad \text{(M-LINA)}$$

$$\frac{\Gamma =_{1,2} \Gamma_1 \circ \Gamma_2}{\Gamma, \mathtt{x:lin\ P} =_{1,2} \Gamma_1 \circ (\Gamma_2, \mathtt{x:lin\ P})} \quad \text{(M-LINB)}$$

$$\frac{\Gamma =_{1,2} \Gamma_1 \circ \Gamma_2}{\Gamma, \mathtt{x:un\ P} =_{1,2} (\Gamma_1, \mathtt{x:un\ P}) \circ (\Gamma_2, \mathtt{x:un\ P})} \quad \text{(M-UN)}$$

Figure 1-20: Ordered lambda calculus: Context splitting

the tricky elements of the type system. The rules for pairs illustrate how this is done. The rule for introducing pairs (T-OPAIR) splits the incoming context into two parts, Γ_1 and Γ_2; any ordered assumptions in Γ_2 will represent data closer to the top of the stack than Γ_1. Therefore, if the pair (x) and its two components $\mathtt{x}_1$ and $\mathtt{x}_2$ are all allocated on the stack, then the pointer x will end up on top, $\mathtt{x}_2$ next and $\mathtt{x}_1$ on the bottom. The elimination rule for pairs (T-OSPLIT) is careful to maintain the proper ordering of the context. As above, the rule splits the context into Γ_1 and Γ_2, where Γ_2, which represents data on top of the stack, is used in a computation $\mathtt{t}_1$ that generates a pair. The context $\Gamma_1, \mathtt{x}_1\mathtt{:T}_1, \mathtt{x}_2\mathtt{:T}_2$ is used to check $\mathtt{t}_2$. Notice that if both components of the pair, $\mathtt{x}_1$ and $\mathtt{x}_2$, were allocated on the stack when the pair was introduced, they reappear back in the context in the appropriate order.

Consider the following function, taking a boolean and a pair allocated sequentially at the top of the stack. The boolean is at the very top of the stack and the integer pair is next (the top is to the right). If the boolean is true, it leaves the components of the pair (two unrestricted integers) in the same order as given; otherwise, it swaps them.

```
λx:ord (ord (int * int) * bool).
  split x as p,b in
  if b then
    p
  else
    split p as i1,i2 in
    ord <i2,i1>
```

Typing $\boxed{\Gamma \vdash \mathtt{t} : \mathtt{T}}$

$$\frac{\mathtt{un}\ (\Gamma_1,\Gamma_2)}{\Gamma_1, \mathtt{x}:\mathtt{T}, \Gamma_2 \vdash \mathtt{x} : \mathtt{T}} \quad \text{(T-OVAR)}$$

$$\frac{\mathtt{un}\ (\Gamma)}{\Gamma \vdash \mathtt{q\ b} : \mathtt{q\ Bool}} \quad \text{(T-OBOOL)}$$

$$\frac{\Gamma_2 \vdash \mathtt{t}_1 : \mathtt{q\ Bool} \qquad \Gamma_1 \vdash \mathtt{t}_2 : \mathtt{T} \qquad \Gamma_1 \vdash \mathtt{t}_3 : \mathtt{T}}{\Gamma_1 \circ \Gamma_2 \vdash \mathtt{if}\ \mathtt{t}_1\ \mathtt{then}\ \mathtt{t}_2\ \mathtt{else}\ \mathtt{t}_3 : \mathtt{T}} \quad \text{(T-OIF)}$$

$$\frac{\Gamma_1 \vdash \mathtt{x}_1 : \mathtt{T}_1 \qquad \Gamma_2 \vdash \mathtt{x}_2 : \mathtt{T}_2 \qquad \mathtt{q}(\mathtt{T}_1) \qquad \mathtt{q}(\mathtt{T}_2)}{\Gamma_1 \circ \Gamma_2 \vdash \mathtt{q} \mathtt{<x}_1\mathtt{,x}_2\mathtt{>} : \mathtt{q}\ (\mathtt{T}_1 * \mathtt{T}_2)} \quad \text{(T-OPAIR)}$$

$$\frac{\Gamma_2 \vdash \mathtt{t}_1 : \mathtt{q}\ (\mathtt{T}_1 * \mathtt{T}_2) \qquad \Gamma_1, \mathtt{x}_1:\mathtt{T}_1, \mathtt{x}_2:\mathtt{T}_2 \vdash \mathtt{t}_2 : \mathtt{T}}{\Gamma_1 \circ \Gamma_2 \vdash \mathtt{split}\ \mathtt{t}_1\ \mathtt{as}\ \mathtt{x}_1\mathtt{,x}_2\ \mathtt{in}\ \mathtt{t}_2 : \mathtt{T}} \quad \text{(T-OSPLIT)}$$

$$\frac{\mathtt{q}(\Gamma) \qquad \Gamma, \mathtt{x}:\mathtt{T}_1 \vdash \mathtt{t}_2 : \mathtt{T}_2}{\Gamma \vdash \mathtt{q}\ \lambda \mathtt{x}:\mathtt{T}_1\mathtt{.t}_2 : \mathtt{q}\ \mathtt{T}_1 \to \mathtt{T}_2} \quad \text{(T-OABS)}$$

$$\frac{\Gamma_1 \vdash \mathtt{x}_1 : \mathtt{q}\ \mathtt{T}_{11} \to \mathtt{T}_{12} \qquad \Gamma_2 \vdash \mathtt{x}_2 : \mathtt{T}_{11}}{\Gamma_1 \circ \Gamma_2 \vdash \mathtt{x}_1\ \mathtt{x}_2 : \mathtt{T}_{12}} \quad \text{(T-OAPP)}$$

$$\frac{\Gamma_2 \vdash \mathtt{t}_1 : \mathtt{T}_1 \qquad \Gamma_1, \mathtt{x}:\mathtt{T}_1 \vdash \mathtt{t}_2 : \mathtt{T}_2}{\Gamma_1 \circ \Gamma_2 \vdash \mathtt{let}\ \mathtt{x} = \mathtt{t}_1\ \mathtt{in}\ \mathtt{t}_2 : \mathtt{T}_2} \quad \text{(T-OLET)}$$

Figure 1-21: Ordered lambda calculus: Typing

Operational Semantics

To define the operational semantics for our new ordered type system, we will divide our previous stores into two parts, a heap H and a stack K. Both are just a list of bindings as stores were before (see Figure 1-22). We also define a couple of auxiliary functions. The first says what it means to add a binding to the store. This is straightforward: unrestricted and linear bindings are added to the heap and ordered bindings are added to the top of the stack.

$$\begin{aligned}
\mathtt{(H;K),x} \mapsto \mathtt{ord\ w} &= \mathtt{(H;K,x} \mapsto \mathtt{ord\ w)} \\
\mathtt{(H;K),x} \mapsto \mathtt{lin\ w} &= \mathtt{(H,x} \mapsto \mathtt{lin\ w;K)} \\
\mathtt{(H;K),x} \mapsto \mathtt{un\ w} &= \mathtt{(H,x} \mapsto \mathtt{un\ w;K)}
\end{aligned}$$

The second function specifies how to remove a binding from the store. Notice that ordered deallocation will only remove the object at the top of the stack.

$$\begin{aligned}
\mathtt{(H;K,x} \mapsto \mathtt{v)} \overset{\mathtt{ord}}{\sim} \mathtt{x} &= \mathtt{H;K} \\
\mathtt{(H_1,x} \mapsto \mathtt{v,H_2;K)} \overset{\mathtt{lin}}{\sim} \mathtt{x} &= \mathtt{H_1,H_2;K} \\
\mathtt{(H;K)} \overset{\mathtt{un}}{\sim} \mathtt{x} &= \mathtt{H;K}
\end{aligned}$$

With these simple changes, the evaluation rules from previous sections can be reused essentially unchanged. However, we do need to add the evaluation context for sequencing (let x = E in t) and its evaluation rule:

$$\mathtt{(S;let\ x = x_1\ in\ t_2)} \longrightarrow_\beta \mathtt{(S;[x} \mapsto \mathtt{x_1]t_1)} \qquad \text{(E-LET)}$$

S ::=		*stores:*
	H;K	*complete store*
H ::=		*heap:*
	∅	*empty heap*
	H, x ↦ lin w	*linear heap binding*
	H, x ↦ un w	*unrestricted heap binding*

K ::=		*stack:*
	∅	*empty stack*
	K, x ↦ ord w	*stack binding*

Figure 1-22: Ordered lambda calculus: Operational semantics

1.4.1 EXERCISE [RECOMMENDED, ★]: Write a program that demonstrates what can happen if the syntax of pair formation is changed to allow programmers to write nested subexpressions (i.e., we allow the term ord <t_1,t_2> rather than the term ord <x,y>). □

1.4.2 EXERCISE [RECOMMENDED, ★★]: Demonstrate the problem with allowing ordered functions (i.e., admitting the syntax ord λx:T_1.t and ord $T_1 \to T_2$) by writing a well-typed program that uses ordered functions and gets stuck. □

1.4.3 EXERCISE [★★★]: Modify the language so that programmers can use stack-allocated, ordered functions. There are many solutions to this problem, some more sophisticated than others. □

1.5 Further Applications

Memory management applications make good motivation for substructural type systems and provides a concrete framework for studying their properties. However, substructural types systems, and their power to control the number and order of uses of data and operations, have found many applications outside of this domain. In the following paragraphs, we informally discuss a few of them.

Controlling Temporal Resources

We have studied several ways that substructural type systems can be used to control physical resources such as memory and files. What about controlling the temporal resources? Amazingly, substructural type systems can play a role here as well: Careful crafting of a language with an *affine* type system, where values are used at most once, can ensure that computations execute in polynomial time.

To begin, we will allow our polynomial time language to contain affine booleans, pairs and (non-recursive) functions. In addition, to make things interesting, we will add affine lists to our language, which have constructors `nil` and `cons` and a special iterator to recurse over objects with list type. Such iterators have the following form.

```
iter (stop ⇒ t1 | x with y ⇒ t2)
```

If t_1 has type T and t_2 also has type T (under the assumption that x has type T_1 and y has type T_1 `list`), our iterator defines a function from T_1 lists to objects with type T. Operationally, the iterator does a case to see whether its input list is `nil` or `cons(hd,tl)` and executes the corresponding branch. We can define the operation of iterators using two simple rules.[1]

$$\texttt{iter (stop} \Rightarrow t_1 \mid \texttt{hd with rest} \Rightarrow t_2\texttt{) nil} \longrightarrow_\beta t_1 \qquad \text{(E-ITERNIL)}$$

$$\frac{\texttt{iter (stop} \Rightarrow t_1 \mid \texttt{hd with rest} \Rightarrow t_2\texttt{)}\ v_2 \longrightarrow_\beta^* v_2'}{\begin{array}{c}\texttt{iter (stop} \Rightarrow t_1 \mid \texttt{hd with rest} \Rightarrow t_2\texttt{) cons(}v_1\texttt{,}v_2\texttt{)} \longrightarrow_\beta \\ \texttt{[hd} \mapsto v_1\texttt{][rest} \mapsto v_2'\texttt{]}t_2\end{array}} \qquad \text{(E-ITERCONS)}$$

In the second rule, the iterator is invoked inductively on v_2, giving the result v_2', which is used in term t_2. The familar append function below illustrates the use of iterators.

```
val append : T list→T list→T list =
  iter (
    stop ⇒ λ(l:T list).l
  | hd with rest ⇒ λ(l:T list).cons(hd,rest l))
```

When applied to a list l_1, append builds up a function that expects a second list l_2 and concatenates l_2 to the end of l_1. Clearly, append is a polynomial time function, a linear-time one in fact, but it is straightforward to write exponential time algorithms in the language as we have defined it so far. For instance:

```
val double : T list→T list =
  iter (stop ⇒ nil | hd with rest ⇒ cons(hd,cons(hd,rest)))

val exp : T list→T list =
  iter (stop ⇒ nil | hd with rest ⇒ double (cons(hd,rest)))
```

1. Since we are not interested in memory management here, we have simplified our operational semantics from previous parts of this chapter by deleting the explicit store and using substitution instead. The operational judgment has the form $t \longrightarrow_\beta t'$ and, in general, is defined similarly to the operational systems in *TAPL*.

The key problem here is that it is trivial to write iterators like double that increase the size of their arguments. After constructing one of these, we can use it as the inner loop of another, like exp, and cause an exponential blow-up in running time. But this is not the only problem. Higher-order functions make it even easier to construct exponential-time algorithms:

```
val compose =
  λ(fg:(T list→T list) * (T list→T list)).
    λ(x:T list).
      split fg as f,g in f (g x)

val junk : T

val exp2 : T list→T list→T list =
  iter (
    stop ⇒ λ(l:T list).cons(junk,l)
  | hd with rest ⇒ λ(l:T list).compose <rest,rest> l)
```

Fortunately, a substructural type system can be used to eliminate both problems by allowing us to define a class of *non-size-increasing* functions and by preventing the construction of troublesome higher-order functions, such as exp_2.

The first step is to demand that all user-defined objects have affine type. They can be used zero or one times, but not more. This restriction immediately rules out programs such as exp_2. System defined operators like cons can be used many times.

The next step is to put mechanisms in place to prevent iterators from increasing the size of their inputs. This can be achieved by altering the cons constructor so that it can only be applied when it has access to a special resource with type R.

```
operator cons : (R,T,T list) → T list
```

There is no constructor for resources with type R so they cannot be generated out of thin air; we can only apply fcons as many times as we have resources. We also adapt the syntax for iterators as follows.

```
iter (stop ⇒ t1 | hd with tl and r ⇒ t2)
```

Inside the second clause of the iterator, we are only granted a single resource (r) with which to allocate data. Consequently, we can allocate at most one cons cell in t_2. This provides us with the power to rebuild a list of the same size, but we cannot write a function such as double that doubles the length of the list or exp that causes an exponential increase in size. To ensure that a single resource from an outer scope does not percolate inside the iterator and get reused on each iteration of the loop, we require that iterators be closed, mirroring the containment rules for recursive functions defined in earlier sections of this chapter.

Although restricted to polynomial time, our language permits us to write many useful functions in a convenient fashion. For instance, we can still write append much like we did before. The resource we acquire from destructing the list during iteration can be used to rebuild the list later.

```
val append : T list → T list → T list =
  iter (
    stop ⇒ λ(l:T list).l
  | hd with rest and r ⇒ λ(l:T list). cons(r,hd,rest l))
```

We can also write `double` if our input list comes with appropriate credits, in the form of unused resources.

```
val double : (T*R) list → T list =
  iter (
    stop ⇒ nil
  | hd with rest and r1 ⇒
     split hd as x,r2 in cons(r1,hd,cons(r2,hd,rest)))
```

Fortunately, we will never be able to write `exp`, unless, of course, we are given an exponential number of credits in the size of the input list. In that case, our function `exp` would still only run in linear time with respect to our overall input (list and resources included).

The proof that all (first-order) functions we can define in this language run in polynomial time uses some substantial domain theory that lies outside the scope of this book. However, the avid reader should see Section 1.6 for references to the literature where these proofs can be found.

Compiler Optimizations

Many compiler optimizations are enabled when we know that there will be *at most one use* or *at least one use* of a function, expression or data structure. If there is at most one use of an object then we say that object has *affine* type. If there is at least one use then we say the object has *relevant* (or *strict*) type. The following sorts of optimizations employ usage information directly; several of them have been implemented in the Glasgow Haskell Compiler.

- *Floating in bindings.* Consider the expression `let x = e in (λy....x...)`. Is it a good idea to float the binding inside the lambda and create the new expression `λy.let x = e in (...x...)`? The answer depends in part on how many times the resulting function is used. If it is used at most once, the optimization might be a good one: we may avoid computing e and will never compute it more than once.

- *Inlining expressions.* In the example above, if we have the further information that x itself is used at most once inside the body of the function, then we might want to substitute the expression e for x. This may give rise to further local optimizations at the site where e is used. Moreover, if it turns out that e is used zero times (as opposed to one time) we will have saved ourselves the trouble of computing it.
- *Thunk update avoidance.* In lazy functional languages such as Haskell, evaluation of function parameters is delayed until the parameter is actually used in the function body. In order to avoid recomputing the value of the parameter each time it is used, implementers make each parameter a *thunk*—a reference that may either hold the computation that needs to be run or the value itself. The first time the thunk is used, the computation will be run and will produce the necessary result. In general, this result is stored back in the thunk for all future uses of the parameter. However, if the compiler can determine that the data structure is used as most once, this thunk update can be avoided.
- *Eagerness.* If we can tell that a Haskell expression is used at least once, then we can evaluate it right away and avoid creating a thunk altogether.

The optimizations described above may be implemented in two phases. The first phase is a program analysis that may be implemented as affine and/or relevant type inference. After the analysis phase, the compiler uses the information to transform programs. Formulating compiler optimizations as type inference followed by type-directed translation has a number of advantages over other techniques. First, the language of types can be used to communicate optimization information across modular boundaries. This can facilitate the process of scaling intra-procedural optimizations to inter-procedural optimizations. Second, the type information derived in one optimization pass can be maintained and propagated to future optimization passes or into the back end of the compiler where it can be used to generate Typed Assembly Language or Proof-Carrying Code, as discussed in Chapters 4 and 5.

1.6 Notes

Substructural logics are very old, dating back to at least Orlov (1928), who axiomatized the implicational fragment of relevant logic. Somewhat later, Moh

(1950) and Church (1951) provided alternative axiomatizations of the relevant logic now known as R. In the same time period, Church was developing his theory of the lambda calculus at Princeton University, and his λI calculus (1941), which disallowed abstraction over variables that did not appear free in the body of the term, was the first substructural lambda calculus. Lambek (1958) introduced the first "ordered logic," and used it to reason about natural language sentence structure. More recently, Girard (1987) developed linear logic, which gives control over both contraction and weakening, and yet provides the full power of intuitionistic logic through the unrestricted modality "!". O'Hearn and Pym (1999) show that the logic of bunched implications provides another way to recapture the power of intuitionistic logic while giving control over the structural rules.

For a comprehensive account of the history of substructural logics, please see Došen (1993), who is credited with coining the phrase "substructural logic," or Restall (2005). Restall's textbook on substructural logics (2000) provides good starting point to those looking to study the technical details of either the proof theory or model theory for these logics.

Reynolds pioneered the study of substructural type systems for programming languages with his development of syntactic control of interference (1978; 1989), which prevents two references from being bound to the same variable and thereby facilitates reasoning about Algol programs. Later, Girard's development of linear logic inspired many researchers to develop functional languages with linear types. One of the main applications of these new type systems was to control effects and enable in-place update of arrays in pure functional languages.

Lafont (1988) was the one of the first to study programming languages with linear types, developing a linear abstract machine. He was soon followed by many other researchers, including Baker (1992) who informally showed how to compile Lisp into a linear assembly language in which all allocation, deallocation and pointer manipulation is completely explicit, yet safe. Another influential piece of work is due to Chirimar, Gunter, and Riecke (1996) who developed an interpretation of linear logic based on reference counting. The reference counting scheme described here is directly inspired by the work of Chirimar et al., but the technical setup is slightly different; we have explicit operations to increment and decrement reference counts whereas incrementing and decrementing counts in Chirimar's system is done implicitly. Stephanie Weirich suggested the invariant for proving our reference counting system sound. Turner and Wadler (1999) summarize two computational interpretations that arise directly through the Curry-Howard isomorphism from Girard's linear logic. They differ from the account given in this chapter as neither account has both shared, usable data structures and deallocation. Unfortunately, these two features together appear incompatible with a type system derived directly from linear logic and its single unrestricted modality.

The development of practical linear type systems with two classes of type, one linear and one unrestricted, began with Wadler's work (1990) in the early nineties. The presentation given in this chapter is derived from Wadler's work and is also inspired by work from Wansbrough and Peyton Jones (1999) and Walker and Watkins (2001). Wansbrough and Peyton Jones included qualifier subtyping and bounded parametric polymorphism in their system in addition to many of the features described here. Walker and Watkins added reference counting features to a language with linear types and also memory regions. The idea of formulating the system with a generic context splitting operator was taken from Cervesato and Pfenning's presentation of Linear LF (2002).

The algorithmic type system described in section 1-5 solves what is commonly known in the linear logic programming and theorem proving literature, as the *resource management problem*. Many of the ideas for the current presentation came from work by Cervesato, Hodas, and Pfenning (2000), who solve the more general problem that arises when linear logic's additive connectives are considered. Hofmann takes a related approach when solving the type inference problem for a linearly-typed functional language (1997a).

The ordered type system developed here is derived from Polakow and Pfenning's ordered logic (1999), in the same way that the practical linear type systems mentioned above emerged from linear logic. It was also inspired by the ordered lambda calculus of Petersen, Harper, Crary, and Pfenning (2003), though there are some technical differences. Ahmed and Walker (2003) and Ahmed, Jia, and Walker (2003) use an ordered, modal logic to specify memory invariants and have integrated the logical specifications into a low-level typed language. Igarashi and Kobayashi (2002) have used ordered types to explore the more general problem of resource usage analysis. In addition, they have developed effective type inference algorithms for their type systems.

Recently, O'Hearn (2003) has proposed *bunched typing*, a new form of substructural typing, to control interference between mutable variables, generalizing Reynolds's earlier work on syntactic control of interference. These bunched types were derived from earlier work by O'Hearn and Pym (1999) on bunched logic. Together, Reynolds, Ishtiaq, and O'Hearn (Reynolds, 2000; Ishtiaq and O'Hearn, 2001) have used bunched logic to develop a system for verifying programs that explicitly allocate and deallocate data.

Analysis and reasoning about the time and space complexity of programs has always been an important part of computer science. However, the use of programming language technology, and type systems in particular, to automatically constrain the complexity of programs is somewhat more recent. For instance, Bellantoni and Cook (1992) and Leivant (1993) developed predicative systems that control the use and complexity of recursive functions.

It is possible to write all, and only, the polynomial-time functions in their system. However, it is not generally possible to compose functions and therefore many "obviously" polynomial-time algorithms cannot be coded naturally in their system. Girard (1998), Hofmann (2000; 1999), and Bellantoni, Niggl, and Schwichtenberg (2000) show how linear type systems can be used to alleviate some of these difficulties. The material presented in this chapter is derived from Hofmann's work.

One of the most successful and extensive applications of substructural type systems in programming practice can be found in the Concurrent Clean programming language (Nöcker, Smetsers, van Eekelen, and Plasmeijer, 1991). Clean is a commercially developed, pure functional programming language. It uses *uniqueness types* (Barendsen and Smetsers, 1993), which are a variant of linear types, and strictness annotations (Nöcker and Smetsers, 1993) to help support concurrency, I/O and in-place update of arrays. The implementation is fast and is fully supported by a wide range of program development tools including an Integrated Development Environment for project management and GUI libraries, all developed in Clean itself.

Substructural type systems have also found gainful employment in the intermediate languages of the Glasgow Haskell Compiler. For instance, Turner, Wadler, and Mossin (1995) and Wansbrough and Peyton Jones (1999) showed how to use affine types and affine type inference to optimize programs as discussed earlier in this chapter. They also use extensive strictness analysis to avoid thunk creation.

Recently, researchers have begun to investigate ways to combine substructural type systems with dependent types and effect systems such as those described in Chapters 2 and 3. The combination of both dependent and substructural types provides a very powerful tool for enforcing safe memory management and more general resource-usage protocols. For instance, DeLine and Fähndrich developed Vault (2001; 2002), a programming language that uses static capabilities (Walker, Crary, and Morrisett, 2000) (a hybrid form of linear types and effects) to enforce a variety of invariants in Microsoft Windows device drivers including locking protocols, memory management protocols and others. Cyclone (Jim et al., 2002; Grossman et al., 2002), a completely type-safe substitute for C, also uses linear types and effects to grant programmers fine-grained control over memory allocation and deallocation. In each of these cases, the authors do not stick to the pure linear types described here. Instead, they add coercions to the language to allow linearly-typed objects to be temporarily aliased in certain contexts, following a long line of research on this topic (Wadler, 1990; Odersky, 1992; Kobayashi, 1999; Smith, Walker, and Morrisett, 2000; Aspinall and Hofmann, 2002; Foster, Terauchi, and Aiken, 2002; Aiken, Foster, Kodumal, and Terauchi, 2003).

2 Dependent Types

David Aspinall and Martin Hofmann

In the most general sense, dependent types are type-valued functions. This definition includes, for example, the type operators of F^{ω} such as `Pair`. When applied to two types `S` and `T`, this yields the type `Pair S T` whose elements are pairs `(s,t)` of elements `s` from `S` and `t` from `T` (see *TAPL*, Chapter 29). However, the terminology "dependent types" is usually used to indicate a particular class of type-valued functions: those functions which send *terms* to types. In this chapter we study this kind of dependency.

2.1 Motivations

We begin the chapter by looking at a few representative examples of where type-term dependency occurs naturally.

Programming with Vectors and Format Strings

The prototypical example of programming with dependent types is introduced by the *type family* of vectors (one-dimensional arrays):

```
Vector :: Nat → *
```

This kinding assertion states that `Vector` maps a natural number `k:Nat` to a type. The idea is that the type `Vector k` contains vectors of length `k` of elements of some fixed type, say `data`.

To use vectors, we need a way of introducing them. A useful initialization function takes a length `n`, a value `t` of type `data`, and returns a vector with `n`

The system studied in this chapter is the dependently typed lambda-calculus, λLF (Figures 2-1, 2-2), extended with Σ-types (Figure 2-5) and the Calculus of Constructions (Figure 2-7). The associated OCaml implementation, called `deptypes`, can be found on the book's web site.

elements all set to t. The typing of such an init function is written like this,

init : Πn:Nat. data → Vector n

and the application init k t has type Vector k.

The type of init introduces the *dependent product type* (or "Pi type"), written Πx:S.T. This type generalizes the arrow type of the simply typed lambda-calculus. It is the type of functions which map elements s:S to elements of [x ↦ s]T. In contrast to the simply-typed case, the result type of a function with a Π-type can vary according to the argument supplied. According to Seldin (2002), the Π-type goes back to Curry and is thus almost as old as the lambda calculus itself.

A more interesting way of building up vectors is given by the constant empty vector empty : Vector 0 and a constructor for building longer vectors:

cons : Πn:Nat. data → Vector n → Vector (n+1).

The typing of cons expresses that cons takes three arguments: a natural number n, an element of type data, and a vector of length n. The result is a vector of length n+1. This means that, for example, if v : Vector 5 and x : data, then cons 5 x v : Vector 6.

The dependent product type Πx:S.T is somewhat analogous to the universal type ∀X.T of System F. The type of a term t with type ∀X.T also varies with the argument supplied; but in the case of a type abstraction, the argument is a type rather than a term. If A is a type, then t A:[X ↦ A]T. In System F (and F^{ω}), type variation occurs only with type arguments, whereas in dependent type theory it may occur with term-level arguments.

The reader familiar with programming with ordinary arrays will have realized that by using a type of arrays instead of vectors we could avoid dependent typing. The initialization function for one-dimensional arrays could be given the simple type Nat → data → Array, where Array is the type of arrays with entries of type data. The point of the dependent typing is that it reveals more information about the behavior of a term, which can be exploited to give more precise typings and exclude more of the badly behaved terms in a type system. For example, with the dependent type of vectors, we can type a function that returns the first element of a non-empty vector:

first : Πn:Nat.Vector(n+1) → data

The function first can never be applied to an empty vector—non-emptiness is expressed within the type system itself! This is a useful gain. With ordinary arrays instead of dependently-typed vectors, we would need some special way to deal with the case when first is applied to the empty array. We could return an ad-hoc default element, or we might use a language-based exception mechanism to indicate the error. Either mechanism is more clumsy than simply prohibiting illegal applications of `first` from being written.

We suggested that `Πx:S.T` generalizes the function space `S→T` of simply typed lambda calculus. In fact, we can treat `S→T` simply as an abbreviation:

`S→T` = `Πx:S.T` *where* `x` *does not appear free in* `T`

For example, `Πx:Nat.Nat` is exactly equivalent to `Nat → Nat`. We will continue to write the arrow → whenever possible, to increase readability.

Another favorite example of a function with a useful dependent typing is `sprintf` of the C language.[1] Recall that `sprintf` accepts a format string and list of arguments whose types must correspond to the declarations made in the format string. It then converts the given arguments into a string and returns it. A simplified form of `sprintf` might have the typing:

```
sprintf : Πf:Format. Data(f) → String
```

where we suppose that `Format` is a type of valid print formats (for example, considered as character lists) and that `Data(f)` is the type of data corresponding to format `f`. The function `Data(f)` evaluates the type that the format string describes, which might include clauses like these:

```
Data([])         =  Unit
Data("%d"::cs)   =  Nat * Data(cs)
Data("%s"::cs)   =  String * Data(cs)
Data(c::cs)      =  Data(cs)
```

This example is rather different to the case of vectors. Vectors are uniform: we introduce operations that are parametric in the length `n`, and the family of types `Vector n` is indexed by `n`. In the case of format strings, we use case analysis over values to construct the type `Data(f)` which depends on `f` in an arbitrary way. Unsurprisingly, this non-uniform kind of dependent type is more challenging to deal with in practical type systems for programming.

2.1.1 EXERCISE [★]: Suggest some dependent typings for familiar data types and their operations. For example, consider matrices of size `n * m` and the typing of matrix multiplication, and a type of dates where the range of the day is restricted according to the month. □

1. A `sprintf`-like formating function can also be typed in ML without dependent types if formats are represented as appropriate higher-order functions rather than strings. For details see Danvy (1998).

The Curry-Howard Correspondence

A rather different source for dependent typing is the Curry-Howard correspondence, also known by the slogan *propositions-as-types* (Howard, 1980). Under this correspondence simple types correspond to propositions in the implicational fragment of constructive logic. A formula has a proof if and only if the corresponding type is inhabited. For instance, the formula

$$((A \to B) \to A) \to (A \to B) \to B$$

is valid in constructive logic and at the same time is inhabited, namely by $\lambda f.\lambda u.u(f\ u)$. The underlying philosophical idea behind this correspondence is that a constructive proof of an implication $A \implies B$ ought to be understood as a procedure that transforms any given proof of A into a proof of B.

If propositions are types, then proofs are terms. We can introduce a type constructor Prf which maps a formula A (understood as a type) into the type of its proofs Prf A, and then a proof of $A \implies B$ becomes a λ-term of type $\text{Prf}\ A \to \text{Prf}\ B$. Often the type constructor Prf is omitted, notationally identifying a proposition with the type of its proofs. In that case, a proof of $A \implies B$ is simply any term of type $A \to B$.

Generalizing the correspondence to first-order predicate logic naturally leads to dependent types: a predicate B over type A is viewed as a type-valued function on A; a proof of the universal quantification $\forall x{:}A.B(x)$ is—constructively—a procedure that given an arbitrary element x of type A produces a proof of $B(x)$. Hence under the Curry-Howard correspondence we should identify universal quantification with dependent product: a proof of $\forall x{:}A.B(x)$ is a member of $\Pi x{:}A.B(x)$. Indeed, Per Martin-Löf, one of the protagonists of dependent typing (1984), was motivated by this extension. In particular, he introduced type-theoretic equivalents to existential quantification (Σ-types) and equality (identity types), used in the next example.

An important application of the Curry-Howard correspondence is that it allows one to freely mix propositions and (programming language) types. For example, an indexing function ith(n) to access elements of vectors of length n could be given the type

$$\Pi n{:}\text{Nat}.\Pi l{:}\text{Nat}.\text{Lt}(l,n) \to \text{Vector}(n) \to T$$

where $\text{Lt}(l,n)$ is the proposition asserting that l is less than n. Perhaps more interestingly, we can package up types with axioms restricting their elements. For instance, the type of binary, associative operations on some type T may be given as

$$\Sigma m{:}T \to T \to T.\Pi x{:}T.\Pi y{:}T.\Pi z{:}T.\text{Id}\ (m(x,m(y,z)))\ (m(m(x,y),z))$$

Here Σx:A.B(x) is the type of pairs (a,b) where a:A and b:B(a) and Id t_1 t_2 is the type of proofs of the equality t_1=t_2. In Martin-Löf's type theory existential quantification is rendered with Σ-types, the idea being that a constructive proof of $\exists$x:A.B(x) would consist of a member a of type A and a proof, thus a member, of B(a)—in other words, an element of Σa:A.B(a).

2.1.2 EXERCISE [★]: Write down a type which represents a constructive version of the axiom of choice, characterised by: *if for every element* a *of a type* A *there exists an element* b *of* B *such that* P(a,b) *then there exists a function* f *mapping an arbitrary* x:A *to an element of* B *such that* P(x, f x). □

2.1.3 EXERCISE [★]: Suppose that f : A→C, g : B→C are two functions with equal target domain. Using set-theoretic notation we can form their *pullback* as $\{(a,b) \in A \times B \mid f\,a = g\,b\}$. Define an analogous type using Σ and Id. □

Logical Frameworks

Dependent types have also found application in the representation of other type theories and formal systems. Suppose that we have an implementation of dependent types and want to get a rough-and-ready typechecker for simply typed lambda calculus. We may then make the following declarations:

```
Ty    :: *
Tm    :: Ty → *
base  : Ty
arrow : Ty → Ty → Ty
app   : ΠA:Ty.ΠB:Ty.Tm(arrow A B) → Tm A →Tm B
lam   : ΠA:Ty.ΠB:Ty.(Tm A → Tm B) → Tm(arrow A B)
```

Here Ty represents the type of simple type expressions and for A:Ty the type Tm A represents the type of lambda terms of type A. We have a constant base:Ty representing the base type and a function arrow representing the formation of arrow types. As for terms we have a function app that accepts to types A,B, a term of type arrow A B, a term of type A and yields a term of type B: the application of the two.

Somewhat intriguingly, the function corresponding to lambda abstraction takes a "function" mapping terms of type A to terms of type B and returns a term of type arrow A B. This way of using functions at one level to represent dependencies at another level is particularly useful for representing syntax with binders, and the technique is known as *higher-order abstract syntax.*

We can now represent familiar terms such as the identity on A:Ty by

```
idA = lam A A (λx:Tm A.x)
```

or the Church numeral 2 on type A by

```
two = λA:Ty.lam A (arrow (arrow A A) A)
          (λx:Tm A.lam _ _ (λf:Tm(arrow A A).
                 app _ _ f (app _ _ f x)))
```

(replacing some obvious type arguments by underscores to aid readability).

Logical frameworks are systems which provide mechanisms for representing syntax and proof systems which make up a logic. The exact representation mechanisms depend upon the framework, but one approach exemplified in the Edinburgh Logical Framework (Harper, Honsell, and Plotkin, 1993) is suggested by the slogan *judgments-as-types*, where types are used to capture the judgments of a logic.[2]

2.1.4 EXERCISE [★]: Write down some typing declarations which introduce a judgment expressing an evaluation relation for the representation of simply typed terms shown above. You should begin with a type family `Eval` which is parameterized on a simple type `A` and two terms of type `Tm A`, and declare four terms which represent the rules defining the compatible closure of one-step beta-reduction. □

2.2 Pure First-Order Dependent Types

In this section we introduce one of the simplest systems of dependent types, in a presentation called λLF. As the name suggests, this type system is based on a simplified variant of the type system underlying the Edinburgh LF, mentioned above. The λLF type theory generalizes simply typed lambda-calculus by replacing the arrow type $S \to T$ with the dependent product type $\Pi x{:}S.T$ and by introducing type families. It is pure, in the sense that it has only Π-types; it is first-order, in the sense that it does not include higher-order type operators like those of F^{ω}. Under the Curry-Howard correspondence, this system corresponds to the ∀, →-fragment of first-order predicate calculus.

Syntax

The main definition of λLF appears in Figure 2-1 and 2-2. The terms are the same as those of the simply typed lambda calculus $\lambda_{\to}$. The types include type variables X which can be declared in the context but never appear bound. Type variables range over proper types as well as type familes such as

2. Judgments are the statements of a logic or a type system. For example, well-formedness, derivability, well-typedness. In LF these judgments are represented as types and derivations of a judgment are represented as members.

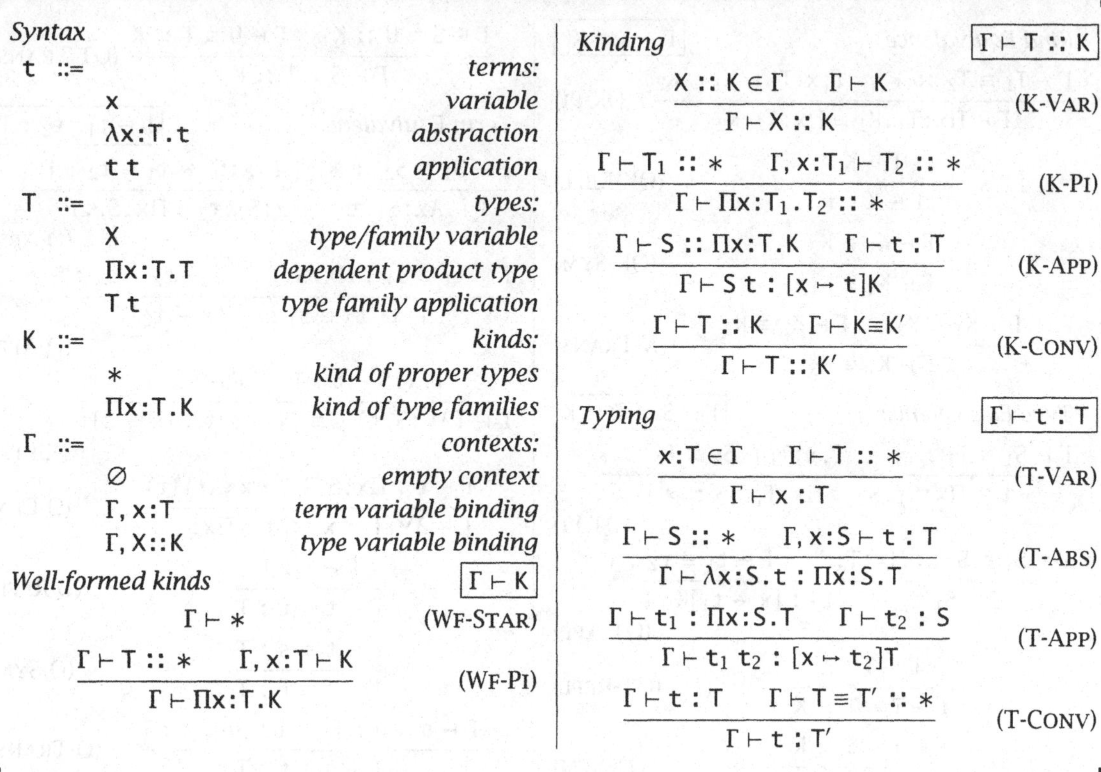

Figure 2-1: First-order dependent types (λLF)

Vector :: Nat → *. We may use type and term variables declared in a fixed initial context to simulate the built-in types and operators of a programming language.[3] Apart from variables, types may be dependent products or type family applications. The latter allow us to instantiate families, for example, to give types such as Vector k for k:Nat.

Kinds allow us to distinguish between proper types and type families. Proper types have kind $*$ while type families have dependent product kinds of the form Πx:T.K.

Contexts may bind term variables and type variables.

3. Strictly speaking, we should consider a *signature* as a special form of context and consider the term and type variables declared in it to be the constants of the language. This isn't necessary when we move to richer type theories in which it is possible to define data types.

λLF

Kind Equivalence $\boxed{\Gamma \vdash K \equiv K'}$

$$\frac{\Gamma \vdash T_1 \equiv T_2 :: * \qquad \Gamma, x{:}T_1 \vdash K_1 \equiv K_2}{\Gamma \vdash \Pi x{:}T_1.K_1 \equiv \Pi x{:}T_2.K_2} \quad \text{(QK-PI)}$$

$$\frac{\Gamma \vdash K}{\Gamma \vdash K \equiv K} \quad \text{(QK-REFL)}$$

$$\frac{\Gamma \vdash K_1 \equiv K_2}{\Gamma \vdash K_2 \equiv K_1} \quad \text{(QK-SYM)}$$

$$\frac{\Gamma \vdash K_1 \equiv K_2 \qquad \Gamma \vdash K_2 \equiv K_3}{\Gamma \vdash K_1 \equiv K_3} \quad \text{(QK-TRANS)}$$

Type Equivalence $\boxed{\Gamma \vdash S \equiv T :: K}$

$$\frac{\Gamma \vdash S_1 \equiv T_1 :: * \qquad \Gamma, x{:}T_1 \vdash S_2 \equiv T_2 :: *}{\Gamma \vdash \Pi x{:}S_1.S_2 \equiv \Pi x{:}T_1.T_2 :: *} \quad \text{(QT-PI)}$$

$$\frac{\Gamma \vdash S_1 \equiv S_2 :: \Pi x{:}T.K \qquad \Gamma \vdash t_1 \equiv t_2 : T}{\Gamma \vdash S_1\ t_1 \equiv S_2\ t_2 : [x \mapsto t_1]K} \quad \text{(QT-APP)}$$

$$\frac{\Gamma \vdash T : K}{\Gamma \vdash T \equiv T :: K} \quad \text{(QT-REFL)}$$

$$\frac{\Gamma \vdash T \equiv S :: K}{\Gamma \vdash S \equiv T :: K} \quad \text{(QT-SYM)}$$

$$\frac{\Gamma \vdash S \equiv U :: K \qquad \Gamma \vdash U \equiv T :: K}{\Gamma \vdash S \equiv T :: K} \quad \text{(QT-TRANS)}$$

Term Equivalence $\boxed{\Gamma \vdash t_1 \equiv t_2 : T}$

$$\frac{\Gamma \vdash S_1 \equiv S_2 :: * \qquad \Gamma, x{:}S_1 \vdash t_1 \equiv t_2 : T}{\Gamma \vdash \lambda x{:}S_1.t_1 \equiv \lambda x{:}S_2.t_2 : \Pi x{:}S_1.T} \quad \text{(Q-ABS)}$$

$$\frac{\Gamma \vdash t_1 \equiv s_1 : \Pi x{:}S.T \qquad \Gamma \vdash t_2 \equiv s_2 : S}{\Gamma \vdash t_1\ t_2 \equiv s_1\ s_2 : [x \mapsto t_2]T} \quad \text{(Q-APP)}$$

$$\frac{\Gamma, x{:}S \vdash t : T \qquad \Gamma \vdash s : S}{\Gamma \vdash (\lambda x{:}S.t)\ s \equiv [x \mapsto s]t : [x \mapsto s]T} \quad \text{(Q-BETA)}$$

$$\frac{\Gamma \vdash t : \Pi x{:}S.T \qquad x \notin FV(t)}{\Gamma \vdash \lambda x{:}T.t\,x \equiv t : \Pi x{:}S.T} \quad \text{(Q-ETA)}$$

$$\frac{\Gamma \vdash t : T}{\Gamma \vdash t \equiv t : T} \quad \text{(Q-REFL)}$$

$$\frac{\Gamma \vdash t \equiv s : T}{\Gamma \vdash s \equiv t : T} \quad \text{(Q-SYM)}$$

$$\frac{\Gamma \vdash s \equiv u : T \qquad \Gamma \vdash u \equiv t : T}{\Gamma \vdash s \equiv t : T} \quad \text{(Q-TRANS)}$$

Figure 2-2: First-order dependent types (λLF)—Equivalence rules

Typechecking Rules

The rules in Figure 2-1 define three judgment forms, for checking kind formation, kinding, and typing.

The characteristic typing rules of the system are the abstraction and application rules for terms, altered to use Π-types. The abstraction introduces a dependent product type, checking that the domain type S is well-formed:

$$\frac{\Gamma \vdash S :: * \qquad \Gamma, x{:}S \vdash t : T}{\Gamma \vdash \lambda x{:}S.t : \Pi x{:}S.T} \quad \text{(T-ABS)}$$

The term application rule eliminates a term with this type, substituting the operand in the Π-type:

$$\frac{\Gamma \vdash t_1 : \Pi x{:}S.T \qquad \Gamma \vdash t_2 : S}{\Gamma \vdash t_1\ t_2 : [x \mapsto t_2]T} \quad \text{(T-APP)}$$

The well-formedness check in T-ABS uses the kinding rules to ensure that S is a type. Notice that this check may again invoke the typing rules, in the rule K-APP, which checks the instantiation of a type family. The kind formation judgment also invokes the well-formedness of types (in the first premise of WF-PI), so the three judgment forms are in fact mutually defined. One consequence is that proofs of properties in this system typically proceed by simultaneous proofs for the different judgment forms, using derivation height as an overall measure or alternatively simultaneous structural induction.

There are two conversion rules, K-CONV and T-CONV, which allow us to replace a kind or type with another one that is equivalent.

Kinds have the general form $\Pi x_1 : T_1 . \ldots x_n : T_n . *$ but in the typing rules we only ever need to check for proper types with kind $*$. Nevertheless, we include the K-CONV to ensure that kinding is closed under conversion within the T_i. There is no mechanism for forming kinds by abstraction, so the only way to construct an object of a kind other than $*$ is by declaring it in the context.

Equivalence Rules

One of the main questions in any type system is when two types should be considered equivalent. Type equivalence is in particular needed in the application rules T-APP and K-APP. To show that some actual argument has an acceptable type for a function or type family, we may need to use the rule T-CONV to convert the type. In fact, the algorithmic typing rules introduced later on show that this is the only place where type equivalence is needed.

But what should our notion of type equivalence be? Without adding special equality axioms, we can consider natural notions of equality which arise from the type structure. With dependent types, a natural notion is to equate types that differ only in their term components, when those term components themselves should be considered equal. So the question is reduced to considering notions of term equality.

A first example is a type-family application containing a β-redex, since we consider β-equivalent λ-terms to be equal: $T\ ((\lambda x{:}S.x)\ z) \equiv T\ z$. A slightly different and more concrete example is two different applications of the `Vector` family: `Vector (3 + 4)` $\equiv$ `Vector 7`. It seems reasonable that a typechecker should accept each of these pairs of types as being equivalent. But we quickly come across more complex equivalences involving more computation, or even, requiring proof in the general case. For example, supposing `x` is an unknown value of type `Nat` and `f:Nat → Nat` is a function whose behavior is known. If it happens that `f x=7` for all `x` then we have `Vector (f x)` $\equiv$ `Vector 7`, but this equality could be more difficult to add to an automatic typechecker.

The question of what form of type equivalence to include in a system of dependent types is therefore a central consideration in the design of the system. Many different choices have been studied, leading to systems with fundamentally different character. The most notable distinction between systems is whether or not typechecking is decidable.

In the first case, we may choose to include only basic equalities which are manifestly obvious. This is the viewpoint favored by Martin-Löf, who considers *definitional equality* to be the proper notion of equivalence. The first two equalities above are definitional: 3 + 4 is definitionally equal to 7 by the rules of computation for addition. Alternatively, one may prefer to include as many equalities as possible, to make the theory more powerful. This is the approach followed, for example, in the type theory implemented by the NuPrl system (1986). This formulation of type theory includes type equivalences like the third example above, which may require arbitrary computation or proof to establish. In such a type system, typechecking is undecidable.

For λLF, we axiomatize definitional equality based on the type structure, which includes β and η equality on lambda terms. It is possible to define this using a relation of equality defined via compatible closure of untyped reduction (this is the approach followed by Pure Type Systems, see Section 2.7). Instead, we give a declarative, typed definition of equivalence, using rules which follow the same pattern as the typing rules. The advantage of this approach is that it is more extensible than the "untyped" approach and avoids the need to establish properties of untyped reduction. See Chapter 6 in this volume for further explanation of the issues here.

The rules for equivalence are shown in Figure 2-2. Again there are three judgments, for equivalence of each of the syntactic categories of terms, types, and kinds. The only interesting rules are Q-BETA and Q-ETA which introduce β and η-equivalence on terms; the remaining rules are purely structural and express that equivalence is a congruence.

2.3 Properties

In this section we mention some basic properties of λLF. We don't go very far: in Section 2.4 we introduce an algorithmic presentation of λLF which allows us to establish further properties indirectly but rather more easily.

Basic Properties

The following properties use some additional notation. Inclusion is defined between contexts as $\Gamma \subseteq \Delta$ iff $\mathtt{x}{:}\mathtt{T} \in \Gamma$ implies $\mathtt{x}{:}\mathtt{T} \in \Delta$, in other words,

$\Gamma \subseteq \Delta$ means that Δ is a permutation of an extension of Γ. We write $\Gamma \vdash J$ for an arbitrary judgment, amongst the six defined in Figures 2-1 and 2-2. We write $\Gamma \vdash K, K'$ to stand for both $\Gamma \vdash K$ and $\Gamma \vdash K'$, and similarly for other judgments.

2.3.1 **Lemma [Permutation and Weakening]**: Suppose $\Gamma \subseteq \Delta$. Then $\Gamma \vdash J$ implies $\Delta \vdash J$. □

2.3.2 **Lemma [Substitution]**: If Γ, $\mathtt{x{:}S}$, $\Delta \vdash J$ and $\Gamma \vdash \mathtt{s} : \mathtt{S}$, then Γ, $[\mathtt{x} \mapsto \mathtt{s}]\Delta \vdash [\mathtt{x} \mapsto \mathtt{s}]J$. □

2.3.3 **Lemma [Agreement]**: Judgments in the system are in agreement, as follows:

1. If $\Gamma \vdash \mathtt{T} :: \mathtt{K}$ then $\Gamma \vdash \mathtt{K}$.

2. If $\Gamma \vdash \mathtt{t} : \mathtt{T}$ then $\Gamma \vdash \mathtt{T} :: *$.

3. If $\Gamma \vdash \mathtt{K} \equiv \mathtt{K'}$ then $\Gamma \vdash \mathtt{K}, \mathtt{K'}$.

4. If $\Gamma \vdash \mathtt{T} \equiv \mathtt{T'} :: \mathtt{K}$ then $\Gamma \vdash \mathtt{T}, \mathtt{T'} :: \mathtt{K}$.

5. If $\Gamma \vdash \mathtt{t} \equiv \mathtt{t'} : \mathtt{T}$ then $\Gamma \vdash \mathtt{t}, \mathtt{t'} : \mathtt{T}$. □

2.3.4 **Exercise [★★, ↛]**: Prove the lemmas above. □

Strong Normalization

As an auxiliary device for the soundness and completeness of algorithmic typechecking we will now introduce general beta reduction which permits reductions within the scope of abstractions.

We define beta reduction on λLF terms by the four rules:

$$\frac{\mathtt{t}_1 \longrightarrow_\beta \mathtt{t}_1'}{\lambda\mathtt{x{:}T}_1\mathtt{.t}_1 \longrightarrow_\beta \lambda\mathtt{x{:}T}_1\mathtt{.t}_1'} \qquad \text{(Beta-Abs)}$$

$$\frac{\mathtt{t}_1 \longrightarrow_\beta \mathtt{t}_1'}{\mathtt{t}_1\ \mathtt{t}_2 \longrightarrow_\beta \mathtt{t}_1'\ \mathtt{t}_2} \qquad \text{(Beta-App1)}$$

$$\frac{\mathtt{t}_2 \longrightarrow_\beta \mathtt{t}_2'}{\mathtt{t}_1\ \mathtt{t}_2 \longrightarrow_\beta \mathtt{t}_1\ \mathtt{t}_2'} \qquad \text{(Beta-App2)}$$

$$(\lambda\mathtt{x{:}T}_1\mathtt{.t}_1)\ \mathtt{t}_2 \longrightarrow_\beta [\mathtt{x} \mapsto \mathtt{t}_2]\mathtt{t}_1 \qquad \text{(Beta-AppAbs)}$$

Notice that this reduction does not go inside the type labels of λ abstractions.

The following central result is required to ensure completeness and termination of typechecking, proved in the next section.

2.3.5 THEOREM [STRONG NORMALIZATION]: The relation $\longrightarrow_\beta$ is strongly normalizing on well-typed terms. More precisely, if $\Gamma \vdash \mathtt{t}:\mathtt{T}$ then there is no infinite sequence of terms $(\mathtt{t}_i)_{i\geq 1}$ such that $\mathtt{t} = \mathtt{t}_1$ and $\mathtt{t}_i \longrightarrow_\beta \mathtt{t}_{i+1}$ for $i \geq 1$. □

Proof: This can be proved by defining a reduction-preserving translation from λLF to the simply-typed lambda-calculus as follows. First, for every type variable X, no matter of what kind, we introduce a simple type variable $\mathtt{X}^\natural$. Second, for each type expression T, no matter of what kind, we define a simple type expression $\mathtt{T}^\natural$ by $\Pi\mathtt{x}:\mathtt{S}.\mathtt{T}^\natural = \mathtt{S}^\natural \to \mathtt{T}^\natural$ and $(\mathtt{T}\ \mathtt{t})^\natural = \mathtt{T}^\natural$. Finally, the mapping $-^\natural$ is extended to terms and contexts by applying it to all type expressions occurring within.

Now we can show by induction on typing derivations in λLF that $\Gamma \vdash \mathtt{t}:\mathtt{T}$ implies $\Gamma^\natural \vdash \mathtt{t}^\natural:\mathtt{T}^\natural$, from which the result follows by the strong normalization theorem for β-reduction of the simply typed lambda calculus. □

Since $\longrightarrow_\beta$ is finitely branching, this implies that for each term t there exists a number $\mu(\mathtt{t})$ such that if $(\mathtt{t}_i)_{1\leq i\leq k}$ is a reduction sequence starting from t, that is, $\mathtt{t}=\mathtt{t}_1$ and $\mathtt{t}_i \longrightarrow_\beta \mathtt{t}_{i+1}$ for $1 \leq i < k$ then $k \leq \mu(\mathtt{t})$. A term t′ such that $\mathtt{t} \longrightarrow_\beta^* \mathtt{t}'$ and $\mathtt{t}' \not\longrightarrow_\beta$ is called a (β) *normal form* of t. Since $\longrightarrow_\beta$ is confluent, see below, normal forms are unique and we may write $\mathtt{t}' = \mathrm{nf}(\mathtt{t})$.

2.3.6 THEOREM: The relation $\longrightarrow_\beta$ is confluent. □

2.3.7 EXERCISE [★★★, ↛]: Prove the theorem in the following way: first show that $\longrightarrow_\beta$ is *locally confluent* in the sense that if $\mathtt{t} \longrightarrow_\beta \mathtt{t}_1$ and $\mathtt{t} \longrightarrow_\beta^* \mathtt{t}_2$ then $\mathtt{t}_1 \longrightarrow_\beta^* \mathtt{t}'$ and $\mathtt{t}_2 \longrightarrow_\beta \mathtt{t}'$ for some t′. Then conclude confluence using the fact that $\longrightarrow_\beta$ is strongly normalizing. This last part is a standard result from term rewriting known as Newman's Lemma.

Alternatively, you can prove confluence directly using Tait-Martin-Löf's method of parallel reduction, see *TAPL*, Chapter 30. □

2.4 Algorithmic Typing and Equality

To implement λLF, we need to find a formulation of the system that is closer to an algorithm. As usual, we follow the strategy of reformulating the rules to be *syntax-directed*, so that they can be used to define an algorithm going from conclusion to premises (see the description of the implementation in Section 2.9) . We also need an algorithm for deciding type equivalence.

The algorithmic presentation of λLF is shown in Figures 2-3 and 2-4. The judgments mirror the defining presentation, with the addition of a context checking judgment. (This is used only to check an initial context: the rules otherwise maintain context well-formation when extending contexts going from conclusion to premises.)

The non-syntax-directed rules K-CONV and T-CONV are removed. To replace T-CONV, we add equivalence testing in the algorithmic rules for applications, KA-APP and TA-APP.

The equivalence testing rules in Figure 2-4 assume that they are invoked on well-typed phrases. We show these rules with contexts Γ to facilitate extensions to type-dependent equalities or definitions in the context (used in the implementation), although in the rules for pure λLF, the context plays no role in equivalence testing.

The equivalence testing algorithm on terms that is suggested by these rules is similar to the one described in Chapter 6, but we do not make use of type information. (Similarly, the type equivalence rules do not record kinds.) The algorithmic judgment $\Gamma \mapsto \mathtt{s} \equiv \mathtt{t}$ for arbitrary terms is defined mutually with $\Gamma \mapsto \mathtt{s} \equiv_{wh} \mathtt{t}$ which is defined between *weak head normal forms.* Weak head reduction is a subset of the β reduction $\longrightarrow_\beta$, defined by the rules:

$$\frac{\mathtt{t}_1 \longrightarrow_{wh} \mathtt{t}_1'}{\mathtt{t}_1\ \mathtt{t}_2 \longrightarrow_{wh} \mathtt{t}_1'\ \mathtt{t}_2} \qquad \text{(WH-APP1)}$$

$$(\lambda \mathtt{x}{:}\mathtt{T}_1.\mathtt{t}_1)\ \mathtt{t}_2 \longrightarrow_{wh} [\mathtt{x} \mapsto \mathtt{t}_2]\mathtt{t}_1 \qquad \text{(WH-APPABS)}$$

Weak head reduction only applies β-reduction in the head position. The implementation described in Section 2.9 adds expansion of definitions to this reduction; see Chapter 9 for a thorough treatment of how to do this.

2.4.1 THEOREM [WEAK HEAD NORMAL FORMS]: If $\Gamma \vdash \mathtt{t}{:}\mathtt{T}$ then there exists a unique term $\mathtt{t}' = \text{whnf}(\mathtt{t})$ such that $t \longrightarrow_{wh}{}^* \mathtt{t}' \not\longrightarrow_{wh}$. □

The theorem is a direct consequence of Theorem 2.3.5 and of the fact that $\longrightarrow_{wh}$ is deterministic (a partial function).

Correctness of the Algorithm

We will now show that the typechecking algorithm defined by the algorithmic rules is sound, complete, and terminates on all inputs.

Since the algorithm checks the context only as it is extended, and (for efficiency) does not check the type of variables in the leaves, we can only expect to show soundness for contexts which are well-formed. The soundness lemma makes use of an auxiliary algorithmic judgment for context formation:

$$\mapsto \emptyset \qquad \text{(WFA-EMPTY)}$$

$$\frac{\mapsto \Gamma \qquad \Gamma \mapsto \mathtt{T} :: *}{\mapsto \Gamma, \mathtt{x}{:}\mathtt{T}} \qquad \text{(WFA-TM)}$$

$$\frac{\mapsto \Gamma \qquad \Gamma \mapsto \mathtt{K}}{\mapsto \Gamma, \mathtt{X}{::}\mathtt{K}} \qquad \text{(WFA-TY)}$$

Algorithmic kind formation $\boxed{\Gamma \mapsto \mathsf{K}}$

$$\Gamma \mapsto * \qquad \text{(WFA-STAR)}$$

$$\frac{\Gamma \mapsto \mathsf{T} :: * \qquad \Gamma, \mathsf{x}{:}\mathsf{T} \mapsto \mathsf{K}}{\Gamma \mapsto \Pi \mathsf{x}{:}\mathsf{T}.\mathsf{K}} \qquad \text{(WFA-PI)}$$

Algorithmic kinding $\boxed{\Gamma \mapsto \mathsf{T} :: \mathsf{K}}$

$$\frac{\mathsf{X} :: \mathsf{K} \in \Gamma}{\Gamma \mapsto \mathsf{X} :: \mathsf{K}} \qquad \text{(KA-VAR)}$$

$$\frac{\Gamma \mapsto \mathsf{T}_1 :: * \qquad \Gamma, \mathsf{x}{:}\mathsf{T}_1 \mapsto \mathsf{T}_2 :: *}{\Gamma \mapsto \Pi \mathsf{x}{:}\mathsf{T}_1.\mathsf{T}_2 :: *} \qquad \text{(KA-PI)}$$

$$\frac{\Gamma \mapsto \mathsf{S} :: \Pi \mathsf{x}{:}\mathsf{T}_1.\mathsf{K} \qquad \Gamma \mapsto \mathsf{t} : \mathsf{T}_2 \qquad \Gamma \mapsto \mathsf{T}_1 \equiv \mathsf{T}_2}{\Gamma \mapsto \mathsf{S}\ \mathsf{t} : [\mathsf{x} \mapsto \mathsf{t}]\mathsf{K}} \qquad \text{(KA-APP)}$$

Algorithmic typing $\boxed{\Gamma \mapsto \mathsf{t} : \mathsf{T}}$

$$\frac{\mathsf{x}{:}\mathsf{T} \in \Gamma}{\Gamma \mapsto \mathsf{x} : \mathsf{T}} \qquad \text{(TA-VAR)}$$

$$\frac{\Gamma \mapsto \mathsf{S} :: * \qquad \Gamma, \mathsf{x}{:}\mathsf{S} \mapsto \mathsf{t} : \mathsf{T}}{\Gamma \mapsto \lambda \mathsf{x}{:}\mathsf{S}.\mathsf{t} : \Pi \mathsf{x}{:}\mathsf{S}.\mathsf{T}} \qquad \text{(TA-ABS)}$$

$$\frac{\Gamma \mapsto \mathsf{t}_1 : \Pi \mathsf{x}{:}\mathsf{S}_1.\mathsf{T} \qquad \Gamma \mapsto \mathsf{t}_2 : \mathsf{S}_2 \qquad \Gamma \mapsto \mathsf{S}_1 \equiv \mathsf{S}_2}{\Gamma \mapsto \mathsf{t}_1\ \mathsf{t}_2 : [\mathsf{x} \mapsto \mathsf{t}_2]\mathsf{T}} \qquad \text{(TA-APP)}$$

Figure 2-3: Algorithmic presentation of λLF

Algorithmic kind equivalence $\boxed{\Gamma \mapsto \mathsf{K} \equiv \mathsf{K}'}$

$$\Gamma \mapsto * \equiv * \qquad \text{(QKA-STAR)}$$

$$\frac{\Gamma \mapsto \mathsf{T}_1 \equiv \mathsf{T}_2 \qquad \Gamma, \mathsf{x}{:}\mathsf{T}_1 \mapsto \mathsf{K}_1 \equiv \mathsf{K}_2}{\Gamma \mapsto \Pi \mathsf{x}{:}\mathsf{T}_1.\mathsf{K}_1 \equiv \Pi \mathsf{x}{:}\mathsf{T}_2.\mathsf{K}_2} \qquad \text{(QKA-PI)}$$

Algorithmic type equivalence $\boxed{\Gamma \mapsto \mathsf{S} \equiv \mathsf{T}}$

$$\Gamma \mapsto \mathsf{X} \equiv \mathsf{X} \qquad \text{(QTA-VAR)}$$

$$\frac{\Gamma \mapsto \mathsf{S}_1 \equiv \mathsf{T}_1 \qquad \Gamma, \mathsf{x}{:}\mathsf{T}_1 \mapsto \mathsf{S}_2 \equiv \mathsf{T}_2}{\Gamma \mapsto \Pi \mathsf{x}{:}\mathsf{S}_1.\mathsf{S}_2 \equiv \Pi \mathsf{x}{:}\mathsf{T}_1.\mathsf{T}_2} \qquad \text{(QTA-PI)}$$

$$\frac{\Gamma \mapsto \mathsf{S}_1 \equiv \mathsf{S}_2 \qquad \Gamma \mapsto \mathsf{t}_1 \equiv \mathsf{t}_2}{\Gamma \mapsto \mathsf{S}_1\ \mathsf{t}_1 \equiv \mathsf{S}_2\ \mathsf{t}_2} \qquad \text{(QTA-APP)}$$

Algorithmic term equivalence $\boxed{\Gamma \mapsto \mathsf{s} \equiv \mathsf{t}}$

$$\frac{\Gamma \mapsto \mathsf{whnf}(\mathsf{s}) \equiv_{\mathsf{wh}} \mathsf{whnf}(\mathsf{t})}{\Gamma \mapsto \mathsf{s} \equiv \mathsf{t}} \qquad \text{(QA-WH)}$$

$$\Gamma \mapsto \mathsf{x} \equiv_{\mathsf{wh}} \mathsf{x} \qquad \text{(QA-VAR)}$$

$$\frac{\Gamma, \mathsf{x}{:}\mathsf{S} \mapsto \mathsf{t}_1 \equiv \mathsf{t}_2}{\Gamma \mapsto \lambda \mathsf{x}{:}\mathsf{S}.\mathsf{t}_1 \equiv_{\mathsf{wh}} \lambda \mathsf{x}{:}\mathsf{S}.\mathsf{t}_2} \qquad \text{(QA-ABS)}$$

$$\frac{\Gamma \mapsto \mathsf{s}_1 \equiv_{\mathsf{wh}} \mathsf{s}_2 \qquad \Gamma \mapsto \mathsf{t}_1 \equiv_{\mathsf{wh}} \mathsf{t}_2}{\Gamma \mapsto \mathsf{s}_1\ \mathsf{t}_1 \equiv_{\mathsf{wh}} \mathsf{s}_2\ \mathsf{t}_2} \qquad \text{(QA-APP)}$$

$$\frac{\Gamma, \mathsf{x}{:}\mathsf{S} \mapsto \mathsf{s}\ \mathsf{x} \equiv \mathsf{t} \qquad \text{s not a } \lambda}{\Gamma \mapsto \mathsf{s} \equiv_{\mathsf{wh}} \lambda \mathsf{x}{:}\mathsf{S}.\mathsf{t}} \qquad \text{(QA-NABS1)}$$

$$\frac{\Gamma, \mathsf{x}{:}\mathsf{S} \mapsto \mathsf{s} \equiv \mathsf{t}\ \mathsf{x} \qquad \text{t not a } \lambda}{\Gamma \mapsto \lambda \mathsf{x}{:}\mathsf{S}.\mathsf{s} \equiv_{\mathsf{wh}} \mathsf{t}} \qquad \text{(QA-NABS2)}$$

Figure 2-4: Algorithmic presentation of λLF—Equivalence rules

2.4.2 **Lemma [Soundness of algorithmic λLF]:** Each of the algorithmic judgments is sound, in the following sense:

1. If $\Gamma \mapsto K$ then $\Gamma \vdash K$.

2. If $\Gamma \mapsto T :: K$ then $\Gamma \vdash T :: K$.

3. If $\Gamma \mapsto t : T$ then $\Gamma \vdash t : T$.

4. If $\Gamma \mapsto K, K'$ and $\Gamma \mapsto K \equiv K'$, then $\Gamma \vdash K \equiv K'$.

5. If $\Gamma \mapsto T, T' :: K$ and $\Gamma \mapsto T \equiv T'$ then $\Gamma \vdash T \equiv T' :: K$.

6. If $\Gamma \mapsto t, t' : T$ and $\Gamma \mapsto t \equiv t'$ then $\Gamma \vdash t \equiv t' :: K$.

where in each case, we additionally assume $\mapsto \Gamma$. □

Proof: By induction on algorithmic derivations. □

To establish completeness of algorithmic subtyping and later on termination we need to induct on the length of normalization sequences which we formalize as follows.

Recall that $\mu(s)$ denotes an upper bound on the length of any $\longrightarrow_\beta$ reduction sequence starting from s. We write $|s|$ for the size of the term s.

2.4.3 **Definition:** We associate an ω^2-valued weight to each judgment arising in a possible derivation of an equality judgment by

$$w(\Delta \mapsto s_1 \equiv s_2) = w(\Delta \mapsto s_1 \equiv_{wh} s_2) + 1$$
$$w(\Delta \mapsto s_1 \equiv_{wh} s_2) = \omega \cdot (\mu(s_1) + \mu(s_2)) + |s_1| + |s_2| + 1.$$ □

2.4.4 **Lemma [Completeness of algorithmic λLF]:** Each of the algorithmic judgments is complete, in the following sense:

1. If $\Gamma \vdash K$ then $\Gamma \mapsto K$.

2. If $\Gamma \vdash T : K$ then for some K', we have $\Gamma \mapsto T : K'$ and $\Gamma \mapsto K \equiv K'$ and $\Gamma \mapsto K'$.

3. If $\Gamma \vdash t : T$ then for some T', we have $\Gamma \mapsto t : T'$ and $\Gamma \mapsto T \equiv T'$ and $\Gamma \mapsto T' :: *$.

4. If $\Gamma \vdash t_1 \equiv t_2 : T$ then $\Gamma \mapsto t_1 \equiv t_2$.

5. If $\Gamma \vdash T_1 \equiv T_2 :: K$ then $\Gamma \mapsto T_1 \equiv T_2$. □

Proof: One first proves that each of the declarative rules is admissible in the algorithmic system. The result then follows by induction on derivations in the declarative system. The only rules that are not immediately obvious are the transitivity rules for equivalence of kinds, types, and terms, and the rule Q-APP. These two are left as exercises. □

2.4.5 EXERCISE [★★★, ↛]: Show that rule QT-TRANS is admissible for the algorithmic system in the sense that whenever $\Gamma \vdash t_i : T$ for $i = 1, 2, 3$ and $\Gamma \mapsto t_1 \equiv t_2$ and $\Gamma \mapsto t_2 \equiv t_3$ then $\Gamma \mapsto t_1 \equiv t_3$. □

2.4.6 EXERCISE [★★★, ↛]: Show that rule Q-APP is admissible for the algorithmic system in the sense that whenever $\Gamma \vdash t_1\ t_2 : T$ and $\Gamma \vdash s_1\ s_2 : T$ and $\Gamma \mapsto t_1 \equiv s_1$ and $\Gamma \mapsto t_2 \equiv s_2$ then $\Gamma \mapsto t_1\ t_2 \equiv s_1\ s_2$. □

Given soundness and completeness, we also want to know that our algorithm terminates on all inputs. This also demonstrates the decidability of the original judgments.

2.4.7 THEOREM [TERMINATION OF TYPECHECKING]: The algorithmic presentation yields a terminating algorithm for typechecking. □

We highlight the crucial ideas of the proof of Theorem 2.4.7 here; the details are left to the diligent reader (Exercise 2.4.9 below). The equivalence judgment $\Gamma \mapsto t_1 \equiv t_2$ introduces a possible source of nontermination when invoked on non-well-typed terms (for example, $\Omega = \Delta\Delta$ where $\Delta = \lambda x{:}A.x\ x$). Here, computation of weak head normal form runs into an infinite loop. We must be careful that equivalence testing is called only on well-typed terms.

The crucial termination property for term equality that we need is captured by the following lemma.

2.4.8 LEMMA: Suppose that $\Gamma \vdash t_1 : T_1$ and $\Gamma \vdash t_2 : T_2$. Then the syntax-directed backwards search for a derivation of $\Gamma \mapsto t_1 \equiv t_2$ always terminates. Equivalently, there is no infinite derivation ending in $\Gamma \mapsto t_1 \equiv t_2$. □

Proof: We claim that the weight of any premise of a rule is always less than the weight of the conclusion which excludes any infinite derivation tree. In other words we argue by induction on the length of reduction sequences and, subordinately, on the size of terms. This property is obviously satisfied for QA-WH, QA-ABS, QA-APP. To deal with rule QA-NABS1 (and similarly, QA-NABS2) note that s must be of the form $y\ u_1\ \ldots\ u_n$ whereby $\mu(s\ x) = \mu(s)$. The size, however, goes down, as the λ-symbol has disappeared. □

2.4.9 EXERCISE [★★★, ↛]: Complete the proof of 2.4.2, 2.4.4, and 2.4.7. □

Properties of λLF

We can use the algorithmic presentation of λLF to prove additional properties enjoyed by the main definition. We just mention one example: type preservation under β-reduction.

2.4.10 THEOREM [PRESERVATION]: If $\Gamma \vdash \mathtt{t} : \mathsf{T}$ and $\mathtt{t} \longrightarrow_\beta \mathtt{t}'$, then $\Gamma \vdash \mathtt{t}' : \mathsf{T}$ also. □

Proof: We show a slightly restricted form of the theorem, for well-formed contexts Γ. More precisely, well-formed contexts are those which can be built using the same rules as for $\mapsto \Gamma$ (page 57), but in the declarative system; the corresponding assertion is written $\vdash \Gamma$. It is easy to extend the completeness lemma to show that $\vdash \Gamma$ implies $\mapsto \Gamma$.

The crucial case is that of an outermost β-reduction (BETA-APPABS), when $\mathtt{t} = (\lambda \mathtt{x}{:}\mathsf{T}_1.\mathtt{t}_1)\ \mathtt{t}_2$ for some T_1, $\mathtt{t}_1$, $\mathtt{t}_2$.

By Lemma 2.4.4, we know that $\Gamma \mapsto (\lambda \mathtt{x}{:}\mathsf{T}_1.\mathtt{t}_1)\ \mathtt{t}_2 : \mathsf{T}'$ for some T' with $\Gamma \mapsto \mathsf{T} \equiv \mathsf{T}'$ and $\Gamma \mapsto \mathsf{T}' :: *$. The first judgment must have been derived with TA-APP preceded by TA-ABS, so we have the derivability of

$$\Gamma \mapsto \mathsf{T}_1 :: * \qquad \Gamma \mapsto \mathsf{T}_1 \equiv \mathsf{S}_1 \qquad \Gamma, \mathtt{x}{:}\mathsf{T}_1 \mapsto \mathtt{t}_1 : \mathsf{S}_2 \qquad \Gamma \mapsto \mathtt{t}_2 : \mathsf{S}_1$$

in the algorithmic system, with $\mathsf{T}' = [\mathtt{x} \mapsto \mathtt{t}_2]\mathsf{S}_2$.

By the above and the assumptions about Γ, we have $\mapsto \Gamma, \mathtt{x}{:}\mathsf{T}_1$. Hence by Lemma 2.4.2, we can go back to get analogs of the statements above in the declarative system. For the last case, to establish the equivalence $\Gamma \vdash \mathsf{T}_1 \equiv \mathsf{S}_1 :: *$ we use Lemma 2.3.3 to get $\Gamma \vdash \mathsf{S}_1 :: *$ and then $\Gamma \mapsto \mathsf{S}_1 :: *$.

Now by T-CONV we have $\Gamma \vdash \mathtt{t}_2{:}\mathsf{T}_1$ and so with substitution, Lemma 2.3.2, we get $\Gamma \vdash [\mathtt{x} \mapsto \mathtt{t}_2]\mathtt{t}_1 : [\mathtt{x} \mapsto \mathtt{t}_2]\mathsf{S}_2$ and then the result follows using T-CONV again, with another hop between the systems and Lemma 2.3.3, to show the equivalence $\Gamma \vdash [\mathtt{x} \mapsto \mathtt{t}_2]\mathsf{S}_2 \equiv \mathsf{T} :: *$. □

2.4.11 EXERCISE [★★★, ↛]: Generalize the proof above to arbitrary contexts Γ. □

2.5 Dependent Sum Types

Figure 2-5 shows extensions to λLF to add dependent sum (or "Sigma") types, written $\Sigma \mathtt{x}{:}\mathsf{T}_1.\mathsf{T}_2$. Dependent sums were motivated briefly in the introduction. They generalize ordinary product types in a similar way to the way that dependent products generalize ordinary function spaces. The degenerate non-dependent case, when $\mathtt{x}$ does not appear free in T_2, amounts to the ordinary product, written as $\mathsf{T}_1 \times \mathsf{T}_2$.

We extend the terms and types of λLF given in Figure 2-1 with pairs, projection operations, and the type constructor itself. Notice that the pair $(\mathtt{t}_1,\mathtt{t}_2)$

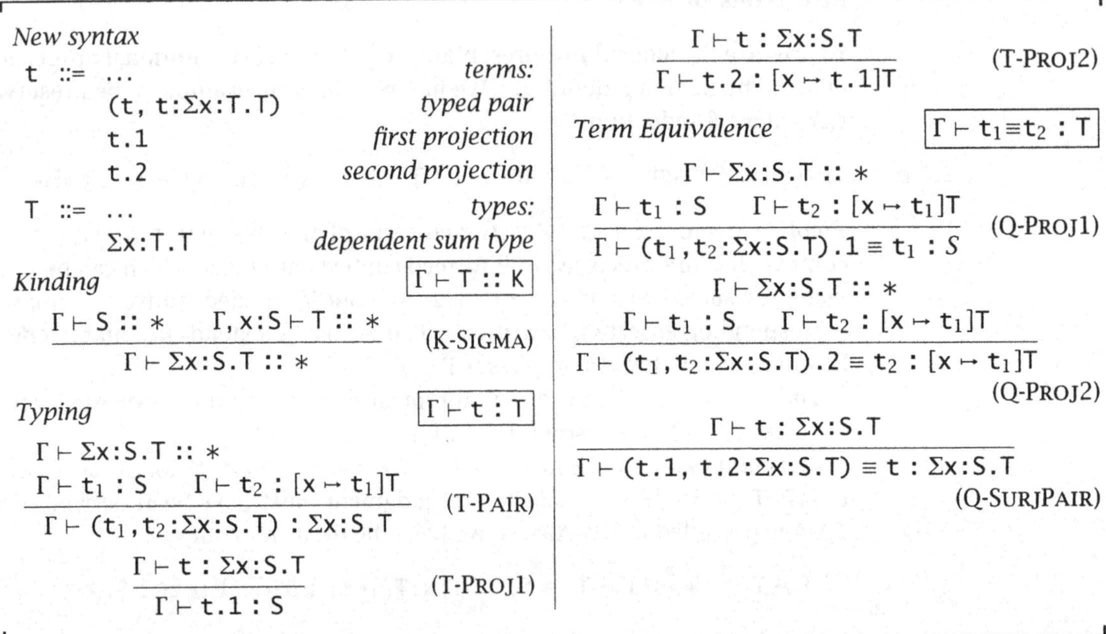

Figure 2-5: Dependent sum types

is annotated explicitly with a type Σ`x:T`$_1$`.T`$_2$ in the syntax. The reason for this is that the type of such a pair cannot be reconstructed from the types of t_1 and t_2 alone. For example, if `S::T→*` and `x:T` and `y:S x` the pair `(x,y)` could have both `Σz:T.S z` and `Σz:T.S x` as a type.

The most cluttered typing rule is the one which introduces a dependent pair, T-PAIR. It must check first that the Σ-type itself is allowed, and then that each component has the requested type. The projection rules are straightforward: compare the second projection with the rule T-APP in Figure 2-1.

The equality relation on terms is extended to Σ-types by three rules. The first two define the elimination behavior of projections on a pair (compare with the beta rule for Π-types). The third rule, Q-SURJPAIR, is known as *surjective pairing*. This rule is a form of eta rule for Σ-types: it states that every pair can be formed using the pair constructor.

Algorithmic Typing with Dependent Sum Types

To extend the algorithm to deal with Σ-types, we first extend the notions of beta and weak-head reduction. In both, the main clause is projection on a

Extends λLF algorithm (2-3 and 2-4)

Algorithmic kinding $\boxed{\Gamma \mapsto \mathtt{T} :: \mathtt{K}}$

$$\frac{\Gamma \mapsto \mathtt{T}_1 :: * \qquad \Gamma, \mathtt{x}{:}\mathtt{T}_1 \mapsto \mathtt{T}_2 :: *}{\Gamma \mapsto \Sigma\mathtt{x}{:}\mathtt{T}_1.\mathtt{T}_2 :: *} \quad \text{(KA-SIGMA)}$$

Algorithmic typing $\boxed{\Gamma \mapsto \mathtt{t} : \mathtt{T}}$

$$\frac{\begin{array}{l}\Gamma \mapsto \Sigma\mathtt{x}{:}\mathtt{T}_1.\mathtt{T}_2 :: * \\ \Gamma \mapsto \mathtt{t}_1 : \mathtt{T}_1' \qquad \Gamma \mapsto \mathtt{T}_1' \equiv \mathtt{T}_1 \\ \Gamma \mapsto \mathtt{t}_2 : \mathtt{T}_2' \qquad \Gamma \mapsto \mathtt{T}_2' \equiv [\mathtt{x} \mapsto \mathtt{t}_1]\mathtt{T}_2\end{array}}{\Gamma \mapsto (\mathtt{t}_1,\mathtt{t}_2{:}\Sigma\mathtt{x}{:}\mathtt{T}_1.\mathtt{T}_2) : \Sigma\mathtt{x}{:}\mathtt{T}_1.\mathtt{T}_2} \quad \text{(TA-PAIR)}$$

$$\frac{\Gamma \mapsto \mathtt{t} : \Sigma\mathtt{x}{:}\mathtt{T}_1.\mathtt{T}_2}{\Gamma \mapsto \mathtt{t}.1 : \mathtt{T}_1} \quad \text{(TA-PROJ1)}$$

$$\frac{\Gamma \mapsto \mathtt{t} : \Sigma\mathtt{x}{:}\mathtt{T}_1.\mathtt{T}_2}{\Gamma \mapsto \mathtt{t}.2 : [\mathtt{x} \mapsto \mathtt{t}.1]\mathtt{T}_2} \quad \text{(TA-PROJ2)}$$

Algorithmic type equivalence $\boxed{\Gamma \mapsto \mathtt{S} \equiv \mathtt{T}}$

$$\frac{\Gamma \mapsto \mathtt{S}_1 \equiv \mathtt{T}_1 \qquad \Gamma, \mathtt{x}{:}\mathtt{T}_1 \mapsto \mathtt{S}_2 \equiv \mathtt{T}_2}{\Gamma \mapsto \Sigma\mathtt{x}{:}\mathtt{S}_1.\mathtt{S}_2 \equiv \Sigma\mathtt{x}{:}\mathtt{T}_1.\mathtt{T}_2} \quad \text{(QTA-SIGMA)}$$

Algorithmic term equivalence $\boxed{\Gamma \mapsto \mathtt{t} \equiv_{\mathrm{wh}} \mathtt{t}'}$

$$\frac{\Gamma \mapsto \mathtt{t}_i \equiv \mathtt{t'}_i}{\Gamma \mapsto (\mathtt{t}_1,\mathtt{t}_2{:}\mathtt{T}) \equiv_{\mathrm{wh}} (\mathtt{t'}_1,\mathtt{t'}_2{:}\mathtt{T'})} \quad \text{(QA-PAIR)}$$

$$\frac{\Gamma \mapsto \mathtt{t}_i \equiv \mathtt{t}.i \qquad \mathtt{t}\text{ not a pair}}{\Gamma \mapsto (\mathtt{t}_1,\mathtt{t}_2{:}\mathtt{T}) \equiv_{\mathrm{wh}} \mathtt{t}} \quad \text{(QA-PAIR-NE)}$$

$$\frac{\Gamma \mapsto \mathtt{t}.i \equiv \mathtt{t}_i \qquad \mathtt{t}\text{ not a pair}}{\Gamma \mapsto \mathtt{t} \equiv_{\mathrm{wh}} (\mathtt{t}_1,\mathtt{t}_2{:}\mathtt{T})} \quad \text{(QA-NE-PAIR)}$$

Figure 2-6: Algorithmic typing for Σ-types

pair. Beta reduction also allows reduction inside the components of a pair.

$$(\mathtt{t}_1,\mathtt{t}_2{:}\mathtt{T}).i \longrightarrow_\beta \mathtt{t}_i \quad \text{(BETA-PROJPAIR)}$$

$$\frac{\mathtt{t} \longrightarrow_\beta \mathtt{t}'}{\mathtt{t}.i \longrightarrow_\beta \mathtt{t}'.i} \quad \text{(BETA-PROJ)}$$

$$\frac{\mathtt{t}_1 \longrightarrow_\beta \mathtt{t}_1'}{(\mathtt{t}_1,\mathtt{t}_2{:}\mathtt{T}) \longrightarrow_\beta (\mathtt{t}_1',\mathtt{t}_2{:}\mathtt{T})} \quad \text{(BETA-PAIR1)}$$

$$\frac{\mathtt{t}_2 \longrightarrow_\beta \mathtt{t}_2'}{(\mathtt{t}_1,\mathtt{t}_2{:}\mathtt{T}) \longrightarrow_\beta (\mathtt{t}_1,\mathtt{t}_2'{:}\mathtt{T})} \quad \text{(BETA-PAIR2)}$$

Weak head reduction just has two new cases:

$$(\mathtt{t}_1,\mathtt{t}_2{:}\mathtt{T}).i \longrightarrow_{\mathrm{wh}} \mathtt{t}_i \quad \text{(WH-PROJPAIR)}$$

$$\frac{\mathtt{t} \longrightarrow_{\mathrm{wh}} \mathtt{t}'}{\mathtt{t}.i \longrightarrow_{\mathrm{wh}} \mathtt{t}'.i} \quad \text{(WH-PROJ)}$$

Using the weak head reduction, the algorithmic typing and equality judgments are extended with the rules in Figure 2-6 to deal with Σ-types.

2.5.1 EXERCISE [★★★, ↛]: Extend Lemmas 2.4.2, 2.4.4 and 2.4.7 to Σ-types. (No surprises are to be expected.) □

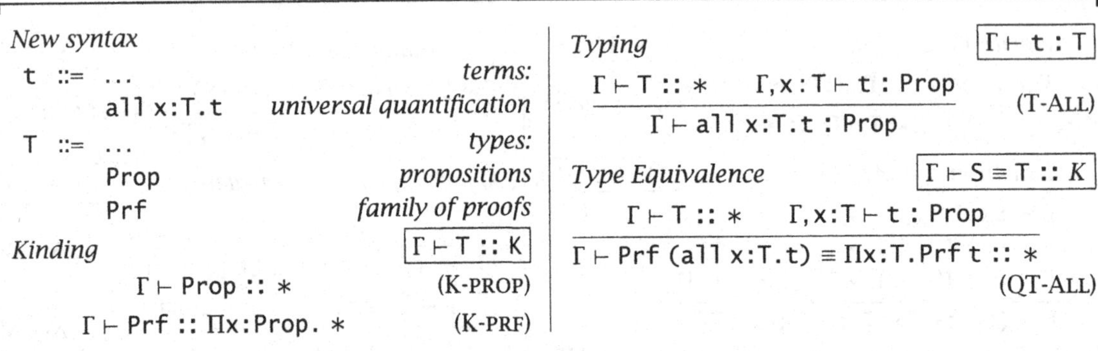

Figure 2-7: The Calculus of Constructions (CC)

2.6 The Calculus of Constructions

The Calculus of Constructions (CC), one of the most famous systems of dependent types, was introduced by Coquand and Huet (1988) as a setting for all of constructive mathematics. While it has turned out that CC needs to be extended with certain features (in particular inductive types [Mohring, 1986]), its simplicity in relationship to its expressivity is unprecedented.

In our framework CC can be formulated as an extension of λLF which has a new basic type `Prop` and a new type family `Prf`. Elements of the type `Prop` represent propositions, and also "datatypes" such as the type of natural numbers (we use the term "datatype" to refer to usual programming language types, as opposed to types of proofs of a proposition). Propositions and datatypes are identified in CC by taking the Curry-Howard isomorphism as an identity. The type family `Prf` assigns to each proposition or datatype `p : Prop` the type `Prf p` of its proofs, or, in the case of datatypes, its members. CC has one new term former `all x:T.t`, and two rules which relate it to `Prf`. The additions to λLF are shown in Figure 2-7.

In most presentations and implementations of CC the type `Prf t` is notationally identified with the term `t`. This is convenient and enhances readability, however, we will not adopt it for the sake of compatibility. The original formulation of CC went as far as using the same notation, namely `(x:A)` for all three binders: `Π,all,λ`. That did not enhance readability at all and was thus given up after some time!

CC contains F^{ω} as a subsystem by an obvious translation. For example, here is the type of an encoding of natural numbers in CC:

```
nat = all a:Prop.all z:Prf a.all s:Prf a →Prf a. a
```

(recall that `A→B` abbreviates `Πx:A.B`). Notice that `nat` is a member of type `Prop`. The natural numbers inhabit the type `Prf nat`. Accordingly, we have

```
zero = λa:Prop.λz:Prf a.λs:Prf a → Prf a.z : Prf nat

succ = λn:Prf nat.λa:Prop.λz:Prf a.
          λs:Prf a → Prf a.s(n a z s) : Prf nat → Prf nat

add = λm:Prf nat.λn:Prf nat.m nat n succ :
                                    Prf nat → Prf nat → Prf nat
```

Regarding higher-order polymorphism, here is how we define existential types in CC:

```
exists = λf:A→Prop.all c:Prop.all m:(Πx:A.Prf (f x)→Prf c).c
```

Here `A` is any type; we obtain System F's existential types with `A=Prop`; we obtain existential quantification over natural numbers with `A=Prf nat`.

2.6.1 Exercise [⋆, ↛]: Define the term corresponding to existential introduction of type: `Πf:A→Prop.Πa:A.Πi:Prf (f a).Prf (exists f)`. □

Conversely, existential elimination corresponds to applying a term of type `exists f` to an appropriately typed argument.

2.6.2 Exercise [⋆⋆⋆, ↛]: Formalize the translation from F^ω into CC. □

The combination of type dependency and impredicativity à la System F yields an astonishing expressive power. For example, we can define Leibniz equality as follows:

```
eq = λa:Prop.λx:Prf a.λy:Prf a.
          all p:Prf a→Prop.all h:Prf (p x).p y
   : Πa:Prop.Prf a → Prf a → Prop
```

We can now prove reflexivity of equality by exhibiting an inhabitant of the type `Πa:Prop. Πx:Prf a. Prf (eq a x x)`. Indeed,

```
eqRefl = λa:Prop. λx:Prf a. λp:Prf a → Prop. λh:Prf (p x).h
```

is such a term.

2.6.3 Exercise [⋆⋆, ↛]: State and prove symmetry and transitivity of equality. □

In a similar way, we can define other logical primitives such as boolean connectives and quantifiers and then prove mathematical theorems. Occasionally we have to assume additional axioms. For example, induction for the natural numbers can be stated, but not proved; it is thus convenient to work under the assumption:

```
natInd : Πp:Prf nat →Prop.Prf (p zero)
                  → (Πx:Prf nat.Prf (p x) → Prf (p(succ x)))
                   → Πx:Prf nat.Prf (p x)
```

With that assumption in place we can for example prove associativity of addition in the form of a term of type:

```
Πx:Prf nat.Πy:Prf nat.Πz:Prf nat.
                Prf (eq nat (add x (add y z)) (add (add x y) z))
```

2.6.4 EXERCISE [★★★]: Find such a term. □

The task of finding proof terms inhabiting types is greatly simplified by an interactive goal-directed theorem prover such as LEGO (Luo and Pollack, 1992; Pollack, 1994) or Coq (Barras et al., 1997), or a structure-driven text editor for programming, such as Agda or Alfa (Coquand, 1998; Hallgren and Ranta, 2000).

Algorithmic Typing and Equality for CC

We will now consider algorithmic typechecking for the pure CC. The beta reduction relation is extended with a clause for `all`:

$$\frac{\mathtt{t} \longrightarrow_{\beta} \mathtt{t}'}{\mathtt{all\ x{:}T.t} \longrightarrow_{\beta} \mathtt{all\ x{:}T.t}'} \qquad \text{(BETA-ALL)}$$

2.6.5 THEOREM: The relation $\longrightarrow_{\beta}$ is strongly normalizing on well-typed terms of CC. □

Proof: One can prove this directly using Tait's reducibility method; see, for example, Coquand and Huet (1988) or Luo and Pollack (1992). Alternatively, we can define a reduction-preserving mapping from CC into F^{ω} by "forgetting" type dependency—e.g., by mapping `eq a` $\mathtt{t}_1$ $\mathtt{t}_2$ to $\forall P.P \to P$. Therefore, an alleged infinite reduction sequence in CC would entail an infinite reduction sequence in F^{ω}. The details are beyond the scope of this survey. □

With this result in place it is now possible to establish soundness, completeness, and termination of algorithmic typing. The additional rules for the algorithm (extending those for λLF) are presented in Figure 2-8.

The Calculus of Inductive Constructions

The fact that induction cannot be proved is a flaw of the impredicative encoding of datatypes. Not only is it aesthetically unappealing to have to make

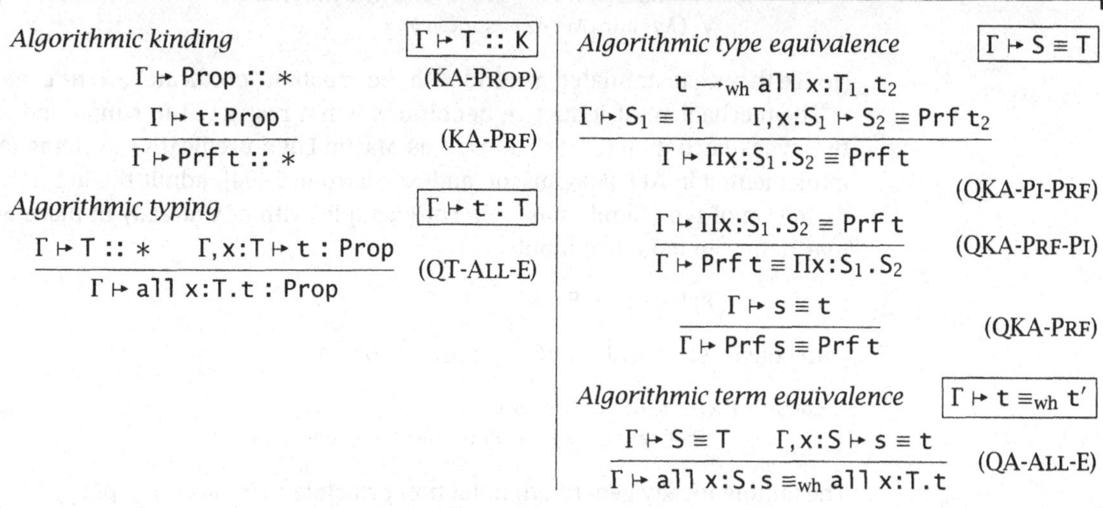

Figure 2-8: Algorithmic typing for CC

assumptions on an encoding; more seriously, the assumption of `natInd` destroys the analog of the progress theorem (see *TAPL*, §8.3). For example, the following term does not reduce to a canonical form:

```
natInd (λx:Prf nat.nat) zero (λx:Prf nat.λy:Prf nat.zero) zero
```

For these reasons, Mohring (1986) and subsequent authors (Werner, 1994; Altenkirch, 1993) have combined CC with inductive definitions as originally proposed (for a predicative system) by Martin-Löf (1984). In the thus obtained *Calculus of Inductive Constructions* (CIC) as implemented in the Coq theorem prover (Barras et al., 1997) we can declare the type `nat:Prop` as an inductive type with constructors `zero:Prf nat` and `succ:Prf nat→Prf nat`. This generates a constant:

```
natInd : Πp:Prf nat→Prop.Prf (p zero) →
           (Πx:Prf nat.Prf (p x) → Prf (p(succ x))) →
            Πx:Prf nat.Prf (p x)
```

which obeys the following equality rules:

```
natInd p hz hs zero ≡ hz
natInd p hz hs (succ n) ≡ hs n (natInd p hz hs n)
```

This clearly provides induction, but it also allows us to define primitive recursive functions such as addition by

```
add = λx:Prf nat.λy:Prf nat.natInd (λx:nat.nat)
        y (λy:nat.λr:nat.succ r) x
```

Notice that we instantiated natInd with the constant "predicate" λx:nat.nat.

The mechanism of inductive definitions is not restricted to simple inductive types such as nat. CIC, as well as Martin-Löf's predicative systems (as implemented in ALF [Magnusson and Nordström, 1994]) admit the inductive definition of type families as well. For example, with nat already in place we may define an inductive family

```
vector : Prf nat → Prop
```

with constructors nil : Prf (vector zero) and

```
cons : Πx:Prf nat. Prf nat →
        Prf (vector x) → Prf (vector(succ x))
```

The (automatically generated) induction principle then has the typing

```
vecInd : Πp:Πx:nat.Prf (vector x) → Prop.
    Prf (p zero nil) →
    (Πx:Prf nat.Πy:Prf (vector x).
        Πa:Prf nat.Prf (p x y)→Prf (cons x a y)) →
    Πx:Prf nat.Πy:Prf (vector x).Prf (p x y)
```

2.6.6 Exercise [★★, ↛]: What are the equality rules for this induction principle by analogy with the equations for natInd? □

Let us see how we can define the exception-free first function from the introduction for these vectors. We first define an auxiliary function first′ that works for arbitrary vectors by

```
first' = vecInd (λx:Prf nat.λv:Prf (vector x).nat)
  zero
  (λx:Prf nat.λy:Prf (vector x).
      λa:Prf nat.λprev:Prf nat.a) :
  Πx:Prf nat.Πv:Prf (vector x).Prf nat
```

This function obeys the equations:

```
first' zero nil = zero
first' (succ x) (cons x a y) = a
```

We obtain the desired function first by instantiation

```
first = λx:Prf nat.λy:Prf (vector (succ x)).
              first' (succ x) y
```

The default value zero can be omitted in a system like ALF which allows the definition of dependently-typed functions by pattern matching. In that system one would merely declare the type of first and write down the single pattern

```
first x (cons x a y) = a
```

ALF can then work out that this defines a total function. The extension of pattern matching to dependent types was introduced in Coquand (1992) which also contains beautiful examples of proofs (as opposed to programs) defined by pattern matching. McBride (2000) has studied translations of such pattern matching into traditional definitions using recursion/induction principles like vecInd.

2.6.7 EXERCISE [★★★, ↛]: Define using vecInd a function

```
concat : Πx:Prf nat.Πy:Prf nat.Prf (vector x) →
                                  Prf (vector y) →
                                  Prf (vector (add x y))
```

How does it typecheck? □

As a matter of fact, the CIC goes beyond the type system sketched here in that it allows quantification over *kinds*, so, for example, the "predicate" p in natInd may be an arbitrary type family. This means that using the constant family p = λx:nat.Prop we can define a function eqZero: Prf nat → Prop which equals true when applied to zero and false on all other arguments. This facility turns out to be useful to define the exception-free first function on vectors which was presented in the introduction.

Another additional feature of the CIC is the separation of propositions and datatypes into two disjoint universes Prop and Set. Both behave like our Prop, the difference lies in a program extraction feature that maps developments in the CIC to programs in an extension of F^{ω} with inductive types and general recursion. Types and terms residing in Prop are deleted by this translation; only types and terms in Set are retained. In this way, it is possible to extract correct programs from formal correctness proofs. Details can be found in Paulin-Mohring (1989).

Sigma Types in CC

It is unproblematic and useful to combine CC with Σ-types as described in Section 2.5 and Figure 2-5. This allows one to form types of algebraic structures, for instance

```
Semigrp = Σa:Prop.Σop:Prf a → Prf a → Prf a.
            Πx:Prf a.Πy:Prf a.Πz:Prf a.
              Prf (eq a (op x (op y z)) (op (op x y) z));
```

This system is contained in Luo's *Extended Calculus of Constructions* (ECC) (1994) which additionally permits Π and Σ quantification over kinds. For consistency reasons which we will briefly describe next this requires an infinite hierarchy of ever higher kinds $*_0, *_1, *_2, \ldots$. For instance, in ECC one has

$$\Sigma X{:}*_3.\ X : *_4$$

ECC has been implemented in the LEGO system (Luo and Pollack, 1992).

It is quite another matter to ask for a reflection of Σ-types into the universe `Prop` of datatypes and propositions, by analogy with the way `all` is treated. The temptation is to introduce a term former `ex y:T.t : Prop` when `x:T` ⊢ `t:Prop`, together with an equality rule asserting that

$$\texttt{Prf (ex y:T.t)} \equiv \Sigma\texttt{y:T.Prf t}.$$

Coquand (1986) has shown that the resulting system is unsound in the sense that all types are inhabited and strong normalization fails. Intuitively, the reason is that in this system we are able to define

```
prop = ex x:Prop.nat
```

and now have a mapping `i:Prop→Prf prop` defined by

```
i = λx:Prop.(x,zero:Prf nat)
```

as well as a left inverse `j:Prf prop →Prop` given by

```
j = λx:Prf prop.x.1.
```

Thus, we have reflected the universe `Prop` into one of its members, which allows one to encode (after some considerable effort) one of the set-theoretic paradoxes showing that there cannot be a set of all sets.

This must be contrasted with the impredicative existential quantifier `exists` defined on page 65. The difference between `exists` and the hypothetical term former `ex` is that `exists` does not allow one to project out the existential witness in case it is of type `Prop`.

An existential quantifier which does not provide first and second projections, but only the impredicative elimination rule known from System F is called a *weak sum, weak Σ-type*, or *existential.* In contrast, the Σ-types with projections are sometimes called *strong.*

We conclude this section by remarking that it is unproblematic to have "small" strong Σ-types in the CC, that is, if $\texttt{t}_1\texttt{:Prop}$ and $\texttt{x:Prf t}_1 \vdash \texttt{t}_2\texttt{:Prop}$ then $\sigma\texttt{x:Prf t}_1\texttt{.t}_2\texttt{:Prop}$ with the equivalence

$$\texttt{Prf}(\sigma\ \texttt{x:Prf t}_1\texttt{.t}_2) \equiv \Sigma\texttt{x:Prf t}_1\texttt{.Prf t}_2.$$

2.6.8 EXERCISE [★★★, ↛]: An "approximation" for σ `x:Prf t1.t2` is given by

```
exists = all c:Prop.all b:Πx:Prf t1.Prf t2 → Prf c.c.
```

Define pairing and first projection for `exists`. Unfortunately, it is not possible to define a second projection. □

2.7 Relating Abstractions: Pure Type Systems

The Calculus of Constructions is a very expressive system, but at first sight, somewhat difficult to understand because of the rich mix of different "levels" of typing (especially in its original formulation with `Prf` implicit). Given a lambda term $\lambda x : S.t$, we cannot tell without (possibly lengthy) further analysis of S and t whether this is a term-level function, a type abstraction, a type family, a type operator, or something else.

Partly as an attempt to explain the fine structure of CC, Barendregt introduced the *lambda cube* of typed calculi (briefly introduced in *TAPL*, Chapter 30), illustrated below:

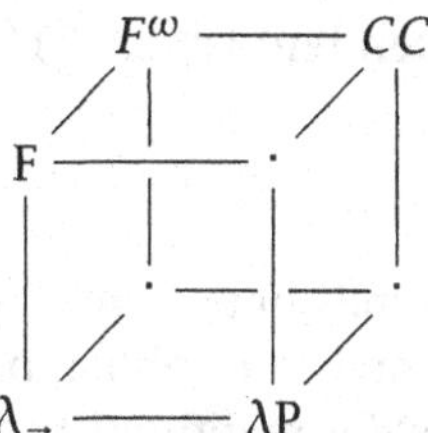

The cube relates previously known typed lambda calculi (recast within a uniform syntax) to CC, by visualizing three "dimensions" of abstraction. In the bottom left corner, we have $\lambda_\to$ with ordinary term-term abstraction. Moving rightwards, we add the type-term abstraction characteristic of dependent types: λP is the Lambda Cube's version of our λLF. Moving upwards, we add the term-type abstraction of System F, capturing polymorphism. Finally, moving towards the back plane of the cube, we add the higher-order type-type abstraction characteristic of F^ω.

Pure Type Systems

The type systems of the Lambda Cube, and many others besides, can be described in the setting of *pure type systems* (Terlouw, 1989; Berardi, 1988; Barendregt, 1991, 1992; Jutting, McKinna, and Pollack, 1994; McKinna and Pollack, 1993; Pollack, 1994). There is an simple and elegant central definition of Pure Type System (PTS) using just six typing rules, which captures a

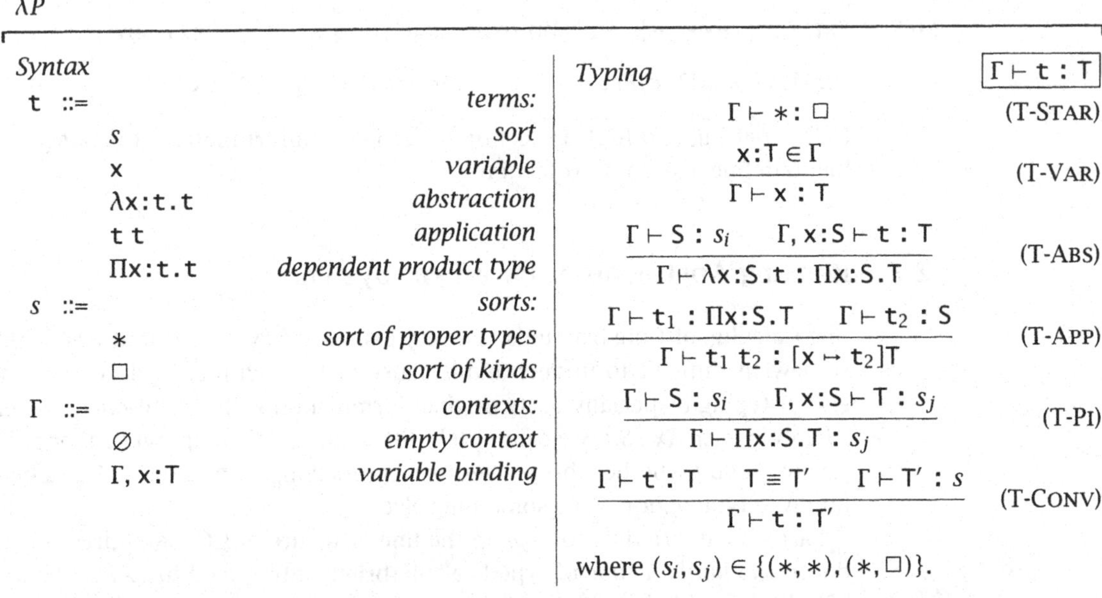

Figure 2-9: First-order dependent types, PTS-style (λP)

large family of systems constructed using Π-types. This uniform presentation allows one to establish basic properties for many systems at once, and also to consider mappings between type systems (so-called *PTS morphisms*).

A presentation of λLF as a Pure Type System is given in Figure 2-9.

The first thing to notice about PTSs is that there is a single syntactic category of terms, used to form types, terms, and abstractions and applications of different varieties. Although formally there is a single syntactic category, we use the same meta-variables as before, to aid intuition. (So the letters T and K and also range over the syntactic category of terms, but the system will determine that they are types and kinds, respectively).

To allow levels of types and kinds to be distinguished, the PTS framework uses tokens called *sorts* to classify different categories of term, within the formal system itself. The system λP requires two sorts: first, $*$, which is the kind of all proper types, as used before, and second, $\square$, which is the sort that classifies well-formed kinds. Judgments of the form $\Gamma \vdash T : *$ replace $\Gamma \vdash T :: *$ from Figure 2-1, and judgments $\Gamma \vdash K : \square$ replace $\Gamma \vdash K$.

The rule T-Pi controls formation of Π-types, by restricting which sorts we are allowed to quantify over. In turn, this restricts which λ-abstractions can be introduced by T-Abs. For λLF, there are two instances of λ-abstraction and two instances of Π-formation. In the PTS presentation, these are captured by the two pairs of sorts allowed in T-PI. When $s_i = s_j = *$, we have the first-order dependent product type, and when $s_j = \Box$ we have the kind of type families, corresponding respectively to K-PI and WF-PI in Figure 2-1.

The conversion rule is the main point of departure. The equivalence relation $\mathtt{s} \equiv \mathtt{t}$ in Pure Type Systems is defined between untyped terms, as the compatible closure of β-reduction. This has a strong effect on the metatheory.

2.7.1 EXERCISE [★★★★]: Using the obvious mapping from the syntax of λLF into the syntax of λP, give a proposition stating a connection between the two presentations. Try to prove your proposition. □

Systems of the Lambda Cube and Beyond

The other systems of the Lambda Cube can be expressed using the same rules as in Figure 2-9, with the single difference of changing the combinations of pairs of sorts (s_i, s_j) allowed in T-PI. This controls which kind of abstractions we can put into the context. The table below characterises the systems of the Lambda Cube:

System	PTS formation rules				
$\lambda_{\rightarrow}$	{ (∗,∗)				}
λP	{ (∗,∗),	(∗,□)			}
F	{ (∗,∗),		(□,∗)		}
F^{ω}	{ (∗,∗),		(□,∗),	(□, □)	}
CC	{ (∗,∗),	(∗,□),	(□,∗),	(□, □)	}

Further PTSs are given by adjusting the axiom T-STAR of Figure 2-9, which is another parameter in the formal definition of PTS. For example, if we take the axiom to be

$$\Gamma \vdash * : * \qquad \text{(T-TYPETYPE)}$$

(together with the T-PI restriction of $\{(*,*)\}$), we obtain a system where $*$ is the sort of all types including itself. In this system, all types are inhabited and there are non-normalizing terms (as in the result of Coquand, 1986 mentioned on page 70). Though this renders the logical interpretation of the system meaningless, it is debatable whether such systems may nonetheless be useful in some situations as type systems for programming languages.

For further details of Pure Type Systems, we refer the reader to the references given at the end of the chapter.

2.8 Programming with Dependent Types

The task of building practical programming languages with dependent types is a topic of current research. Early languages include Pebble (Lampson and Burstall, 1988) and Cardelli's Quest (Cardelli and Longo, 1991). Programming in Martin-Löf's type theory is described in the monograph (Smith, Nordström, and Petersson, 1990). More recently, Augustsson introduced a language called Cayenne (1998), with a syntax based on the functional programming language Haskell, and Xi and Pfenning studied the language Dependent ML, based around a fragment of Standard ML (1998; 1999). The difference between Cayenne and Dependent ML goes beyond the choice of underlying language, and serves to illustrate a fundamental design decision for practical programming with dependent types.

Languages with Undecidable Typechecking

Given the expressivity of dependent types as illustrated in previous sections it is natural and tempting to add them to a programming language. The price for this expressivity is, however, the complexity of typechecking. As we have explained, typechecking dependent types requires deciding equality of terms as a subtask which in turn requires the underlying term language to be strongly normalizing. On the other hand, most practical programming languages provide general recursion with possible nontermination. Simply adding dependent types to a Turing-complete term language invariably leads to undecidable typechecking.

Of course, typechecking remains semi-decidable, so one can simply wait for an answer for a reasonable amount of time before giving up and turning the typechecker off. This is basically the (surprisingly successful) approach undertaken in Cayenne. Another example is the theorem prover PVS (1996) which includes a dependently-typed programming language (at the time of writing, in an experimental stage), and also has semi-decidable typechecking. In PVS, however, it is possible to resort to interactive theorem proving to aid the type checker.

Undecidable typechecking is not to the taste of all programming language designers, and for reasons such as scalability, may not be suitable for general application. The alternative is to consider dependently typed languages built around standard programming language features, yet with low-complexity typechecking algorithms. To achieve this one must sacrifice some of the generality of dependent types. Dependent ML (DML) is a proposal which follows this approach, which we will investigate in more detail in the remainder of this section. A type system closely related to that of DML, but aimed at Haskell, was studied by Zenger, under the name *indexed types* (1997).

Exactly because this class of type systems have the desirable feature that they provide "static" typechecking independently from execution or equivalence checking of terms, some authors prefer not to call them "dependent" at all. The definition of dependent types given in Chapter 8 is slightly stricter than ours, and contrasts statically typed languages like DML and Indexed Types with languages where there is a lack of *phase distinction* between the compilation and execution of a program (see page 305).

A Simplified Version of Dependent ML

The crucial idea behind DML is that type dependency on terms is not allowed for arbitrary types, but only for certain *index sorts*. Typechecking gives rise to well-behaved constraint systems on terms belonging to index sorts. Typechecking and even (to an extent) type inference can then be reduced to a constraint-solving problem over the index sorts, which is decidable.

In this presentation we fix the index sorts to be integer numbers and linear subsets thereof, although Pfenning and Xi consider richer possibilities. We also base the language on the lambda-calculi we have studied so far, rather than a form of Standard ML.

Before going into details we will look at some simple examples concerning vectors. We write `int` for the index sort of integers and assume a basic type `data` and a basic type family `Vector : int→*` where `Vector[n]` denotes arrays over `data` of length `n` as usual. Note that, for example, `Vector[-1]` will be empty. Next, we introduce the constants

```
nil  : Vector[0]
cons : Πn:int.data → Vector[n] → Vector[n+1]
```

and a construct for pattern matching obeying the following typing rule:

$$\frac{\Gamma \vdash \mathtt{t}_1 : \mathtt{Vector[i]} \qquad \Gamma, \mathtt{i=0} \vdash \mathtt{t}_2 : \mathtt{T} \qquad \Gamma, \mathtt{n:int}, \mathtt{x:data}, \mathtt{l:Vector[n]}, \mathtt{i=n+1} \vdash \mathtt{t}_3 : \mathtt{T}}{\Gamma \vdash \mathtt{match}\ \mathtt{t}_1\ \mathtt{with}\ \mathtt{nil} \rightarrow \mathtt{t}_2 \mid \mathtt{cons[n](x,l)} \rightarrow \mathtt{t}_3 : \mathtt{T}} \quad \text{(MATCH-VECTOR)}$$

There are several things to notice here. Types distinguish between ordinary non-dependent function spaces $\mathtt{T}_1 \rightarrow \mathtt{T}_2$ and type families indexed by index sorts, $\Pi\mathtt{x:I.T}$. Application for Π-types is written using square brackets. Contexts contain bindings of index variables to index sorts, type variables to types, and constraints over terms of index sort. Here the constraints are equations; in general they may be propositions of some restricted form so as to retain decidability.

In our setting, nil, cons, and match are just interesting for their typing behaviors. We might postulate the obvious conversion rules for instances of match, to define a term equality judgment as studied earlier. But it is important to realize that we needn't do this for the purpose of typechecking, since for DML-style systems term equality is completely decoupled from typing.

In examples we will allow the definition of recursive functions by first declaring them with their type and then giving an accordingly typed implementation which may involve calls to the function being defined.[4]

Example: Appending Vectors

We want to define a function for appending two vectors. It should obey the following typing:

```
append : Πm:int.Πn:int.Vector[m] → Vector[n] → Vector[m+n]
```

To do this we define the body of append as follows:

```
append-body = λm:int.λn:int.λl:Vector[m].λt:Vector[n].
    match l with
        nil → t
      | cons[r](x,y) → cons[r+n](x,append[r][n](y,t))
```

We should prove that append-body has the same type as append. Let Γ = m:int, n:int, l:Vector[m], t:Vector[n]. After applying the rule MATCH-VECTOR backwards we are required to show that

$$\Gamma, \texttt{m=0} \vdash \texttt{t : Vector[m+n]}$$

and

$$\Gamma, \texttt{r:int, x:data, y:Vector[r], m=r+1} \vdash \texttt{cons[r+n](x,append[r][n](y,t)) : Vector[m+n]}$$

For the first requirement, we notice that Γ, m=0 ⊢ n=m+n:int from which the claim will follow by the type conversion rule and the obvious type equivalence which equates instances of Vector indexed by equal index terms:

$$\frac{\Gamma \vdash \texttt{i=j}}{\Gamma \vdash \texttt{Vector[i]=Vector[j]}}$$

This rule is an instance of QT-APP for DML families.

For the second requirement, we first notice that, given the purported typing of append, the append-subterm has type Vector[r+n], thus, by the typing of cons the term itself has type Vector[r+n+1], but in the given context, this is equal to Vector[m+n] hence the required typing follows by type conversion again.

4. One can achieve this effect with a constant $\texttt{fix}_T$: (T→T) → T for any type T.

Example: Splitting a Vector

This example illustrates DML's restricted form of Σ-types. Again, we have both dependent sums indexed by index sorts, and non-dependent sums (i.e., ordinary cartesian products). We will use the following type abbreviation:

```
T(m) = Σp:int.Σq:{ i | p+i=m }.Vector[p] * Vector[q]
```

The type `T(m)` has elements of the form `(p,(q,(k,l)))`, which we shall write as `(p,q,k,l)` to avoid excessive parentheses. The terms `p` and `q` are integer indices, obeying the constraint $\mathtt{p} + \mathtt{q} = \mathtt{m}$.

Now we can define a `split` function that partitions a vector into two pieces of given lengths:

```
split : Πm:int.Vector[m] → T(m)

split-body = λm:int.λl:Vector[m].
    match l with
       nil ⇒ (0,0,nil,nil) : T(0)
     | cons[r](x,y) ⇒ let (p,q,u,v) = split[r](y) in
              if test(x) then (p+1, q, cons[p](x,u), v) : T(r+1)
                         else (p, q+1, u, cons[q](x,v)) : T(r+1)
```

where `test(x)` is some unspecified boolean-valued term. The typing of `split` guarantees that the result vectors could be appended to form a vector with the same length as the input. Notice that we can say that there is *some* pair `p` and `q` such that `p+q=m` where `m` is the length of the input, but with the restricted form of predicates in DML, we cannot say that `p` is equal to the number of elements `x` from the input for which `test(x)` is true.

To see how `split` is typed, let Γ = `m:int, l:Vector[m]`. We have Γ, `m=0` ⊢ `T(0)=T(m)` which deals with the first case of the match. For the second case, we need to show

```
Γ,p:int, q:int, p+q=r, u:Vector[p], v:Vector[q], r+1=m ⊢
    (p+1, q, cons[p](x,u), v) : T(r+1) = T(m)
```

and similarly for the `else`-branch of the `if` statement. Again this follows from trivial equational reasoning, and the expected rules for sum types.

Definition of Simplified DML

Figure 2-10 summarizes the syntax of our simplified form of DML. Most of the typing rules are routine, so we leave completing the system to exercises.

The definition of DML is closely related to λLF with Σ-types, except that dependencies are restricted to special terms of index sorts, so there is a partitioning of the syntax. Index sorts comprise the integers and subsets of index

DML

I ::=		*index sorts:*
	int	*index sort of integers*
	{x:I | P}	*subset sort*
P ::=		*propositions:*
	P ∧ P	*conjunction*
	i<=i	*index inequality*
i ::=		*index terms:*
	x	*variable*
	q	*constant* $q \in \mathbb{Z}$
	*q*i	*multiplication by* $q \in \mathbb{Z}$
	i+i	*addition*
t ::=		*terms:*
	x	*variable*
	λx:I.t	*index abstraction*
	t[i]	*index application*
	λx:T.t	*abstraction*
	t t	*application*
	(i, t)	*index pairing*
	(t, t)	*term pairing*
	let (x, y)=t in t	*projection*
T ::=		*types:*
	X	*type/family variable*
	Πx:I.T	*indexed product*
	Σx:I.T	*indexed sum*
	T[i]	*type family application*
	$T_1 \to T_2$	*function type*
	$T_1 * T_2$	*cartesian product*
K ::=		*kinds:*
	*	*kind of proper types*
	Πx:I.K	*kind of type families*
Γ ::=		*contexts:*
	∅	*empty context*
	Γ, x:T	*term variable binding*
	Γ, x:I	*index variable binding*
	Γ, P	*constraint*

Figure 2-10: Simplified Dependent ML (DML)

sorts. Subset formation is permitted only with respect to a restricted set of predicates. In our case, these are conjunctions of linear inequalities (equality of two indices, $\mathtt{i_1{=}i_2}$, can be defined as $\mathtt{i_1{<=}i_2} \wedge \mathtt{i_2{<=}i_1}$). Index terms themselves are restricted to variables, constants, addition of terms and multiplication by constants. Given an index sort, proposition, or index term $\mathcal{I}$, we write *FIV*($\mathcal{I}$) to stand for the free (index) variables of $\mathcal{I}$. We use the same category of variables for index variables and ordinary variables, but we can tell from a typing context whether a variable ranges over index terms or ordinary terms. Given a context Γ, let *IV*(Γ) stand for the set of index variables declared in Γ. A term $\mathcal{I}$ in the index syntax is well-formed in Γ just in case *FIV*($\mathcal{I}$) ⊆ *IV*(Γ); no typing rules are needed to check well-formedness in the index syntax. For contexts, we assume as usual that no variable is bound more than once, and moreover, that the free variables appearing in declarations x:I and constratints P are declared earlier in the context.

Ordinary terms include index terms in application position and in the first component of pairs. There are types depending on index terms, but there are no types depending on ordinary terms. As a result, function space and cartesian product cannot be defined as special cases of Π and Σ-types, but must be included as primitives. Kinds are just as in LF, except that dependency is restricted to index sorts I.

In the typing rules we assume given two semantically defined judgments:

$\Gamma \models \mathtt{P}$	P *is a consequence of* Γ
$\Gamma \models \mathtt{i : I}$	i:I *follows from the assumptions of* Γ

These judgments depend only on the index assumptions and propositions in Γ, and their intention should be clear. For example, we have:

$$\mathtt{x:\{y:int \mid y>=8\},\ z:int,\ z>=9} \ \models\ \mathtt{x+z >= 13}$$

The judgments can be defined formally using the obvious interpretation of the index syntax in $\mathbb{Z}$ (see Exercise 2.8.1).

In practice we are of course interested an algorithm for deriving the two judgments. In our simplified version of DML, both judgments $\Gamma \models \mathtt{P}$ and $\Gamma \models \mathtt{i:I}$ are decidable, and there are well-known methods which we can use for handling linear equalities over the integers. In the case of a more complicated index language the judgments might both be undecidable; for instance, if we allow multiplication of index terms and existential quantification in propositions then undecidability follows from the undecidability of Hilbert's 10th problem.

In the typing rules, the semantic judgment is used whenever we need to check that an index term belongs to an index sort. For example, the rule for type family application becomes:

$$\frac{\Gamma \vdash \mathtt{S :: \Pi x{:}I.K} \qquad \Gamma \models \mathtt{i : I}}{\Gamma \vdash \mathtt{S[i] : [x \mapsto i]K}} \qquad \text{(DML-K-App)}$$

The typing rules for the remainder of the language are defined similarly to λLF and the simply-typed lambda calculus. For instance, we have the following rule for index abstraction:

$$\frac{\Gamma, \mathtt{x{:}I} \vdash \mathtt{t : T}}{\Gamma \vdash \mathtt{\lambda x{:}I.t : \Pi x{:}I.T}} \qquad \text{(DML-I-Abs)}$$

but for ordinary abstraction we introduce the arrow:

$$\frac{\Gamma, \mathtt{x{:}S} \vdash \mathtt{t : T}}{\Gamma \vdash \mathtt{\lambda x{:}S.t : S \to T}} \qquad \text{(DML-T-Abs)}$$

There are similarly two rules for pairing and for projections. For the projection of an indexed pair, we have the dependent case:

$$\frac{\Gamma \vdash \mathtt{t : \Sigma x{:}I.T} \qquad \Gamma, \mathtt{x{:}I}, \mathtt{y{:}T} \vdash \mathtt{t' : T'}}{\Gamma \vdash \mathtt{let\ (x,y)=t\ in\ t' : T'}} \qquad \text{(DML-I-Proj)}$$

We can also follow the same procedure as for λLF to formulate an algorithmic version of typing; the difference is that algorithmic type equality amounts to checking of index constraints which can be performed semantically by constraint solving, without any normalization. In particular, equality of terms is not intertwined with typechecking at all. The crucial rule for algorithmic equality is

$$\frac{\Gamma \mapsto \mathtt{S}_1 \equiv \mathtt{S}_2 \qquad \Gamma \models \mathtt{i}_1 = \mathtt{i}_2}{\Gamma \mapsto \mathtt{S}_1\ \mathtt{i}_1 \equiv \mathtt{S}_2\ \mathtt{i}_2} \quad \text{(DML-QIA-APP)}$$

where the second judgment is an instance of the semantic consequence judgment $\Gamma \models \mathtt{P}$.

2.8.1 EXERCISE [★★]: Give a semantic interpretation of DML index syntax. Considering only the index variables in Γ, an *index environment* η is a function from index variables to integers. Given this notion, we can define $\Gamma \models \mathtt{P}$ as $\forall \eta.\ \eta \models \Gamma.\ \Longrightarrow \eta \models \mathtt{P}$. Complete the definition. □

2.8.2 EXERCISE [★★★, ↛]: Complete the presentation of DML by defining the typechecking judgments and give an algorithm for typechecking. □

Closing Example: Certifying Parameters

Several motivating application examples have been given for DML in the literature, including eliminating array bounds checks and unnecessary cases from pattern matches. Rather than repeat those examples, we give a slightly different kind of example to illustrate the use of DML-style typing to certify that constraints are met on parameters of functions.[5]

The scenario is that we are programming for an embedded system which is providing safety features for an onboard computer in an automobile. We are provided with a system call:

```
brake : int * int → unit
```

where it is safety critical that whenever `brake` is called with parameters `(x,y)` then some proposition $P(x,y)$ must be satisfied, for example, a conjunction of linear inequalities describing some "safe window."

To guarantee this, we should try to type our main program under the following assumed typing for `brake`. Notice that `brake` is provided as a system call, so we can assume an arbitrary typing for it.

```
brake : {(x,y) : int * int | P} → unit
```

5. This example is taken from the project *Mobile Resource Guarantees* (EU IST-2001-33149); see `http://www.lfcs.inf.ed.ac.uk/mrg`.

where P encodes $P(x, y)$. Unfortunately, this typing does not quite fit into the DML-framework since it unduly mixes index sorts and ordinary types. To repair this, we introduce a type family Int : int → ∗ with the intuition that Int(x) is a singleton type containing just the integer x, as a "run-time" integer rather than an index term. We also need special typings for run-time integers:

```
0 : Int(0)
1 : Int(1)
plus : Πx,y:int.Int(x) → Int(y) → Int(x+y)
times_q : Πx:int.Int(x) → Int(qx)
```

where q is a fixed integer. These typings allow us to reflect the index terms in ordinary terms. Moreover, we need a type family Bool:int→∗ with the intuition that Bool(x) contains true if 1<=x and Bool(x) contains false if x<=0. Now we can suppose constants:

```
true  : Πx:int|1<=x. Bool(x)
false : Πx:int|x<=0. Bool(x)
leq   : Πx,y:int. Int(x) → Int(y) → Bool(1+y-x)
```

(where we write Πx:int|P.T as an abbreviation of Πx:{x:int | P}. T).

We also need a construct for case distinction obeying the following typing rule:

$$\frac{\Gamma \vdash \mathtt{t_1 : Bool(i)} \qquad \Gamma, \mathtt{1<=i} \vdash \mathtt{t_2 : T} \qquad \Gamma, \mathtt{i<=0} \vdash \mathtt{t_3 : T}}{\Gamma \vdash \mathtt{if\ t_1\ then\ t_2\ else\ t_3 : T}}$$

Notice that if we define boolean negation in terms of if-then-else then we would obtain the typing:

```
not : Πx:int. Bool(x) → Bool(1-x)
```

because 1<=x ⊨ 1-x<=0 and x<=0 ⊨ 1<=1-x. Unfortunately, the derived typings for conjunction and disjunction are rather weak:

```
andalso,orelse : Πx,y:int.Bool(x)→Bool(y) → Σz:int.Bool(z)
```

Xi introduces a separate index sort of booleans with the usual operations on the index level. This gives tighter typings for the boolean operations like

```
andalso : Πx,y:bool.Bool(x)→Bool(y)→Bool(x ∧ y).
```

The price is that constraint solving for such a combined theory is much more complex.

Returning to the example with the system call, let us suppose that the linear constraint P simply states x+y<=10 and that the main function is just a wrapper around brake that makes sure the constraint is actually met, i.e.

```
main(x,y) = if x+y<=10 then call brake(x,y) else call brake(0,0)
```

Here is the corresponding DML version. We assume that the system call `brake` satisfies the typing

```
brake : Πx,y:int|x+y<=10.Int(x) → Int(y) → unit

main : Πx,y:int.Int(x) → Int(y) → unit
main-body = λx,y:int.λxx:Int(x).λyy:Int(y).
                if leq[x+y,10](plus[x,y](xx,yy),10)
                     then brake[x,y](xx,yy)
                     else brake[0,0](0,0)
```

Although this example is rather simple, it illustrates the general technique for connecting index sort constraints to function calls. The fact that this definition is type correct guarantees that the required safe window for calls to `brake` is indeed always obeyed.

Summary and Outlook

We have shown the theory of a simplified fragment of Pfenning and Xi's DML demonstrating the important feature that typechecking amounts to constraint solving, for example, in the domain of integers, rather than normalizing terms. In this way, it becomes possible to retain decidability of typechecking in the presence of general recursion.

The DML examples show that index annotations are quite heavy. Fortunately, most can be inferred automatically by a process known as *elaboration*. It is plausible that in the examples we can reconstruct the annotations by replacing them by indeterminate linear terms in the index variables in scope and then solving for the coefficients. In Xi's thesis (1998), elaboration is presented in detail as a logic program in the style of our algorithmic subtyping.

One of the design criteria behind the original DML was to allow ordinary Standard ML programs to be extended with additional type annotations. Current research in dependent type systems for programming seeks further advances at the programming language level. The aim is to provide more comfortable high-level notations and new programming language abstractions for applying dependent type theory. One example of this is by enriching pattern matching, see McBride (2000) and McBride and McKinna (2004).

Underlying type theories such as CIC are amply expressive for this purpose; the challenge lies in making these systems more convenient to use, by adding programming language constructions, notational conveniences and advanced inference techniques. Present implementations, oriented towards mathematical interactive proof development, need to be adapted to programming language settings. These exciting developments leave much to be expected for the future of programming with dependent types.

2.9 Implementation of Dependent Types

In this final section we describe an OCaml implementation of the dependent type theory described in preceding sections. The implementation allows declarations and definitions of both terms and types. Typechecking occurs as soon as a declaration or definition is given. A term may be given with a type, which will be checked, or without, in which case one will be inferred. Similarly for kinds. Finally, we can ask to normalise well-typed terms.

The typechecking algorithm proceeds by evaluating the rules in Figures 2-4 and 2-3 and the later tables extending these judgments. More precisely, we have (simultaneously defined) functions:

```
val whnf : term → term
val typeof : context → term → ty
val kindof : context → ty → kind
val checkkind :  context → kind → unit
val tyeqv : context → ty → ty → bool
val kindeqv : context → ty → ty → bool
val tmeqv : context → ty → ty → bool
```

These functions are implemented by encoding the algorithmic rules using pattern matching. For example, the definition of `tmeqv` begins like so:

```
 tmeqv ctx tm1 tm2 =
   let tm1' = whred true ctx tm1 in
   let tm2' = whred true ctx tm2 in
   match (tm1',tm2') with
     (TmVar(fi,i,j), TmVar(fi',i',j')) → i=i'
   | (TmAbs(_,x,tyS1,tmS2),TmAbs(_,y,tyT1,tmT2))→
       let ctx' = addbinding ctx x (VarBind(tyS1)) in
       tmeqv ctx'  tmS2 tmT2
...
```

(the first argument of `whred` is a flag indicating whether to allow definitions in the context to be expanded).

We stress that the implementation is a direct rendition of the syntax and rules described earlier. It does not include any of the numerous desirable features that make programming with dependent types more convenient, such as argument synthesis (Harper and Pollack, 1991) or interactive, goal-directed construction of terms. Conversely, because the implementation is simple, it should be straightforward to experiment with extensions. The program is built on the F^{ω} implementation from *TAPL* and uses the same design and data structures (see *TAPL*, Chapters 6, 7, and 30).

We illustrate the use of the implementation by way of some examples. Notice that the ASCII input to the system to produce a type like `Πx:A.B` is `Pi x:A.B`.

Examples

With the commands

```
A : *;
Nat : *;
zero : Nat;
succ : Πn:Nat.Nat;
Vector : Πn:Nat.*;
```

we declare variables `A`, `Nat`, constants `zero` and `succ` intended to denote zero and successor on the natural numbers, and a type `Vector` depending on type `Nat`. Note that the implementation does not support →; we must use Π-types throughout. Next, we declare functions to form vectors by

```
nil : Vector zero
cons : Πn:Nat. Πx:A. Πv:Vector n. Vector (succ n)
```

allowing us to define a function for forming vectors of length three:

```
one = succ zero;two = succ one;
mkthree = λx:A.λy:A.λz:A.
        cons two z (cons one y (cons zero x nil));
```

The implementation will respond by inferring the type of `mkthree`:

```
mkthree : Πx:A. Πy:A. Πz:A. Vector (succ two)
```

We can now partially apply `mkthree` to two elements of type `A` by

```
a:A; b:A;
mkthree a b;
```

resulting in the response

```
λz:A.
 cons (succ (succ zero)) z
 (cons (succ zero) b (cons zero a nil)) :
     Πz:A.Vector(succ (succ (succ zero)))
```

This response exhibits two weaknesses of the implementation. First, definitions are always expanded in results; this will in practice almost always lead to unreadable outpt. Second, the first arguments to cons must be given explicitly and are printed out while they could be inferred from the types of the second arguments. Practical implementations of dependent types overcome both these problems. For instance, in LEGO (Luo and Pollack, 1992), `mkthree` would be defined (in our notation) as

```
mkthree = λx:A.λy:A.λz:A. cons z (cons y (cons x nil));
```

and the response to `mkthree a b` would be

```
λz:A.cons z (cons  b (cons a nil))) :  Πz:A.Vector three
```

For LEGO to know that the first argument to `cons` is implicit we must declare `cons` by

```
Πn|Nat. Πx:A. Πv:Vector n. Vector (succ n)
```

where the bar indicates implicitness for argument synthesis.

Returning to our experimental checker, let us illustrate Σ-types. We declare three types

```
A:∗; B:Πx:A.∗; C:Πx:A.Πy:B x.∗;
```

and define

```
S = Σx:A.Σy:B x.C x y;
```

Supposing

```
a:A; b:B a; c: C a b;
```

then we can form

```
 (a,(b,c:Σy:B a.C a y):S);
```

which is an element of `S`. The first type annotation is actually redundant and the implementation allows one to abbreviate the above by

```
(a,b,c:S)
```

If we declare

```
Q : Πx:S.∗;
x:S; y:Q x;
```

Then the following typecast succeeds

```
y:Q (x.1,x.2.1,x.2.2:S);
```

thus illustrating the built-in surjective pairing.

Here, finally, is the definition of natural numbers in CC:

```
nat = all a:Prop.all z:Prf a.all s:Πx:Prf a.Prf a. a;
```

Note that `Prf` always requires parentheses in the implementation.

We also remark that by default the implementation prints the weak-head normal form of input terms. The β-normal form of a term `t` is printed with the command `Normal t`.

2.10 Further Reading

Dependent type theories have been widely investigated, much of the development building on the pioneering work of Per Martin-Löf. This is not the place for a comprehensive overview of the literature; rather we provide a few pointers into work related to the developments in this chapter.

The Edinburgh Logical Framework and its type system are described in Harper, Honsell, and Plotkin (1993). Our definition of λLF has the same type structure, but omits signatures, and includes declarative equality judgments rather than an untyped equivalence relation. A more complete recent development which also includes equality judgments is in Harper and Pfenning (2004).

Richer type theories than LF are considered in many places. The calculus of constructions was introduced in Coquand and Huet (1988) and further developed in related type theories (Mohring, 1986; Luo, 1994; Pollack, 1994). Algorithms for typechecking with dependent types were first considered by Coquand (1991), Cardelli (1986; 1988b), and also within the closely related AUTOMATH system of de Bruijn (1980).

The best survey of Pure Type Systems remains Barendregt's handbook article (1992), which includes a description of the Lambda Cube. Although the definition of PTS is elegant and short, developing the meta-theory for PTSs has been surprisingly challenging. Several important results and improvements have been made since Barendregt's article. For example, Pollack (1994), studied formalization of the meta-theory of PTSs in type theory itself, Poll (1998) established the *expansion postponement* property for the class of normalizing PTSs, and Zwanenburg (1999) studied the addition of subtyping to PTSs.

Type theories which combine inductive types and quantification over kinds, such as CIC, do not permit an easy normalization proof by translation into a simply-typed normalizing sytem as was the case for the pure CC. Therefore, strong normalization must be proved from scratch for those systems. So far only partial proofs have been published for CIC as it is implemented in Coq; the closest work so far is in the recent PhD thesis of Miquel (2001). For UTT as implemented in LEGO, a strong normalization proof is given in Goguen (1994), which introduces the idea of a *typed operational semantics* as a more controlled way of managing reduction in a typed setting.

A topic we have not considered here is the semantics of dependent types. There has been considerable study; see Hofmann (1997b) for a particular approach and some comparison with the literature. Notable contributions include Cartmell (1986), Erhard (1988), Streicher (1991), and Jacobs (1999).

3 *Effect Types and Region-Based Memory Management*

Fritz Henglein, Henning Makholm, and Henning Niss

Type-based program analysis is program analysis based on the concepts, theories and technologies developed for type systems and employed in the definition of programming languages. It is a vast field of research with numerous applications and considerable practical impact. Applications include strictness analysis, data representation analysis, binding-time analysis, soft typing (also called dynamic typing inference), boxing analysis, pointer aliasing, value flow analysis (and all its applications), region-based memory management, communication topology analysis, Year 2000 type analysis, cryptographic protocol verification, locking, race detection, and others; see Palsberg (2001) for an overview of additional applications.

This chapter presents type-based program analysis based on *type and effect systems* (or *effect type systems*) and illustrates their application in *region-based memory management*, which is the chapter's ultimate focus. Classical type systems express properties of values, not the computations leading to those values. *Effect types* describe all important effects of computation, not just their results. Region-based memory management refers to programming where heap data is allocated in individually managed regions that are explicitly allocated and deallocated. As we shall see, state-of-the-art region-based memory management employs effect type systems to ensure *region safety*, which guarantees that no accesses to unallocated or deallocated regions occur at run time.

3.1 Introduction and Overview

Region-based memory management has a well-developed theory, has been subject to practice-oriented engineering, and is deployed in industrial-quality language implementations and prototype systems. We provide a consolidated review of the state of the art in region-based memory management and use it as an application domain to develop fundamental concepts of effect type systems step by step.

Value Flow and Simple Effect Analyses

In §3.2, we introduce BL, a standard typed higher-order functional language. Then we present an TL, an extension of BL, with atomic labels p (tags, names) and corresponding *tagging* and *untagging* operations `t at p` and `t ! p`. Evaluation of `t at p` equips the value v of `t` with label p resulting in a *tagged value* $\langle v \rangle_p$; correspondingly, evaluation of `t ! p'` simply checks that p in the value $\langle v \rangle_p$ of `t` equals label p′ before returning v. We present a type system which ensures that the check in `t ! p'` always succeeds. Thus, the labels and their operations can be thought of as *annotations* that let us trace where values are created and used at run-time; they express and make explicit *value flow information* of the underlying BL program. The connection of TL and the value flow information expressed in it to region-based memory management is a reinterpretation of labels as regions and tagging/untagging operations as region access operations. An expression `t at p` is then reinterpreted as "evaluate `t`, allocate it in the region bound to p, and return the corresponding pointer," and `t ! p` is reinterpreted as "evaluate `t` to a pointer into the region bound to p and load its contents from there." This leaves the problem of figuring out when to allocate and deallocate a region. The basic idea is extracting lifetime information about values living in a region ρ from typing derivations: If a (sub)term `t` that contains uses of a region ρ can be typed such that ρ neither occurs in the typing assumptions nor in the result, we take this to mean that ρ does not need to exist before evaluating `t` or after. So we can evaluate `t` by first allocating a new region ρ, then evaluating `t`, and finally deallocating ρ. To express this we extend TL with a construct newρ.t and add straightforward evaluation and typing rules to give language STL. §3.2 concludes with the observation that STL is *unsound* because the typing judgments do not capture accesses to regions from the environment part in lexical closures; that is, important properties of the computation (evaluation) itself are not reflected in (the types of) the values produced by those computations.

The unsoundness motivates the use of effect type systems to capture accesses to regions during an evaluation. In §3.3, we introduce *effect types* (types and effects), which represent relevant effects (accesses to regions) of an evaluation together with the type of its result. The basic lifetime interpretation of typing judgments for region allocation and deallocation with explicit effects is then sound since all accesses to regions are represented in the effect of an expression, as are those from the environment part of a lexical closure.

Region-Based Effect Analyses

The development in §3.2 and §3.3 is focused on the conceptual roles of types, effects, value flow information, and lifetime interpretation of typing judgments. In particular, the type systems are monomorphic, and regions cannot be passed as parameters. Turning our attention to realistic region-based memory management, §3.4 extends the region annotations by adding region abstraction and region application. This extension provides the basis for region polymorphism, which is crucial for practicality. The key result of this section is *conditional correctness*: If a region annotated program does not run into an error (in particular, does not access an unallocated or deallocated region) then it has the same result as the underlying program without region annotations. This result by itself shows that region annotations may introduce errors during evaluation, but do not otherwise change the semantics of the underlying program. It is noteworthy that conditional correctness holds for all region-annotated terms independent of any type system.

§3.5 presents TT, the Tofte–Talpin region type system, in a simplified form and adapted to our setting. The main result in this section is type *soundness*: no TT-annotated term can go wrong. Combining soundness with conditional correctness we obtain *correctness*: A TT-annotated program produces the same result as the underlying unannotated program. This section highlights the role of the type system: its job is to ensure soundness; conditional correctness is already taken care of.

Region-Based Systems: Inference and Systems

There are usually many different well-annotated versions of a given underlying program, all of which are correct. They do not have the same efficiency characteristics: Some retain regions substantially longer during execution than others. In §3.6 we turn to the question of how to automatically infer "good" region annotations. Region inference is technically complex. The section discusses the algorithmic techniques that have been used for TT inference and a number of restricted cases, providing pointers to the relevant literature for detailed descriptions.

The Tofte–Talpin type system enforces a stack discipline on region allocation and deallocation driven by a lexically scoped region-creation expression. §3.7 presents refinements of its standard implementation to accomplish better region performance for lexically scoped regions: region resetting and delayed allocation/early deallocation. Furthermore, it discusses region lifetime subtyping and systems where region allocation and deallocation are decoupled altogether: calculus of capabilities for continuation passing style programs and imperative regions.

Finally, §3.8 surveys implementations with statically checked region-based memory management: ML Kit with Regions, a Standard ML compiler; Cyclone and Vault, which are type-safe C-like languages with explicit region management and other novel extensions; and prototype systems for Java and Prolog. It briefly reviews systems and libraries for region-based programming with no static region safety guarantees, but with dynamic or no-region fault detection.

3.2 Value Flow by Typing with Labels

The language BL, also called *Finitary PCF* (Jung and Stoughton, 1993; Loader, 2001), is a simply typed lambda-calculus with general recursion (fix), Boolean values and call-by-value semantics. It is the underlying language, for which we shall develop region-based memory management based on effect type systems in this section. Its syntax and small-step operational semantics are given in Figure 3-1.

Tagged Language

In this subsection we introduce TL, which is BL extended with explicit tagging and untagging operations. Syntax and operational semantics are defined in Figure 3-2, extending the definitions for BL in Figure 3-1.

The category of label variables ρ designates a denumerable set of label variables $\rho_0, \rho_1, \ldots$. Like ordinary program variables, label variables are atomic and have no internal structure. For convenience we may abbreviate *label expression* to *label.* Labels p can only consist of label variables for now. We shall extend p later. Anticipating their reinterpretation later, we shall also call label variables *region variables* and labels *regions* or *places.*

Operationally, evaluation of `t at p` consists of *tagging* the value of `t` with label p. We write the result of tagging value v with p as $\langle \mathsf{v} \rangle_{\mathsf{p}}$. The untagging operation `t at p'` evaluates `t` to a tagged value $\langle \mathsf{v} \rangle_{\mathsf{p}}$, checks that its label p matches p' and, if so, returns the underlying value v. If the label does not match, the evaluation gets stuck—it *goes wrong.* As we shall see, the typing rules of TL guarantee that evaluation never goes wrong in this way for well-typed terms.

The tagging and untagging operations serve to *name* certain sets of values and to mark where such values are constructed and used. Note the following:

- Multiple subterms of a term may have the same label.
- Even though a label may occur only once in a program, it may tag multiple values at run time; for example, in $\lambda \mathsf{x}_0.(\mathsf{x}_0$ `at` $\rho_0)$ the same label ρ_0 will

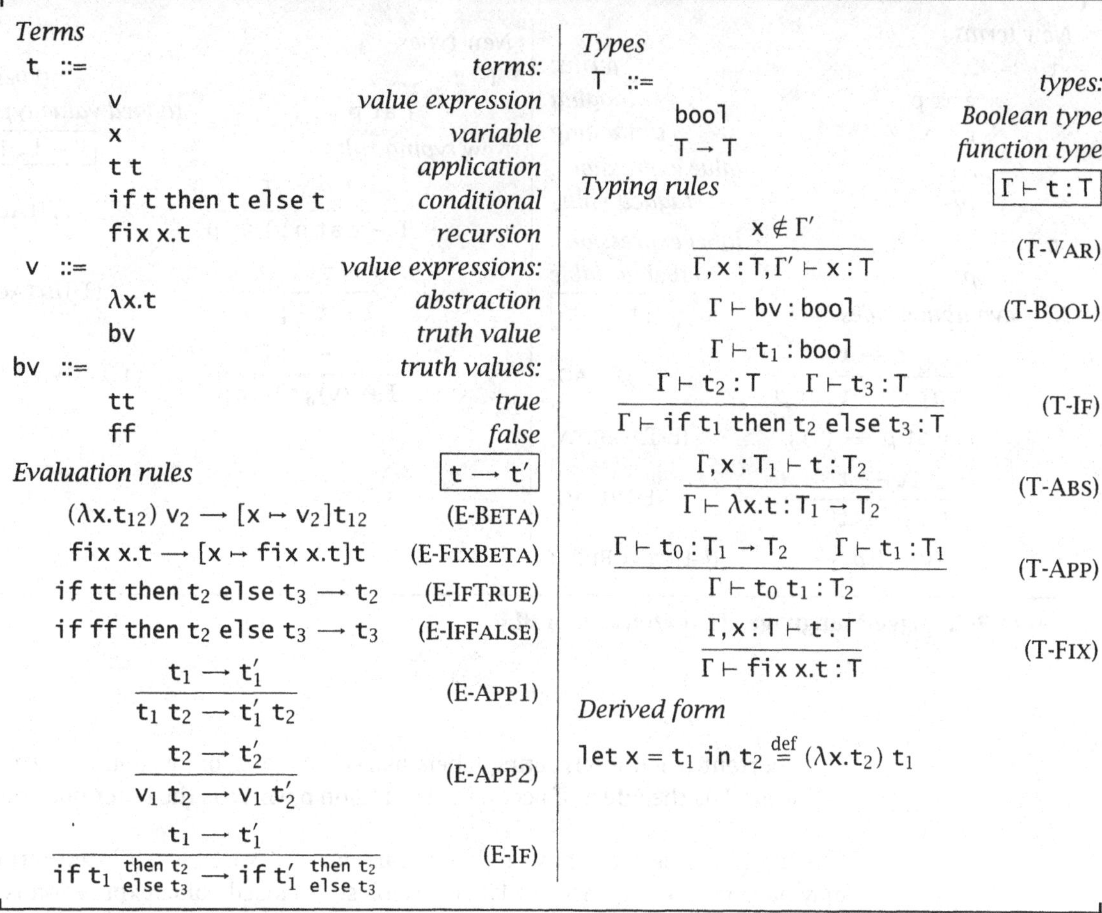

Figure 3-1: Base language BL

tag multiple values if the function is called multiple times with different argument values.

- Labels let us distinguish values produced in different places even though they are extensionally equal; for example, in a call $\mathtt{f}$ $(\mathtt{tt}\ \mathtt{at}\ \rho_0)$ $(\mathtt{tt}\ \mathtt{at}\ \rho_1)$ we can keep track of the uses of both arguments separately even though they are the same values.

- We distinguish between $\mathtt{v}$ $\mathtt{at}$ $\mathtt{p}$ and $\langle \mathtt{v} \rangle_{\mathtt{p}}$. The former denotes an unevaluated expression, where $\mathtt{v}$ has not been tagged with $\mathtt{p}$ yet, and the latter denotes the result of performing the tagging. This distinction will be

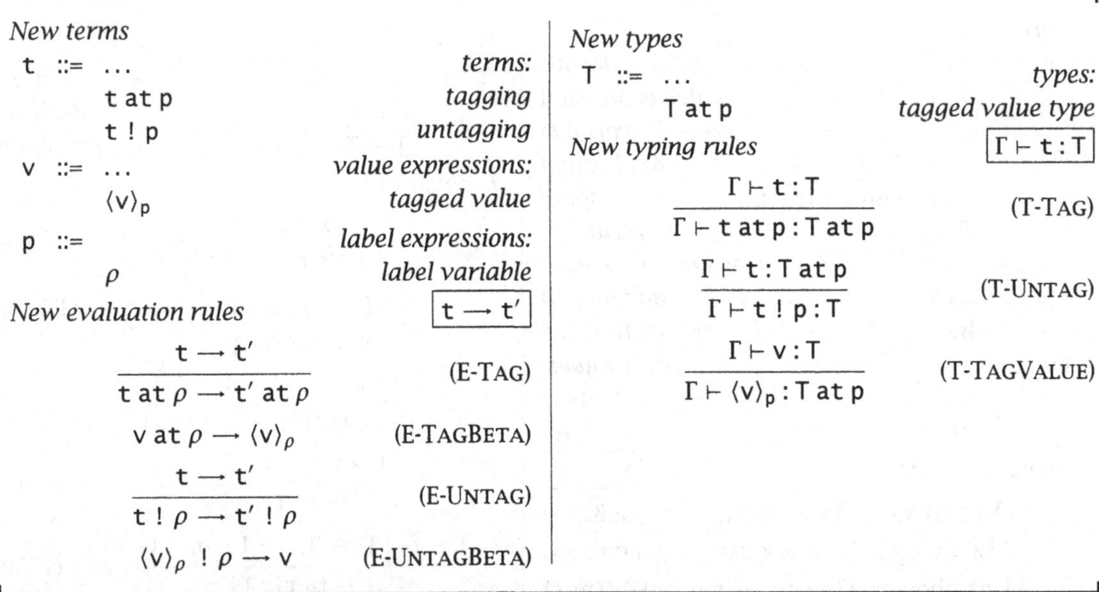

Figure 3-2: Tagged language, TL (extension of BL)

important when interpreting labels as regions later on: evaluation of the former has the effect of accessing the region p whereas the latter does not.

A term is *closed* if it has no free occurrences of variables. (Closed terms may have free occurrences of label variables.) A closed value expression is a *value*.

We write $\mathtt{t} \xrightarrow{\mathrm{T}} \mathtt{t}'$ if $\mathtt{t} \longrightarrow \mathtt{t}'$ can be derived from the TL evaluation rules; that is, the evaluation rules of both Figures 3-1 and 3-2. A term t is *final* (or a *final state*) if there is no term t′ such that $\mathtt{t} \xrightarrow{\mathrm{T}} \mathtt{t}'$. Each value expression is final. We call all final states that are not value expressions *stuck* (or *stuck states*).

We write $\mathtt{t} \downarrow \mathtt{t}'$ if $\mathtt{t} \xrightarrow{\mathrm{T}}{}^{*} \mathtt{t}'$ and t′ is final. We write $\mathtt{t}\downarrow$ if there exists t′ such that $\mathtt{t} \downarrow \mathtt{t}'$. If t has no final state and thus does not terminate we write $\mathtt{t}\uparrow$.

For simplicity we shall think of BL as a subset of TL. This is justified since all BL-terms are also TL-terms and both evaluation and typing relations for TL are conservative over BL. For emphasis we may write $\mathtt{t} \xrightarrow{\mathrm{BL}} \mathtt{t}'$ if $\mathtt{t} \xrightarrow{\mathrm{T}} \mathtt{t}'$ and t, t′ are BL-terms.

Labels as Value Flow Information

The label erasure (or simply erasure) of a TL-term is the BL-term we obtain by erasing all occurrences of `at p`, `! p` and $\langle . \rangle_p$ in it. More precisely, we define erasure and its inverse, completion, as follows:

3.2.1 DEFINITION [ERASURE, COMPLETION]: Let $\mathtt{t} \in$ TL. Then the *erasure* $\|\mathtt{t}\|$ of term t is defined as follows:

$$\begin{array}{rcl} \|\mathtt{x}\| & = & \mathtt{x} \\ \|\mathtt{t}_1\ \mathtt{t}_2\| & = & \|\mathtt{t}_1\|\ \|\mathtt{t}_2\| \\ \|\mathtt{if}\ \mathtt{t}_1\ \mathtt{then}\ \mathtt{t}_2\ \mathtt{else}\ \mathtt{t}_3\| & = & \mathtt{if}\ \|\mathtt{t}_1\|\ \mathtt{then}\ \|\mathtt{t}_2\|\ \mathtt{else}\ \|\mathtt{t}_3\| \\ \|\mathtt{fix}\ \mathtt{x}.\mathtt{t}\| & = & \mathtt{fix}\ \mathtt{x}.\|\mathtt{t}\| \\ \|\lambda\mathtt{x}.\mathtt{t}\| & = & \lambda\mathtt{x}.\|\mathtt{t}\| \\ \|\mathtt{tt}\| & = & \mathtt{tt} \\ \|\mathtt{ff}\| & = & \mathtt{ff} \\ \|\mathtt{t}\ \mathtt{at}\ \mathtt{p}\| & = & \|\mathtt{t}\| \\ \|\mathtt{t}\ !\ \mathtt{p}\| & = & \|\mathtt{t}\| \\ \left\|\langle\mathtt{v}\rangle_{\mathtt{p}}\right\| & = & \|\mathtt{v}\| \end{array}$$

Conversely, we call a TL-term t′ a *completion* of BL-term t if $\|\mathtt{t}'\| = \mathtt{t}$. □

Note that erasures are BL-terms. Note also that erasures are closed under substitution:

3.2.2 PROPOSITION: $\|[\mathtt{x} \mapsto \mathtt{t}_2]\mathtt{t}_1\| = [\mathtt{x} \mapsto \|\mathtt{t}_2\|]\|\mathtt{t}_1\|$ □

A *constructor/deconstructor completion* (or *con/decon completion)* is a completion where each value expression is tagged and untagging takes place in each destructive context; labels must not occur anywhere else. Formally, *con/decon completions* are generated from t in Figure 3-3.

In a con/decon completion each value gets tagged when it is created, and every such tag is checked and removed immediately before the underlying untagged value is destructed—that is, when it is needed as the function in a function application or as the Boolean test in a conditional. In this fashion the label p in `t ! p` tells us which value expressions could have constructed the value of t.

For this to be true, however, evaluations of TL-terms must not get stuck due to label mismatch in a redex $\langle \mathtt{v} \rangle_\rho\ !\ \rho'$. Intuitively, the reason for this is as follows. It would be clearly wrong to conclude that evaluation of $\mathtt{t}\ !\ \rho_1$ uses a value constructed by a value expression labeled ρ_1 in the original source

Con/decon completion templates				
t ::=		*:*	v ::=	*:*
	v		(λx.t) at p	*abstraction*
	x		bv at p	*truth value*
	(t ! p) t		bv ::=	*truth values:*
	if (t ! p) then t else t		tt	*true*
	fix x.t		ff	*false*

Figure 3-3: Con/decon completions

program if t evaluates to $\langle \texttt{tt}\rangle_{\rho_0}$. Note, however, that $\langle \texttt{tt}\rangle_{\rho_0}\ !\ \rho_1$ is stuck, which means $\texttt{t}\ !\ \rho_1$ gets stuck. Conversely, if an evaluation does not get stuck, all its computation steps of the form $\langle \texttt{tt}\rangle_{\rho}\ !\ \rho'$ succeed, which is only possible if $\rho = \rho'$. In that case a subterm $\texttt{t}\ !\ \rho$ expresses that the value of t is constructed from one of the value expressions labeled ρ.

As we shall see, the type system of TL guarantees that no stuck states can occur during evaluation of (well-typed) TL-terms. So the label information in TL-terms can be soundly interpreted as value flow information.

3.2.3 EXAMPLE: Consider the BL-program $\texttt{t}_0$:

```
let fst= λu.λv.u in
    (let x = λp.p tt ff in λy.λq.q (x fst) y)
    tt
```

Value flow analysis should tell us that x may be applied to fst (which is rather easy to see), fst may be applied to tt (which is not immediately obvious from the source code), and the λ-abstraction λy.λp.p (x fst) y may be applied to tt, but λp.p (x fst) y is not applied anywhere.

The following con/decon completion $\texttt{t}_1$ of $\texttt{t}_0$ captures this:

$$
\begin{array}{l}
\texttt{let fst= } \lambda_{l_K}\texttt{u}.\lambda_{l_b}\texttt{v.u in}\\
\quad (\texttt{let x} = \lambda_{l_x}\texttt{p}.((\texttt{p}^{l_K}\ \texttt{tt}_{l_t})^{l_b}\ \texttt{ff}_{l_f})\ \texttt{in}\\
\quad\quad \lambda_{l_f}\texttt{y}.\lambda_{l_c}\texttt{q}.((q^{l_q}\ (\texttt{x}^{l_x}\ \texttt{fst}))^{l_d}\ \texttt{y}))\\
\quad \texttt{tt}_{l_t}
\end{array}
$$

To make the completion more readable, we have written $\lambda_{\texttt{p}}\texttt{x.t}$ for (λx.t) at p, $\texttt{bv}_{\texttt{p}}$ for bv at p, and $(\texttt{t}^{\texttt{p}}\ \texttt{t}')$ for $(\texttt{t}\ !\ \texttt{p})\ \texttt{t}'$. □

3.2.4 EXERCISE [★, ↛]: Show that $\texttt{t}_1$ is a TL-term by giving a TL-typing derivation for it. □

3.2.5 EXERCISE [★, ↛]: Give a reduction sequence $t_1 \xrightarrow{T} \dots \xrightarrow{T} t_k$ such that t_k is final. Which (E-UNTAGBETA) reduction steps occur in it? Which labels occur in those steps? □

3.2.6 EXERCISE [★, ↛]: Note that t_0 is the erasure of t_1: $\|t_1\| = t_0$. Give a reduction sequence $\|t_1\| \xrightarrow{BL} \dots \xrightarrow{BL} t'_m$ such that t'_m is final. How are t_k from Exercise 3.2.5 and t'_m related to each other? How long is the reduction sequence for t_0 to t_k in comparison to the reduction sequence for t_1? (Generalize to arbitrary TL-terms and their erasures.) □

3.2.7 EXERCISE [★★]: Let S be a substitution mapping the labels occurring in t_1 to (not necessarily different) labels. Consider the term $S(t_1)$, which is t_1 with its labels substituted according to S. Is $S(t_1)$ TL-typable? If so, does closure under all substitutions hold for all closed TL-terms? If not, for which subset of the closed TL-terms does it hold? □

Correctness

A TL-term can be thought of as an instrumented version of the underlying BL-term. Intuitively, this is because an evaluation of a TL-term performs the same proper computation steps as its erasure (the underlying BL-term), with interspersed auxiliary label reduction steps (E-TAGBETA) and (E-UNTAGBETA).

Correctness means that evaluation of TL-terms gives the "same" results as evaluation of their underlying BL-terms. It is factored into two orthogonal parts:

1. Conditional correctness, which states that TL-terms produce the same results as their underlying BL-terms unless they get stuck. Conditional correctness is a property of the evaluation rules for TL and BL alone; it is independent of their typing rules.

2. Soundness, which states that TL-terms do not get stuck.

It is instructive to see how this method works in a technically very simple setting such as TL. For this reason we shall introduce it below. The same results for more expressive languages with effect typing, region scoping and polymorphism will be proved later on in §3.4 and §3.5.

3.2.8 DEFINITION: Define relations $. \xrightarrow{T_1} .$ and $. \xrightarrow{T_2} .$ on TL-terms as follows:

1. $t_1 \xrightarrow{T_2} t_2$ if $t_1 \longrightarrow t_2$ is derived by application of Axiom (E-TAGBETA) or (E-UNTAGBETA) from Figure 3-2.

2. $t_1 \xrightarrow{T_1} t_2$ if $t_1 \longrightarrow t_2$ is derived from all evaluation rules of Figures 3-1 and 3-2, but without application of Axioms (E-TAGBETA) or (E-UNTAGBETA). □

Each $\xrightarrow{T_1}$ reduction step corresponds to a reduction step in the underlying BL-term whereas $\xrightarrow{T_2}$ reductions do not change the underlying BL-term at all. This is captured in the following lemma.

3.2.9 **Lemma [Simulation]:** Let t, t_1, t_2 range over TL-terms.

1. If v is a value expression then so is $\|v\|$.
2. $\xrightarrow{T_2}$ is strongly normalizing.
3. If $t_1 \xrightarrow{T_1} t_2$ then $\|t_1\| \xrightarrow{BL} \|t_2\|$.
4. If $t_1 \xrightarrow{T_2} t_2$ then $\|t_1\| = \|t_2\|$. □

3.2.10 **Exercise [★★, ↛]:** Prove Lemma 3.2.9. □

Using Lemma 3.2.9 we can prove the following theorem. It states that evaluation of a TL-term performs basically the same computation steps as the underlying BL-term until it gets stuck or arrives at a value expression.

3.2.11 **Theorem [Conditional Correctness]:** For TL-terms t, t' we have:

1. If $t \xrightarrow{T}{}^{*} t'$ then $\|t\| \xrightarrow{BL}{}^{*} \|t'\|$.
2. If $t \uparrow$ then $\|t\| \uparrow$.
3. If $\|t\|$ gets stuck then t gets stuck, too. □

3.2.12 **Exercise [★]:** Prove Theorem 3.2.11. □

The next lemma says that the type of a term is preserved under evaluation.

3.2.13 **Lemma [Subject Reduction (Preservation)]:** Let t, t' be TL-terms. If $\Gamma \vdash t : T$ and $t \xrightarrow{T} t'$ then $\Gamma \vdash t' : T$. □

3.2.14 **Exercise [★★, ↛]:** Prove Lemma 3.2.13 in standard fashion: by induction on $t \xrightarrow{T} t'$ and formulating the requisite substitution lemma. □

3.2.15 **Lemma [Progress]:** If $\vdash t : T$ then either $t = v$ for some value (closed value expression) v or there exists t' such that $t \xrightarrow{T} t'$. □

Proof: (Sketch) The lemma follows from the following statement: For all derivable $\Gamma \vdash t : T$, if $\Gamma = \varnothing$ then

1. there exists t' such that $t \xrightarrow{T} t'$, or

2. (a) if $\mathtt{T}$ is of the form $\mathtt{T}' \to \mathtt{T}''$ then $\mathtt{t} = \lambda\mathtt{x}.\mathtt{t}''$ for some $\mathtt{x}, \mathtt{t}''$, and

   (b) if $\mathtt{T} = \mathtt{bool}$ then $\mathtt{t} \in \{\mathtt{tt}, \mathtt{ff}\}$.

This statement can be proved by rule induction on $\Gamma \vdash \mathtt{t} : \mathtt{T}$. □

The Progress Lemma says that a well-typed closed term is not stuck. Together with the Subject Reduction Lemma it says that, since all its reducts are well-typed, too, it never gets stuck.

3.2.16 Theorem [Soundness]: If $\vdash \mathtt{t} : \mathtt{T}$ then evaluation of $\mathtt{t}$ does not get stuck. □

Putting the Conditional Correctness Theorem and the Soundness Theorem together we obtain as a corollary the correctness of TL relative to BL:

3.2.17 Corollary [Correctness]: Let $\mathtt{t}$ be a closed TL-term and $\mathtt{v}$ a TL-value.

1. $\mathtt{t} \uparrow$ iff $\|\mathtt{t}\| \uparrow$.

2. $\|\mathtt{t}\| \xrightarrow{\text{BL}}{}^{*} \|\mathtt{v}\|$ iff there exists a TL-value $\mathtt{v}'$ with $\|\mathtt{v}'\| = \|\mathtt{v}\|$ and $\mathtt{t} \xrightarrow{\text{T}}{}^{*} \mathtt{v}'$. □

3.2.18 Exercise [★★]: Prove Corollary 3.2.17. □

Inference of Value Flow Information

Given a BL-term $\mathtt{t}$ we are interested in finding a con/decon completion to obtain value flow information about $\mathtt{t}$. Note, however, that a BL-term $\mathtt{t}$ may have many different con/decon completions, and while each provides sound value flow information, some provide better information than others. For example, the trivial completion in which each label operation in a term has the same label ρ_h contains no useful value flow information: it says that any value created anywhere may be used anywhere. Correct, but trivial. Intuitively, we are interested in a con/decon completion with a maximal number of distinct labels, as this gives the most fine-grained value flow information.

3.2.19 Exercise: Consider $\mathtt{t}_0$ =

```
let fst = λu.λv.u in
    (let x = λp.p tt ff in λy.λq.q (x fst) y)
    tt
```

again and its con/decon completion $\mathtt{t}_1$ =

$$
\begin{array}{l}
\mathtt{let\ fst} = \lambda_{l_K}\mathtt{u}.\lambda_{l_b}\mathtt{v.u\ in} \\
\quad (\mathtt{let\ x} = \lambda_{l_x}\mathtt{p}.((\mathtt{p}^{l_K}\ \mathtt{tt}_{l_t})^{l_b}\ \mathtt{ff}_{l_f})\ \mathtt{in}\ \ \lambda_{l_f}\mathtt{y}.\lambda_{l_c}\mathtt{q}.((q^{l_q}\ (\mathtt{x}^{l_x}\ \mathtt{fst}))^{l_d}\ \mathtt{y})) \\
\quad \mathtt{tt}_{l_t}.
\end{array}
$$

Does there exist another con/decon completion of t_0 with more distinct labels or is t_1 maximal in this sense? □

Indeed, it can be shown that each BL-term has a con/decon completion such that any other of its con/decon completions can be obtained by applying a label substitution to it. We call it a *principal completion* of the given BL-term. In particular, principal completions have the maximal possible number of distinct labels. Furthermore, they are unique up to renaming of labels.

We shall not go into any technical details on how to infer principal completions, but present the basic ideas.

A con/decon completion template for a BL-term t is a con/decon completion of t in which each label variable occurs exactly once. Clearly, each con/decon completion that satisfies the TL-typing rules is a substitution instance (mapping labels to labels) of this template. Furthermore, it can be shown that a substitution gives rise to a well-typed con/decon completion if and only if it satisfies a set of equational constraints between the template labels. That set can be computed in linear time from the con/decon completion, and a most general solution of the constraints can likewise be computed in linear time. The most general solution, in turn, gives rise to a principal completion when applied to the con/decon completion template. What we have described is the standard method for simple type inference by equational constraint extraction and solution; see, for example, Wand (1987b) and Henglein (1989) for simple type inference and Mossin (1997, Section 2) for its application to value flow analysis.

The pleasant properties of processing sets of equational constraints—in particular, existence of most general/principal solutions and efficient incremental algorithms for computing them (unification)—have led to type systems whose design has been driven to a considerable degree by a desire to deploy efficient unification technology for automatic inference, not only by semantic or logical analysis for capturing relevant semantic information.

Labels as Regions

We can think of region variables as being bound to memory regions and (re)interpret tagging and untagging operations as follows. The value $\langle v \rangle_p$ denotes a(ny) pointer into region p where v is stored. The tagging operation t at p is implemented by storing the value of t in region p. Its result is the pointer to where the value is stored. The untagging operation t ! p is implemented as evaluating t to a pointer, checking that it points into region p and, if it does, retrieving the pointer's value. The TL type system guarantees that all checks succeed and so can be elided at run time.

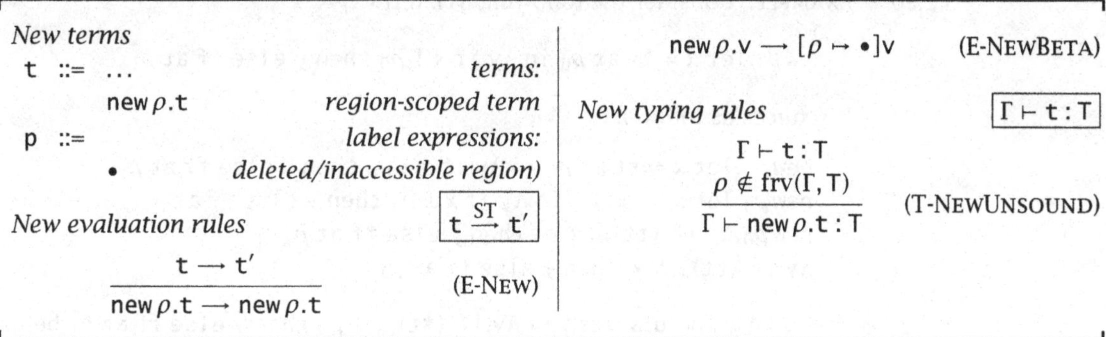

Figure 3-4: Scoped tagged language (unsound), STL (basis: TL)

Now consider the (derivable) judgment $\Gamma \vdash \mathtt{t} : \mathsf{T}$ for a subterm `t` in a program. Assume that ρ occurs in `t` in tagging and/or untagging operations. If ρ does not occur in Γ then, intuitively, the environment in which `t` evaluates contains no values in ρ; it is empty. Furthermore, if ρ does not occur in T either, then no values stored in ρ are needed by the context of `t`; all the values stored in ρ can be deleted.

This leads us to the introduction of terms with *(lexically) scoped regions*: $\mathtt{new}\,\rho.\mathtt{t}$. Here $\mathtt{new}\,\rho.\mathtt{t}$ binds region variable ρ in `t`. The semantics of $\mathtt{new}\,\rho.\mathtt{t}$ is as follows: allocate a new region, bind it to ρ, evaluate `t` and, finally, deallocate the region bound to ρ. This results in a stack-oriented memory management discipline: the most recently allocated region is deallocated first.

Figure 3-4 shows $\mathtt{new}\,\rho.\mathtt{t}$ and corresponding evaluation and typing rules, which extend TL to STL. In rule (T-NewUnsound) function $\mathrm{frv}(\Gamma, \mathsf{T})$ denotes the set of region variables that occur freely in Γ and T.

Rule (E-New) expresses that a region-scoped term $\mathtt{new}\,\rho.\mathtt{t}$ is evaluated by reducing `t` to a value `v`. During this reduction, it is possible that region ρ is accessed. After evaluation is complete $\mathtt{new}\,\rho.\mathtt{v}$ is reduced to $[\rho \mapsto \bullet]\mathtt{v}$ by rule (E-NewBeta), where $\bullet$ is substituted for all occurrences of ρ in `v`. In particular, all occurrences in `v` of the form $\langle \mathtt{v}' \rangle_\rho$ are replaced by $\langle \mathtt{v}' \rangle_\bullet$. Since rule (E-UntagBeta) from Figure 3-2 requires a proper region variable, any access to such a value gets stuck. Note, in particular, that the term $\langle \mathtt{v}' \rangle_\bullet \;!\; \bullet$ is stuck. In this fashion the substitution of $\bullet$ for ρ makes all values stored in ρ inaccessible in ensuing computation steps, which models deleting the whole region of values stored in ρ.

The bad news is that STL is unsound: Stuck states can occur. The reason for this is that a term `t` with derivable judgment $\Gamma \vdash \mathtt{t} : \mathsf{T}$ may still access region ρ during evaluation even if ρ occurs neither in Γ nor T.

3.2.20 EXAMPLE: Consider the following STL-term $\mathtt{t}_f$ =:

$$\mathtt{new}\,\rho_0.\mathtt{let}\ \mathtt{x} = \mathtt{tt}\ \mathtt{at}\ \rho_0\ \mathtt{in}\ \lambda\mathtt{y}.\mathtt{if}\ \mathtt{x}\ !\ \rho_0\ \mathtt{then}\ \mathtt{y}\ \mathtt{else}\ \mathtt{ff}\ \mathtt{at}\ \rho_1$$

It reduces as follows:

$$\begin{array}{ll} \mathtt{new}\,\rho_0.\mathtt{let}\ \mathtt{x} = \mathtt{tt}\ \mathtt{at}\ \rho_0\ \mathtt{in}\ \lambda\mathtt{y}.\mathtt{if}\ x\ !\ \rho_0\ \mathtt{then}\ \mathtt{y}\ \mathtt{else}\ \mathtt{ff}\ \mathtt{at}\ \rho_1 & \longrightarrow \\ \mathtt{new}\,\rho_0.\mathtt{let}\ \mathtt{x} = \langle\mathtt{tt}\rangle_{\rho_0}\ \mathtt{in}\ \lambda\mathtt{y}.\mathtt{if}\ x\ !\ \rho_0\ \mathtt{then}\ \mathtt{y}\ \mathtt{else}\ \mathtt{ff}\ \mathtt{at}\ \rho_1 & \longrightarrow \\ \mathtt{new}\,\rho_0.\lambda\mathtt{y}.\mathtt{if}\ \langle\mathtt{tt}\rangle_{\rho_0}\ !\ \rho_0\ \mathtt{then}\ \mathtt{y}\ \mathtt{else}\ \mathtt{ff}\ \mathtt{at}\ \rho_1 & \longrightarrow \\ \lambda\mathtt{y}.\mathtt{if}\ \langle\mathtt{tt}\rangle_{\bullet}\ !\ \bullet\ \mathtt{then}\ \mathtt{y}\ \mathtt{else}\ \mathtt{ff}\ \mathtt{at}\ \rho_1 & \end{array}$$

Note that ρ_0 occurs freely in $\lambda\mathtt{y}.\mathtt{if}\ \langle\mathtt{tt}\rangle_{\rho_0}\ !\ \rho_0\ \mathtt{then}\ \mathtt{y}\ \mathtt{else}\ \mathtt{ff}\ \mathtt{at}\ \rho_1$ before performing the last reduction step. Its type $\mathtt{bool}\ \mathtt{at}\ \rho_1 \to \mathtt{bool}\ \mathtt{at}\ \rho_1$, however, does not mention ρ_0. Note that

$$\lambda\mathtt{y}.\mathtt{if}\ \langle\mathtt{tt}\rangle_{\bullet}\ !\ \bullet\ \mathtt{then}\ \mathtt{y}\ \mathtt{else}\ \mathtt{ff}\ \mathtt{at}\ \rho_1$$

is a value; it is *not* stuck. It is easy to see, however, how it can give rise to a stuck state. The program $\mathtt{t}_f\ (\mathtt{tt}\ \mathtt{at}\ \rho_1)$ is a well-typed STL-program of type $\mathtt{bool}\ \mathtt{at}\ \rho_1$, yet evaluation gets stuck:

$$\begin{array}{ll} \mathtt{t}_f\ (\mathtt{tt}\ \mathtt{at}\ \rho_1) & \xrightarrow{*} \\ (\lambda\mathtt{y}.\mathtt{if}\ \langle\mathtt{tt}\rangle_{\bullet}\ !\ \bullet\ \mathtt{then}\ \mathtt{y}\ \mathtt{else}\ \mathtt{ff}\ \mathtt{at}\ \rho_1)\ (\mathtt{tt}\ \mathtt{at}\ \rho_1) & \longrightarrow \\ \mathtt{if}\ \langle\mathtt{tt}\rangle_{\bullet}\ !\ \bullet\ \mathtt{then}\ \mathtt{ff}\ \mathtt{at}\ \rho_1\ \mathtt{else}\ \mathtt{ff}\ \mathtt{at}\ \rho_1 & \end{array}$$

To continue evaluation would require reduction of $\langle\mathtt{tt}\rangle_{\bullet}\ !\ \bullet$ to a Boolean value; $\langle\mathtt{tt}\rangle_{\bullet}\ !\ \bullet$, however, is stuck. □

In §3.3 we introduce explicit effects into types to capture the accesses to regions needed for evaluation. This is the path taken by Tofte and Talpin (1997) in their ground-breaking work on region-based memory management.

Notes on Value Flow Analysis

Although Reynolds (1969) was the first to look at the problem of computing flow for structured data and called it *data set computation,* we follow Schwartz (1975) in using the term *value flow* to emphasize its general applicability to primitive, structured, and higher-order data. Schwartz (1975) developed value flow analysis for structured values in the context of SETL and was the first to suggest exploiting lifetime analysis based on value flow analysis for region-based memory management. *Closure analysis,* the term introduced by Sestoft (1989), and *control flow analysis,* the term used by Shivers (1988; 1991), focus on the flow of function values (function closures). Note that data and control flow are interdependent for higher-order languages; see Mossin (1997, Section 1.4) for a discussion of this. Shivers coined the term 0CFA, which in other literature is also used for the monovariant value flow analyses above (which is different from Shivers' 0CFA, however; see Mossin [1997] for a discussion). Another form of monovariant value flow analysis is set-based analysis (Heintze, 1994).

Palsberg and O'Keefe (1995) showed that safety analysis, a constraint-based analysis, characterizes typability in Amadio and Cardelli's type system (1993) with recursive subtyping, providing a type theoretic characterization of monovariant value flow analysis. Constraint-based value flow analysis for object-oriented languages was pioneered by Palsberg and Schwartzbach (1990, 1994). See Nielson, Nielson, and Hankin (1999) for a presentation of monovariant value flow analysis based on flow logic and abstract interpretation.

Classical data flow analysis corresponds to value flow analysis for primitive data (only); it has been used in compilers already in the early 1960s. See Aho, Sethi, and Ullman (1986) for its history.

Monovariant value flow analysis is directional: values flow from constructor points (value expressions) to uses, but not the other way around. The value flow information for BL as expressed in TL-completions corresponds to a very simple (and inexpressive) value flow analysis: equational flow analysis, in which value flows are treated symmetrically (Heintze, 1995). Intuitively, this means all flows are bidirectional: values do not only "flow" from their creation points to their uses, as in monovariant value flow analysis (0CFA), but somewhat weirdly, also the other way around. The type-based presentation of equational value flow analysis in this section owes greatly to Mossin (1997, Section 2), where it is called *simple flow analysis*.

Polymorphic value flow analysis was developed by Mossin (1997), extending earlier work by Dussart, Henglein, and Mossin (1995) and Henglein and Mossin (1994) on combining subtyping, parametric polymorphism and polymorphic recursion for binding-time analysis. Polymorphic value flow analysis is modular and can be computed asymptotically in the same time as monomorphic value flow analysis. Transitive closure is the algorithmic bottleneck in both. Efficient algorithms are given by Fähndrich, Rehof, and Das (2000), Rehof and Fähndrich (2001), and Gustavsson and Svenningsson (2001).

Polymorphic equational value flow analysis underlies Tofte–Talpin style region-based memory management; see §3.5. Region-based memory management based on directional value flow analysis appears possible, but has not been explored. The recognition that region inference performs a form of value flow and dependency analysis is folklore; it has been exploited by Helsen and Thiemann (2004) for polymorphic specialization. Deriving region-based memory management systematically from type-based value flow analysis appears to be new, however. The syntactic modeling of region deallocation by • is due to Helsen and Thiemann (2000) and Calcagno (2001).

See §3.4 and the following sections for more references on region-based memory management.

3.3 Effects

We have seen in the previous subsection that the soundness of a typing rule may depend not only on the results of evaluations, but on certain aspects of the evaluation itself, in other words on how a value is computed, not just which value is computed. To capture properties of evaluation we introduce *effects*.

Effect Type Judgments

The basic effect type judgment is

$$\Gamma \vdash \mathtt{t} :^{\varphi} \mathsf{T}$$

where φ is an *effect expression* (henceforth simply called *effect*) and ${}^{\varphi}\mathsf{T}$ is an *effect type* or *type and effect*. The judgment should be read informally as "Under the assumptions Γ, the evaluation of $\mathtt{t}$ may have the observable effect φ, and it eventually yields a value of type T, if any." For program analysis purposes *observable* may also be understood as *interesting*. When an evaluation has no observable effect, we say it has the *empty effect*, written $\emptyset$, and ${}^{\emptyset}\mathsf{T}$ is abbreviated to T.

In a call-by-name language, Γ is a sequence of *effect type assumptions* of the form $\mathtt{x} : {}^{\varphi}\mathsf{T}$, since $\mathtt{x}$ may be bound to unevaluated thunks, whereas in a call-by-value language we have *type assumptions* of the form $\mathtt{x} : \mathsf{T}$ since variables are bound to *values*, whose evaluation is guaranteed to always have the empty effect. Analogously, in a call-by-name language we have general functional types of the form ${}^{\varphi_1}\mathsf{T}_1 \to {}^{\varphi_2}\mathsf{T}_2$; in a call-by-value language, however, we can restrict ourselves to functional types of the form $\mathsf{T}_1 \to {}^{\varphi}\mathsf{T}_2$.[1]

1. The syntax ${}^{\varphi}\mathsf{T}$ has been chosen here for several reasons:

- It expresses that yielding a value of type T is the last "effect" of evaluation; that is it occurs after φ.
- Functional types in a call-by-value language end up being written $\mathsf{T}_1 \to {}^{\varphi}\mathsf{T}_2$, which is consistent with the notation used in the literature where the *delayed effect* φ is written above the function type arrow.
- It is consistent with the syntax $M^{\varphi}\mathsf{T}$ used in monadic interpretations of type and effect systems in the literature.

Terms

$\mathtt{t}$ ::=		*terms:*
	$\mathtt{v}$	*value expression*
	$\mathtt{x}$	*variable*
	$\mathtt{t\ t}$	*application*
	$\mathtt{if\ t\ then\ t\ else\ t}$	*conditional*
	$\mathtt{t\ at\ p}$	*tagging*
	$\mathtt{t\ !\ p}$	*untagging*
	$\mathtt{new}\ \rho.\mathtt{t}$	*label-scoped term*
	$\mathtt{fix\ x.t}$	*recursion*
$\mathtt{v}$ ::=		*value expressions:*
	$\lambda\mathtt{x.t}$	*abstraction*
	$\mathtt{bv}$	*truth value*
	$\langle\mathtt{v}\rangle_{\mathtt{p}}$	*tagged value*
$\mathtt{bv}$ ::=		*truth values:*
	$\mathtt{tt}$	*true*
	$\mathtt{ff}$	*false*
$\mathtt{p}$ ::=		*label/region expressions:*
	ρ	*label/region variable*
	$\bullet$	*deleted/inaccessible label/region*

Effect expressions

φ ::=	$\{\rho, \dots, \rho\}$	*effect expressions:*

Types

$\mathtt{T}$ ::=		*types:*
	$\mathtt{bool}$	*Boolean type*
	$\mathtt{T} \to^{\varphi} \mathtt{T}$	*function type*
	$\mathtt{T\ at\ p}$	*tagged value type*

Effect typing rules $\boxed{\Gamma \vdash \mathtt{t} :^{\varphi} \mathtt{T}}$

$$\frac{\mathtt{x} \notin \Gamma'}{\Gamma, \mathtt{x} : \mathtt{T}, \Gamma' \vdash \mathtt{x} :^{\varphi} \mathtt{T}} \quad \text{(TE-VAR)}$$

$$\Gamma \vdash \mathtt{bv} :^{\varphi} \mathtt{bool} \quad \text{(TE-BOOL)}$$

$$\frac{\Gamma \vdash \mathtt{t_1} :^{\varphi} \mathtt{bool} \qquad \Gamma \vdash \mathtt{t_2} :^{\varphi} \mathtt{T} \qquad \Gamma \vdash \mathtt{t_3} :^{\varphi} \mathtt{T}}{\Gamma \vdash \mathtt{if\ t_1\ then\ t_2\ else\ t_3} :^{\varphi} \mathtt{T}} \quad \text{(TE-IF)}$$

$$\frac{\Gamma, \mathtt{x} : \mathtt{T_1} \vdash \mathtt{t} :^{\varphi_2} \mathtt{T_2}}{\Gamma \vdash \lambda \mathtt{x.t} :^{\varphi_1} \mathtt{T_1} \to^{\varphi_2} \mathtt{T_2}} \quad \text{(TE-ABS)}$$

$$\frac{\Gamma \vdash \mathtt{t_0} :^{\varphi} \mathtt{T_1} \to^{\varphi} \mathtt{T_2} \qquad \Gamma \vdash \mathtt{t_1} :^{\varphi} \mathtt{T_1}}{\Gamma \vdash \mathtt{t_0\ t_1} :^{\varphi} \mathtt{T_2}} \quad \text{(TE-APP)}$$

$$\frac{\Gamma \vdash \mathtt{t} :^{\varphi} \mathtt{T} \qquad \mathtt{p} \in \varphi}{\Gamma \vdash \mathtt{t\ at\ p} :^{\varphi} \mathtt{T\ at\ p}} \quad \text{(TE-AT)}$$

$$\frac{\Gamma \vdash \mathtt{t} :^{\varphi} \mathtt{T\ at\ p} \qquad \mathtt{p} \in \varphi}{\Gamma \vdash \mathtt{t\ !\ p} :^{\varphi} \mathtt{T}} \quad \text{(TE-FROM)}$$

$$\frac{\Gamma \vdash \mathtt{v} :^{\varphi} \mathtt{T}}{\Gamma \vdash \langle \mathtt{v} \rangle_{\mathtt{p}} :^{\varphi} \mathtt{T\ at\ p}} \quad \text{(TE-CELL)}$$

$$\frac{\Gamma \vdash \mathtt{t} :^{\varphi} \mathtt{T} \qquad \rho \notin \mathrm{frv}(\Gamma, \mathtt{T})}{\Gamma \vdash \mathtt{new}\ \rho.\mathtt{t} :^{\varphi - \{\rho\}} \mathtt{T}} \quad \text{(TE-NEW)}$$

$$\frac{\Gamma, \mathtt{x} : \mathtt{T} \vdash \mathtt{t} :^{\varphi} \mathtt{T}}{\Gamma \vdash \mathtt{fix\ x.t} :^{\varphi} \mathtt{T}} \quad \text{(TE-FIX)}$$

Figure 3-5: Scoped effect typed language ETL(sound)

Effect Typed Language ETL

We shall now present an effect typing system for language ETL. ETL has the same source terms and evaluation rules as STL. The only difference to STL is its effect type system. Syntax and effect typing rules for ETL are given in Figure 3-5.

An effect is a finite set of region variables. Note that it must not contain $\bullet$. A judgment $\Gamma \vdash \mathtt{t} :^{\varphi} \mathtt{T}$ is intended to express that, assuming the free variables of t are bound to values of types according to Γ, the regions that t accesses during evaluation are included in φ and the result of the evaluation has type T if it terminates.

The typing rules of Figure 3-5 are basically those corresponding to the monomorphic subset of the Tofte-Talpin system, which we shall encounter in §3.5.[2] They are inspired by a desire to employ equational constraint solving for effect expressions as much as possible.

Since we are only interested in whether a particular region may be accessed during evaluation of a term or not, our effect system does not record the order in which effects take place. We simply record the set of region variables that may be accessed during evaluation of t. In this sense our effect type system is *control-flow insensitive.* Effect type systems that capture evaluation order in their effects are discussed briefly later.

Soundness

Effects make the region variables accessed during evaluation sufficiently "visible" to ensure that the typing rule for new ρ.t is sound.

3.3.1 EXAMPLE: Consider the term

$$\mathtt{t}_f = \mathtt{new}\,\rho_0.\mathtt{let}\ \mathtt{x} = \mathtt{tt}\ \mathtt{at}\ \rho_0\ \mathtt{in}\ \lambda\mathtt{y}.\mathtt{if}\ \mathtt{x}\ !\ \rho_0\ \mathtt{then}\ \mathtt{y}\ \mathtt{else}\ \mathtt{ff}\ \mathtt{at}\ \rho_1$$

from Example 3.2.20 again. Whereas it is typable in STL even though it gets stuck when applied to an argument, it is not typable in ETL. To see this, consider the let-expression $\mathtt{t}_l$

$$\mathtt{let}\ \mathtt{x} = \mathtt{tt}\ \mathtt{at}\ \rho_0\ \mathtt{in}\ \lambda\mathtt{y}.\mathtt{if}\ \mathtt{x}\ !\ \rho_0\ \mathtt{then}\ \mathtt{y}\ \mathtt{else}\ \mathtt{ff}\ \mathtt{at}\ \rho_1$$

inside $\mathtt{t}_f$. Its ETL effect type T_l is ${}^{\{\rho_0\}}(\mathtt{bool}\ \mathtt{at}\ \rho_1 \rightarrow {}^{\{\rho_0\}}\mathtt{bool}\ \mathtt{at}\ \rho_1)$. Note that ρ_0 occurs in the effect, but in neither the function type's domain nor its range type. This reflects the fact that an application of $\mathtt{t}_l$ may access region ρ_0. Since $\rho_0 \in \mathrm{frv}(\mathtt{bool}\ \mathtt{at}\ \rho_1 \rightarrow {}^{\{\rho_0\}}\mathtt{bool}\ \mathtt{at}\ \rho_1)$, rule (TE-NEW) is *not* applicable, and so there is no way of inferring a type for $\mathtt{t}_f$, which indeed would be unsound. □

3.3.2 EXERCISE [★★, ↛]: Give a derivation of $\vdash \mathtt{t}_l : \mathsf{T}_l$. Argue that any ETL-derivable type T for $\mathtt{t}_l$ must contain an occurrence of ρ_0. □

2. The only substantial difference is rule (TE-APP). It is more restrictive than the corresponding rule (RT-APP) in the sense that it requires $\varphi_2 \subseteq \varphi$ in rule (RT-APP) to be solved equationally. Note that, in general, the typing rules of TT in §3.5 are for con/decon completions (only). They can be derived from ETL by merging rules (TE-FROM) and (TE-CELL) into the other rules.

Generally, we can prove the following soundness theorem.

3.3.3 THEOREM [SOUNDNESS OF ETL]: If $\vdash \mathtt{t} :^{\varphi} \mathsf{T}$ then evaluation of t does not get stuck. □

We shall not prove this result here. The techniques will be presented in §3.5 for a more general type system.

3.3.4 EXERCISE [★★★★, ↛]: Prove correctness for ETL. Do so by extending the Conditional Correctness Theorem and the Soundness Theorem for TL to ETL. □

Notes on Effect Type Systems

Type and effect systems are introduced by Lucassen, Gifford and Jouvelot (Gifford and Lucassen, 1986; Lucassen, 1987; Lucassen and Gifford, 1988; Jouvelot and Gifford, 1989) for integrating imperative operations, notably updatable references and control effects, into functional languages. Type and effect inference using unification technology, which is the basis for region inference, is developed by Jouvelot and Gifford (1991) and Talpin and Jouvelot; Talpin and Jouvelot (1992; 1994). Tofte and Talpin (1997) develop it into region inference for region-based memory management.

Nielson and Nielson (1994, 1996) pioneered type and effect systems with *behaviors* or *causal* effects, where effect types model order of evaluation. In such systems the language of effect expressions has operators for sequential composition and choice. They also provide for recursively defined effect expressions. The sequential composition operator captures the sequential order of the execution of effects. The choice operator corresponds to choice of one effect or another. This changes the nature of effects substantially as they basically turn into process algebras, with their own nontrivial theory. Modeling order of execution is key to capturing synchronization properties of concurrent processes, where atomic effects include sending and receiving messages. See Amtoft, Nielson, and Nielson (1999) and Nielson, Nielson, and Hankin (1999) for references on soundness, inference and applications.

The applications of type and effect systems include verification of cryptographic protocols by effect type checking (Gordon and Jeffrey, 2001b,a, 2002), behavioral type systems for asynchronous programming (Igarashi and Kobayashi, 2001; Rajamani and Rehof, 2001; Chaki, Rajamani, and Rehof, 2002; Rajamani and Rehof, 2002), and interference analysis for concurrent threads (see Flanagan and Qadeer [2003] for references).

In terms of the computational λ-calculus of Moggi (1989), types are associated with values and effect types with *computations*; that is, intuitively, an effect type ${}^{\varphi}\mathsf{T}$ corresponds to an (effect indexed) monad type $\mathcal{M}^{\varphi}\mathsf{T}$. This connection is investigated by Semmelroth and Sabry (1999), Wadler (2003), and Fluet (2004).

3.4 Region-Based Memory Management

Region-based memory management is a particular way to manage the dynamically (or *heap-*) allocated memory of a program. Traditionally, the heap is managed either explicitly by the programmer using constructs such as C's `malloc` and `free`, or automatically by a garbage collector leaving the programmer with only the responsibility of when to allocate memory. Region-based memory management uses explicit instructions for the allocation and deallocation of memory, but the safety of the explicit deallocations is guaranteed by a type system, and in some cases a compile-time analysis called "region inference" (§3.6) can insert the allocation and deallocation instructions automatically.

Basically a *region* is a sub-heap containing a number of heap-allocated values, and the heap is a collection of regions. A region starts out empty and grows when a value is allocated in it. A region can grow independently of the other regions constituting the heap; that is, one can allocate values in all regions currently available. Regions can only shrink when the complete region is deallocated; one does not deallocate individual values.

In summary, we use three region primitives: (1) allocation of a new region, (2) allocation of a value in a region, and (3) deallocation of a complete region (and thereby all values allocated in the region). In contrast to TL in §3.2 we simply elide dereferencing.

A Region-Annotated Language

Our region-annotated language RAL is a lambda calculus with a fixed-point operator and (Boolean) constants, extended with explicit region annotations. Its syntax and evaluation semantics are defined in Figure 3-6. As usual, λx.t and fix x.u binds the variable x in t and u, respectively. Similarly, $\lambda\rho$.u and new ρ.t binds the region variable ρ in u and t, respectively.

By analogy with §3.2, we define basic semantic notions for RAL. We write $t \overset{RAL}{\longrightarrow} t'$ if $t \longrightarrow t'$ can be derived from the RAL evaluation rules in Figure 3-6. A RAL-term t is *final* if there is no term t′ such that $t \overset{RAL}{\longrightarrow} t'$. Note that each value expression is final. All other final terms are *stuck*.

We write $t \longrightarrow^* t'$ if $t \overset{RAL}{\longrightarrow}{}^* t'$ and t′ is final and t $\downarrow$ if there exists t′ such that t $\downarrow$ t′. If t has no final state and thus does not terminate, we write t $\uparrow$. The relation $\longrightarrow^{*!}$ on terms is defined by: $t \longrightarrow^{*!} t'$ if $t \longrightarrow^* t'$ and t′ is final.

Terms

$\mathtt{t}$	::=		*terms:*
		$\mathtt{u}$	*value or almost-value*
		$\mathtt{x}$	*variable*
		$\mathtt{if\ t\ then\ t\ else\ t}$	*conditional*
		$\mathtt{fix\ x.u}$	*recursion*
		$\mathtt{t\ t}$	*application*
		$\mathtt{t}\ [[\mathtt{p}]]$	*region application*
		$\mathtt{new}\ \rho.\mathtt{t}$	*region creation*
$\mathtt{u}$	::=		*almost-values:*
		$\mathtt{v}$	*value*
		$(\lambda\mathtt{x.t})\ \mathtt{at\ p}$	*abstraction*
		$(\lambda\rho.\mathtt{u})\ \mathtt{at\ p}$	*region abstraction*
$\mathtt{v}$	::=		*value expressions:*
		$\mathtt{bv}$	*truth value*
		$\langle\lambda\mathtt{x.t}\rangle_{\mathtt{p}}$	*closure*
		$\langle\lambda\rho.\mathtt{u}\rangle_{\mathtt{p}}$	*region closure*
$\mathtt{bv}$	::=		*truth values:*
		$\mathtt{tt}$	*true*
		$\mathtt{ff}$	*false*
$\mathtt{p}$	::=		*places:*
		ρ	*region variable*
		$\bullet$	*deallocated*

Evaluation $\quad \boxed{\mathtt{t} \xrightarrow{\text{RAL}} \mathtt{t}'}$

$$\frac{\mathtt{t}_1 \longrightarrow \mathtt{t}_1'}{\mathtt{if}\ \mathtt{t}_1\ \begin{smallmatrix}\mathtt{then}\ \mathtt{t}_2\\ \mathtt{else}\ \mathtt{t}_3\end{smallmatrix} \longrightarrow \mathtt{if}\ \mathtt{t}_1'\ \begin{smallmatrix}\mathtt{then}\ \mathtt{t}_2\\ \mathtt{else}\ \mathtt{t}_3\end{smallmatrix}} \quad \text{(RE-IF)}$$

$$\mathtt{if\ tt\ then}\ \mathtt{t}_2\ \mathtt{else}\ \mathtt{t}_3 \longrightarrow \mathtt{t}_2 \quad \text{(RE-IFTRUE)}$$

$$\mathtt{if\ ff\ then}\ \mathtt{t}_2\ \mathtt{else}\ \mathtt{t}_3 \longrightarrow \mathtt{t}_3 \quad \text{(RE-IFFALSE)}$$

$$\frac{\mathtt{t}_1 \longrightarrow \mathtt{t}_1'}{\mathtt{t}_1\ \mathtt{t}_2 \longrightarrow \mathtt{t}_1'\ \mathtt{t}_2} \quad \text{(RE-APP1)}$$

$$\frac{\mathtt{t}_2 \longrightarrow \mathtt{t}_2'}{\mathtt{v}_1\ \mathtt{t}_2 \longrightarrow \mathtt{v}_1\ \mathtt{t}_2'} \quad \text{(RE-APP2)}$$

$$\lambda\mathtt{x.t}\ \mathtt{at}\ \rho \longrightarrow \langle\lambda\mathtt{x.t}\rangle_\rho \quad \text{(RE-CLOS)}$$

$$\langle\lambda\mathtt{x.t}\rangle_\rho\ \mathtt{v} \longrightarrow [\mathtt{x} \mapsto \mathtt{v}]\mathtt{t} \quad \text{(RE-BETA)}$$

$$\frac{\mathtt{u} \longrightarrow \mathtt{u}'}{\mathtt{fix\ x.u} \longrightarrow \mathtt{fix\ x.u}'} \quad \text{(RE-FIX)}$$

$$\mathtt{fix\ x.v} \longrightarrow [\mathtt{x} \mapsto \mathtt{fix\ x.v}]\mathtt{v} \quad \text{(RE-FIXBETA)}$$

$$\frac{\mathtt{t} \longrightarrow \mathtt{t}'}{\mathtt{t}\ [[\mathtt{p}]] \longrightarrow \mathtt{t}'\ [[\mathtt{p}]]} \quad \text{(RE-RAPP)}$$

$$\lambda\rho_1.\mathtt{u}\ \mathtt{at}\ \rho_2 \longrightarrow \langle\lambda\rho_1.\mathtt{u}\rangle_{\rho_2} \quad \text{(RE-RCLOS)}$$

$$\langle\lambda\rho_1.\mathtt{u}\rangle_{\rho_2}\ [[\mathtt{p}]] \longrightarrow [\rho_1 \mapsto \mathtt{p}]\mathtt{u} \quad \text{(RE-RBETA)}$$

$$\frac{\mathtt{t}_1 \longrightarrow \mathtt{t}_1'}{\mathtt{new}\ \rho.\mathtt{t}_1 \longrightarrow \mathtt{new}\ \rho.\mathtt{t}_1'} \quad \text{(RE-NEW)}$$

$$\mathtt{new}\ \rho.\mathtt{v} \longrightarrow [\rho \mapsto \bullet]\mathtt{v} \quad \text{(RE-DEALLOC)}$$

Figure 3-6: Region-annotated language, RAL

3.4.1 DEFINITION: Let the function "$\mathrm{eval}_{\mathrm{R}}(\cdot)$" from terms to $\{\mathtt{tt}, \mathtt{ff}, \bot, \mathtt{wrong}\}$ be:

a) $\mathrm{eval}_{\mathrm{R}}(\mathtt{t}_0) = \mathtt{bv}$ iff $\mathtt{t}_0 \to_{\mathrm{R}}^{*!} \mathtt{bv}$.

b) $\mathrm{eval}_{\mathrm{R}}(\mathtt{t}_0) = \bot$ iff there is an infinite sequence $\mathtt{t}_1, \mathtt{t}_2, \ldots, \mathtt{t}_i, \ldots$ such that $\mathtt{t}_i \xrightarrow{\text{RAL}} \mathtt{t}_{i+1}$ for $0 \le i$.

c) $\mathrm{eval}_{\mathrm{R}}(\mathtt{t}_0) = \mathtt{wrong}$ iff $\mathtt{t}_0 \to^{*!} \mathtt{t}$ where $\mathtt{t}$ is not a value. □

Recall that the new ρ.t construct introduces a new region variable ρ. The variable ρ can be used to annotate value-producing terms within t. The allocation of the new region in our system is implicit; it happens automatically when the execution focus moves inside the new binder. Implicit alpha-conversion makes sure that the new does not capture any foreign region variables before the allocation. On the other hand, deallocation is explicit in the evaluation semantics. The (RE-DEALLOC) rule records the fact that a value stored in the deallocated region is no longer available by replacing the region variable with the special marker $\bullet$. The "dangling pointers" to deallocated values can be manipulated freely as long as one does not attempt to read the values they point to. At that point execution will get stuck, because there is no reduction rule for an expression of the form "$\langle\lambda$x.t$\rangle_\bullet$ v." Rule (RE-BETA) that would ordinarily reduce it applies only when the place is a ρ, which explicitly does not include $\bullet$ as in the effect typed language ETL.

Observe that the substitution $[\rho \mapsto \bullet]$ in (RE-DEALLOC) can affect allocation expressions $(\cdots)$ at ρ as well as already allocated values $\langle\cdots\rangle_\rho$. In the former case we end up with a "$(\cdots)$ at $\bullet$" expression which asks to allocate something in a region that does not exist anymore. This is impossible, of course, but the occurrence of such a subterm is not an error. The error happens if the expression is eventually executed, in which case execution will get stuck because (RE-CLOS) and (RE-RCLOS) demand a ρ rather than a p after the "at." Similarly a $\bullet$ can appear as the actual parameter in a region application, and the application can even be reduced without an error.

A novel aspect of the region-annotated language, compared to the tagged language described previously, is the presence of *region abstractions.* The intention is that a region abstraction "$\lambda\rho$.u," where u is an "almost-value (see Figure 3-6) ranging over normal values and yet-to-be-allocated abstractions, is the natural counterpart to a normal abstraction only at the level of regions. One can apply such an abstraction to an actual place parameter p in which case evaluation proceeds by substituting the place p for the formal parameter ρ in u, and then evaluates the result of this substitution. Region abstractions allow one to parameterize a function over the regions necessary for the evaluation of the function. Typically, this means parameterizing over the regions containing the input to the function and the regions in which the output should be stored. We say that such a function is *region polymorphic* in the region parameters.

For example, consider the following program computing Fibonacci numbers.[3]

3. In examples we shall allow ourselves to use features such as integers allocated in regions even though they are not part of the formal development.

```
fix fib. λn.
  if n<2 then 1
  else fib(n-2)+fib(n-1)
```

One possible region annotation of this program is (ignore everything but the first line for now):

```
fix fib. (λρ_i. (λρ_o. (λn.
    if new ρ. (n < (2 at ρ) then 1 at ρ_o)
    else new ρ_1.
            new ρ_2.fib[[ρ_2]][[ρ_1]] (new ρ.n -_{at ρ_2} (2 at ρ))
        +_{at ρ_o}new ρ_3.fib[[ρ_3]][[ρ_1]] (new ρ.n -_{at ρ_3} (1 at ρ))
    ) at ρ_i) at ρ_i) at ρ_f
```

The point is that the `fib` function expects two region parameters at runtime: one, ρ_i, in which the input `n` is stored, and one, ρ_o, in which the function is supposed to store its result. Thus, any caller of `fib` is required to choose appropriate actual regions for these as witnessed in the two calls to `fib` in the body.

Observe that, since the only way to allocate and deallocate a region is via the `new` construct, it is not possible for the function to deallocate a region associated with a parameter, and similarly, the function cannot itself allocate such a region. The consequence is that the lifetime of regions passed as parameters to a function encompasses the lifetime of the complete function invocation. In order to avoid large, long-lived regions, it is therefore important to allow the body of a recursive function to use actual parameters to recursive invocations different from the formal parameters. This is referred to as *region polymorphic recursion* in the literature, as it allows us to choose different instantiations of the polymorphically bound region parameters for different invocations.

Continuing the Fibonacci example above, it is crucial that the two recursive calls to `fib` can each supply their own actual parameters (in this case ρ_2, ρ_1 and ρ_3, ρ_1). Thus, for each call we store the arguments in separate regions whose lifetimes are just the duration of the function call. The results need slightly longer lifetimes, since we need to add those up to give the result of the original call, but they can be stored in the same region. (The example is taken from Tofte and Talpin [1997].)

3.4.2 EXERCISE [★★]: What would happen to the region-behavior of the Fibonacci program if region polymorphic recursion were disallowed (that is, if the recursive calls were required to use the formal region parameters as actual region parameters)? □

The original calculus proposed by Tofte and Talpin (let us call it the TT calculus) differs from our RAL in a number of ways. The most conspicuous difference is that the region-creation construct "new ρ.t" is written "letregion ρ in t." A more subtle one is that TT restricts the places where region abstractions and recursive function definitions can occur. Region abstractions are only allowed in the definition of recursive functions, and a recursive function definition must appear in a let binding. These restrictions are implicit in the syntax of TT—it combines recursion and region abstraction in a single combined construction

$$t ::= \texttt{letrec}\ f[\rho_1,\ldots,\rho_k](x)\ \texttt{at}\ \rho = t_1\ \texttt{in}\ t_2$$

which corresponds to the RAL expression

$$\texttt{let}\ f = \texttt{fix}\ f.(\lambda\rho_1,\ldots,\rho_k,\rho'.(\lambda x.t_1)\ \texttt{at}\ \rho')\ \texttt{at}\ \rho\ \texttt{in}\ t_2$$

Using the letrec as an abbreviation, we can rewrite the Fibonacci example to the following program:

```
letrec fib[ρi,ρo] (n) at ρf =
  if new ρ. (n < (2 at ρ) then 1 at ρo)
  else
    new ρ1.
         new ρ2. fib[ρ2,ρ1] (new ρ. n -at ρ2 (2 at ρ))
    +at ρo new ρ3. fib[ρ3,ρ1] (new ρ. n -at ρ3 (1 at ρ))
```

3.4.3 EXERCISE [★★]: This unfolding of the TT letrec uses abstraction over multiple regions at once, which is not actually part of the RAL calculus. Show how n-ary region abstractions can be simulated using our unary ones. □

3.4.4 EXERCISE [★]: What is the role of the ρ' parameter in the above RAL expansion of TT's letrec construction? Can you guess why it is not part of the original TT syntax? □

3.4.5 EXERCISE [★]: What is the role of ρ in the letrec construction? Is it really operationally necessary? □

The dynamic semantics presented by Tofte and Talpin (1997) stresses that regions are allocated and deallocated according to a stack discipline. A *runtime configuration* contains a *region environment* that maps region variables to concrete regions (denoted by r), and a *store* that maps (concrete) regions to the values stored in them. Evaluation of a new ρ.t then proceeds as follows: (1) first choose a fresh (concrete) region r and extend the region environment with a binding $\rho \mapsto$ r and the store with a binding r $\mapsto \emptyset$ where $\emptyset$ is the empty region containing no values; (2) then proceed with the evaluation of t in this extended runtime configuration; (3) complete the evaluation of the entire term by removing the bindings for ρ and r from the configuration.

That original formulation is closer to an operational understanding of how the region operations work than the store-less semantics we use here. On the other hand, the store-less semantics is easier to reason about, a trick due to Helsen and Thiemann (2000) and Calcagno (2001). See Calcagno et al. (2002) for a proof that the two styles of semantics are indeed equivalent.

Reusing Deallocated Memory

Intuitively it should be safe to reuse deallocated memory (indicated by the special place •) while executing a region-safe program. More formally, assume that t• is a term containing deallocated values and that t is constructed from t• by replacing some of these with new values. Then if t• evaluates to some value or loops indefinitely (that is, it does not go wrong), then so does t.

3.4.6 PROPOSITION: Let *Val* be the set of values and *Dead* be the subset of values of the form "⟨...⟩•." Let the relation $\preceq$ between terms be the compatible closure of $Dead \times Val$. That is, t• $\preceq$ t if t arises from t• by replacing some (zero or more) deallocated values by arbitrary new values.

If t• $\preceq$ t and eval_R(t•) $= Y \neq$ wrong, then eval_R(t) $= Y$, too. □

Proof: Left as an exercise (★★, ↛). □

Annotating Programs with Regions Preserves Meanings

Region annotating a program is the process of adding region annotations to it to make the memory management explicit (see §3.6 for how to do this automatically). Thus, the process takes a program written in BL and produces a program written in RAL. The intention is, of course, that the region-annotated program is supposed to have the same behavior as the original program. In other words, we shall prove that adding region annotations preserves the meaning of the program. We make this precise in the present section. We do so by starting with a region-annotated program and showing that it behaves the same as the program obtained by removing all region annotations (thereby obtaining a program in BL, Figure 3-1).

By analogy with erasure for TL-terms, going from a term in the region-annotated language RAL to a term in the underlying base language BL is a matter of erasing all region annotations.

$$
\begin{array}{rcl}
\|\mathtt{bv}\| & = & \mathtt{bv} \\
\left\|\mathtt{if}\ \mathtt{t_0}\ \begin{array}{l}\mathtt{then}\ \mathtt{t_1}\\ \mathtt{else}\ \mathtt{t_2}\end{array}\right\| & = & \mathtt{if}\ \|\mathtt{t_0}\|\ \begin{array}{l}\mathtt{then}\ \|\mathtt{t_1}\|\\ \mathtt{else}\ \|\mathtt{t_2}\|\end{array} \\
\|\mathtt{x}\| & = & \mathtt{x} \\
\|(\lambda\mathtt{x.t})\ \mathtt{at}\ \mathtt{p}\| & = & \lambda\mathtt{x}.\|\mathtt{t}\| \\
\|\langle\lambda\mathtt{x.t}\rangle_{\mathtt{p}}\| & = & \lambda\mathtt{x}.\|\mathtt{t}\|
\end{array}
\qquad
\begin{array}{rcl}
\|\mathtt{t_1}\ \mathtt{t_2}\| & = & \|\mathtt{t_1}\|\ \|\mathtt{t_2}\| \\
\|\mathtt{fix}\ \mathtt{x.u}\| & = & \mathtt{fix}\ \mathtt{x}.\|\mathtt{u}\| \\
\|\mathtt{new}\ \rho\mathtt{.t}\| & = & \|\mathtt{t}\| \\
\|(\lambda\rho\mathtt{.u})\ \mathtt{at}\ \mathtt{p}\| & = & \|\mathtt{u}\| \\
\|\langle\lambda\rho\mathtt{.u}\rangle_{\mathtt{p}}\| & = & \|\mathtt{u}\| \\
\|\mathtt{t}\ [[\mathtt{p}]]\| & = & \|\mathtt{t}\|
\end{array}
$$

Figure 3-7: Definition of the erasure function

3.4.7 DEFINITION: The *erasure* $\|\mathtt{t}\|$ of a region-annotated term $\mathtt{t}$ is the BL-term defined by removing the region annotations, as shown in Figure 3-7. □

The ideal meaning-preservation statement would be: For any region-annotated program $\mathtt{t}$, if $\mathrm{eval_R}(\mathtt{t}) = Y$ then $\mathrm{eval}(\|\mathtt{t}\|) = Y$ and vice versa. Unfortunately that is not true, since $\mathtt{t}$ can go wrong due to memory-management errors (such as trying to read a value after it has been deallocated) that have no counterpart in $\|\mathtt{t}\|$. What we can prove, however, is the following theorem:

3.4.8 THEOREM [CONDITIONAL CORRECTNESS]: Let $\mathtt{t}$ be a region-annotated program (i.e., formally, any term), and assume $\mathrm{eval_R}(\mathtt{t}) \neq \mathtt{wrong}$. Then $\mathrm{eval_R}(\mathtt{t}) = \mathrm{eval}(\|\mathtt{t}\|)$. □

In other words, a region-annotated program behaves the same as the original unannotated program, unless it goes wrong. Our semantics for region-annotated programs does not allow us to distinguish between going wrong because of memory-management errors and going wrong due to plain old type errors, but it would be straightforward (though tedious) to extend the semantics with such a notion and then prove that if $\mathrm{eval}(\|\mathtt{t}\|) \neq \mathrm{eval}(\mathtt{t})$ then $\mathrm{eval}(\mathtt{t})$ is memory-wrong rather than type-wrong. Since we are primarily concerned with well-typed programs, we will not pursue that further.

The proof of the theorem proceeds through a series of lemmas:

3.4.9 LEMMA: Assume that $\mathtt{t}$ is a value $\mathtt{v}$ *or* an almost-value $\mathtt{u}$. Then $\|\mathtt{t}\|$ is a value for BL. □

Proof: By structural induction on $\mathtt{t}$. The induction hypothesis is used in the case of region abstractions and closures, which disappear during erasure. (This is why the body of a region abstraction is restricted to be an almost-value rather than an arbitrary term.) □

3.4.10 LEMMA [SIMULATION]: Assume $\mathtt{t} \xrightarrow{\text{RAL}} \mathtt{t}'$. Then either (a) $\|\mathtt{t}\| \longrightarrow \|\mathtt{t}'\|$ or (b) $\|\mathtt{t}\| = \|\mathtt{t}'\|$. □

Proof: By induction on the derivation of $\mathtt{t} \xrightarrow{\text{RAL}} \mathtt{t}'$.

For the rules (RE-IF), (RE-APP1), and (RE-APP2), apply the induction hypothesis. If this application yields case (a), use the corresponding context rule from BL. In the case of (RE-APP2), Lemma 3.4.9 ensures that erasure of the function expression is still a value, such that the corresponding BL rule is available.

For the rule (RE-FIX), first observe that since the body of the fix is an almost-value, the only rules that can establish the reduction $\mathtt{u} \xrightarrow{\text{RAL}} \mathtt{u}'$ are (RE-CLOS) and (RE-RCLOS). Then, by inspection of each of these rules we find $\|\mathtt{u}\| = \|\mathtt{u}'\|$, and thus also $\|\mathtt{fix\ x.u}\| = \|\mathtt{fix\ x.u}'\|$.

For (RE-IFTRUE), (RE-IFFALSE), (RE-BETA), and (RE-FIXBETA), the $\|\mathtt{t}\| \longrightarrow \|\mathtt{t}'\|$ case applies through the corresponding BL reductions.

For (RE-RAPP) and (RE-NEW), use the induction hypothesis directly.

For (RE-CLOS) and (RE-RCLOS), $\|\mathtt{t}\| = \|\mathtt{t}'\|$ holds trivially. The case is similar for (RE-RBETA) and (RE-DEALLOC), because the erasure hides the effect of region substitutions. □

3.4.11 LEMMA [SIMULATED PROGRESS]: Assume $\mathtt{t} \xrightarrow{\text{RAL}} \mathtt{t}'$ yet not $\|\mathtt{t}\| \longrightarrow \|\mathtt{t}'\|$. Then $\mathtt{t}'$ is strictly smaller than $\mathtt{t}$ under a size measure where unevaluated abstractions are considered "larger" (for example, twice as large) than closures. □

Proof: From the proof of Lemma 3.4.10 it is clear that the derivation of $\mathtt{t} \xrightarrow{\text{RAL}} \mathtt{t}'$ must consist of a stack of context rules with one of the axioms (RE-CLOS), (RE-RCLOS), (RE-RBETA), or (RE-DEALLOC) at the top. Because the context rules do not themselves add material to the term, it is sufficient to check the lemma for those four axioms. For (RE-CLOS) and (RE-RCLOS), the size measure is explicitly defined to make the lemma true. For (RE-RBETA) or (RE-DEALLOC), the region substitution does not change the size of its argument, whereas the reductions remove either the λ or the new binder. □

3.4.12 LEMMA: Assume $\mathrm{eval}_{\mathrm{R}}(\mathtt{t}) = \mathtt{bv}$. Then $\mathrm{eval}(\|\mathtt{t}\|) = \mathtt{bv}$, too. □

Proof: We have that $\mathtt{t} \longrightarrow^{*!} \mathtt{bv}$. By applying Lemma 3.4.10 to each of the reduction steps in turn, we get $\|\mathtt{t}\| \xrightarrow{\text{BL}}{}^{*} \|\mathtt{bv}\| = \mathtt{bv}$. Since bv has no successor, $\mathrm{eval}(\|\mathtt{t}\|) = \mathtt{bv}$. □

3.4.13 LEMMA: Assume $\mathrm{eval}_{\mathrm{R}}(\mathtt{t}_0) = \bot$. Then $\mathrm{eval}(\|\mathtt{t}_0\|) = \bot$, too. □

Proof: The assumption gives us an infinite series of reductions $\mathtt{t}_0 \xrightarrow{\text{RAL}} \mathtt{t}_1 \xrightarrow{\text{RAL}} \cdots \xrightarrow{\text{RAL}} \mathtt{t}_i \ldots$. By Lemma 3.4.10, we get for each $i \geq 0$ that either $\|\mathtt{t}_i\| = \|\mathtt{t}_{i+1}\|$

or $\|\mathtt{t}_i\| \xrightarrow{\mathrm{BL}} \|\mathtt{t}_{i+1}\|$. Lemma 3.4.11 guarantees that there does not exist an N such that $\|\mathtt{t}_i\| \not\xrightarrow{\mathrm{BL}} \|\mathtt{t}_{i+1}\|$ for all $i > N$. Therefore, by choosing certain i's, we get an infinite series of BL reductions $\|\mathtt{t}_0\| \xrightarrow{\mathrm{BL}} \|\mathtt{t}_{i_1}\| \xrightarrow{\mathrm{BL}} \cdots \xrightarrow{\mathrm{BL}} \left\|\mathtt{t}_{i_j}\right\| \ldots$. Hence eval$(\|\mathtt{t}_0\|) = \bot$. □

Proof: [of Theorem 3.4.8] Assume that $\mathrm{eval}_\mathrm{R}(\mathtt{t}) \neq \mathtt{wrong}$. Then $\mathrm{eval}_\mathrm{R}(\mathtt{t})$ is either bv or $\bot$, and one of the last two lemmas gives us eval$(\|\mathtt{t}\|) = \mathrm{eval}_\mathrm{R}(\mathtt{t})$. □

3.5 The Tofte–Talpin Type System

One of the features that differentiates Tofte and Talpin's region language from other region-based systems (such as Hanson [1990], Ross [1967], and Schwartz [1975]) is the presence of a *type system*. The type system is sound (page 117) and thus well-typed programs do not go wrong at runtime. In the present setting, this means that if the term t is well-typed then $\mathrm{eval}_\mathrm{R}(\mathtt{t}) \neq \mathtt{wrong}$. In particular, well-typed programs are memory safe. In contrast to this, in the other systems mentioned above, the programmer has to establish memory safety manually, and this is essentially just as hard as establishing memory safety of C-like `malloc/free` programs.

In Figure 3-8, we define a region type system for RAL, called RTL for "Region-Typed Language." The judgment $\Gamma \vdash \mathtt{t} :^{\varphi} \mathtt{T}$ reads: in type environment Γ the term t has type T and effect φ. The effect captures the regions that have to be live (that is, allocated) for the term to evaluate without memory problems. In types, $\forall$X.T binds the type variable X in T, $\Pi\rho.^{\varphi}\mathtt{T}$ binds the region variable ρ in T and φ, and $\forall\epsilon$.T binds the effect variable ϵ in T. We denote the sets of free type variables, free region variables, and free effect variables of a type T by ftv(T), frv(T), and fev(T), respectively. These are extended to typing contexts in the obvious manner. We write $[\mathtt{X} \mapsto \mathtt{T}]$, $[\rho \mapsto \mathtt{p}]$, and $[\epsilon \mapsto \varphi]$ for the capture-avoiding substitutions of type T for the type variable X, place p for the region variable ρ, and effect φ for the effect variable ϵ, respectively.

The typing rules in Figure 3-8 are natural extensions of the typing rules for the effect typed language in Figure 3-5 (page 103). The region-annotated language, is however, both type polymorphic and effect polymorphic. The type system includes standard rules for introducing and eliminating type polymorphism and the obvious variations for effect polymorphism. Compared to System *F* (*TAPL*, Chapter 23) we do not have explicit syntax for these introductions and eliminations. As already mentioned, the language also contains region polymorphism. Region polymorphism is explicit in the syntax because it has operational significance.

Effect polymorphism is the natural complement to type polymorphism and higher-order functions. Consider a higher-order polymorphic function such

Type expressions

$$\begin{array}{llll}
\mathtt{p} & \in & \text{Place} & \textit{places} \\
\epsilon & \in & \text{EffVar} & \textit{effect variables} \\
\varphi & \in & \mathcal{P}_{\text{fin}}(\text{Place} \cup \text{EffVar}) & \textit{effects} \\
\mathtt{T} & ::= & & \textit{type expressions:} \\
& & \mathtt{X} & \textit{type variable} \\
& & \mathtt{bool} & \textit{Boolean type} \\
& & (\mathtt{T} \rightarrow {}^{\varphi}\mathtt{T}, \mathtt{p}) & \textit{function type} \\
& & (\Pi\rho.{}^{\varphi}\mathtt{T}, \mathtt{p}) & \textit{region function} \\
& & \forall \mathtt{X}.\mathtt{T} & \textit{type polymorphism} \\
& & \forall \epsilon.\mathtt{T} & \textit{effect polymorphism}
\end{array}$$

Typing rules $\boxed{\Gamma \vdash \mathtt{t} :^{\varphi} \mathtt{T}}$

$$\frac{\Gamma(\mathtt{x}) = \mathtt{T}}{\Gamma \vdash \mathtt{x} :^{\varphi} \mathtt{T}} \quad \text{(RT-VAR)}$$

$$\Gamma \vdash \mathtt{bv} :^{\varphi} \mathtt{bool} \quad \text{(RT-BOOL)}$$

$$\frac{\Gamma \vdash \mathtt{t}_1 :^{\varphi} \mathtt{bool} \qquad \Gamma \vdash \mathtt{t}_2 :^{\varphi} \mathtt{T} \qquad \Gamma \vdash \mathtt{t}_3 :^{\varphi} \mathtt{T}}{\Gamma \vdash \mathtt{if}\ \mathtt{t}_1\ \mathtt{then}\ \mathtt{t}_2\ \mathtt{else}\ \mathtt{t}_3 :^{\varphi} \mathtt{T}} \quad \text{(RT-IF)}$$

$$\frac{\Gamma, \mathtt{x}:\mathtt{T}_1 \vdash \mathtt{t} :^{\varphi_2} \mathtt{T}_2 \qquad \mathtt{p} \in \varphi}{\Gamma \vdash (\lambda \mathtt{x}.\mathtt{t})\ \mathtt{at}\ \mathtt{p} :^{\varphi} (\mathtt{T}_1 \rightarrow {}^{\varphi_2}\mathtt{T}_2, \mathtt{p})} \quad \text{(RT-ABS)}$$

$$\frac{\Gamma, \mathtt{x}:\mathtt{T}_1 \vdash \mathtt{t} :^{\varphi_2} \mathtt{T}_2}{\Gamma \vdash \langle \lambda \mathtt{x}.\mathtt{t} \rangle_{\mathtt{p}} :^{\varphi} (\mathtt{T}_1 \rightarrow {}^{\varphi_2}\mathtt{T}_2, \mathtt{p})} \quad \text{(RT-CLOS)}$$

$$\frac{\Gamma \vdash \mathtt{t}_0 :^{\varphi} (\mathtt{T}_1 \rightarrow {}^{\varphi_2}\mathtt{T}_2, \mathtt{p}) \qquad \Gamma \vdash \mathtt{t}_1 :^{\varphi} \mathtt{T}_1 \qquad \mathtt{p} \in \varphi \qquad \varphi_2 \subseteq \varphi}{\Gamma \vdash \mathtt{t}_0\ \mathtt{t}_1 :^{\varphi} \mathtt{T}_2} \quad \text{(RT-APP)}$$

$$\frac{\Gamma, \mathtt{x}:\mathtt{T} \vdash \mathtt{u} :^{\varphi} \mathtt{T}}{\Gamma \vdash \mathtt{fix}\ \mathtt{x}.\mathtt{u} :^{\varphi} \mathtt{T}} \quad \text{(RT-FIX)}$$

$$\frac{\Gamma \vdash \mathtt{u} :^{\varphi'} \mathtt{T} \qquad \rho \notin \text{frv}(\Gamma) \qquad \mathtt{p} \in \varphi}{\Gamma \vdash (\lambda \rho.\mathtt{u})\ \mathtt{at}\ \mathtt{p} :^{\varphi} (\Pi\rho.{}^{\varphi'}\mathtt{T}, \mathtt{p})} \quad \text{(RT-RABS)}$$

$$\frac{\Gamma \vdash \mathtt{u} :^{\varphi'} \mathtt{T} \qquad \rho \notin \text{frv}(\Gamma)}{\Gamma \vdash \langle \lambda \rho.\mathtt{u} \rangle_{\mathtt{p}} :^{\varphi} (\Pi\rho.{}^{\varphi'}\mathtt{T}, \mathtt{p})} \quad \text{(RT-RCLOS)}$$

$$\frac{\Gamma \vdash \mathtt{t} :^{\varphi} (\Pi\rho.{}^{\varphi'}\mathtt{T}, \mathtt{p}) \qquad \mathtt{p} \in \varphi \qquad [\rho \mapsto \mathtt{p}']\varphi' \subseteq \varphi}{\Gamma \vdash \mathtt{t}\ [[\mathtt{p}']] :^{\varphi} [\rho \mapsto \mathtt{p}']\mathtt{T}} \quad \text{(RT-RAPP)}$$

$$\frac{\Gamma \vdash \mathtt{t} :^{\varphi,\rho} \mathtt{T} \qquad \rho \notin \text{frv}(\Gamma, \mathtt{T})}{\Gamma \vdash \mathtt{new}\ \rho.\mathtt{t} :^{\varphi} \mathtt{T}} \quad \text{(RT-NEW)}$$

$$\frac{\Gamma \vdash \mathtt{t} :^{\varphi} \mathtt{T} \qquad \mathtt{X} \notin \text{ftv}(\Gamma)}{\Gamma \vdash \mathtt{t} :^{\varphi} \forall \mathtt{X}.\mathtt{T}} \quad \text{(RT-TGEN)}$$

$$\frac{\Gamma \vdash \mathtt{t} :^{\varphi} \forall \mathtt{X}.\mathtt{T}}{\Gamma \vdash \mathtt{t} :^{\varphi} [\mathtt{X} \mapsto \mathtt{T}']\mathtt{T}} \quad \text{(RT-TINST)}$$

$$\frac{\Gamma \vdash \mathtt{t} :^{\varphi} \mathtt{T} \qquad \epsilon \notin \text{fev}(\Gamma, \varphi)}{\Gamma \vdash \mathtt{t} :^{\varphi} \forall \epsilon.\mathtt{T}} \quad \text{(RT-EGEN)}$$

$$\frac{\Gamma \vdash \mathtt{t} :^{\varphi} \forall \epsilon.\mathtt{T}}{\Gamma \vdash \mathtt{t} :^{\varphi} [\epsilon \mapsto \varphi']\mathtt{T}} \quad \text{(RT-EINST)}$$

Figure 3-8: The RTL region type system

as list map: it takes a function and a list as arguments and applies the function to each element in the list. In the region-free base language, map has type $\forall \alpha, \beta.(\alpha \rightarrow \beta) \times \alpha\ \mathtt{list} \rightarrow \beta\ \mathtt{list}$. What is the effect of applying the equivalent of map in the region-annotated language to such arguments? It certainly has to include the effect, φ say, of applying the argument function, and thus the type of the region-annotated map function would have to reflect that in the latent effect of the complete function:

$$\forall \alpha, \beta.(\alpha \rightarrow {}^{\varphi}\beta) \times (\alpha\ \mathtt{list}, \rho) \rightarrow {}^{\{\rho,\rho'\}\cup\varphi}(\beta\ \mathtt{list}, \rho')$$

(see page 121 for the typing rules concerning lists). However, that would only allow us to apply map to functions with latent effect φ. We could of course inspect the complete program and make sure that all effects were large enough that this is not a problem, but this approach would unnecessarily keep many regions alive. Instead, we can employ effect polymorphism to propagate the effect of the functional argument to the effect of the complete evaluation of map as in $\forall\alpha,\beta.\forall\epsilon.(\alpha \to^{\epsilon} \beta) \times (\alpha\ \mathtt{list},\rho) \to^{\{\rho,\rho'\}\cup\epsilon} (\beta\ \mathtt{list},\rho')$.

The RTL type system is based on the type system of the TT calculus in Tofte and Talpin (1997).[4] Compared to TT, RTL has moved effect enlargement upwards in the derivation tree so that the axioms are responsible for introducing proper effects. This simplifies both the presentation of the rules and the soundness proof slightly, and it is possible to establish a meta-property of the type system that allows effects to be enlarged. Moreover, the RTL system, with its System-*F*-like polymorphism in types, regions, and effects, is more permissive than the TT system with its let-polymorphism. The restrictions present in the original system were there to simplify the region inference algorithm.

The typing rules of RTL can be applied in sequence to obtain a typing of the letrec construction in the TT system. Recall, that a TT letrec

$$\mathtt{letrec}\ \mathtt{f}[\rho_1,\ldots,\rho_k](\mathtt{x})\ \mathtt{at}\ \rho = \mathtt{t}_1\ \mathtt{in}\ \mathtt{t}_2$$

is expressed in RAL as

$$\mathtt{let}\ \mathtt{f} = \mathtt{fix}\ \mathtt{f}.(\lambda\rho_1,\ldots,\rho_k,\rho'.(\lambda\mathtt{x}.\mathtt{t}_1)\ \mathtt{at}\ \rho')\ \mathtt{at}\ \rho\ \mathtt{in}\ \mathtt{t}_2$$

The combined construction can be typed by a stack of RTL rules:

$$\dfrac{\dfrac{\dfrac{\Gamma,\mathtt{f}\mapsto T_{12},\mathtt{x}\mapsto T \vdash \mathtt{t}_1 :^{\varphi_1} T_1}{\Gamma,\mathtt{f}\mapsto T_{12} \vdash \mathtt{t}_{14} :^{\rho'} T_{14}}\ \text{(RT-ABS)}}{\Gamma,\mathtt{f}\mapsto T_{12} \vdash \mathtt{t}_{13} :^{\varphi} T_{13}}\ \text{(RT-RABS)}}{\vdots}\ \text{(RT-EGEN)}$$

$$\dfrac{\dfrac{\dfrac{}{\Gamma,\mathtt{f}\mapsto T_{12} \vdash \mathtt{t}_{13} :^{\varphi} T_{12}}\ \text{(RT-EGEN)}}{\Gamma \vdash \mathtt{t}_{11} :^{\varphi} T_{12}}\ \text{(RT-FIX)}}{\vdots}\ \text{(RT-TGEN)}$$

$$\dfrac{\dfrac{}{\Gamma \vdash \mathtt{t}_{11} :^{\varphi} T_{11}}\ \text{(RT-TGEN)} \qquad \Gamma,\mathtt{f}\mapsto T_{11} \vdash \mathtt{t}_2 :^{\varphi} T_2}{\Gamma \vdash \mathtt{letrec}\ \mathtt{f}[\rho_1,\ldots,\rho_k](\mathtt{x})\ \mathtt{at}\ \rho = \mathtt{t}_1\ \mathtt{in}\ \mathtt{t}_2 :^{\varphi} T_2}\ \text{(RT-LET)}$$

4. The type system in that paper is not defined explicitly. The paper presents a typed translation from a language resembling our Base Language BL to the TT calculus. From this translation one can extract a type system for TT.

where

$$
\begin{array}{ll}
t_{14} = (\lambda x.t_1) \text{ at } \rho' & T_{14} = (T \to^{\varphi_1} T_1, \rho') \\
t_{13} = (\lambda \rho_1,\ldots,\rho_k,\rho'.t_{14}) \text{ at } \rho & T_{13} = (\Pi \rho_1,\ldots,\rho_k,\rho'.^{\rho'} T_{14}, \rho) \\
 & T_{12} = \forall \epsilon_1 \ldots \forall \epsilon_n.T_{13} \\
t_{11} = \text{fix } f.t_{13} & T_{11} = \forall X_1 \ldots \forall X_m.T_{12}.
\end{array}
$$

As usual with let-polymorphism, each time f is mentioned in t_2, its type scheme must immediately be fully instantiated. This principle is extended to the effect and region abstractions; these must also be fully instantiated (applied, in the case of region abstraction) each time f is mentioned in t_2 or in t_1. Thus, the original TT type system does not allow expressions in general to have type $(\Pi\rho.^{\varphi}T, p)$; in particular, region abstractions cannot be passed as parameters to, or returned from, functions.

Syntactic Type Soundness

We will now prove that typable programs are memory safe. We do so by establishing *type soundness*—that is, that well-typed programs do not go wrong. The type soundness proof is structured as a standard sequence of substitution, subject reduction, and progress lemmas. This approach was pioneered by Helsen and Thiemann (2000) in the context of region-based languages, and apparently independently discovered by Calcagno (2001) for a big-step semantics. Tofte and Talpin (1997) also proved type soundness, albeit not directly but as a consequence of their correctness theorem of region inference and using a complex co-inductive proof technique.

As usual, we start by showing that one can massage derivations so that the typing context only mentions the free variables of the term and so that the derivation does not end with one of the instantiation rules.

3.5.1 LEMMA: If $\Gamma \vdash t :^{\varphi} T$, $dom(\Gamma') = fv(t)$, and Γ and Γ' agree when both are defined, then $\Gamma' \vdash t :^{\varphi} T$. □

Proof: Straightforward induction on the typing derivation. □

3.5.2 LEMMA: Let S be a substitution of the form $[\rho \mapsto p]$, $[\epsilon \mapsto \varphi]$, or $[X \mapsto T]$. If $\Gamma \vdash t :^{\varphi} T$ can be derived in n steps, then likewise can $S\Gamma \vdash St :^{S\varphi} ST$. □

Proof: Left as an exercise (★). □

3.5.3 LEMMA: Assume that $\Gamma \vdash v :^{\varphi} T$ has a derivation in n steps. Then it has a derivation in at most n steps where the last rule used is neither (RT-TINST) nor (RT-EINST). □

Proof: By induction on n. All but the cases for (RT-TINST) and (RT-EINST) either are direct or are simple applications of the induction hypothesis. Thus, assume that the derivation ends with (RT-EINST) (the case for (RT-TINST) is similar). Apply the induction hypothesis to the derivation of its premise; this gives a derivation that concludes in a type with the shape $\forall\epsilon.T'$ yet does not end with (RT-EINST) or (RT-TINST). It cannot end with (RT-VAR), (RT-IF), (RT-APP), (RT-FIX), (RT-RAPP), or (RT-NEW) either, because variables, conditionals, applications, fixed-points, region applications, and region creations are not values. The only other rule that can conclude $\forall\epsilon.T'$ is (RT-EGEN), so the whole derivation now must end with

$$\dfrac{\dfrac{\Gamma \vdash v :^{\varphi} T' \qquad \epsilon \notin \mathrm{fev}(\Gamma,\varphi)}{\Gamma \vdash v :^{\varphi} \forall\epsilon.T'}\ \text{(RT-EGEN)}}{\Gamma \vdash v :^{\varphi} T}\ \text{(RT-EINST)}$$

where $T = [\epsilon \mapsto \varphi']T'$ for some φ'.

Lemma 3.5.2 now gives a derivation of $[\epsilon \mapsto \varphi']\Gamma \vdash v :^{[\epsilon\mapsto\varphi']\varphi} [\epsilon \mapsto \varphi']T'$ in $n-2$ steps. But since $\epsilon \notin \mathrm{fev}(\Gamma,\varphi)$, this conclusion is the same as $\Gamma \vdash v :^{\varphi} T$, so we can use that instead of the original derivation. Now apply the induction hypothesis to this new derivation. □

3.5.4 LEMMA [CANONICAL FORMS]:

1. if v is a value of type bool, then v is of the form bv;
2. if v is a value of type $(T_1 \to^{\varphi} T_2, p)$ then v is of the form $\langle\lambda x.t\rangle_p$;
3. if v is a value of type $(\Pi\rho.^{\varphi}T, p)$ then v is of the form $\langle\lambda\rho.u\rangle_p$. □

Proof: Left as an exercise (★, ↛). □

We next prove some lemmas about effects. First, one can always enlarge the effect attributed to a term and obtain a derivable typing. Second, if a value can be typed, then it can also be typed with an empty effect; that is, evaluation of values does not cause any observable effects.

3.5.5 LEMMA: If $\Gamma \vdash t :^{\varphi} T$ and $\varphi \subseteq \varphi'$, then $\Gamma \vdash t :^{\varphi'} T$. □

Proof: Straightforward induction on the typing derivation. □

3.5.6 LEMMA: Let v be a value. If $\Gamma \vdash v :^{\varphi} T$ then $\Gamma \vdash v :^{\emptyset} T$. □

Proof: From Lemma 3.5.3 we get a derivation of $\Gamma \vdash v :^{\varphi} T$ that ends with neither (RT-TINST) nor (RT-EINST). Therefore, the derivation must end with one of the typing rules for values. By inspecting each of the rules (RT-BOOL), (RT-CLOS), and (RT-RCLOS) for values we see that we can construct a derivation of $\Gamma \vdash v :^{\emptyset} T$ (by choosing the effect to be empty in each case). □

Having established these basic lemmas we can now prove the lemmas leading to the type soundness result.

3.5.7 LEMMA [SUBSTITUTION]: If $\Gamma, x_1 : T_1 \vdash t :^{\varphi} T$ and $\Gamma \vdash t_1 :^{\emptyset} T_1$, then $\Gamma \vdash [x_1 \mapsto t_1]t :^{\varphi} T$. □

Proof: By induction on the typing derivation for t. The cases are all standard, except for (RT-VAR) where $t = x_1$. By (RT-VAR) itself, $T = T_1$ and since $[x_1 \mapsto t_1]x_1 = t_1$, the second assumption combined with Lemma 3.5.5 gives us the desired derivation. □

3.5.8 PROPOSITION [SUBJECT REDUCTION]: If $\Gamma \vdash t :^{\varphi} T$ and $t \xrightarrow{\text{RAL}} t'$ then $\Gamma \vdash t' :^{\varphi} T$. □

Proof: By induction over the typing derivation.

The rules (RT-VAR), (RT-BOOL), (RT-CLOS), and (RT-RCLOS) cannot occur; these rules require t to have a shape that makes $t \xrightarrow{\text{RAL}} t'$ impossible.

The cases for the rules (RT-ABS) and (RT-RABS) are immediate; the evaluation step must be by rule (RE-CLOS) or (RE-RCLOS), and we can immediately construct typings for the reduct using (RT-CLOS) or (RT-RCLOS).

For the rule (RT-IF), use case analysis on the last step in the derivation of $t \xrightarrow{\text{RAL}} t'$. The only possibilities are (RE-IF), (RE-IFTRUE), and (RE-IFFALSE). In the two latter cases, t′ is one of the branches of the conditional, and the sought-for conclusion is already one of the premises of (RT-IF). In the case of (RE-IF), use the induction hypothesis on the typing of the condition; by reusing the existing typing derivations for the branches, we can produce a typing for t′ using (RT-IF) again.

For the rule (RT-APP), again use case analysis on the derivation of $t \xrightarrow{\text{RAL}} t'$. The possible rules are now (RE-APP1), (RE-APP2), and (RE-BETA). The two former are analogous to (RE-IF) above, so consider (RE-BETA). The term t must be of the form $\langle\lambda x.t_b\rangle_\rho$ v, and the premises to (RT-APP) are (1) $\Gamma \vdash \langle\lambda x.t_b\rangle_\rho :^{\varphi} (T' \xrightarrow{\varphi'} T, \rho)$ and (2) $\Gamma \vdash v :^{\varphi} T'$, where further $\rho \in \varphi$ and $\varphi' \subseteq \varphi$. Now, $\langle\lambda x.t_b\rangle_\rho$ is a value and thus by Lemma 3.5.3 there exists a derivation of (1) ending with (RT-CLOS) which must include a (sub-)derivation of (3) $\Gamma, x : T' \vdash t_b :^{\varphi'} T$. Applying first Lemma 3.5.6 to (2) yields $\Gamma \vdash v :^{\emptyset} T'$ and then applying Lemma 3.5.7 to (3) above and this, we get a derivation of $\Gamma \vdash [x \mapsto v]t_b :^{\varphi'} T$ as required because $\varphi' \subseteq \varphi$ and we can enlarge the effect (Lemma 3.5.5).

For the rule (RT-FIX), the reduction must be by (RE-FIX) or (RE-FIXBETA). Again, the case for (RE-FIX) is analogous to (RE-IF), so assume (RE-FIXBETA). The term t must be of the form `fix` x.v and the typing derivation has a sub-derivation of (1) $\Gamma, x : T \vdash v :^{\varphi} T$. First, apply Lemma 3.5.6 to get $\Gamma, x : T \vdash v :^{\emptyset} T$ and use this and (RT-FIX) to construct a derivation of (2) $\Gamma \vdash$ `fix` $x.v :^{\emptyset} T$. Now, Lemma 3.5.7 applied to (1) and (2) yields $\Gamma \vdash [x \mapsto$ `fix` $x.v]v :^{\varphi} T$.

For the rule (RT-RAPP), the reduction must be by (RE-RAPP) (similar to the other context rules above) or (RE-RBETA). The term t must be of the form $\langle \lambda\rho_1.u\rangle_\rho$ [[p]], and the typing derivation has a sub-derivation of (1) $\Gamma \vdash \langle\lambda\rho_1.u\rangle_\rho :^{\varphi} (\Pi\rho_1.^{\varphi'}T', \rho)$ where further $\rho \in \varphi$, $[\rho_1 \mapsto p]\varphi' \subseteq \varphi$, and $T = [\rho_1 \mapsto p]T'$. Now, $\langle\lambda\rho_1.u\rangle_\rho$ is a value and thus by Lemma 3.5.3 there exists a derivation of (1) ending with (RT-RCLOS) which must include a sub-derivation of (2) $\Gamma \vdash u :^{\varphi'} T'$ where $\rho_1 \notin frv(\Gamma)$. Applying Lemma 3.5.2 to (2) and $[\rho_1 \mapsto p]$, we get a derivation of $[\rho_1 \mapsto p]\Gamma \vdash [\rho_1 \mapsto p]u :^{[\rho_1 \mapsto p]\varphi'} [\rho_1 \mapsto p]T'$ as required because $[\rho_1 \mapsto p]\Gamma = \Gamma$ (since $\rho_1 \notin frv(\Gamma)$), $[\rho_1 \mapsto p]\varphi' \subseteq \varphi$ which we can enlarge (Lemma 3.5.5), and $T = [\rho_1 \mapsto p]T'$.

For the rule (RT-NEW), t reduces by (RE-NEW) or (RE-DEALLOC). Only the latter case is interesting. The term t must be of the form newρ.v and the typing derivation must include a derivation of $\Gamma \vdash v :^{\varphi,\rho} T$ where $\rho \notin frv(\Gamma, T)$. Then, by Lemma 3.5.6 we have $\Gamma \vdash v :^{\emptyset} T$. Applying Lemma 3.5.2 we thus get a derivation of $[\rho \mapsto \bullet]\Gamma \vdash [\rho \mapsto \bullet]v :^{[\rho\mapsto\bullet]\emptyset} [\rho \mapsto \bullet]T$, that is $\Gamma \vdash [\rho \mapsto \bullet]v :^{\emptyset} T$ (since $\rho \notin frv(\Gamma, T)$). Now use Lemma 3.5.5 to recover the original effect φ.

For the rule (RT-TGEN) (the case for rule (RT-EGEN) is analogous) we have a derivation of $\Gamma \vdash t :^{\varphi} T'$ where $X \notin ftv(\Gamma)$ and $T = \forall X.T'$. Apply the induction hypothesis to this to get $\Gamma \vdash t' :^{\varphi} T'$. Since still $X \notin ftv(\Gamma)$ we can use (RT-TGEN) to construct a derivation of $\Gamma \vdash t' :^{\varphi} T$ where $T = \forall X.T'$ as required.

For the rule (RT-TINST) (the case for rule (RT-EINST) is analogous) we have a derivation of $\Gamma \vdash t :^{\varphi} \forall X.T'$ where $T = [X \mapsto T'']T'$ for some T''. Again apply the induction hypothesis to this and get $\Gamma \vdash t' :^{\varphi} \forall X.T'$ and use (RT-TINST) to construct a derivation of $\Gamma \vdash t' :^{\varphi} T$ where $T = [X \mapsto T'']T'$ as required. □

3.5.9 PROPOSITION [PROGRESS]: If $\emptyset \vdash t :^{\varphi} T$ and $\bullet \notin \varphi$, then either t is a value or there is some t′ such that $t \xrightarrow{RAL} t'$. □

Proof: By induction over the typing derivation of $\emptyset \vdash t :^{\varphi} T$.

If the last rule in the derivation is (RT-TGEN), (RT-EGEN), (RT-TINST), or (RT-EINST), the conclusion follows directly from the induction hypothesis (since the typing context remains empty and the effect remains the same in each premise). For example, for (RT-TGEN) we have a derivation of $\emptyset \vdash t :^{\varphi} T'$ where $T = \forall X.T'$. Applying the induction hypothesis to this we get that either t is a value, or there exists some t′ such that $t \xrightarrow{RAL} t'$ as required.

The case (RT-VAR) is impossible (since Γ is empty by assumption).

The cases for (RT-BOOL), (RT-CLOS), and (RT-RCLOS) are immediate.

For (RT-ABS) and (RT-RABS), there are immediate reductions by (RE-CLOS) or (RE-RCLOS), respectively.

For (RT-FIX): If u in `fix` x.u is a value v then (RE-FIXBETA) applies and we have a reduction. If u is an abstraction or a region abstraction, then it itself reduces (by either (RE-CLOS) or (RE-RCLOS)), and we obtain a reduction by (RE-FIX). This exhausts the possible syntactic forms of a non-value u.

For (RT-APP), t is an application $t_0\ t_1$, and we we have derivations of $\varnothing \vdash t_0 :^{\varphi} (T_1 \rightarrow^{\varphi_2} T, p)$ and $\varnothing \vdash t_1 :^{\varphi} T_1$ for some $p \in \varphi$ and $\varphi_2 \subseteq \varphi$. Apply the induction hypothesis to each of these. This either gives a reduction for at least one of them (in which case we can reduce t by (RE-APP1) or (RE-APP2)), or shows that t_1 and t_2 are both values. In this latter case, by Lemma 3.5.4, t_0 must have the form $\langle \lambda x_0.t_0' \rangle_p$. Now we can apply the (RE-BETA) rule to obtain a reduction, because $p \in \varphi$ cannot be • and so must be a region variable.

The cases for (RT-RAPP) and (RT-IF) are similar, but simpler.

For (RT-NEW), t is $\texttt{new}\,\rho.t_1$, and we have a derivation of $\varnothing \vdash t_1 :^{\varphi,\rho} T$. Since ρ is (by definition) not •, the induction hypothesis applies to t_1. We get that either t_1 is a value, in which case we get a reduction using (RE-DEALLOC), or t_1 reduces to another term t_1', in which case we get a reduction using (RE-NEW). □

3.5.10 THEOREM: If $\varnothing \vdash t :^{\varnothing} T$, then either (1) there is some value v such that $t \rightarrow^* v$ and $\varnothing \vdash v :^{\varnothing} T$, or (2) for each t′ such that $t \rightarrow^* t'$ there is some t″ such that $t' \rightarrow^+ t''$. □

Proof: Straightforward consequence of Propositions 3.5.8 and 3.5.9. □

3.5.11 COROLLARY [TYPE SOUNDNESS]: If $\varnothing \vdash t :^{\varnothing} \texttt{bool}$, then it is not the case that $\text{eval}_R(t) = \texttt{wrong}$. □

Extensions

The region-annotated language that we have presented only has Booleans and functions, but it is straightforward to add most other common types of data to it. As an example, in Figure 3-9 we give the necessary rules for extending the system with lists. The proofs of the metaproperties (in particular type soundness and conditional correctness) carry through to this extended system without any changes to the existing cases.

Rule (RT-CONS) implies that when adding a new element in front of a list, it must have the same type as the elements already there. That is hardly surprising, but note that it implies that the region part of the type must also be the same. Thus, the different elements of a list are always allocated in the same region and therefore will be deallocated at the same time. If a single element of the list turns out to have a long lifetime, the region type system propagates that long lifetime to all the other elements!

3.5.12 EXERCISE [RECOMMENDED, ★★, ↛]: Using Figure 3-9 as a guideline, write rules to extend the system with one or more of: Let bindings (a lambda abstraction

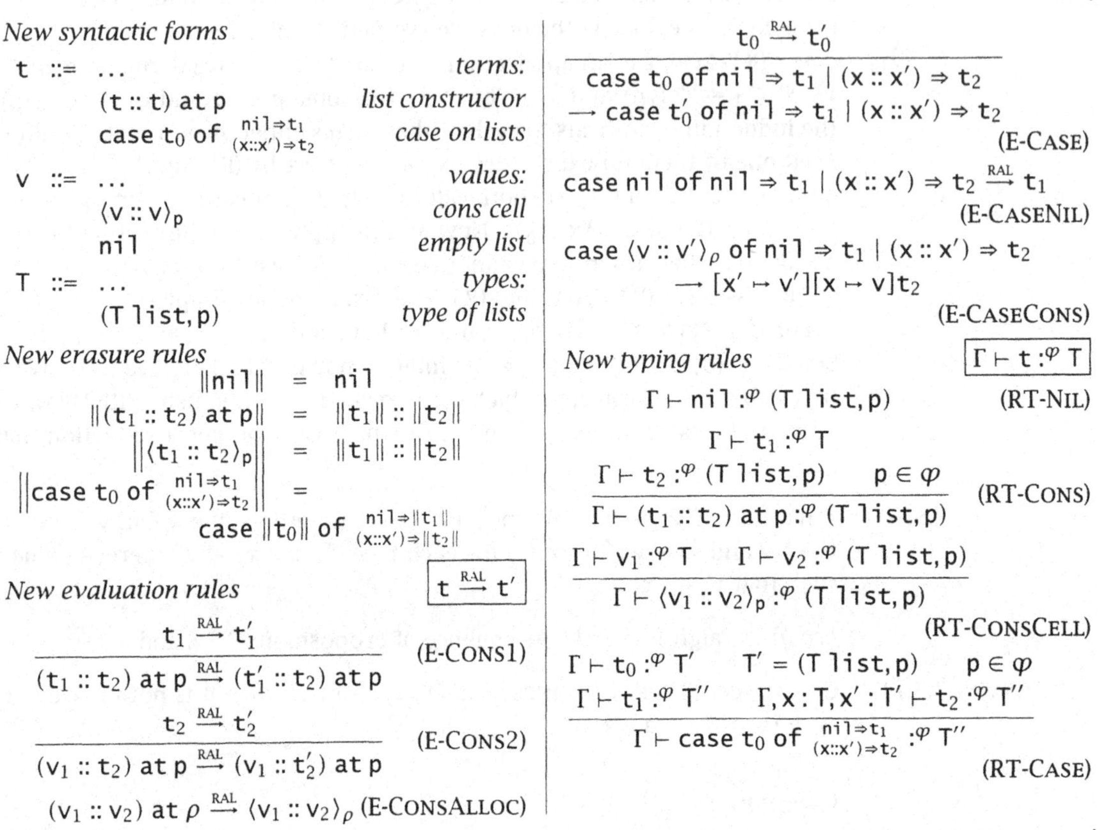

Figure 3-9: Extending the system with a list type

allocates a closure on the heap, so a let binding cannot simply be simulated as a β-redex); pairs and records; sums and variants; and general recursive types (equi- or iso-). Verify that the Conditional Correctness and Type Soundness theorems still hold for your rules. □

3.5.13 EXERCISE [★★★★]: References can be added easily to the type system with rules like

$$\frac{\Gamma \vdash \mathtt{t} :^{\varphi} \mathtt{T} \qquad \mathtt{p} \in \varphi}{\Gamma \vdash \mathtt{ref\ t\ at\ p} :^{\varphi} (\mathtt{T\ ref}, \mathtt{p})} \quad \text{(RT-REF)}$$

$$\frac{\Gamma \vdash \mathtt{t} :^{\varphi} (\mathtt{T\ ref}, \mathtt{p}) \qquad \mathtt{p} \in \varphi}{\Gamma \vdash \mathtt{!t} :^{\varphi} \mathtt{T}} \quad \text{(RT-DEREF)}$$

$$\frac{\Gamma \vdash \texttt{t} :^{\varphi} (\texttt{T ref}, \texttt{p}) \qquad \Gamma \vdash \texttt{t}' :^{\varphi} \texttt{T} \qquad \texttt{p} \in \varphi}{\Gamma \vdash \texttt{t:=t}' :^{\varphi} \texttt{unit}} \qquad \text{(RT-ASSIGN)}$$

Of course, these rules need to be combined with the usual value restriction on type *and effect* polymorphism, as discussed on pages 335–336 in *TAPL*. Which extensions to the semantics and soundness proofs are necessary for proving these rules sound? □

The typing rules presented in the above exercise correspond exactly to the way updatable references are handled in the ML Kit. Observe that since the (RT-ASSIGN) rule demands equality between the type of the value stored in the reference and the type of the new value, the rule forces the two values to have the same lifetime. For long-lived references, such as those found with container classes in object-oriented programs, this behavior is inadequate. No better solution has, however, been proposed yet.

3.6 Region Inference

So far, we have said a lot about the region type system and how region-annotated programs are supposed to be executed, but next to nothing about where the region annotations come from.

One easy answer would be, "why, the programmer wrote them"—but alas, this answer would not be easy for the programmer. Realistic programs usually need quite a lot of region abstractions and applications in order to distribute their data over several regions while still being region typable, and it is not always obvious exactly where they should be put. While it just might be possible to write a nontrivial well-typed program in the region-annotated language, it would be quite impossible to maintain it.

Thus, the idea of using a region type system to check the safety of region annotations goes hand in hand with the idea that the region annotations themselves are the product of an automatic compile-time analysis. The human programmer writes a program `t` in BL, whereupon the compiler will construct a region-annotated program `t'` such that $\|\texttt{t}'\| = \texttt{t}$ and `t'` is well-typed in RTL. This process is known as *region inference*, because Tofte and Talpin (1994) viewed it as akin to a type reconstruction ("inference") problem.

3.6.1 EXERCISE [RECOMMENDED, ★]: One can easily formulate a trivial region inference: Just choose a single fixed ρ, annotate each lambda abstraction (and other allocating expressions) in the input program with "`at` ρ," and then wrap the entire program in a single `new` construction. This evidently always produces a region-annotated program that erases to the input program, but will it always be RTL-typable? □

Of course, the trivial region inference is worthless from a memory-management point of view. It produces a region-annotated program that never deallocates anything until the entire computation is finished. What we want is the opposite: region annotations that deallocate data as soon as allowed by the region type system. Unfortunately it is not known whether "best possible region annotations" in this sense always exist, but good approximate solutions are available.

The articles by Tofte and Talpin (1994, 1997) do not themselves present an algorithm for region inference, but the nondeterministic region inference system they present has evidently been constructed with an inference algorithm in mind. The inference algorithm was published by Tofte and Birkedal (1998). We do not have the space to describe it in detail, but instead show how it works in the context of an example. Consider the term

```
letrec m(f) = if f(0) then 0 else m(λx.f(x+1)) + 1
in m(λx.x=10)
```

Let us initially assume an that oracle has told us that the "correct" region-polymorphic type scheme for `m` is

$$\forall \epsilon_1, \epsilon_2 . \Pi \rho_1, \rho_2 .^{\{\rho_2\}}((\texttt{int} \to^{\{\epsilon_1\}} \texttt{bool}, \rho_1) \to^{\{\epsilon_2, \epsilon_1, \rho_1\}} \texttt{int}, \rho_2).$$

The driving force in the region inference algorithm is an attempt to construct the RTL typing tree for the region-annotated program. The search proceeds much like the familiar Algorithm $\mathcal{W}$, unifying types as well as region variables and effect positions as we go. We don't know yet what to do with typing-rule premises of the form $\rho \in \varphi$ or $\varphi \subseteq \varphi'$, so let us initially just collect them for further processing.

By the time we have analyzed the subexpression `m(λx.f(x+1))`, the unification-based inference has built the typing tree shown in Figure 3-10. (For bevity, we assume a primitive rule for adding one to an integer—it allows concluding $\Gamma \vdash \texttt{t+1} :^{\varphi} \texttt{int}$ from $\Gamma \vdash \texttt{t} :^{\varphi} \texttt{int}$).

A set of collected effect constraints are also shown on the figure. Luckily, the effect polymorphism in the oracle's type scheme has a form that allows the possible instantiations of the effect fields in it to be descibed with subset and inclusion constraints; in this case $\varphi_4 \subseteq \varphi_5$ and $\rho_4 \in \varphi_5$.

3.6.2 **Exercise** [★, ↛]: Locate where in the proof tree the other collected constraints come from. □

Whenever we choose concrete substitutions for the symbols φ, φ_3, φ_4, and φ_5 that satisfy the constraints, we get a valid proof. What it is proof *of* depends on the substitutions we choose for φ and φ_3, because these effect

$$\dfrac{\vdots}{\Gamma \vdash \mathtt{m}\,[[\rho_4,\rho_5]] :^{\varphi} ((\mathtt{int} \xrightarrow{\varphi_4} \mathtt{bool},\rho_4) \xrightarrow{\varphi_5} \mathtt{int},\rho_5)} \quad \dfrac{\dfrac{\Gamma' \vdash \mathtt{f} :^{\varphi_1} (\mathtt{int} \xrightarrow{\varphi_3} \mathtt{bool},\rho_3) \quad \dfrac{}{\Gamma' \vdash \mathtt{x} :^{\varphi_4} \mathtt{int}}}{\Gamma' \vdash \mathtt{x+1} :^{\varphi_4} \mathtt{int}} \; }}{\Gamma' \vdash \mathtt{f(x+1)} :^{\varphi_4} \mathtt{bool}}$$

$$\dfrac{\Gamma \vdash \mathtt{m}\,[[\rho_4,\rho_5]] :^{\varphi} ((\mathtt{int} \xrightarrow{\varphi_4} \mathtt{bool},\rho_4) \xrightarrow{\varphi_5} \mathtt{int},\rho_5) \qquad \Gamma \vdash (\lambda\mathtt{x.f(x+1)})\ \mathtt{at}\ \rho_4 :^{\varphi} (\mathtt{int} \xrightarrow{\varphi_4} \mathtt{bool},\rho_4)}{\Gamma \vdash \mathtt{m}\,[[\rho_4,\rho_5]]((\lambda\mathtt{x.f(x+1)})\ \mathtt{at}\ \rho_4) :^{\varphi} \mathtt{int}}$$

where Γ is $\mathtt{m} : \forall\epsilon_1,\epsilon_2.\Pi\rho_1,\rho_2.^{\{\rho_2\}}((\mathtt{int} \xrightarrow{\{\epsilon_1\}} \mathtt{bool},\rho_1) \xrightarrow{\{\epsilon_2,\epsilon_1,\rho_1\}} \mathtt{int},\rho_2), \mathtt{f} : (\mathtt{int} \xrightarrow{\varphi_3} \mathtt{bool},\rho_3)$ and Γ' is $\Gamma, \mathtt{x} : \mathtt{int}$. Collected effect constraints: $\varphi_4 \subseteq \varphi_5$, $\rho_4 \in \varphi_5$, $\{\rho_5\} \subseteq \varphi$, $\varphi_3 \subseteq \varphi_4$, $\rho_3 \in \varphi_4$, $\rho_4 \in \varphi$, $\varphi_5 \subseteq \varphi$, $\rho_5 \in \varphi$.

Figure 3-10: A partially region-inferred proof tree

meta-variables occur in the conclusion. On the other hand, φ_4 and φ_5 do not occur in the conclusion, so we can eliminate them from the constraint set and simplify it to $\{\rho_4 \in \varphi, \rho_5 \in \varphi, \rho_3 \in \varphi, \varphi_3 \subseteq \varphi\}$. Much of (Tofte and Birkedal, 1998) is concerned with giving precise rules for such manipulations.

Observe now that the constaints imply that ρ_4 and ρ_5 must appear in the effect position of the concluding statement, but there is no reason for any of them to appear in either the type or the environment. Therefore, we are allowed to insert a new around the expression, and thus deallocate the closure for $\mathtt{m}\,[[\rho_4,\rho_5]]$ as well as the one for $\lambda\mathtt{x.f(x+1)}$ after the call returns. By doing so, we make ρ_4 and ρ_5 invisible from outside the expression, so constraints that mention them can be dropped from the constraint set. On the other hand, ρ_3 cannot be finished off in this way yet, because it occurs (explicitly) in the environment Γ.

The final result of the analysis of the expression is thus the judgment

$$\Gamma \vdash \mathtt{new}\,\rho_4,\rho_5.(\mathtt{m}\,[[\rho_4,\rho_5]]((\lambda\mathtt{x.f(x+1)})\ \mathtt{at}\ \rho_4)) :^{\varphi} \mathtt{int}$$

plus the (simplified) constraint set $\{\rho_3 \in \varphi, \varphi_3 \subseteq \varphi\}$.

3.6.3 Exercise [★★]: Why didn't the region inference insert a $\mathtt{new}\,\rho_5.\cdots$ around the subexpression $(\lambda\mathtt{x.f(x+1)})\ \mathtt{at}\ \rho_4$? □

The analysis of the rest of the body of m is unsurprising; it ends with

$$\mathtt{m} : \cdots, \mathtt{f} : (\mathtt{int} \xrightarrow{\varphi_3} \mathtt{bool},\rho_3) \vdash \mathtt{if}\ \mathtt{f(0)}\ \mathtt{then}\ 0\ \mathtt{else}\ (\cdots)\mathtt{+1} :^{\varphi} \mathtt{int}$$

and still with the same constraint set $\{\rho_3 \in \varphi, \varphi_3 \subseteq \varphi\}$ (another copy of each of these constraints was produced by the analysis of `f(0)`).

This gives the immediate type $((\texttt{int} \to^{\varphi_3} \texttt{bool}, \rho_3) \to^{\varphi} \texttt{int}, \rho')$ for `m`, where ρ' was added by the `letrec` construction itself. Since neither ρ_3 nor ρ' appears in the (empty) environment for `letrec`, we can abstract over them and make them region parameters. Finally we can abstract over effects by introducing an effect variable for each effect meta-variable in the simplified constraint set that is not connected to the environment by subset constraints. In the effect-polymorphic type, each φ position becomes the set of effect and region variables that must be in the effect, according to the constraints.[5] Thus the effect abstraction simply encapsulates the (transitive closure of the) simplified constraint set.

It turns out our oracle was right! The abstracted type of `m` is exactly what it said it would be, with ϵ_1 corresponding to φ_3, ϵ_2 to φ, ρ_1 to ρ_3, and ρ_2 to ρ'. Now the analysis of the body of the `letrec` is unsurprising; we get the following region-annotated program:

```
letrec m[ρ1](f) =
  if f(0) then 0
  else new ρ4,ρ5.(m [[ρ4]] at ρ5((λx.f(x+1)) at ρ4)) + 1
in new ρ6,ρ7.(m [[ρ6]] at ρ7((λx.x=10) at ρ6))
```

Where did the oracle get its prediction of `m`'s type from? Tofte and Birkedal (1998) construct it by *Mycroft iteration*: First, `m`'s body is analyzed under the optimistic assumption that `m` itself will have the type scheme

$$\forall\epsilon_1,\epsilon_2.\Pi\rho_1,\rho_2.^{\{\rho_2\}}((\texttt{int} \to^{\{\epsilon_1\}} \texttt{bool}, \rho_1) \to^{\{\epsilon_2\}} \texttt{int}, \rho_2)$$

that is, with no constraints at all between the various region and effect parts of polymorphic instances. If the type scheme constructed after the initial iteration does not match (which in this case it doesn't), a new iteration is tried with the new type scheme as assumption, and so forth until a fixpoint is reached.

The trick, of course, lies in ensuring that a fixpoint is eventually reached; it might well be that it just produces a list of ever larger type schemes. The original region inference algorithm (Tofte and Birkedal, 1998) solved this problem by heuristically omitting certain opportunities for region and effect

5. The way this is done in the published formulation of the algorithm includes considering one effect variable in each latent effect to be special; it is called the *handle* and is the one that corresponds to the entire effect. The distinction between the handle and other effect variables is present in the original TT calculus even though it has no special role in the soundness and correctness proofs.

abstractions such that the iterative computation of a fixpoint for the recursive function's type scheme could be guaranteed to terminate. The cost of this approach is that completeness fails: Example programs can be constructed for which the region inference algorithm leads to region annotations that are not the best possible.

Later Birkedal and Tofte (2001) rephrased the algorithm in terms of constraint solving. This reworked algorithm seems to be complete in the sense that for any region-annotated term `t` that can be TT-typed, the inference algorithm's output on ‖`t`‖ will have as least as good space behavior as `t`. However, Birkedal and Tofte prove only a weaker "restricted completeness" result; full completeness in the sense described here was not considered in the article.

Another restricted case with an easy region inference problem is known. It is when the input program can be typed with *first order types*, that is, such that neither the argument nor the return type for any function includes a function type itself. Then there is no reason to use effect polymorphism, and one never needs to generalize over region variables that appear only in latent effects. (For since there is only one arrow in each type, such a variable could just as well have been discharged by a `new` within the lambda abstraction.) These two facts lead to a bounded representation of the latent effect: We simply need to know for each of the `p` positions in the argument and return types whether the actual `p` is in the latent effect. That solves the termination problem, and with a bit of ingenuity one does not even need fixpoint iteration for finding the best type scheme.

This principle has been used to derive a region inference for an adaptation of the Tofte–Talpin system for a Prolog dialect which is naturally first order; see Makholm (2000, Chapter 10).

3.6.4 Exercise [★]: Why does effect polymorphism not make sense in a first-order program? □

3.7 More Powerful Models for Region-Based Memory Management

Unfortunately, even with region-polymorphic recursion, the Tofte–Talpin model (as expressed either as RTL or the original TT) is not quite strong enough to achieve reasonable object lifetimes. At fault is the very idea of `new`—that the lifetime of a region must coincide with the time it takes to execute some subexpression of the original program. To see how this is a problem, let us look at how the Tofte-Talpin system treats the classic "Game of Life" example. The task is to simulate a cellular automaton for n generations, starting from a specified state. This is a typical case of iterative programming, and the problems we will discover are common for iterative programs in general.

The standard way of programming an iteration in a functional language is to use tail recursion:

```
let rec nextgen(g)  = ⟨read g; create and return new generation⟩
let rec life(n,g)  = if n=0 then g
                          else life(n-1,nextgen(g))
```

We shall leave the details of nextgen unspecified here and in the following discussion. We assume, for simplicity, that a single region holds all the pieces of a generation description, and, for the sake of the argument, that the iteration count n needs to be heap-allocated, too.

The ordinary TT region inference algorithm annotates the Game of Life example as follows:

```
letrec nextgen[ρ](g)  = ⟨read g from ρ; create new gen. at ρ⟩
letrec life[ρn,ρg](n,g)  =
       if n=0 then g
       else new ρ'n
            in life[ρ'n,ρg]((n-1) at ρ'n, nextgen[ρg](g))
```

There are two major problems here. First, the recursive call of life is not a tail call anymore because it takes some work to deallocate a region at the end of new. Therefore all the ρ'_n regions will pile up on the call stack during the iteration and be deallocated only when the final result has been found. Second, any typable region annotation of the program must let the nextgen function construct its result in the same region that contains its input. This means that the program has a serious space leak: all the intermediate-generation data will be deallocated only when the result of the iteration is deallocated.

Both of these problems are caused by the fact that new aligns the lifetime of its region with the hierarchical expression evaluation. Several solutions for this have been proposed, but because their formal properties have not been as thoroughly explored as the TT calculus, we will only present them briefly.

Region Resetting in the ML Kit

The ML Kit's region implementation (Birkedal et al., 1996; Tofte et al., 2001b) is based on the TT system. Its solution to the tail recursion problem is based on a concept of *resetting* a region, meaning that its entire contents are deallocated whereas the region itself continues existing.

After a TT region inference, a special *storage-mode analysis* (Birkedal, Tofte, and Vejlstrup, 1996) that runs after region inference amends the region annotations to control resetting: Each "at ρ" annotation gets replaced by either "atbot ρ," meaning first reset the region and then allocate the new object as the new oldest object in the region, or "attop ρ," meaning allocate without resetting the region.

With this system one can rewrite the original Life program as follows to obtain better region behavior:

```
let rec copy(g) = ⟨read g; make fresh copy⟩
let rec life'((n,g) as p)
        = if n=0 then p
          else life'(n-1,copy(nextgen(g)))
let rec life(p) = snd (life' (p))
```

where copy (whose body is omitted here for brevity) takes apart a generation description and constructs a fresh, identical copy. Region inference and storage-mode analysis will then produce the region annotations

```
letrec nextgen[ρ,ρ'](g) = ⟨read g from ρ; new gen. at ρ'⟩
letrec copy[ρ',ρ](g) = ⟨read g from ρ'; fresh copy atbot ρ⟩
letrec life'[ρn,ρg]((n,g) as p)
      = if n=0 then p
        else life'[ρn,ρg]((n-1) atbot ρn,
                               new ρ'g
                               in copy[ρ'g,atbot ρg]
                                  (nextgen[ρg,ρ'g](g)))
letrec life[ρn,ρg](p) = snd (life'[ρn,ρg](p))
```

Letting life′ return the entire p instead of just g forces region inference to place all of the ns in ρ_n. A memory leak in ρ_n is prevented by the atbot allocation, whose effect is that the region ρ_n is reset prior to placing n-1 in it.

The memory leak in ρ_g is prevented with the introduction of the copy function. Now the new generation can be constructed in a temporary region ρ'_g that gets deallocated before the recursive call; once the old generation is not needed anymore, the new generation is copied into ρ_g with the atbot mode, which frees the old generation. (The atbot annotation in the passing of the region parameter serves to allow copy to actually reset the region; the need for this extra annotation has to do with aliasing between region variables.)

The storage-mode analysis works by changing the region annotation for an allocation to atbot if the value to be allocated is the only live value whose type includes the region name, as determined by a simple local liveness analysis. Neither a formal definition of the storage-mode analysis nor a proof that it is safe has appeared in the literature, but it is described briefly by Birkedal,

Tofte, and Vejlstrup (1996), together with a number of other analyses that the ML Kit uses to implement the region model efficiently.

This solution does make it possible for iterative computations to run in constant space (assuming, in the Life example, that the size of a single g is bounded), but it is by no means obvious that precisely these were the changes one needed to make to the original unannotated program to improve the space behavior. Furthermore, inserting such region optimizations in the program impede maintainability because they obscure the intended algorithm.

Aiken–Fähndrich–Levien's Analysis for Early Deallocation

Aiken, Fähndrich, and Levien (1995) extend the TT system in another direction, decoupling dynamic region allocation and deallocation from the introduction of region variables with the new construct.

In the AFL system, entry into a new block introduces a region variable, but does not allocate a region for it. During evaluation of the body of new, a region variable goes through precisely three states: unallocated, allocated, and finally deallocated. After a TT region inference (and possibly also storage-mode analysis as in the ML Kit), a constraint-based analysis—guided by a higher-order data-flow analysis for region variables—is used to insert explicit region allocation [[alloc ρ]] and deallocation commands [[free ρ]] into the program. Ideally the [[alloc ρ]] happens right before the first allocation in the region, and [[free ρ]] just after the last read from the region, but sometimes they need to be pushed farther away from the ideal placements because the same region annotations on a function body must match all call sites.

With this system, the Life example can be improved by rewriting the original program to

```
let rec copy(g)  =  ⟨read g; make fresh copy⟩
let rec life(n,g) = if n=0 then copy(g)
                         else life(n-1,nextgen(g)),
```

making the base case return a fresh copy of its input rather than the input itself. This program is analyzed as[6]

```
letrec nextgen[ρ,ρ'](g)
        = [[alloc ρ']] ⟨read g from ρ; new gen. at ρ'⟩ [[free ρ]]
letrec copy[ρ,ρ'](g)
        = [[alloc ρ']] ⟨read g from ρ; fresh copy at ρ'⟩ [[free ρ]]
```

6. The syntax here is not identical with the one used by Aiken, Fähndrich, and Levien (1995); for example, they write "free_after ρ t" for what we write as "t [[free ρ]]."

```
letrec life[ρ_n,ρ_g,ρ'](n,g)
  = if n=0
    then [[free ρ_n]] copy[ρ_g,ρ'](g)
    else new ρ'_n,ρ'_g
         in life[ρ'_n,ρ'_g,ρ']
              ([[alloc ρ'_n]] (n-1) at ρ'_n [[free ρ_n]],
               nextgen[ρ_g,ρ'_g](g))
```

Because deallocation of each region is done explicitly and not by new, the body of new is a tail call context, and the regions containing the old n and g can be freed as soon as n-1 and nextgen(g) have been computed. Without rewriting the original program this would not be the case, because a function must either always free one of its input regions or never do it.

Imperative Regions: The Henglein-Makholm-Niss Calculus

Recently Henglein, Makholm, and Niss (2001) published a region system that completely severs the connection between region lifetimes and expression structures by eliminating the new construct. Instead, the region annotations form an imperative sublanguage manipulating region handles asynchronously with respect to the expression structure.

The HMN system does not, as the two previously sketched solutions, build on top of the Tofte-Talpin model and its region inference algorithm; instead it has its own region type system (proved sound by Niss, 2002) and inference algorithm (Makholm, 2003). Starting anew means that the system is conceptually simpler while still incorporating the essential features of ML Kit-like resetting and AFL-style early deallocation as special cases. On the other hand, the theory has not yet been extended to higher-order functions.

In the HMN system it is possible to handle the Game of Life with no rewriting at all. A function can pass regions as output (indicated by o: below) as well as receive them as input (indicated by i:); HMN region inference produces

```
letrec nextgen[i:ρ;o:ρ'](g)
      = [[new ρ']] ⟨read g from ρ; new gen. at ρ'⟩ [[release ρ]]
letrec life[i:ρ_n,ρ_g;o:ρ'](n,g)
      = if n=0 then [[release ρ_n]] g [[ρ' := ρ_g]]
               else life[i:ρ'_n,ρ'_g;o:ρ']
                      ([[new ρ'_n]] (n-1) at ρ'_n [[release ρ_n]],
                       nextgen[i:ρ_g;o:ρ'_g](g))
```

where each iteration of life decides for itself whether to release the region it gets as its second parameter or to return it back to the caller.

The $[[\rho' := \rho_g]]$ operation serves the same purpose as the copy operation in the AFL solution, but is very cheap at runtime—it just renames the region that was previously called ρ_g to ρ', whereupon it is returned to the caller.

The renaming of regions means that the region-annotated types of values can change during the execution of the program. To manage that, the HMN region type system is based around a typing judgment with the shape

$$\Psi \vdash \{\Delta_1;\Gamma_1\}\ \mathtt{t} : \mathtt{T}\ \{\Delta_2;\Gamma_2\}$$

where the contexts Γ_1 and Γ_2 describe the types of the local variables before and after t is evaluated. The sets of region variables Ψ, Δ_1, and Δ_2 describe the available region variables.

Other advanced features of the HMN system include reference-counted regions with a linear type discipline for region handles, "constant" region parameters that correspond to the region abstraction of the Tofte–Talpin model, and a subtyping discipline for regions that allows extensive manipulation of dangling pointers.

Other Models

A number of more powerful region models and associated region type systems have been proposed without an accompanying inference algorithm.

Walker, Crary, and Morrisett (2000) have developed a region model with a region type-system for a continuation-passing style language, intended to be used for translating the Tofte–Talpin execution model to certified machine code. To handle the CPS transformation of region abstractions, a very advanced type system with bounded quantification over regions and effects was necessary. The final system is much stronger than the Tofte–Talpin system itself, but little is known about how to make automatic region inference utilize this extra strength.

Walker and Watkins (2001) have developed a region type system in which region references can be stored in data structures such as lists. They are still not completely first class, because they must have linear types (see Chapter 1), but the system is strong enough to reason about heterogeneous lists (i.e., lists whose elements are allocated in different regions).

Another, more restricted, way of allowing heterogeneous structures is found in the system (Grossman et al., 2002). Cyclone employs a kind of subtyping on region lifetimes and a simpler notion of effects: A region variable ρ outlives another region variable ρ' if the lifetime of ρ encompasses the lifetime of ρ'. In that event, a value allocated in the region denoted by ρ can safely be used instead of the same value allocated in the region denoted by ρ'. Cyclone supports subtyping of values according to this principle.

3.8 Practical Region-Based Memory Management Systems

The ML Kit

The ML Kit[7] essentially implements the theory described in §3.4 to §3.6 with two important extensions: first, it includes region resetting and storage-mode analysis as described in §3.7, and, second, it includes a multiplicity inference allowing the compiler to allocate finite regions on the runtime stack (Birkedal, Tofte, and Vejlstrup, 1996). The *multiplicity analysis* is a type-based analysis that determines, whether each region is finite or infinite. A *finite region* is one into which the analysis can determine that only one value will ever be written; all other regions are *infinite*. The importance of finite regions is that they can be stack-allocated since it is known in advance how large they are. Furthermore, since regions in the Tofte and Talpin region language follow a stack-discipline aligned with the expression structure of the program, such regions can even be allocated on the normal runtime stack, giving a particularly simple, efficient implementation. The latest incarnation of the ML Kit even includes a garbage collector (Hallenberg, Elsman, and Tofte, 2002), which is useful in situations where it is not practical to make a program more region friendly. See Tofte et al. (2001b) for a comprehensive introduction to programming with regions in the ML Kit, and Tofte et al. (2001a) for a survey of the interplay between theory and practice in the ML Kit.

Cyclone

Cyclone,[8] a dialect of C designed to prevent safety violations, uses regions both as a memory management discipline and as a way to guarantee safety (through type soundness). Cyclone includes three kinds of regions: a single *global* (or *heap*) region; *stack* regions (corresponding to stack frames allocated from statement blocks); and *dynamic* regions (corresponding to our lexically scoped regions).

Instead of having effect variables as in the Tofte and Talpin system, Cyclone uses an operator on types (with no operational significance). The `regions_of` operator represents the region variables that occur free in a type; the crucial trick is that the `regions_of` operator applied to a type variable is simply left abstract until the type variable is instantiated. Intuitively, instead of propagating the effect of functional arguments via effect variables, they are propagated via the `regions_of` operator. Returning to the `map` example on

7. http://www.it-c.dk/research/mlkit
8. http://www.cs.cornell.edu/projects/cyclone/

page 115 we get the following Cyclone type for map:

$$\forall \alpha, \beta.(\alpha \to \beta) \times (\alpha\ \mathtt{list}, \rho) \xrightarrow{\{\rho,\rho'\}\cup \mathtt{regions_of}(\alpha\to\beta)} (\beta\ \mathtt{list}, \rho').$$

For practical reasons, a major aspect in the design of Cyclone was to make it easy for C programmers to write Cyclone applications and to port legacy C code to Cyclone. In particular, requiring programmers to write region-annotations as seen in the present chapter is out of the question. Cyclone addresses this by combining inference of region annotations with defaults that work in many cases.

Cyclone began as a compiler for producing *typed assembly language* (see Chapter 4) and as such can be seen as one way to realize *proof-carrying code* (see Chapter 5). The region aspects of Cyclone are described by Grossman et al. (2002); a system overview is given by Jim et al. (2002).

Other Systems

The ML Kit and Cyclone are both mature systems. Several research prototypes demonstrating various principles for region-based memory management have been described in the literature.

One trend has been to adapt Tofte and Talpin's system (and its spirit) to other languages. Christiansen and Velschow (1998) describe RegJava, which is a simple, region-annotated core subset of Java and an accompanying implementation. Makholm and Sagonas (2002) extend a Prolog compiler with region-based memory management and region inference based on Henglein, Makholm, and Niss (2001).

Another trend has been to vary the fundamental assumption that regions should be allocated and deallocated according to a stack-discipline. In this direction the present authors have constructed a prototype implementation of the system of Henglein et al. (2001) for a small functional language with function pointers (but not lexical closures containing free variables). Cyclone can also be seen as the practical realization of some of the ideas in the Calculus of Capabilities (Walker, Crary, and Morrisett, 2000).

Finally, region-based memory management without the memory safety guarantees offered by region types has a long history. The basic idea, of gaining extra efficiency by bulk allocations and deallocations, is certainly natural. Systems using region-like abstractions for their memory management date as far back as 1967 (Ross, 1967; Schwartz, 1975; Hanson, 1990). In contrast to these special purpose region abstractions, the GNU C Library provides an abstraction, called *obstacks*, to application programmers (GNU, 2001).

Also in this line of work is Gay and Aiken's *RC* compiler translating region annotated C programs to ordinary C programs with library support for regions (2001). At runtime, each region is equipped with a reference count keeping track of the number of (external) references to objects in the region. The operation for deleting a region can then flag instances that attempt to delete a region with non-zero reference count. A type system provides the compiler the opportunity to remove some of the reference count operations, but it does not guarantee memory safety as the type systems discussed in this chapter do.

PART II

Types for Low-Level Languages

Types for Low-Level Languages

The next two chapters explore a number of techniques that can be used to extend high-level typing ideas to programs written in low-level languages. This problem is interesting for a number of reasons. It seems natural to assume that low-level code obtained by compiling well-typed high-level programs should have the same semantics and similar typing properties. Yet, it is not immediately clear how to write a type-checker for low-level programs.

Type checking is a convenient way to ensure that a program has certain semantic properties, such as memory safety. Type checking has gained acceptance as a major component of the security infrastructure in distributed systems that share code between hosts that do not trust each other. Notable examples are the Java Virtual Machine (JVM) (Lindholm and Yellin, 1997) and the Microsoft Common Language Infrastructure (CLI) (Gordon and Syme, 2001; Gough, 2002), both of which feature type checkers for intermediate languages used for the distribution of code in distributed systems. Such distribution schemes rely on low-level languages in order to delegate to the untrusted code producer most or all of the compilation effort, and to reduce or eliminate the need for a trusted compiler on the receiving side. This strategy also has the potential to give the code producer some flexibility in the choice of the high-level language in which the development of the code takes place.

The distribution of untrusted mobile code is the main scenario that we will use to guide our design choices. We refer to a system that receives and executes untrusted code as a *host* and to the untrusted code itself as an *agent*. Hosts want to have strong guarantees about the safety of the agent's execution. Probably the most basic guarantee is memory safety, which ensures that the agent does not attempt to dereference memory addresses to which it has not been given access. But often hosts need to have stronger guarantees, such as type safety with respect to a certain type system, or bounded execution and resource usage, or proper use of the provided APIs. We shall start to address the memory safety and type safety aspects first and then show how the techniques that we develop can be applied to more complex safety policies.

It is worth pointing out that, in the absence of type checking, alternative mechanisms for ensuring the memory safety of untrusted code are based on coarse-grained memory protection, enforced either by hardware or by software. Hardware memory protection is used when the untrusted code is run in a separate address space. A software equivalent is *software fault isolation* (SFI) (Wahbe et al., 1993), in which the untrusted code is instrumented with run-time checks that prevent memory accesses outside a pre-configured memory range. In both of these cases, the communication between the untrusted code and the host system is expensive because it must involve copying of data into the untrusted-code address space.

Most of the challenges in typing low-level languages arise because we cannot abstract details of how high-level features are implemented. In JVM and CLI, these problems are attenuated by keeping in the intermediate language the most troublesome high-level features, such as exceptions and dynamic dispatch.

In these two chapters, we examine instead an extreme situation, in which the untrusted code is written in assembly language. Correspondingly, the type system must be more expressive than would be necessary for similar programs written in a high-level language. In essence, a type checker for a low-level language verifies not only the well-typedness of the corresponding high-level constructs but also that the construct has been compiled correctly. Most of the mechanisms that we'll need can be expressed using types. Indeed, Chapter 4 describes a type system that is appropriate for assembly language. Since such a large part of low-level type checking is closer to program verification than type checking, we use in Chapter 5 a method based on logic. Besides being an instructive alternative presentation of type systems and type checking, that approach will allow us to move seamlessly beyond type checking and into checking more complex properties of the untrusted code.

4 Typed Assembly Language

Greg Morrisett

How can we ensure that when we download some code that the code will not do something "bad" when we execute it? One idea is to leverage the principle of *proof-carrying code* introduced by Necula and Lee. The principle of PCC is that we can eliminate the need to trust a piece of code by requiring a formal, machine-checkable proof that the code has some desired properties. The key insight is that checking a proof is usually quite easy, and can be done with a relatively small (and hence trustworthy) proof-checking engine.

If we are to effectively use PCC to build trustworthy systems, then we must solve two problems:

1. What properties should we require of the code?
2. How do code producers construct a formal proof that their code has the desired properties?

The first question is extremely context and application dependent. It requires that we somehow rule out all "bad" things without unduly restricting "good" things, and make both "bad" and "good" formal. The second question is impossible to solve automatically for arbitrary code assuming non-trivial safety properties. So, how are we to take advantage of PCC?

One approach is based on *type-preserving* compilation. The idea here is to focus on some form of type safety as the desired property. The advantage of focusing on type safety is that programmers are willing to do the hard part—construct a proof that some code is type-safe. The way they do this is by writing the code in a high-level language (e.g., Java or ML). If the source they write doesn't type-check, then they rewrite the code until it does. In this respect, they are engaging in a form of interactive theorem proving.

Once the initial proof is done, a type-preserving compiler takes over, mapping the type-safe source code through a series of successively lower-level intermediate languages to target code. As it transforms the code, it also (conceptually) transforms the proof. It is usually much easier to do this sort of transformation than to prove type safety directly on the generated code.

Of course, such a methodology demands that as part of the compilation process, we design a series of typed intermediate languages, culminating with typed machine code. Intermediate languages such as the Java Virtual Machine Language (JVML) and Microsoft's Common Language Infrastructure (CLI) are targets of type-preserving compilers for a number of high-level languages, including Java, C#, and ML.

However, both the JVM and CLI are relatively high-level "CISC-like" abstract machines. That is, they have pre-conceived notions of methods and objects which may be incompatible with an efficient encoding for a given language. For instance, the JVM does not support tail-calls, making the implementation of functional languages impractical. The CLI does support tail-calls, but there are other features that it lacks. For instance, arrays are treated as covariant in the type system, and thus require a run-time check upon update.

Of course, there will never be a universal, portable typed intermediate language (TIL) that supports all possible languages and implementation strategies. Nonetheless, we seek a principled approach to the design of TILs that minimizes the need to add new features and typing rules. In particular, we seek a more "RISC-like" design for type systems that makes it possible to encode high-level language features and to support a variety of optimizations.

4.1 TAL-0: Control-Flow-Safety

We begin our design for a "RISC"-style typed assembly language by focusing on one safety property, known as *control-flow safety.* Informally, we wish to ensure that a program does not jump to arbitrary machine addresses throughout its execution, but only to a well-defined subset of possible entry points. Control-flow safety is a crucial building block for building dynamic checks into a system. For instance, before performing a system call, such as a file read, we might need to check that the arguments to the call have the right properties (e.g., the file has been opened for reading and the destination buffer is sufficiently large.) Without control-flow safety, a malicious client could jump past these checks and directly into the underlying routine.

A focus on control-flow safety will also let us start with an extremely simple abstract machine and demonstrate the key ideas of adapting a type system to machine code. In subsequent sections, we will expand this machine and its type system to accommodate more features.

The syntax for our control-flow-safe assembly language, which we will call TAL-0, is given in Figure 4-1. We assume a fixed set of k general-purpose

r ::=	registers:	ι ::=	instructions:
r1 | r2 | ··· | rk		r_d:=v	
v ::=	operands:	r_d:=r_s+v	
n	integer literal	if r jump v	
ℓ	label or pointer	I ::=	instruction sequences:
r	registers	jump v	
		ι;I	

Figure 4-1: Instructions and operands for TAL-0

registers and a few representative instructions based on a subset of MIPS assembly language. To keep the language readable, we use a somewhat more familiar notation for instructions than the usual cryptic "mov," "add," etc. Intuitively, each instruction uses the value in a source register (r_s) and an operand to compute a value which is placed in the destination register (r_d). In this setting, an operand is either another register, a word-sized immediate integer,[1] or a label. We use "value" to refer to an operand that is not a register.

For our purposes, it is also useful to define instruction sequences (I) as lists of instructions terminated by an explicit, unconditional control transfer (i.e., a jump). Of course, when the assembly code is mapped down to machine code, jumps to adjacent blocks can be eliminated since the code will fall through. We could make the order of instruction sequences and hence fall-throughs explicit, but we prefer a simpler, more uniform assembly language to present the key ideas.

Here is an example TAL-0 code fragment that computes the product of registers r1 and r2, placing the final result in r3 before jumping to a return address assumed to be in r4.

```
prod: r3 := 0;          // res := 0
      jump loop

loop: if r1 jump done; // if a = 0 goto done
      r3 := r2 + r3;    // res := res + b
      r1 := r1 + -1;    // a := a - 1
      jump loop

done: jump r4           // return
```

1. As we are dealing with an assembly language, we ignore the issue of fitting a full word-sized integer into a single instruction.

R ::=	*register files:*	H ::=	*heaps:*
$\{\mathtt{r}_1 = v_1, \ldots, \mathtt{r}_k = v_k\}$		$\{\ell_1 = h_1, \ldots, \ell_m = h_m\}$	
h ::=	*heap values:*	M ::=	*machine states:*
$\mathtt{I}$	code	(H, R, I)	

Figure 4-2: TAL-0 abstract machine syntax

We model evaluation of TAL-0 assembly programs using a rewriting relation between *abstract* machine states. Rather than model the execution of a concrete machine, we use a higher-level representation for machine states which maintains certain distinctions. For instance, in a real machine, labels are resolved during program loading to some machine address which is also represented as an integer. In our abstract machine, we maintain the distinction between labels and arbitrary integers because this will allow us to easily state and then prove our desired safety property—that any control flow instruction can only branch to a valid, labelled entry point. Indeed, our abstract machine will get stuck if we try to transfer control to an integer as opposed to a label. So, the problem of enforcing the safety property now reduces to ensuring that our abstract machine cannot get stuck.

However, to support this level of abstraction, we must worry about the situation where a label is added to an integer, or where a test is done on a label. One possibility is to assume a coercion function `intof` which maps labels to integers, and use `intof`(ℓ) whenever ℓ appears as an operand to an arithmetic instruction. Though a perfectly reasonable approach, there are a number of reasons one might avoid it: First, it violates the abstraction that we are attempting to provide which may lead to subtle information flows. In some security contexts, this could be undesirable. Second, such a coercion would make it harder to prove the equivalence of two program states, where labels are α-converted. In turn, this would restrict an implementation's freedom to re-arrange code or recycle its memory.[2] Finally, it simplifies the type system if we simply treat labels as abstract. In particular, if we included such a coercion, we would need some form of subtyping to validate the coercion. However, we emphasize that it is possible to expose labels as machine integers if desired.

The syntax for TAL-0 abstract machines is given in Figure 4-2. An abstract machine state M contains three components: (1) A heap H which is a finite,

2. The problem can be avoided by assuming a coercion relation between labels and integers that respects the alpha-equivalence class of labels.

partial map from labels to heap values (h), (2) a register file R which is a total map from registers to values, and (3) a current instruction sequence I. The instruction sequence is meant to model the sequence of instructions pointed to by the program counter in a concrete machine. One way to think of the machine's operation is that it pre-fetches sequences of instructions up to the nearest `jump` whenever a control-transfer is made.

We consider heaps and register files to be equivalent up to re-ordering. We also consider the labels in the domain of H to bind the free occurrences of those labels in the rest of the abstract machine. Finally, we consider abstract machine states to be equivalent up to alpha-conversion of bound labels.

The rewriting rules for TAL-0 are as follows:

$$\frac{H(\hat{R}(v)) = I}{(H, R, \texttt{jump}\ v) \longrightarrow (H, R, I)} \quad \text{(JUMP)}$$

$$(H, R, r_d\texttt{:=}v; I) \longrightarrow (H, R[r_d = \hat{R}(v)], I) \quad \text{(MOV)}$$

$$\frac{R(r_s) = n_1 \qquad \hat{R}(v) = n_2}{(H, R, r_d\texttt{:=}r_s\texttt{+}v; I) \longrightarrow (H, R[r_d = n_1 + n_2], I)} \quad \text{(ADD)}$$

$$\frac{R(r) = 0 \qquad H(\hat{R}(v)) = I'}{(H, R, \texttt{if}\ r\ \texttt{jump}\ v; I) \longrightarrow (H, R, I')} \quad \text{(IF-EQ)}$$

$$\frac{R(r) = n \qquad n \neq 0}{(H, R, \texttt{if}\ r\ \texttt{jump}\ v; I) \longrightarrow (H, R, I)} \quad \text{(IF-NEQ)}$$

The rules make use of $\hat{R}$ which simply lifts R from operating on registers to operands:

$$\begin{aligned}\hat{R}(r) &= R(r)\\ \hat{R}(n) &= n\\ \hat{R}(\ell) &= \ell\end{aligned}$$

Notice that for `jump` and a successful `if-jump` we simply load a new instruction sequence from the heap and begin executing it. Of course, this assumes that the destination operand evaluates to some label ℓ (as opposed to an integer), and that the heap provides a binding for ℓ. Otherwise, the machine cannot make the transition and becomes stuck. For instance, if we attempted to evaluate `jump 42`, then no transition could occur. In other words, if we can devise a type system that rules out such stuck machine states, then we can be assured that all control transfers must go to properly labelled instruction sequences.

Of course, there are other ways this particular abstract machine can get stuck. For instance, if we attempt to add an integer to a label, or test a label using `if`, then the machine will get stuck. This reflects our choice to leave labels abstract.

4.1.1 EXERCISE [★, ↛]: Taking H to be a heap that maps the labels `prod`, `loop`, and `done` to their respective instruction sequences above, and taking R_0 = `{r1=2,r2=2,r3=0,r4=exit}` where `exit` is some unspecified label, show that ($H, R_0,$ `jump prod`) steps to a state ($H, R,$ `jump r4`) with R(`r3`) = 4. □

4.1.2 EXERCISE [RECOMMENDED, ★★★, ↛]: Build an interpreter for the TAL-0 abstract machine in your favorite programming language. □

4.1.3 EXERCISE [★★★, ↛]: Formulate a semantics for a concrete machine based on the TAL-0 instruction set. The concrete machine should manipulate only integers and have states of the form (M, R, pc) where M is a memory mapping 32-bit integers to 32-bit integers, R is a register file, and pc holds a 32-bit integer for the next instruction to execute. You should assume an isomorphism `encode` and `decode` that maps instructions to and from distinct integers.

Then, prove that the TAL-0 abstract machine is faithful to the concrete machine by establishing a simulation relation between abstract and concrete machine states and by showing that this relation is preserved under evaluation. □

4.2 The TAL-0 Type System

The goal of the type system for TAL-0 is to ensure that any well-formed abstract machine M cannot get stuck—that is, there always exists an M' such that $M \longrightarrow M'$. Obviously, our type system is going to have to distinguish labels from integers to ensure that the operands of a control transfer are labels. But we must also ensure that, no matter how many steps are taken by the abstract machine, it never gets into a stuck state (i.e., typing is preserved.) Thus, when we transfer control to a label, we need to know what kinds of values it expects to have in the registers.

To this end, we define our type syntax in Figure 4-3. There are four basic type constructors. Obviously, `int` will be used to classify integer values and `code` types will classify labels. Furthermore, `code`(Γ) will classify those labels which, when jumped to, expect to have values described by Γ in the associated register. Here, Γ is a *register file type*—a total function from registers to types. In this respect, we can think of a label as a continuation which takes a record of values described by Γ as an argument.

We also support universal polymorphism in TAL-0 through the addition of type variables (α) and quantified types ($\forall\alpha.\tau$). As usual, we consider types

τ ::=		*operand types:*	Γ ::=	*register file types:*
	`int`	*word-sized integers*	$\{\mathtt{r}_1 : \tau_1, \ldots, \mathtt{r}_k : \tau_k\}$	
	$\mathtt{code}(\Gamma)$	*code labels*	Ψ ::=	*heap types:*
	α	*type variables*	$\{\ell_1 : \tau_1, \ldots, \ell_n : \tau_n\}$	
	$\forall\alpha.\tau$	*universal polymorphic types*		

Figure 4-3: TAL-0 type syntax

up to alpha-equivalence of bound type variables. Finally, we consider register file types and heap types to be equivalent up to re-ordering.

With these static constructs in hand, we can now formalize the type system using the inference rules in Figure 4-4. The first judgment, $\Psi \vdash v : \tau$, is used to determine the type of a value. Recall that a value is a register-free operand, so there is no need for a register context in the judgment. Integer literals are given type `int`, whereas labels are given the type assigned to them by the heap type context Ψ. Note that this rule only applies when the label is in the domain of Ψ.

The second judgment, $\Psi;\Gamma \vdash v : \tau$ lifts value typing to operands. A register is given the type assigned by the register file type Γ. In addition, a polymorphic operand can be instantiated with any type, in a fashion similar to ML.[3]

The next judgment, $\Psi \vdash \iota : \Gamma_1 \to \Gamma_2$ is used to check instructions. The notation is meant to suggest that the instruction expects a register file described by Γ_1 on input, and produces a register file described by Γ_2 on output. Note that for the `if` instruction, we must ensure that the destination operand v is a code pointer that expects a register file described by the same Γ as any subsequent instruction. This ensures that, no matter which way the branch goes, the resulting machine state will be well-formed.

The judgment $\Psi \vdash I : \mathtt{code}(\Gamma)$ assigns an instruction sequence I the type $\mathtt{code}(\Gamma)$ when the sequence expects to be given a register file described by Γ. In particular, a `jump` instruction's type is dictated by the type of its operand. The code type for a sequence of instructions is determined from composition. Most importantly, we can generalize the type of an instruction sequence by abstracting any type variables. Note that there is no need to prevent abstraction of type variables which occur free in the context Ψ, as is the case with generalization in ML. This is because Ψ will only contain closed types (see below). Thus, generalization is always possible.

3. We could also include instantiation for values, but to keep things simple, we have omitted that rule.

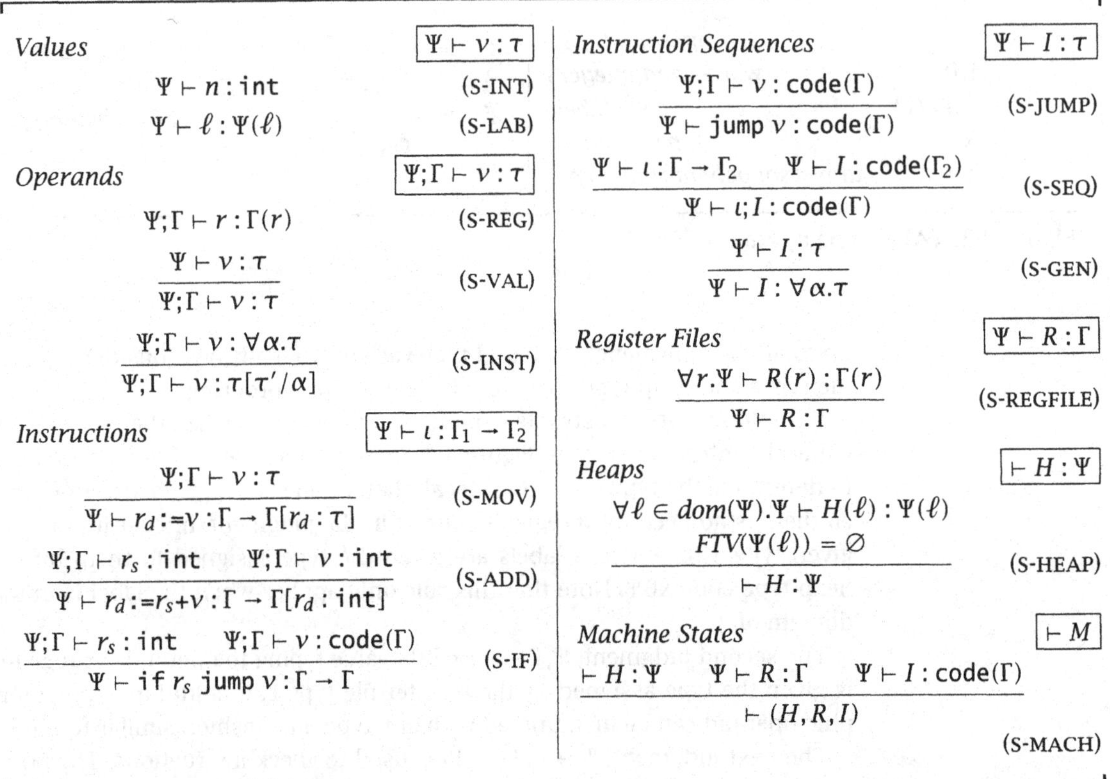

Figure 4-4: TAL-0 typing rules

The judgment $\Psi \vdash R : \Gamma$ asserts that the register file R is accurately described by Γ, under the assumptions of Ψ. Similarly, the judgment $\vdash H : \Psi$ asserts that the heap H is accurately described by Ψ. This is essentially the same rule as a "letrec" for declarations in a conventional functional language: We get to assume that the labels have their advertised type, and then check for any inconsistencies within their definitions. This allows labels to refer to one another directly. Note also that we require the types in Ψ to be closed so that generalization remains valid.

Finally, the judgment $\vdash (H, R, I)$ puts the pieces together: We must have some type assignment Ψ that describes the heap H, a register file typing Γ that describes R consistent with Ψ, and I must be a continuation with a precondition of Γ on the register file, under the assumptions of Ψ.

Some Examples and Subtleties

As a simple example of the type system in action, let us revisit the `prod` example:

```
prod: r3 := 0;              // res := 0
      jump loop

loop: if r1 jump done;      // if a = 0 goto done
      r3 := r2 + r3;        // res := res + b
      r1 := r1 + (-1);      // a := a - 1
      jump loop

done: jump r4               // return
```

Let Γ be the register file type:

$$\texttt{\{r1,r2,r3:int,r4:}\forall\alpha\texttt{.code\{r1,r2,r3:int,r4:}\alpha\texttt{\}\}}$$

Registers `r1`, `r2`, and `r3` are assigned the type `int`, and `r4` is assigned a polymorphic code type for reasons revealed below. Let Ψ be the label type assignment that maps `prod`, `loop`, and and `done` to `code`(Γ). Let I be the instruction sequence associated with `loop` and let us verify that it is indeed well-formed with the type that we have assigned it.

We must show that $\Psi \vdash I : \texttt{code}(\Gamma)$. It suffices to show that each instruction preserves Γ, since the final `jump` is to loop, which expects Γ. For the first instruction, we must show $\Psi \vdash \texttt{if r1 jump done} : \Gamma \to \Gamma$ using the S-IF rule:

$$\frac{\dfrac{}{\Psi;\Gamma \vdash \texttt{r1} : \Gamma(\texttt{r1}) = \texttt{int}}\,\text{S-REG} \qquad \dfrac{\dfrac{}{\Psi \vdash \texttt{done} : \Psi(\texttt{done}) = \texttt{code}(\Gamma)}\,\text{S-LAB}}{\Psi;\Gamma \vdash \texttt{done} : \texttt{code}(\Gamma)}\,\text{S-VAL}}{\Psi \vdash \texttt{if r1 jump done} : \Gamma \to \Gamma}$$

Next, we must show that adding `r2` to `r3` preserves Γ:

$$\frac{\dfrac{}{\Psi;\Gamma \vdash \texttt{r2} : \Gamma(\texttt{r2}) = \texttt{int}}\,\text{S-REG} \qquad \dfrac{}{\Psi;\Gamma \vdash \texttt{r3} : \Gamma(\texttt{r3}) = \texttt{int}}\,\text{S-REG}}{\Psi \vdash \texttt{r3 := r2 + r3} : \Gamma \to \Gamma}$$

Then, we must show that subtracting 1 from `r1` preserves Γ:

$$\frac{\dfrac{}{\Psi;\Gamma \vdash \texttt{r1} : \Gamma(\texttt{r2}) = \texttt{int}}\,\text{S-REG} \qquad \dfrac{\dfrac{}{\Psi \vdash \texttt{-1} : \texttt{int}}\,\text{S-INT}}{\Psi;\Gamma \vdash \texttt{-1} : \texttt{int}}\,\text{S-VAL}}{\Psi \vdash \texttt{r1 := r1 + (-1)} : \Gamma \to \Gamma}$$

Finally, we must show that the `jump` which terminates the sequence has type `code`(Γ), using the S-JUMP rule:

$$\dfrac{\dfrac{\dfrac{}{\Psi;\Gamma \vdash \texttt{loop} : \Psi(\texttt{loop}) = \texttt{code}(\Gamma)}\text{ S-LAB}}{\Psi;\Gamma \vdash \texttt{loop} : \texttt{code}(\Gamma)}\text{ S-VAL}}{\Psi \vdash \texttt{jump loop} : \texttt{code}(\Gamma)}$$

Stringing the sub-proofs together using the S-SEQ rule, we can thus confirm that $\Psi \vdash I : \texttt{code}(\Gamma)$.

Carrying on, we can show that each label's code has the type associated with it. However, there is a major subtlety with the last `jump r4` instruction and the type that we have assigned `r4` throughout the code. To understand this, consider the following:

```
foo: r1 := bar;
     jump r1

bar: ...
```

What type can we assign to `bar`? Without the polymorphism, it must be a code type `code`(Γ) such that $\Gamma(\texttt{r1}) = \texttt{code}(\Gamma)$, since the label `bar` will be in register `r1` when we jump to it. But with only simple types (i.e., no subtyping, polymorphism, or recursive types), there is no solution to this equation.

With our support for polymorphism, the problem can be averted. In particular, we can assign `bar` a polymorphic type τ of the form $\forall\alpha.\texttt{code}\{\texttt{r1} : \alpha, \ldots\}$. At the `jump` instruction, we have a register file context of the form $\Gamma = \{\texttt{r1} : \tau, \ldots\}$ and we must show that $\Gamma \vdash \texttt{r1} : \texttt{code}(\Gamma)$. Using S-INST, we can instantiate the type of `r1`, which is τ, with τ to derive $\Gamma \vdash \texttt{r1} : \texttt{code}\{\texttt{r1} : \tau, \ldots\}$.

This explains why we have used a polymorphic type for `r4` in the `prod` example above. Of course, this problem can be solved in other ways. Clearly, adding recursive types provides a solution to the problem. An alternative is to add some type *Top* which is greater than or equal to all other types, and use this to forget the type of a register as we jump through it. Yet another solution is to treat register file types as partial maps, and provide a form of subtyping that lets you forget the type of a register, thereby making it unusable as an operand until it is assigned a value. This last approach was the one used by the original TAL. We prefer the approach based on polymorphism, because there are many other compelling uses of this feature.

4.2.1 EXERCISE [★, ↛]: Draw the derivation of well-formedness for the instruction sequences associated with `prod` and `done`. □

For instance, polymorphism can also be used to achieve a type for "join-points" in a control-flow graph. Consider the situation where we have two jumps from distinct contexts to the same label:

```
{r1:int,...}
jump baz

...
{r1:code{...},...}
jump baz
```

What type should `baz` require of register `r1`? Again, without support for some form of polymorphism or subtyping, we would be forced to make the types the same, in which case this code would be rejected. The problem could be worked around by, for instance, always loading an integer into `r1` before jumping to this label. But that would slow down the program with unnecessary instructions. Fortunately, polymorphism saves us again. In particular, we can assign `baz` a type of the form $\forall\alpha.$`code{r1:`α`,...}`. Then, at the first `jump`, we would instantiate α to `int`, whereas at the second `jump`, we would instantiate α with the appropriate `code` type. Of course, the addition of *Top* would also provide a convenient mechanism for typing join points.

One other feature that polymorphism provides which cannot be captured through simple subtyping, is the idea of *callee-saves* registers. A callee-save register is a register whose value should remain the same across a procedure call. If the procedure wishes to use that register, then it is responsible for saving and restoring its value before returning to the caller. Of course, we don't yet have a way to save and restore registers to memory, but a procedure could shuffle values around into different registers.

Suppose we wish to call a procedure, such as `prod`, and guarantee that the register `r5` is preserved across the call. We can accomplish this by requiring the procedure's entry label to have a type of the form:

$\forall\alpha.$`{r5:`α`,r4:`$\forall\beta.$`code{r5:`α`,r4:`β`,...},...}`

where `r4` is the register which is meant to hold the return address for the procedure, and "..." does not contain a free occurrence of α. Note that the return address's type specifies that `r5` must have the same type (α) upon return as was originally passed in. Furthermore, the procedure is required to treat `r5` uniformly since its type is abstract. Since there is no way to manufacture values of abstract type, and since we've only passed in one α value, it must be that if the procedure ever returns, then `r5` has the same value in it as it did upon entry (see Exercise 4.2.5.) Note that the procedure is free to move `r5`'s value into some other register, and to use `r5` to hold other values. But before it can return, it must restore the original value.

So, it is clear that polymorphism can play a unifying role in the design of type systems for low-level languages. It provides a way for us to conveniently "forget" types, which is necessary for jumps through registers and join points. But it also provides an ability to capture critical compiler invariants, such as callee-saves registers.

4.2.2 EXERCISE [RECOMMENDED, ★, ↛]: Suppose we change the `done` instruction sequence from `jump r4` to `jump r1`. Show that there is no way to prove the resulting code is well-typed. □

4.2.3 EXERCISE [RECOMMENDED, ★★★, ↛]: Reformulate the type system by eliminating type variables and universal polymorphism in favor of a *Top* type and subtyping. Then show how the product example can be typed under your rules. □

4.2.4 EXERCISE [★★★, ↛]: Reformulate the type system by using recursive types in lieu of polymorphism. Then show how the product example can be typed under your rules. □

4.2.5 EXERCISE [★★★★, ↛]: Prove that the approach to callee-saves registers actually preserves values. Hint: one relatively easy way to prove this is suggested by Crary (1999). Another possible solution is to adapt Reynolds' relational semantics for the polymorphic lambda calculus (1983) to the TAL setting. The result should follow as a "free theorem" (Wadler, 1989). □

Proof of Type Soundness for TAL-0

We now wish to show that the type system given in the previous section actually enforces our desired safety property. In particular, we wish to show that, given a well-typed machine state M, then M cannot get stuck (i.e., jump to an integer or undefined label.) It suffices to show that a well-typed machine state is not immediately stuck (progress), and that when it steps to a new machine state M', that state is also well-typed (preservation). For then, by induction on the length of an evaluation sequence, we can argue that there is no stuck M' such that $M \longrightarrow^* M'$.

Our first step is to establish a set of substitution lemmas which show that derivations remain possible after substituting types for type variables:

4.2.6 LEMMA [TYPE SUBSTITUTION]: If:

1. $\Psi;\Gamma \vdash v : \tau_1$, then $\Psi;\Gamma[\tau/\alpha] \vdash v : \tau_1[\tau/\alpha]$.
2. $\Psi \vdash \iota : \Gamma_1 \rightarrow \Gamma_2$ then $\Psi \vdash \iota : \Gamma_1[\tau/\alpha] \rightarrow \Gamma_2[\tau/\alpha]$.

3. $\Psi \vdash I : \tau_1$, then $\Psi \vdash I : \tau_1[\tau/\alpha]$.

4. $\Psi \vdash R : \Gamma$, then $\Psi \vdash R : \Gamma[\tau/\alpha]$. □

The register substitution lemma ensures that typing is preserved when we look up a value in the register file. It corresponds to the value substitution lemma in a soundness proof for a conventional lambda calculus.

4.2.7 LEMMA [REGISTER SUBSTITUTION]: If $\vdash H : \Psi$, $\Psi \vdash R : \Gamma$ and $\Psi;\Gamma \vdash v : \tau$ then $\Psi;\Gamma \vdash \hat{R}(v) : \tau$ □

As usual, we shall need a Canonical Values lemma that tells us what kind of value we have from its type:

4.2.8 LEMMA [CANONICAL VALUES]: If $\vdash H : \Psi$ and $\Psi \vdash v : \tau$ then:

1. If $\tau = \texttt{int}$ then $v = n$ for some n.

2. If $\tau = \texttt{code}(\Gamma)$ then $v = \ell$ for some $\ell \in dom(H)$ and $\Psi \vdash H(\ell) : \texttt{code}(\Gamma)$. □

This extends to operands as follows:

4.2.9 LEMMA [CANONICAL OPERANDS]: If $\vdash H : \Psi$, $\Psi \vdash R : \Gamma$, and $\Psi;\Gamma \vdash v : \tau$ then:

1. If $\tau = \texttt{int}$ then $\hat{R}(v) = n$ for some n.

2. If $\tau = \texttt{code}(\Gamma)$ then $\hat{R}(v) = \ell$ for some $\ell \in dom(H)$ and $\Psi \vdash H(\ell)$: $\texttt{code}(\Gamma)$. □

4.2.10 THEOREM [SOUNDNESS OF TAL-0]: If $\vdash M$, then there exists an M' such that $M \longrightarrow M'$ and $\vdash M'$. □

Proof: Suppose $M = (H, R, I)$ and $\vdash M$. By inversion of the S-MACH rule, there exists a Ψ and Γ such that (a) $\vdash H : \Psi$, (b) $\Psi \vdash R : \Gamma$, and (c) $\Psi \vdash I : \texttt{code}(\Gamma)$. The proof proceeds by induction on I.

case $I = \texttt{jump}\ v$*:* From (c) and inversion of S-JUMP, we have $\Psi;\Gamma \vdash v$: $\texttt{code}(\Gamma)$. From the Canonical Operands lemma, we know that there exists an I' such that $H(\hat{R}(v)) = I'$ and $\Psi \vdash I' : \texttt{code}(\Gamma)$. Taking $M' = (H, R, I')$, we can show $M \longrightarrow M'$ via the JUMP rule. We must now show $\vdash (H, R, I')$, but this follows immediately.

case $I = r_d\texttt{:=}v; I'$*:* From inversion of the S-SEQ rule, we have $\Psi \vdash r_d\texttt{:=}v : \Gamma \to \Gamma_2$ and $\Psi \vdash I' : \texttt{code}(\Gamma_2)$ for some Γ_2. Then, by inversion of the S-MOV rule, we have $\Psi;\Gamma \vdash v : \tau$ and $\Gamma_2 = \Gamma[r_d : \tau]$ for some τ. By the Register Substitution lemma, we have $\Psi;\Gamma \vdash \hat{R}(v) : \tau$. Taking $M' = (H, R[r_d = \hat{R}(v)], I')$, we see that $M \longrightarrow M'$ via the MOV rule. From the S-REGFILE rule, we conclude that $\Psi \vdash R[r_d = \hat{R}(v)] : \Gamma[r_d : \tau]$.

case $I = r_d\texttt{:=}r_s\texttt{+}v\texttt{;}I'$: From inversion of S-SEQ, we have $\Psi \vdash r_d\texttt{:=}r_s\texttt{+}v : \Gamma \to \Gamma_2$ and $\Psi \vdash I' : \texttt{code}(\Gamma_2)$ for some Γ_2. Then, by inversion of the S-ADD rule, we have $\Psi;\Gamma \vdash r_s : \texttt{int}$, $\Psi;\Gamma \vdash v : \texttt{int}$ and $\Gamma_2 = \Gamma[r_d : \texttt{int}]$. From the and Canonical Operand lemma, we know that there exists integers n_1 and n_2 such that $R(r_s) = n_1$ and $\hat{R}(v) = n_2$. Taking $n = n_1 + n_2$ and $M' = (H, R[r_d = n], I')$, we see that $M \longrightarrow M'$ via the ADD rule. By the S-INT and S-VAL rules, $\Psi;\Gamma[r_d : int] \vdash n : int$. Thus, by the S-REGFILE rule, we conclude that $\Psi \vdash R[r_d = n] : \Gamma[r_d : \texttt{int}]$.

case $I = \texttt{if}\ r_s\ \texttt{jump}\ v\texttt{;}I'$: From inversion of the S-SEQ rule, we have $\Psi \vdash \texttt{if}\ r_s\ \texttt{jump}\ v : \Gamma \to \Gamma_2$ and $\Psi \vdash I' : \texttt{code}(\Gamma_2)$ for some Γ_2. Then, by inversion of the S-IF rule, we have $\Psi;\Gamma \vdash r_s : \texttt{int}$, $\Psi;\Gamma \vdash v : \texttt{code}(\Gamma)$ and $\Gamma_2 = \Gamma$. By the Canonical Operands lemma, there exists an ℓ and I_2 such that $\hat{R}(v) = \ell$, $H(\ell) = I_2$, and $\Psi \vdash I_2 : \texttt{code}(\Gamma)$. Also by Canonical Operands, $R(r_s) = n$ for some integer n. If $n = 0$ then $M \longrightarrow (M, R, I_2)$ via IF-EQ. If $n \neq 0$ then $M \longrightarrow (M, R, I')$ via IF-NEQ. In either case, the well-formedness of the resulting machine state follows from the S-MACH rule. □

Proof Representation and Checking

It is not clear whether type inference for TAL-0 machine states is decidable. That is, given a machine state (H, R, I), does there exist a Ψ and Γ such that $\vdash H : \Psi$, $\Psi \vdash R : \Gamma$, and $\Psi \vdash : \texttt{code}(\Gamma)$? On the one hand, this seems possible since the type system is so simple. On the other hand, the system, as presented, supports polymorphic recursion for which inference is known to be undecidable in the context of the lambda calculus. Furthermore, as we progress to more advanced typing features, the decidability of type reconstruction will surely vanish. Thus, in any practical realization, we must require some help for constructing a proof that the code is indeed type-correct.

In the case of TAL-0, it is sufficient to provide types for the labels (i.e., Ψ). Indeed, it is even possible to omit types for some labels and keep reconstruction decidable. We really only need enough type information to cut each loop in the control-flow graph, or for those labels that are moved into registers. Minimizing the type information is an important goal in any practical system, since the size of the types can often be larger than the code itself! However, it is desirable to keep the type checker as simple as possible so that we can trust it is properly enforcing the type system.

One way to keep the type checker simple is to modify the syntax so that type reconstruction is entirely syntax directed. By this, we mean simply that for any given term, at most one rule should apply. Furthermore, the checker should not have to "guess" any of the sub-goal components. For TAL-0, this could be accomplished by (a) requiring types on all labels and (b) adding a form of explicit type instantiation to operands (e.g., $v[\tau]$).

An alternative approach is to force the code provider to ship an explicit representation of the complete proof of well-formedness, along with the code, and make sure that the proof and the code have the same instructions, labels, etc. Of course, these proof will tend to be much larger than the code itself, but we can use various techniques to reduce the size of the proof representation (see for instance Necula and Lee, 1998b).

Such a separation of proofs and code is advantageous because we can ship the *binary* machine code (as opposed to the assembly code), disassemble it, and then compare it against the assembly-level proof. If everything checks out, then we can load the binary and execute it directly. Such an approach is called *proof-carrying code* (Necula, 1997, 1998) and was first used by Necula's Touchstone compiler (Necula and Lee, 1998a), and the Special-J compiler (Colby et al., 2000), both of which are described more fully in the next chapter.

Indeed, we could even go so far as to pass along the proof of soundness for the entire type system, and a proof that the abstract machine is faithful to the concrete machine's semantics! This would ensure that the code consumer has to trust nothing but (a) the formalization of the concrete machine semantics, and (b) the proof checker. This is the approach proposed by Appel and Felty and is called *foundational proof-carrying code* (2000).

In the rest of this chapter, we will remain vague about how proofs are to be represented. The key thing to note is that we are not limited in the choice of type constructors by issues of inference. Rather, we will require that the code producer provide us with enough evidence that we can easily reconstruct and check the proof of well-formedness. Therefore, our only limitation will be the incompletenesses of the resulting proof system.

4.2.11 EXERCISE [★★★★, ↛]: Build a type-checker for TAL-0 in your favorite programming language. Assume that you are given as input a set of labels, their associated types, and instruction sequences. Furthermore, assume that operands are augmented with explicit syntax for polymorphic instantiation. □

4.3 TAL-1: Simple Memory-Safety

TAL-0 includes registers and heap-allocated code, but provides no support for allocated *data*. In this section, we will add primitive support for allocated objects that can be shared by reference (i.e., pointer) and extend our safety property to include a notion of object-level memory safety: No memory access should read or write a data object at a given location unless the program has been granted access to that location.

From a typing perspective, the critical issue will be how to accommodate locations that hold values of different types at different times during the execution of the program. We need such a facility to at least support the construction of compound values, such as tuples, records, datatype constructors, or objects. A high-level language, such as ML, provides mechanisms to allocate and initialize data structures as a single expression. For instance, `{x = 3, y = 4}` is an expression that builds a record with two components. At the assembly level, such high-level compound expressions must be broken into machine-level steps. We must first allocate space for the object, and then initialize the components by storing them in that space. To prevent someone from treating an uninitialized component as if it holds a valid value, we must use a different type. But obviously, once we initialize that component, its type should change to reflect that it is now valid for use.

Already, we have support for storing values of different types in registers. For instance, nothing prevents us from moving a `code` value into a register currently holdingan `int`. However, when we add allocated data objects, we can no longer track the changes easily due to *aliasing*. Let `ptr(τ)` denote a pointer to a data object of type τ and consider this sequence of instructions:

```
    {r1:ptr(code(...))}
1.  r3 := 0;
2.  Mem[r1] := r3;
3.  r4 := Mem[r1];
4.  jump r4
```

We assume upon entry that `r1` is a pointer to a data location that contains a code label. The first two instructions overwrite the contents of memory at the location in `r1` with the integer 0. The third instruction loads the value from the location in `r1` and jumps to it. Clearly, this code should be rejected by the type-checker as it violates our control-flow safety property. To ensure this, we might require that the type system update the type of `r1` whenever we store through it. For instance, after the second instruction, the type of `r1` would change from `ptr(code(...))` to `ptr(int)`. Then at instruction four, the code would be rejected because of an attempt to jump to an integer.

Now consider this sequence:

```
    {r1:ptr(code(...)),r2:ptr(code(...))}
1.  r3 := 0;
2.  Mem[r1] := r3;
3.  r4 := Mem[r2];
4.  jump r4
```

The code is exactly the same except that instead of loading the value pointed to by `r1`, we load the value pointed to by `r2`. Should this code type-check?

The answer depends on whether or not `r1` and `r2` hold the same value—that is, whether or not they are aliases for the same location. There is no problem when they are not aliases, but when they are, the code behaves the same as in the previous example (i.e., attempts to jump to the integer 0.) It becomes clear that to prevent this problem, whenever we update a memory location with a value of a different type, we must update the types of *all* aliases to that location. To do so, the type system must track whether or not two values are the same and, more generally, whether or not two code labels behave the same.

Of course, there is no complete logic for tracking the equalities of values and computations, but it is possible to construct a powerful type system that allows us to conservatively track equality of *some* values. For instance see the work on *alias types* (Smith, Walker, and Morrisett, 2000; Walker and Morrisett, 2001; DeLine and Fähndrich, 2001). But all of these systems are, in my opinion, technically daunting. Furthermore, certifying compilers for high-level languages rarely need such complex machinery.

Nonetheless, we need some support for (a) allocating and initializing data structures that are to be shared, and (b) stack-allocating procedure frames. Therefore, we will focus on typing principles that try to strike a balance between expressiveness and complexity. After all, our goal is to provide a simple but expressive structure for implementing type-safe, high-level languages on conventional architectures.

In particular, we will use the type system to separate locations into one of two classes: The first class, called *shared pointers*, will support arbitrary aliasing. However, the types of the contents of shared pointers must remain invariant. That is, we can never write a value of a different type into the contents of a shared location. This is the same basic principle that ML-style `refs` and other high-level languages follow.

The second class of locations, called *unique pointers*, will support updates that change the type of the contents. However, unique pointers cannot be aliased. In particular, we will prevent unique pointers from being copied. Thus, they will behave much the same way as registers.

The combination of unique and shared pointers will provide us with a simple, but relatively flexible framework for dealing with memory. In particular, we will be able to use unique pointers to handle the thorny problem of allocating and initializing shared data structures. We will also be able to use unique pointers to model data structures whose lifetime is controlled by the compiler, such as stack frames.

r ::=		*registers:*		`sfree` n	*free n stack words*
	`r1` | `r2` | ··· | `rk`	*gp registers*	v ::=		*operands:*
	`sp`	*stack pointer*		r	*registers*
ι ::=		*instructions:*		n	*integer literals*
	...	*as in TAL-0*		ℓ	*code or shared data pointers*
	r_d`:= Mem[`$r_s + n$`]`	*load from memory*		`uptr(`h`)`	*unique data pointers*
	`Mem[`$r_d + n$`] :=` r_s	*store to memory*	h ::=		*heap values:*
	r_d`:= malloc` n	*allocate n heap words*		I	*instruction sequences*
	`commit` r_d	*become shared*		$\langle v_1, \ldots, v_n \rangle$	*tuples*
	`salloc` n	*allocate n stack words*			

Figure 4-5: TAL-1 syntax additions

The TAL-1 Extended Abstract Machine

Figure 4-5 gives a set of syntactic extensions to TAL-0 which are used in the definition of TAL-1. We have added six new instructions: Two of the instructions can be used to load a value from memory into a register, or to store a register's value to memory respectively. The effective address for both instructions is calculated as a word-level offset from a base register. The other instructions are non-standard. The `malloc` instruction is used to allocate an object with n words. A (unique) reference to the object is placed in the destination register. Typically, `malloc` will be implemented by the concrete machine using a small sequence of inlined instructions or a procedure call. We abstract from these details here so that our abstract machine can support a wide variety of allocation techniques. The `commit` instruction is used to coerce a unique pointer to a shared pointer. It has no real run-time effect but it makes it easier to state and prove the invariants of the type system.

The `salloc` and `sfree` constructs manipulate a special unique pointer which is held in a distinguished register called `sp` (stack pointer). The instruction `salloc` attempts to grow the stack by n words, whereas `sfree` shrinks the stack by n words. The type system will prevent the stack from underflowing, so in principle, `sfree` could be implemented by a simple arithmetic operation (e.g., `sp := sp +` n.) Unfortunately, stack overflow will not be captured by this type system. Therefore, we assume that the `salloc` instruction checks for overflow and aborts the computation somehow.

As before, we will model machine states using a triple of a heap, register file, and instruction sequence. And, as before, register files will map registers to word-sized values, while heaps will map labels to heap-values. We extend heap values to include tuples of word-sized values. Thus, a label can refer to either code or data. We could also use the heap to store unique data values, but this would make it more difficult to prove that the pointers to these values are indeed unique. Instead, we will extend operands with terms of the form uptr(h) and use such a term to represent a unique pointer to a heap value h.

The rewriting rules for the instructions of TAL-1 that overlap with TAL-0 remain largely the same. However, we must prevent unique pointers from being copied. More precisely, we must prevent the situation where we have two references to the same unique data. Note that, for the addition and `if` instructions, the use of a unique pointer as an operand will cause the machine to get stuck since the operands must be integers to make progress. However, the typing for assignment (r:=v) must be changed to prevent copies of unique pointers:

$$\frac{\hat{R}(v) \neq \mathtt{uptr}(h)}{(H,R,r_d\mathtt{:=}v;I) \longrightarrow (H,R[r_d = v],I)} \quad \text{(MOV-1)}$$

This rule can only fire when the source operand is not a unique pointer.

We must now give the rewriting rules for the new instructions:

$$(H,R,r_d\mathtt{:=}\ \mathtt{malloc}\ n;I) \longrightarrow (H,R[r_d = \mathtt{uptr}\langle m_1,\ldots,m_n\rangle],I) \quad \text{(MALLOC)}$$

$$\frac{r_d \neq \mathtt{sp} \qquad \ell \notin dom(H)}{(H,R[r_d = \mathtt{uptr}(h)],\mathtt{commit}\ r_d;I) \longrightarrow (H[\ell = h],R[r_d = \ell],I)} \quad \text{(COMMIT)}$$

$$\frac{R(r_s) = \ell \qquad H(\ell) = \langle v_0,\ldots,v_n,\ldots,v_{n+m}\rangle}{(H,R,r_d\mathtt{:=}\ \mathtt{Mem}[r_s + n];I) \longrightarrow (H,R[r_d = v_n],I)} \quad \text{(LD-S)}$$

$$\frac{R(r_s) = \mathtt{uptr}\langle v_0,\ldots,v_n,\ldots,v_{n+m}\rangle}{(H,R,r_d\mathtt{:=}\ \mathtt{Mem}[r_s + n];I) \longrightarrow (H,R[r_d = v_n],I)} \quad \text{(LD-U)}$$

$$\frac{R(r_d) = \ell \qquad H(\ell) = \langle v_0,\ldots,v_n,\ldots,v_{n+m}\rangle \qquad R(r_s) = v \qquad v \neq \mathtt{uptr}(h)}{(H,R,\mathtt{Mem}[r_d + n]\ \mathtt{:=}\ \mathtt{r}_s;I) \longrightarrow (H[\ell = \langle v_0,\ldots,v,\ldots,v_{n+m}\rangle],R,I)} \quad \text{(ST-S)}$$

$$\frac{R(r_d) = \mathtt{uptr}\langle v_0,\ldots,v_n,\ldots,v_{n+m}\rangle, \qquad R(r_s) = v \qquad v \neq \mathtt{uptr}(h)}{(H,R,\mathtt{Mem}[r_d + n]\ \mathtt{:=}\ \mathtt{r}_s;I) \longrightarrow (H,R[r_d = \mathtt{uptr}\langle v_0,\ldots,v,\ldots,v_{n+m}\rangle],I)} \quad \text{(ST-U)}$$

$$\frac{R(\mathtt{sp}) = \mathtt{uptr}\langle v_0,\ldots,v_p\rangle \qquad p + n \leq \mathsf{MAXSTACK}}{(H,R,\mathtt{salloc}\ n) \longrightarrow (H,R[\mathtt{sp} = \mathtt{uptr}\langle m_1,\ldots,m_n,v_0,\ldots,v_p\rangle])} \quad \text{(SALLOC)}$$

$$\frac{R(\mathtt{sp}) = \mathtt{uptr}\langle m_1,\ldots,m_n,v_0,\ldots,v_p\rangle}{(H,R,\mathtt{sfree}\ n) \longrightarrow (H,R[\mathtt{sp} = \mathtt{uptr}\langle v_0,\ldots,v_p\rangle])} \quad \text{(SFREE)}$$

The `malloc` instruction places a unique pointer to a tuple of n words in the destination register. We assume that the memory management subsystem has initialized the tuple with some arbitrary integer values $m_1, \ldots, m_n$. Recall that the rewriting rules prevent these unique pointers from being copied. However, the `commit` instruction allows us to move a unique pointer into the heap where it can be shared. As we will see, however, shared pointers must have invariant types, whereas unique pointers' types can change.

The memory-load instruction has two variants, depending upon whether the source register holds a value that is shared or unique. If it is shared, then we must look up the binding in the heap to get the heap value. If it is unique, then the heap value is immediately available. Then, in both cases, the heap value should be a tuple. We extract the nth word and place it in the destination register.

The memory-store instruction is the dual and is used to update the nth component of a tuple. Note that the machine gets stuck on an attempt to store a unique pointer, thereby preventing copies from leaking into a data object.

As a simple example of the use of these constructs, consider the following code:

```
copy: {r1:ptr(int,int), r2,r3:int}
        r2 := malloc 2;
        r3 := Mem[r1];
        Mem[r2] := r3;
        r3 := Mem[r1+1];
        Mem[r2+1] := r3;
        commit r2;
        {r1:ptr(int,int), r2:ptr(int,int), r3:int }
```

The code is meant to do a deep copy of the data structure pointed to by `r1` and place the copy in register `r2`. Suppose that $r1$ holds a label ℓ_1 and $H(\ell_1) = \langle 3, 5 \rangle$. After executing the malloc instruction, `r2` will hold a unique pointer to a pair of (arbitrary) integers of the form $\mathtt{uptr}\langle m_1, m_2 \rangle$. After the load and store, the first integer component of `r1` will have been copied into the first component of `r2`. Thus, the contents of ℓ_2 will have changed to $\mathtt{uptr}\langle 3, m_2 \rangle$. After the second load and store, the second component will have been copied, so `r2` will hold the value $\mathtt{uptr}\langle 3, 5 \rangle$. Finally, after the `commit` instruction, `r2` will hold a fresh, shared label ℓ_2 and the heap will have been extended so that it maps ℓ_2 to the heap value $\langle 3, 5 \rangle$.

Here is an example program which uses `salloc` and `sfree`:

```
foo: {sp : uptr(int), r1 : code{...}}
        salloc 2;         // {sp : uptr(int,int,int)}
        Mem[sp] := r1; // {sp : uptr(code{...},int,int)}
        sfree 1           // {sp : uptr(int,int)}
```

τ ::=	*operand types:*	σ ::=	*allocated types:*
...	*as in TAL-0*	ϵ	*empty*
ptr(σ)	*shared data pointers*	τ	*value type*
uptr(σ)	*unique data pointers*	σ_1, σ_2	*adjacent*
$\forall\rho.\tau$	*quantification over allocated types*	ρ	*allocated type variable*

Figure 4-6: TAL-1 types

On input, the stack has one integer element and `r1` has a code pointer. The first instruction grows the stack by two words. The second instruction stores the value in `r1` into the top of the stack. The third instruction frees one of the words. Note that `salloc` becomes stuck if we attempt to allocate more than MAXSTACK (total) words and that `sfree` becomes stuck if we attempt to shrink the stack by more words than are on the stack. Finally, note that our stacks grow "up" (indexing is positive) whereas the common convention is to have stacks that grow down. The only reason for this choice is that it unifies unique pointers to tuples with stacks. If we wanted to support downward stacks, then we could introduce a new kind of data structure (e.g., `stptr`.)

4.3.1 EXERCISE [RECOMMENDED, ★, ↛]: Show how stack-push and stack-pop instructions can be explained using the primitives provided by TAL-1. Explain how a sequence of pushes or a sequence of pops can be optimized. □

4.3.2 EXERCISE [★★★, ↛]: Modify the abstract machine so that unique pointers are allocated in the heap, just like shared pointers, but are represented as a tagged value of the form uptr(ℓ). Then show that the machine maintains the invariant that there is at most one copy of a unique pointer. □

4.4 TAL-1 Changes to the Type System

What changes and additions are needed to the type system to ensure that the new abstract machine won't get stuck? In particular, how do we ensure that when we do a load, the source register contains a data pointer (as opposed to an integer or code label), and the data pointer points to a heap value that has at least as many components as the offset requires? Similarly, how do we ensure that for a store, the destination register is a data pointer to a large enough heap value? And how do we ensure that the stack does not underflow? How do we ensure that we don't try to copy a unique pointer? In short, how do we ensure progress?

Heap Values $\boxed{\Psi \vdash v : \tau}$

$$\frac{\Psi;\Gamma \vdash v_i : \tau_i}{\Psi \vdash \langle v_1,\ldots,v_n\rangle : \tau_1,\ldots,\tau_n} \quad \text{(S-TUPLE)}$$

Operands $\boxed{\Psi \vdash v : \tau}$

$$\frac{\Psi;\Gamma \vdash h : \sigma}{\Psi;\Gamma \vdash \mathtt{uptr}(h) : \mathtt{uptr}(\sigma)} \quad \text{(S-UPTR)}$$

Figure 4-7: TAL-1 typing rules (heap values and operands)

Figure 4-6 gives a new set of types for classifying TAL-1 values. The τ types are used to classify values and operands, whereas the σ types are used to classify heap-allocated data. We have added three new operand types corresponding to shared pointers ($\mathtt{ptr}(\sigma)$), unique pointers ($\mathtt{uptr}(\sigma)$), and polymorphism over allocated types ($\forall\rho.\tau$.)

The allocated types (σ) consist of sequences of operand types. The syntax supports nesting structure (i.e., trees) but we implicitly treat adjacency as associative with ϵ as a unit. So, for instance:

$$\mathtt{ptr}(\mathtt{int},(\rho,(\mathtt{int},\epsilon))) = \mathtt{ptr}((\mathtt{int},\rho),\mathtt{int})$$

Allocated types also support variables (ρ) which are useful for abstracting a chunk of memory. That is, α can be used to abstract a single word-sized type, whereas ρ can be used to abstract a type of arbitrary size. As we will see, polymorphism over allocated types is the key to efficient support for procedures.

Figures 4-7 and 4-8 give the new typing rules. As in TAL-0, we take Γ to be a total map from registers to operand types. We are also assuming that Ψ is a finite partial function from labels to allocated operand types (i.e., `code` or `ptr` types.)

The well-formedness rules for tuples and unique pointers are straightforward. The S-MOV-1 rule defines the new type for the move instruction. It has as a pre-condition that the value being moved should not be a unique pointer.

The typing rule for `malloc` requires a non-negative integer argument, and updates the destination register's type with a unique pointer of an n-tuple of integers. The `commit` instruction expects a unique pointer in the given register, and simply changes its type to a shared pointer.

The load and store instructions require two rules each, depending upon whether they are operating on unique pointers. Notice that for the store rules, we are not allowed to place a unique pointer into the data structure. Notice also that that when storing into a unique pointer, there is no requirement that the new value have the same type as the old value. In contrast, for shared pointers, the old and new values must have the same type.

Instructions $\boxed{\Psi \vdash \iota : \Gamma_1 \to \Gamma_2}$

$$\frac{\Psi;\Gamma \vdash v : \tau \qquad \tau \neq \mathtt{uptr}(\sigma)}{\Psi \vdash r_d \mathtt{:=} v : \Gamma \to \Gamma[r_d : \tau]} \quad \text{(S-MOV-1)}$$

$$\frac{n \geq 0}{\Psi \vdash r_d \mathtt{:=}\ \mathtt{malloc}\ n : \Gamma \to \Gamma[r_d : \mathtt{uptr}\langle\underbrace{\mathtt{int},\ldots,\mathtt{int}}_{n}\rangle]} \quad \text{(S-MALLOC)}$$

$$\frac{\Psi;\Gamma \vdash r_d : \mathtt{uptr}(\sigma) \qquad r_d \neq \mathtt{sp}}{\Psi \vdash \mathtt{commit}\ r_d : \Gamma \to \Gamma[r_d : \mathtt{ptr}(\sigma)]} \quad \text{(S-COMMIT)}$$

$$\frac{\Psi;\Gamma \vdash r_s : \mathtt{ptr}(\tau_1,\ldots,\tau_n,\sigma)}{\Psi \vdash r_d \mathtt{\ :=\ Mem}[r_s + n] : \Gamma \to \Gamma[r_d : \tau_n]} \quad \text{(S-LDS)}$$

$$\frac{\Psi;\Gamma \vdash r_s : \mathtt{uptr}(\tau_1,\ldots,\tau_n,\sigma)}{\Psi \vdash r_d \mathtt{\ :=\ Mem}[r_s + n] : \Gamma \to \Gamma[r_d : \tau_n]} \quad \text{(S-LDU)}$$

$$\frac{\Psi;\Gamma \vdash r_s : \tau_n \qquad \tau_n \neq \mathtt{uptr}(\sigma') \qquad \Psi;\Gamma \vdash r_d : \mathtt{ptr}(\tau_1,\ldots,\tau_n,\sigma)}{\Psi \vdash \mathtt{Mem}[r_d + n] \mathtt{\ :=\ } r_s : \Gamma \to \Gamma} \quad \text{(S-STS)}$$

$$\frac{\Psi;\Gamma \vdash r_s : \tau \qquad \tau \neq \mathtt{uptr}(\sigma') \qquad \Psi;\Gamma \vdash r_d : \mathtt{uptr}(\tau_1,\ldots,\tau_n,\sigma)}{\Psi \vdash \mathtt{Mem}[r_d + n] \mathtt{\ :=\ } r_s : \Gamma \to \Gamma[r_d : \mathtt{uptr}(\tau_1,\ldots,\tau,\sigma)]} \quad \text{(S-STU)}$$

$$\frac{\Psi;\Gamma \vdash \mathtt{sp} : \mathtt{uptr}(\sigma) \qquad n \geq 0}{\Psi \vdash \mathtt{salloc}\ n : \Gamma \to \Gamma[\mathtt{sp} : \mathtt{uptr}(\underbrace{\mathtt{int},\ldots,\mathtt{int}}_{n},\sigma)]} \quad \text{(S-SALLOC)}$$

$$\frac{\Psi;\Gamma \vdash \mathtt{sp} : \mathtt{uptr}(\tau_1,\ldots,\tau_n,\sigma)}{\Psi \vdash \mathtt{sfree}\ n : \Gamma \to \Gamma[\mathtt{sp} : \mathtt{uptr}(\sigma)]} \quad \text{(S-SFREE)}$$

Figure 4-8: TAL-1 typing rules (instructions)

The rules for `salloc` and `sfree` are straightforward. For `sfree` n we check that there are at least n *values* on the stack to avoid underflow. Note that the rule does not allow allocated type variables (ρ) to be eliminated, reflecting the fact that, in general, we do not know how many words are occupied by ρ. For instance, ρ could be instantiated with ϵ in which case there are no values. A similar restriction holds for loads and stores—we must at least know the sizes up through the word component we are projecting or storing.

To prevent the machine from becoming stuck, salloc would ideally check that adding n words to the stack would not exceed MAXSTACK. But alas, we cannot always determine the current length of the stack. In particular, if its type contains an allocated variable ρ, then we are in trouble. One way around this problem is to change the abstract machine so that it does not get stuck upon overflow by defining a transition (e.g., by jumping to a pre-defined label). This would correspond to a machine trap due to an illegal access.

It is possible to extend our soundness proof for TAL-0 to cover the new constructs in TAL-1 and show that a well-formed machine state cannot get stuck, except when the stack overflows. In the proof of soundness, one critical property we must show is that any typing derivation remains valid under an extension of the heap. In particular, if $\vdash H : \Psi$ and $\Psi \vdash h : \tau$, then $\vdash H[\ell = h] : \Psi[\ell : \tau]$. Another critical property is that we would have to show that a given label ℓ that occurs in the heap has exactly one type throughout the execution of the program. In other words, once we have committed a pointer so that it can be shared, its type must remain invariant.

4.4.1 EXERCISE [★★★★, ↛]: Extend the proof of soundness to cover the new features in TAL-1. □

4.5 Compiling to TAL-1

At this point, TAL-1 provides enough mechanism that we can use it as a target language for the compiler of a polymorphic, procedural language with integers, tuples, records, and function pointers (but not yet lexically nested closures.) As a simple example, let us start with the following C code:

```
int prod(int x, int y) {
  int a = 0;
  while (x != 0) {
    a = a + y;
    x = x - 1;
  }
  return a;
}

int fact(int z) {
  if (z != 0) return prod(fact(z-1),z);
  else return 1;
}
```

and show how it may be compiled to TAL-1, complete with typing annotations on the code labels. We assume a calling convention where arguments are passed on the stack, and the return address is passed in r4. We also assume that results are returned in register r1, and arguments are popped off the stack by the callee. Finally, we assume that registers r2 and r3 are freely available as scratch registers.

Let us first translate the prod function under these conventions:

```
prod: ∀a,b,c,s.
        code{r1:a,r2:b,r3:c,sp:uptr(int,int,s),
             r4:∀d,e,f.code{r1:int,r2:d,r3:e,r4:f,sp:uptr(s)}}
       r2 := Mem[sp];      // r2:int, r2 := x
       r3 := Mem[sp+1];    // r3:int, r3 := y
       r1 := 0             // r1:int, a := 0
       jump loop

loop: ∀s.code{r1,r2,r3:int,sp:uptr(int,int,s),
                r4:∀d,e,f.code{r1:int,r2:d,r3:e,r4:f,sp:uptr(s)}}
       if r2 jump done;    // if x ↔ 0 goto done
       r1 := r1 + r3;      // a := a + y
       r2 := r2 + (-1);    // x := x - 1
       jump loop

done: ∀s.code{r1,r2,r3:int,sp:uptr(int,int,s),
                r4:∀d,e,f.code{r1:int,r2:d,r3:e,r4:f,sp:uptr(s)}}
       sfree 2;          // sp:uptr(s)
       jump r4
```

The code itself is rather straightforward. What is most interesting is the types we have placed on the labels. Note that, upon input to prod, r1, r2, and r3 can have any types, since we have abstracted their types. Note also that the stack pointer has type uptr(int,int,s) and thus has two integers at the front, but can have any sequence of values following, since we have abstracted the tail with an allocated type variable s. The return address in r4 is polymorphic for r2 and r3 to allow values of any type in those registers upon return. As discussed earlier, the type of r4 is abstracted by the return address to allow jumping through that register. Furthermore, the return address demands that the stack have type uptr(s), reflecting that the callee should pop the arguments before jumping to the return address. Thus, the contents of the rest of the stack is guaranteed to be preserved since s is abstract.

In general, a source-level procedure that takes arguments of types $\tau_1, \ldots, \tau_n$ and returns a value of type τ would translate to a label with the same type as prod's, except that the stack pointer would have type uptr($\tau_1, \ldots, \tau_n, s$), and r4's return code type would expect r1 to have type τ.

The types for the loop and done labels are similar to prod's, except that registers r1,r2, and r3 must hold integers. The reader is encouraged to check that the resulting code is well-formed according to the typing rules for TAL-1.

Now let us translate the recursive factorial procedure using the same calling conventions:

```
fact: ∀a,b,c,s.
        code{r1:a,r2:b,r3:c,sp:uptr(int,s),
             r4:∀d,e,f.code{r1:int,r2:d,r3:e,r4:f,sp:uptr(s)}}
       r1 := Mem[sp];      // r1:int, r1 := z
       if r1 jump retn     // if z = 0 goto retn
       r2 := r1 + (-1);    // r2:int, r2 := z-1
       salloc 2            // sp:uptr(int,int,int,s)
       Mem[sp+1] := r4;    // sp:uptr(int,(∀d,e,f.code{...}),int,s)
       Mem[sp] := r2;      // sp:uptr(int,(∀d,e,f.code{...}),int,s)
       r4 := cont;
       jump fact           // r1 := fact(z-1)

cont: ∀c,s',d,e,f.
        code{r1:int,r2:d,r3:e,r4:f,
             sp:uptr(∀d,e,f.code{...},int,s')}
       r4 := Mem[sp];     // restore original return address
       Mem[sp] := r1;     // sp:uptr(int,int,s')
       jump prod          // tail call prod(fact(z-1),z)

retn: ∀b,c,s.
        code{r1:int,r2:b,r3:c,sp:uptr(int,s),
             r4:∀d,e,f.code{r1:int,r2:d,r3:e,r4:f,sp:uptr(s)}}
       r1 := 1;
       sfree 1;         // sp:uptr(s)
       jump  r4         // return 1
```

The first couple of instructions load the argument from the stack, test if it is zero, and if so, jump to the `retn` block where the argument is popped off the stack and the value 1 is returned. If the argument `z` is non-zero, then we must calculate `z-1`, pass it in a recursive call to `fact`, and then pass the result along with `z` to the `prod` function.

To do the recursive call, we must allocate stack space for the return address (`r4`) and the argument `z-1`, and save those values on the stack. Then we must load a new return address into `r4`, namely `cont` and finally jump to `fact`. When the recursive call returns, control will transfer to the `cont` label. Notice that `cont` expects the stack to hold the original return address and the value of `z`. We restore the original return address by loading it from the stack. We then overwrite the same stack slot with the result of `fact(z-1)`. Finally, we do a tail-call to `prod`.

It is important to recognize that the calling conventions we chose are not specific to the abstract machine. For instance, we could have chosen a convention where the return address is pushed on the stack, or where arguments are passed in registers, introduced callee-saves registers, etc. In contrast, virtual machines languages such as the JVML and CLI bake the notion of procedure and procedure call into the language. To add support for different calling conventions (e.g., tail-calls, or a tailored convention for leaf procedures) requires additions and changes to the abstract machine and its type system. In contrast, by focusing on a more primitive set of type constructors (e.g., $\forall$, `code`, and `uptr` types), we are able to accommodate many conventions without change to the type system.

4.5.1 EXERCISE [RECOMMENDED, ★★, ↛]: Rewrite the `fact` procedure with a calling convention where the arguments and return address are placed on the stack. Include typing annotations on the labels and convince yourself that the code type-checks. □

4.6 Scaling to Other Language Features

TAL-1 only supports simple tuple or record-like data structures. Thus, it is insufficient for compiling real-world high-level languages which provide data abstraction mechanisms such as closures, algebraic datatypes, objects, and/or arrays.

Simple Objects and Closures

Support for closures and simple forms of objects is readily accommodated by adding *existential* abstraction for both operand and allocated types:

$$\tau \quad ::= \quad \ldots \mid \exists\alpha.\tau \mid \exists\rho.\tau$$

The rules for introducing and eliminating existentials on operands are extremely simple:

$$\frac{\Psi;\Gamma \vdash v : \tau[\tau'/\alpha]}{\Psi;\Gamma \vdash v : \exists\alpha.\tau} \qquad \text{(S-PACK)}$$

$$\frac{\Psi;\Gamma \vdash v : \exists\alpha.\tau \qquad \alpha \notin FTV(\Gamma)}{\Psi;\Gamma \vdash v : \tau} \qquad \text{(S-UNPACK)}$$

(There are two similar rules for existentials that abstract allocated types.) The first rule allows us to abstract a common type for some components of a data structure. For instance, if r has type

```
ptr(code{r1:int,r2:int,...},int)
```

then we can use the S-PACK rule to treat the value as if it has type

```
∃α.ptr(code{r1:α,r2:int,...},α).
```

Now, such a value can only be used by eliminating the existential using the S-UNPACK rule. However, we are required to continue treating α as abstract and distinct from any other type that may be in our context.

As suggested by Pierce and Turner (1993), we can use existentials to encode very simple forms of objects. For example, consider an object interface that looks like this, written in a Java-style:

```
interface Point {
  int getX();
  int getY();
}
```

and consider two classes that implement this interface:

```
class C1 implements Point {
  int x = 0, y = 0;
  int getX() { return x; }
  int getY() { return y; }
}

class C2 implements Point {
  int x = 0, y = 0 , n = 0;
  int getX() { n++; return x; };
  int getY() { n++; return y; }
}
```

We can think of objects as pairs of a method table and an instance variable frame. The methods take the instance variable frame as an implicit "self" argument. For instance, the C1 class would have an instance frame that holds two integers, whereas the C2 class would have an instance frame that holds three integers. Thus, at an intermediate language level, C1's get operations would have type:

```
ptr(int,int) → int
```

while C2's operations would have type:

```
ptr(int,int,int) → int
```

When we build a C1 object or a C2 object, we need to hide the type of the instance frame so that only the methods can gain access to and manipulate the values of the instance variables. We also need to hide the type of the instance frames so that we can give the objects a common type. We can achieve this by using an existential to abstract the type of the instance frame and pairing the methods with the instance frame. At an intermediate level, the type of a `Point` object would thus be something like:

$$\exists\alpha.\mathtt{ptr}(\mathtt{ptr}(\alpha \to \mathtt{int}, \alpha \to \mathtt{int}), \alpha)$$

Note that for any value with this type, we cannot directly access the instance variables because their type is abstract (i.e., α). However, once such an object is unpacked, we can project out a method and the instance frame, and pass the frame to the method because the methods expect an α value as an argument.

Closures are simple forms of objects where the instance frame holds the environment, and there is a single method for applying the closure to its arguments. Thus, with the simple addition of existential types, we have the ability to encode the primary features of modern languages, notably closures and objects. Indeed, the original TAL paper (Morrisett, Walker, Crary, and Glew, 1999) showed how a polymorphic, core functional language could be mapped to a version of typed assembly with support for existentials. This translation was based on previous work of Minamide, Morrisett, and Harper (1996).

Of course, in a more realistic implementation, we might represent objects without the level of indirection on instance variables, and instead of passing only the instance variables to methods, we could pass the whole object to a method. With the addition of recursive types ($\mu\alpha.\tau$) and the usual isomorphism ($\mu\alpha.\tau = \tau[\mu\alpha.\tau/\alpha]$), this becomes possible:

$$\exists\rho.\mu\alpha.\mathtt{ptr}(\mathtt{ptr}(\alpha \to \mathtt{int}, \alpha \to \mathtt{int}), \rho)$$

Notice that in the above encoding, we have abstracted an allocated type (ρ) which is used to describe the rest of the object after the method pointer. Furthermore, the methods in the method table expect to take values of type α which is isomorphic to the type of the (unpacked) object. That is, the methods take in the whole object (including the method table) instead of just the instance variables.

This last encoding of objects is closely based on ideas of Bruce (1995; 2002). There are many other potential encodings (see Bruce, Cardelli, and Pierce, 1997, for a nice overview.) In short, it is possible to draw upon the wealth of literature on object and closure encodings to find a small set of re-usable type constructors, such as F-bounded existentials, to provide your typed assembly language with enough power to support compilation of modern object-oriented or functional languages, without baking in a particular object model. Again, this contrasts with the JVM and CLI which fix on a single object model and provide poor support for encoding languages outside that model.

One problem with these object encodings is that they do not readily support a form of "down-casting" where we perform a run-time test to determine whether an object implements a given interface. Such operations are common in languages such as Java, where the lack of parametric polymorphism and the erroneous addition of covariant arrays requires dynamic type tests. In general, dynamic type tests can be accomplished by using some form of representation types (Crary, Weirich, and Morrisett, 1998), but these encodings are relatively heavyweight and do not support the actual representations used by implementations. Glew (1999) suggested and implemented extensions to TALx86 that better supports practical implementations.

Arrays, Arithmetic, and Dependent Types

In TAL-1, we are restricted to using *constant* offsets to access the data components of an object. Similarly, we can only allocate objects whose size is known at compile time. Thus, we cannot directly encode arrays.

The simplest way to add arrays is to revert to high-level, CISC-like instructions. We could imagine adding a primitive r_d := `newarray`(r_i, r_s) which would allocate an array with r_i elements, and initialize all of the components with the value in r_s, returning a pointer to the array in register r_d. To read components out of an array, we might have an operation r_d := `ldarr`(r_s, r_i) which would load the r_i^{th} component of array r_s, placing the result in r_d. Dually, the operation `starr`(r_s, r_d, r_i) would store the value in r_s into the r_i^{th} component of array r_d.

To ensure type safety for the `ldarr` and `starr` operations, we would need to check that the element offset r_i did not exceed the number of elements in the array and jump to an exception handler if this constraint is not met. In turn, this would demand that we (implicitly) maintain the size of the array somewhere. For instance, we could represent an array with n elements as a tuple of $n + 1$ components with the size in the first slot.

4.6.1 EXERCISE [RECOMMENDED, ★★, ↛]: Extend the TAL-1 abstract machine with rewriting rules for arrays as described above and provide typing rules for the new instructions. □

The advantage of the approach sketched above is that it leaves the type system simple. However, it has a number of drawbacks: First, there is no way to eliminate the check that an offset is in bounds, even if we know and can prove that this is the case. Second, this approach requires that we maintain the size of the array at runtime, even though the size might be statically apparent. Third, the real machine-level operations that make up the primitive subscript and update operations would not be subject to low-level optimizations (e.g., instruction scheduling, strength reduction, and induction variable elimination.)

An alternative approach based on *dependent types* was suggested by Xi and Harper (2001) and implemented (to some degree) in TALx86. The key idea behind the approach, called DTAL, is to first add a form of *compile-time* expressions to the type system:

$$e \ ::= \ n \mid e_1 + e_2 \mid e_1 - e_2 \mid e_1 * e_2 \mid \mathtt{i} \mid \cdots$$

A compile-time expression is made up of constants (n), arithmetic operations, and compile-time integer variables (`i`). We then allow type constructors to depend upon (i.e., be indexed by) a compile time expression. For instance, the type $\mathtt{arr}(\tau, 30 + 12)$ would classify those arrays that have 42 components, each of which is a value of type τ. Similarly, the type `int(36)` would classify those integer values that are equal to 36—in other words, `int(36)` is a singleton type.

To support integers whose value is unknown, or arrays whose number of elements are unknown, we can use a suitably quantified compile-time variable. For instance, the type `∃i.int(i)` would classify any integer value, and the type $\exists \mathtt{i}.\mathtt{arr}(\tau,\mathtt{i*2})$ would classify arrays of τ values with an even number of components. More importantly, the type

$$\forall \mathtt{i}_1,\mathtt{i}_2.\mathtt{code}\{\mathtt{r1{:}int}(\mathtt{i}_1),\mathtt{r2{:}arr}(\mathtt{T},\mathtt{i}_1),\mathtt{r3{:}int}(\mathtt{i}_2)\}$$

would classify code that expects `r2` to hold an array with i_1 elements, `r1` to hold an integer equal to i_1, and `r3` to hold some other integer equal to i_2. Thus, we can use this limited form of dependent types to track an important relation between two values—that one register holds the number of elements in the array pointed to by another register.

To support the elimination of array bounds checks, we need to go beyond equality relations and track refinements of values as we perform tests. For instance, in a context with the code type above, if we wanted to use `r3` to index into array `r2`, it should be sufficient to check that the value in `r3` is greater than or equal to 0, and less than `r1`:[4]

```
sub:  ∀i1,i2.code{r1:int(i1),r2:arr(T,i1),r3:int(i2), ...}
  if r3<0 jump L;
  rt := r3 - 1;
  if rt>=0 jump L;
  rd := ldarr(r2,r3)    // rd := Mem[r2+r3]
```

4. In practice, this can be determined using a single unsigned comparison.

In other words, the `ldarr` operation above should type-check since we are in a context where `r2` is an array of size i_1, `r3` is an integer equal to i_2, and the predicate $(i_2 \geq 0) \wedge (i_2 < i_1)$ is true. To support this validation, DTAL checked instructions under a typing context of the form $(\Gamma; P)$ where P was a predicate that was assumed to be true. Tests, such as the `blt r3, ERROR` instruction, would typically add conjuncts to the context's predicate.

For example, type-checking for the fragment above would proceed as follows:

```
1. sub:  ∀i1,i2.(...; true)
2.   if r3<0 jump L;  // ({...}; true ∧ (i2 >= 0))
3.   rt := r3 - 1;    // ({...,rt:int(i2-i1)};(i2 >= 0))
4.   if rt>=0 jump L; // ({...,rt:int(i2-i1)};(i2 >= 0)∧(i2-i1 < 0))
5.   rd := ldarr(r2,r3)
```

After checking line 2, the context's predicate (`true`) has been refined by adding the conjunct $i_2 >= 0$ since `r3` has type $\mathtt{int}(i_2)$ and the test can only fall through when `r3` is greater than or equal to zero. At line 3, `rt` is given the type $\mathtt{int}(i_2 - i_1)$ since `r1` has type $\mathtt{int}(i_1)$ and `r3` has type $\mathtt{int}(i_2)$ and the operation places `r3` - `r1` into `rt`. Then, at line 4, the test adds the conjunct $i_1 - i_1 < 0$ to the fall-through continuation's context. Finally, at line 5, we are able to satisfy the pre-condition of the `ldarr` construct since we are in a context where the index lies between 0 and the size of the array.

In DTAL, the predicates used for refinements were restricted to linear inequalities so as to keep type-checking decidable. But in general, we could add support for arbitrary predicates, and simply require that the code producer provide an explicit proof that the current (inferred) predicate implied the necessary pre-conditions. In other words, we can fall back to a very general proof-carrying code framework, as described in the following chapter.

However, as the designer of the type system, we would still be responsible for providing the code producer a set of sound (and relatively complete) inference rules for proving these relations. Though this is possible, it is nowhere as easy as the simple proofs that we have presented here.

4.7 Some Real World Issues

Clearly, TAL-1 and the extensions described earlier provide the mechanisms needed to implement only very simple languages. Furthermore, most of the operations of the machine have a one-to-one correspondence with the operations of a typical RISC-style machine. Some operations, such as `commit` could be pushed into the proof representation since they have no run-time effect.

And abstracting other operations, such as `malloc`, insulates us from details of the memory management runtime.

Of course, there are a number of simple extensions that could be made to make the type system a little more useful. For instance, we could annotate primitive memory type components with flags to control whether that component supports read-only, write-only, or read-write access.

4.7.1 EXERCISE [$\star$, $\nrightarrow$]: Assuming you added type qualifiers for read-only and write-only access to tuple components. How would you change the abstract machine so that you captured their intended meaning? □

We could also add support for subtyping in a number of ways. For instance, we could take: $\mathtt{ptr}(\sigma, \sigma') \leq \mathtt{ptr}(\sigma)$. That is, we can safely forget the tail of a sequence of values, for both `ptr` and `uptr` types. We can also consider a read-write component to be a subtype of a read-only or a write-only component. For shared, read-only components, we can support covariant deep subtyping, and for write-only components, we can have contra-variant subtyping. Interestingly, it is sound to have covariant subtyping on read-write components of unique pointers. All of these extensions were supported in some form for TALx86.

An issue not addressed here is support for primitive values of sizes less than a machine word (e.g., a `char` or `short`). But this too is relatively easy to accommodate. The key thing is that we need some function from operand types to their sizes so that we can determine whether or not a `ld` or `st` is used at the right offset. A slightly more troublesome problem is the issue of alignment. On many architectures (e.g., the MIPS, SPARC, and Alpha), primitive datatypes must be naturally aligned. For instance, a 64-bit value (e.g., a `double`) should be placed on a double-word boundary. Of course, the compiler can arrange to insert padding to ensure this property, if we assume that `malloc` places objects on maximally aligned boundaries. Still, we might need to add a well-formedness judgment to memory types to ensure that they respect alignment constraints.

The approach to typing the stack is powerful enough to accommodate standard procedure calls, but cannot handle nested procedures, even if they are "downward-only" as in Pascal. To support this, we would, in general, need some form of static pointers back into the stack (or display.) The STAL type system supports a limited form of such pointers which also provides the mechanisms needed to implement exceptions (Morrisett et al., 2002). These extensions were used in the TALx86 implementation. An alternative approach, based on intersection types, is suggested by Crary's TALT (Crary, 2003) which has the advantage that it better supports stack-allocated objects. A more general approach is to integrate support for *regions* into the type system in the style of Cyclone (Grossman, Morrisett, Jim, Hicks, Wang, and Cheney, 2002) or one of the other region-based systems described in Chapter 3.

The original TAL used a different mechanism, based on initialization flags and subtyping, to support shared-object initialization. More recently, the work of Petersen et al. (2003) provides an approach to initialization based on a "fuse" calculus. The approach based on initialization flags has the advantage that uninitialized objects are first class, which is useful in some contexts, such as "tail-allocation" (Minamide, 1998). Neither our approach based on unique pointers nor the fuse calculus supports this. Furthermore, neither approach supports the initialization of circular data structures, which is important when building recursive closures. These concerns motivated the design of alias types (Smith, Walker, and Morrisett, 2000) which handles all of these concerns and more, and which were implemented in TALx86. Recently, Ahmed and Walker (2003) have suggested yet another approach based on an embedding of the logic of bunched implications within a type system.

It is possible to add a `free` instruction to TAL-1 which takes a unique pointer and returns it to the runtime for re-use. In some sense, `free` is the ultimate type-changing operation, for it is simply a way to recycle memory so that it can later be used to hold values of a different type. Unfortunately, it is not so easy to provide a `free` operation for shared pointers.

4.7.2 EXERCISE [RECOMMENDED, ★, ↛]: Given an example program that could "go wrong" if we allowed `free` to operate on shared pointers. □

As noted earlier, the type system is closed under extensions to the heap, but not necessarily a shrinking heap. It can be shown that if a location is not reachable from the registers (or from reachable code) then a heap value can be safely thrown away. But discovering that this property is true requires more than a single machine instruction. Indeed, it requires a run-time examination of the pointer-graph to determine the unreachable objects.

Therefore, with the introduction of shared data pointers, we are essentially buying into the need for a garbage collector to effectively recycle memory. Of course, to support accurate garbage collection requires that we provide enough information that the collector can determine pointers from other data values at run-time. Furthermore, the collector requires knowledge of the size of heap objects. Finally, many collectors require a number of subtle properties to hold (e.g., no pointers to the interior of heap objects) before they can be invoked. Capturing all of these constraints in a useful type system is still somewhat of a challenge.

TALx86 and the proposed TALT use a *conservative* collector to recycle memory. Conservative collectors do not require precise information about which objects are pointers. However, they tend to have leaks, since they sometimes think an integer is a pointer to an unreachable object. Like other collectors, a number of invariants must hold in order for the collection to be sound. The TALT system formalizes these constraints as part of its type system.

Another possibility is to integrate the Capability types which provide a general support for regions at the TAL level (Walker, Crary, and Morrisett, 2000). With this type system, it is possible to code up a copying collector within the language as suggested by Wang and Appel (2001). However, doing an efficient copying collector requires a bit more technical machinery. Some of these issues are resolved by Monnier, Saha, and Shao (2001).

Finally, note that, at this point, a paper and pencil proof of the soundness of a system that incorporates these extensions becomes quite large (and tedious) and we are therefore likely to make mistakes. To avoid such pitfalls, we would be wise to encode the abstract machine and type system in some formal system where the proof can be verified. For example, Crary encodes his TALT abstract machine and typing rules using the LF framework (2003) whereas Hamid et al. have done this using Coq (2002). Another approach championed by Appel and Felty (2000) is called Foundational Proof Carrying Code, whereby the types are semantically constructed using higher-order logic in such a way that they are by definition sound with respect to the (concrete) machine's semantics.

4.8 Conclusions

Type systems for low-level code, including compiler intermediate languages and target languages, are an exciting area of research. In part, this is because the "human constraint" is lifted since the typing annotations are produced and consumed by machines instead of humans. That is, we do not have to worry about the type system being too complicated for the average programmer, or that it requires too many typing annotations. These concerns often dominate the design of type systems for high-level languages. Of course, it is still important to keep the design as simple and orthogonal as possible so that we can construct proofs of soundness and have confidence in the implementation. Ideally, proofs should be carried out in a machine-checked environment.

Low-level languages also present new challenges to type system designers. For instance, the issues of initialization and memory recycling are of little concern in high-level languages, since these details are meant to be handled by the compiler and run-time system. Yet, the nitty-gritty details of the run-time system are crucial for the proper functioning of the system.

5 *Proof-Carrying Code*

George Necula

In the previous chapter we saw that one can adapt many of the ideas from type systems for high-level languages to assembly language. In this chapter, we describe yet another technique that can be used to type check assembly language programs. This time, however, we are going to depart from traditional type-checking approaches and see how one can adapt ideas from program verification to this problem. In the process of doing so, we are going to obtain a framework that can be adapted more easily to the verification of code properties that go beyond type safety.

5.1 Overview of Proof Carrying Code

Proof-Carrying Code (PCC) (Necula, 1997; Necula and Lee, 1996) is a *general* framework that allows the host to check *quickly* and *easily* that the agent has certain safety properties. The key technical detail that makes PCC powerful is a requirement that the agent producer cooperates with the host by attaching to the agent code an "explanation" of why the code complies with the safety policy. Then all that the host has to do to ensure the safe execution of the agent is to define a framework in which the "explanation" must be conducted, along with a simple yet sufficiently strong mechanism for checking that (a) the explanation is acceptable (i.e., is within the established framework), that (b) the explanation pertains to the safety policy that the host wishes to enforce, and (c) that the explanation matches the actual code of the agent.

There are a number of possible forms of explanations each with its own advantages and disadvantages. Safety explanations must be precise and comprehensive, just like formal proofs. In fact, in this chapter, the explanations are going to be formal proofs encoded in such a way that they can be checked easily and reliably by a simple proof checker.

There are several ways to implement the PCC concept, and all share the common requirement that the untrusted code contains information whose purpose is to simplify the verification task. At one extreme, we have the JVML and CLI verifiers, which rely on typing declarations present in the untrusted code to check the safety of the code. The KVM (Sun) implementation of the JVML verifier does further require that the code contains loop invariants in order to simplify and speed up the verification. Typed Assembly Language (described in Chapter 4) pushes these ideas to the level of assembly language. The most general instance of PCC, called Foundational Proof-Carrying Code (FPCC) (Appel, 2001; Appel and Felty, 2000), reduces to a minimum the size of the verifier and puts almost the entire burden of verification on the agent producer, who now has to produce and send with the agent detailed proofs of safety. In this chapter, we describe an instantiation of PCC that is similar to TAL in that it operates on agents written in assembly language, and is similar to FPCC in that it requires detailed proofs of safety to accompany the agent code. However, the architecture that we describe here uses a verifier that is more complex than that of FPCC, and thus somewhat less trustworthy. However, the advantage of this architecture is that is places a smaller burden on the agent producer than FPPC, and has been shown to scale to verifying even very large programs (Colby et al., 2000). We are going to refer to this architecture as the Touchstone PCC architecture.

A high-level view of the architecture of the Touchstone PCC system is shown in Figure 5-1. The agent contains, in addition to its executable content, checking-support data that allows the PCC infrastructure resident on the receiving host to check the safety of the agent. The PCC infrastructure is composed of two main modules. The verification-condition generator (VCGen) scans the executable content of the agent and checks directly simple syntactic conditions (e.g., that direct jumps are within the code boundary). Each time VCGen encounters an instruction whose execution could violate the safety policy, it asks the Checker module to verify that the dangerous instruction executes safely in the actual current context.

In order to construct a formal proof of a program, we need to reason about them using mathematical concepts. VCGen "compiles" programs to logical formulae in such a way that the aspects of the execution of the program that are relevant to the security policy are brought out.

VCGen can be quite simple because it relies on the Checker to verify complex safety requirements. There are some cases, however, when VCGen might have to understand complex invariants of the agent code in order to follow its control and data flow. For example, VCGen must understand the loop structure of the agent in order to avoid scanning the loop body an unbounded number of times. Also, VCGen must be able to understand even obscure con-

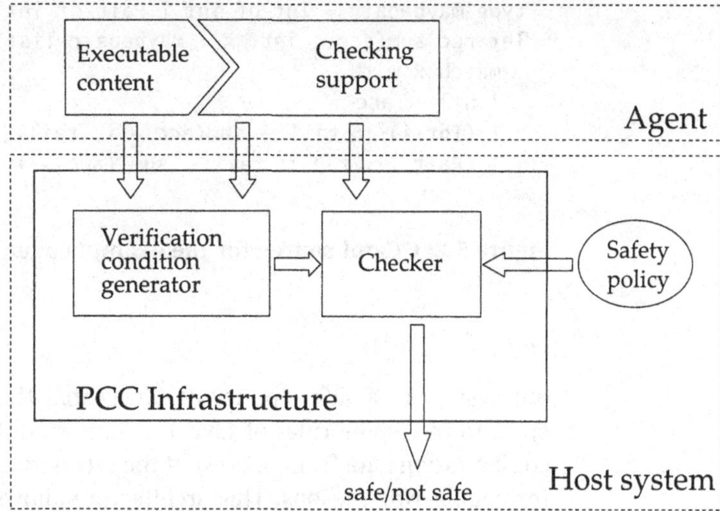

Figure 5-1: The Touchstone PCC architecture

trol flow, as in the presence of indirect jumps or function pointers. In such situations, VCGen relies on *code annotations* that are part of the checking support and are packaged with the agent. This puts most of the burden of handling the complex control-flow issues on the agent producer and keeps the VCGen simple.

The Checker module verifies for VCGen that all dangerous instructions are used in a safe context. The Checker module described in this chapter requires that VCGen formulates the safety preconditions of the dangerous instructions as formulas in a logic. We call these formulas the *verification conditions.* The Checker expects to find in the checking-support data packaged with the agent a formal proof that the safety precondition is met. For the verification to succeed, the Checker must verify the validity of the verification-condition proofs for all dangerous instructions identified by VCGen.

The Touchstone PCC infrastructure described here can be customized to check various safety policies. The "Safety Policy" element in Figure 5-1 is a collection of configuration data that specifies the precise logic that VCGen uses to encode the verification conditions, along with the trusted proof rules that can be used in the safety proofs supplied by the agent producer. For example, the host might require that the untrusted code interacts correctly with the runtime system of a Java Virtual Machine. This can be enforced in

```
type maybepair = Int of int | Pair of int * int
let rec sum(acc : int, x : maybepair list) =
  match x with
  | nil → acc
  | (Int i) :: tail → sum(acc + i, tail)
  | (Pair (l, r)) :: tail → sum (acc + l + r, tail)
```

Figure 5-2: OCaml source for the example agent

our system by a safety policy requiring that the code is well-typed with respect to the typing rules of Java. It is important to separate the safety policy configuration data from the rest of the infrastructure both for conceptual and for engineering reasons. This architecture allows the infrastructure to work with multiple safety policies, without changing most of the implementation.

An Example Agent

In the rest of this chapter, we explore the design and implementation details of the PCC infrastructure. The infrastructure can be configured to check many safety policies. In the example that we use here, we check a simple type-safety policy for an agent written in a generic assembly language. The agent is a function that adds all the elements in a list containing either integers or pairs of integers. If this agent were written in OCaml, its source code might be as shown Figure 5-2.

In order to write the agent in assembly language, we must decide what is the representation strategy for lists and for the `maybepair` type. For the purpose of this example, we represent a list as either the value 0 (for the empty list), or a pointer to a two-word memory area. The first word of the memory area contains a list element, and the second element contains the tail of the list. In order to represent an element of type `maybepair` in an economical way we ensure that any element of kind `Pair`(x, y) is an even-valued pointer to a two-word memory area containing x and y. We represent an element of kind `Int` x as the integer $2x + 1$ (to ensure that it is odd and thus distinguishable from a pair). For example, the representation of the list `[Int 2; Pair (3, 4)]` has the concrete representation shown in Figure 5-3. Notice the tagged representation of the `Int 2` element of the list.

In our examples, we will use the simple subset of a generic assembly language shown below. The expressions e contain arithmetic and logic operations involving constants and registers. This is the same assembly language

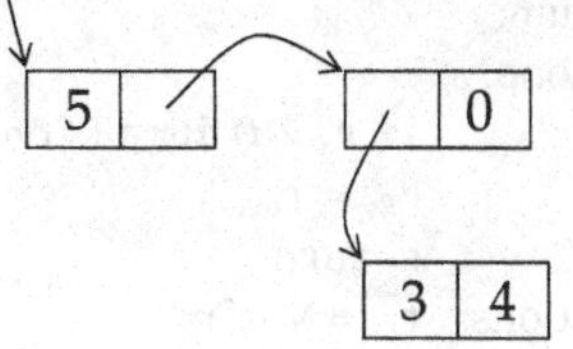

Figure 5-3: Concrete representation of the list `[Int 2; Pair (3, 4)]`

that was used in Chapter 4, except that we relax slightly the syntax of memory addresses, and we replace the general form of indirect jump with a return instruction.

$\mathtt{r}_x := e$	assign the result of e to register $\mathtt{r}_x$
$\mathtt{r}_x :=$ `Mem`$[e]$	load $\mathtt{r}_x$ from address e
`Mem`$[e'] := e$	store the result of e to address e'
`jump` L	jump to a label L
`if` e `jump` L	branch to label L if e is true
`return`	return from the current function

Given our representation strategy and the choice of assembly language instructions, the code for the agent is shown in Figure 5-4. On entry to this code fragment, registers $\mathtt{r}_x$ and $\mathtt{r}_{acc}$ contain the value of the formal arguments `x` and `acc` respectively. The code fragment also uses temporary registers $\mathtt{r}_t$ and $\mathtt{r}_s$. To simplify the handling of the return instruction, we use the convention that the return value is always contained in the register $\mathtt{r}_R$.

The safety policy in this case requires that all memory reads be from pointers that are either non-null lists, in which case we can read either the first or the second field of a list cell, or from pointers to elements of the `Pair` kind. In the case of a memory write, the safety policy constrains the values that can be written to various addresses as follows: in the first word of a list cell we can write either an odd value or an even value that is a pointer to an element of `Pair` kind, and in the second word of a list cell we can write either zero or a pointer to some list cell. There are no constraints on what we can write to the elements of a `Pair`. The restrictions on memory writes ensure that the contents of the accessible memory locations is consistent with the type assigned to their addresses.

The safety policy specifies not only requirements on the agent behavior but can also specify assumptions that the agent can make about the context of the execution. In the case of our agent, the safety policy might specify that the contents of the register $\mathtt{r}_x$ on entry is either zero or a pointer to a list

```
sum:                                                ;r_x : maybepair list
Loop:
          if r_x ≠ 0 jump LCons                      ; Is r_x empty?
          r_R := r_acc
          return
LCons:    r_t := Mem[r_x]                            ; Load the first data
          if even(r_t) jump LPair
          r_t := r_t div 2
          r_acc := r_acc + r_t
          jump LTail
LPair:    r_s := Mem[r_t]                            ; Get the first pair element
          r_acc := Mem[r_acc + r_s]
          r_t := Mem[r_t + 4]                        ; and the second element
          r_acc := r_acc + r_t
LTail:    r_x := Mem[r_x + 4]
          jump Loop
```

Figure 5-4: Assembly code for the function in Figure 5-2

cell. Also, the safety policy can allow the agent to assume that the value read from the first word of a list cell is either odd or otherwise a pointer to a Pair cell. Similarly, the agent can assume that the value it reads from the second word of a cell is either null or else a pointer to a list cell. We formalize this safety policy in the next section.

5.2 Formalizing the Safety Policy

At the core of a safety policy is a list of instructions whose execution may violate safety. The safety policy specifies, for each one, what is the verification condition that guarantees its safe execution. In the variant of PCC described here, the instructions that are handled specially are the memory operations along with the function calls and returns. This choice is hard coded in the verification-condition generator. However, the specific verification condition for each of these instructions is customizable. In such an implementation, we can control very precisely what memory locations can be read, what memory locations can be written and what can be written into them, what functions we call and in what context, and in what context we return from a function. This turns out to be sufficient for a very large class of safety policies. We shall explore in Section 5.7 a safety policy for which this is not sufficient and for which we must change the verification condition generator.

The customizable elements of the safety policy are the following:

- A language of symbolic expressions and formulas that can be used to express verification conditions.
- A set of function preconditions and postconditions for all functions that form the interface between the host and the agent.
- A set of proof rules for verification conditions.

In the rest of this section we describe in turn these elements.

The Syntax of the Logic

For this presentation we use a first-order language of symbolic expressions and formulas, as shown below:

$$\begin{array}{llll} \text{Formulas} & F & ::= & \mathtt{true} \mid F_1 \wedge F_2 \mid F_1 \vee F_2 \mid F_1 \Rightarrow F_2 \mid \forall x.F \mid \exists x.F \\ & & & \mid \mathtt{addr}\, E_a \mid E_1 = E_2 \mid E_1 \neq E_2 \mid f\, E_1 \ldots E_n \\ \text{Expressions} & E & ::= & x \mid \mathtt{sel}\, E_m\, E_a \mid \mathtt{upd}\, E_m\, E_a\, E_v \mid f\, E_1 \ldots E_n \end{array}$$

We consider here only the subset of logical connectives that we need for examples. In practice, a full complement of connectives can be used. The formula ($\mathtt{addr}\ E_a$) is produced by VCGen as a verification condition for a memory read or a memory write to address E_a. This formula holds whenever E_a denotes a valid address. Formulas can also be constructed using a set of formula constructors that are specific to each safety policy.

The language of expressions contains variables and a number of constructors that includes integer numerals and arithmetic operators, and can also be extended by safety policies. A notable expression construct is ($\mathtt{sel}\ E_m\ E_a$) that is used to denote the contents of memory address denoted by E_a in memory state E_m. The construct ($\mathtt{upd}\ E_m\ E_a\ E_v$) denotes a new memory state that is obtained by storing the value E_v at address E_a in memory state E_m. For example, the contents of the address c in a memory that is obtained from memory state m after writing the value 1 at address a followed by writing of value 2, can be written:

$$\mathtt{sel}\ (\mathtt{upd}\ (\mathtt{upd}\ m\ a\ 1)\ b\ 2)\ c$$

A safety policy extends the syntax of the logic by defining new expression and formula constructors. In particular, for our example agent we add constructors for encoding types and a predicate constructor for encoding the typing judgment:

$$\begin{array}{llll} \text{Word types} & W & ::= & \mathtt{int} \mid \mathtt{ptr}\,\{S\} \mid \mathtt{list}\, W \mid \{x \mid F(x)\} \\ \text{Structure types} & S & ::= & W \mid W; S \\ \text{Formulas} & F & ::= & \ldots \mid E : W \mid \mathtt{listinv}\, E_m \end{array}$$

We distinguish among types the *word types*, whose values fit in a machine register or memory word. Pointers can point to an area of memory containing a sequence of words. The word type $\{x \mid F(x)\}$ contains all those values for which the formula F is true (this type is sometimes called a comprehension or set type). The typing formula constructor ":" is written in infix notation. We also add the `listinv` formula constructor that will be used to state that the contents of the memory satisfies the representation invariant for lists of pairs. The precise definition of the typing and the `listinv` formulas will be given on page 200, with respect to a predetermined mapping of values and memory addresses to types. Informally, we say that `listinv` M holds when each memory address that is assigned a pointer type contains values that are assigned appropriate types.

Using these constructors we can write the low-level version of the ML typing judgment x : `maybepair list` as

$$x : \texttt{list}\ \{y \mid (\texttt{even}\ y) \Rightarrow y : \texttt{ptr}\ \{\texttt{int};\ \texttt{int}\}\}$$

In the rest of this section we use the abbreviation `mp_list` for the type `maybepair list`. Notice that we have built-in the recursive type of lists in our logic, in order to avoid the need for recursion at the level of the logic, but we choose to express the union and tuple types explicitly.

5.2.1 Exercise [Recommended, ★]: The singleton type is a type populated by a single value. Write a formula in the above logic corresponding to the assertion that x has type singleton for the value v. Show also how you can write using our language of types the singleton type for the value v. □

5.2.2 Exercise [Recommended, ★]: Consider an alternative representation for the `maybepair` type. A value of this type is a pointer to a tagged memory area containing a tag word followed either by another word encoding an `Int` if the tag value if 0, or by two words encoding a `Pair` if the tag value is 1. Write the formula corresponding to the assertion that x has this representation. □

The Preconditions and Postconditions

A PCC safety policy contains preconditions and postconditions for the functions that form the interface between the agent and the host. These are either functions defined by the agent and invoked by the host or library functions exported by the host for use by the agent. These preconditions and postconditions are expressed as logic formulas that use a number of formula and expression constructors specific to the safety policy.

Function preconditions and postconditions at the level of the assembly language are expressed in terms of argument and return registers, and thus specify also the calling convention. For verification purposes, we model the memory as a pseudo-register r_M.

The function precondition and postcondition for our agent are:

$$\begin{aligned} \mathtt{Pre}_{\mathtt{sum}} &= r_x : \mathtt{mp_list} \wedge \mathtt{listinv}\ r_M \\ \mathtt{Post}_{\mathtt{sum}} &= \mathtt{listinv}\ r_M \end{aligned}$$

The safety policy requires that the memory state be well-typed after the agent returns and allows the agent to assume that the memory state is well-typed when the host invokes it. Notice that we do not specify constraints on the integer arguments and results. This reflects our decision that any value whatsoever can be used as an integer.

Technically, the preconditions and postconditions are not well-formed formulas in our logic because they use register names as expressions. However, we can obtain valid formulas from them once we have a substitution of register names with expressions. We shall see later how this works out in detail.

5.2.3 EXERCISE [RECOMMENDED, ★]: Write the precondition and postcondition of a function of OCaml type `(int * int) * int list → int list`. The first argument is represented as a pointer to a sequence of two integers; the second is a list. Consider that the return value is placed in register r_R. □

5.2.4 EXERCISE [RECOMMENDED, ★]: Consider a function that takes in register r_1 a pointer to a sequence of integer lists. The length of the sequence is passed in register r_2. The function does not return anything. Write the precondition and postcondition for this function. □

The Proof Rules

The last part of the safety policy is a set of proof rules that can be used to reason about formulas in our logic in general and about verification conditions in particular. In Figure 5-5 we show, in natural deduction form, a selection of the derivation rules for the first-order logical connectives. We show the conjunction introduction (ANDI) and the two conjunction eliminations (ANDEL, ANDER), and the similar rules for implication. We also have two rules (MEM0 and MEM1) that allow us to reason about the `sel` and `upd` constructors for memory expressions. These two rules should not be necessary for most type-based safety policies because in those cases all we care to know about the contents of a memory location is its type, not its value.

Note that in this set of base proof rules we do not yet specify when we can prove that `addr` holds. This is the prerogative of the safety-policy specific rules that we describe next.

$$\frac{F_1 \quad F_2}{F_1 \wedge F_2}\ \text{(ANDI)} \qquad \frac{F_1 \wedge F_2}{F_1}\ \text{(ANDEL)} \qquad \frac{F_1 \wedge F_2}{F_2}\ \text{(ANDER)}$$

$$\frac{\begin{array}{c}F_1\\ \vdots \\ F_2\end{array}}{F_1 \Rightarrow F_2}\ \text{(IMPI)} \qquad \frac{F_1 \Rightarrow F_2 \quad F_1}{F_2}\ \text{(IMPE)}$$

$$\frac{A = A'}{\texttt{sel (upd } M\ A\ V\texttt{)}\ A' = V}\ \text{(MEM0)} \qquad \frac{A \neq A'}{\texttt{sel (upd } M\ A\ V\texttt{)}\ A' = \texttt{sel}\ M\ A'}\ \text{(MEM1)}$$

Figure 5-5: Built-in proof rules

Each safety policy can extend the built-in proof rules with new rules. In fact, this is necessary if the safety policy uses formula constructors beyond the built-in ones. The rules specific to our safety policy are shown in Figure 5-6. We have rules for reasoning about the type constructors: lists (NIL, CONS), set types (SET) and pointers to sequences (THIS and NEXT). These are similar to corresponding rules from type systems with recursive types and tuples. Next come two rules for reasoning about the typing properties of reading and writing from pointers. The rule SEL says that the location referenced by a pointer to a word type in a well-typed memory state has the given word type. The rule UPD is used to prove that a well-typed write preserves well-typedness of memory. These rules are similar to corresponding rules for reference types.

Notice that these proof rules are exposing more concrete implementation details than the corresponding source-level rules. For example, the CONS rule specifies that a list cell is represented as a pointer to a pair of words, of which the first one stores the data and the second the tail of the list.

Finally, the PTRADDR rule relates the safety-policy specific formula constructors with the built-in `addr` memory safety formula constructor. This rule says that addresses that can be proved to have pointer type in our type system are valid addresses. And since this is the only rule whose conclusion uses the `addr` constructor, the safety policy is essentially restricting memory accesses to such addresses.

5.2.5 EXERCISE [RECOMMENDED, ★★]: Add a new `array` type constructor to our safety policy and write the proof rules for its usage. An array is represented

$$\frac{}{0 : \texttt{list}\ W}\ (\text{NIL}) \qquad \frac{E : \texttt{ptr}\ \{W; S\}}{E + 4 : \texttt{ptr}\ \{S\}}\ (\text{NEXT})$$

$$\frac{E : \texttt{list}\ W \quad E \neq 0}{E : \texttt{ptr}\ \{W; \texttt{list}\ W\}}\ (\text{CONS}) \qquad \frac{A : \texttt{ptr}\ \{W\} \quad \texttt{listinv}\ M}{(\texttt{sel}\ M\ A) : W}\ (\text{SEL})$$

$$\frac{E : \{y \mid F(y)\}}{F(E)}\ (\text{SET}) \qquad \frac{\texttt{listinv}\ M \quad A : \texttt{ptr}\ \{W\} \quad V : W}{\texttt{listinv}\ (\texttt{upd}\ M\ A\ V)}\ (\text{UPD})$$

$$\frac{E : \texttt{ptr}\ \{W; S\}}{E : \texttt{ptr}\ \{W\}}\ (\text{THIS}) \qquad \frac{A : \texttt{ptr}\ \{W\}}{\texttt{addr}\ A}\ (\text{PTRADDR})$$

Figure 5-6: Proof rules specific to the example safety policy

as a pointer to a memory area that contains the number of elements in the array in the first word and then the array elements in order. Consider first the case where each element is a word type (as in OCaml), and then the case when each element can be a structure (as in C). □

We have shown here just a few of the rules for a simple safety policy. A safety policy for a full language can easily have hundreds of proof rules. For example, the Touchstone implementation of PCC for the Java type system (Colby et al., 2000) has about 150 proof rules.

5.3 Verification-Condition Generation

So far, we have shown how to set up the safety policy; now we need to describe a method for enforcing it. An analogous situation in the realm of high-level type systems is when we have setup a type system, with a language of types and a set of typing rules, and we need to design a type checker for it. A type checker must scan the code and must know what typing rule to apply at each point in the code. In fact, some type checkers work by explicitly collecting typing constraints that are solved in a separate module. Our PCC infrastructure accomplishes a similar task, and separates the scanning of the code from the decision of what safety policy proof rules to apply. The scanning is done by the verification-condition generator, which also identifies *what* must be checked for each instruction. *How* the check is performed is decided by the Checker module, with considerable help from the proof that accompanies the code. In a regular type checker, there is no pressing need to separate code scanning from the construction of the typing derivation, since the scanning process is often simple and the structure of the typing derivation closely follows that of the code. This is not true for low-level type checking. In fact, programs written in assembly language may have very little structure.

To illustrate some of the difficulties of type checking low-level code, consider the following fragment of code written in ML, where x is a variable of type T `list` and the variable t occurs in the expression e also with type T `list`:

```
match x with
  _ :: t → e
```

A type checker for ML parses this code, constructs an abstract syntax tree (AST) and then it verifies its well-typedness in a relatively simple manner by traversing the AST. This is possible because the `match` expression packages in one construction all the elements that are needed for type checking: the expression to be matched, the patterns with the variables they define, and the bodies of the cases.

Consider now one particular compilation of this code fragment:

$$
\begin{array}{l}
\mathtt{r}_t := \mathtt{r}_x \\
\mathtt{r}_t := \mathtt{r}_t + 4 \\
\mathtt{if}\ \mathtt{r}_x = 0\ \mathtt{jump\ LNil} \\
\mathtt{r}_t := \mathtt{Mem}[\mathtt{r}_t] \\
\ldots
\end{array}
$$

We assume that the variable x is allocated to register $\mathtt{r}_x$ and that the expression e is compiled with the assumption that, on entry, the variable t is allocated to the register $\mathtt{r}_t$. We observe that the code for compiling the `match` construct is spread over several non-contiguous instructions mixed with the instructions that implement the cases themselves. This is due to the intrinsically sequential nature of assembly language. It would be hard to implement a type checker for assembly language that identifies the code for the `match` by recognizing patterns, as a source-level type checker does. Also, such a type checker would be sensitive to code generation and optimization choices.

Another difficulty is that some high-level operations are split into several small operations. For example the extraction of the tail of the list is separated into the computation of an address in register $\mathtt{r}_t$ and a memory load. We cannot check one of the two instructions in isolation of the other because they both can be used in other contexts as well. Furthermore, it is not sufficient to type check the addition $\mathtt{r}_t + 4$ as we would do in a high-level language (i.e., verify that both operands have compatible arithmetic types). Instead we need to remember that we added the constant 4 to the contents of register $\mathtt{r}_x$, so that when we reach the load instruction, we can determine that we are loading the second word from a list cell. Additionally, our type-checking algorithm has to be flow sensitive and path sensitive because the outcomes of conditional expressions sometimes determine the type of values. In our example, if the conditional falls through then we know that r_x points to a list cell and therefore that r_t points to the second element in a list cell. If, however, the conditional jumps to `LNil`, then we cannot even assign a type to r_t after the addition.

Yet another complication with assembly language is that, unlike in high-level languages, we cannot count on a variable having a single type throughout its scope. In assembly language the registers play the role of variables and since there is a finite number of them, compilers reuse them aggressively to hold different data at different program points. In our example, the register r_t is used before the load to hold both a pointer to a memory location containing a list and after the load instruction to hold a list. We must thus keep different types for registers for different program points. Chapter 4 discusses these problems extensively.

There are a number of approaches for overcoming these difficulties. All of them do maintain different types for registers at different program points but differ on how they handle the dependency on conditionals and the splitting of high-level operations into several instructions. At one extreme is the Java Bytecode Verifier (Lindholm and Yellin, 1997), which typechecks programs written in the Java Virtual Machine Language (JVML). The JVML is relatively high-level and maintains complicated operations bundled in high-level constructs. For instance, in JVML you cannot separate the address computation from the memory access itself. In the context of our example, this means that the addition and the load instruction would be expressed as one bytecode instruction. The JVML is designed such that the outcome of conditionals does not matter for type checking. For example, array-bounds checks and pointer null-checks are bundled with the memory access in high-level bytecode instructions. This approach simplifies the type-checking problem but has the disadvantage that the agent producer cannot really do much optimization. Also this approach puts more burden on the code receiver for compiling and optimizing the code.

Another approach is Typed Assembly Language (TAL), described in Chapter 4, where a more sophisticated type system is used to keep track of the intermediate result of unbundled instructions. But even in TAL some low-level instructions are treated as bundles for the purpose of verification. Examples are memory allocation and array accesses.

Here we are going to describe a type checking method that can overcome the difficulties described above. The method is based on *symbolic evaluation*, and it was originally used in the context of program verification. The method is powerful enough to verify full correctness of a program, not just its well-typedness, which will come in handy when we consider safety policies beyond type safety.

Symbolic Evaluation

In order to introduce symbolic evaluation, consider the code fragment from above but without the conditional.

$$\mathtt{r}_t := \mathtt{r}_x$$
$$\mathtt{r}_t := \mathtt{r}_t + 4$$
$$\mathtt{r}_t := \mathtt{Mem}[\mathtt{r}_t]$$

This fragment exhibits the problems due to reuse of registers with different types and the splitting of high-level operations into low-level instructions. We have already observed that it is more important to remember the effect of the addition instruction than it is to type check it immediately as we see it. In fact, we are going to postpone all checking as much as possible and are going to focus on "remembering" the effect of instructions instead. Observe that if we allow arbitrary complex operands in our instructions, we can rewrite the above code sequence as follows:

$$\mathtt{r}_t := \mathtt{Mem}[\mathtt{r}_x + 4]$$

In this variant, the address computation is bundled with the memory access, and we can actually perform the usual pattern matching to recognize what typing rule to apply. Symbolic evaluation is a technique that has the effect of collecting the results of intermediate computations to create the final result as a complex expression whose meaning is equivalent to the entire computation. A symbolic evaluator is an interpreter that maintains for each register a symbolic expression. We will use the symbol σ to range over *symbolic states*, which are mappings from register names to symbolic expressions. The symbolic state is initialized with a distinct fresh variable for each register, to model the lack of information about the initial values of the registers. For our example the initial symbolic state is:

$$\sigma_0 = \{\mathtt{r}_t = t, \mathtt{r}_x = x, \mathtt{r}_M = m\}$$

where t and x are distinct fresh variables. Technically, this symbolic state says that at the given program point the following invariant holds:

$$\exists t.\exists x.\exists m.\mathtt{r}_t = t \wedge \mathtt{r}_x = x \wedge \mathtt{r}_M = m$$

The symbolic evaluator proceeds forward to interpret the instructions and modifies the symbolic state as specified by the instruction. We show below the sequence of symbolic states during symbolic evaluation.

$$\sigma = \{\mathsf{r}_t = t, \mathsf{r}_x = x, \mathsf{r}_M = m\}$$

$\mathsf{r}_t := \mathsf{r}_x$

$$\sigma = \{\mathsf{r}_t = x, \mathsf{r}_x = x, \mathsf{r}_M = m\}$$

$\mathsf{r}_t := \mathsf{r}_t + 4$

$$\sigma = \{\mathsf{r}_t = x + 4, \mathsf{r}_x = x, \mathsf{r}_M = m\}$$

$\mathsf{r}_t := \mathsf{Mem}[\mathsf{r}_t]$

$$\sigma = \{\mathsf{r}_t = (\mathtt{sel}\ m\ (x + 4)), \mathsf{r}_x = x, \mathsf{r}_M = m\}$$

When the instruction "$\mathsf{r}_t := \mathsf{r}_x$" is processed, the symbolic evaluator looks up the value of r_x in the current symbolic state and then sets r_t to that value. Notice how at the time the load instruction is processed, the symbolic evaluator can figure out that the address being accessed is $x + 4$.

In order to handle memory reads and writes we use a pseudo-register r_M and the `sel` and `upd` constructors introduced in Section 5.2. For memory loads and writes, the symbolic evaluator also emits the required verification conditions using the `addr` constructor. For example, the verification condition for the load instruction would be $(\mathtt{addr}\ (x + 4))$.

Another element of interest is the handling of conditionals. In order to allow for path sensitive checking the symbolic evaluator maintains, in addition to the symbolic state, a list of assumptions about the state. These assumptions are simply formulas involving the same existentially quantified variables that the symbolic state uses. As the symbolic evaluator follows the branches of a conditional, it extends the list of assumptions with formulas that capture the outcome of the conditional expression.

If we now add back the conditional instruction in our example, the symbolic state and the set of assumptions (initially A) at each point are shown below:

$$\sigma = \{\mathsf{r}_t = t, \mathsf{r}_x = x, \mathsf{r}_M = m\}, A$$

$\mathsf{r}_t := \mathsf{r}_x$

$$\sigma = \{\mathsf{r}_t = x, \mathsf{r}_x = x, \mathsf{r}_M = m\}, A$$

$\mathsf{r}_t := \mathsf{r}_t + 4$

$$\sigma = \{\mathsf{r}_t = x + 4, \mathsf{r}_x = x, \mathsf{r}_M = m\}, A$$

$\mathtt{if}\ \mathsf{r}_x = 0\ \mathtt{jump\ LNil}$

$$\sigma = \{\mathsf{r}_t = x + 4, \mathsf{r}_x = x, \mathsf{r}_M = m\}, A \wedge x \neq 0$$

$\mathsf{r}_t := \mathsf{Mem}[\mathsf{r}_t]$

$$\sigma = \{\mathsf{r}_t = \mathtt{sel}\ m\ (x + 4), \mathsf{r}_x = x, \mathsf{r}_M = m\}, A \wedge x \neq 0$$

...

LNil:

$$\sigma = \{\mathsf{r}_t = x + 4, \mathsf{r}_x = x, \mathsf{r}_M = m\}, A \wedge x = 0$$

The symbolic state immediately before the load instruction essentially states that the following invariant holds at that point:

$$\exists t.\exists x.\exists m.\mathsf{r}_t = x \wedge \mathsf{r}_x = x + 4 \wedge \mathsf{r}_M = m \wedge A \wedge x \neq 0$$

This means that the Checker module would have to check the following verification condition for the load instruction:

$$\forall t.\forall x.\forall m.(\mathsf{r}_t = x \wedge \mathsf{r}_x = x + 4 \wedge \mathsf{r}_M = m \wedge A \wedge x \neq 0) \Rightarrow \mathsf{addr}\ (x + 4)$$

Symbolic evaluation has many applications in program analysis. In the following two exercises you can explore how one can use symbolic evaluation to verify easily the correctness of some code transformations.

5.3.1 **Exercise [Recommended, ★]:** Consider the following two code fragments. The one on the right has been obtained from the one on the left by performing a few simple local optimizations. First, we did register allocations, by renaming register r_a, r_b, r_c, and r_d to r_1, r_2, r_3 and r_4 respectively. Then we removed the dead instruction from line 1. We performed copy propagation followed by common subexpression elimination in line 5. Finally, we performed instruction scheduling by moving the instruction from line 3 to be the last in the block.

1	$\mathsf{r}_a := 2$	$\mathsf{r}_1 := \mathsf{r}_2 + 1$
2	$\mathsf{r}_a := \mathsf{r}_b + 1$	$\mathsf{r}_4 := \mathsf{r}_1$
3	$\mathsf{r}_c := \mathsf{r}_a + 2$	$\mathsf{r}_3 := \mathsf{r}_1 + 2$
4	$\mathsf{r}_d := 1$	
5	$\mathsf{r}_d := \mathsf{r}_b + \mathsf{r}_d$	

Show that the result of symbolic evaluation for the registers live at the end of the two basic blocks is identical if you start with symbolic states $\{\mathsf{r}_b = b\}$ and $\{\mathsf{r}_2 = b\}$ respectively. This suggests that symbolic evaluation is insensitive to some common optimizations. □

5.3.2 **Exercise [Recommended, ★]:** Now consider the first code fragment shown in Exercise 5.3.1 and add the instruction "$\mathsf{r}_a := 3$" immediately before line 5. In this case it is not correct to perform common-subexpression elimination. Show now that the result of symbolic evaluation is different for the modified code fragment and the transformed code from Exercise 5.3.1. This suggests that symbolic evaluation can be use to verify the result of compiler optimizations. This technique is in fact so powerful that it can be used to verify most optimizations that the GNU C compiler performs (Necula, 2000). □

Before we can give a complete formal definition of the VCGen, we must consider what happens in the cases when the symbolic evaluator should not follow directly the control-flow of the program. Two such cases are for loops (when following the control-flow would make VCGen loop forever) and for functions (when it is desirable to scan the body of a function only once). In order to handle those cases, VCGen needs some assistance from the agent producer, in the form of code annotations.

The Role of Program Annotations

The VCGen module attempts to execute the untrusted program symbolically in order to signal all potentially unsafe operations. To make this execution possible in finite time and without the need for conservative approximations on the part of VCGen, we require that the program be annotated with invariant predicates. At least one such invariant must be specified for each cycle in the program's control-flow graph. An easy but conservative way to enforce such a constraint is to require an invariant annotation for every backward branch target.

The agent code shown in Figure 5-4 has one loop whose body starts at the label `Loop`. There must be one invariant annotation somewhere in that loop. Let us say that the agent producer places the following invariant at label `Loop`:

$$\texttt{Loop:}\ \texttt{INV} = r_x : \texttt{mp_list} \wedge \texttt{listinv}\ r_M$$

The invariant annotation says that whenever the execution reaches the label `Loop` the contents of register r_x is a list. It also says that the contents of the memory satisfies the representation invariants of lists. Just like the preconditions and postconditions, the invariants can refer to register names.

A valid question at this point is who discovers this annotation and how. There are several possibilities. First, annotations can be inserted by hand by the programmer. This is the only alternative when the agent code is programmed directly in assembly language or when the programmer wants to hand-optimize the output of a compiler. It is true that this method does not scale well, but it is nevertheless a feature of PCC that the code receiver does not care whether the code is produced by a trusted compiler, and will gladly accept code that was written or optimized by hand.

Another possibility is that the annotations can be produced automatically by a certifying compiler. For our simple type safety policy the only annotations that are necessary consist of type declarations for the live registers at that point. See Necula (1998) for more details.

Finally, note that the invariant annotations are required but cannot be trusted to be correct as they originate from the same possibly untrusted source as the code itself. Nevertheless, VCGen can still use them safely, as described in the next section.

The Verification-Condition Generator

Now we have all the elements necessary to describe the verification-condition generator for the case of one function whose precondition and postcondition are specified by the safety policy. We will assume that each invariant annotation occupies one instruction slot, even though in practice they are stored in a separate region of the agent. Let *Inv* be the partial mapping from program counters to invariant predicates. If $i \in Dom(Inv)$, then there is an invariant Inv_i at program counter i. Next, for a more uniform treatment of functions and loops, we will consider that the first instruction in each agent function is an invariant annotation with the precondition predicate. In our example, this means that $Inv_1 = \mathtt{r}_x : \mathtt{mp_list} \wedge \mathtt{listinv}\ \mathtt{r}_M$. This, along with the loop invariant (with the same predicate) at index 2 are all the loop invariants in the example. Thus, $Dom(Inv) = \{1, 2\}$, and the first few lines of our agent example are modified as follows:

```
1 sum:    INV rx : mp_list ∧ listinv rM
2 Loop:   INV rx : mp_list ∧ listinv rM
3         if rx ≠ 0 jump LCons                   ; list is empty
```

Given a symbolic state σ and an expression e that contains references to register names, we write $(\sigma\ e)$ to denote the result of substituting the register names in e with the expressions given by σ. We extend this notation to formulas F that refer to register names (e.g., function preconditions or postconditions, or loop invariants). We also write $\sigma[r \leftarrow e]$ to denote a symbolic state that is the same as σ but with register r mapped to e.

We write Π_i for the instruction (or annotation) at the program counter i.

The core of the verification-condition generator is a symbolic evaluation function *SE* that given a value i for the program counter and a symbolic state σ, produces a formula that captures all of the verification conditions from the given program counter until the next return instruction or invariant. The definition of the *SE* function is shown below:

$$
SE(i,\sigma) = \begin{cases}
SE(i+1, \sigma[r \leftarrow \sigma\ e]) & \text{if } \Pi_i = r := e \\
(\sigma\ e) \Rightarrow SE(L,\sigma) \wedge & \text{if } \Pi_i = \mathtt{if}\ e\ \mathtt{jump}\ \mathtt{L} \\
\quad (\mathtt{not}\ (\sigma\ e)) \Rightarrow SE(i+1,\sigma) & \\
\mathtt{addr}\ (\sigma\ a) \wedge & \text{if } \Pi_i = r := \mathtt{Mem}[a] \\
\quad SE(i+1, \sigma[r \leftarrow (\sigma\ (\mathtt{sel}\ \mathtt{r}_M\ a))]) & \\
\mathtt{addr}\ (\sigma\ a) \wedge & \text{if } \Pi_i = \mathtt{Mem}[a] := e \\
\quad SE(i+1, \sigma[\mathtt{r}_M \leftarrow (\sigma\ (\mathtt{upd}\ \mathtt{r}_M\ a\ e))] & \\
\sigma\ Post & \text{if } \Pi_i = \mathtt{return} \\
\sigma\ I & \text{if } \Pi_i = \mathtt{INV}\ I
\end{cases}
$$

Symbolic evaluation is defined by case analysis of the instruction contained at a given program counter. Symbolic evaluation is undefined for values of the program counter that do not contain a valid instruction. In the case of a `set` instruction, the symbolic evaluator substitutes the current symbolic state into the right-hand side of the instruction and then uses the result as the new value of the destination register. Then the symbolic evaluator continues with the following instruction. For a conditional, the symbolic evaluator adds the proper assumption about the outcome of the conditional expression. Memory operations are handled like assignments but with the generation of additional verification conditions.

When either the return instruction or an invariant is encountered, the symbolic evaluator stops with a predicate obtained by substituting the current symbolic state into the postcondition or the invariant formula. The symbolic evaluator also ensures (using a simple check not shown here) that each loop in the code has at least one invariant annotation. This ensures the termination of the *SE* function.

What remains to be shown is how the verification-condition generator uses the *SE* function. For each invariant in the code, VCGen starts a symbolic evaluation with a symbolic state initialized with distinct variables. Assuming that the set of registers is $\{\mathtt{r}_1, \ldots, \mathtt{r}_n\}$, we define the *global verification condition VC* as follows:

$$\begin{array}{rcl} VC & = & \bigwedge_{i \in Dom(Inv)} \forall x_1 \ldots x_n.\ \ \sigma_0\, Inv_i \Rightarrow SE(i+1, \sigma_0) \\ & & \text{where } \sigma_0 = \{\mathtt{r}_1 = x_1, \ldots, \mathtt{r}_n = x_n\} \end{array}$$

Essentially the VCGen evaluates symbolically every path in the program that connects two invariants or an invariant and a return instruction. In Figure 5-7 we show the operation of the VCGen algorithm on the agent code from Figure 5-4 (after we have added the invariant annotations for the precondition and the loop, as explained at the beginning of this section). We show on the left the program points and a brief description of each action. Some actions result in extending the stack of assumptions that the Checker is allowed to make. These assumptions are shown underlined and with an indentation level that encodes the position in the stack of each assumption. Thus an assumption at a given indentation level implicitly discards all previously occurring assumptions at the same or larger indentation level. Finally, we show right-justified and boxed the checking goals submitted to the Checker.

There are two invariants (in lines 1 and 2) and for each one we generate fresh new variables for registers, we assume that the invariant holds, and then we start the symbolic evaluator. For the first invariant, the symbolic evaluator when starting in line 2 encounters an invariant and terminates.

Every boxed formula shown flushed right in Figure 5-7 is a verification condition that VCGen produces and the Checker module has to verify for some arbitrary values of the initial variables.

Notice that the invariant formulas are used both as assumptions and as verification conditions. There is a strong similarity between the role of invariants and that of predicates in a proof by induction. In the latter case the

1: Generate fresh values $\mathtt{r}_M = m_0$, $\mathtt{r}_R = r_0$, $\mathtt{r}_x = x_0$, $\mathtt{r}_{acc} = acc_0$, $\mathtt{r}_t = t_0$ and $\mathtt{r}_s = s_0$		
1: Assume Invariant	x_0 : mp_list listinv m_0	
2: Invariant		x_0 : mp_list listinv m_0
2: Generate fresh values $\mathtt{r}_M = m_1$, $\mathtt{r}_R = r_1$, $\mathtt{r}_x = x_1$, $\mathtt{r}_{acc} = acc_1$, $\mathtt{r}_t = t_1$ and $\mathtt{r}_s = s_1$		
2: Assume Invariant	x_1 : mp_list listinv m_1	
3: Branch 3 taken	$x_1 \neq 0$	
6: Check load		addr x_1
7: Branch 7 taken	even (sel m_1 x_1)	
11: Check load		addr (sel m_1 x_1)
13: Check load		addr ((sel m_1 x_1) + 4)
15: Check load		addr (x_1 + 4)
16: Goto Loop		
2: Invariant		(sel m_1 (x_1 + 4)) : mp_list listinv m_1
7: Branch 7 not taken	odd (sel m_1 x_1)	
10: Goto LTail		
15: Check load		addr (x_1 + 4)
16: Goto Loop		
2: Invariant		(sel m_1 (x_1 + 4)) : mp_list listinv m_1
3: Branch 3 not taken	$x_1 = 0$	
5: Return		listinv m_1

Figure 5-7: The sequence of actions taken by VCGen

$$
\frac{\dfrac{\dfrac{\texttt{listinv}\ m_1 \qquad \dfrac{\dfrac{x_1 : \texttt{mp_list} \quad x_1 \neq 0}{x_1 : \texttt{ptr}\ \{\texttt{maybepair;mp_list}\}}\ \text{CONS}}{x_1 : \texttt{ptr}\ \{\texttt{maybepair}\}}\ \text{THIS}}{(\texttt{sel}\ m_1\ x_1) : \texttt{maybepair}}\ \text{SEL}}{\texttt{even}\ (\texttt{sel}\ m_1\ x_1) \Rightarrow (\texttt{sel}\ m_1\ x_1) : \texttt{ptr}\ \{\texttt{int;int}\}}\ \text{SET} \qquad \texttt{even}\ (\texttt{sel}\ m_1\ x_1)}{\dfrac{\dfrac{(\texttt{sel}\ m_1\ x_1) : \texttt{ptr}\ \{\texttt{int;int}\}}{(\texttt{sel}\ m_1\ x_1) : \texttt{ptr}\{\texttt{int}\}}\ \text{THIS}}{\texttt{addr}\ (\texttt{sel}\ m_1\ x_1)}\ \text{PTRADDR}}\ \text{IMPE}
$$

Figure 5-8: Proof of a verification condition

predicate is assumed to hold and with this assumption we must prove that it holds for a larger value in a well founded order. This effectively ensures that the invariant formulas are preserved through an arbitrary execution from one invariant point to another.

Let us consider now how one proves the verification conditions. The first interesting one is the addr from line 6. Let

$$\texttt{maybepair} \stackrel{def}{=} \{y \mid \texttt{even}(y) \Rightarrow y : \texttt{ptr}\ \{\texttt{int; int}\}\}$$

To construct its proof, we first derive $x_1 : \texttt{ptr}\ \{\texttt{maybepair;mp_list}\}$ using the rule CONS with the assumptions $x_1 : \texttt{mp_list}$ and $x_1 \neq 0$. Then we can derive $\texttt{addr}\ x_1$ using the rule PTRADDR.

A more interesting case is that of proving $\texttt{addr}\ (\texttt{sel}\ m_1\ x_1)$ from the assumptions $x_1 : \texttt{mp_list}$, $\texttt{listinv}\ m_1$, $x_1 \neq 0$, and $\texttt{even}\ (\texttt{sel}\ m_1\ x_1)$. This proof is shown in Figure 5-8.

5.3.3 EXERCISE [★★, ↛]: Construct the the proof of the verification condition corresponding to the loop invariant from line 2. You must prove that $\texttt{sel}\ m_1\ (x_1 + 4) : \texttt{mp_list}$ from the assumptions $x_1 : \texttt{mp_list}$, $\texttt{listinv}\ m_1$, $x_1 \neq 0$, and $\texttt{even}\ (\texttt{sel}\ m_1\ x_1)$. □

5.3.4 EXERCISE [★★★]: Notice that we have to prove that $\texttt{sel}\ m_1\ x_1 : \texttt{ptr}\ \{\texttt{int}\}$ several times as a step in proving those verification conditions from Figure 5-7 that refer to $(\texttt{sel}\ m_1\ x_1)$. Show how you can add an invariant to the program to achieve the effect of proving this fact only once. □

We have been arguing that symbolic evaluation is just an alternative method for type checking, with additional benefits for checking more complex safety policies. Since there is a simple type checker at the source level for our type system, it seems reasonable to wonder whether we could hope to build automatically the proofs of these verification conditions. This is indeed possible for such type-based safety policies. Consider for instance how the proof shown in Figure 5-8 could be constructed through a goal-directed manner. The goal is an `addr` formula, and we observe that only the PTRADDR among our rules (shown in Figure 5-6) has a conclusion that matches the goal. The subgoal now is (`sel` m_1 x_1) : `ptr {int}`. In order to prove that the result of reading from a memory location has a certain type, we must prove that the memory is well-typed and the address has some pointer type. When we try to prove that x_1 has a pointer type, we find among the assumptions that x_1 : `mp_list`. The remaining steps can be easily constructed by a theorem prover that knows the details of the type system. This general strategy was used successfully to construct a simple theorem prover that can build automatically and efficiently proofs of verification conditions for the entire Java type safety policy (Colby et al., 2000).

5.3.5 **Exercise** [★★★]: Extend the verification-condition generator approach shown here to handle a function call instruction `call L`, where L is a label that is considered the start of a function. For each such function there is a precondition and a postcondition. Make the simplifying assumption that the `call` instruction saves the return address and a set of callee-save registers on a special stack that cannot be manipulated directly by the program. A `ret` instruction always returns to the last return address saved on the stack and also restores the callee-save registers. □

5.3.6 **Exercise** [★★]: It is sometimes useful to use more kinds of annotations in addition to the loop invariants. For example, the agent producer might know that a certain point in the code is not reachable, as is the case for the label `L1` in the code fragment shown below:

```
    call exit
L1: UNREACHABLE
    ...
```

In such a case it is useful to add an annotation `UNREACHABLE` to signal to the symbolic evaluator that it can stop the evaluation at that point. Show how you can change the symbolic evaluator to handle these annotation without allowing the agent producer to "lie" about reachability of code. □

5.3.7 **Exercise** [★★]: Extend the symbolic evaluator to handle the indirect jump instruction `jump at` e, where e must evaluate to a valid program counter.

Indirect jumps are often used to implement efficiently `switch` statements, in which case the destination address is one of a statically-known set of labels. Assume that immediately after the indirect jump instruction there is an annotation of the form `JUMPDEST(L1, L2)` to declare that the destination address is one of `L1` or `L2`. □

5.3.8 EXERCISE [★★★★, ↛]: Extend the symbolic evaluator to handle stack frames. The basic idea is that there is a dedicated stack pointer register r_{SP} that always points at the last used stack word. This register can only be incremented or decremented by a constant amount. You can ignore stack overflow issues. The stack frame for a function has a fixed size that is declared with an annotation. The only accesses to it are through the stack pointer register along with a constant offset. The key insight is that since there is no aliasing to the stack frame slots they can be treated as pseudo registers. Make sure you handle properly the overlapping of stack frames at function calls. □

This completes our simplified account of the operation of VCGen. Note that the VCGen defined here constructs a global verification condition that it then passes to the Checker module. This approach, while natural and easy to describe, turns out to be too wasteful. For large examples on the order of millions of instructions it is quite common for this monolithic formula to require hundreds of megabytes for storage, slowing down the checking process considerably. A high-level type checker that would construct an explicit typing derivation would be just as wasteful. A more efficient VCGen architecture passes to the Checker module each verification condition as it is produced. After the checker validates it, the verification condition is discarded and the symbolic evaluation resumes. This optimization might not seem interesting from a scientific point of view, but it is illustrative of a number of engineering details that must be addressed to make PCC scalable.

5.4 Soundness Proof

In this section we prove that the type checking technique presented so far is sound, in the sense that "well-typed programs cannot go wrong." More precisely, we prove that if the global verification condition for a program is provable using the proof rules given by the safety policy, then the program is guaranteed to execute without violating memory safety. The method we use is similar to those used for type systems for high-level languages. We define formally the operational semantics of the assembly language, along with the notion of "going wrong." It is a bit more difficult to formalize the notion of well-typed programs. In high-level type systems there is a direct connection between the typing derivations and the abstract-syntax tree of the program. In our case, the connection is indirect: we first use a verification-condition generator and then we exhibit a derivation of the global verification condition using the safety policy proof rules. In order to reflect this staging in the operation of our type checker, we split the soundness proof into a proof of soundness of the set of safety policy rules and a proof of soundness of the VCGen algorithm.

Soundness of the Safety Policy

The ultimate goal of our safety policy is to provide memory safety. In order to prove that our typing rules enforce memory safety, we must first define the semantics of the expression and formula constructors that we have defined.

The semantic domain for the expressions is the set of integers,[1] except for the memory expressions that we model using partial maps from integers to integers.

Next we observe that the typing formulas involving pointer types and the `listinv` formulas have a well-defined meaning only in a given context that assigns types to addresses. The necessary context is a mapping $\mathcal{M}$ from a *valid* address to the word type of the value stored at that address. Since we do not consider allocation or deallocation, our type system ensures that the mapping $\mathcal{M}$ remains constant throughout the execution of the program.

We write $\models_{\mathcal{M}} F$ when the formula F holds in the memory typing $\mathcal{M}$. A few of the most interesting cases from the definition of $\models_{\mathcal{M}}$ are shown below:

$$
\begin{array}{lll}
\models_{\mathcal{M}} F_1 \wedge F_2 & \texttt{iff} & \models_{\mathcal{M}} F_1 \text{ and } \models_{\mathcal{M}} F_2 \\
\models_{\mathcal{M}} F_1 \Rightarrow F_2 & \texttt{iff} & \text{whenever } \models_{\mathcal{M}} F_1 \text{ then } \models_{\mathcal{M}} F_2 \\
\models_{\mathcal{M}} \forall x.F(x) & \texttt{iff} & \forall e \in \mathbb{Z}.\ \models_{\mathcal{M}} F(e) \\
 & & \\
\models_{\mathcal{M}} a : \texttt{int} & \texttt{iff} & a \in \mathbb{Z} \\
\models_{\mathcal{M}} a : \texttt{list}\ W & \texttt{iff} & a = 0 \vee (\mathcal{M}(a) = W \wedge \mathcal{M}(a+4) = \texttt{list}\ W) \\
\models_{\mathcal{M}} a : \texttt{ptr}\ \{S\} & \texttt{iff} & \forall i.0 \le i < |S| \Rightarrow \mathcal{M}(a + 4 * i) = S_i \\
\models_{\mathcal{M}} a : \{y \mid F(y)\} & \texttt{iff} & \models_{\mathcal{M}} F(a) \\
 & & \\
\models_{\mathcal{M}} \texttt{listinv}\ m & \texttt{iff} & \forall a \in Dom(\mathcal{M}).a \in Dom(m) \text{ and } \models_{\mathcal{M}} m\ a : \mathcal{M}(a) \\
\models_{\mathcal{M}} \texttt{addr}\ a & \texttt{iff} & a \in Dom(\mathcal{M})
\end{array}
$$

In the above definition we used the notation $|S|$ for the length of a sequence of word types S, and S_i for the ith element of the sequence.

---

1. A more accurate model would use integers modulo 2^{32} in order to reflect the finite range of integers that are representable as machine words.

With these definitions we can now start to prove the soundness of the derivation rules. Given a rule with variables $x_1, \ldots, x_n$, premises $H_1, \ldots, H_m$ and conclusion C, we must prove

$$\models_{\mathcal{M}} \forall x_1 . \forall x_2 . \ldots \forall x_n . (H_1 \wedge \cdots \wedge H_m) \Rightarrow C$$

For example, the soundness of rule SEL requires proving the following fact:

$$\models_{\mathcal{M}} \forall a . \forall W . \forall m . (a : \texttt{ptr}\ \{W\}) \wedge (\texttt{listinv}\ m) \Rightarrow (\texttt{sel}\ m\ a) : W$$

From the first assumption we derive that $\mathcal{M}(a) = W$. From the second assumption we derive that $\models_{\mathcal{M}} m\ a : W$ and since $\models_{\mathcal{M}} (\texttt{sel}\ m\ a) = m\ a$ we obtain the desired conclusion.

5.4.1 EXERCISE [RECOMMENDED, ★]: Prove that CONS and NEXT are sound. □

5.4.2 EXERCISE [★★, ↛]: Prove the soundness of the remaining rules shown in Figure 5-6. □

An Operational Semantics for Assembly Language

Next we formalize an operational semantics for the assembly language. We model the execution state as a mapping ρ from register names to values. Just like in the previous chapter, the domain of values is $\mathbb{Z}$, except for the r_M register, which takes as values partial mappings from $\mathbb{Z}$ to $\mathbb{Z}$. Since we do not consider allocation and deallocation, the domain of the memory mapping does not change. Let $\mathcal{A}ddr$ be that domain. The operational semantics is defined only for programs whose memory accesses are only to addresses in the $\mathcal{A}ddr$ domain.

We write $(\rho\ e)$ for the result of evaluating in the register state ρ the expression e, which can refer to register names. We write $\rho[r_r \leftarrow v]$ for the new register state obtained after setting register r_r to value v in state ρ.

The operational semantics is defined in Figure 5-9 in the form of a small-step transition relation $(i, \rho) \rightsquigarrow (i, \rho')$ from a given program counter and register state to another such pair. Notice that the transition relation is defined for memory operations only if the referenced addresses are valid.

We follow the usual convention and leave the transition relation undefined for those states where the execution is considered unsafe. For instance, the transition relation is not defined if the program counter is outside the code area or if it points to an unrecognized instruction. More importantly, the transition relation is not defined if a memory access is attempted at an invalid address.

$$
(i,\rho) \rightsquigarrow \begin{cases}
(i+1,\rho[\mathtt{r}_d \leftarrow \rho\ e]), & \textit{if}\quad \Pi_i = \mathtt{set}\ \mathtt{r}_d\ \mathtt{to}\ e \\
(i+1,\rho[\mathtt{r}_d \leftarrow \rho\ (\mathtt{sel}\ \mathtt{r}_M\ e)]), & \textit{if}\quad \Pi_i = \mathtt{load}\ \mathtt{r}_d\ \mathtt{from}\ e \\
 & \qquad \textit{and}\quad \rho\ e \in \mathcal{A}ddr \\
(i+1,\rho[\mathtt{r}_M \leftarrow \rho\ (\mathtt{upd}\ \mathtt{r}_M\ e_2\ e_1)]), & \textit{if}\quad \Pi_i = \mathtt{write}\ e_1\ \mathtt{to}\ e_2 \\
 & \qquad \textit{and}\quad \rho\ e_2 \in \mathcal{A}ddr \\
(L,\rho), & \textit{if}\quad \Pi_i = \mathtt{if}\ e\ \mathtt{goto}\ L \\
 & \qquad \textit{and}\quad \rho\ e \\
(i+1,\rho), & \textit{if}\quad \Pi_i = \mathtt{if}\ e\ \mathtt{goto}\ L \\
 & \qquad \textit{and}\quad \rho\ (\mathtt{not}\ e) \\
(i+1,\rho), & \textit{if}\quad \Pi_i = \mathtt{INV}\ I
\end{cases}
$$

Figure 5-9: The abstract machine for the soundness proof

Soundness of Verification-Condition Generation

The soundness theorem for VCGen states that if the verification condition holds, and all addresses that are in *Dom*($\mathcal{M}$) are valid addresses (i.e., they belong to $\mathcal{A}ddr$), then the execution starting at the beginning of the agent in a state that satisfies the precondition will make progress either forever or until it reaches a return instruction in a state that satisfies the postcondition. What this theorem rules out is the possibility that the execution gets stuck either because it tries to execute an instruction at an invalid program counter, or it tries to dereference an invalid address. The formal statement of the theorem is the following:

5.4.3 THEOREM [SOUNDNESS OF VCGEN]: Let ρ_1 be a state such that $\models_{\mathcal{M}} \rho_1\ \mathit{Pre}$. If $\mathit{Dom}(\mathcal{M}) \subseteq \mathcal{A}ddr$ and if $\models_{\mathcal{M}} \mathit{VC}$ then the execution starting at $(1, \rho_1)$ can make progress either forever, or until it reaches a `return` instruction in state ρ, in which case $\models_{\mathcal{M}} \rho\ \mathit{Post}$. □

We prove by induction on the number of execution steps that either we have reached the return instruction, or else we can make further progress. As in all proofs by induction, the most delicate issue is the choice of the induction hypothesis. Informally, our induction hypothesis is that for each execution state there is a "corresponding" state of the symbolic evaluator.

In order to express the notion of correspondence, we must consider the differences between the concrete execution states ρ (mapping register names to values) and the symbolic evaluation states σ (mapping register names to symbolic expressions that use expression constructors and variables). To bridge these two notions of states we need a mapping ϕ from variables that appear in σ, to values. For a symbolic expression e that contains variables, we write $(\phi\ e)$ for the result of replacing the variables in e as specified by ϕ and evaluating the result. Consequently, we write $\phi \circ \sigma$ for a mapping from register names to values that maps each register name $\mathtt{r}_i$ to the value $\phi\ (\sigma\ \mathtt{r}_i)$. Thus $\phi \circ \sigma$ is a concrete execution state.

The main relationship that we impose between ρ and σ is that there exists a mapping ϕ such that $\rho = \phi \circ \sigma$. The full induction hypothesis relates these states with the program counter i, and is defined as follows:

$$IH(i, \rho, \sigma, \phi) \stackrel{\text{def}}{=} \rho = \phi \circ \sigma \text{ and } \models_{\mathcal{M}} \phi\ (SE(i, \sigma))$$

The core of the soundness proof is the following lemma:

5.4.4 THEOREM [PROGRESS]: Let Π be a program such that $\models_{\mathcal{M}} VC$ and $Dom(\mathcal{M}) \subseteq \mathcal{A}ddr$. For any execution state (i, ρ) and σ and ϕ such that $IH(i, \rho, \sigma, \phi)$ then either:

- Π_i = `return`, and $\models_{\mathcal{M}} \rho\ Post$, or
- there exist new states ρ', σ' and a mapping ϕ' such that $(i, \rho) \to (i', \rho')$ and $IH(i', \rho', \sigma', \phi')$. □

Proof: The proof is by case analysis on the current instruction. Since we have that $\models_{\mathcal{M}} \phi\ SE(i, \sigma)$ we know that $SE(i, \sigma)$ is defined, hence the program counter is valid and Π_i is a valid instruction. We show here only the most interesting cases.

Case: Π_i = `return`. In this case $SE(i, \sigma) = \sigma\ Post$ and from $\models_{\mathcal{M}} \phi\ SE(i, \sigma)$ along with $\rho = \phi \circ \sigma$ we can infer that $\models_{\mathcal{M}} \rho\ Post$.

Case: Π_i = `load` $\mathtt{r}_d$ `from` e. In this case $SE(i, \sigma) = \mathtt{addr}\ (\sigma\ e) \wedge SE(i + 1, \sigma[\mathtt{r}_d \leftarrow \sigma\ (\mathtt{sel}\ \mathtt{r}_M\ e)])$. Let $\sigma' = \sigma[\mathtt{r}_d \leftarrow \sigma\ (\mathtt{sel}\ \mathtt{r}_M\ e)]$, $\rho' = \rho[\mathtt{r}_d \leftarrow \rho\ (\mathtt{sel}\ \mathtt{r}_M\ e)]$, $i' = i + 1$ and $\phi' = \phi$. In order to prove progress, we must prove $\rho\ e \in \mathcal{A}ddr$. The induction hypothesis $IH(i, \rho, \sigma, \phi)$ ensures that $\models_{\mathcal{M}} (\mathtt{addr}\ (\phi(\sigma\ e)))$, which in turn means that $(\rho\ e) \in Dom(\mathcal{M})$. Since we require that the memory typing be defined only on valid addresses we obtain the progress condition.

Next we have to prove that the induction hypothesis is preserved. The only interesting part of this proof is that $\phi' \circ \sigma' = \rho'$, which in turn requires proving that $\phi(\sigma\ (\mathtt{sel}\ \mathtt{r}_M\ e)) = \rho\ (\mathtt{sel}\ \mathtt{r}_M\ e)$. This follows from $\phi \circ \sigma = \rho$.

Case: Π_i = `INV` I. In this case $SE(i, \sigma) = \sigma\ I$. We know that $\models_{\mathcal{M}} \phi(\sigma\ I)$ and therefore $\models_{\mathcal{M}} \rho\ I$. The execution can always make progress for an invariant instruction and we must choose $i' = i + 1$ and $\rho' = \rho$. We know that $\models_{\mathcal{M}} VC$ and hence

$$\models_{\mathcal{M}} \forall x_1.\dots.\forall x_n.\sigma_0\, I \Rightarrow SE(i+1, \sigma_0)$$

where $\sigma_0 = \{r_1 = x_1, \dots, r_n = x_n\}$. We choose $\sigma' = \sigma_0$ and ϕ' as follows:

$$\phi' = \{x_1 = \rho\ r_1, \dots, x_n = \rho\ r_n\}$$

This ensures that $\rho = \phi' \circ \sigma'$ and also that $\models_{\mathcal{M}} \phi'\ SE(i+1, \sigma')$, which completes this case of the proof. □

5.4.5 Exercise [Recommended, ★, ↛]: Finish the proof of Theorem 5.4.4 by proving the remaining cases (assignment, conditional branch and memory write). □

The progress theorem constitutes the inductive case of the proof of the soundness theorem 5.4.3.

5.4.6 Exercise [★]: Prove Theorem 5.4.3. □

5.5 The Representation and Checking of Proofs

In previous sections, we showed how verification-condition generation can be used to verify certain properties of low-level code. The soundness theorem states that VCGen constructs a valid verification condition for an agent program only if the agent meets the safety policy. One way to verify the validity of the verification condition is to witness a derivation using a sound system of proof rules. In PCC such a derivation must be attached to the untrusted code so that the Checker module can find and check it. For this to work properly in practice, we need a framework for encoding proofs of logical formulas so that they are relatively compact and easy to check. We would like to have a framework and not just one proof checker for a given logic because we want to be able to change the set of axioms and inference rules as we adapt PCC to different safety policies. We would like to be able to adapt proof checking to other safety policies with as few changes to the infrastructure as possible. In this section we present a logical framework derived from the Edinburgh Logical Framework (Harper, Honsell, and Plotkin, 1993), along with associated proof representation and proof checking algorithms, that have the following desirable properties:

- The framework can be used to encode judgments and derivations from a wide variety of logics, including first-order and higher-order logics.
- The implementation of the proof checker is parameterized by a high-level description of the logic. This allows a unique implementation of the proof checker to be used with many logics and safety policies.

- The proof checker performs a directed, one-pass inspection of the proof object, without having to perform search. This leads to a simple implementation of the proof checker that is easy to trust and install in existing extensible systems.

- Even though the proof representation is detailed, it is also compact.

The above desiderata are important not only for proof-carrying code but for any application where proofs are represented and manipulated explicitly. One such application is a proof-generating theorem prover. A theorem prover that generates an explicit proof object for each successfully proved predicate enables a distrustful user to verify the validity of the proved theorem by checking the proof object. This effectively eliminates the need to trust the soundness of the theorem prover at the relatively small expense of having to trust a much simpler proof checker.

The first impulse when designing efficient proof representation and validation algorithms is to specialize them to a given logic or a class of related logics. For example, we might define the representation and validation algorithms by cases, with one case for each proof rule in the logic. This approach has the major disadvantage that new algorithms must be designed and implemented for each logic. To make matters worse, the size of such proof checking implementations grow with the number of proof rules in the logic. We would prefer instead to use general algorithms parameterized by a high-level description of the particular logic of interest.

We choose the Edinburgh Logical Framework (LF) as the starting point in our quest for efficient proof manipulation algorithms because it scores very high on the first three of the four desirable properties listed above. Edinburgh LF is a simple variant of λ-calculus with the property that, if a predicate is represented as an LF type then any LF expression of that type is a proof of that predicate. Thus, the simple logic-independent LF type-checking algorithm can be used for checking proofs.

The Edinburgh Logical Framework

The Edinburgh Logical Framework (also referred to as LF) has been introduced by Harper, Honsell, and Plotkin (1993) as a metalanguage for high-level specification of logics. LF provides natural support for the management of binding operators and of the hypothetical and schematic judgments through LF bound variables. Consider for example, the usual formulation of the implication introduction rule IMPI in first-order logic, shown in Figure 5-5. This rule is hypothetical because the proof of the right-hand side of the implication can use the assumption that the left-hand side holds. However, there is a side condition requiring that this assumption not be used elsewhere in the proof. As we shall see below, LF can represent this side condition in a natural way by representing the assumption as a local variable bound in the proof of the right side of the implication. The fact that these techniques are supported directly by the logical framework is a crucial factor for the succinct formalization of proofs.

The LF type theory is a language with entities at three levels: objects, types and kinds, whose abstract syntax is shown below:

Kinds	K	::=	$\mathtt{Type} \mid \Pi x{:}A.K$
Types	A	::=	$a \mid A\,M \mid \Pi x{:}A_1.A_2$
Objects	M	::=	$x \mid c \mid M_1 M_2 \mid \lambda x{:}A.M$

Types are used to classify objects and similarly, kinds are used to classify types. The type $\Pi x{:}A.B$ is a dependent function type with x bound in B. In the special case when x does not occur in B, we use the more familiar notation $A \to B$. Also, Type is the base kind, a is a type constant and c is an object constant. Dependent types are covered in detail in Chapter 2.

The encoding of a logic in LF is described by an *LF signature* Σ that contains declarations for a set of LF type constants and object constants corresponding to the syntactic formula constructors and to the proof rules. For a more concrete discussion, I describe in this section the LF representation of the safety policy that we have developed for our example agent.

The syntax of the logic is described in Figure 5-10. This signature defines an LF type constant for each kind of syntactic entity in the logic: expressions (ι), formulas (o), word types (w), and structure types (s). Then, there is an LF constant declaration for each syntactic constructor, whose LF type describes the arity of the constructor and the types of the arguments and constructed value. Two of these are worth explaining. The `settype` constructor, used to represent word types of the form $\{y \mid F(y)\}$, has one argument, the function F from expressions to formulas; similarly, the `all` constructor encodes universally quantified formulas. In both of these cases, we are representing a binding in the object logic (i.e., the logic that is being represented) with a binding in LF. The major advantage of this representation is that α-equivalence and β-reduction in the object logic are supported implicitly by the similar mechanisms in LF. This *higher-order representation* strategy is essential for a concise representation of logics with binding constructs.

The LF representation function $\ulcorner\cdot\urcorner$ is defined inductively on the structure of expressions, types and formulas. For example:

$$\ulcorner P \Rightarrow (P \wedge P)\urcorner = \mathtt{imp}\ \ulcorner P\urcorner\ (\mathtt{and}\ \ulcorner P\urcorner\ \ulcorner P\urcorner)$$
$$\ulcorner \forall x.\mathtt{addr}\ x\urcorner = \mathtt{all}\ (\lambda x : \iota.\mathtt{addr}\ x)$$

ι	: Type		`true`	: o
o	: Type		`and`	: $o \to o \to o$
w	: Type		`impl`	: $o \to o \to o$
s	: Type		`all`	: $(\iota \to o) \to o$
			`eq`	: $\iota \to \iota \to o$
`zero`	: ι		`neq`	: $\iota \to \iota \to o$
`sel`	: $\iota \to \iota \to \iota$		`addr`	: $\iota \to o$
`upd`	: $\iota \to \iota \to \iota \to \iota$		`hastype`	: $\iota \to w \to o$
			`ge`	: $\iota \to \iota \to o$
`int`	: w			
`list`	: $w \to w$			
`seq1`	: $w \to s$			
`seq2`	: $w \to s \to s$			
`ptr`	: $s \to w$			
`settype`	: $(\iota \to o) \to w$			
	(*a*)			(*b*)

Figure 5-10: LF signature for the syntax of first-order predicate logic with equality and subscripted variables, showing expression (a) and predicate (b) constructors

5.5.1 EXERCISE [★]: Write the LF representation of the predicate $\forall a.a$: `ptr {int}` $\Rightarrow$ `addr` a. □

The strategy for representing proofs in LF is to define a type family "`pf`" indexed by representation of formulas. Then, we represent the proof of "F" as an LF expression having type "`pf` F." This representation strategy is called "judgments as types and derivations as objects" and was first used in the work of Harper, Honsell, and Plotkin (1993). Note that the dependent types of LF allow us to encode not only that an expression encodes a proof but also which formula it proves.

One can view the axioms and inference rules as proof constructors. This justifies representing the axioms and inference rules in a manner similar to the syntactic constructors, by means of LF constants. The signature shown in Figure 5-11 contains a fragment of the proof constructors required for the proof rules shown in Figure 5-5 (for first-order logic) and Figure 5-6 (for our safety policy). Note how the dependent types of LF can define precisely the meaning of each rule. For example, the declaration of the constant "`andi`"

$$
\begin{array}{lll}
\texttt{pf} & : & o \to \texttt{Type} \\
\\
\texttt{truei} & : & \texttt{pf true} \\
\texttt{andi} & : & \Pi p{:}o.\Pi r{:}o.\texttt{pf}\ p \to \texttt{pf}\ r \to \texttt{pf}\ (\texttt{and}\ p\ \ r) \\
\texttt{andel} & : & \Pi p{:}o.\Pi r{:}o.\texttt{pf}\ (\texttt{and}\ p\ \ r) \to \texttt{pf}\ p \\
\texttt{ander} & : & \Pi p{:}o.\Pi r{:}o.\texttt{pf}\ (\texttt{and}\ p\ \ r) \to \texttt{pf}\ r \\
\texttt{impi} & : & \Pi p{:}o.\Pi r{:}o.(\texttt{pf}\ p \to \texttt{pf}\ r) \to \texttt{pf}\ (\texttt{impl}\ \ p\ \ r) \\
\texttt{impe} & : & \Pi p{:}o.\Pi r{:}o.\texttt{pf}\ (\texttt{impl}\ \ p\ \ r) \to \texttt{pf}\ p \to \texttt{pf}\ r \\
\texttt{alli} & : & \Pi p{:}\iota \to o.(\Pi v{:}\iota.\texttt{pf}\ (p\ v)) \to \texttt{pf}\ (\texttt{all}\ \ p) \\
\texttt{alle} & : & \Pi p{:}\iota \to o.\Pi e{:}\iota.\texttt{pf}\ (\texttt{all}\ \ p) \to \texttt{pf}\ (p\ e) \\
\texttt{mem0} & : & \Pi m{:}\iota.\Pi a{:}\iota.\Pi v{:}\iota.\Pi a'{:}\iota.\texttt{pf}\ (\texttt{eq}\ a\ a') \to \texttt{pf}\ (\texttt{eq}\ (\texttt{sel}\ \ (\texttt{upd}\ m\ a\ v)\ a')\ v) \\
 & & \Pi m{:}\iota.\Pi a{:}\iota.\Pi v{:}\iota.\Pi a'{:}\iota. \\
\texttt{mem1} & : & \qquad \texttt{pf}\ (\texttt{neq}\ a\ a') \to \texttt{pf}\ (\texttt{eq}\ (\texttt{sel}\ \ (\texttt{upd}\ m\ a\ v)\ a')\ (\texttt{sel}\ \ m\ a')) \\
\\
\texttt{cons} & : & \Pi E{:}\iota.\Pi W{:}w. \\
 & & \texttt{pf}\ (\texttt{hastype}\ E\ (\texttt{list}\ W)) \to \texttt{pf}\ (\texttt{neq}\ E\ \texttt{zero}) \to \\
 & & \texttt{pf}\ (\texttt{hastype}\ E\ (\texttt{ptr}\ (\texttt{seq2}\ W\ (\texttt{seq1}\ (\texttt{list}\ W))))). \\
\texttt{set} & : & \Pi E{:}\iota.\Pi F{:}\iota \to o.\texttt{pf}\ (\texttt{hastype}\ E\ (\texttt{settype}\ F)) \to \texttt{pf}\ (F\ E).
\end{array}
$$

Figure 5-11: LF signature for safety policy proof rules

says that, in order to construct the proof of a conjunction of two predicates, one can apply the constant "andi" to four arguments, the first two being the two conjuncts and the other two being the representations of proofs of the conjuncts respectively.

The LF representation function $\ulcorner\cdot\urcorner$ is extended to derivations and is defined recursively on the derivation, as shown in the following examples (the letters $\mathcal{D}$ are used to name sub-derivations):

$$\ulcorner \frac{\begin{array}{cc}\mathcal{D}_1 & \mathcal{D}_2 \\ F_1 & F_2\end{array}}{F1 \wedge F_2} \urcorner = \texttt{andi}\ \ulcorner F_1 \urcorner\ \ulcorner F_2 \urcorner\ \ulcorner \mathcal{D}_1 \urcorner\ \ulcorner \mathcal{D}_2 \urcorner$$

$$\ulcorner \frac{\begin{array}{c} F_1 \\ \vdots\ \mathcal{D}^u \\ F_2 \end{array}}{F_1 \Rightarrow F_2} \urcorner = \texttt{impi}\ \ulcorner F_1 \urcorner\ \ulcorner F_2 \urcorner\ (\lambda u{:}\texttt{pf}\ \ulcorner F_1 \urcorner.\ulcorner \mathcal{D}^u \urcorner)$$

$$M \;=\; \texttt{impi}\ \ulcorner F\urcorner\ (\texttt{and}\ \ulcorner F\urcorner\ \ulcorner F\urcorner)\ (\lambda x{:}\texttt{pf}\ \ulcorner F\urcorner.\texttt{andi}\ \ulcorner F\urcorner\ \ulcorner F\urcorner\ x\ x)$$

Figure 5-12: LF representation of a proof of $F \Rightarrow (F \wedge F)$

In the representation of the implication introduction proof rule, the letter u is the name of the assumption that F_1 holds. Note how the representation encodes the constraint that this assumptions must be local to the proof of F_2.

To conclude the presentation of the LF representation, consider the proof of the formula "$F \Rightarrow (F \wedge F)$." The LF representation of this proof is shown in Figure 5-12.

5.5.2 EXERCISE [★]: Write the LF representation of the proof of the formula $\forall a.a$: `ptr {int}` $\Rightarrow$ `addr` a, using the proof rules from our safety policy. □

The LF Type System

The main advantage of using LF for proof representation is that proof validity can be checked by a simple type-checking algorithm. That is, to check that the LF object M is the representation of a valid proof of the predicate F we use the LF typing rules (to be presented below) to verify that M has type `pf` $\ulcorner F\urcorner$ in the context of the signature Σ declaring the valid proof rules.

Type checking in the LF type system is defined by means of four judgments described below:

$\Gamma \overset{LF}{\vdash} A : K$	A is a valid type of kind K
$\Gamma \overset{LF}{\vdash} M : A$	M is a valid object of type A
$A \equiv_{\beta\eta} B$	type A is $\beta\eta$-equivalent to type B
$M \equiv_{\beta\eta} N$	object M is $\beta\eta$-equivalent to object N

where Γ is a typing context assigning types to LF variables. These typing judgment are with respect to a given signature Σ.

The derivation rules for the LF typing judgments are shown in Figure 5-13. For the $\beta\eta$-equivalence judgments we omit the rules that define it to be an equivalence and a congruence.

As an example of how LF type checking is used to perform proof checking, consider LF term M shown in Figure 5-12, representing a proof of the predicate $F \Rightarrow (F \wedge F$ by implication introduction followed by conjunction introduction. It is easy to verify, given the LF typing rules and the declaration of the

Types $\boxed{\Gamma \overset{LF}{\vdash} A : K}$

$$\frac{\Sigma(a) = K}{\Gamma \overset{LF}{\vdash} a : K}$$

$$\frac{\Gamma \overset{LF}{\vdash} A : \Pi x{:}B.K \qquad \Gamma \overset{LF}{\vdash} M : B}{\Gamma \overset{LF}{\vdash} A\, M : [^{M}/_{x}]K}$$

$$\frac{\Gamma \overset{LF}{\vdash} A : \mathsf{Type} \qquad \Gamma, x : A \overset{LF}{\vdash} B : \mathsf{Type}}{\Gamma \overset{LF}{\vdash} \Pi x{:}A.B : \mathsf{Type}}$$

Objects $\boxed{\Gamma \overset{LF}{\vdash} M : A}$

$$\frac{\Sigma(c) = A}{\Gamma \overset{LF}{\vdash} c : A}$$

$$\frac{\Gamma(x) = A}{\Gamma \overset{LF}{\vdash} x : A}$$

$$\frac{\Gamma, x : A \overset{LF}{\vdash} M : B}{\Gamma \overset{LF}{\vdash} \lambda x{:}A.M : \Pi x{:}A.B}$$

$$\frac{\Gamma \overset{LF}{\vdash} M : \Pi x{:}A.B \qquad \Gamma \overset{LF}{\vdash} N : A}{\Gamma \overset{LF}{\vdash} MN : [^{N}/_{x}]B}$$

$$\frac{\Gamma \overset{LF}{\vdash} M : A \qquad A \equiv_{\beta\eta} B}{\Gamma \overset{LF}{\vdash} M : B}$$

Equivalence $\boxed{M \equiv_{\beta\eta} N}$

$$(\lambda x{:}A.M)N \equiv_{\beta\eta} [^{N}/_{x}]M$$

Figure 5-13: The LF type system

constants involved, that this proof has the LF type "pf (imp$\ulcorner F \urcorner$ (and$\ulcorner F \urcorner$ $\ulcorner F \urcorner$))." The adequacy of LF type checking for proof checking in the logic under consideration is stated formally in the Theorems 5.5.3 and 5.5.4 below. These theorems follow immediately from lemmas proved in Harper, Honsell, and Plotkin (1993). They continue to hold if the logic is extended with new expression and predicate constructors.

5.5.3 **Theorem [Adequacy of syntax representation]:**

1. If E is a closed expression, then $\cdot \overset{LF}{\vdash} \ulcorner E \urcorner : \iota$. If M is a closed LF object such that $\cdot \overset{LF}{\vdash} M : \iota$, then there exists an expression E such that $\ulcorner E \urcorner \equiv_{\beta\eta} M$.
2. If W is a word-type, then $\cdot \overset{LF}{\vdash} \ulcorner W \urcorner : w$. If M is a closed LF object such that $\cdot \overset{LF}{\vdash} M : w$, then there exists a word type W such that $\ulcorner W \urcorner \equiv_{\beta\eta} M$.
3. If S is a structured type, then $\cdot \overset{LF}{\vdash} \ulcorner S \urcorner : s$. If M is a closed LF object such that $\cdot \overset{LF}{\vdash} M : s$, then there exists a structured type S such that $\ulcorner S \urcorner \equiv_{\beta\eta} M$.
4. If F is a closed formula, then $\cdot \overset{LF}{\vdash} \ulcorner F \urcorner : o$. If M is a closed LF object such that $\cdot \overset{LF}{\vdash} M : o$, then there exists a formula F such that $\ulcorner F \urcorner \equiv_{\beta\eta} M$. □

5.5.4 **Theorem [Adequacy of Derivation Representation]:**

1. If $\mathcal{D}$ is a derivation of F then $\cdot \overset{LF}{\vdash} \ulcorner \mathcal{D} \urcorner :$ pf $\ulcorner F \urcorner$.

2. If M is a closed LF object such that $\cdot \overset{LF}{\vdash} M : \mathtt{pf}\ \ulcorner F \urcorner$, then there exists a derivation $\mathcal{D}$ of F such that $\ulcorner \mathcal{D} \urcorner \equiv_{\beta\eta} M$. □

In the context of PCC, Theorem 5.5.4(2) says that if the agent producer can exhibit an LF object having the type "$\mathtt{pf}\ \ulcorner VC \urcorner$" then there is a derivation of the verification condition within the logic, which in turn means that the verification condition is valid and the agent code satisfies the safety policy.

Owing to the simplicity of the LF type system, the implementation of the type checker is simple and easy to trust. Furthermore, because all of the dependencies on the particular object logic are separated in the signature, the implementation of the type checker can be reused directly for proof checking in various first-order or higher-order logics. The only logic-dependent component of the proof checker is the signature, which is usually easy to verify by visual inspection.

Unfortunately, the above-mentioned advantages of LF representation of proofs come at a high price. The typical LF representation of a proof is large, due to a significant amount of redundancy. This fact can already be seen in the proof representation shown in Figure 5-12, where there are six copies of F as opposed to only three in the predicate to be proved. The effect of redundancy observed in practice increases non-linearly with the size of the proofs. Consider for example, the representation of the proof of the n-way conjunction $F \wedge \ldots \wedge F$. Depending on how balanced is the binary tree representing this predicate, the number of copies of F in the proof representation ranges from an expected value of $n \log n$ (when the tree is perfectly balanced) to a worse case value of $n^2/2$ (when the tree degenerates into a list). The redundancy of representation is not only a space problem but also leads to inefficient proof checking, because all of the redundant copies have to be type checked and then checked for equivalence with instances of F from the predicate to be proved.

The proof representation and checking framework presented in the next section is based on the observation that it is possible to retain only the skeleton of an LF representation of a proof and to use a modified LF type-checking algorithm to reconstruct on the fly the missing parts. The resulting *implicit LF* (or LF_i) representation inherits the advantages of the LF representation (i.e., small and logic-independent implementation of the proof checker) without the disadvantages (i.e., large proof sizes and slow proof checking).

Implicit LF

The solution to the redundancy problem is to eliminate the redundant subterms from the proof. In most cases we can eliminate all copies of a given subterm from the proof and rely instead on the copy that exists within the predicate to be proved, which is constructed by the VCGen and is trusted to be well formed. But now the code receiver will be receiving proofs with missing subterms. One possible strategy is for the code receiver to reconstruct the original form of the proof and then to use the simple LF type checking algorithm to validate it. But this does not save proof-checking time and requires significantly more working memory than the size of the incoming LF_i proof. Instead, we modify the LF type-checking algorithm to reconstruct the missing subterms while it performs type checking. One major advantage of this strategy is that terms that are reconstructed based on copies from the verification condition do not need to be type checked themselves.

We will not show the formal details of the type reconstruction algorithm but will show instead how it operates on a simple example. For expository purposes, the missing proof subterms are marked with placeholders, written as $*$. Consider now the proof of the predicate $F \Rightarrow (F \wedge F)$ of Figure 5-12. If we replace all copies of "F" with placeholders we get the following LF_i object:

$$\texttt{impi}\ *_1\ *_2\ (\lambda u{:}*_3.\texttt{andi}\ *_4\ *_5\ u\ u)$$

This implicit proof captures the structure of the proof without any redundant information. The subterms marked with placeholders can be recovered while verifying that the term has type "pf (impl$\ulcorner F \urcorner$ (and$\ulcorner F \urcorner$ $\ulcorner F \urcorner$))," as described below.

Reconstruction starts by recognizing the top-level constructor impi. The expected type of the entire term, "pf (impl $\ulcorner F \urcorner$ (and $\ulcorner F \urcorner$ $\ulcorner F \urcorner$))," is "matched" against the result type of the impi constant, as given by the signature Σ. The result of this matching is an instantiation for placeholders 1 and 2 and a residual type-checking constraint for the explicit argument of impi, as follows:

$$\begin{array}{rcl} *_1 & \equiv & \ulcorner F \urcorner \\ *_2 & \equiv & \texttt{and}\ \ulcorner F \urcorner\ \ulcorner F \urcorner \\ \vdash\ (\lambda u{:}*_3.\texttt{andi}\ *_4\ *_5\ u\ u) & : & \texttt{pf}\ \ulcorner F \urcorner \to \texttt{pf}\ (\texttt{and}\ \ulcorner F \urcorner\ \ulcorner F \urcorner) \end{array}$$

Reconstruction continues with the remaining type-checking constraint. From its type we can recover the value of placeholder 3 and a typing constraint for the body:

$$\begin{array}{rcl} *_3 & \equiv & \texttt{pf}\ \ulcorner F \urcorner \\ u{:}\texttt{pf}\ \ulcorner F \urcorner \vdash\ \texttt{andi}\ *_4\ *_5\ u\ u & : & \texttt{pf}\ (\texttt{and}\ \ulcorner F \urcorner\ \ulcorner F \urcorner) \end{array}$$

Now andi is the top-level constant and by matching its result type as declared in the signature with the goal type of the constraint we get the instantiation for placeholders 4 and 5 and two residual typing constraints:

$$
\begin{array}{rcl}
*_4 & \equiv & \ulcorner F \urcorner \\
*_5 & \equiv & \ulcorner F \urcorner \\
u{:}\mathtt{pf}\,\ulcorner F \urcorner \vdash u & : & \mathtt{pf}\,\ulcorner F \urcorner \\
u{:}\mathtt{pf}\,\ulcorner F \urcorner \vdash u & : & \mathtt{pf}\,\ulcorner F \urcorner
\end{array}
$$

The remaining two constraints are solved by the variable typing rule. Note that this step involves verifying the equivalence of the objects $\ulcorner F \urcorner$ from the assumption and the goal. This concludes the reconstruction and checking of the entire proof. We reconstructed the full representation of the proof by instantiating all placeholders with well-typed LF objects. We know that these instantiations are well-typed because they are ultimately extracted from the original constraint type, which is assumed to contain only well-typed subterms.

The formalization of the reconstruction algorithm described informally above is in two stages. First, we show a variant of the LF type system, called implicit LF or LF$_i$, that extends LF with placeholders. This type system has the property that all well-typed LF$_i$ terms can be reconstructed to well-typed LF terms. However, unlike the original LF type system, the LF$_i$ type system is not amenable to a direct implementation of deterministic type checking. Instead, we use a separate reconstruction algorithm.

An object M is fully reconstructed, or fully explicit, when it is placeholder free. We write PF(M) to denote this property. We extend this notation to type environments and write PF(Γ) to denote that all types assigned in Γ to variables are placeholder free.

The LF$_i$ typing rules are an extension of the LF typing rules with two new typing rules for dealing with implicit abstraction and placeholders, and one new β-equivalence rule dealing with implicit abstraction. These additions are shown in Figure 5-14. The LF$_i$ typing judgment is written $\Gamma \overset{i}{\vdash} M : A$.

Note that according to the LF$_i$ type system placeholders cannot occur on a function position, but only as arguments in an application. This restriction allows us to simplify the reconstruction algorithm by avoiding higher-order unification. Note also that several LF$_i$ rules require that the types involved do not contain placeholders. This restriction simplifies greatly the proofs of soundness of the reconstruction algorithms and does not seem to diminish the effectiveness of the LF$_i$ representation.

A quick analysis of the LF$_i$ typing rules reveals that they are not directly useful for type checking or type inference. The main reason is that type checking an application involves "guessing" appropriate A and N. The type A can sometimes be recovered from the type of the application head, but the term

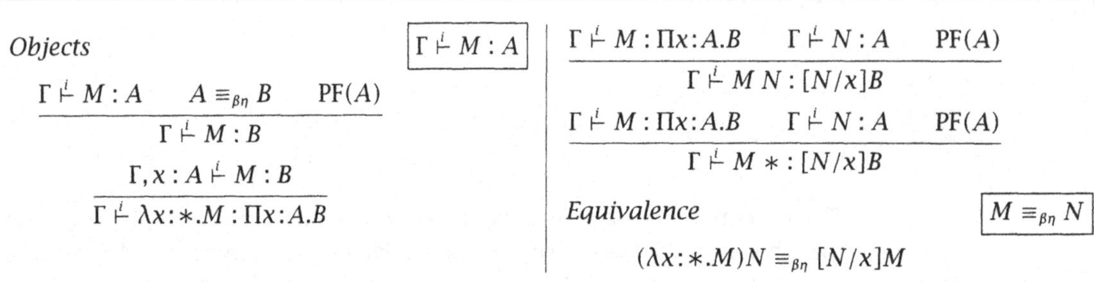

Figure 5-14: The rules that are new in the LF_i type system

N in an application to a placeholder cannot be found easily in general. This is not a problem for us because we need the LF_i type-system only as a step in proving the correctness of the type-reconstruction algorithm, and not as the basis for an implementation of a type-checking algorithm.

The only property of interest of the LF_i type system is that once we have a typing derivation we can reconstruct the object involved and a corresponding LF typing derivation for it. To make this more precise we introduce the notation $M \nearrow M'$ to denote that M' is a fully-reconstructed version of the implicit object M (i.e., $\text{PF}(M')$). This means that M' can be obtained from M by replacing all of its placeholders with fully-explicit LF objects. Note that the reconstruction relation is not a function as there might be several reconstructions of a given implicit object or type.

5.5.5 THEOREM [SOUNDNESS OF LF_i TYPING]: If $\Gamma \overset{i}{\vdash} M : A$ and $\text{PF}(\Gamma)$, $\text{PF}(A)$, then there exists M' such that $M \nearrow M'$ and $\Gamma \overset{LF}{\vdash} M' : A$. □

5.5.6 EXERCISE [★★, ↛]: Prove Theorem 5.5.5 □

5.6 Proof Generation

We have seen that a successfully checked proof of the verification condition guarantees that the verification condition is valid, which in turn guarantees that the code adheres to the safety policy. The PCC infrastructure is simple, easy-to-trust and automatic. But this is only because all the difficult tasks have been delegated to the code and proof producers. The first difficult task, besides writing code that is indeed safe, is to generate the code annotations consisting of loop invariants for all loops and of function specifications for all

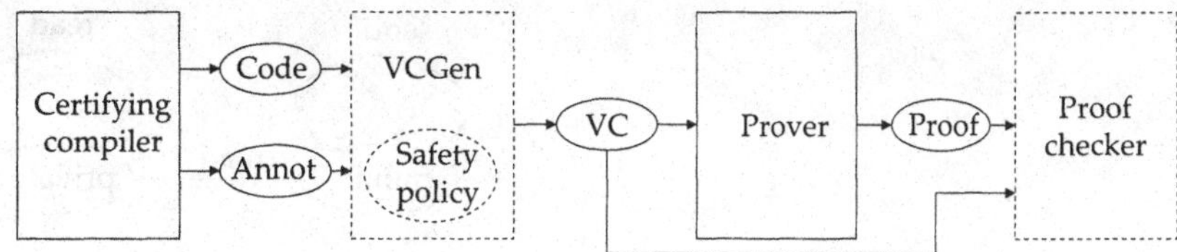

Figure 5-15: Interaction between untrusted PCC tools (continuous lines) and trusted PCC infrastructure (interrupted lines)

local functions. The other difficult task is to prove the verification condition produced by the verification-condition generator.

Fortunately there are important situations when both the generation of the annotations and of the proof can be automated. Consider the situation in which there exists a high-level language, perhaps a domain-specific one, in which the safety policy is guaranteed to be satisfied by a combination of static and run-time checks. For example, if the safety policy is memory safety then any memory-safe high-level language can be used. The key insight is that in these systems the safety policy is guaranteed to hold by the design of the static and run-time checks. In essence, the high-level type checker acts as a theorem prover. All we have to do is to show that a sufficient number and kind of static and run-time checks have been performed.

Figure 5-15 shows the interaction between the untrusted PCC tools used by the code producer and the trusted PCC infrastructure used by the code receiver. The annotations are generated automatically by a *certifying compiler* from high-level language to assembly language. For safety policies that follow closely the high-level type system, it is surprisingly easy for a compiler to produce the loop invariants, which are essentially conjunctions of type declarations for the live registers at the given program point. This is information that the compiler can easily maintain and emit.

Before it can generate the required proofs, the code producer must pass the annotated code to a local copy of VCGen. The proof itself is generated by a theorem prover customized for the specific safety policy. As discussed in Section 5.3, such a theorem prover is little more than a type checker. However, unlike a regular type checker or theorem prover, the PCC theorem prover must generate explicit representation of the proofs. The architecture shown in Figure 5-15 is described in detail in Necula (1998).

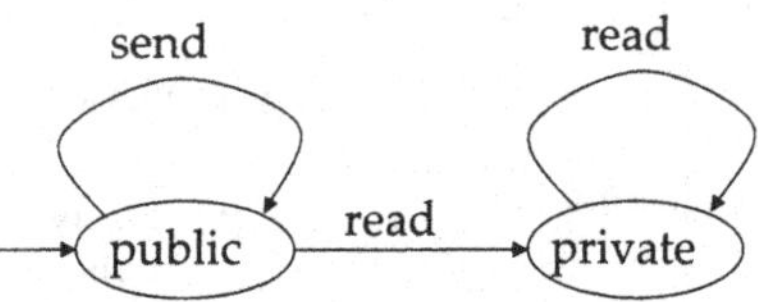

Figure 5-16: A privacy policy

5.7 PCC beyond Types

The presentation of PCC so far has focused on type-based safety policies. We have shown that verification condition generation followed by theorem proving can overcome many of the difficulties of type checking programs written in low-level languages. It should be obvious that we can take the example that we used so far and change the type system by simply changing the proof rules, with no changes to the infrastructure itself. But the machinery we have constructed in the process can be used to enforce more complex safety policies than are usually associated with types. And we can do this with very few changes, thanks both to the modular design of the infrastructure and to the choice of using the lower-level mechanism of logic rather than committing to a high-level type system. However, every time the set of proof rules is changed, one must redo the proof of soundness. In this section, we explore one example of a safety policy that goes beyond types.

Consider a safety policy that allows access to two host services: *read* the contents of a local file and *send* data over the network. The host wishes to enforce the policy that the agent cannot send data after it has read local files. This is a conservative way to ensure that no local file contents will be leaked. This example is taken from Schneider (2000).

This safety policy can be described using the state machine shown in Figure 5-16. Initially the agent is in the `public` state in which it can use both the `send` and the `read` services. However, once it uses the `read` service the agent transitions in the `private` state, in which it can use only the `read` service.

In order to enforce such a safety policy, it is sufficient to check that the `send` service cannot be used after the `read` service has been used. At the level of assembly language, these services would be most likely implemented as function calls. In that case the privacy safety policy can be implemented as a precondition on the `send` function. Instead of introducing a general mechanism for handling function calls (see Exercise 5.3.5), we use a special-purpose handling of the instructions `call read` and `call send`.

In the presentation of PCC from previous sections, there is no element of the state of the computation that reflects whether a certain function has been invoked or not. One way to address this issue is to require that the agent code keep track of its own public/private state at run-time, presumably in a register or a memory location. Then the postcondition of `read` would require that this state element reflect the `private` state and the precondition of `send` would require that the state element reflect the `public` state. This strategy is appropriate when the producer of the agent code wishes to use run-time checking to enforce the safety policy, in which case it would have to prove that the appropriate checks have been inserted. This strategy also has the benefit of not requiring any changes in the PCC infrastructure.

We will pursue another alternative. We will modify VCGen and the symbolic evaluator to keep track of the public/private state. And since we prefer to extend the PCC infrastructure with a general-purpose mechanism rather than a specific policy, the VCGen extension should be able to record any information about the *history* of the execution, not just its public/private state.

For this purpose we extend the symbolic evaluation state with another pseudo-register, called $\mathtt{r}_H$ to store a sequence of interesting events in the past of the computation. The set of symbolic expressions that this register can have are shown below:

$$\begin{array}{llcl} \text{Histories} & H & ::= & x \mid \mathtt{event}\ V\ H \\ \text{Events} & V & ::= & \mathtt{init} \mid \mathtt{read} \mid \mathtt{send} \end{array}$$

Additionally we add a number of formulas that we can use for stating properties of the history of execution:

$$\text{Formulas} \quad F \quad ::= \quad \ldots \mid \mathtt{publicState}\ H \mid \mathtt{privateState}\ H$$

As usual when we extend the language of formulas we must also extend the proof rules. For our safety policy we add the following three proof rules:

$$\mathtt{publicState}\ (\mathtt{event}\ \mathtt{init}\ H) \qquad \text{(INIT)}$$

$$\frac{\mathtt{publicState}\ H}{\mathtt{publicState}\ (\mathtt{event}\ \mathtt{send}\ H)} \qquad \text{(SEND)}$$

$$\mathtt{privateState}\ (\mathtt{event}\ \mathtt{read}\ H) \qquad \text{(READ)}$$

The definition of the VCGen and the symbolic evaluator can remain unchanged for the instructions considered so far, except that the $\mathtt{r}_H$ register can be used in loop invariants and function preconditions and postconditions. In particular, for the privacy safety policy the invocations of the `read` and send services can be handled in the symbolic evaluator as follows:

$$SE(i,\sigma) = \begin{cases} \ldots & \\ SE(i+1, \sigma[\mathtt{r}_H \leftarrow (\sigma\ (\mathtt{event\ read\ r}_H))]) & \text{if } \Pi_i = \mathtt{call\ read} \\ \mathtt{publicState}\ (\sigma\ \mathtt{r}_H) \wedge & \text{if } \Pi_i = \mathtt{call\ send} \\ SE(i+1, \sigma[\mathtt{r}_H \leftarrow (\sigma\ (\mathtt{event\ send\ r}_H))]) & \end{cases}$$

The symbolic evaluator extends the history state with information about the services that were used. Additionally, the send call requires through its precondition that the history of the computation be consistent with the public state of the safety policy. A realistic symbolic evaluator would support a general-purpose function call instruction, in which case the effect of the read and send functions could be achieved by appropriate function preconditions and postconditions.

5.7.1 EXERCISE [★★, ↛]: Add two actions lock *e* and unlock *e* that can be used to acquire and release a lock that is denoted by the expression *e*. Define a PCC safety policy (extensions to the logic, new proof rules and changes to the symbolic evaluator) that requires correct use of locks: a lock cannot be acquired or released twice in a row, and the agent must release all locks upon return. □

5.7.2 EXERCISE [★★, ↛]: The verification-condition generator that we described in Section 5.3 cannot enforce a safety policy that allows the agent to "probe" the accessibility of a memory page by attempting a read from an address within that page. This is a common way to check for stack overflow in many systems. Show how you can change the symbolic evaluator to use the history register for the purpose of specifying such a safety policy. □

This example shows how to use PCC for safety policies that go beyond type checking. In fact, PCC is extremely powerful in this sense. Any safety policy that could be enforced by an interpreter using run-time checking could in principle be enforced by PCC. A major advantage of PCC over interpreters is that it can check properties that would be very expensive to check at run time. Consider, for example, how complicated it would be to write an interpreter that enforces at run-time a fine grained memory safety policy. Each memory word would have to be instrumented with information whether it is accessible or not. By comparison, we can use PCC along with a strong type system to achieve the same effect, with no run-time penalty.

5.8 Conclusion

Below is a list of the most important ways in which PCC improves over other existing techniques for enforcing safe execution of untrusted code:

- PCC operates at **load time** before the agent code is installed in the host system. This is in contrast with techniques that enforce the safety policy by relying on extensive run-time checking or even interpretation. As a result PCC agents run at native-code speed, which can be ten times faster than interpreted agents (written for example using Java bytecode) or 30% faster than agents whose memory operations are checked at run time.

  Additionally, by doing the checking at load time it becomes possible to enforce certain safety policies that are hard or impossible to enforce at run time. For example, by examining the code of the agent and the associated "explanation" PCC can verify that a certain interrupt routine terminates within a given number of instructions executed or that a video frame rendering agent can keep up with a given frame rate. Run-time enforcement of timing properties of such fine granularity is hard.

- The trusted computing base in PCC is **small**. PCC is simple and small because it has to do a relatively simple task. In particular, PCC does not have to discover on its own whether and why the agent meets the safety policy.
- For the same reason, PCC can operate even on agents expressed in **native-code** form. And because PCC can verify the code after compilation and optimization, the checked code is ready to run without needing an additional interpreter or compiler on the host. This has serious software engineering advantages since it reduces the amount of security critical code and it is also a benefit when the host environment is too small to contain an interpreter or a compiler, such as is the case for many embedded software systems.

- PCC is **general.** All PCC has to do is to verify safety explanations and to match them with the code and the safety policy. By standardizing a language for expressing the explanations and a formalism for expressing the safety policies, it is possible to implement a single algorithm that can perform the required check, for any agent code, any valid explanation and a large class of safety policies. In this sense a single implementation of PCC can be used for checking a variety of safety policies.

The PCC infrastructure is designed to complement a cryptographic authentication infrastructure. While cryptographic techniques such as digital signatures can be used by the host to verify external properties of the agent program, such as freshness and authenticity, or the author's identity, the PCC infrastructure checks internal semantic properties of the code such as what the code does and what it does not do. This enables the host to prevent safety breaches due to either malicious intent (for agents originating from untrusted sources) or due to programming errors (for agents originating from trusted sources).

However, proof-carrying code is not without costs. The most notable challenge to using PCC is the difficulty of producing code annotations and proofs. In some cases, these can be produced automatically based on some high-level language invariants. But in general a human is required to be involved and the more complex the safety policy the more onerous the burden of proof can be expected to be. All that PCC offers in this direction is a way to shift this burden from the code received to the code producer who can be expected to have more computational power, and especially more knowledge of why the code satisfies the safety policy.

Proof-carrying code is a witness to the fact that programming language technology and type theory are the basis of valuable techniques for solving practical engineering problems. However, in the process of applying these techniques for the design of a PCC infrastructure, it became necessary to adapt the off-the-shelf techniques in non-trivial ways to the particular application domain. Some of that adaptation can be carried out in a theoretical setting, such as the extension of Edinburgh LF to implicit LF, while other parts involve real engineering.

Part III

Types and Reasoning about Programs

6 *Logical Relations and a Case Study in Equivalence Checking*

Karl Crary

Logical relations are a fundamental technique for proving properties of programming languages. Logical relations arise when a property is to be proven of all well-formed terms in the language, but that property is not preserved by one or more of the language's elimination forms. For example, one such property is termination: if a function expression t_{fun} and its argument t_{arg} both terminate, it does not follow that the application of t_{fun} to t_{arg} necessarily terminates.

In cases such as this, it is impossible to prove directly by induction on typing derivations that all well-formed terms enjoy the property in question. However, such a property may nevertheless be true; for example, normalization holds for all well-typed terms in the simply typed lambda-calculus (*TAPL*, Chapter 12). Logical relations surmount this difficulty by proving a stronger property based on a term's type. In the example above, for t_{fun} one would show (informally speaking) not only that t_{fun} itself terminates, but also that any application of t_{fun} to a terminating argument also terminates.

The classic application of logical relations is to prove various sorts of termination properties, especially *strong normalization* (Tait, 1967). A very simple example of a logical relation argument is given in *TAPL*, Chapter 12, to prove a simple termination result. However, the technique has wide applicability beyond just termination properties. This chapter will develop the technique of logical relations via a case study in decision procedures for equivalence of terms. Then, the next chapter will exploit this technique in developing a powerful theory of typed operational reasoning.

This chapter draws on material from *TAPL*, Chapters 1 through 12, 23, and 29. As usual, we will identify terms that differ only in the names of bound variables, and our substitution is capture avoiding. (Recall *TAPL*, §5.3.)

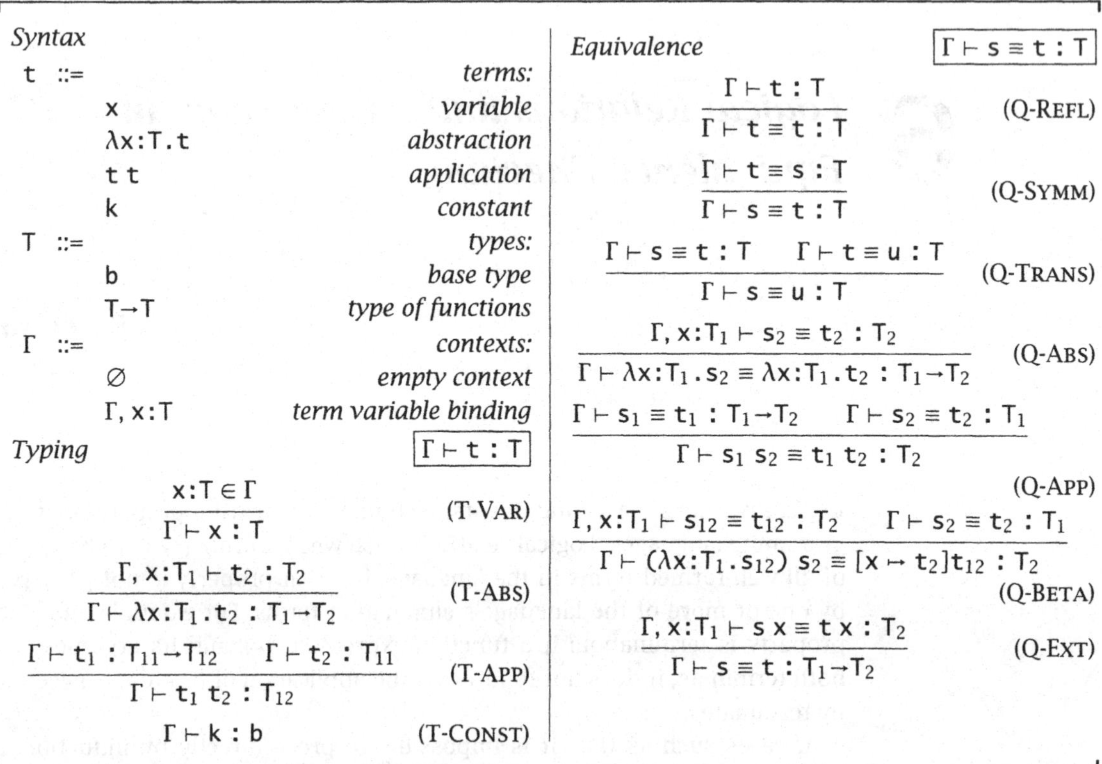

Figure 6-1: Simply typed lambda-calculus with a base type ($\lambda_{\to b}$)

6.1 The Equivalence Problem

We are concerned with the problem of determining whether or not two terms in the simply typed lambda calculus are equivalent. The system we will consider is formulated in Figure 6-1. In order that the problem not be trivial, the system includes a single base type b that is inhabited by an unspecified set of constants. The constants are ranged over by the metavariable k.

The equivalence judgment, which will be our key subject of concern, is written $\Gamma \vdash s \equiv t : T$, meaning that (in context Γ) the terms s and t are equivalent, when considered as members of the type T. (The alert reader may observe that the type T at which terms are compared does not play an important role in the rules in Figure 6-1; however, it will be of critical importance in our future developments.) It is important to observe that this notion of equivalence is defined directly, rather than by an appeal to an operational semantics. For this reason, this form of equivalence is often referred to as *definitional equivalence.*

The equivalence system consists of seven rules. The first three rules express that term equivalence is an equivalence relation, and the next two rules express that it is a congruence with respect to abstraction and application. Finally, there are two substantiative rules. The first expresses that a beta redex is equivalent to its contractum. The second is an *extensionality* principle; it says that two functions (i.e., terms of type $T_1 \to T_2$) are equivalent if all applications to an argument are equivalent.[1] (A variable is used to stand in for all possible arguments.)

Motivation

Term equivalence is important for a variety of reasons, but one of the most important applications of the system relates not to the equivalence of terms, but of *types.* Recall the language λ_ω from *TAPL,* Chapter 29. In λ_ω the type system provided type expressions of higher kind in order to provide a facility for type operators. As a result, the type system of λ_ω was essentially a copy of the simply typed lambda calculus "one level up," in which terms became types and types became kinds.

Conversely, we may view the simply typed lambda calculus as the type system of λ_ω viewed "one level down," in which types become terms and kinds become types. Thus, the type b in $\lambda_{\to b}$ corresponds to the kind $*$ of types in λ_ω. By solving the problem of checking equivalence of terms, we also learn how to check equivalence of types, which is in turn essential to the problem of type checking.

Note that $\lambda_{\to b}$ contains no *actual* terms standing for types such as Nat; they correspond to the uninterpreted constants k of type b. Terms standing for built-in type operators such as $\to$ would correspond to constants of type b$\to$b$\to$b. For simplicity, we include no such built-in operators, but they would be easy to add.

6.2 Non-Type-Directed Equivalence Checking

The most common strategy for checking for term equivalence is *normalize-and-compare.* To determine whether two well-typed terms, say s and t, are

1. Although extensionality considerably broadens definitional equivalence, many systems prefer to omit extensionality because it can sometimes complicate equivalence checking. However, for the approach to equivalence checking we discuss in this chapter, extensionality actually simplifies matters, so we do not hesitate to include it.

equal, the strategy computes their normal forms s' and t' using a reduction relation derived from the equivalence rules and then compares to see if s' and t' are identical.[2] The original terms s and t are equivalent if and only if the normal forms s' and t' are identical.

Normalize-and-compare relies on three facts:

- One must be able to derive a reduction relation $s \Rightarrow t$ from the equivalence rules. This relation must be suitable in the sense that, if $\Gamma \vdash s : T$ and $\Gamma \vdash t : T$, then $\Gamma \vdash s \equiv t : T$ iff $s \Leftrightarrow^* t$, where $\Leftrightarrow^*$ is the symmetric, transitive closure of $\Rightarrow$. For $\lambda_{\to b}$ a suitable relation is given in Figure 6-2.

- The reduction relation must be *confluent,* meaning that if $r \Rightarrow^* s$ and $r \Rightarrow^* t$ then there exists some term u such that $s \Rightarrow^* u$ and $t \Rightarrow^* u$. If the relation is confluent, then its symmetric, transitive closure may be decided by comparing normal forms, as stated by Lemma 6.2.1 below.

- The reduction relation must be *normalizing,* meaning that every term must have a normal form, and those normal forms must be effectively computable. Given the existence and computability of normal forms, one may use the preceding two facts to show that two terms are equivalent exactly when their normal forms coincide.

6.2.1 LEMMA: Suppose $\Rightarrow$ is confluent and the normal forms of s and t are s' and t'. Then $s \Leftrightarrow^* t$ iff $s' = t'$. □

Proof: Exercise [★★, ↛]. □

In summary, to employ the normalize-and-compare strategy, one must define a suitable reduction relation, and prove that it is suitable, confluent, and normalizing. In some cases, the strategy is not applicable, either because the suitable relation fails to be confluent and normalizing, or because no suitable relation can be defined in the first place. It is this latter case that will arise in the next section. In fact, many proofs of normalization employ a logical relation (such as those in the presence of polymorphism [Girard, Lafont, and Taylor, 1989]), so the normalize-and-compare strategy, even when applicable, often still involves logical relations.

6.2.2 EXERCISE [★★]: Prove one half of the suitability of $\Rightarrow$ for definitional equivalence: if $\Gamma \vdash s \equiv t : T$ then $s \Leftrightarrow^* t$. (Hint: in the case for Q-EXT, use the reduction rule QR-ETA.) □

2. Actually, nearly all implementations of equivalence checkers refine this strategy to interleave comparison with the computation of normal forms. This is done for two reasons: First, if the terms are inequivalent, it can be detected earlier. Second, once any corresponding components of the normal forms are determined to be equivalent, they can be discarded. Thus, one can avoid storing the entire normal forms, which can be large.

Parallel reduction $\boxed{s \Rightarrow t}$

$$t \Rightarrow t \qquad \text{(QR-REFL)}$$

$$\frac{s_2 \Rightarrow t_2}{\lambda x{:}T_1.s_2 \Rightarrow \lambda x{:}T_1.t_2} \qquad \text{(QR-ABS)}$$

$$\frac{s_1 \Rightarrow t_1 \qquad s_2 \Rightarrow t_2}{s_1\ s_2 \Rightarrow t_1\ t_2} \qquad \text{(QR-APP)}$$

$$\frac{s_1 \Rightarrow t_1 \qquad s_2 \Rightarrow t_2}{(\lambda x{:}T_1.s_1)\ s_2 \Rightarrow [x \mapsto t_2]t_1} \qquad \text{(QR-BETA)}$$

$$\frac{s \Rightarrow t \qquad x \text{ not free in } s}{\lambda x{:}T.s\ x \Rightarrow t} \qquad \text{(QR-ETA)}$$

Figure 6-2: Parallel reduction of terms

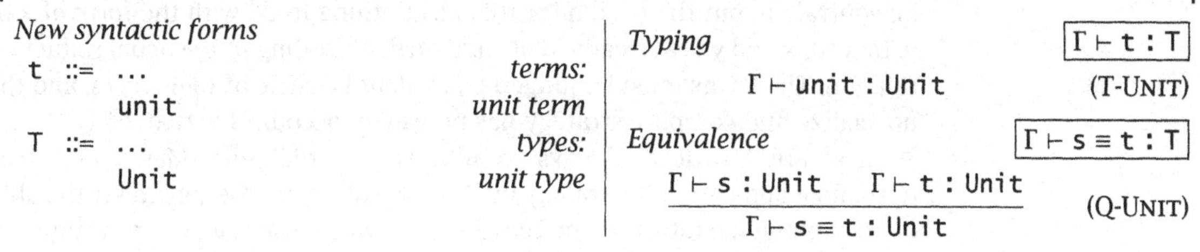

Figure 6-3: Unit type ($\lambda_{\to b1}$)

6.2.3 EXERCISE [★★]: Because of the rule QR-ETA, the reduction relation $\Rightarrow$ is confluent only for well-typed terms. Give an example of an ill-typed term for which confluence fails. □

6.3 Type-Driven Equivalence

One case in which the normalize-and-compare strategy is inapplicable is when the definition of equivalence is type sensitive. The example we will work with arises when we add a second base type corresponding to `Unit` (recall *TAPL*, §11.2). The important thing about this type is that it contains exactly one element; the sole element of `Unit` is written `unit`. These additions are summarized in Figure 6-3.

The interesting facet of the extension with unit is its equivalence rule:

$$\frac{\Gamma \vdash s : \text{Unit} \qquad \Gamma \vdash t : \text{Unit}}{\Gamma \vdash s \equiv t : \text{Unit}} \qquad \text{(Q-UNIT)}$$

This rule expresses the fact that, since the type `Unit` contains exactly one element, any two elements of `Unit` must actually be the same. It is important to note that this rule is strictly stronger than the alternative rule:

$$\Gamma \vdash \texttt{unit} \equiv \texttt{unit} : \texttt{Unit} \qquad \text{(Q-UNIT-WEAK)}$$

Although Q-UNIT-WEAK is sound (indeed, it is derivable from either Q-UNIT or Q-REFL), it cannot derive equivalences involving unit *variables*, such as:

$$\dfrac{\dfrac{}{\texttt{x:Unit, y:Unit} \vdash \texttt{x : Unit}}\text{T-UNIT} \qquad \dfrac{}{\texttt{x:Unit, y:Unit} \vdash \texttt{y : Unit}}\text{T-UNIT}}{\texttt{x:Unit, y:Unit} \vdash \texttt{x} \equiv \texttt{y : Unit}}\text{Q-UNIT}$$

This example also illustrates why the normalize-and-compare strategy is inapplicable once the unit type is added. The terms x and y must be judged to be equivalent, but the reason for this has nothing to do with the *form* of x or y. Indeed, x and y are already in normal form according to the usual reduction relation. The terms must be judged equivalent because of their *types*, and the normalize-and-compare strategy has no way to account for that.

There are a variety of ways to address this difficulty. Many repair the normalize-and-compare strategy by, in one way or another, giving it the ability to exploit type information. However, we will consider an entirely different strategy, an algorithm that tests for equivalence directly, without computing normal forms.

6.3.1 EXERCISE [★]: The need for types in deciding equivalence is not limited to open terms. Give two *closed* terms that are equivalent but have distinct normal forms. □

6.4 An Equivalence Algorithm

We wish to devise an algorithm for the equivalence problem. Stated precisely, the problem is this: Supposing $\Gamma \vdash \texttt{s} : \texttt{T}$ and $\Gamma \vdash \texttt{t} : \texttt{T}$, determine whether or not $\Gamma \vdash \texttt{s} \equiv \texttt{t} : \texttt{T}$.

To solve this problem, we will employ a type-driven algorithm. This algorithm is based on two main observations:

1. If T is Unit, we can immediately return true. This is because we then have $\Gamma \vdash \texttt{s : Unit}$ and $\Gamma \vdash \texttt{t : Unit}$ from our assumptions, and $\Gamma \vdash \texttt{s} \equiv \texttt{t : Unit}$ follows directly by Q-UNIT.

2. If T is $\texttt{T}_1 \to \texttt{T}_2$, we can reduce the problem to a related problem where T is just $\texttt{T}_2$. To do so, we replace any query of the form:

$$\Gamma \vdash \texttt{s} \overset{?}{\equiv} \texttt{t} : \texttt{T}_1 \to \texttt{T}_2$$

with the equivalent query:

$$\Gamma, x{:}T_1 \vdash s\ x \stackrel{?}{\equiv} t\ x : T_2$$

These queries are equivalent because the latter judgment immediately implies the former using the Q-Ext rule, and the former implies the latter using the Q-App rule and a weakening lemma:

6.4.1 Lemma [Weakening]: If $\Gamma \vdash s \equiv t : T$ then $\Gamma, x{:}S \vdash s \equiv t : T$. □

Proof: Straightforward induction on equivalence and typing derivations. (Recall *TAPL* Lemma 9.3.7.) □

The significance of these observations is that they give us a means to reduce an equivalence problem at an arbitrary type to one at the base type b. Therefore, it remains only to find an algorithm that decides equivalence at type b.

Equivalence at Base Type

At type b we can use a variant of the normalize-and-compare strategy. Informally, this is because we address elsewhere the type Unit, which mandated type-directed consideration. The normalization phase (discussed in detail below) will place the equivalence problem in one of five forms (or a symmetric form):[3]

1. $\Gamma \vdash x\ s_1\ \dots\ s_n \stackrel{?}{\equiv} x\ t_1\ \dots\ t_n : b$
2. $\Gamma \vdash k \stackrel{?}{\equiv} k : b$
3. $\Gamma \vdash x\ s_1\ \dots\ s_m \stackrel{?}{\equiv} y\ t_1\ \dots\ t_n : b$ (where $x \neq y$)
4. $\Gamma \vdash x\ s_1\ \dots\ s_n \stackrel{?}{\equiv} k : b$
5. $\Gamma \vdash k \stackrel{?}{\equiv} k' : b$ (where $k \neq k'$)

Clearly, in case 2 we may immediately return true, and in case 5 we may immediately return false. We may also return false in case 3, since we know nothing about what the variables x and y represent, and therefore they could return distinct types. Similarly, we can return false for case 4.

3. Note that in case 1, x must be applied to the same number of arguments on each side, since both sides have the same type.

However, in case 1, a subtlety remains: Suppose, for example, that we wish to determine whether x s ≡ x t : b, where x has the type T→b, and s and t have type T. Since we know nothing about what the variable x represents, this equivalence holds exactly when s ≡ t : T. Thus, although x s ≡ x t : b is an equivalence problem at type b, to decide it we must still decide an equivalence problem at type T (which could be anything, such as Unit), and we have seen that we cannot do so with a simple syntactic comparison.

Thus, if the normalization portion of the normalize-and-compare phase writes the problem in the form:

$$\Gamma \vdash \mathtt{x}\ \mathtt{s}_1\ \ldots\ \mathtt{s}_n \stackrel{?}{\equiv} \mathtt{x}\ \mathtt{t}_1\ \ldots\ \mathtt{t}_n : \mathtt{b}$$

the comparisons of s_i to t_i should be done using the entire type-driven algorithm, and not simple syntactic comparison.

Weak Head Normalization

One additional insight is necessary to understand the algorithm. Since the comparison portion works on a term of the form x t_1 ... t_n by using the entire algorithm on the subterms t_i, there is no point in normalizing the term any more than is required to put it in that form.

For example, if we wish to determine whether x s ≡ x t : b, where x has the type Unit→b, and s and t have type Unit, the answer will always be true, so any effort spent normalizing s or t is wasted.

Consequently, our algorithm will employ a less aggressive form of normalization called *weak head normalization.* In weak head normalization, the leftmost, outermost redex is always selected for reduction, and the process is halted as soon as the term begins with something other than a lambda abstraction.

Such terms of type b will always either be a constant k or be in the form x t_1 ... t_n. These terms are called *paths.* (Although some other terms—such as abstractions—are also weak head normal, those other terms cannot have type b so they will not arise.)

The Algorithm

An algorithm based on the preceding observations is given in Figure 6-4. The algorithm is given in the form of rules defining four relations:

1. Algorithmic term equivalence: $\Gamma \vdash$ s ⇔ t : T. This portion of the algorithm is directed by the type T. It works by driving the type T down to b. All of Γ, s, t, and T are inputs to this relation.

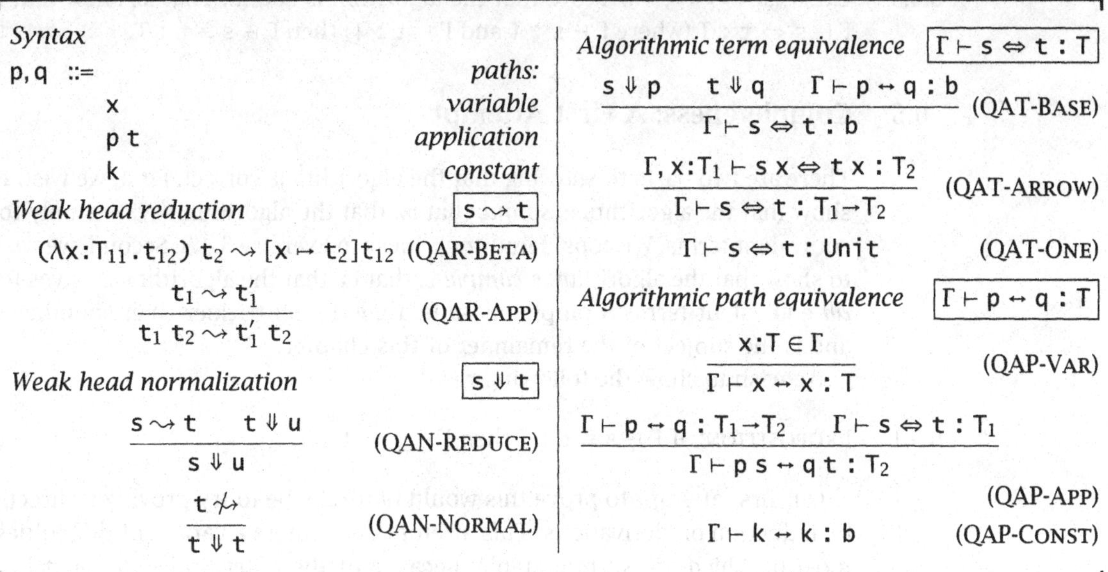

Figure 6-4: Equivalence algorithm for $\lambda_{\to b1}$

2. Algorithmic path equivalence: $\Gamma \vdash \mathsf{p} \leftrightarrow \mathsf{q} : \mathsf{T}$. This portion of the algorithm is directed by the structure of the paths p and q. It works by checking that the head variables of p and q are the same (or that p and q are the same constant), and then comparing corresponding subterms of the path for algorithmic term equivalence. The type T is an *output* of this relation, and Γ, p, and q are inputs.

3. Weak head reduction: $\mathsf{s} \rightsquigarrow \mathsf{t}$. This portion of the algorithm reduces one redex at the head of the term s. It implements one step of weak head normalization.

4. Weak head normalization: $\mathsf{s} \Downarrow \mathsf{t}$. This portion of the algorithm computes weak head normal forms by performing weak head reductions until no more can be performed. (We write $\mathsf{t} \not\rightsquigarrow$ to mean that there exists no term t' such that $\mathsf{t} \rightsquigarrow \mathsf{t}'$.)

6.4.2 Exercise [★★, ↛]: Hand-execute the algorithm on:

$$\mathsf{f{:}(Unit{\to}Unit){\to}b} \vdash \mathsf{f\ (\lambda x{:}Unit.unit)} \overset{?}{\Leftrightarrow} \mathsf{f\ (\lambda x{:}Unit.x)} : \mathsf{b{\to}b}$$

□

6.4.3 EXERCISE [★★★★, ↛]: Prove that the algorithm is sound. That is, show that if $\Gamma \vdash \mathtt{s} \Leftrightarrow \mathtt{t} : \mathtt{T}$ (where $\Gamma \vdash \mathtt{s} : \mathtt{T}$ and $\Gamma \vdash \mathtt{t} : \mathtt{T}$) then $\Gamma \vdash \mathtt{s} \equiv \mathtt{t} : \mathtt{T}$. □

6.5 Completeness: A First Attempt

There are two parts to showing that the algorithm is correct. First, we wish to show that the algorithm is *sound;* that is, that the algorithm says yes only for equivalent terms. We considered soundness in Exercise 6.4.3. Second, we wish to show that the algorithm is *complete;* that is, that the algorithm says yes for *all* equivalent terms. Completeness is a good deal trickier than soundness, and is the subject of the remainder of this chapter.

We wish to show the following result:

6.5.1 PROPOSITION: If $\Gamma \vdash \mathtt{s} \equiv \mathtt{t} : \mathtt{T}$ then $\Gamma \vdash \mathtt{s} \Leftrightarrow \mathtt{t} : \mathtt{T}$. □

Our first attempt to prove this would naturally be to try proving it directly by induction on derivations. This attempt encounters a variety of difficulties, most of which are surmountable. Because of the Q-REFL rule, we must first prove something about typing:

6.5.2 PROPOSITION: If $\Gamma \vdash \mathtt{t} : \mathtt{T}$ then $\Gamma \vdash \mathtt{t} \Leftrightarrow \mathtt{t} : \mathtt{T}$. □

With this addition, several cases for the two propositions go through without difficulty: for Proposition 6.5.1, T-CONST and T-UNIT; and for Proposition 6.5.2, Q-REFL, Q-EXT, and Q-UNIT. Four other rules are more difficult, but can be dealt with, as follows:

- *Cases* Q-SYMM *and* Q-TRANS*:* For these cases, we must prove lemmas stating that the algorithm is symmetric and transitive (Lemmas 6.5.3 and 6.5.4 below).
- *Case* Q-ABS *(*T-ABS *is similar):* Here we wish to show that $\Gamma \vdash \lambda \mathtt{x}{:}\mathtt{T}_1.\mathtt{s}_2 \Leftrightarrow \lambda \mathtt{x}{:}\mathtt{T}_1.\mathtt{t}_2 : \mathtt{T}_1 {\to} \mathtt{T}_2$, for which we must prove that:

  $$\Gamma, \mathtt{x}{:}\mathtt{T}_1 \vdash (\lambda \mathtt{x}{:}\mathtt{T}_1.\mathtt{s}_2)\mathtt{x} \Leftrightarrow (\lambda \mathtt{x}{:}\mathtt{T}_1.\mathtt{t}_2)\mathtt{x} : \mathtt{T}_2$$

  However, the induction hypothesis provides us a related but different fact:

  $$\Gamma, \mathtt{x}{:}\mathtt{T}_1 \vdash \mathtt{s}_2 \Leftrightarrow \mathtt{t}_2 : \mathtt{T}_2$$

  To conclude this case from the available information, we need another lemma stating that the algorithm is closed under weak head expansion (Lemma 6.5.5 below).

6.5.3 Lemma [Algorithmic Symmetry]: If $\Gamma \vdash s \Leftrightarrow t : T$ then $\Gamma \vdash t \Leftrightarrow s : T$. □

6.5.4 Lemma [Algorithmic Transitivity]: If $\Gamma \vdash s \Leftrightarrow t : T$ and $\Gamma \vdash t \Leftrightarrow u : T$ then $\Gamma \vdash s \Leftrightarrow u : T$. □

Proof: Both proofs are by induction on derivations, with a simultaneous induction showing the analogous property for algorithmic path equivalence. □

6.5.5 Lemma [Algorithmic Weak Head Closure]: If $\Gamma \vdash s \Leftrightarrow t : T$ and $s' \rightsquigarrow^* s$ and $t' \rightsquigarrow^* t$ then $\Gamma \vdash s' \Leftrightarrow t' : T$. □

Proof: By induction on the derivation of algorithmic term equivalence. □

6.5.6 Exercise [★, ↛]: Verify Lemma 6.5.5. □

Trouble with Application

This leaves four rules: two dealing with application (T-App and Q-App), and two dealing with variables and substitution (T-Var and Q-Beta). It is the application rules that bring the proof attempt to a standstill.[4]

The essential problem is that the induction hypothesis gives us no information about what happens when a term is applied to an argument. Consider the case Q-App:

$$\frac{\Gamma \vdash s_1 \equiv t_1 : T_1 \to T_2 \qquad \Gamma \vdash s_2 \equiv t_2 : T_1}{\Gamma \vdash s_1\ s_2 \equiv t_1\ t_2 : T_2} \qquad \text{(Q-App)}$$

The induction hypothesis gives us that $\Gamma \vdash s_1 \Leftrightarrow t_1 : T_1 \to T_2$ and $\Gamma \vdash s_2 \Leftrightarrow t_2 : T_1$. We wish to conclude that $\Gamma \vdash s_1\ s_2 \Leftrightarrow t_1\ t_2 : T_2$, but we cannot.

By inversion on $\Gamma \vdash s_1 \Leftrightarrow t_1 : T_1 \to T_2$ we obtain the fact that $\Gamma, x{:}T_1 \vdash s_1\ x \Leftrightarrow t_1\ x : T_2$, but that is as close as we get, since the behavior of the algorithm comparing $s_1\ x$ to $t_1\ x$ is entirely different from its behavior comparing $s_1\ s_2$ to $t_1\ t_2$.

6.6 Logical Relations

The problem discussed above arises because the algorithmic equivalence relation is not *logical,* in the following sense:[5]

4. The variable and substitution rules could be addressed using a device we develop in Section 6.9, but we will not bother to employ it here, since this proof attempt is doomed by application.

5. Actually, it is more precise to say that algorithmic term equivalence is not *evidently* logical; that is, we cannot prove it at this stage in the proof. (See Exercise 6.9.12.)

6.6.1 DEFINITION: Suppose $R(\mathtt{s},\mathtt{t},\mathtt{T})$ is a relation indexed by types T, such that s and t are terms having type T. Then R is *logical* if whenever $R(\mathtt{s}_1,\mathtt{t}_1,\mathtt{T}_1\to\mathtt{T}_2)$ and $R(\mathtt{s}_2,\mathtt{t}_2,\mathtt{T}_1)$ hold, it follows that $R(\mathtt{s}_1\ \mathtt{s}_2,\mathtt{t}_1\ \mathtt{t}_2,\mathtt{T}_2)$ also holds. □

That is, a relation is logical when the relatedness of two applications $\mathtt{s}_1\ \mathtt{s}_2$ and $\mathtt{t}_1\ \mathtt{t}_2$ is inherited from the pairwise relatedness of their constituent function and argument ($\mathtt{s}_1$ with $\mathtt{t}_1$, and $\mathtt{s}_2$ with $\mathtt{t}_2$). Such a relation is called "logical" because it respects the actions of the logical operators (in this case implication) that correspond to the language's type constructors.

The idea behind proof by logical relations is to circumvent problems resulting from the absence of logicality by defining another relation that *is* logical, and that also implies the desired property (in this case algorithmic equivalence). The new, logical relation is then used in the induction hypothesis in the proof.

Our overall proof strategy, then, consists of three stages:

1. Define a suitable logical relation. When two terms are related by the logical relation, we will say that they are *logically equivalent*.

2. Show that logical equivalence implies algorithmic equivalence.

3. Show that definitional equivalence implies logical equivalence.

A Logical Relation

A direct way to define a logical relation is essentially by fiat. The definition proceeds inductively by cases on the index type, asserting algorithmic equivalence at base types, and asserting exactly the necessary property at function types. This gives us the following first attempt at a definition of *logical equivalence:*

$\Gamma \vdash \mathtt{s}$ is $\mathtt{t} : \mathtt{T}$ if and only if either:
 T=Unit,
 or T=b and $\Gamma \vdash \mathtt{s} \Leftrightarrow \mathtt{t} : \mathtt{b}$,
 or $\mathtt{T}=\mathtt{T}_1\to\mathtt{T}_2$ and for all s′, t′,
  if $\Gamma \vdash \mathtt{s}'$ is $\mathtt{t}' : \mathtt{T}_1$
  then $\Gamma \vdash \mathtt{s}\ \mathtt{s}'$ is $\mathtt{t}\ \mathtt{t}' : \mathtt{T}_2$.

Note that the first clause of the definition could equivalently be "T=Unit *and* $\Gamma \vdash \mathtt{s} \Leftrightarrow \mathtt{t} : \mathtt{Unit}$," since the algorithmic equivalence at Unit always holds.

Monotonicity

This relation is clearly logical, and at base types it just as clearly implies algorithmic equivalence. The question is, does it imply algorithmic equivalence at function types? The answer turns out to be *almost, but not quite*:

Suppose $\Gamma \vdash \mathtt{s}$ is $\mathtt{t} : \mathsf{T}_1 \to \mathsf{T}_2$. We wish to show that $\Gamma \vdash \mathtt{s} \Leftrightarrow \mathtt{t} : \mathsf{T}_1 \to \mathsf{T}_2$, for which it is sufficient to show:

$$\Gamma, \mathtt{x}{:}\mathsf{T}_1 \vdash \mathtt{s}\ \mathtt{x} \Leftrightarrow \mathtt{t}\ \mathtt{x} : \mathsf{T}_2$$

Since T_2 is smaller than $\mathsf{T}_1 \to \mathsf{T}_2$, we can conclude by induction that the desired algorithmic equivalence follows from the corresponding logical equivalence. Thus it remains to show:

$$\Gamma, \mathtt{x}{:}\mathsf{T}_1 \vdash \mathtt{s}\ \mathtt{x} \text{ is } \mathtt{t}\ \mathtt{x} : \mathsf{T}_2$$

From the definition of logical equivalence, we can deduce the desired logical equivalence from:

1. $\Gamma, \mathtt{x}{:}\mathsf{T}_1 \vdash \mathtt{s}$ is $\mathtt{t} : \mathsf{T}_1 \to \mathsf{T}_2$, and

2. $\Gamma, \mathtt{x}{:}\mathsf{T}_1 \vdash \mathtt{x}$ is $\mathtt{x} : \mathsf{T}_1$.

The latter is not obvious, but we will be able to prove it (for our final definition). The former, on the other hand, is very similar to our assumption, $\Gamma \vdash \mathtt{s}$ is $\mathtt{t} : \mathsf{T}_1 \to \mathsf{T}_2$. All we need to know is that logical equivalence is preserved when bindings are added to the context. This property is called *monotonicity* (or, *preservation under weakening*).

Failure of Monotonicity

Unfortunately, monotonicity fails for our current definition of logical equivalence. It is not difficult to show monotonicity for the algorithm:

6.6.2 LEMMA [ALGORITHMIC MONOTONICITY]: Suppose $\Gamma' \supseteq \Gamma$. Then:

1. If $\Gamma \vdash \mathtt{s} \Leftrightarrow \mathtt{t} : \mathsf{T}$ then $\Gamma' \vdash \mathtt{s} \Leftrightarrow \mathtt{t} : \mathsf{T}$.

2. If $\Gamma \vdash \mathtt{p} \leftrightarrow \mathtt{q} : \mathsf{T}$ then $\Gamma' \vdash \mathtt{p} \leftrightarrow \mathtt{q} : \mathsf{T}$. □

Proof: By induction on derivations. □

The lemma gives us monotonicity of logical equivalence for type `b`, and logical equivalence is trivially monotone for type `Unit`. That leaves $\mathsf{T}_1 \to \mathsf{T}_2$, where monotonicity fails.

To see why, let us attempt to prove the special case where the context is extended with a single binding. We suppose $\Gamma \vdash$ s is t : $T_1 \to T_2$ and attempt to show Γ, x:S $\vdash$ s is t : $T_1 \to T_2$. By the definition, it is sufficient to show that if Γ, x:S $\vdash$ s′ is t′ : T_1 then Γ, x:S $\vdash$ s s′ is t t′ : T_2. Since T_2 is smaller than $T_1 \to T_2$, induction gives us monotonicity for T_2, so it is sufficient to show that $\Gamma \vdash$ s s′ is t t′ : T_2. This follows from our original supposition by the definition of logical equivalence, *provided* that $\Gamma \vdash$ s′ is t′ : T_1. Unfortunately, our second supposition provides only Γ, x:S $\vdash$ s′ is t′ : T_1. Thus, at type T_1 we need not monotonicity (which induction could provide), but the converse, *antitonicity* (or, *preservation under strengthening*), which is certainly false.

6.6.3 EXERCISE [★]: Let antitonicity be the property that if Γ, x:S $\vdash$ s is t : T then $\Gamma \vdash$ s is t : T. Produce a counterexample for antitonicity. □

6.6.4 EXERCISE [★★★]: Suppose the language contains exactly one constant k. Produce a counterexample for monotonicity and give the proof. □

6.7 A Monotone Logical Relation

Earlier we addressed the problem of logicality by fiat, crafting a definition that provided exactly the necessary property. We can address the problem of monotonicity in essentially the same manner. The problem is that the definition's clause for function types could hold for a context Γ, but not evidently hold for a larger context Γ'.

To resolve this difficulty, we revise the definition so that the clause for function types must hold not only for the current context Γ, but also for any extended context $\Gamma' \supseteq \Gamma$. This gives us our final definition of logical equivalence:

6.7.1 DEFINITION [LOGICAL EQUIVALENCE]:
$\Gamma \vdash$ s is t : T if and only if either:
T=Unit,
or T=b and $\Gamma \vdash$ s $\Leftrightarrow$ t : b,
or T=$T_1 \to T_2$ and, for all s′, t′ and all $\Gamma' \supseteq \Gamma$,
if $\Gamma' \vdash$ s′ is t′ : T_1
then $\Gamma' \vdash$ s s′ is t t′ : T_2. □

With this definition, we can easily prove the monotonicity of logical equivalence:

6.7.2 LEMMA [LOGICAL MONOTONICITY]: If $\Gamma \vdash$ s is t : T and $\Gamma' \supseteq \Gamma$ then $\Gamma' \vdash$ s is t : T. □

Proof: By induction on T, appealing to algorithmic monotonicity in the case where T = b. □

An Aside

A logical relation made monotone in this manner is often called a *Kripke* logical relation, by analogy to Kripke models for modal logic. Modal logic is a form of logic designed for reasoning about the differences between various degrees or forms of truth, typically including *contingent* truths—truths that happen to hold given the existing state of affairs—and *necessary* (or "categorical") truths, which must hold in *any* reasonable state of affairs.

A Kripke model for modal logic is based on a set of "worlds," where each world supports a different set of truths. The set of worlds is additionally structured by a notion of which worlds are "reachable" from which other worlds. In such a model, a contingent truth is one that holds in the current world, and a necessary truth is one that holds in all worlds reachable from the current world. (Any world not reachable from the current world is ignored, since there is no way to observe its existence.)

The connection to Kripke models arises in the logical relation's use of a context Γ, which we may view as specifying a world. Each world provides a different set of variables, and we may reach another world by adding variables to the current context. Thus, when we require that our logical relation be monotone (that is, that it continues to hold in all reachable contexts), we are saying that we are interested in *necessary* equivalence, not accidental (i.e., contingent) equivalence.[6]

6.8 The Main Lemma

With a monotone logical relation in hand, we are now ready to prove the completeness of the algorithm. Recalling our proof strategy from page 234, we have accomplished the first step, the definition of a suitable logical relation. We now wish to show that logical equivalence implies algorithmic equivalence. It will then remain to show that definitional equivalence implies logical equivalence.

The former fact is established by the following "main lemma." The Main Lemma actually establishes two facts simultaneously. First, it shows that logical equivalence implies algorithmic equivalence. To appreciate the second fact, recall (from page 235) that to show that logical implies algorithmic

6. Exercise 6.6.4 in essence asks you to produce an example of an accidental equivalence, one that holds only in a certain world.

equivalence, we also need to establish that variables are logically equivalent to themselves. To do so, we prove the stronger result that algorithmically equivalent paths are logically equivalent. The necessary result for variables follows, since a variable is always algorithmically path equivalent to itself (rule QAP-VAR).

In the following proof, observe how inseparably the two induction hypotheses of the lemma are intertwined. It is typical of logical relations proofs to use a lemma such as this, wherein one clause of the lemma establishes the logical relation and the other clause exploits it. This structure of the proof usually results from the definition of the logical relation in the arrow case, where the relation appears on both the left and the right of the implication.

6.8.1 LEMMA [MAIN LEMMA]:

1. If $\Gamma \vdash \mathtt{s}$ is $\mathtt{t} : \mathtt{T}$ then $\Gamma \vdash \mathtt{s} \Leftrightarrow \mathtt{t} : \mathtt{T}$.

2. If $\Gamma \vdash \mathtt{p} \leftrightarrow \mathtt{q} : \mathtt{T}$ then $\Gamma \vdash \mathtt{p}$ is $\mathtt{q} : \mathtt{T}$. □

Proof: By induction on T.

Case: $\mathtt{T} = \mathtt{b}$

1. Suppose $\Gamma \vdash \mathtt{s}$ is $\mathtt{t} : \mathtt{b}$. By definition, $\Gamma \vdash \mathtt{s} \Leftrightarrow \mathtt{t} : \mathtt{b}$.

2. Suppose $\Gamma \vdash \mathtt{p} \leftrightarrow \mathtt{q} : \mathtt{b}$. Since p and q are paths, it follows that $\mathtt{p} \not\rightsquigarrow$ and $\mathtt{q} \not\rightsquigarrow$, so $\mathtt{p} \Downarrow \mathtt{p}$ and $\mathtt{q} \Downarrow \mathtt{q}$ by QAN-NORMAL. Therefore $\Gamma \vdash \mathtt{p} \Leftrightarrow \mathtt{q} : \mathtt{b}$ by QAT-BASE, and $\Gamma \vdash \mathtt{p}$ is $\mathtt{q} : \mathtt{b}$ follows by the definition.

Case: $\mathtt{T} = \mathtt{Unit}$

1. For any s and t, $\Gamma \vdash \mathtt{s} \Leftrightarrow \mathtt{t} : \mathtt{Unit}$ by QAT-ONE.

2. For any p and q, $\Gamma \vdash \mathtt{p}$ is $\mathtt{q} : \mathtt{Unit}$ by the definition.

Case: $\mathtt{T} = \mathtt{T}_1 \rightarrow \mathtt{T}_2$

1. Suppose $\Gamma \vdash \mathtt{s}$ is $\mathtt{t} : \mathtt{T}_1 \rightarrow \mathtt{T}_2$. We wish to show that $\Gamma \vdash \mathtt{s} \Leftrightarrow \mathtt{t} : \mathtt{T}_1 \rightarrow \mathtt{T}_2$. It is sufficient to show that $\Gamma, \mathtt{x}{:}\mathtt{T}_1 \vdash \mathtt{s}\ \mathtt{x} \Leftrightarrow \mathtt{t}\ \mathtt{x} : \mathtt{T}_2$. This will follow by induction, if we can show that $\Gamma, \mathtt{x}{:}\mathtt{T}_1 \vdash \mathtt{s}\ \mathtt{x}$ is $\mathtt{t}\ \mathtt{x} : \mathtt{T}_2$.

   By induction (using the second clause), since $\Gamma, \mathtt{x}{:}\mathtt{T}_1 \vdash \mathtt{x} \leftrightarrow \mathtt{x} : \mathtt{T}_1$ (by QAP-VAR), we may deduce that $\Gamma, \mathtt{x}{:}\mathtt{T}_1 \vdash \mathtt{x}$ is $\mathtt{x} : \mathtt{T}_1$. Therefore, since $(\Gamma, \mathtt{x}{:}\mathtt{T}_1) \supseteq \Gamma$, we may conclude that $\Gamma, \mathtt{x}{:}\mathtt{T}_1 \vdash \mathtt{s}\ \mathtt{x}$ is $\mathtt{t}\ \mathtt{x} : \mathtt{T}_2$, as desired.

2. Suppose $\Gamma \vdash \mathtt{p} \leftrightarrow \mathtt{q} : \mathtt{T}_1 \rightarrow \mathtt{T}_2$. We wish to show that $\Gamma \vdash \mathtt{p}$ is $\mathtt{q} : \mathtt{T}_1 \rightarrow \mathtt{T}_2$. Suppose further that $\Gamma' \supseteq \Gamma$ and $\Gamma' \vdash \mathtt{s}$ is $\mathtt{t} : \mathtt{T}_1$. Then we wish to show

that $\Gamma' \vdash \mathtt{p\ s}$ is $\mathtt{q\ t} : \mathsf{T}_2$. This will follow by induction, if we can show that $\Gamma' \vdash \mathtt{p\ s} \leftrightarrow \mathtt{q\ t} : \mathsf{T}_2$.

By induction (using the first clause), $\Gamma' \vdash \mathtt{s} \Leftrightarrow \mathtt{t} : \mathsf{T}_1$. By algorithmic monotonicity (Lemma 6.6.2), $\Gamma' \vdash \mathtt{p} \leftrightarrow \mathtt{q} : \mathsf{T}_1 \rightarrow \mathsf{T}_2$. Therefore, by rule QAP-APP, $\Gamma' \vdash \mathtt{p\ s} \leftrightarrow \mathtt{q\ t} : \mathsf{T}_2$, as required. □

6.9 The Fundamental Theorem

The final step in the completeness proof is to show that definitional equivalence implies logical equivalence. We will refer to the theorem showing this fact as the "Fundamental Theorem."

Recall our attempted proof from Section 6.5. The principal problem we encountered was with application; we could not deduce from the algorithmic equivalence of two functions anything about the equivalence of their applications to arguments. We have solved that problem by using a logical relation, which explicitly provides the necessary conclusions about applications.

Structural Properties of Logical Equivalence

Since we are now using logical equivalence in place of algorithmic equivalence, we must revisit some of our other devices from Section 6.5. To address the Q-SYMM, Q-TRANS, Q-ABS, and T-ANS, we showed that the algorithm is symmetric, transitive, and closed under weak head reduction (Lemmas 6.5.3, 6.5.4, and 6.5.5). We will now require analogs of these lemmas applicable to logical equivalence:

6.9.1 LEMMA [LOGICAL SYMMETRY]: If $\Gamma \vdash \mathtt{s}$ is $\mathtt{t} : \mathsf{T}$ then $\Gamma \vdash \mathtt{t}$ is $\mathtt{s} : \mathsf{T}$. □

Proof: By induction on T, appealing to algorithmic symmetry (Lemma 6.5.3) in the case where $\mathsf{T} = \mathsf{b}$. □

6.9.2 LEMMA [LOGICAL TRANSITIVITY]: If $\Gamma \vdash \mathtt{s}$ is $\mathtt{t} : \mathsf{T}$ and $\Gamma \vdash \mathtt{t}$ is $\mathtt{u} : \mathsf{T}$ then $\Gamma \vdash \mathtt{s}$ is $\mathtt{u} : \mathsf{T}$. □

Proof: Exercise [RECOMMENDED, ★★, ↛]. □

6.9.3 LEMMA [LOGICAL WEAK HEAD CLOSURE]: If $\Gamma \vdash \mathtt{s}$ is $\mathtt{t} : \mathsf{T}$ and $\mathtt{s}' \rightsquigarrow^* \mathtt{s}$ and $\mathtt{t}' \rightsquigarrow^* \mathtt{t}$ then $\Gamma \vdash \mathtt{s}'$ is $\mathtt{t}' : \mathsf{T}$. □

Proof: By induction on T; in the case where $\mathsf{T} = \mathsf{b}$, we appeal to algorithmic weak head closure (Lemma 6.5.5). □

Closure under Substitution

There remain two more cases we did not consider in Section 6.5, T-VAR and Q-BETA. We could deal with T-VAR immediately, since a consequence of the Main Lemma is that variables are logically equivalent to themselves. However, we will actually end up dealing with T-VAR somewhat differently in light of one last remaining complication. (See the T-VAR case of Theorem 6.9.8.)

That final complication stems from the rule Q-BETA:

$$\frac{\Gamma, \mathtt{x}{:}\mathtt{T}_1 \vdash \mathtt{s}_{12} \equiv \mathtt{t}_{12} : \mathtt{T}_2 \qquad \Gamma \vdash \mathtt{s}_2 \equiv \mathtt{t}_2 : \mathtt{T}_1}{\Gamma \vdash (\lambda \mathtt{x}{:}\mathtt{T}_1.\mathtt{s}_{12})\ \mathtt{s}_2 \equiv [\mathtt{x} \mapsto \mathtt{t}_2]\mathtt{t}_{12} : \mathtt{T}_2} \qquad \text{(Q-BETA)}$$

Suppose we employ the obvious induction hypothesis: if $\Gamma \vdash \mathtt{s} \equiv \mathtt{t} : \mathtt{T}$ then $\Gamma \vdash \mathtt{s}$ is $\mathtt{t} : \mathtt{T}$. Then, for the Q-BETA case, we need to show that:

$$\Gamma \vdash (\lambda \mathtt{x}{:}\mathtt{T}_1.\mathtt{s}_{12})\ \mathtt{s}_2 \text{ is } [\mathtt{x} \mapsto \mathtt{t}_2]\mathtt{t}_{12} : \mathtt{T}_2$$

Using logical weak head closure (Lemma 6.9.3), it is sufficient to show that:

$$\Gamma \vdash [\mathtt{x} \mapsto \mathtt{s}_2]\mathtt{s}_{12} \text{ is } [\mathtt{x} \mapsto \mathtt{t}_2]\mathtt{t}_{12} : \mathtt{T}_2$$

Induction provides us with $\Gamma, \mathtt{x}{:}\mathtt{T}_1 \vdash \mathtt{s}_{12} \equiv \mathtt{t}_{12} : \mathtt{T}_2$ and $\Gamma \vdash \mathtt{s}_2 \equiv \mathtt{t}_2 : \mathtt{T}_1$.

Thus, we could complete the proof by showing that logical equivalence is closed under logically equivalent substitutions. Unfortunately, it is not clear how to prove such a proposition at this stage in the completeness proof, as the form of the logical relation gives us no leverage on the matter.

The Theorem

Fortunately, we can work around this difficulty by building this notion of equivalent substitutions into the Fundamental Theorem itself. First we require a few definitions:

6.9.4 DEFINITION [SUBSTITUTIONS]: A substitution is a function from some set of variables to terms. □

6.9.5 DEFINITION [SUBSTITUTIONS AND TERMS]: Suppose γ is a substitution and $\mathtt{t}$ is a term such that the free variables of $\mathtt{t}$ are contained in $dom(\gamma)$. Then we write $\gamma(t)$ to refer to the term resulting from simultaneously carrying out on $\mathtt{t}$ all the substitutions specified by γ. □

6.9.6 DEFINITION [SUBSTITUTION EXTENSION]: Suppose $\mathtt{x} \notin dom(\gamma)$. Then we define $\gamma[\mathtt{x} \mapsto \mathtt{t}]$ as the substitution with domain $dom(\gamma) \cup \{\mathtt{x}\}$ such that:

$$(\gamma[\mathtt{x} \mapsto \mathtt{t}])(\mathtt{y}) = \begin{cases} \gamma(\mathtt{y}) & \mathtt{x} \neq \mathtt{y} \\ \mathtt{t} & \mathtt{x} = \mathtt{y} \end{cases}$$

□

6.9.7 **Definition [Logically Equivalent Substitutions]:** Logical equivalence of substitutions is defined as follows:

> $\Gamma' \vdash \gamma$ is $\delta : \Gamma$ if $dom(\gamma) = dom(\delta) = dom(\Gamma)$ and for every $x{:}T \in \Gamma$ we have $\Gamma' \vdash \gamma(x)$ is $\delta(x) : T$. □

Now we can state the Fundamental Theorem by uniformly considering all equivalences under the application of equivalent substitutions. Since typing never depends on equivalence, we can separate the Fundamental Theorem into two parts (one for typing and one for equivalence) and prove each in turn.

6.9.8 **Theorem [Fundamental Theorem 1]:** If $\Gamma \vdash t : T$ and $\Gamma' \vdash \gamma$ is $\delta : \Gamma$ then $\Gamma' \vdash \gamma(t)$ is $\delta(t) : T$. □

Proof: By induction on derivations. We show several cases; the rest are left as exercises.

Case T-Var: $t = x$
with $x{:}T \in \Gamma$

By assumption, $\Gamma' \vdash \gamma(x)$ is $\delta(x) : T$.

Case T-Abs: $t = \lambda x{:}T_1.t_2$
$T = T_1 \to T_2$

We wish to show that $\Gamma' \vdash \gamma(\lambda x{:}T_1.t_2)$ is $\delta(\lambda x{:}T_1.t_2) : T_1 \to T_2$. Suppose $\Gamma'' \supseteq \Gamma'$ and $\Gamma'' \vdash s'$ is $t' : T_1$. We wish to show that $\Gamma'' \vdash (\lambda x{:}T_1.\gamma(t_2))s'$ is $(\lambda x{:}T_1.\delta(t_2))t' : T_2$. By logical weak head closure (Lemma 6.9.3), it is sufficient to show that $\Gamma'' \vdash [x \mapsto s']\gamma(t_2)$ is $[x \mapsto t']\delta(t_2) : T_2$.

By logical monotonicity, $\Gamma'' \vdash \gamma$ is $\delta : \Gamma$. Thus, $\Gamma'' \vdash \gamma[x \mapsto s']$ is $\delta[x \mapsto t'] : (\Gamma, x{:}T_1)$. Therefore, by induction, $\Gamma'' \vdash \gamma[x \mapsto s'](t_2)$ is $\delta[x \mapsto t'](t_2) : T_2$, which is equivalent to the desired conclusion.

Case T-App: $t = t_1\ t_2$
$T = T_{12}$

By induction, $\Gamma' \vdash \gamma(t_1)$ is $\delta(t_1) : T_1 \to T_2$ and $\Gamma' \vdash \gamma(t_2)$ is $\delta(t_2) : T_1$. By the definition of the logical relation, since $\Gamma' \supseteq \Gamma$, we may conclude $\Gamma' \vdash \gamma(t_1)\gamma(t_2)$ is $\delta(t_1)\delta(t_2) : T_2$. That is, $\Gamma' \vdash \gamma(t_1\ t_2)$ is $\delta(t_1\ t_2) : T_2$. □

6.9.9 **Theorem [Fundamental Theorem 2]:** If $\Gamma \vdash s \equiv t : T$ and $\Gamma' \vdash \gamma$ is $\delta : \Gamma$ then $\Gamma' \vdash \gamma(s)$ is $\delta(t) : T$. □

Proof: By induction on derivations. We show one case; the rest are left as exercises.

Case Q-BETA: $s = (\lambda x{:}T_1.s_{12})\ s_2$
$t = [x \mapsto t_2]t_{12} : T_2$
$T = T_2$

By induction, $\Gamma' \vdash \gamma(s_2)$ is $\delta(t_2) : T_1$. Thus $\Gamma' \vdash \gamma[x \mapsto \gamma(s_2)]$ is $\delta[x \mapsto \delta(t_2)] : (\Gamma, x{:}T_1)$. Therefore, by induction:

$$\Gamma' \vdash \gamma[x \mapsto \gamma(s_2)](s_{12}) \text{ is } \delta[x \mapsto \delta(t_2)](t_{12}) : T_2$$

By rearranging substitutions:

$$\Gamma' \vdash [x \mapsto \gamma(s_2)]\gamma(s_{12}) \text{ is } \delta([x \mapsto t_2]t_{12}) : T_2$$

Finally, by logical weak head closure (Lemma 6.9.3):

$$\Gamma' \vdash (\lambda x{:}T_1.\gamma(s_{12}))\gamma(s_2) \text{ is } \delta([x \mapsto t_2]t_{12}) : T_2$$

That is:

$$\Gamma' \vdash \gamma((\lambda x{:}T_1.s_{12})\ s_2) \text{ is } \delta([x \mapsto t_2]t_{12}) : T_2$$ □

6.9.10 EXERCISE [RECOMMENDED, ★★★]: Complete the proof of Theorems 6.9.8 and 6.9.9. □

Now we can establish the algorithm's completeness, using the Fundamental Theorem with an identity substitution:

6.9.11 COROLLARY [COMPLETENESS]: If $\Gamma \vdash s \equiv t : T$ then $\Gamma \vdash s \Leftrightarrow t : T$. □

Proof: Suppose $\Gamma \vdash s \equiv t : T$. Let γ be the identity substitution on *dom*(Γ). For all $x{:}T$ in Γ, observe that $\Gamma \vdash x$ is $x : T$ by the Main Lemma. Therefore $\Gamma \vdash \gamma$ is $\gamma : \Gamma$. By the Fundamental Theorem, $\Gamma \vdash \gamma(s)$ is $\gamma(t) : T$, which is to say $\Gamma \vdash s$ is $t : T$. Therefore $\Gamma \vdash s \Leftrightarrow t : T$ by the Main Lemma. □

6.9.12 EXERCISE [★]: An irony arises from the use logical relations to show completeness: it turns out that algorithmic equivalence actually is logical after all (at least for well-formed terms); we just cannot prove it until we have already proven the algorithm to be sound and complete. Show that if $\Gamma \vdash s_1 \Leftrightarrow t_1 : T_1 \to T_2$ and $\Gamma \vdash s_2 \Leftrightarrow t_2 : T_1$ (where $\Gamma \vdash s_1 : T_1 \to T_2$, $\Gamma \vdash t_1 : T_1 \to T_2$, $\Gamma \vdash s_2 : T_1$, and $\Gamma \vdash t_2 : T_1$), then $\Gamma \vdash s_1\ s_2 \Leftrightarrow t_1\ t_2 : T_2$. □

6.9.13 EXERCISE [★★★★]: We have shown that the equivalence algorithm is sound and complete. To show that the algorithm decides the equivalence problem, it remains to show that it terminates on all well-formed inputs. Show that if $\Gamma \vdash s : T$ and $\Gamma \vdash t : T$ then there exists no infinite proof search rooted in $\Gamma \vdash s \Leftrightarrow t : T$.

Hint: Termination is a corollary of completeness. You will not need to prove any additional non-trivial facts about the algorithm. □

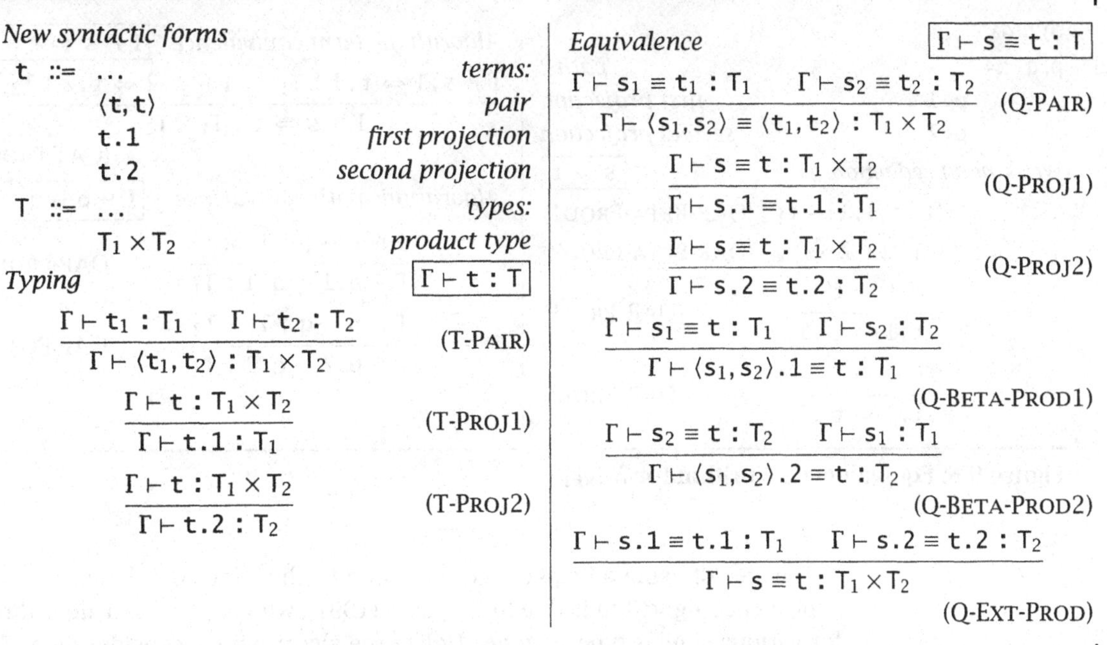

Figure 6-5: Product types ($\lambda_{\to\times b1}$)

6.9.14 EXERCISE [RECOMMENDED, ★★★★]: Our language can be extended straightforwardly with pairs. Figure 6-5 gives the extended syntax and type system, and Figure 6-6 extends the equivalence algorithm to account for pairs. Extend the completeness proof to cover the extended language and algorithm. □

6.9.15 EXERCISE [★★★]: Unfortunately, some extensions of the technique of logical relations, such as for universal types, are not as simple as that for pairs. Suppose our language and algorithm are extended in the natural manner to support universal types as in System F (*TAPL*, Chapter 23). To prove the algorithm complete involves defining a logical relation. However, to define the necessary logical relation is not straightforward. Observe what goes wrong. □

6.10 Notes

The ideas behind logical relations were first developed by Tait (1967) and Howard (1973), and were refined further by Plotkin (1980). Logical relations were first proposed as a general proof technique by Statman (1985).

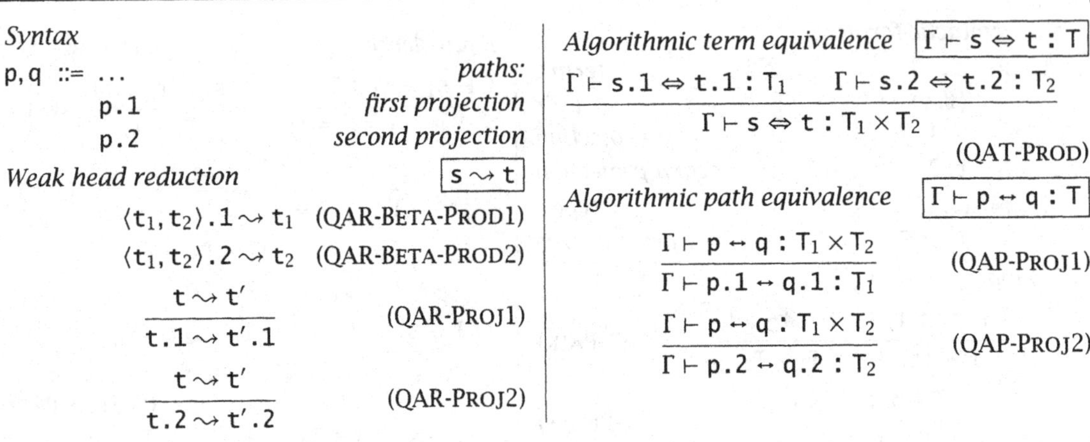

Figure 6-6: Equivalence algorithm for $\lambda_{\to\times b1}$

The idea of using a Kripke logical relation to show the completeness of an equivalence algorithm is due to Coquand (1991), who applies it to algorithms for various similar type systems. Unlike the algorithm we consider here, Coquand's algorithms are not type-directed. Coquand's technique was adopted by Stone and Harper (2000), who use a more sophisticated form of logical relation to show the completeness of an equivalence algorithm for a language with singleton kinds. (Singleton kinds arise from a form of type definitions, and are discussed in §9.3.)

A broader survey of applications of logical relations appears in Mitchell's *Foundations for Programming Languages* (1996). A good introductory text on modal logic and Kripke models is Sally Popkorn's *First Steps in Modal Logic* (1994). A shorter introduction to modal logic from a different perspective (leaving out connections to Kripke models) is given by Pfenning and Davies (2001).

7 Typed Operational Reasoning

Andrew Pitts

The aim of this chapter is to explain, by example, some methods for reasoning about equivalence of programs based directly upon a type system and an operational semantics for the programming language in question. We will concentrate on methods for reasoning about equivalence of representations of abstract data types. This provides an excellent example: it is easy to appreciate why such methods are useful and at the same time non-trivial problems have to be solved to get a sound reasoning principle in the presence of non-termination and recursion. Rather than just treat abstract data types, we will cover full existential types, using a programming language combining a pure fragment of ML (including records and recursive functions) with System F.

7.1 Introduction

As explained in *TAPL*, Chapter 24, type systems involving existentially quantified type variables provide a useful foundation for explaining and relating various features of programming languages to do with information hiding. To establish the properties of such type-theoretic interpretations of information hiding requires a theory of semantic equivalence for expressions of existential type. Methods involving type-indexed families of *relations* between between expressions have proved very useful in this respect. Study of relational properties of typed calculi goes back to the *logical relations* for simply typed lambda calculus in Plotkin (1973) and Statman (1985) and discussed in Chapter 6, and the notion of *relational parametricity* for polymorphic types in Reynolds (1983). More relevant to the kind of example considered in this chapter is Mitchell's principle for establishing the denotational equivalence of programs involving higher-order functions and different implementations of an abstract datatype in terms of the existence of a *simulation* relation between the implementations (Mitchell, 1991a). This principle was extended by Plotkin and Abadi (1993) to encompass all the (possibly impredicative) existential types of the Girard-Reynolds polymorphic lambda calculus.

One feature of these works is that they develop proof principles for *denotational* models of programming languages. The relevance of such principles to the operational behavior of programs relies upon 'goodness of fit' results (some published, some not) connecting operational and denotational semantics. Another feature of the above works is that they do not treat the use of general recursive definitions; and so the languages considered are not Turing powerful. It is folklore that a proof principle for denotational equality at existential type, phrased in terms of the existence of certain simulation relations, is still valid in the presence of recursively defined functions of higher type, provided one imposes some *admissibility* conditions on the notion of relation. In fact using techniques for defining operationally based logical relations developed in Pitts (2000), we will see in this chapter that suitable admissibility conditions for relations and an associated proof principle for operational equivalence at existential type can be phrased directly, and quite simply, in terms of the syntax and operational semantics of a programming language combining existential types with recursively defined, higher-order functions. The programming language we work with combines a pure fragment of ML (including records and recursive functions) with the polymorphic lambda calculus of Girard (1972) and Reynolds (1974).

7.2 Overview

In order to get the most out of this chapter you should have some familiarity with *TAPL*, Chapters 23 and 24. The material in this chapter is technically quite intricate (especially the definition and properties of the logical relation in §7.6) and it is easy to lose sight of the wood for the trees. So here is an overview of the chapter.

Equivalence of programs One application of formal semantics of programming languages is to give a mathematically precise definition of what it means for one program to be semantically equal to another. In this chapter we use operational semantics and discuss a notion of program equivalence called *contextual equivalence* (§7.5).

Extensionality principles In order to reason about program equivalence, it is useful to establish the validity of proof methods for it. The most basic method uses the congruence property—reasoning by "replacing equals by equals"—which holds of contextual equivalence by construction. In §7.1

we discuss informally some methods for proving contextual equivalence of implementations of abstract datatypes. The discussion culminates with the Extensionality Principle 7.3.6. One goal of this chapter is to give a mathematically precise formulation of this principle and to establish its validity.

Logical relations The Extensionality Principle is phrased in terms of type-respecting *relations* between the terms of our example language. In order to formulate this principle precisely and then prove it we develop an alternative characterisation of contextual equivalence in terms of a certain "logical relation" (§7.6). The combination of features in our language—higher-order recursive functions and fully impredicative polymorphic types—force us to use a form of logical relation with quite a difficult definition. Chapter 6 presents another use of logical relations with a simpler definition; as such, that chapter provides a useful warm-up for this one.

7.3 Motivating Examples

In this section we motivate the use of logical relations for reasoning about existential types by giving some examples.

To begin, let us recall the syntax for expressions involving existentially quantified type variables from *TAPL*, Chapter 24. If T is a type expression and X is a type variable, then we write `{∃X,T}` for the corresponding existentially quantified type. Free occurrences of X in T become bound in this type expression. We write `[X ↦ S]T` for the result of substituting a type S for all free occurrences of X in T, renaming bound type variables as necessary to avoid capture.[1] It t is a term of type `[X ↦ S]T`, then we can "pack" the type S and the term t together to get a term

`{*S,t} as {∃X,T}` (7.1)

of the indicated existential type. To eliminate such terms we use the form

`let {*X,x}=`t_1 `in` t_2 (7.2)

This is a binding construct: free occurrences of the type variable X and the value variable x in t_2 become bound in the term. The typing of such terms goes as follows:

> if t_1 has type `{∃X,T}` and t_2 has type T_2 when we assume the variable x has type T, then *provided* X *does not occur free in* T_2, we can conclude that the term in (7.2) has type T_2.

1. Throughout this chapter we will always identify expressions, be they types or terms, up to renaming of bound variables.

(Such rules are better presented symbolically, but we postpone doing that until we give a formal definition of the language we will be using, in the next section.) The italicized restriction on free occurrences of X in T_2 in the above rule is what distinguishes an existential type from a type-indexed dependent sum, where there is free access both to the type component as well as the term component of a "packed" term: see Mitchell and Plotkin (1988), p. 474 *et seq*, for a discussion of this point.

Since we wish to consider existential types in the context of an ML-like language, we adopt an eager strategy for evaluating expressions like (7.1) and (7.2). Thus to evaluate the first, one evaluates t to canonical form, v say, and returns the canonical form {*S,v} as {∃X,T}; to evaluate the second, one evaluates t_1 to canonical form, {*S,v} as {∃X,T} say, and then evaluates $[X \mapsto S][x \mapsto v]t_2$.

7.3.1 EXAMPLE: Consider the existentially quantified record type

```
type Counter = {∃X, {mk:X, inc:X→X, get:X→Int}}
```

where Int is a type of integers. Values of type Counter consist of some type together with values of the appropriate types implementing mk, inc, and get. For example

```
val counter1 = {*Int, {mk  = 0,
                       inc = λx:Int.x+1,
                       get = λx:Int.x   } as Counter
```

and

```
val counter2 = {*Int, {mk  = 0,
                        inc = λx:Int.x-1,
                        get = λx:Int.0-x } as Counter
```

are both values of type Counter. The terms

```
let {*X,x} = counter1  in x.get(x.inc(x.mk))
let {*X,x} = counter2 in x.get(x.inc(x.mk))
```

(where we use the syntax r.f for selecting field f of record r) are both terms of type Int which evaluate to 1. By contrast, of the terms

```
let {*X,x} = counter1  in x.get(x.inc(1))
let {*X,x} = counter2 in x.get(x.inc(1))
```

the first evaluates to 2, whereas the second evaluates to 0; but in this case neither term is well-typed. Indeed, it is the case that *any* well-typed closed term involving occurrences of the term $\texttt{counter}_1$ will exhibit precisely the same evaluation behavior if we replace those occurrences by $\texttt{counter}_2$. In other words, $\texttt{counter}_1$ and $\texttt{counter}_2$ are equivalent in the following sense. □

7.3.2 **Definition [Contextual equivalence, informally]:** We write $\mathtt{t}_1 =_{\text{ctx}} \mathtt{t}_2 \mathtt{:T}$ to indicate that two terms $\mathtt{t}_1$ and $\mathtt{t}_2$ of the same type T are *contextually equivalent*. By definition, this means that for all well-typed terms $\mathtt{t[t}_1\mathtt{]}$ containing instances of $\mathtt{t}_1$, if $\mathtt{t[t}_2\mathtt{]}$ is the term obtained by replacing those instances by $\mathtt{t}_2$, then $\mathtt{t[t}_1\mathtt{]}$ and $\mathtt{t[t}_2\mathtt{]}$ give exactly the same observable results when evaluated. □

This notion of program equivalence assumes we have already fixed upon a definition of the "observable results" of evaluating terms. It also presupposes that the meaning of a well-typed term should only depend upon the final result (if any) of evaluating it. This is reasonable for deterministic and non-interactive programming even in the presence of computational effects like side-effecting state or raising exceptions, provided we include those effects as part of the observable results of evaluation. Certainly, contextual equivalence is a widely used notion of program equivalence in the literature and it is the one we adopt here.

For the terms in Example 7.3.1, it is the case that

$$\mathtt{counter}_1 =_{\text{ctx}} \mathtt{counter}_2 \mathtt{:Counter} \tag{7.3}$$

but the quantification over all possible contexts $\mathtt{t[-]}$ in the definition of $=_{\text{ctx}}$ makes a direct proof of this and similar facts rather difficult. Thus one is led to ask whether there are proof principles for contextual equivalence that make proving such equivalences at existential types more tractable. Since values `{*S,v} as {∃X,T}` of a given existential type `{∃X,T}` are specified by pairs of data S and v, as a first stab at such a proof principle one might try componentwise equivalence. Equivalence in the second component will of course mean contextual equivalence; but in the first component, where the expressions involved are types, what should equivalence mean? If we take it to mean syntactic identity, =, (which for us includes renaming of bound variables) we obtain the following proof principle.[2]

7.3.3 **Principle [Extensionality for ∃-types, Version I]:** For an existential type $\mathtt{E} \overset{\text{def}}{=} \mathtt{\{\exists X,T\}}$, types $\mathtt{T}_1$, $\mathtt{T}_2$, and values $\mathtt{v}_1$, $\mathtt{v}_2$, if $\mathtt{T}_1 = \mathtt{T}_2$ and $\mathtt{v}_1 =_{\text{ctx}} \mathtt{v}_2 \mathtt{:[X} \mapsto \mathtt{T}_2\mathtt{]T}$, then $\mathtt{(\{*T}_1\mathtt{,v}_1\mathtt{\}\ as\ E)} =_{\text{ctx}} \mathtt{(\{*T}_2\mathtt{,v}_2\mathtt{\}\ as\ E):\{\exists X,T\}}$. □

The hypotheses of Principle 7.3.3 are far too strong for it to be very useful. For example, it cannot be used to prove (7.3), since in this case $\mathtt{T}_1 = \mathtt{Int} = \mathtt{T}_2$, but

2. This and subsequent proof principles for `{∃X,T}` are called *extensionality* principles by analogy with the familiar extensionality principle for functions; it is a convenient terminology, but perhaps the analogy is a little stretched.

```
val v₁ = {mk=0, inc=λx:Int.x+1, get=λx:Int.x}
```

and

```
val v₂ = {mk=0, inc=λx:Int.x-1, get=λx:Int.0-x}
```

are clearly not contextually equivalent values of the record type

```
{mk:Int,inc:Int→Int,get:Int→Int}
```

(for example, we get different integers when evaluating $\mathtt{t[v_1]}$ and $\mathtt{t[v_2]}$ when t[−] is (−.inc)0). However, they do become contextually equivalent if in the second term we use a variant of integers in which the roles of positive and negative are reversed. Such "integers" are of course in bijection with the usual ones and this leads us to our second version of an extensionality principle for existential types—in which the use of syntactic identity as the notion of type equivalence is replaced by the more flexible one of *bijection*. A bijection $\mathtt{i} : \mathtt{T_1} \cong \mathtt{T_2}$ means a closed term $\mathtt{i} : \mathtt{T_1}\to\mathtt{T_2}$ for which there is a closed term $\mathtt{i^{-1}} : \mathtt{T_2}\to\mathtt{T_1}$ which is a two-sided inverse up to contextual equivalence: $\mathtt{i^{-1}(i\ x_1)} =_{\mathrm{ctx}} \mathtt{x_1} : \mathtt{T_1}$ and $\mathtt{i(i^{-1}\ x_2)} =_{\mathrm{ctx}} \mathtt{x_2} : \mathtt{T_2}$.

7.3.4 PRINCIPLE [EXTENSIONALITY FOR ∃-TYPES, VERSION II]: For each existential type $\mathtt{E} \overset{\mathrm{def}}{=} \{\exists\mathtt{X},\mathtt{T}\}$, types $\mathtt{T_1}$, $\mathtt{T_2}$, and values $\mathtt{v_1}$, $\mathtt{v_2}$, if there is a *bijection* $\mathtt{i} : \mathtt{T_1} \cong \mathtt{T_2}$ such that $\mathtt{T(i)\ v_1} =_{\mathrm{ctx}} \mathtt{v_2} : [\mathtt{X} \mapsto \mathtt{T_2}]\mathtt{T}$, then

$$(\{^*\mathtt{T_1},\mathtt{v_1}\}\ \mathtt{as\ E}) =_{\mathrm{ctx}} (\{^*\mathtt{T_2},\mathtt{v_2}\}\ \mathtt{as\ E}) : \{\exists\mathtt{X},\mathtt{T}\}.$$

In stating this principle we have used the notation T(i) for the "action" of types T on bijections i: given a type T, possibly containing free occurrences of a type variable X, one can define an induced bijection $\mathtt{T(i)} : [\mathtt{X} \mapsto \mathtt{T_1}]\mathtt{T} \cong [\mathtt{X} \mapsto \mathtt{T_2}]\mathtt{T}$ (with inverse $\mathtt{T(i^{-1})}$). For example, if T is the type

```
{mk:X, inc:X→X, get:X→Int}
```

then T(i) is

```
λx:{ mk:T₁, inc:T₁→T₁, get:T₁→Int}.
    { mk = i(x.mk),
      inc = λx₂:T₂.i(x.inc(i⁻¹ x₂)),
      get = λx₂:T₂.x.get(i⁻¹ x₂)) }
```

and $\mathtt{T(i^{-1})}$ is

```
λx:{ mk:T₂, inc:T₂→T₂, get:T₂→Int}.
    { mk = i⁻¹(x.mk),
      inc = λx₁:T₁.i⁻¹(x.inc(i x₁)),
      get = λx₁:T₁.x.get(i x₁)) }.
```

(In general, if T is a simple type then the definition of T(i) and T(i^{-1}) can be done by induction on the structure of T; for recursively defined types, the definition of the induced bijection is not so straightforward.) □

We can use this second version of the extensionality principle for existential types to prove the contextual equivalence in (7.3), using the bijection

$$\mathtt{i} \overset{\text{def}}{=} (\lambda\mathtt{x}:\mathtt{Int}.\mathtt{0}\text{-}\mathtt{x}) : \mathtt{Int} \cong \mathtt{Int}.$$

This does indeed satisfy $\mathtt{T(i)}\ \mathtt{v}_1 =_{\text{ctx}} \mathtt{v}_2 : \mathtt{Int}$ when $\mathtt{v}_1$, $\mathtt{v}_2$, and T are defined as above. (Of course these contextual equivalences, and indeed the fact that this particular term i is a bijection, all require proof; but the methods developed in this chapter render this straightforward.) However, the use of bijections between types is still too restrictive for proving many common examples of contextual equivalence of abstract datatype implementations, such as the following.

7.3.5 **Example:** Consider the following existentially quantified record type, where Bool is a type of booleans.

```
type Semaphore = {∃X, {bit:X, flip:X→X, read:X→Bool}}
```

The following terms have type Semaphore:

```
val semaphore₁ =
    {*Bool, {bit  = true
             flip = λx:Bool.not x,
             read = λx:Bool.x       } as Semaphore;
val semaphore₂ =
    {*Int,  {bit  = 1,
             flip = λx:Int.0-2*x,
             read = λx:Int.x >= 0} as Semaphore
```

There is no bijection Bool ≅ Int, so one cannot use Principle 7.3.4 to prove

$$\mathtt{semaphore}_1 =_{\text{ctx}} \mathtt{semaphore}_2 : \mathtt{Semaphore}. \tag{7.4}$$

Nevertheless, this contextual equivalence does hold. An informal argument for this makes use of the following relation $r : \mathtt{Bool} \leftrightarrow \mathtt{Int}$ between values of type Bool and of type Int.

$$\begin{aligned} r \overset{\text{def}}{=} &\quad \{(\mathtt{true},\mathtt{m}) \mid m = (-2)^n \text{ for some even } n \geq 0\} \\ &\cup \ \{(\mathtt{false},\mathtt{m}) \mid m = (-2)^n \text{ for some odd } n \geq 0\}. \end{aligned}$$

Write $\mathtt{s}_i$ for the second component of $\mathtt{semaphore}_i$ ($i = 1,2$). Then

- $\mathtt{s_1.bit}$ evaluates to true; $\mathtt{s_2.bit}$ evaluates to 1; and $(\mathtt{true}, 1) \in r$;
- if $(\mathtt{t_1}, \mathtt{t_2}) \in r$, then $(\mathtt{s_1.flip})\mathtt{t_1}$ and $(\mathtt{s_2.flip})\mathtt{t_2}$ evaluate to a pair of values which are again r-related;
- if $(\mathtt{t_1}, \mathtt{t_2}) \in r$, then $(\mathtt{s_1.read})\mathtt{t_1}$ and $(\mathtt{s_2.read})\mathtt{t_2}$ evaluate to the same boolean value.

The informal argument for the contextual equivalence (7.4) goes as follows: "any context t[−] which is well-typed whenever its hole '−' is filled with a term of type Semaphore can only make use of a term placed in its hole by opening it as an abstract pair {X,x} and applying the methods bit, flip, and read in some combination; therefore the above observations about r are enough to show that $\mathtt{t[semaphore_1]}$ and $\mathtt{t[semaphore_2]}$ always have the same evaluation behavior." □

The validity of this informal argument and in particular the assumptions it makes about the way a context can "use" its hole are far from immediate and need formal justification. Leaving that for later, at least we can state the relational principle a bit more precisely.

7.3.6 PRINCIPLE [EXTENSIONALITY FOR ∃-TYPES, FINAL VERSION]: For each existential type $\mathtt{E} \stackrel{\text{def}}{=} \{\exists\mathtt{X},\mathtt{T}\}$, types $\mathtt{T_1}$, $\mathtt{T_2}$, and values $\mathtt{v_1}$, $\mathtt{v_2}$, if there is a *relation* $r : \mathtt{T_1} \leftrightarrow \mathtt{T_2}$ between terms of type $\mathtt{T_1}$ and of type $\mathtt{T_2}$, such that $(\mathtt{v_1}, \mathtt{v_2}) \in \mathtt{T}[r]$, then $(\{{*}\mathtt{T_1},\mathtt{v_1}\}\ \mathtt{as}\ \mathtt{E}) =_{\mathrm{ctx}} (\{{*}\mathtt{T_2},\mathtt{v_2}\}\ \mathtt{as}\ \mathtt{E}) : \{\exists\mathtt{X},\mathtt{T}\}$. □

Evidently this principle presupposes the existence of an "action" of types on term-relations that sends relations $r : \mathtt{T_1} \leftrightarrow \mathtt{T_2}$ to relations $\mathtt{T}[r] : [\mathtt{X} \mapsto \mathtt{T_1}]\mathtt{T} \leftrightarrow [\mathtt{X} \mapsto \mathtt{T_2}]\mathtt{T}$ and with certain other properties. It is the definition of this action that is at the heart of the matter. It has to be phrased with some care in order for the above extensionality principle to be valid for languages involving non-termination of evaluation (through the presence of fixpoint recursion for example). We will give a precise definition in §7.6 (Definition 7.6.9) for a language combining impredicative polymorphism with fixpoint recursion at the level of terms. How best to define such relational actions in the presence of recursion at the level of types is still a matter for research (see Exercise 7.8.1).

7.3.7 NOTE: Principle 7.3.4 generalizes Principle 7.3.3, because if $\mathtt{T_1} = \mathtt{T_2}$, then the identity function $\mathtt{i} \stackrel{\text{def}}{=} \lambda\mathtt{x{:}T_1.x}$ is a bijection $\mathtt{T_1} \cong \mathtt{T_2}$ satisfying

$$(\mathtt{T(i)\ v}) =_{\mathrm{ctx}} \mathtt{v} \quad \text{(for any v)}$$

so that $v_1 =_{ctx} v_2$ implies $(T(i)\ v_1) =_{ctx} v_2$. Principle 7.3.6 generalizes Principle 7.3.4, because each bijection $i : T_1 \cong T_2$ can be replaced by its *graph*

$$r_i \stackrel{\text{def}}{=} \{(u_1, u_2) \mid i\ u_1 =_{ctx} u_2\}$$

which in fact has the property that $(v_1, v_2) \in T[r_i]$ if and only if $(T(i)\ v_1)$ is contextually equivalent to v_2. □

As mentioned in the Introduction, Principle 7.3.6 is an operational generalization of similar principles for the denotational semantics of abstract datatypes over the simply typed lambda calculus (Mitchell, 1991a) and relationally parametric models of the polymorphic lambda calculus (Plotkin and Abadi, 1993). It permits many examples of contextual equivalence at existential types to be proved rather easily. Nevertheless, we will see in §7.7 that it is incomplete for the particular ML-like language we consider here, in the sense that $(\{{*}T_1, v_1\}\ \text{as}\ E) =_{ctx} (\{{*}T_2, v_2\}\ \text{as}\ E) : \{\exists X, T\}$ can hold even though there is no relation r for which $(v_1, v_2) \in T[r]$ holds (see Example 7.7.4).

7.4 The Language

In this section we define a small, ML-like programming language that we will use in the rest of the chapter. It combines Girard's *System F* (1972) (in other words, the *polymorphic lambda calculus* of Reynolds [1974]) with recursively defined functions, record types and ground types; in common with ML (Milner, Tofte, Harper, and MacQueen, 1997), evaluation order is strict (i.e., left-to-right, call-by-value). We will call the language F_{ML}. Its syntax and type system are specified in Figure 7-1 and its operational semantics in Figure 7-2.

Syntax

In Figure 7-1, X and x respectively range over disjoint countably infinite sets of *type variables* and *value variables*; `l` ranges over a countably infinite set of *field labels*; `c` ranges over the constants `true`, `false` and `n` (for $n \in \mathbb{Z}$); `Gnd` is either the type of booleans `Bool` or the type of integers `Int`; and `op` ranges over a fixed collection of arithmetic and boolean operations (such as +, =, `not`, etc).

To simplify the definition of the language's operational semantics we employ the now quite common device of using a syntax for terms that is in a "reduced" (or "A-normal") form, with all sequential evaluation expressed via `let`-expressions. For example, the general form of (left-to-right, call-by-value) function application is coded by

$$t_1\ t_2 \stackrel{\text{def}}{=} \text{let}\ x_1{=}t_1\ \text{in}\ (\text{let}\ x_2{=}t_2\ \text{in}\ x_1\ x_2). \tag{7.5}$$

Syntax

t ::=		*terms:*
	`v`	*value*
	`if v then t else t`	*conditional*
	$\mathtt{op}(\mathtt{v}_i\ ^{i\in 1..n})$	*operation*
	`v v`	*application*
	`v.l`	*projection*
	`v T`	*type application*
	`let {*X,x}=v in t`	*unpacking*
	`let x=t in t`	*sequencing*
v ::=		*values:*
	`x`	*value variable*
	`c`	*constant*
	`fun x(x:T)=t:T`	*recursive function*
	$\{\mathtt{l}_i\mathtt{=v}_i\ ^{i\in 1..n}\}$	*record value*
	`λX.v`	*type abstraction*
	`{*T,v} as {∃X,T}`	*package value*
T ::=		*types:*
	`X`	*type variable*
	`Gnd`	*ground type*
	`T→T`	*function type*
	$\{\mathtt{l}_i\mathtt{:T}_i\ ^{i\in 1..n}\}$	*record type*
	`∀X.T`	*universally quantified type*
	`{∃X,T}`	*existentially quantified type*
Γ ::=		*typing contexts:*
	$\emptyset$	*empty context*
	Γ, x:T	*non-empty context*
	Γ, X	*non-empty context*

Typing terms $\boxed{\Gamma \vdash \mathtt{t} : \mathtt{T}}$

$$\frac{\mathtt{x}:\mathtt{T} \in \Gamma}{\Gamma \vdash \mathtt{x} : \mathtt{T}} \quad \text{(T-VAR)}$$

$$\Gamma \vdash \mathtt{c} : \mathit{Typeof}(\mathtt{c}) \quad \text{(T-CONST)}$$

$$\frac{\Gamma, \mathtt{f}:\mathtt{T}, \mathtt{x}:\mathtt{T}_1 \vdash \mathtt{t} : \mathtt{T}_2 \qquad \mathtt{T} = \mathtt{T}_1 \to \mathtt{T}_2}{\Gamma \vdash \mathtt{fun\ f(x:T_1)=t:T_2} : \mathtt{T}} \quad \text{(T-FUN)}$$

$$\frac{(\Gamma \vdash \mathtt{v}_i : \mathtt{T}_i)\ ^{i\in 1..n}}{\Gamma \vdash \{\mathtt{l}_i\mathtt{=v}_i\ ^{i\in 1..n}\} : \{\mathtt{l}_i\mathtt{:T}_i\ ^{i\in 1..n}\}} \quad \text{(T-RCD)}$$

$$\frac{\Gamma, \mathtt{X} \vdash \mathtt{v} : \mathtt{T} \qquad \mathtt{X} \notin \mathit{ftv}(\Gamma)}{\Gamma \vdash \lambda \mathtt{X}.\mathtt{v} : \forall \mathtt{X}.\mathtt{T}} \quad \text{(T-TABS)}$$

$$\frac{\Gamma \vdash \mathtt{v}_1 : [\mathtt{X} \mapsto \mathtt{T}_1]\mathtt{T} \qquad \mathtt{T}' = \{\exists \mathtt{X}, \mathtt{T}\}}{\Gamma \vdash \{{*}\mathtt{T}_1, \mathtt{v}_1\}\ \mathtt{as}\ \mathtt{T}' : \mathtt{T}'} \quad \text{(T-PACK)}$$

$$\frac{\Gamma \vdash \mathtt{v} : \mathtt{Bool} \qquad \Gamma \vdash \mathtt{t}_1 : \mathtt{T} \qquad \Gamma \vdash \mathtt{t}_2 : \mathtt{T}}{\Gamma \vdash \mathtt{if\ v\ then\ t_1\ else\ t_2} : \mathtt{T}} \quad \text{(T-IF)}$$

$$\frac{\mathtt{op}:\mathtt{Gnd}_1, \ldots, \mathtt{Gnd}_n \to \mathtt{Gnd} \qquad (\Gamma \vdash \mathtt{v}_i : \mathtt{Gnd}_i)\ ^{i\in 1..n}}{\Gamma \vdash \mathtt{op}(\mathtt{v}_i\ ^{i\in 1..n}) : \mathtt{Gnd}} \quad \text{(T-OP)}$$

$$\frac{\Gamma \vdash \mathtt{v}_1 : \mathtt{T}_1 \to \mathtt{T}_2 \qquad \Gamma \vdash \mathtt{v}_2 : \mathtt{T}_1}{\Gamma \vdash \mathtt{v}_1\ \mathtt{v}_2 : \mathtt{T}_2} \quad \text{(T-APP)}$$

$$\frac{\Gamma \vdash \mathtt{v} : \{\mathtt{l}_i\mathtt{:T}_i\ ^{i\in 1..n}\}}{\Gamma \vdash \mathtt{v}.\mathtt{l}_j : \mathtt{T}_j} \quad \text{(T-PROJ)}$$

$$\frac{\Gamma \vdash \mathtt{v} : \forall \mathtt{X}.\mathtt{T}}{\Gamma \vdash \mathtt{v}\ \mathtt{T}_1 : [\mathtt{X} \mapsto \mathtt{T}_1]\mathtt{T}} \quad \text{(T-TAPP)}$$

$$\frac{\Gamma, \mathtt{X}, \mathtt{x}:\mathtt{T} \vdash \mathtt{t} : \mathtt{T}_1 \qquad \mathtt{X} \notin \mathit{ftv}(\Gamma, \mathtt{T}_1) \qquad \Gamma \vdash \mathtt{v} : \{\exists \mathtt{X}, \mathtt{T}\}}{\Gamma \vdash \mathtt{let}\ \{{*}\mathtt{X}, \mathtt{x}\}\mathtt{=v}\ \mathtt{in}\ \mathtt{t} : \mathtt{T}_1} \quad \text{(T-UNPACK)}$$

$$\frac{\Gamma \vdash \mathtt{t}_1 : \mathtt{T}_1 \qquad \Gamma, \mathtt{x}:\mathtt{T}_1 \vdash \mathtt{t}_2 : \mathtt{T}_2}{\Gamma \vdash \mathtt{let\ x=t_1\ in\ t_2} : \mathtt{T}_2} \quad \text{(T-SEQ)}$$

Figure 7-1: F_{ML} syntax and typing

As a further simplification, function abstraction and recursive function declaration have been rolled into the one form fun $\mathtt{f(x{:}T_1) = t{:}T_2}$, which corresponds to the expressions

$$\begin{array}{lll} & \mathtt{let\ fun\ f\ (x{:}T_1) = t{:}T_2\ in\ f\ end} & \text{in Standard ML} \\ \text{or} & \mathtt{let\ rec\ f\ (x{:}T_1) = t{:}T_2\ in\ f} & \text{in Ocaml.} \end{array}$$

Ordinary function abstraction can be coded as

$$\lambda \mathtt{x{:}T_1.t} \stackrel{\text{def}}{=} \mathtt{fun\ f(x{:}T_1) = t{:}T_2} \tag{7.6}$$

where f does not occur freely in t (and T_2 is the type of t, given f has type $T_1 \rightarrow T_2$ and x has type T_1). In what follows we shall use the abbreviations (7.5) and (7.6) without further comment. We shall also use infix notation for application of constant arithmetic and boolean operators such as +, =, etc.

7.4.1 Remark [Value-restriction]: Note that the operation $\lambda X.(-)$ of polymorphic generalization is restricted to apply only to values. This is a real restriction since for a non-value term t, one cannot define $\lambda X.t$ to be the term let x=t in $\lambda X.x$, since the latter will in general be an ill-typed term. In an ML-like language $\lambda X.t$ is not yet fully evaluated if t is a non-value; and thus evaluation must go under type abstraction $\lambda X.(-)$ and work on terms at types with free type variables. By imposing the restriction that $\lambda X.t$ is only well-formed when t is a value we can restrict attention to the evaluation of closed terms of *closed* type, simplifying the technical development. The restriction does not seem to affect the expressiveness of F_{ML} in practice and is comparable to the "value restriction" on let-bound polymorphism used in the 1997 revision of Standard ML (Milner et al., 1997) and in Objective Caml (Leroy, 2000). However, this restriction does have an effect on the properties of F_{ML}. For example, with the restriction the type $\forall X.X$ contains no closed values (see Exercise 7.7.6); whereas without the restriction there are closed values of that type, such as $\lambda X.$ (fun f(x:Bool) = f x : X) true. The "emptiness" of $\forall X.X$ plays a role in the properties explored in Example 7.7.4 and Remark 7.7.7. □

Operational Semantics

Although we do not do so, the operational semantics of F_{ML} could be specified in the style of the *Definition of Standard ML* (Milner, Tofte, Harper, and MacQueen, 1997) as a syntax-directed, inductively defined relation between terms and values.[3] Here we are interested primarily in the notion of contex-

3. That Definition uses environments assigning values to value variables. For reasons of technical convenience we eliminate the use of environments by substituting them into the term and only considering the evaluation relation between *closed* terms and values.

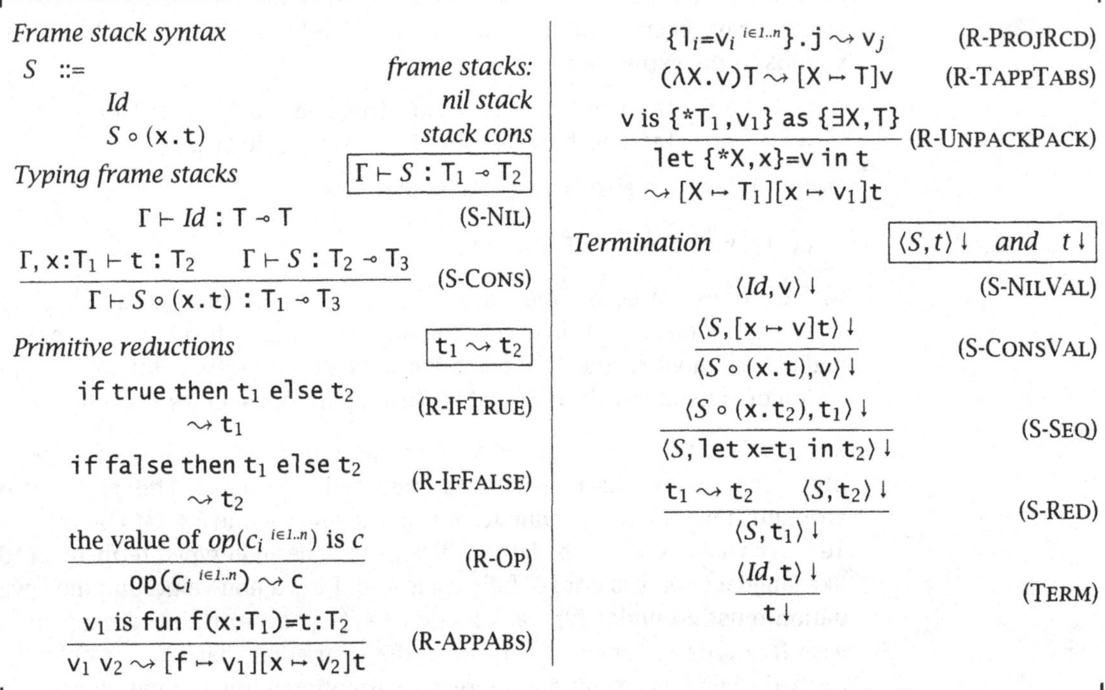

Figure 7-2: F_{ML} operational semantics

tual equivalence (Definition 7.3.2) that this evaluation relation determines by observing the results of evaluating terms in context. Because evaluation in F_{ML} is strict and the language has a sufficiently expressive collection of constructs for deconstructing values, it turns out that the notion of contextual equivalence is not affected much by the choice of what to observe of evaluation. Most reasonable choices give rise to the same equivalence as the one we adopt (see Exercise 7.5.10 below), which is based upon observing *termination*: whether or not a term evaluates to some value, we care not which. So instead of defining the relation of evaluation between terms and values, we proceed directly to a definition of the termination relation, $\mathtt{t}\!\downarrow$, for F_{ML}. This is given in Figure 7-2, using an auxiliary notion of *frame stack*. (The conventions and notations used in Figure 7-2 in connection with binding, free variables and substitution are summarized in Figure 7-3.)

Frame stacks are finite lists of individual "evaluation frames." They provide a convenient syntax for the notion of *evaluation context* E[−] (Felleisen and Hieb, 1992; Wright and Felleisen, 1994). Every closed term can be decomposed

Binding constructs

$\texttt{let \{*X,x\}=v in (-)}$
$\texttt{let x=t in (-)}$
$\texttt{fun f(x:T}_1\texttt{)=(-:T}_2\texttt{)}$
$\lambda\texttt{X.(-)}$
$\forall\texttt{X.(-)}$
$\texttt{\{}\exists\texttt{X,(-)\}}$
$S \circ \texttt{(x.(-))}$

We identify expressions up to renaming of bound value and type variables.

Notation for free variable sets

$ftv(E)$ is the finite set of free type variables of the expression E (a type, a term, or a frame stack);

$fv(E)$ is the finite set of free value variables of an expression E (a term, or a frame stack, but not a type, since types do not contain occurrences of value variables).

Closed types, terms and frame stacks

A type T is *closed* if $ftv(\mathsf{T}) = \emptyset$.

A term or frame stack E is *closed* if $fv(\mathsf{E}) = \emptyset$ (even if $ftv(\mathsf{E}) \neq \emptyset$).

Notation for substitution

$[\mathsf{X} \mapsto \mathsf{T}]E$ denotes the result of capture-avoiding substitution of a type T for all free occurrences of a type variable X in E (a type, a term, or a frame stack);

$[\mathsf{x} \mapsto \mathsf{v}]E$ denotes the result of capture-avoiding substitution of a value v for all free occurrences of the value variable x in a term or frame stack E.

(Note that as their name suggests, value variables stand for unknown *values*—the substitution of a non-value term for a variable makes no sense syntactically, in that it may result in an ill-formed expression.)

Figure 7-3: Binding, free variables and substitution

uniquely as E[t] where the evaluation context E[−] is a context with a unique hole (−) occurring in the place where the next step of evaluation (called a *primitive reduction* in Figure 7-2), if any, will take place. With F_{ML}'s reduced syntax, such evaluation contexts turn out to be just nested sequences of the `let`-construct

$$\mathsf{E}[-] = \texttt{let } \mathsf{x}_1\texttt{=(...(let } \mathsf{x}_n\texttt{=(-) in } \mathsf{t}_n\texttt{)...) in } \mathsf{t}_1.$$

The corresponding frame stack

$$S = Id \circ (\mathsf{x}_1 . \mathsf{t}_1) \circ \cdots \circ (\mathsf{x}_n . \mathsf{t}_n)$$

records this sequence as a list of *evaluation frames*, $\mathsf{x}_i . \mathsf{t}_i$ (with free occurrences of x_i in t_i being bound in $\mathsf{x}_i . \mathsf{t}_i$). Under this correspondence it can be shown that E[t] evaluates to some value in the standard evaluation-style (or "big-step") structural operational semantics if and only if $\langle S, \mathsf{t}\rangle\downarrow$ holds, for the relation $\langle -, -\rangle\downarrow$ defined in Figure 7-2. Not only does the use of frame stacks enable a conveniently syntax-directed inductive definition of termination, but also frame stacks play a big role in §7.6 when defining the logical relation that we use to establish properties of F_{ML} contextual equivalence.

7.4.2 EXERCISE [RECOMMENDED, ★★]: Consider a relation $\langle S_1, \mathtt{t}_1\rangle \longrightarrow \langle S_2, \mathtt{t}_2\rangle$ defined by cases according to the structure of the term $\mathtt{t}_1$ and the frame stack S_1, as follows:

- $\langle S \circ (\mathtt{x.t}), \mathtt{v}\rangle \longrightarrow \langle S, [\mathtt{x} \mapsto \mathtt{v}]\mathtt{t}\rangle$
- $\langle S, \mathtt{let\ x=t_1\ in\ t_2}\rangle \longrightarrow \langle S \circ (\mathtt{x.t_2}), \mathtt{t}_1\rangle$
- $\langle S, \mathtt{t}_1\rangle \longrightarrow \langle S, \mathtt{t}_2\rangle$, if $\mathtt{t}_1 \rightsquigarrow \mathtt{t}_2$.

Show that

$$\langle S'@S, \mathtt{t}\rangle\downarrow \quad\Leftrightarrow\quad (\exists \mathtt{v})\ \langle S, \mathtt{t}\rangle \longrightarrow^* \langle Id, \mathtt{v}\rangle\ \&\ \langle S', \mathtt{v}\rangle\downarrow \tag{7.7}$$

where $\longrightarrow^*$ denotes the reflexive-transitive closure of the $\longrightarrow$ relation, and $S'@S$ is the frame stack obtained by appending the two lists of evaluation frames S' and S. Deduce that $\mathtt{t}\downarrow$ holds if and only if there is some value $\mathtt{v}$ with $\langle Id, \mathtt{t}\rangle \longrightarrow^* \langle Id, \mathtt{v}\rangle$. □

Typing

We will consider the termination relation only for frame stacks and terms that are *well-typed.* A term $\mathtt{t}$ is well-typed with respect to a particular typing context Γ if a typing judgment

$$\Gamma \vdash \mathtt{t} : \mathtt{T} \tag{7.8}$$

can be derived for some type $\mathtt{T}$ using the rules in Figure 7-1. We identify typing contexts Γ up to rearranging their constituent hypotheses ("$\mathtt{X}$" or "$\mathtt{x} : \mathtt{X}$") and eliminating duplicates. Thus a typical typing context looks like

$$\Gamma = \mathtt{X}_1, \ldots, \mathtt{X}_m, \mathtt{x}_1 : \mathtt{T}_1, \ldots, \mathtt{x}_n : \mathtt{T}_n$$

where the type variables $\mathtt{X}_i$ and the value variables $\mathtt{x}_j$ are all distinct (and $m = 0$ or $n = 0$ is allowed). The typing judgments that are derivable from the rules all have the property that the free type variables of $\mathtt{T}$ and each $\mathtt{T}_j$ occur in the set $\{\mathtt{X}_1, \ldots, \mathtt{X}_m\}$, and the free value variables of $\mathtt{t}$ occur in the set $\{\mathtt{x}_1, \ldots, \mathtt{x}_n\}$. This is ensured by including some explicit side-conditions about free variable occurrences in the typing rules (T-ABS) and (T-UNPACK). In *TAPL*, Chapters 23 and 24, such side-conditions are implicit, being subsumed by extra well-formedness conditions for typing judgments. Also, we have chosen to include sufficient explicit type information in terms to ensure that for any given Γ and t, there is at most one T for which (7.8) holds. Apart from such minor differences, the rules in Figure 7-1 for inductively generating the valid F_{ML} typing judgments are all quite standard.

The judgment for typing frame stacks takes the form

$$\Gamma \vdash S : \mathsf{T}_1 \multimap \mathsf{T}_2 \tag{7.9}$$

where, in terms of the evaluation context corresponding to S, T_2 is the overall type of the context, given that T_1 is the type of the hole. The rules for generating this judgment are given in Figure 7-2. Unlike for terms, we have not included explicit type information in the syntax of frame stacks; for example, *Id* is not tagged with a type. However, it is not hard to see that, given Γ, S, and T_1, there is at most one T_2 for which (7.9) holds. This property is enough for our purposes, since the argument type of a frame stack will always be supplied in any particular situation in which we use it.

7.4.3 EXERCISE [★, ↛]: Write $\Gamma \vdash \langle S, \mathtt{t}\rangle : \mathsf{T}$ to mean that $\Gamma \vdash S : \mathsf{T}' \multimap \mathsf{T}$ and $\Gamma \vdash \mathtt{t} : \mathsf{T}'$ hold for some type T′. Using the relation $\longrightarrow$ from Exercise 7.4.2, show that if $\emptyset \vdash \langle S_1, \mathtt{t}_1\rangle : \mathsf{T}$ and $\langle S_1, \mathtt{t}_1\rangle \longrightarrow \langle S_2, \mathtt{t}_2\rangle$, then $\emptyset \vdash \langle S_2, \mathtt{t}_2\rangle : \mathsf{T}$. □

Unwinding Recursive Functions

In what follows we will need a finiteness property of recursively defined functions with respect to the termination relation. This *unwinding property*, as it is called, is a syntactic analog of the fact that the denotation of a recursively defined function is constructed as the least upper bound (*lub*) of finite approximations obtained by successively unfolding its definition starting with the *bottom* denotation, i.e., the totally undefined partial function. This gives rise to the useful principle of *Scott induction* in denotational semantics: given an *admissible* property of denotations, i.e., one closed under the formation of lubs of increasing chains, to show that it holds of the denotation of recursively defined data it suffices to show that it holds of bottom and is closed under application of the function that defines the data as a fixed point. Here we use a syntactic analog of Scott induction for recursively defined functions, $\mathtt{fun\ f(x{:}T_1) = u{:}T_2}$, in order to prove the "fundamental property" (Lemma 7.6.17) of the logical relation constructed in §7.6.

The proof of the unwinding property that we give here is made easier by our syntax-directed definition of termination using frame stacks. For statements and proofs of similar properties see for example: Mason, Smith, and Talcott (1996), Section 4.3, Pitts and Stark (1998), Theorem 3.2, Birkedal and Harper (1999), Section 3.1, and Lassen (1998), Section 4.5.

7.4.4 THEOREM [UNWINDING]: Given any closed recursive function value F of the form fun f(x:T_1)=u:T_2, define the followings abbreviations[4] :

$$F_0 \stackrel{\text{def}}{=} \texttt{fun f(x:}T_1\texttt{) = (f x) : }T_2$$
$$F_{n+1} \stackrel{\text{def}}{=} \texttt{fun f(x:}T_1\texttt{) = [f} \mapsto F_n\texttt{]u : }T_2$$

Thus F_0 is a closed function value describing a function of type $T_1 \to T_2$ that diverges when applied to any argument, and the F_n are obtained from this by repeatedly substituting for the the value variable f in the body u of the original function value F. Then for all terms t containing at most f free we have $[f \mapsto F]t\downarrow$ if and only if $(\exists n)\ [f \mapsto F_n]t\downarrow$. □

Proof: By definition of the relation $t\downarrow$ in terms of the relation $\langle S, t\rangle\downarrow$ (via rule (TERM) in Figure 7-2), it suffices to prove the more general property that for all terms t and frame stacks S (containing at most f free) we have

$$\langle [f \mapsto F]S, [f \mapsto F]t\rangle\downarrow \;\Leftrightarrow\; (\exists n)\ \langle [f \mapsto F_n]S, [f \mapsto F_n]t\rangle\downarrow \tag{7.10}$$

The proof of (7.10) is via a series of straightforward, if somewhat tedious, inductions that we leave as an exercise. □

7.4.5 EXERCISE [★★★, ↛]: This exercise leads you through a proof of (7.10). First prove that

$$\langle [f \mapsto F_n]S, [f \mapsto F_n]t\rangle\downarrow \;\Rightarrow\; \langle [f \mapsto F]S, [f \mapsto F]t\rangle\downarrow \tag{7.11}$$

holds for all n, S and t by induction on the derivation of $\langle [f \mapsto F_n]S, [f \mapsto F_n]t\rangle\downarrow$ from the rules in Figure 7-2. Conversely show that

$$\langle [f \mapsto F]S, [f \mapsto F]t\rangle\downarrow \;\Rightarrow\; (\exists n)\ \langle [f \mapsto F_n]S, [f \mapsto F_n]t\rangle\downarrow \tag{7.12}$$

holds for all S and t, by induction on the derivation of $\langle [f \mapsto F]S, [f \mapsto F]t\rangle\downarrow$ from the rules. To do this, you will first need to prove by induction on n that

$$\langle [f \mapsto F_n]S, [f \mapsto F_n]t\rangle\downarrow \;\Rightarrow\; \langle [f \mapsto F_{n+1}]S, [f \mapsto F_{n+1}]t\rangle\downarrow \tag{7.13}$$

holds for all n, S and t; the base case $n = 0$ involves yet another induction, this time over the derivation of $\langle [f \mapsto F_0]S, [f \mapsto F_0]t\rangle\downarrow$ from the rules. □

4. Note that in the definition of F_{n+1}, the outer binding instance of f is a dummy, since f does not occur free in $[f \mapsto F_n]$u.

7.5 Contextual Equivalence

Definition 7.3.2 gave an informal definition of the notion of *contextual equivalence* that applies to any (typed) programming language. In giving a precise definition of this notion for the F_{ML} language we will take the more abstract, relational approach of Gordon (1998) and Lassen (1998) that avoids the explicit use of program contexts `t[-]` in favor of congruence relations. For one thing, program contexts are an inconveniently concrete notion, because substitution of terms `t'` for the hole "–" in a context `t[-]` to produce a term `t[t']` may involve the capture of free variables in `t'` by binders in `t[-]`. For example, when we replace the hole "–" in the context `fun f(x:T) = f [-]` by the term `f x`, its free value variables are captured by the `fun`-binder. Consequently, contexts have to be treated more concretely than terms since renaming their bound variables may not preserve their meaning. For example, if we identified `fun f(x:T) = f [-]` with `fun g(x:T) = g [-]` (where `f` and `g` are distinct value variables), then we should have to identify the results of filling the hole with `f x`, that is, we should have to identify the syntactically unequal terms `fun f(x:T) = f(f x)` and `fun g(x:T) = g(f x)`. But more than this, the abstract treatment of contextual equivalence that we use focuses attention upon the key features of this kind of program equality, namely that it is a congruence and is "adequate" for observing termination. In a nutshell, we will define contextual equivalence to be the largest type-respecting congruence relation between F_{ML} terms that is adequate for observing termination.

7.5.1 DEFINITION: A *type-respecting binary relation* between F_{ML} terms is a set R of quadruples (Γ, t, t', T), each consisting of a typing context, two terms and a type satisfying $\Gamma \vdash t : T$ and $\Gamma \vdash t' : T$. Figure 7-4 defines the properties of *reflexivity*, *symmetry*, *transitivity*, *substitutivity*, and *compatibility* for such relations; R has one of these properties if it is closed under the axioms and rules under the corresponding heading in the figure. In these figures, and elsewhere, we write $\Gamma \vdash t \mathrel{R} t' : T$ instead of $(\Gamma, t, t', T) \in R$. We say that R is

- an *equivalence relation* if it has the reflexivity, symmetry and transitivity properties;
- a *congruence relation* if it is an equivalence relation with the *substitutivity* and *compatibility* properties;
- *adequate* (for the termination relation $\downarrow$ defined in Figure 7-2) if whenever $\emptyset \vdash t \mathrel{R} t' : T$ holds, then $t\downarrow$ holds if and only if $t'\downarrow$ does. □

7.5.2 DEFINITION: We will need to use the following constructions on type-respecting binary relations.

Reflexivity

$$\frac{\Gamma \vdash \mathtt{t} : \mathtt{T}}{\Gamma \vdash \mathtt{t}\,R\,\mathtt{t} : \mathtt{T}}$$

Symmetry

$$\frac{\Gamma \vdash \mathtt{t}\,R\,\mathtt{t}' : \mathtt{T}}{\Gamma \vdash \mathtt{t}'\,R\,\mathtt{t} : \mathtt{T}}$$

Transitivity

$$\frac{\Gamma \vdash \mathtt{t}\,R\,\mathtt{t}' : \mathtt{T} \qquad \Gamma \vdash \mathtt{t}'\,R\,\mathtt{t}'' : \mathtt{T}}{\Gamma \vdash \mathtt{t}\,R\,\mathtt{t}'' : \mathtt{T}}$$

Substitutivity

$$\frac{\Gamma \vdash \mathtt{v}\,R\,\mathtt{v}' : \mathtt{T}_1 \qquad \Gamma, \mathtt{x} : \mathtt{T}_1 \vdash \mathtt{t}\,R\,\mathtt{t}' : \mathtt{T}_2}{\Gamma \vdash [\mathtt{x} \mapsto \mathtt{v}]\mathtt{t}\,R\,[\mathtt{x} \mapsto \mathtt{v}']\mathtt{t}' : \mathtt{T}_2}$$

$$\frac{\Gamma, \mathtt{X} \vdash \mathtt{t}\,R\,\mathtt{t}' : \mathtt{T}}{\Gamma \vdash [\mathtt{X} \mapsto \mathtt{T}_1]\mathtt{t}\,R\,[\mathtt{X} \mapsto \mathtt{T}_1]\mathtt{t}' : [\mathtt{X} \mapsto \mathtt{T}_1]\mathtt{T}}$$

Compatibility

$$\frac{(\mathtt{x}{:}\mathtt{T}) \in \Gamma}{\Gamma \vdash \mathtt{x}\,R\,\mathtt{x} : \mathtt{T}}$$

$$\Gamma \vdash \mathtt{c}\,R\,\mathtt{c} : \mathit{Typeof}(\mathtt{c})$$

$$\frac{\Gamma, \mathtt{f}{:}\mathtt{T}_1 \to \mathtt{T}_2, \mathtt{x}{:}\mathtt{T}_1 \vdash \mathtt{t}\,R\,\mathtt{t}' : \mathtt{T}_2}{\begin{array}{c}\Gamma \vdash \mathtt{fun\ f(x{:}T_1){=}t{:}T_2}\ R \\ \mathtt{fun\ f(x{:}T_1){=}t'{:}T_2} : \mathtt{T}_1 \to \mathtt{T}_2\end{array}}$$

$$\frac{(\Gamma \vdash \mathtt{v}_i\,R\,\mathtt{v}_i' : \mathtt{T}_i)^{\,i \in 1..n}}{\begin{array}{c}\Gamma \vdash \{\mathtt{l}_i{=}\mathtt{v}_i{}^{\,i \in 1..n}\}\,R\,\{\mathtt{l}_i{=}\mathtt{v}_i'{}^{\,i \in 1..n}\} \\ : \{\mathtt{l}_i{:}\mathtt{T}_i{}^{\,i \in 1..n}\}\end{array}}$$

$$\frac{\Gamma, \mathtt{X} \vdash \mathtt{v}\,R\,\mathtt{v}' : \mathtt{T} \qquad \mathtt{X} \notin \mathit{ftv}(\Gamma)}{\Gamma \vdash \lambda\mathtt{X.v}\,R\,\lambda\mathtt{X.v}' : \forall\mathtt{X.T}}$$

$$\frac{\Gamma \vdash \mathtt{v}_1\,R\,\mathtt{v}_1' : [\mathtt{X} \mapsto \mathtt{T}_1]\mathtt{T}}{\begin{array}{c}\Gamma \vdash \{{*}\mathtt{T}_1,\mathtt{v}_1\}\ \mathtt{as}\ \{\exists\mathtt{X},\mathtt{T}\}\ R \\ \{{*}\mathtt{T}_1,\mathtt{v}_1'\}\ \mathtt{as}\ \{\exists\mathtt{X},\mathtt{T}\} : \{\exists\mathtt{X},\mathtt{T}\}\end{array}}$$

$$\frac{\begin{array}{c}\Gamma \vdash \mathtt{v}\,R\,\mathtt{v}' : \mathtt{Bool} \\ \Gamma \vdash \mathtt{t}_1\,R\,\mathtt{t}_1' : \mathtt{T} \qquad \Gamma \vdash \mathtt{t}_2\,R\,\mathtt{t}_2' : \mathtt{T}\end{array}}{\begin{array}{c}\Gamma \vdash \mathtt{if\ v\ then\ t_1\ else\ t_2}\ R \\ \mathtt{if\ v'\ then\ t_1'\ else\ t_2'} : \mathtt{T}\end{array}}$$

$$\frac{\begin{array}{c}\mathtt{op{:}Gnd_1,\ldots,Gnd_n{\to}Gnd} \\ (\Gamma \vdash \mathtt{v}_i\,R\,\mathtt{v}_i' : \mathtt{Gnd}_i)^{\,i \in 1..n}\end{array}}{\Gamma \vdash \mathtt{op}(\mathtt{v}_i{}^{\,i \in 1..n})\,R\,\mathtt{op}(\mathtt{v}_i'{}^{\,i \in 1..n}) : \mathtt{Gnd}}$$

$$\frac{\Gamma \vdash \mathtt{v}_1\,R\,\mathtt{v}_1' : \mathtt{T}_1 \to \mathtt{T}_2 \qquad \Gamma \vdash \mathtt{v}_2\,R\,\mathtt{v}_2' : \mathtt{T}_1}{\Gamma \vdash \mathtt{v}_1\ \mathtt{v}_2\,R\,\mathtt{v}_1'\ \mathtt{v}_2' : \mathtt{T}_2}$$

$$\frac{\Gamma \vdash \mathtt{v}\,R\,\mathtt{v}' : \{\mathtt{l}_i{:}\mathtt{T}_i{}^{\,i \in 1..n}\}}{\Gamma \vdash \mathtt{v.l}_j\,R\,\mathtt{v}'\mathtt{.l}_j : \mathtt{T}_j}$$

$$\frac{\Gamma \vdash \mathtt{v}\,R\,\mathtt{v}' : \forall\mathtt{X.T}}{\Gamma \vdash \mathtt{v}\ \mathtt{T}_1\,R\,\mathtt{v}'\ \mathtt{T}_1 : [\mathtt{X} \mapsto \mathtt{T}_1]\mathtt{T}}$$

$$\frac{\begin{array}{c}\Gamma, \mathtt{X}, \mathtt{x}{:}\mathtt{T} \vdash \mathtt{t}\,R\,\mathtt{t}' : \mathtt{T}_1 \\ \mathtt{X} \notin \mathit{ftv}(\Gamma, \mathtt{T}_1) \qquad \Gamma \vdash \mathtt{v}\,R\,\mathtt{v}' : \{\exists\mathtt{X},\mathtt{T}\}\end{array}}{\begin{array}{c}\Gamma \vdash \mathtt{let}\ \{{*}\mathtt{X},\mathtt{x}\}{=}\mathtt{v}\ \mathtt{in}\ \mathtt{t}\ R \\ \mathtt{let}\ \{{*}\mathtt{X},\mathtt{x}\}{=}\mathtt{v}'\ \mathtt{in}\ \mathtt{t}' : \mathtt{T}_1\end{array}}$$

$$\frac{\Gamma \vdash \mathtt{t}_1\,R\,\mathtt{t}_1' : \mathtt{T}_1 \qquad \Gamma, \mathtt{x}{:}\mathtt{T}_1 \vdash \mathtt{t}_2\,R\,\mathtt{t}_2' : \mathtt{T}_2}{\Gamma \vdash \mathtt{let\ x{=}t_1\ in\ t_2}\,R\,\mathtt{let\ x{=}t_1'\ in\ t_2'} : \mathtt{T}_2}$$

Figure 7-4: Properties of a type-respecting relation R between F_{ML} terms

(i) The *identity* relation is $Id \stackrel{\text{def}}{=} \{(\Gamma, \mathtt{t}, \mathtt{t}, \mathtt{T}) \mid \Gamma \vdash \mathtt{t} : \mathtt{T}\}$.

(ii) The *reciprocal* of the relation R is $R^{op} \stackrel{\text{def}}{=} \{(\Gamma, \mathtt{t}', \mathtt{t}, \mathtt{T}) \mid \Gamma \vdash \mathtt{t}\,R\,\mathtt{t}' : \mathtt{T}\}$.

(iii) The *composition* of relations R_1 and R_2 is
$R_1 \circ R_2 \stackrel{\text{def}}{=} \{(\Gamma, \mathtt{t}, \mathtt{t}'', \mathtt{T}) \mid \exists \mathtt{t}'.\, \Gamma \vdash \mathtt{t}\,R_1\,\mathtt{t}' : \mathtt{T}\ \&\ \Gamma \vdash \mathtt{t}'\,R_2\,\mathtt{t}'' : \mathtt{T}\}$.

(iv) The *transitive closure* of the relation R is the countable union $R^+ \stackrel{\text{def}}{=} \bigcup_{i \in \mathbb{N}} R_i$, where $R_0 = R$ and $R_{i+1} = R \circ R_i$.

(v) The *open extension* of the relation R is denoted R° and consists of all quadruples $(\Gamma, \mathtt{t}, \mathtt{t}', \mathsf{T})$ such that $\emptyset \vdash \sigma(\mathtt{t})\ R\ \sigma(\mathtt{t}') : \sigma(\mathsf{T})$ holds for all Γ-closing substitutions σ. If $\Gamma = \mathsf{X}_1, \ldots, \mathsf{X}_m, \mathtt{x}_1 : \mathsf{T}_1, \ldots, \mathtt{x}_n : \mathsf{T}_n$, then a Γ-*closing substitution* is given by a function $[\mathsf{X}_i \mapsto \mathsf{T}_i \mid i = 1..m]$ mapping the type variables X_i to closed types T_i and by a function $[\mathtt{x}_j \mapsto \mathtt{v}_j \mid j = 1..n]$ mapping the value variables $\mathtt{x}_j$ to closed values $\mathtt{v}_j$ of appropriate type, namely satisfying $\emptyset \vdash \mathtt{v}_j : [\mathsf{X}_i \mapsto \mathsf{T}_i \mid i = 1..m]\mathsf{T}_j$.

(Note that R° only depends on the quadruples of the form $(\emptyset, \mathtt{t}, \mathtt{t}', \mathsf{T})$ in R.) □

We wish to define contextual equivalence to be the largest adequate congruence relation, but it is not immediately clear why a largest such relation exists. Therefore we give a theorem rather than a definition.

7.5.3 Theorem [F_{ML} contextual equivalence, $=_{\mathrm{ctx}}$]: There exists a largest type-respecting binary relation between F_{ML} terms that is a congruence and adequate. We call it *contextual equivalence* and write it $=_{\mathrm{ctx}}$. □

Proof: The proof makes use of the following series of facts, only the last of which is not entirely straightforward to prove (see Exercise 7.5.4).

(i) The identity relation *Id* is an adequate congruence relation.

(ii) The collection of adequate relations is closed under taking unions.

(iii) Every compatible relation is reflexive, i.e., contains *Id*.

(iv) The set of all of compatible relations is closed under the operations of composition and reciprocation; similarly for the set of all substitutive relations and the set of all adequate relations.

(v) If the union of a non-empty family of compatible relations is transitive, it is also compatible; similarly, if the union of a non-empty family of reflexive and substitutive relations is transitive, it is also (reflexive and) substitutive.

Let $=_{\mathrm{ctx}}$ be the union of the family of relations that are adequate, compatible and substitutive. Note that this family is non-empty by (i). By (ii), $=_{\mathrm{ctx}}$ is adequate. So it suffices to show that it is a congruence relation. It is certainly reflexive by (i); and (iv) implies that it is also symmetric and transitive. So it just remains to show that it is compatible and substitutive, and this follows from (v), whose proof needs (iii). □

7.5.4 EXERCISE [★★]: Prove properties (iii) and (v) stated in the above proof. □

It is not easy to use either the formulation in terms of contexts in Definition 7.3.2 or the more abstract characterisation of Theorem 7.5.3 to prove that a particular pair of terms are contextually equivalent. For example, it is not easy to see from these characterisations that terms in the primitive reduction relation of Figure 7-2 are contextually equivalent (Corollary 7.5.8). That this is so follows from the coincidence of $=_{\text{ctx}}$ with a notion of equivalence popularized by Mason and Talcott (1991).

7.5.5 DEFINITION [CIU-EQUIVALENCE, $=_{\text{ciu}}$]: Two closed F_{ML} terms belonging to the same (closed) type are *ciu-equivalent* if they have the same termination behavior when they are paired with any frame stack (a "use" of the terms); the relation is extended to open terms via closing substitutions (or "closed instantiations"—thus we arrive at an explanation of the rather cryptic name for this equivalence).

More formally, we define $=_{\text{ciu}}$ to be the type-respecting relation R° (using the operation from Definition 7.5.2(v)), where R consists of quadruples $(\varnothing, \mathtt{t}, \mathtt{t}', \mathtt{T})$ satisfying $\varnothing \vdash \mathtt{t} : \mathtt{T}$, $\varnothing \vdash \mathtt{t}' : \mathtt{T}$, and $\forall S.\ \langle S, \mathtt{t}\rangle\downarrow \Leftrightarrow \langle S, \mathtt{t}'\rangle\downarrow$. □

7.5.6 LEMMA: For any frame stack S and term $\mathtt{t}$, define a term $S[\mathtt{t}]$ by induction of the length of the stack S as follows:

$$\left.\begin{array}{rcl} Id[\mathtt{t}] & \stackrel{\text{def}}{=} & \mathtt{t} \\ S \circ (\mathtt{x}.\mathtt{t}')[\mathtt{t}] & \stackrel{\text{def}}{=} & S[\mathtt{let\ x=t\ in\ t'}] \end{array}\right\} \tag{7.14}$$

Then $\langle S, \mathtt{t}\rangle\downarrow$ if and only if $S[\mathtt{t}]\downarrow$ (i.e., $\langle Id, S[\mathtt{t}]\rangle\downarrow$). □

Proof: This is proved by induction on the length of S. The base case $S = Id$ is trivial. The induction step follows from the fact that $\langle S, \mathtt{let\ x=t\ in\ t'}\rangle\downarrow$ holds if and only if it was derived using rule (S-SEQ) in Figure 7-4, if and only if $\langle S \circ (\mathtt{x}.\mathtt{t}'), \mathtt{t}\rangle\downarrow$ holds. □

7.5.7 THEOREM [CIU THEOREM FOR F_{ML}]: The contextual and ciu-equivalence relations coincide. □

Proof: We first show that $=_{\text{ctx}}$ is contained in $=_{\text{ciu}}$. Suppose

$$\Gamma \vdash \mathtt{t} =_{\text{ctx}} \mathtt{t}' : \mathtt{T}. \tag{7.15}$$

Since $=_{\text{ctx}}$ satisfies the substitutivity and reflexivity properties from Figure 7-4, it follows that

$$\varnothing \vdash \sigma(\mathtt{t}) =_{\text{ctx}} \sigma(\mathtt{t}') : \sigma(\mathtt{T}) \tag{7.16}$$

for any Γ-closing substitution σ. For any frame stack S, since $=_{\text{ctx}}$ satisfies the compatibility (and reflexivity) properties from Figure 7-4, from (7.16) we deduce that $\emptyset \vdash S[\sigma(\texttt{t})] =_{\text{ctx}} S[\sigma(\texttt{t}')] : \sigma(\texttt{T})$ (using the notation of (7.14)). Since $=_{\text{ctx}}$ is adequate, this means that $S[\sigma(\texttt{t})]\downarrow$ if and only if $S[\sigma(\texttt{t}')]\downarrow$; hence by Lemma 7.5.6, $\langle S, \sigma(\texttt{t})\rangle\downarrow$ if and only if $\langle S, \sigma(\texttt{t}')\rangle\downarrow$. As this holds for all σ and S, we have $\Gamma \vdash \texttt{t} =_{\text{ciu}} \texttt{t}' : \texttt{T}$, as required.

To complete the proof of the theorem we have to show conversely that $=_{\text{ciu}}$ is contained in $=_{\text{ctx}}$. We can deduce this as a corollary of a stronger characterisation of $=_{\text{ctx}}$ in terms of logical relations (Theorem 7.6.25) that we establish later; so we postpone the rest of this proof until then. □

7.5.8 Corollary [Conversions]: The following are valid contextual equivalences:

(i) $\Gamma \vdash \texttt{if true then } \texttt{t}_1 \texttt{ else } \texttt{t}_2 =_{\text{ctx}} \texttt{t}_1 : \texttt{T}$ and
$\Gamma \vdash \texttt{if false then } \texttt{t}_1 \texttt{ else } \texttt{t}_2 =_{\text{ctx}} \texttt{t}_2 : \texttt{T}$, where $\Gamma \vdash \texttt{t}_i : \texttt{T}$ for $i = 1, 2$.

(ii) $\Gamma \vdash \texttt{op}(\texttt{c}_i{}^{i\in 1..n}) =_{\text{ctx}} \texttt{c} : \texttt{Gnd}$, where c is the value of $op(c_i{}^{i\in 1..n})$ and $Typeof(\texttt{c}) = \texttt{Gnd}$.

(iii) $\Gamma \vdash \texttt{v}_1\ \texttt{v}_2 =_{\text{ctx}} [\texttt{f} \mapsto \texttt{v}_1][\texttt{x} \mapsto \texttt{v}_2]\texttt{t} : \texttt{T}_2$,
where $\texttt{v}_1 = \texttt{fun f(x:T}_1\texttt{)=t:T}_2$.

(iv) $\Gamma \vdash \{\texttt{l}_i\texttt{=v}_i{}^{i\in 1..n}\}\texttt{.j} =_{\text{ctx}} \texttt{v}_j : \texttt{T}_j$,
where $\Gamma \vdash \{\texttt{l}_i\texttt{=v}_i{}^{i\in 1..n}\} : \{\texttt{l}_i\texttt{:T}_i{}^{i\in 1..n}\}$.

(v) $\Gamma \vdash (\lambda \texttt{X.v})\texttt{T}_1 =_{\text{ctx}} [\texttt{X} \mapsto \texttt{T}_1]\texttt{v} : [\texttt{X} \mapsto \texttt{T}_1]\texttt{T}$, where $\Gamma \vdash \texttt{v} : \forall \texttt{X.T}$.

(vi) $\Gamma \vdash \texttt{let \{*X,x\}=(\{*T}_1\texttt{,v}_1\texttt{\} as \{}\exists\texttt{X,T\}) in t} =_{\text{ctx}} [\texttt{X} \mapsto \texttt{T}_1][\texttt{x} \mapsto \texttt{v}_1]\texttt{t} : \texttt{T}_2$, where $\Gamma, \texttt{X}, \texttt{x:T} \vdash \texttt{t} : \texttt{T}_2$ with $\texttt{X} \notin ftv(\Gamma, \texttt{T}_2)$.

(vii) $\Gamma \vdash \texttt{let x=v in t} =_{\text{ctx}} [\texttt{x} \mapsto \texttt{v}]\texttt{t} : \texttt{T}_2$, where $\Gamma \vdash \texttt{v} : \texttt{T}_1$ and $\Gamma, \texttt{x:T}_1 \vdash \texttt{t} : \texttt{T}_2$.

(viii) $\Gamma \vdash \texttt{let x}_1\texttt{=t}_1\texttt{ in (let x}_2\texttt{=t}_2\texttt{ in t)} =_{\text{ctx}}$
$\texttt{let x}_2\texttt{=(let x}_1\texttt{=t}_1\texttt{ in t}_2\texttt{) in t} : \texttt{T}$, where $\Gamma \vdash \texttt{t}_1 : \texttt{T}_1$,
$\Gamma, \texttt{x}_1\texttt{:T}_1 \vdash \texttt{t}_2 : \texttt{T}_2$ and $\Gamma, \texttt{x}_2\texttt{:T}_2 \vdash \texttt{t} : \texttt{T}$. □

Proof: These are all ciu-equivalences, so we can just apply Theorem 7.5.7 (using the difficult half of the theorem whose proof we have postponed to §7.6!). The ciu-equivalences all follow easily from the definition of the termination relation (Figure 7-2) except for the last one, where one can apply property (7.7) from Exercise 7.4.2 to reduce proving (viii) for $=_{\text{ciu}}$ to the special case when $\texttt{t}_1$ is a value: see the following exercise. □

7.5.9 **Exercise** [★, ↛]: Given

$$\begin{aligned} \emptyset &\vdash \mathtt{t}_1 : \mathsf{T}_1 \\ \mathtt{x}_1{:}\mathsf{T}_1 &\vdash \mathtt{t}_2 : \mathsf{T}_2 \\ \mathtt{x}_2{:}\mathsf{T}_2 &\vdash \mathtt{t} : \mathsf{T} \end{aligned}$$

use property (7.7) to show for all frame stacks S that

$$\langle S \circ (\mathtt{x}_1.\mathtt{let}\ \mathtt{x}_2\mathtt{=t}_2\ \mathtt{in}\ \mathtt{t}), \mathtt{t}_1 \rangle \downarrow \quad \text{iff} \quad \langle S \circ (\mathtt{x}_2.\mathtt{t}) \circ (\mathtt{x}_1.\mathtt{t}_2), \mathtt{t}_1 \rangle \downarrow.$$

Deduce part (viii) of Corollary 7.5.8. □

7.5.10 **Exercise** [★★]: Recall from Definition 7.5.1 the notion of an adequate type-respecting binary relation. Let us call a type-respecting binary relation R `true`-*adequate* if, whenever $\emptyset \vdash \mathtt{t}\ R\ \mathtt{t}' : \mathtt{Bool}$ holds, $\langle Id, \mathtt{t} \rangle \longrightarrow^* \langle Id, \mathtt{true} \rangle$ holds if and only if $\langle Id, \mathtt{t}' \rangle \longrightarrow^* \langle Id, \mathtt{true} \rangle$ does. Here $\longrightarrow^*$ is the relation defined in Exercise 7.4.2. One can adapt the proof of Theorem 7.5.3 to show that there is a largest type-respecting binary relation $=_{ctx}^{\mathtt{true}}$ between F_{ML} terms that is a congruence and `true`-adequate. Show that $=_{ctx}^{\mathtt{true}}$ coincides with contextual equivalence, $=_{ctx}$. □

7.6 An Operationally Based Logical Relation

We now have a precise definition of contextual equivalence for F_{ML} terms. Before showing that the Extensionality Principle 7.3.6 holds for existential types in F_{ML}, we need a precise definition of the action of types on term-relations, $r \mapsto \mathsf{T}[r]$, mentioned in the principle. That is the topic of this section. We will end up with a characterisation of $=_{ctx}$ in terms of a logical relation, yielding several useful extensionality properties of contextual equivalence.

7.6.1 **Notation**: Let *Typ* denote the set of closed F_{ML} types. Given $\mathsf{T} \in Typ$, let

- *Term*(T) denote the set of closed terms of type T, i.e., those terms `t` for which $\emptyset \vdash \mathtt{t} : \mathsf{T}$ holds;
- *Val*(T) denote the subset of *Term*(T) whose elements are values; and
- *Stack*(T) denote the set of closed frame stacks whose argument type is T, i.e., those frame stacks S for which $\emptyset \vdash S : \mathsf{T} \multimap \mathsf{T}'$ for some $\mathsf{T}' \in Typ$.

Given $\mathsf{T}, \mathsf{T}' \in Typ$, let

- *TRel*(T, T′) denote the set of all subsets of *Term*(T) × *Term*(T′); we call its elements *term-relations*;

- $VRel(\mathsf{T},\mathsf{T}')$ denote the set of all subsets of $Val(\mathsf{T}) \times Val(\mathsf{T}')$; we call its elements *value-relations*;

- $SRel(\mathsf{T},\mathsf{T}')$ denote the the set of all subsets of $Stack(\mathsf{T}) \times Stack(\mathsf{T}')$; we call its elements *stack-relations*. □

Note that every value-relation is also a term-relation (since values are particular sorts of term): $VRel(\mathsf{T},\mathsf{T}') \subseteq TRel(\mathsf{T},\mathsf{T}')$. On the other hand we can obtain a value-relation from a term-relation just by restricting attention to values: given $r \in TRel(\mathsf{T},\mathsf{T}')$, define $r^{v} \in VRel(\mathsf{T},\mathsf{T}')$ by

$$r^{v} \stackrel{\text{def}}{=} \{(\mathsf{v},\mathsf{v}') \in Val(\mathsf{T}) \times Val(\mathsf{T}') \mid (\mathsf{v},\mathsf{v}') \in r\}. \tag{7.17}$$

We will be particularly interested in term-relations r that are indistinguishable, as far as termination properties are concerned, from their value restrictions, r^{v}. Definition 7.6.3 makes this precise, using a Galois connection between term-relations and stack-relations. The definition may appear to be rather mysterious; its nature will emerge as we develop the action of types on term-relations and its properties. First we recall for the reader what is meant in general by a "Galois connection."

7.6.2 DEFINITION: A *Galois connection* between partially ordered sets $(P, \leq_P)$ and $(Q, \leq_Q)$ is specified by a pair of functions $f : P \to Q$ and $g : Q \to P$ satisfying $q \leq_Q f(p)$ if and only if $p \leq_P g(q)$, for all $p \in P$ and $q \in Q$. □

7.6.3 DEFINITION [CLOSED AND VALUABLE TERM-RELATIONS]: Let $\mathsf{T} \in Typ$ and $\mathsf{T}' \in Typ$ be closed types. Given a term-relation $r \in TRel(\mathsf{T},\mathsf{T}')$, define a stack-relation $r^{s} \in SRel(\mathsf{T},\mathsf{T}')$ by

> $(S, S') \in r^{s}$ if and only if for all $(\mathsf{t},\mathsf{t}') \in r$, $\langle S, \mathsf{t}\rangle \downarrow$ holds if and only if $\langle S', \mathsf{t}'\rangle \downarrow$ does.

Conversely, given a stack-relation $s \in SRel(\mathsf{T},\mathsf{T}')$, define a term-relation $s^{t} \in TRel(\mathsf{T},\mathsf{T}')$ by

> $(\mathsf{t},\mathsf{t}') \in s^{t}$ if and only if for all $(S, S') \in s$, $\langle S, \mathsf{t}\rangle \downarrow$ holds if and only if $\langle S', \mathsf{t}'\rangle \downarrow$ does.

Call a term-relation $r \in TRel(\mathsf{T},\mathsf{T}')$ *closed* if it satisfies $r = r^{st}$ and *valuable* if it satisfies $r = r^{vst}$. □

7.6.4 NOTE: The operator $(-)^{st}$ is denoted $(-)^{\top\top}$ in Pitts (1998; 2000). □

7.6.5 LEMMA: The operations $(-)^s$ and $(-)^t$ for turning term-relations into stack-relations and *vice versa*, form a Galois connection:

$$s \subseteq r^s \quad \text{if and only if} \quad r \subseteq s^t. \tag{7.18}$$

Hence the operator $(-)^{st}$ on term-relations is monotone ($r_1 \subseteq r_2$ implies $(r_1)^{st} \subseteq (r_2)^{st}$), inflationary ($r \subseteq r^{st}$), and idempotent ($(r^{st})^{st} = r^{st}$). □

Proof: If $s \subseteq r^s$, then for any $(\mathtt{t},\mathtt{t}') \in r$ we have for all $(S,S') \in s$ that $(S,S') \in r^s$, so $\langle S,\mathtt{t}\rangle\downarrow$ iff $\langle S',\mathtt{t}'\rangle\downarrow$; hence $(\mathtt{t},\mathtt{t}') \in s^t$. Thus $s \subseteq r^s$ implies $r \subseteq s^t$. The converse implication holds by a similar argument. Once we have (7.18), the other properties follow by standard arguments true of any Galois connection, which we give in case the reader has not seen them before.

Thus for any term-relation r, since $r^s \subseteq r^s$, from (7.18) we conclude that $r \subseteq r^{st}$; so $(-)^{st}$ is inflationary (and symmetrically, so is the operator $(-)^{ts}$ on stack-relations).

Now we can deduce that $(-)^s$ and $(-)^t$ are order-reversing. For if $r_1 \subseteq r_2$, then $r_1 \subseteq r_2 \subseteq r_2^{st}$, so by (7.18), $r_2^s \subseteq r_1^s$. Similarly, $s_1 \subseteq s_2$ implies $s_2^t \subseteq s_1^t$. Hence $(-)^{st}$ is monotone (and so is $(-)^{ts}$).

Finally, for idempotence, in view of the inflationary property we just have to show $(r^{st})^{st} \subseteq r^{st}$. But applying (7.18) to $r^{st} \subseteq r^{st}$ we get $r^s \subseteq (r^{st})^s$; applying the order-reversing operator $(-)^t$ to this yields $(r^{st})^{st} \subseteq r^{st}$, as required. □

7.6.6 COROLLARY: Every valuable term-relation is—in particular—a closed term-relation. □

Proof: Note that because $(-)^{st}$ is idempotent (by the above lemma), any term-relation of the form r^{st} is closed. Thus valuable term-relations (ones satisfying $r = r^{vst}$) are in particular closed. □

The following exercise establishes a supply of valuable term-relations that we will need later.

7.6.7 EXERCISE [RECOMMENDED, ★★]: Given any value-relation $r \in \mathit{VRel}(\mathtt{T},\mathtt{T}')$, show that r^{st} is valuable, i.e., satisfies $r^{st} = (r^{st})^{vst}$. □

Closed term-relations (and hence also valuable term-relations) have excellent "admissibility" properties that we record in the following lemma.

7.6.8 LEMMA: If $r \in \mathit{TRel}(\mathtt{T},\mathtt{T}')$ satisfies $r = r^{st}$ (and in particular if it is valuable), then it has the following properties.

Equivalence-respecting If $(\mathtt{t},\mathtt{t}') \in r$, $\varnothing \vdash \mathtt{t} =_{\text{ciu}} \mathtt{t}_1 : \mathtt{T}$, and $\varnothing \vdash \mathtt{t}' =_{\text{ciu}} \mathtt{t}_1' : \mathtt{T}$, then $(\mathtt{t}_1,\mathtt{t}_1') \in r$.

Admissibility Given recursive function values $\mathsf{F} \stackrel{\text{def}}{=} \texttt{fun f(x:T}_1\texttt{)=u:T}_2$ and $\mathsf{F}' \stackrel{\text{def}}{=} \texttt{fun f(x:T}_1\texttt{)=u':T}_2$, let F_n and F'_n ($n = 0, 1, \ldots$) be their "unwindings," as in Theorem 7.4.4. If $([\mathtt{x} \mapsto \mathsf{F}_n]\mathtt{t}, [\mathtt{x} \mapsto \mathsf{F}'_n]\mathtt{t}') \in r$ for all $n = 0, 1, \ldots$, then $([\mathtt{x} \mapsto \mathsf{F}]\mathtt{t}, [\mathtt{x} \mapsto \mathsf{F}']\mathtt{t}') \in r$. □

Proof: Suppose $(\mathtt{t}, \mathtt{t}') \in r$, $\emptyset \vdash \mathtt{t} =_{\text{ciu}} \mathtt{t}_1 : \mathsf{T}$ and $\emptyset \vdash \mathtt{t}' =_{\text{ciu}} \mathtt{t}'_1 : \mathsf{T}$. To see that $(\mathtt{t}_1, \mathtt{t}'_1) \in r$, since $r = (r^s)^t$, it suffices to show for all $(S, S') \in r^s$ that $\langle S, \mathtt{t}_1 \rangle \downarrow$ iff $\langle S', \mathtt{t}'_1 \rangle \downarrow$. But

$$\begin{array}{lll} \langle S, \mathtt{t}_1 \rangle \downarrow & \text{iff } \langle S, \mathtt{t} \rangle \downarrow & (\text{since } \emptyset \vdash \mathtt{t} =_{\text{ciu}} \mathtt{t}_1 : \mathsf{T}) \\ & \text{iff } \langle S', \mathtt{t}' \rangle \downarrow & (\text{since } (S, S') \in r^s \text{ and } (\mathtt{t}, \mathtt{t}') \in r) \\ & \text{iff } \langle S', \mathtt{t}'_1 \rangle \downarrow & (\text{since } \emptyset \vdash \mathtt{t}' =_{\text{ciu}} \mathtt{t}'_1 : \mathsf{T}). \end{array}$$

For the **Admissibility** property we apply the Unwinding Theorem. Suppose $([\mathtt{x} \mapsto \mathsf{F}_n]\mathtt{t}, [\mathtt{x} \mapsto \mathsf{F}'_n]\mathtt{t}') \in r$ holds for all $n = 0, 1, \ldots$. Then for any $(S, S') \in r^s$ we have

$$\begin{array}{ll} \langle S, [\mathtt{x} \mapsto \mathsf{F}]\mathtt{t} \rangle \downarrow & \\ \text{iff for some } n, \langle S, [\mathtt{x} \mapsto \mathsf{F}_n]\mathtt{t} \rangle \downarrow & (\text{by Theorem 7.4.4}) \\ \text{iff for some } n, \langle S', [\mathtt{x} \mapsto \mathsf{F}'_n]\mathtt{t}' \rangle \downarrow & (\text{since } (S, S') \in r^s \text{ and} \\ & \quad ([\mathtt{x} \mapsto \mathsf{F}_n]\mathtt{t}, [\mathtt{x} \mapsto \mathsf{F}'_n]\mathtt{t}') \in r) \\ \text{iff } \langle S, [\mathtt{x} \mapsto \mathsf{F}']\mathtt{t}' \rangle \downarrow & (\text{by Theorem 7.4.4 again}) \end{array}$$

and therefore $([\mathtt{x} \mapsto \mathsf{F}]\mathtt{t}, [\mathtt{x} \mapsto \mathsf{F}']\mathtt{t}') \in (r^s)^t$; but $r^{st} = r$. □

7.6.9 Definition [Action of types on term-relations]: The action of types on term-relations takes the following form: if $\mathsf{T}(\overline{\mathsf{X}})$ is a type whose free type variables lie among the list $\overline{\mathsf{X}} = \mathsf{X}_1, \ldots, \mathsf{X}_n$, then given a corresponding list of term relations $r_1 \in \mathit{TRel}(\mathsf{T}_1, \mathsf{T}'_1), \ldots, r_n \in \mathit{TRel}(\mathsf{T}_n, \mathsf{T}'_n)$, we define a term relation $\mathsf{T}[\overline{r}] \in \mathit{TRel}([\overline{\mathsf{X}} \mapsto \overline{\mathsf{T}}]\mathsf{T}, [\overline{\mathsf{X}} \mapsto \overline{\mathsf{T}'}]\mathsf{T})$. The definition is by induction on the structure of T as follows.

$$\begin{array}{rcl} \mathsf{X}_i[\overline{r}] & \stackrel{\text{def}}{=} & (r_i)^{vst} \\ \mathsf{Gnd}[\overline{r}] & \stackrel{\text{def}}{=} & (\mathit{Id}_{\mathsf{Gnd}})^{st} \\ (\mathsf{T}_1 \to \mathsf{T}_2)[\overline{r}] & \stackrel{\text{def}}{=} & \mathsf{fun}(\mathsf{T}_1[\overline{r}], \mathsf{T}_2[\overline{r}])^{st} \\ \{\mathtt{l}_i : \mathsf{T}_i\ ^{i \in 1..n}\}[\overline{r}] & \stackrel{\text{def}}{=} & \{\mathtt{l}_i = \mathsf{T}_i[\overline{r}]\ ^{i \in 1..n}\}^{st} \\ (\forall \mathsf{X}.\mathsf{T})[\overline{r}] & \stackrel{\text{def}}{=} & (\lambda r.\mathsf{T}[r, \overline{r}])^{st} \\ \{\exists \mathsf{X}, \mathsf{T}\}[\overline{r}] & \stackrel{\text{def}}{=} & \{\exists r, \mathsf{T}[r, \overline{r}]\}^{st} \end{array}$$

$\boxed{Id_{\mathsf{Gnd}}} \in VRel(\mathsf{Gnd},\mathsf{Gnd})$
is $\{(\mathsf{c},\mathsf{c}) \mid Typeof(\mathsf{c}) = \mathsf{Gnd}\}$.

$\boxed{\mathsf{fun}(r_1,r_2)} \in VRel(\mathsf{T}_1\to\mathsf{T}_2,\mathsf{T}'_1\to\mathsf{T}'_2)$,
given $r_1 \in TRel(\mathsf{T}_1,\mathsf{T}'_1)$ and $r_2 \in TRel(\mathsf{T}_2,\mathsf{T}'_2)$,
is defined by:

> $(\mathsf{v},\mathsf{v}') \in \mathsf{fun}(r_1,r_2)$ if and only if for all $(\mathsf{v}_1,\mathsf{v}'_1) \in (r_1)^{\mathsf{v}}$, it is the case that $(\mathsf{v}\ \mathsf{v}_1,\mathsf{v}'\ \mathsf{v}'_1) \in r_2$.

$\boxed{\{\mathsf{l}_i\mathsf{=}r_i\ ^{i\in 1..n}\}} \in VRel(\{\mathsf{l}_i\mathsf{:T}_i\ ^{i\in 1..n}\}, \{\mathsf{l}_i\mathsf{:T}'_i\ ^{i\in 1..n}\})$
given $(r_i \in TRel(\mathsf{T}_i,\mathsf{T}'_i)\ ^{i\in 1..n})$,
is defined by:

> $(\mathsf{v},\mathsf{v}') \in \{\mathsf{l}_i\mathsf{=}r_i\ ^{i\in 1..n}\}$ if and only if for all $i \in 1..n$, it is the case that $(\mathsf{v}.\mathsf{l}_i,\mathsf{v}'.\mathsf{l}_i) \in r_i$.

$\boxed{\lambda r.R(r)} \in VRel(\forall\mathsf{X.T},\forall\mathsf{X.T}')$,
given $R(r) \in TRel([\mathsf{X}\mapsto\mathsf{T}_1]\mathsf{T},[\mathsf{X}\mapsto\mathsf{T}'_1]\mathsf{T}')$ for $r \in TRel(\mathsf{T}_1,\mathsf{T}'_1)$ and $\mathsf{T}_1,\mathsf{T}'_1 \in Typ$,
is defined by:

> $(\mathsf{v},\mathsf{v}') \in \lambda r.R(r)$ if and only if for all $\mathsf{T}_1,\mathsf{T}'_1 \in Typ$ and all $r \in TRel(\mathsf{T}_1,\mathsf{T}'_1)$, it is the case that $(\mathsf{v}\ \mathsf{T}_1,\mathsf{v}'\ \mathsf{T}'_1) \in R(r)$.

$\boxed{\{\exists r,R(r)\}} \in VRel(\{\exists\mathsf{X,T}\},\{\exists\mathsf{X,T}'\})$,
given $R(r) \in TRel([\mathsf{X}\mapsto\mathsf{T}_1]\mathsf{T},[\mathsf{X}\mapsto\mathsf{T}'_1]\mathsf{T}')$ for $r \in TRel(\mathsf{T}_1,\mathsf{T}'_1)$ and $\mathsf{T}_1,\mathsf{T}'_1 \in Typ$,
is defined by:

> $(\mathsf{v},\mathsf{v}') \in \{\exists r,R(r)\}$ if and only if there exist $\mathsf{T}_1,\mathsf{T}'_1 \in Typ$, $r \in TRel(\mathsf{T}_1,\mathsf{T}'_1)$ and $(\mathsf{v}_1,\mathsf{v}'_1) \in R(r)$ with
> $\mathsf{v} = \{{*}\mathsf{T}_1,\mathsf{v}_1\}\ \mathsf{as}\ \{\exists\mathsf{X,T}\}$ and
> $\mathsf{v}' = \{{*}\mathsf{T}'_1,\mathsf{v}'_1\}\ \mathsf{as}\ \{\exists\mathsf{X,T}'\}$.

Figure 7-5: Type-directed constructions on term-relations

In addition to the operations on term-, value- and stack-relations given in Definition 7.6.3, these definitions make use of the operations for constructing value-relations from term-relations given in Figure 7-5. □

We can use the action of types on term-relations to define a type-respecting binary relation between *open* terms (in the sense of Definition 7.5.1) by insisting that if we substitute related terms for the free value variables, the resulting terms are still related. This "mapping related things to related things" property is the common characteristic of the wide variety of constructs called *logical relations* that have arisen since the seminal work of Plotkin (1973) and Statman (1985) concerning simply typed λ-calculus; see also Chapter 6.

7.6.10 Definition [Logical relation, Δ]: Given $\Gamma \vdash \mathsf{t} : \mathsf{T}$ and $\Gamma \vdash \mathsf{t}' : \mathsf{T}$, with $\Gamma = \mathsf{X}_1,\ldots,\mathsf{X}_m, \mathsf{x}_1 : \mathsf{T}_1,\ldots,\mathsf{x}_n : \mathsf{T}_n$ say, we write $\Gamma \vdash \mathsf{t}\ \Delta\ \mathsf{t}' : \mathsf{T}$ to mean that for all Γ-closing substitutions σ,σ' (cf. Definition 7.5.2(v)) and all families of term-relations $\bar{r} = (r_i \in TRel(\sigma(\mathsf{X}_i),\sigma'(\mathsf{X}_i))\ ^{i\in 1..m})$, if $(\sigma(\mathsf{x}_j),\sigma'(\mathsf{x}_j)) \in \mathsf{T}_j[\bar{r}]^{\mathsf{v}}$ holds for each $j = 1,\ldots,n$, then $(\sigma(t),\sigma'(t')) \in \mathsf{T}[\bar{r}]$. □

7.6.11 Remark: Since it is far from straightforward, the form of Definitions 7.6.9 and 7.6.10 deserves some explanation. These definitions embody certain extensionality and parametricity properties (see §7.7 and Theorem 7.7.8) that we wish to show hold for F_{ML} contextual equivalence: eventually we show that the above logical relation Δ coincides with contextual equivalence (Theorem 7.6.25). To get that coincidence we have to formulate the definition of Δ so that it satisfies the crucial property of Lemma 7.6.17 below (the so-called fundamental property of the logical relation) and is adequate (Lemma 7.6.24). The definition of the action of types on term-relations in Definition 7.6.9 is carefully formulated to ensure these properties hold.

First of all, note the use of closing substitutions to reduce the logical relation for open terms to that for closed ones. This builds in the "instantiation" aspect of ciu-equivalence that we wish to prove of contextual equivalence. (It also means that the logical relation has the "monotonicity" propertymonotonicity *property of logical relations* considered in Chapter 6.)

Secondly, we want $\mathsf{T}[\vec{r}]$ to always be a closed term-relation, because then it has the equivalence-respecting and admissibility properties noted in Lemma 7.6.8. This accounts for the use of $(-)^{st}$ in the definition. The $(-)^{s}$ and $(-)^{t}$ operators build into the logical relation a delicate interplay between terms and frame stacks. Of course this relies on the formulation of the operational semantics of F_{ML} in §7-3: although more traditional "big-step" or "small-step" operational semantics lead to the same termination relation (cf. Exercise 7.4.2), the pairing between frame stacks and terms defined in Figure 7-2 is ideal for our purposes.

Lastly, the call-by-value nature of F_{ML} dictates that relational parametricity properties of polymorphic types should be with respect to term-relations that are valuable; but instead of letting r range over such relations in the definition of $(\forall \mathsf{X}.\mathsf{T})[\vec{r}]$ and $\{\exists \mathsf{X},\mathsf{T}\}[\vec{r}]$ we have used an equivalent formulation in which r ranges over all term-relations (of appropriate type), but type variables X are interpreted using the closure of the value-restriction operator $(-)^{v}$: for in fact as r ranges over all term-relations, r^{vst} ranges over all valuable term-relations. □

The rest of this section is devoted to showing that contextual equivalence and ciu-equivalence coincide with the logical relation.

7.6.12 **Lemma**: Each of the term relations $\mathsf{T}[\vec{r}]$ defined in Definition 7.6.9 is valuable, i.e., satisfies $\mathsf{T}[\vec{r}] = \mathsf{T}[\vec{r}]^{vst}$, and hence in particular by Corollary 7.6.6 is closed. □

Proof: It is immediate from the definition that each $\mathsf{T}[\vec{r}]$ is of the form r^{st} for some *value*-relation r; so just apply Exercise 7.6.7. □

The following lemma helps with calculations involving the action on term-relations of function types. We give its proof in detail since it typifies the kind of reasoning needed when working with the Galois connection given by the $(-)^s$ and $(-)^t$ operators. (For related properties for record and $\forall$-types, see Exercise 7.6.14.)

7.6.13 LEMMA: The operation $\mathtt{fun}(-,-)$ from Definition 7.6.9(ii) satisfies

$$\mathtt{fun}(r_1,(r_2)^{st})^{stv} = \mathtt{fun}(r_1,(r_2)^{st}) \tag{7.19}$$

$$\mathtt{fun}((r_1)^{vst},(r_2)^{st}) = \mathtt{fun}(r_1,(r_2)^{st}). \tag{7.20}$$

Proof: To prove (7.19), first note that since $(-)^{st}$ is inflationary (Lemma 7.6.5) we have $\mathtt{fun}(r_1,(r_2)^{st}) \subseteq \mathtt{fun}(r_1,(r_2)^{st})^{st}$; and since $\mathtt{fun}(r_1,(r_2)^{st})$ is a value-relation, it follows that $\mathtt{fun}(r_1,(r_2)^{st}) \subseteq \mathtt{fun}(r_1,(r_2)^{st})^{stv}$. For the reverse inclusion it suffices to prove

$$\mathtt{fun}(r_1,(r_2)^{st})^{st} \subseteq \mathtt{fun}(r_1,(r_2)^{st}) \tag{7.21}$$

and then apply $(-)^v$ to both sides (noting that $\mathtt{fun}(r_1,(r_2)^{st})$, being a value-relation, is equal to $\mathtt{fun}(r_1,(r_2)^{st})^v$). For (7.21) we use the following simple property of the termination relation (Figure 7-2) with respect to application:

$$\langle S \circ (\mathtt{f.f\ v_1}), \mathtt{v}\rangle\downarrow \;\Leftrightarrow\; \langle S, \mathtt{v\ v_1}\rangle\downarrow$$

and hence

$$(\langle S, \mathtt{v\ v_1}\rangle\downarrow \Leftrightarrow \langle S', \mathtt{v'\ v_1'}\rangle\downarrow) \;\Leftrightarrow\; (\langle S \circ (\mathtt{f.f\ v_1}), \mathtt{v}\rangle\downarrow \Leftrightarrow \langle S' \circ (\mathtt{f.f\ v_1'}), \mathtt{v'}\rangle\downarrow) \tag{7.22}$$

If $(\mathtt{v},\mathtt{v'}) \in \mathtt{fun}(r_1,(r_2)^{st})$ and $(\mathtt{v_1},\mathtt{v_1'}) \in (r_1)^v$, then we have $(\mathtt{v\ v_1},\mathtt{v'\ v_1'}) \in (r_2^s)^t$ by definition of the $\mathtt{fun}(-,-)$ operation on term-relations (Figure 7-5). So if $(S,S') \in (r_2)^s$, then

$$\langle S, \mathtt{v\ v_1}\rangle\downarrow \;\Leftrightarrow\; \langle S', \mathtt{v'\ v_1'}\rangle\downarrow$$

and hence by (7.22)

$$\langle S \circ (\mathtt{f.f\ v_1}), \mathtt{v}\rangle\downarrow \;\Leftrightarrow\; \langle S' \circ (\mathtt{f.f\ v_1'}), \mathtt{v'}\rangle\downarrow.$$

Since this holds for all $(\mathtt{v},\mathtt{v'}) \in \mathtt{fun}(r_1,(r_2)^{st})$, we deduce that

$$(S,S') \in (r_2)^s \;\&\; (\mathtt{v_1},\mathtt{v_1'}) \in (r_1)^v \;\Rightarrow\; (S \circ (\mathtt{f.f\ v_1}), S' \circ (\mathtt{f.f\ v_1'})) \in \mathtt{fun}(r_1,(r_2)^{st})^s.$$

So for any $(S,S') \in (r_2)^s$ and $(\mathtt{v_1},\mathtt{v_1'}) \in (r_1)^v$, since

$$(S \circ (\mathtt{f.f\ v_1}), S' \circ (\mathtt{f.f\ v_1'})) \in \mathtt{fun}(r_1,(r_2)^{st})^s$$

it follows that if

$$(\mathsf{v},\mathsf{v}') \in \mathsf{fun}(r_1,(r_2)^{st})^{st} \tag{7.23}$$

then $\langle S \circ (\mathsf{f}.\mathsf{f}\ \mathsf{v}_1), \mathsf{v}\rangle\downarrow \Leftrightarrow \langle S' \circ (\mathsf{f}.\mathsf{f}\ \mathsf{v}'_1), \mathsf{v}'\rangle\downarrow$, and hence by (7.22) it follows that $\langle S, \mathsf{v}\ \mathsf{v}_1\rangle\downarrow \Leftrightarrow \langle S', \mathsf{v}'\ \mathsf{v}'_1\rangle\downarrow$. Since this holds for all $(S,S') \in (r_2)^s$, it follows that $(\mathsf{v}\ \mathsf{v}_1, \mathsf{v}'\ \mathsf{v}'_1) \in (r_2)^{st}$ whenever $(\mathsf{v}_1,\mathsf{v}'_1) \in (r_1)^v$. So $(\mathsf{v},\mathsf{v}') \in \mathsf{fun}(r_1,(r_2)^{st})$ whenever (7.23) holds; thus we have proved the inclusion in (7.21), as required.

Turning to the proof of (7.20), first note that since since $(-)^{st}$ is inflationary, we have $(r_1)^v \subseteq (r_1)^{vst}$. So since $\mathsf{fun}(-,-)$ is clearly order-reversing in its first argument, we have $\mathsf{fun}((r_1)^{vst},(r_2)^{st}) \subseteq \mathsf{fun}((r_1)^v,(r_2)^{st})$; and $\mathsf{fun}((r_1)^v,(r_2)^{st}) = \mathsf{fun}(r_1,(r_2)^{st})$, because $\mathsf{fun}(-,-)$ only depends upon the values related by its first argument. Thus to prove (7.20), we just have to show

$$\mathsf{fun}(r_1,(r_2)^{st}) \subseteq \mathsf{fun}((r_1)^{vst},(r_2)^{st}). \tag{7.24}$$

For this we use the following fact about termination

$$\langle S \circ (\mathsf{x}.\mathsf{v}\ \mathsf{x}), \mathsf{v}_1\rangle\downarrow \Leftrightarrow \langle S, \mathsf{v}\ \mathsf{v}_1\rangle\downarrow$$

which is immediate from the definition in Figure 7-2. From this it follows that

$$(\langle S, \mathsf{v}\ \mathsf{v}_1\rangle\downarrow \Leftrightarrow \langle S', \mathsf{v}'\ \mathsf{v}'_1\rangle\downarrow) \Leftrightarrow (\langle S \circ (\mathsf{x}.\mathsf{v}\ \mathsf{x}), \mathsf{v}_1\rangle\downarrow \Leftrightarrow \langle S' \circ (\mathsf{x}.\mathsf{v}'\ \mathsf{x}), \mathsf{v}'_1\rangle\downarrow) \tag{7.25}$$

If $(\mathsf{v},\mathsf{v}') \in \mathsf{fun}(r_1,(r_2)^{st})$ and $(\mathsf{v}_1,\mathsf{v}'_1) \in (r_1)^v$, then by definition of $\mathsf{fun}(-,-)$ we have $(\mathsf{v}\ \mathsf{v}_1, \mathsf{v}'\ \mathsf{v}'_1) \in (r_2)^{st}$. So if $(S,S') \in (r_2)^s$, then

$$\langle S, \mathsf{v}\ \mathsf{v}_1\rangle\downarrow \Leftrightarrow \langle S', \mathsf{v}'\ \mathsf{v}'_1\rangle\downarrow$$

and hence by (7.25) we have

$$\langle S \circ (\mathsf{x}.\mathsf{v}\ \mathsf{x}), \mathsf{v}_1\rangle\downarrow \Leftrightarrow \langle S' \circ (\mathsf{x}.\mathsf{v}'\ \mathsf{x}), \mathsf{v}'_1\rangle\downarrow.$$

Since this holds for all $(\mathsf{v}_1,\mathsf{v}'_1) \in (r_1)^v$, we deduce that

$$(S,S') \in (r_2)^s \ \&\ (\mathsf{v},\mathsf{v}') \in \mathsf{fun}(r_1,(r_2)^{st}) \Rightarrow (S \circ (\mathsf{x}.\mathsf{v}\ \mathsf{x}), S' \circ (\mathsf{x}.\mathsf{v}'\ \mathsf{x})) \in (r_1)^{vs}.$$

So for any $(S,S') \in (r_2)^s$ and $(\mathsf{v},\mathsf{v}') \in \mathsf{fun}(r_1,(r_2)^{st})$, since $(S \circ (\mathsf{x}.\mathsf{v}\ \mathsf{x}), S' \circ (\mathsf{x}.\mathsf{v}'\ \mathsf{x})) \in (r_1)^{vs}$, it follows for any $(\mathsf{v}_1,\mathsf{v}'_1) \in ((r_1)^{vst})^v \subseteq ((r_1)^{vs})^t$ that we have $\langle S \circ (\mathsf{x}.\mathsf{v}\ \mathsf{x}), \mathsf{v}_1\rangle\downarrow \Leftrightarrow \langle S' \circ (\mathsf{x}.\mathsf{v}'\ \mathsf{x}), \mathsf{v}'_1\rangle\downarrow$, and hence by (7.25) that $\langle S, \mathsf{v}\ \mathsf{v}_1\rangle\downarrow \Leftrightarrow \langle S', \mathsf{v}'\ \mathsf{v}'_1\rangle\downarrow$. Since this holds for all $(S,S') \in (r_2)^s$, it follows that $(\mathsf{v}\ \mathsf{v}_1, \mathsf{v}'\ \mathsf{v}'_1) \in (r_2)^{st}$. Hence $(\mathsf{v},\mathsf{v}') \in \mathsf{fun}((r_1)^{vst},(r_2)^{st})$ whenever $(\mathsf{v},\mathsf{v}') \in \mathsf{fun}(r_1,(r_2)^{st})$, as required for (7.24). □

7.6.14 EXERCISE [RECOMMENDED, ★]: Show that constructions (iii) and (iv) in Definition 7.6.9 satisfy

$$\{\mathtt{l}_i{=}(r_i)^{st\ i\in 1..n}\}^{stv} = \{\mathtt{l}_i{=}(r_i)^{st\ i\in 1..n}\} \tag{7.26}$$

$$(\lambda r.R(r)^{st})^{stv} = \lambda r.R(r)^{st}. \tag{7.27}$$

(Cf. the proof of Lemma 7.6.13.) □

7.6.15 LEMMA: For all ground types Gnd, $(Id_{\mathsf{Gnd}})^{stv} = Id_{\mathsf{Gnd}}$. □

Proof: Since $(-)^{st}$ is idempotent (Lemma 7.6.5), we have $Id_{\mathsf{Gnd}} \subseteq (Id_{\mathsf{Gnd}})^{st}$; and since Id_{Gnd} is a value-relation it follows that $Id_{\mathsf{Gnd}} \subseteq (Id_{\mathsf{Gnd}})^{stv}$. To prove the reverse inclusion, for each constant c of type Gnd consider

$$\mathtt{diverge} \stackrel{\text{def}}{=} \mathtt{(fun\ f(b{:}Bool) = f\ b : Bool)true}$$

$$S_{\mathtt{c}} \stackrel{\text{def}}{=} Id \circ \mathtt{(x.\ if\ x{=}c\ then\ true\ else\ diverge)}.$$

Note that for all constants c′ of type Gnd

$$\langle S_{\mathtt{c}}, \mathtt{c}' \rangle \downarrow \;\Leftrightarrow\; \mathtt{c} = \mathtt{c}'. \tag{7.28}$$

Furthermore, since $(\mathtt{c}', \mathtt{c}'') \in Id_{\mathsf{Gnd}}$ iff $\mathtt{c}' = \mathtt{c}''$, we have that $(S_{\mathtt{c}}, S_{\mathtt{c}}) \in (Id_{\mathsf{Gnd}})^{s}$; so if the constants c and c′ satisfy $(\mathtt{c}, \mathtt{c}') \in (Id_{\mathsf{Gnd}})^{st}$, then we have $\langle S_{\mathtt{c}}, \mathtt{c}\rangle \downarrow \Leftrightarrow \langle S_{\mathtt{c}}, \mathtt{c}'\rangle \downarrow$. So by (7.28), $(\mathtt{c}, \mathtt{c}') \in (Id_{\mathsf{Gnd}})^{st}$ implies $\mathtt{c} = \mathtt{c}'$; thus $(Id_{\mathsf{Gnd}})^{stv} \subseteq Id_{\mathsf{Gnd}}$. □

7.6.16 LEMMA: The action of types on term-relations of Definition 7.6.9 has the following substitution property. For any types T and T′ with $ftv(\mathsf{T}) \subseteq \mathsf{X}, \overline{\mathsf{X}}$ and $ftv(\mathsf{T}') \subseteq \overline{\mathsf{X}}$, it is the case that $([\mathsf{X} \mapsto \mathsf{T}']\mathsf{T})[\overline{r}] = \mathsf{T}[\mathsf{T}'[\overline{r}], \overline{r}]$. □

Proof: This follows by induction on the structure of the type T; for the base case when T = X, use Lemma 7.6.12. □

7.6.17 LEMMA [FUNDAMENTAL PROPERTY OF THE LOGICAL RELATION]: The logical relation Δ of Definition 7.6.10 has the substitutivity and compatibility properties defined in Figure 7-4. □

Proof: The first substitutivity property in Figure 7-4 (closure under substituting values for value variables) holds for Δ because of the way it is defined in terms of closing substitutions. The second substitutivity property (closure under substituting types for types variables) holds for Δ because of Lemma 7.6.16.

Now consider the compatibility properties given in Figure 7-4. There is one for each clause in the grammar of F_{ML} terms and values (Figure 7-1). We consider each in turn, giving the details in some cases and setting the others as exercises (with solutions).

Value variables: This case is immediate from the definition of Δ in Definition 7.6.10.

Constants: We have to show for each constant c, with $Typeof(\mathsf{c}) = \mathsf{Gnd}$ say, that $(\mathsf{c},\mathsf{c}) \in \mathsf{Gnd}[\overline{r}] = (Id_{\mathsf{Gnd}})^{st}$. But by definition of Id_{Gnd} (Figure 7-5), $(\mathsf{c},\mathsf{c}) \in Id_{\mathsf{Gnd}}$; and $Id_{\mathsf{Gnd}} \subseteq (Id_{\mathsf{Gnd}})^{st}$ by Lemma 7.6.5.

Recursive functions: Using property (7.19) and the fact that each $\mathsf{T}[\overline{r}]$ is valuable and hence closed (Lemma 7.6.12), the compatibility property for recursive functions reduces to proving the property in Exercise 7.6.18.

Record values: This case follows from the property in Exercise 7.6.19.

Type abstractions: This case follows from the property in Exercise 7.6.20.

Package values: This case follows easily from the definition of $\{\exists r, R(r)\}$ in Figure 7-5, using Lemma 7.6.16.

Conditionals: This case follows from the property in Exercise 7.6.21.

Operations: In view of Lemma 7.6.15, this compatibility property follows once we prove $(\mathsf{op}(\mathsf{c}_i\ ^{i\in 1..n}), \mathsf{op}(\mathsf{c}_i\ ^{i\in 1..n})) \in (Id_{\mathsf{Gnd}})^{st}$ for any (suitably typed) constants c_i and operator op. But if the value of $\mathsf{op}(\mathsf{c}_i\ ^{i\in 1..n})$ is the constant c say, then for any S

$$\langle S, \mathsf{op}(\mathsf{c}_i\ ^{i\in 1..n})\rangle\downarrow \;\Leftrightarrow\; \langle S, \mathsf{c}\rangle\downarrow.$$

Hence for any $(S,S') \in (Id_{\mathsf{Gnd'}})^{s}$ (where $\mathsf{Gnd'} = Typeof(\mathsf{c})$), we have

$$\begin{aligned}\langle S, \mathsf{op}(\mathsf{c}_i\ ^{i\in 1..n})\rangle\downarrow &\Leftrightarrow \langle S, \mathsf{c}\rangle\downarrow \\ &\Leftrightarrow \langle S', \mathsf{c}\rangle\downarrow && \text{(since } (\mathsf{c},\mathsf{c}) \in Id_{\mathsf{Gnd'}}\text{)} \\ &\Leftrightarrow \langle S', \mathsf{op}(\mathsf{c}_i\ ^{i\in 1..n})\rangle\downarrow.\end{aligned}$$

So we do indeed have $(\mathsf{op}(\mathsf{c}_i\ ^{i\in 1..n}), \mathsf{op}(\mathsf{c}_i\ ^{i\in 1..n})) \in (Id_{\mathsf{Gnd}})^{st}$.

Applications: This case amounts to proving that if recursive function values v and v' satisfy $(\mathsf{v},\mathsf{v}') \in \mathsf{fun}(r_1,r_2)^{st}$ for some closed term-relations r_1 and r_2, then for any $(\mathsf{v}_1,\mathsf{v}_1') \in r_1$ it is the case that $(\mathsf{v}\ \mathsf{v}_1, \mathsf{v}'\ \mathsf{v}_1') \in r_2$. But this property follows immediately from the definition of $\mathsf{fun}(-,-)$ using the first part of Lemma 7.6.13: for

$$\begin{aligned}(\mathsf{v},\mathsf{v}') \in \mathsf{fun}(r_1,r_2)^{stv} \\ &= \mathsf{fun}(r_1,(r_2)^{st})^{stv} && \text{(since } r_2 \text{ is closed)} \\ &= \mathsf{fun}(r_1,(r_2)^{st}) && \text{(by (7.19))} \\ &= \mathsf{fun}(r_1,r_2) && \text{(since } r_2 \text{ is closed).}\end{aligned}$$

Projections: This case is similar to the previous one, but using property (7.26) from Exercise 7.6.14 rather than (7.19).

Type applications: This case is similar to the previous one, using property (7.27) from Exercise 7.6.14.

Unpacking: This case follows from the property in Exercise 7.6.22.

Sequencing: This case follows from the property in Exercise 7.6.23. □

7.6.18 EXERCISE [RECOMMENDED, ★★★]: Suppose

$$\begin{aligned}
&\mathtt{F} \stackrel{\text{def}}{=} \mathtt{fun\ f(x:T_1)=t:T_2} \in \mathit{Val}(\mathtt{T_1 \to T_2})\\
&\mathtt{F'} \stackrel{\text{def}}{=} \mathtt{fun\ f(x:T'_1)=t':T'_2} \in \mathit{Val}(\mathtt{T'_1 \to T'_2})\\
&r_1 \in \mathit{TRel}(\mathtt{T_1},\mathtt{T'_1})\\
&r_2 \in \mathit{TRel}(\mathtt{T_2},\mathtt{T'_2})
\end{aligned}$$

satisfy $r_2 = (r_2)^{st}$ and

$$\begin{aligned}
&([\mathtt{f} \mapsto \mathtt{v}][\mathtt{x} \mapsto \mathtt{v_1}]\mathtt{t}, [\mathtt{f} \mapsto \mathtt{v'}][\mathtt{x} \mapsto \mathtt{v'_1}]\mathtt{t'}) \in r_2,\\
&\text{for all } (\mathtt{v},\mathtt{v'}) \in \mathtt{fun}(r_1, r_2) \text{ and } (\mathtt{v_1},\mathtt{v'_1}) \in (r_1)^{v}.
\end{aligned} \tag{7.29}$$

Use the admissibility property of valuable term-relations established in Lemma 7.6.8 to show that $(\mathtt{F},\mathtt{F'}) \in \mathtt{fun}(r_1, r_2)$. □

7.6.19 EXERCISE [★★]: Suppose for $i \in 1..n$ that $\mathtt{v}_i \in \mathit{Val}(\mathtt{T}_i)$, $\mathtt{v}'_i \in \mathit{Val}(\mathtt{T}'_i)$ and $r_i \in \mathit{TRel}(\mathtt{T}_i, \mathtt{T}'_i)$ with $r_i = (r_i)^{st}$. Putting

$$\begin{aligned}
&\mathtt{v} \stackrel{\text{def}}{=} \{\mathtt{l}_i\mathtt{=v}_i\ ^{i\in 1..n}\} \in \mathit{Val}(\{\mathtt{l}_i\mathtt{:T}_i\ ^{i\in 1..n}\})\\
&\mathtt{v'} \stackrel{\text{def}}{=} \{\mathtt{l}_i\mathtt{=v}'_i\ ^{i\in 1..n}\} \in \mathit{Val}(\{\mathtt{l}_i\mathtt{:T}'_i\ ^{i\in 1..n}\})
\end{aligned}$$

show that if $(\mathtt{v}_i,\mathtt{v}'_i) \in r_i$ for $i \in 1..n$, then $(\mathtt{v},\mathtt{v'})$ is in the value-relation $\{\mathtt{l}_i\mathtt{=}r_i\ ^{i\in 1..n}\}$ defined in Figure 7-5. □

7.6.20 EXERCISE [★★]: Let T and T′ be types with at most X free. For each $\mathtt{T_1}, \mathtt{T'_1} \in \mathit{Typ}$ and $r \in \mathit{TRel}(\mathtt{T_1},\mathtt{T'_1})$ suppose we are given a closed term-relation $R(r)$ in $\mathit{TRel}([\mathtt{X} \mapsto \mathtt{T_1}]\mathtt{T}, [\mathtt{X} \mapsto \mathtt{T'_1}]\mathtt{T'})$ (i.e., $R(r) = R(r)^{st}$). Show that if the values v and v′ satisfy

$$\begin{aligned}
&\mathtt{X} \vdash \mathtt{v} : \mathtt{T}\\
&\mathtt{X} \vdash \mathtt{v'} : \mathtt{T'}\\
&\forall \mathtt{T_1}, \mathtt{T'_1} \in \mathit{Typ}, r \in \mathit{TRel}(\mathtt{T_1},\mathtt{T'_1}).\ ([\mathtt{X} \mapsto \mathtt{T_1}]\mathtt{v}, [\mathtt{X} \mapsto \mathtt{T'_1}]\mathtt{v'}) \in R(r)
\end{aligned}$$

then $(\lambda\mathtt{X}.\mathtt{v}, \lambda\mathtt{X}.\mathtt{v'})$ is in the value-relation $\lambda r.R(r)$ defined in Figure 7-5. □

7.6.21 **Exercise** [★★]: Suppose $(\mathtt{v},\mathtt{v'}) \in (Id_{\mathtt{Bool}})^{st}$ and $(\mathtt{t}_1,\mathtt{t}'_1),(\mathtt{t}_2,\mathtt{t}'_2) \in r$, where $r \in TRel(\mathtt{T},\mathtt{T'})$ is closed (i.e., $r = (r)^{st}$). Show that

$$(\mathtt{if\ v\ then\ t_1\ else\ t_2}, \mathtt{if\ v'\ then\ t'_1\ else\ t'_2})$$

is in r. □

7.6.22 **Exercise** [★★]: Let T and T′ be types with at most X free. For each $\mathtt{T}_1,\mathtt{T}'_1 \in Typ$ and $r_1 \in TRel(\mathtt{T}_1,\mathtt{T}'_1)$ suppose we are given a closed term-relation $R(r_1) = R(r_1)^{st}$ in $TRel([\mathtt{X}\mapsto\mathtt{T}_1]\mathtt{T},[\mathtt{X}\mapsto\mathtt{T}'_1]\mathtt{T'})$. Suppose we are also given a closed term-relation $r_2 = (r_2)^{st} \in TRel(\mathtt{T}_2,\mathtt{T}'_2)$ for some closed types $\mathtt{T}_2,\mathtt{T}'_2 \in Typ$. Show that if the terms t, t′ satisfy

$$\mathtt{X},\mathtt{x}:\mathtt{T} \vdash \mathtt{t}:\mathtt{T}_2$$
$$\mathtt{X},\mathtt{x}:\mathtt{T'} \vdash \mathtt{t'}:\mathtt{T}'_2$$
$$\forall \mathtt{T}_1,\mathtt{T}'_1 \in Typ, r_1 \in TRel(\mathtt{T}_1,\mathtt{T}'_1), (\mathtt{v}_1,\mathtt{v}'_1) \in (r_1)^{\nu}.$$
$$([\mathtt{X}\mapsto\mathtt{T}_1][\mathtt{x}\mapsto\mathtt{v}_1]\mathtt{t}, [\mathtt{X}\mapsto\mathtt{T}_1][\mathtt{x}\mapsto\mathtt{v}_1]\mathtt{t}) \in r_2$$

then whenever $(\mathtt{v},\mathtt{v'}) \in \{\exists r_1, R(r_1)\}^{st\nu}$, it is also the case that

$$(\mathtt{let\ \{*X,x\}=v\ in\ t}, \mathtt{let\ \{*X,x\}=v'\ in\ t'})$$

is in r_2. □

7.6.23 **Exercise** [★★]: Suppose we are given $r_1 \in TRel(\mathtt{T}_1,\mathtt{T}'_1)$, $r_2 \in TRel(\mathtt{T}_2,\mathtt{T}'_2)$ with r_1 valuable (i.e., $r_1 = (r_1)^{\nu st}$) and r_2 closed (i.e., $r_2 = (r_2)^{st}$). Show that if the terms $\mathtt{t}_2,\mathtt{t}'_2$ satisfy

$$\mathtt{x}:\mathtt{T}_1 \vdash \mathtt{t}_2:\mathtt{T}_2$$
$$\mathtt{x}:\mathtt{T}'_1 \vdash \mathtt{t}'_2:\mathtt{T}'_2$$
$$\forall (\mathtt{v}_1,\mathtt{v}'_1) \in (r_1)^{\nu}. ([\mathtt{x}\mapsto\mathtt{v}_1]\mathtt{t}_2, [\mathtt{x}\mapsto\mathtt{v}'_1]\mathtt{t}'_2) \in r_2$$

then whenever $(\mathtt{t}_1,\mathtt{t}'_1) \in r_1$, it is also the case that

$$(\mathtt{let\ x=t_1\ in\ t_2}, \mathtt{let\ x=t'_1\ in\ t'_2})$$

is in r_2. □

7.6.24 **Lemma** [Adequacy]: The logical relation Δ is adequate (Definition 7.5.1). □

Proof: Suppose $\varnothing \vdash \mathtt{t}\ \Delta\ \mathtt{t'} : \mathtt{T}$; we have to show that $\mathtt{t}\downarrow$ holds iff $\mathtt{t'}\downarrow$ does, or equivalently that

$$\langle Id, \mathtt{t}\rangle\downarrow \quad \text{iff} \quad \langle Id, \mathtt{t'}\rangle\downarrow. \tag{7.30}$$

Unraveling Definition 7.6.10, the assumption that the closed terms $\mathtt{t}$ and $\mathtt{t}'$ of closed type T are Δ-related means that $(\mathtt{t},\mathtt{t}') \in \mathsf{T}[]$, the latter being the action of the type T on the empty list of term-relations. By Lemma 7.6.12, $\mathsf{T}[]$ is valuable; so $(\mathtt{t},\mathtt{t}') \in \mathsf{T}[]^{vst}$. Hence to prove (7.30), it suffices to show that $(Id, Id) \in (\mathsf{T}[]^{v})^{s}$; but for any $(\mathtt{v},\mathtt{v}') \in \mathsf{T}[]^{v}$,

$$\langle Id, \mathtt{v}\rangle\downarrow \quad \text{iff} \quad \langle Id, \mathtt{v}'\rangle\downarrow$$

holds trivially by axiom (S-NILVAL) in Figure 7-2. □

We are finally able to put all the pieces together and prove the main result of this section. At the same time we complete the proof of Theorem 7.5.7.

7.6.25 THEOREM [$=_{ctx}$ EQUALS Δ EQUALS $=_{ciu}$]: F_{ML} contextual equivalence, $=_{ctx}$, (as defined in Theorem 7.5.3) coincides with the logical relation Δ of Definition 7.6.10 and with ciu-equivalence, $=_{ciu}$ (Definition 7.5.5): $\Gamma \vdash \mathtt{t} =_{ctx} \mathtt{t}' : \mathsf{T}$ holds if and only if $\Gamma \vdash \mathtt{t}\ \Delta\ \mathtt{t}' : \mathsf{T}$ does, if and only if $\Gamma \vdash \mathtt{t} =_{ciu} \mathtt{t}' : \mathsf{T}$ does. □

Proof: It suffices to show that the following chain of inclusions holds:

$$=_{ctx} \overset{(1)}{\subseteq} =_{ciu} \overset{(3)}{\subseteq} \Delta \overset{(2)}{\subseteq} =_{ctx}.$$

(1) This is the half of Theorem 7.5.7 that we have already proved in §7.5.

(2) We have not yet shown that Δ is an equivalence relation; and in fact we will only deduce this once we have shown that it coincides with $=_{ctx}$ and $=_{ciu}$ (which are easily seen to be equivalence relations). However, we have shown that Δ is compatible, substitutive and adequate (Lemmas 7.6.17 and 7.6.24). In the proof of Theorem 7.5.3 we constructed $=_{ctx}$ as the union of all such type-respecting relations, without regard to whether they were also equivalence relations; therefore Δ is contained in $=_{ctx}$.

(3) Noting how $=_{ciu}$ and Δ are defined on open terms via substitutions, we can combine the first part of Lemma 7.6.8 with Lemma 7.6.12 to give

$$\Gamma \vdash \mathtt{t} =_{ciu} \mathtt{t}' : \mathsf{T} \ \&\ \Gamma \vdash \mathtt{t}'\ \Delta\ \mathtt{t}'' : \mathsf{T} \Rightarrow \Gamma \vdash \mathtt{t}\ \Delta\ \mathtt{t}'' : \mathsf{T}. \tag{7.31}$$

We noted in the proof of Theorem 7.5.3 that every compatible term-relation is reflexive. (This is easily proved by induction on the structure of terms.) So since Δ is compatible (Lemma 7.6.17) it is in particular reflexive. So we can take $\mathtt{t}' = \mathtt{t}''$ in (7.31) to deduce that $\Gamma \vdash \mathtt{t} =_{ctx} \mathtt{t}' : \mathsf{T}$ implies $\Gamma \vdash \mathtt{t}\ \Delta\ \mathtt{t}' : \mathsf{T}$. □

7.7 Operational Extensionality

In this section we develop some of the consequences of Theorem 7.6.25. Now that we know that contextual equivalence coincides with ciu-equivalence (Theorem 7.5.7), when giving general properties of $=_{\text{ctx}}$ we restrict attention to closed terms of closed type where possible, since the corresponding property for open terms can be obtained via closing substitutions.

7.7.1 THEOREM [EXTENSIONALITY FOR VALUES]: We now give extensionality principles for the various types of value; for package values, the principle is a formalization of the final one discussed in the Introduction (Principle 7.3.6).

1. CONSTANTS: Given constants $\mathtt{c}$, $\mathtt{c}'$ of the same ground type, $\mathtt{Gnd}$ say, $\varnothing \vdash \mathtt{c} =_{\text{ctx}} \mathtt{c}' : \mathtt{Gnd}$ holds if and only if $\mathtt{c} = \mathtt{c}'$.

2. FUNCTIONS: Given $\mathtt{f}{:}\mathtt{T}_1{\to}\mathtt{T}_2, \mathtt{x}{:}\mathtt{T}_1 \vdash \mathtt{t} : \mathtt{T}_2$ and $\mathtt{f}{:}\mathtt{T}_1{\to}\mathtt{T}_2, \mathtt{x}{:}\mathtt{T}_1 \vdash \mathtt{t}' : \mathtt{T}_2$, writing $\mathtt{v}$ and $\mathtt{v}'$ for the recursive function values $\mathtt{fun\ f(x{:}T_1){=}t{:}T_2}$ and $\mathtt{fun\ f(x{:}T_1){=}t'{:}T_2}$ respectively, then $\varnothing \vdash \mathtt{v} =_{\text{ctx}} \mathtt{v}' : \mathtt{T}_1{\to}\mathtt{T}_2$ if and only if for all $\varnothing \vdash \mathtt{v}_1 : \mathtt{T}_1$, it is the case that $\varnothing \vdash [\mathtt{f} \mapsto \mathtt{v}][\mathtt{x} \mapsto \mathtt{v}_1]\mathtt{t} =_{\text{ctx}} [\mathtt{f} \mapsto \mathtt{v}'][\mathtt{x} \mapsto \mathtt{v}_1]\mathtt{t}' : \mathtt{T}_2$.

3. RECORDS: Given values $\varnothing \vdash \mathtt{v}_i : \mathtt{T}_i$ and $\varnothing \vdash \mathtt{v}'_i : \mathtt{T}_i$ for $i \in 1..n$, then $\varnothing \vdash \{\mathtt{l}_i{=}\mathtt{v}_i\ ^{i\in 1..n}\} =_{\text{ctx}} \{\mathtt{l}_i{=}\mathtt{v}'_i\ ^{i\in 1..n}\} : \{\mathtt{l}_i{:}\mathtt{T}_i\ ^{i\in 1..n}\}$ if and only if for each $i \in 1..n$, $\varnothing \vdash \mathtt{v}_i =_{\text{ctx}} \mathtt{v}'_i : \mathtt{T}_i$.

4. TYPE ABSTRACTIONS: Given $\mathtt{X} \vdash \mathtt{v} : \mathtt{T}$ and $\mathtt{X} \vdash \mathtt{v}' : \mathtt{T}$, then $\varnothing \vdash \lambda\mathtt{X}.\mathtt{v} =_{\text{ctx}} \lambda\mathtt{X}.\mathtt{v}' : \forall\mathtt{X}.\mathtt{T}$ if and only if for all closed types $\mathtt{T}'$, $\varnothing \vdash [\mathtt{X} \mapsto \mathtt{T}']\mathtt{v} =_{\text{ctx}} [\mathtt{X} \mapsto \mathtt{T}']\mathtt{v}' : [\mathtt{X} \mapsto \mathtt{T}']\mathtt{T}$.

5. PACKAGES: For any closed existential type $\{\exists\mathtt{X},\mathtt{T}\}$, closed types $\mathtt{T}_1$, $\mathtt{T}_2$, and values $\varnothing \vdash \mathtt{v}_i : [\mathtt{X} \mapsto \mathtt{T}_i]\mathtt{T}$ $(i = 1, 2)$,

$$\varnothing \vdash \{{*}\mathtt{T}_1,\mathtt{v}_1\}\ \mathtt{as}\ \{\exists\mathtt{X},\mathtt{T}\} =_{\text{ctx}} \{{*}\mathtt{T}_2,\mathtt{v}_2\}\ \mathtt{as}\ \{\exists\mathtt{X},\mathtt{T}\} : \{\exists\mathtt{X},\mathtt{T}\}$$

holds if there is some term-relation $r \in \mathit{TRel}(\mathtt{T}_1, \mathtt{T}_2)$ with $(\mathtt{v}_1, \mathtt{v}_2) \in \mathtt{T}[r]$. □

Proof:

1. The property for constants follows from Lemma 7.6.15 combined with Theorem 7.6.25.

2. Suppose for all $\varnothing \vdash \mathtt{v}_1 : \mathtt{T}_1$ that

$$\varnothing \vdash [\mathtt{f} \mapsto \mathtt{v}][\mathtt{x} \mapsto \mathtt{v}_1]\mathtt{t} =_{\text{ctx}} [\mathtt{f} \mapsto \mathtt{v}'][\mathtt{x} \mapsto \mathtt{v}_1]\mathtt{t}' : \mathtt{T}_2 \tag{7.32}$$

where v and v' are as in part 2 of the theorem. To show $\emptyset \vdash v =_{ctx} v' : T_1 \to T_2$, by Theorem 7.6.25 it suffices to show $\emptyset \vdash v \mathrel{\Delta} v' : T_1 \to T_2$, i.e., that $(v, v') \in (T_1 \to T_2)[] = \mathtt{fun}(T_1[], T_2[])^{st}$. In fact we show that $(v, v') \in \mathtt{fun}(T_1[], T_2[])$. For this we have to prove that if $(v_1, v_1') \in T_1[]^{v}$, then $(v\, v_1, v'\, v_1') \in T_2[]$. By Theorem 7.6.25 again, this is the same as showing: if $\emptyset \vdash v_1 =_{ctx} v_1' : T_1$, then $\emptyset \vdash v\, v_1 =_{ctx} v'\, v_1' : T_2$. As noted in Corollary 7.5.8, we can turn the primitive reduction for function application into a ciu-equivalence and hence by Theorem 7.6.25 into a contextual equivalence:

$$\emptyset \vdash v\, v_1 =_{ctx} [f \mapsto v][x \mapsto v_1]t : T_2 \tag{7.33}$$

and similarly for $v'\, v_1'$. Therefore we just need to show: if $\emptyset \vdash v_1 =_{ctx} v_1' : T_1$, then $\emptyset \vdash [f \mapsto v][x \mapsto v_1]t =_{ctx} [f \mapsto v'][x \mapsto v_1']t' : T_2$. But this follows from the assumption (7.32) using the reflexivity and substitutivity properties of $=_{ctx}$. So we have established one half (the difficult half) of the property in 2. For the converse, if $\emptyset \vdash v =_{ctx} v' : T_1 \to T_2$, then for any $\emptyset \vdash v_1 : T_1$, the compatibility properties of $=_{ctx}$ give $\emptyset \vdash v\, v_1 =_{ctx} v'\, v_1 : T_2$; and then as before, we can compose with (7.33) to get (7.32).

3. We leave the extensionality property for records as an exercise (7.7.2).

4. For the property for type abstractions, suppose

$$\forall T' \in \mathit{Typ}.\quad \emptyset \vdash [X \mapsto T']v =_{ctx} [X \mapsto T']v' : [X \mapsto T']T. \tag{7.34}$$

Note that since Δ coincides with $=_{ctx}$ (Theorem 7.6.25) it is reflexive and hence $X \vdash v \mathrel{\Delta} v : T$ holds. According to Definition 7.6.10 this means that for all $T_1, T_1' \in \mathit{Typ}$ and $r \in \mathit{TRel}(T_1, T_1')$, $([X \mapsto T_1]v, [X \mapsto T_1']v) \in T[r]$. Since $T[r]$ is closed (Lemma 7.6.12), we can combine (7.34) with the first part of Lemma 7.6.8 (using $=_{ctx}$ in place of $=_{ciu}$ by virtue of Theorem 7.6.25) to conclude that $([X \mapsto T_1]v, [X \mapsto T_1']v') \in T[r]$ for all r. Then using the equivalence in Corollary 7.5.8(v), we have

$$\forall T_1, T_1' \in \mathit{Typ}, r \in \mathit{TRel}(T_1, T_1').\quad ((\lambda X.v)T_1, (\lambda X.v')T_1') \in T[r]$$

and hence $(\lambda X.v, \lambda X.v')$ is in $\lambda r.T[r]$. Since $\lambda r.T[r] \subseteq (\lambda r.T[r])^{st}$ and the latter is equal to $(\forall X.T)[]$ by definition, we have $\emptyset \vdash \lambda X.v \mathrel{\Delta} \lambda X.v' : \forall X.T$, and hence by Theorem 7.6.25, $\emptyset \vdash \lambda X.v =_{ctx} \lambda X.v' : \forall X.T$. So we have established one half (the difficult half) of the property in 4. The argument for the other half is similar to that for property 2, using Corollary 7.5.8(v) and the congruence properties of $=_{ctx}$.

5. Finally, let us consider the extensionality property for package values. (Note that unlike the other four, this only gives a sufficient condition for contextual equivalence; Example 7.7.4 below shows that the condition is not necessary.) If $(\mathtt{v}_1, \mathtt{v}_2) \in \mathtt{T}[r]$, then from Definition 7.6.9 we have

$$\begin{aligned}(\{{}^*\mathtt{T}_1,\mathtt{v}_1\}\ \mathtt{as}\ \{\exists\mathtt{X},\mathtt{T}\}, \{{}^*\mathtt{T}_2,\mathtt{v}_2\}\ \mathtt{as}\ \{\exists\mathtt{X},\mathtt{T}\}) &\in \{\exists r,\mathtt{T}[r]\}\\ &\subseteq \{\exists r,\mathtt{T}[r]\}^{st}\\ &= \{\exists\mathtt{X},\mathtt{T}\}[].\end{aligned}$$

Thus $\varnothing \vdash \{{}^*\mathtt{T}_1,\mathtt{v}_1\}\ \mathtt{as}\ \{\exists\mathtt{X},\mathtt{T}\}\ \Delta\ \{{}^*\mathtt{T}_2,\mathtt{v}_2\}\ \mathtt{as}\ \{\exists\mathtt{X},\mathtt{T}\} : \{\exists\mathtt{X},\mathtt{T}\}$ and we can apply Theorem 7.6.25 to get the desired contextual equivalence. □

7.7.2 EXERCISE [★★, ↛]: Use Theorem 7.6.25, Corollary 7.5.8 and the definition of the term-relation $\{\mathtt{l}_i\mathtt{=}r_i\ ^{i\in 1..n}\}$ in Definition 7.6.9 to deduce extensionality property 3 of Theorem 7.7.1. □

To see how Theorem 7.7.1(5) can be used in practice, we will apply it to establish the contextual equivalence of Example 7.3.5 from the Introduction.

7.7.3 EXAMPLE: Recall the type Semaphore and its values $\mathtt{semaphore}_1$, $\mathtt{semaphore}_2$ from Example 7.3.5. To show $\varnothing \vdash \mathtt{semaphore}_1 =_{\text{ctx}} \mathtt{semaphore}_2 : \mathtt{Semaphore}$ using Theorem 7.7.1(5), it suffices to show that $(\mathtt{v}_1, \mathtt{v}_2) \in \mathtt{T}[r]$ where

$$\begin{aligned}\mathtt{T} &\stackrel{\text{def}}{=} \{\mathtt{bit{:}X,\ flip{:}X{\to}X,\ read{:}X{\to}Bool}\}\\ \mathtt{v}_1 &\stackrel{\text{def}}{=} \{\mathtt{bit{=}true,\ flip{=}\lambda x{:}Bool.not\ x,\ read{=}\lambda x{:}Int.x}\}\\ \mathtt{v}_2 &\stackrel{\text{def}}{=} \{\mathtt{bit{=}1,\ flip{=}\lambda x{:}Int.0\text{-}2{*}x,\ read{=}\lambda x{:}Int.x >= 0}\}\end{aligned}$$

and $r \in \mathit{VRel}(\mathtt{Bool},\mathtt{Int})$ is

$$\begin{aligned}r \stackrel{\text{def}}{=}\ & \{(\mathtt{true},\mathtt{m}) \mid m = (-2)^n \text{ for some even } n \geq 0\} \cup\\ & \{(\mathtt{false},\mathtt{m}) \mid m = (-2)^n \text{ for some odd } n \geq 0\}.\end{aligned}$$

Since r is a value-relation, we can use Lemma 7.6.13 to slightly simplify $\mathtt{T}[r]$:

$$\begin{aligned}\mathtt{T}[r] &\stackrel{\text{def}}{=} \{\mathtt{bit}{=}r^{st}, \mathtt{flip}{=}\mathtt{fun}(r^{st}, r^{st})^{st}, \mathtt{read}{=}\mathtt{fun}(r^{st}, \mathit{Id}^{st}_{\mathtt{Bool}})^{st}\}^{st}\\ &= \{\mathtt{bit}{=}r^{st}, \mathtt{flip}{=}\mathtt{fun}(r, r^{st})^{st}, \mathtt{read}{=}\mathtt{fun}(r, \mathit{Id}^{st}_{\mathtt{Bool}})^{st}\}^{st}.\end{aligned}$$

So since $(-)^{st}$ is inflationary, to prove $(\mathtt{v}_1, \mathtt{v}_2) \in \mathtt{T}[r]$, it suffices to show

$$\begin{aligned}(\mathtt{true},1) &\in r\\ (\lambda\mathtt{x{:}Bool.not\ x}, \lambda\mathtt{x{:}Int.0\text{-}2{*}x}) &\in \mathtt{fun}(r, r^{st})\\ (\lambda\mathtt{x{:}Int.x}, \lambda\mathtt{x{:}Int.x >= 0}) &\in \mathtt{fun}(r, \mathit{Id}^{st}_{\mathtt{Bool}}).\end{aligned}$$

These follow from the definition of r—the first trivially and the second two once we combine the definition of fun(–,–) with the fact (Lemma 7.6.8) that closed relations such as r^{st} and $Id^{st}_{\mathtt{Bool}}$ respect ciu-equivalence. For example, if $(v_1, v_1') \in r$, then (λx:Bool.not x)v_1 and (λx:Int.0-2*x)v_1' are ciu-equivalent to r-related values v_2 and v_2'; then since $(v_2, v_2') \in r \subseteq r^{st}$ and the latter is closed, we have ((λx:Bool.not x)v_1, (λx:Int.0-2*x)v_1') $\in r^{st}$. As this holds for all $(v_1, v_1') \in r$, we have (λx:Bool.not x, λx:Int.0-2*x) in fun(r, r^{st}). □

Theorem 7.7.1(5) gives a sufficient condition for contextual equivalence of package values, but the condition is not necessary: it can be the case that {* T_1, v_1} as {∃X, T} is contextually equivalent to {* T_2, v_2} as {∃X, T} even though there is no $r \in TRel(T_1, T_2)$ with $(v_1, v_2) \in$ T[r]. The rest of this section is devoted to giving an example of this unpleasant phenomenon (based on a suggestion of Ian Stark arising out of our joint work on logical relations for functions and dynamically allocated names in Pitts and Stark, 1993).

7.7.4 **Example:** Consider the following types and terms.

```
      P  def=  (X→Bool)→Bool
      Q  def=  {∃X,P}
      N  def=  ∀X.X
diverge  def=  (fun f(b:Bool) = f b : Bool)true
      G  def=  fun g(f:N→Bool) = diverge : Bool
     G'  def=  fun g(f:Bool→Bool) =
                   (if f true then
                        if f false then diverge else true
                    else diverge) : Bool.
```

Thus N is a type with no values (Exercise 7.7.6); G is a function that diverges when applied to any value of type N→Bool; and G′ is a function that diverges when applied to any value of type Bool→Bool except ones (such as the identity function) that map true to true and false to false, in which case it returns true. We claim that

(i) there is no $r \in TRel$(N, Bool) for which (G, G′) ∈ P[r] holds,

(ii) but nevertheless ∅ ⊢ {*N,G} as Q $=_{ctx}$ {*Bool,G′} as Q : Q. □

Proof: For (i) note that the definition of N implies that $Val(\mathsf{N}) = \emptyset$, i.e., there are no closed values of type N (Exercise 7.7.6). So any $r \in TRel(\mathsf{N}, \mathsf{Bool})$ satisfies $r^{\nu} = \emptyset$. Now

$$
\begin{aligned}
\mathsf{P}[r]^{\nu} &\stackrel{\text{def}}{=} ((\mathsf{X}\to\mathsf{Bool})\to\mathsf{Bool})[r]^{\nu} \\
&\stackrel{\text{def}}{=} \mathsf{fun}((\mathsf{X}\to\mathsf{Bool})[r], Id^{st}_{\mathsf{Bool}})^{st\nu} \\
&= \mathsf{fun}((\mathsf{X}\to\mathsf{Bool})[r], Id^{st}_{\mathsf{Bool}}) && \text{using (7.19)} \\
&\stackrel{\text{def}}{=} \mathsf{fun}(\mathsf{fun}(r^{\nu st}, Id^{st}_{\mathsf{Bool}})^{st}, Id^{st}_{\mathsf{Bool}}) \\
&= \mathsf{fun}(\mathsf{fun}(r^{\nu st}, Id^{st}_{\mathsf{Bool}})^{st\nu}, Id^{st}_{\mathsf{Bool}}) && \text{by definition of } \mathsf{fun}(-,-) \\
&= \mathsf{fun}(\mathsf{fun}(r^{\nu st}, Id^{st}_{\mathsf{Bool}}), Id^{st}_{\mathsf{Bool}}) && \text{using (7.19)} \\
&= \mathsf{fun}(\mathsf{fun}(r, Id^{st}_{\mathsf{Bool}}), Id^{st}_{\mathsf{Bool}}) && \text{using (7.20)} \\
&= \mathsf{fun}(\mathsf{fun}(r^{\nu}, Id^{st}_{\mathsf{Bool}}), Id^{st}_{\mathsf{Bool}}) && \text{by definition of } \mathsf{fun}(-,-).
\end{aligned}
$$

Since $r^{\nu} = \emptyset$, we have $\mathsf{fun}(r^{\nu}, Id^{st}_{\mathsf{Bool}}) = Val(\mathsf{N}\to\mathsf{Bool}) \times Val(\mathsf{Bool}\to\mathsf{Bool})$; and we know by Theorem 7.6.25 that Id^{st}_{Bool} is the relation $\{(\mathsf{t},\mathsf{t}') \mid \emptyset \vdash \mathsf{t} =_{\text{ctx}} \mathsf{t}' : \mathsf{Bool}\}$. Therefore

$$
\begin{aligned}
\mathsf{P}[r]^{\nu} = \{(\mathsf{v},\mathsf{v}') \mid\ & \emptyset \vdash \mathsf{v}\ \mathsf{v}_1 =_{\text{ctx}} \mathsf{v}'\ \mathsf{v}'_1 : \mathsf{Bool} \\
& \text{for all } \mathsf{v}_1 \in Val(\mathsf{N}\to\mathsf{Bool}) \text{ and } \mathsf{v}'_1 \in Val(\mathsf{Bool}\to\mathsf{Bool})\ \}.
\end{aligned}
$$

However, $\emptyset \vdash \mathsf{G}\ \mathsf{v}_1 =_{\text{ctx}} \mathsf{G}'\ \mathsf{v}'_1 : \mathsf{Bool}$ does not hold if we take v_1 and v'_1 to be the values

$$
\begin{aligned}
\mathsf{v}_1 &\stackrel{\text{def}}{=} \mathsf{fun\ f(x{:}N) = diverge : Bool} \\
\mathsf{v}'_1 &\stackrel{\text{def}}{=} \mathsf{fun\ f(x{:}Bool) = x : Bool}
\end{aligned}
$$

since evaluation of $\mathsf{G}\ \mathsf{v}_1$ does not terminate, whereas evaluation of $\mathsf{G}'\ \mathsf{v}'_1$ does. Therefore $(\mathsf{G},\mathsf{G}') \notin \mathsf{P}[r]^{\nu}$, for any $r \in TRel(\mathsf{N}, \mathsf{Bool})$.

Turning to the proof of (ii), now we know that it cannot be deduced from the extensionality principle for package values in Theorem 7.7.1, we have to prove this contextual equivalence by brute force. The termination relation defined in Fig. 7-2 provides a possible strategy (if rather a tedious one) for proving ciu-equivalences and hence contextual equivalences—by what one might call *termination induction.* Thus to prove (ii) it suffices to prove that the two terms are ciu-equivalent:

$$\forall S.\quad \langle S, \{\mathsf{*N,G}\}\ \mathsf{as\ Q}\rangle\downarrow \;\Leftrightarrow\; \langle S, \{\mathsf{*Bool,G'}\}\ \mathsf{as\ Q}\rangle\downarrow.$$

Attempting to do this by induction on the derivation of terminations $\langle -,-\rangle\downarrow$ (for all S simultaneously), one rapidly realizes that a stronger induction hypothesis is needed: prove for all frame stacks S and terms t that

$\langle$[x ↦ {*N,G} as Q]S, [x ↦ {*N,G} as Q]t$\rangle\downarrow$
if and only if $\langle$[x ↦ {*Bool,G′} as Q]S, [x ↦ {*Bool,G′} as Q]t$\rangle\downarrow$.

It is possible to prove this by induction on the definition of the termination relation in Fig. 7-2 (for all S and t simultaneously). We omit the details except to note that the only difficult induction step is for the primitive reduction (R-UNPACKPACK) in Fig. 7-3 in the case that t is the form let{*X,g}=x in t′. For that step, one can first show for all frame stacks S and terms t that

$\langle$[X ↦ N][g ↦ G]S, [X ↦ N][g ↦ G]t$\rangle\downarrow$
if and only if $\langle$[X ↦ Bool][g ↦ G′]S, [X ↦ Bool][g ↦ G′]t$\rangle\downarrow$.

This also is proved by induction on the definition of the termination relation. Once again we omit the details except to note that now the only difficult induction step is for the primitive reduction (R-APPABS) in the case that t is of the form g v for some value v. To prove that step one can use Lemma 7.7.5 below. This lemma lies at the heart of the reason why the contextual equivalence in (ii) is valid: if an argument supplied to G′ is sufficiently polymorphic (which is guaranteed by the existential abstraction), then when specialized to Bool it cannot have the functionality (true ↦ true, false ↦ false) needed to distinguish G′ from the divergent behavior of G. □

7.7.5 **LEMMA:** For any value v satisfying X, g:P ⊢ v : X→Bool, evaluation of G′([X ↦ Bool][g ↦ G′]v) does not terminate. □

Proof: To prove this we can use the logical relation from the previous section. Consider the following value-relation in *VRel*(Bool, Bool):

$$r \stackrel{\text{def}}{=} \{(\texttt{true},\texttt{true}),(\texttt{false},\texttt{false}),(\texttt{true},\texttt{false})\}.$$

Note that

$$\begin{aligned}(\texttt{X}\to\texttt{Bool})[r]^{v} &\stackrel{\text{def}}{=} \texttt{fun}(r^{vst}, Id^{st}_{\texttt{Bool}})^{stv}\\ &\stackrel{(7.20)}{=} \texttt{fun}(r, Id^{st}_{\texttt{Bool}})^{stv} \stackrel{(7.19)}{=} \texttt{fun}(r, Id^{st}_{\texttt{Bool}})\end{aligned} \qquad (7.35)$$

and hence

$$\begin{aligned}\texttt{P}[r]^{v} &\stackrel{\text{def}}{=} \texttt{fun}((\texttt{X}\to\texttt{Bool})[r], Id^{st}_{\texttt{Bool}})^{stv} = \texttt{fun}((\texttt{X}\to\texttt{Bool})[r]^{v}, Id^{st}_{\texttt{Bool}})^{stv}\\ &\stackrel{(7.35)}{=} \texttt{fun}(\texttt{fun}(r, Id^{st}_{\texttt{Bool}}), Id^{st}_{\texttt{Bool}})^{stv} \stackrel{(7.19)}{=} \texttt{fun}(\texttt{fun}(r, Id^{st}_{\texttt{Bool}}), Id^{st}_{\texttt{Bool}}).\end{aligned} \qquad (7.36)$$

If $(\texttt{v}_1, \texttt{v}_1') \in \texttt{fun}(r, Id^{st}_{\texttt{Bool}})$, since (true, true), (false, false) ∈ r and $Id^{st}_{\texttt{Bool}}$ is contextual equivalence (Theorem 7.6.25) we get

$$\varnothing \vdash \texttt{v}_1\ \texttt{true} =_{\text{ctx}} \texttt{v}_1'\ \texttt{true} : \texttt{Bool}$$
$$\varnothing \vdash \texttt{v}_1\ \texttt{false} =_{\text{ctx}} \texttt{v}_1'\ \texttt{false} : \texttt{Bool}.$$

So using Corollary 7.5.8(iii) and the congruence properties of $=_{\text{ctx}}$, we have

$$\begin{aligned} \mathtt{G'}\ \mathtt{v}_1 &=_{\text{ctx}} (\mathtt{if}\ \mathtt{v}_1\ \mathtt{true}\ \mathtt{then} \\ &\qquad\quad \mathtt{if}\ \mathtt{v}_1\ \mathtt{false}\ \mathtt{then}\ \mathtt{diverge}\ \mathtt{else}\ \mathtt{true} \\ &\qquad \mathtt{else}\ \mathtt{diverge}) \\ &=_{\text{ctx}} (\mathtt{if}\ \mathtt{v}_1'\ \mathtt{true}\ \mathtt{then} \\ &\qquad\quad \mathtt{if}\ \mathtt{v}_1'\ \mathtt{false}\ \mathtt{then}\ \mathtt{diverge}\ \mathtt{else}\ \mathtt{true} \\ &\qquad \mathtt{else}\ \mathtt{diverge}) \\ &=_{\text{ctx}} \mathtt{G'}\ \mathtt{v}_1' \end{aligned}$$

Therefore $(\mathtt{G'}\ \mathtt{v}_1, \mathtt{G'}\ \mathtt{v}_1') \in Id^{st}_{\mathtt{Bool}}$ whenever $(\mathtt{v}_1, \mathtt{v}_1') \in \mathtt{fun}(r, Id^{st}_{\mathtt{Bool}})$; and so $(\mathtt{G'}, \mathtt{G'}) \in \mathtt{P}[r]^{\mathsf{v}}$, by (7.36). Hence using Lemma 7.6.17 we have

$$\begin{aligned} ([\mathtt{X} \mapsto \mathtt{Bool}][\mathtt{g} \mapsto \mathtt{G'}]\mathtt{v}, [\mathtt{X} \mapsto \mathtt{Bool}][\mathtt{g} \mapsto \mathtt{G'}]\mathtt{v}) &\in (\mathtt{X}{\to}\mathtt{Bool})[r]^{\mathsf{v}} \\ &= \mathtt{fun}(r, Id^{st}_{\mathtt{Bool}}) \quad \text{by (7.35).} \end{aligned}$$

So since $(\mathtt{true}, \mathtt{false}) \in r$, we get

$$([\mathtt{X} \mapsto \mathtt{Bool}][\mathtt{g} \mapsto \mathtt{G'}]\mathtt{v}\ \mathtt{true}, [\mathtt{X} \mapsto \mathtt{Bool}][\mathtt{g} \mapsto \mathtt{G'}]\mathtt{v}\ \mathtt{false}) \in Id^{st}_{\mathtt{Bool}}.$$

Thus $([\mathtt{X} \mapsto \mathtt{Bool}][\mathtt{g} \mapsto \mathtt{G'}]\mathtt{v})\mathtt{true}$ and $([\mathtt{X} \mapsto \mathtt{Bool}][\mathtt{g} \mapsto \mathtt{G'}]\mathtt{v})\mathtt{false}$ are contextually equivalent closed terms of type `Bool`. Therefore it cannot be the case that the first evaluates to `true` and the second to `false` (cf. Exercise 7.5.10); but in that case, by definition of G′, it must be that evaluation of $\mathtt{G'}([\mathtt{X} \mapsto \mathtt{Bool}][\mathtt{g} \mapsto \mathtt{G'}]\mathtt{v})$ does not terminate. □

7.7.6 EXERCISE [★, ↛]: By considering the possible typing derivations from the rules in Figure 7-1, show that there is no value v satisfying $\emptyset \vdash \mathtt{v} : \forall \mathtt{X}.\mathtt{X}$. (Note that the syntactic restriction on values of universally quantified type mentioned in Remark 7.4.1 plays a crucial role here.) □

7.7.7 REMARK [THE ROLE OF NON-TERMINATION]: Example 7.7.4 shows that the logical relation presented here is incomplete for proving contextual equivalence of F_{ML} values of existential type. The example makes use of the fact that, because of the presence of recursive function values, evaluation of F_{ML} terms need not terminate. However, it seems that the source of the incompleteness has more to do with the existence of types with no values (such as $\forall \mathtt{X}.\mathtt{X}$) than with non-termination. Eijiro Sumii (private communication) has suggested the following, "terminating" version of Example 7.7.4:

$$\begin{aligned}
\mathtt{P} &\stackrel{\text{def}}{=} \mathtt{(X{\to}Bool){\to}Bool}\\
\mathtt{Q} &\stackrel{\text{def}}{=} \mathtt{\{\exists X,P\}}\\
\mathtt{N} &\stackrel{\text{def}}{=} \mathtt{\forall X.X}\\
\mathtt{H} &\stackrel{\text{def}}{=} \mathtt{\lambda f{:}N{\to}Bool.\ false}\\
\mathtt{H'} &\stackrel{\text{def}}{=} \mathtt{\lambda f{:}Bool{\to}Bool.}\\
&\qquad \mathtt{(if\ f\ true\ then}\\
&\qquad\quad \mathtt{if\ f\ false\ then\ false\ else\ true}\\
&\qquad \mathtt{else\ false)\ :\ Bool.}
\end{aligned}$$

Consider a version of F_{ML} with only non-recursive function abstractions (i.e. with `λx:T.t` rather than `fun f(x:T) = t:T'`). Evaluation is terminating in this version. So to be non-trivial, contextual equivalence should be formulated in terms of observing convergence to the same ground value in all contexts of ground type. Making corresponding changes to the definition of the operations $(-)^s$ and $(-)^t$ on term- and stack-relations, one could develop a logical relation for this terminating version of F_{ML}. It seems that properties (i) and (ii) in Example 7.7.4 are also true of `H` and `H'` in this version (the first by the same argument we gave, but the second by a different argument that nevertheless hinges on the observation at the end of the proof of Example 7.7.4). We leave investigating this as an extended exercise for the reader. □

The proof of Lemma 7.7.5 exploits "relational parametricity" properties of polymorphic types in F_{ML}. In fact Theorem 7.6.25 tells us far more about the properties of type abstraction values than just the extensionality property of Theorem 7.7.1(4).

7.7.8 **Theorem [Relational parametricity for ∀-types]:** Given $X \vdash v : T$ and $X \vdash v' : T$, then $\emptyset \vdash \lambda X.v =_{ctx} \lambda X.v' : \forall X.T$ if and only if for all closed types $T_1, T_1' \in \mathit{Typ}$ and all term-relations $r \in \mathit{TRel}(T_1, T_1')$ it is the case that $([X \mapsto T_1]v, [X \mapsto T_1']v') \in T[r]$. □

Proof: By Theorem 7.6.25, we have that $\emptyset \vdash \lambda X.v =_{ctx} \lambda X.v' : \forall X.T$ iff $\emptyset \vdash \lambda X.v\ \Delta\ \lambda X.v' : \forall X.T$, i.e., iff $(\lambda X.v, \lambda X.v') \in (\forall X.T)[\,] = (\lambda r.T[r])^{st}$. Since $\lambda X.v$ and $\lambda X.v'$ are values, the latter is the case iff $(\lambda X.v, \lambda X.v') \in (\lambda r.T[r])^{stv}$, and by Lemma 7.6.12 and Exercise 7.6.14 $(\lambda r.T[r])^{stv} = \lambda r.T[r]$. Hence $\emptyset \vdash \lambda X.v =_{ctx} \lambda X.v' : \forall X.T$ iff $(\lambda X.v, \lambda X.v') \in \lambda r.T[r]$. By definition (Figure 7-5), this is the case iff for all for all closed types $T_1, T_1' \in \mathit{Typ}$ and all term-relations $r \in \mathit{TRel}(T_1, T_1')$, $((\lambda X.v)T_1, (\lambda X.v')T_1') \in T[r]$; and the latter holds iff $([X \mapsto T_1]v, [X \mapsto T_1']v') \in T[r]$, because $(\lambda X.v)T_1 =_{ciu} [X \mapsto T_1]v$ and $(\lambda X.v')T_1' =_{ciu} [X \mapsto T_1']v'$ (so that we can use Lemmas 7.6.8 and 7.6.12). □

The force of Theorem 7.7.1(4) is to give a method for establishing that two type abstraction values are contextually equivalent. By contrast, the force of Theorem 7.7.8 is to give us useful properties of families of values parameterized by type variables. Given such a value, $X \vdash v : T$, since $=_{ctx}$ is reflexive, we have $\emptyset \vdash \lambda X.v =_{ctx} \lambda X.v : \forall X.T$; hence the theorem has the following corollary.

7.7.9 **Corollary**: Given a value $X \vdash v : T$, for all $T_1, T_1' \in Typ$ and all $r \in TRel(T_1, T_1')$, it is the case that $([X \mapsto T_1]v, [X \mapsto T_1']v) \in T[r]$. □

Such "relational parametricity" properties can often be exploited for proving contextual equivalences: we already saw an example in the proof of Lemma 7.7.5 and other examples can be found in Pitts (2000), Bierman, Pitts, and Russo (2000), and Johann (2002). However, the strict nature of function application and type abstraction in F_{ML} means that it does not satisfy all the parametricity properties one might expect. For example, in Pitts (2000), §7, it is shown that

$$\{\exists X,T\} \cong \forall Y.(\forall X.T\to Y)\to Y$$

holds in the polymorphic version of PCF (Plotkin, 1977) studied in that paper (where $\cong$ is "bijection up to contextual equivalence"—see Principle 7.3.4). However this bijection does not hold in general for F_{ML} (Exercise 7.7.10).

7.7.10 **Exercise** [★★★]: Consider the type $N \stackrel{\text{def}}{=} \forall X.X$ from Example 7.7.4 that you showed has no closed values in Exercise 7.7.6. Show that there cannot exist values

$$i \in Val(\{\exists X,N\}\to\forall Y.(\forall X.N\to Y)\to Y)$$
$$j \in Val((\forall Y.(\forall X.N\to Y)\to Y)\to\{\exists X,N\})$$

that are mutually inverse, in the sense that

$$p{:}\{\exists X,N\} \vdash j(i\ p) =_{ctx} p : \{\exists X,N\}$$
$$y{:}\forall Y.(\forall X.N\to Y)\to Y \vdash i(j\ y) =_{ctx} y : \forall Y.(\forall X.N\to Y)\to Y.$$
□

7.7.11 **Exercise** [★★★, ↛]: Verify the claim made in Note 7.3.7 that Principle 7.3.4 is a special case of Principle 7.3.6. To do so, you will first have to give a definition of the action of F_{ML} types on bijections mentioned in Principle 7.3.4. □

7.8 Notes

This chapter is a revised and expanded version of Pitts (1998) and also draws on material from Pitts (2000).

In discussing typed operational reasoning we have focused on reasoning about *contextual equivalence* of program phrases. Being by construction a congruence, contextual equivalence permits us to use the usual forms of equational reasoning (replacing equals by equals) when deriving equivalences between phrases. However, its definition does not lend itself to establishing the basic laws that are needed to get such reasoning going. We studied two characterisations of contextual equivalence in order to get round this problem: *ciu-equivalence* (Definition 7.5.5) and a certain kind of operationally based *logical relation* (Definition 7.6.10).

contextual equivalence!vs. bisimilarity The informal notion of contextual equivalence (Definition 7.3.2) has been studied for a wide variety of programming languages. If the language's operational semantics involves nondeterminism—usually because the language supports some form of concurrent or interactive computation—then contextual equivalence tends to identify too many programs and various co-inductive notions of *bisimilarity* are used instead (see the textbook by Sangiorgi and David, 2001, for example). But even if we remain within the realm of languages with deterministic operational semantics, one may ask to what extent the results of this chapter are stable with respect to adding further features such as recursive datatypes, mutable state, and object-oriented features à la Objective Caml.

Ciu-equivalence has the advantage of being quite robust in this respect—it can provide a characterisation of contextual equivalence in the presence of such features (Honsell, Mason, Smith, and Talcott, 1995; Talcott, 1998). However, its usefulness is mainly limited to establishing basic laws such as the conversions in Corollary 7.5.8; it cannot be used directly to establish extensionality properties such as those in Theorem 7.7.1 without resorting to tedious "termination inductions" of the kind we sketched in the proof of Example 7.7.4. Ciu-equivalence is quite closely related to some notions of "applicative bisimilarity" that have been applied to functional and object-based languages (Gordon, 1995, 1998), in that their congruence properties can both be established using a clever technique due to Howe (1996). The advantage of applicative bisimilarity is that it has extensionality built into its definition; so when it does coincide with contextual equivalence, this provides a method of establishing some extensionality properties for $=_{\mathrm{ctx}}$ (such as (1)–(4) in Theorem 7.7.1, but not, as far as I know, property (5) for package values).

The kind of operationally based logical relation we developed in this chapter provides a very powerful analysis of contextual equivalence. We used it to prove not only conversions and simple extensionality principles for F_{ML}, but also quite subtle properties of $=_{ctx}$ such as Theorems 7.7.1(5) and 7.7.8. Similar logical relations can be used to prove some properties of ML-style references and of linear types: see Pitts and Stark (1998), Bierman, Pitts, and Russo (2000), and Pitts (2002). Unfortunately, the characteristic feature of logical relations—that functions are related iff they map related arguments to related results—makes it difficult to define them in the presence of "recursive features." I mean by the latter programming language features which in a denotational semantics lead one to have to solve domain equations in which the defined domain occurs both positively (to the left of an even number of function space constructions) and negatively (to the left of an odd number of function space constructions). Recursive datatypes involving function types can lead to such domain equations; as does the use of references to functions in ML. Suitable logical relations can be defined in the denotational semantics of languages with such features using techniques such as those in Pitts (1996), but they tell us properties of denotational equality, which is often a poor (if safe) approximation to contextual equivalence. For this reason people have tried to develop syntactical analogs of these denotational logical relations: see Birkedal and Harper (1999). The unwinding theorem (Theorem 7.4.4) provides the basis for such an approach. However, it seems like a fresh idea is needed to make further progress. Therefore I set a last exercise, whose solution is not included.

7.8.1 EXERCISE [★★★★..., ↛]: Extend F_{ML} with *isorecursive types*, μX.T, as in Figure 20-1 of *TAPL*, Chapter 20. By finding an operationally based logical relation as in §7.6 or otherwise, try to prove the kind of properties of contextual equivalence for this extended language that we developed for F_{ML} in this chapter. (For the special case of iso-recursive types μX.T for which T contains no negative occurrences of X, albeit for a non-strict functional language, see Johann (2002). The generalized ideal model of recursive polymorphic in Vouillon and Melliès (2004) uses the same kind of Galois connection as we used in §7.6 and may well shed light on this exercise. Recent work by Sumii and Pierce [2005] is also relevant.) □

Part IV

Types for Programming in the Large

8 Design Considerations for ML-Style Module Systems

Robert Harper and Benjamin C. Pierce

A programming language for large-scale software development must provide some means of breaking large programs into parts of manageable size, commonly known as modules. The division into modules is chosen to reflect natural divisions of labor within a program, minimizing redundancy and maximizing opportunities for re-use (Parnas, 1972).

The literature on modularity is extensive, covering both *methodology*—how best to decompose programs into modules with a variety of desirable engineering characteristics—and *mechanisms* used to support modular programming. In this chapter, we focus on the latter, laying out a set of core requirements and design issues and developing linguistic mechanisms for addressing them. The heart of our story is the module system found in present-day dialects of ML, but the discussion touches on modularity features from a range of other languages such as C, Modula, and Java.

Our presentation emphasizes type systems for modularity grounded in the framework of *TAPL*. To keep the discussion focused on basic concepts and avoid type-theoretic technicalities, the presentation is informal. However, the material will be easier to follow for readers with some familiarity with basic concepts of subtyping (*TAPL*, Chapter 15), universal polymorphism (*TAPL*, Chapter 23), existential polymorphism and abstract types (*TAPL*, Chapter 24), and type operators (*TAPL*, Chapter 29). Some more advanced typing features are also mentioned in passing, but prior acquaintance with these features is not assumed; these include recursive types (*TAPL*, Chapters 20 and 21), bounded quantification (*TAPL*, Chapters 26 and 28), dependent types (Chapter 2 of this volume) and singletons (Chapter 9).

The chapter begins in §8.1 to §8.3 with a suite of basic modularity mechanisms: modules and signatures, namespace management, separate compilation, inter-module type checking, and principal signatures. §8.4 introduces the central concept of the *phase distinction* and the terminology of *first-* and *second-class* module systems. §8.5 discusses *abstract data types.* Abstract types arise by *sealing* a module with a signature that selectively suppresses the definitions of its type components. Data abstraction raises a number of important technical issues, including *representation independence* and the *avoidance problem.* §8.6 extends the module language with nested hierarchies of modules. §8.7 discusses two alternative mechanisms for representing *families of signatures*—explicitly *parameterized signatures* and the less familiar but more flexible idea of *fibered signatures,* which allow any submodule in a signature to be considered *a posteriori* as the "index" of a signature family. §8.8 extends this discussion to *families of modules* defined by *functors* and raises the issue of *coherence.* We compare two approaches to the coherence problem—*sharing by construction,* which is based on parameterized signatures, and *sharing by specification,* based on fibered signatures—and explain why the latter scales well while the former does not. We then discuss the pragmatic motivations for module families in more depth, exploring several classes of situations in which functors arise naturally. The section closes with a discussion of *generative* and *applicative* functors. §8.9 briefly describes three more advanced topics in module system design: first-class modules, in which modules can be treated as ordinary values; higher-order modules, in which functors are treated on the same footing as other modules; and recursive modules, which permit self-reference. §8.10 relates the modularity concepts of this chapter to the mechanisms found in several well-known languages. §8.11 closes the chapter with historical remarks and additional suggestions for further reading.

8.1 Basic Modularity

Informally, a *module* (or *structure*) is a collection of components, which may include procedure or function definitions, variable declarations, type definitions, and initialization code—specifics will vary from one language to another. A *program* consists of a collection of bindings of module names to modules. One module is specified as the *root*—the main entry point of the program.

One module in a program may refer to another by using the latter's name in an *external reference.* The occurrences of external references between modules determine a dependency ordering in which the referring module depends on the module to which it refers. (We assume for now that cyclic dependencies between modules are not allowed; §8.9 discusses relaxing this restriction.) The job of a linker is to compose a complete program by resolving external references, creating module bindings for each of the external references in the partial program under construction until no unresolved references remain.

To support separate compilation, the dependency of one module on another is mediated by a *signature* (or *interface*) that describes the externally visible components of the latter module. A signature must be sufficiently expressive as to enable clients of a module to be compiled without reference to its implementation. This information typically includes type declarations for procedures and variables and the definitions of type variables.

In practice, most languages support modularity through a mixture of linguistic and extra-linguistic mechanisms. For example, modules are often organized as files, and module naming conventions are often tied to file system naming conventions. To avoid such complications, we concentrate on a module language that emphasizes the central concepts, relegating its realization in specific languages and development environments to informal discussions in §8.10.

Syntax

We employ a notation for modules and signatures that is loosely based on ML. We consider the *module language* to be constructed in terms of some underlying *core language*, whose details we do not care too much about. The principal point of contact between the module and core language consists of references to components of modules from within core language expressions. To account for the type definitions in signatures, it is necessary to enrich the definition of type equivalence to ensure that type components are synonymous with their definitions.

The grammar given in Figure 8-1 defines the syntax of a basic module system that we enrich as further ideas are developed. We use the metavariables x and y to range over term variables, s, t, and u to range over terms, X and Y to range over type variables, S, T, and U to range over types, m and n to range over module variables, M and N to range over module expressions, and I and J to range over signatures and signature variables.[1]

A *program* consists of a sequence of *bindings*, each of which is either a *module binding* or a *signature binding*. A module binding binds a module

1. We are departing slightly from *TAPL*'s metavariable conventions here. In *TAPL*, lowercase identifiers were used consistently for term-level expressions and variables, and uppercase identifiers for type-level expressions and variables. Here, we are using M and N for module-level expressions and m and n for module-level variables. Also, we use I and J to denote both signatures and signature variables. No confusion results from this overlap, since in any case we regard a signature variable as just an abbreviation for its definition.

```
P  ::=                               programs:
       B1 ... Bn              binding sequence
B  ::=                               bindings:
       module m[: I] = M        module binding
       signature J = I       signature binding
M  ::=                                modules:
       m                       module variable
       mod {CB1,...,CBn}          basic module
I  ::=                             signatures:
       J                    signature variable
       sig {CD1,...,CDn}       basic signature
CB ::=                     component bindings:
       type X[>X] = T             type binding
       val x[>x] = t             value binding
```

```
CD ::=                 component declarations:
       type X[>X] = T         type declaration
       val x[>x] : T         value declaration
T  ::= ...                              types:
       m.X                      type selection
t  ::= ...                              terms:
       m.x                     value selection
Γ  ::=                        typing contexts:
       ∅                                 empty
       Γ, D                        declaration
D  ::=                           declarations:
       m : I                module declaration
```

Figure 8-1: Basic module syntax

variable to a module expression, perhaps with a specified signature. A signature binding binds a signature variable to a signature. The scope of a binding in a program is the remainder of the program following that binding. The final module binding is the root module.

Signature bindings are used to give names to signatures: a bound signature variable is simply an abbreviation for the right-hand side of its binding.

A *basic module* consists of a sequence of component bindings, which are either *type bindings* or *value bindings*. A type binding is a binding of a type variable to a type expression. A value binding binds a run-time entity to a term variable. These entities may include procedures, classes, objects, mutable reference cells, and other structures from the core language.

Each component binding has both a *label*, which is underlined, and a *variable*, which is not. The variable governs references to that binding *within* the module; the label governs reference from *outside* of the module. For this reason the label is sometimes called the *external name* of the component, and the variable its *internal name*. The use of a label from outside of a module to designate one of its components is called an *external reference*; the use of a variable from inside the module to designate a preceding binding is called an *internal reference*. If m is a module variable, then m.X is an external reference to the type component of m labeled X, and m.X is an external reference to the value component of m labeled x.

Internal names are bound variables whose scope is the rest of the module in which they occur. As such, internal names may be chosen (and renamed) arbitrarily without affecting the meaning of the module, subject only to the usual requirement that distinct bound variables not be confused in a given scope. In contrast the external name of a component of a module cannot be renamed without affecting the entire program in which that module occurs. This distinction between external and internal names is necessary for both conceptual and technical reasons (detailed in §8.6). In most cases, however, it is not important to emphasize the distinction, so we take the liberty of providing a single name for each component binding with the understanding that it plays a dual role as both the external and internal name of that component.

A *basic signature* consists of a sequence of *component declarations*, either a type declaration or a value declaration. A *type declaration* is a labeled type binding, with the same syntactic form as a type binding in a module. A *value declaration* defines the type of a term variable, but does not give its actual binding. As with bindings, we usually assign a single name to each declaration with the understanding that it serves as both the internal and external name of that component.

Examples

Here is a simple module binding:

```
module m = mod {
  type X = Nat
  val x = 5
}
```

The module bound to m includes one type binding and one value binding. These components are designated, externally, by m.X and m.x. Note that these are, respectively, core-language type and value expressions: the grammar of the core language is enriched to include external references to components of modules.

Here is a more interesting module binding:

```
module n = mod {
  type X = λW:*. W×W
  val f = λy:X(Nat). plus y.1 y.2
}
```

The right-hand side of the type binding X has kind $*{\rightarrow}*$ (i.e., this module is exporting a type *operator*). The right-hand side of the term binding f uses the previously bound operator X. This illustrates the impact of the module language on core-language type checking: in order to check that the core-language expression `λy:X(Nat). plus y.1 y.2` is well typed, we need to use the module-level information that `X` is definitionally equal to `λW:*. W×W`.

The signature I introduced by the binding

```
signature I = sig {
  type X = Nat
  val x : X
}
```

describes the module `m` above, in a sense to be made precise shortly. Similarly,

```
signature J = sig {
  type X = λW:*. W×W
  val f : X(Nat) → Nat
}
```

binds `J` to a signature corresponding to the module `n`.

8.2 Type Checking and Evaluation of Modules

To avoid getting bogged down in formalities, we describe type checking and evaluation throughout the chapter in English prose rather than giving precise, formal definitions. §8.11 offers a number of pointers into the literature for readers interested in a more technical treatment.

Type Checking

Signatures are used to describe modules. If a signature `I` accurately describes a module `M`, then we say that `M` *implements* `I`. This relation may be defined in one of two ways. The direct method simply defines a correspondence between a module and any signature that it may implement. An indirect method is to associate with each module `M` a unique (up to suitable equivalences) *principal signature|seesignatures*, which is the "most precise" (least in the subtyping ordering) signature implemented by `M`. The latter method, though elegant, applies only in languages where every module actually has a principal signature. We start by defining the implementation relation directly and later discuss conditions under which it may be reduced to subtyping.

We say that a basic module `M` implements a basic signature `I` if `M` contains at least the type and value components specified by `I`, up to type equivalence. That is, each type component declared in `I` must be bound in `M` with the same kind and an equivalent definition. (A type definition in a signature is an equational constraint that must be satisfied by any implementation of that signature.) Moreover, each value component declared in `I` must be matched by a value binding in `M` with a subtype of the type specified in `I`. The subtyping relation here is inherited from the core language, enriched to include the expansion of definitions introduced by type bindings in modules and signatures.

When a module binding specifies a signature, the type checker ensures that its right-hand side implements this signature. For example, the following bindings are well-formed because the module bound to m implements the signature I:

```
signature I = sig {
  type T = Int
  type U = Int×Int
  val x : U
}

module m : I = mod {
  type T = Int
  type U = T×T
  val x : T×T = (3,4)
}
```

Since I provides definitions for the types T and U and declares the value x, it follows that m.T and m.U are valid type expressions (equal, respectively, to Int and Int×Int), and m.x is a valid value expression (of type m.T×m.T, which is equivalent to m.U).

To account for external references during type checking, each module variable is assigned a signature by a *typing context*. The assignment of a signature to a module variable amounts to the assumption that it will be bound to a module implementing that signature. This is enforced during linking, which is described in more detail in §8.3.

Signature Matching

Since signatures are descriptions of modules, it is natural to consider a subtyping relation between signatures, called *signature matching* and written I<:J. A signature I may be considered to be a sub-signature of a signature J only if any module implementing I also implements J (this is the ordinary *subsumption principle* from type systems with subtyping). Said differently, if I is a sub-signature of J, then I expresses stronger requirements on an implementation than does J. When I<:J we say that I *matches* J.

There is some room for variation in how the signature matching relation is defined, subject only to the requirement that it validate subsumption. There are two well-known styles of signature matching, which we call *structural* and *nominal*. Structural matching is based entirely on the requirements imposed by the signature, without requiring any declarations. Nominal matching is based on the explicit declaration of subtyping relationships among signatures. Such declarations are often tied to a naming mechanism for modules and signatures, which gives rise to the terminology. (This distinction exactly mirrors the distinction between structural and nominal subtype relations discussed in *TAPL*, §19.3.)

Structural matching affords greater flexibility, since it does not require the programmer to explicitly specify that one signature subsumes another. However, structural matching does not preclude unintended matching relationships; this is at once a strength and a weakness. Nominal matching sacrifices flexibility for simplicity by requiring explicit declaration of matching relationships among signatures. Nominal matching precludes unintended matching relationships, but requires that any intended ones be explicitly stated. This rigidity can sometimes lead to significant problems in practice. For example, in Java, it is impossible to create a new interface `J` that lies above an existing class or interface `I` without modifying the source code of `I`, which may be unavailable, for example, if `I` is part of a commercial library.

The definition of structural matching is guided by purely semantic considerations: it is the largest pre-order on signatures that validates the subsumption principle. That is, `I<:J` iff every module implementing `I` also implements `J`. This is ensured by the following requirements:

1. Every type declaration in `J` must be matched by a corresponding type declaration in `I`. Moreover, their definitions must be equivalent, taking into account the preceding type declarations in `I`.

2. Every value declaration in `J` must be matched by a corresponding value declaration in `I`. Moreover, the type declared in `I` must be a subtype of that declared in `J`, taking account of the preceding type bindings in `I`.

These conditions do not impose any ordering requirements on components and permit the sub-signature to have components not present in the super-signature. (In the terminology of record subtyping from *TAPL*, Chapter 15, the subtype relation between signatures permits width subtyping, depth subtyping, and permutation, with one caveat: in contrast to record subtyping, permutation must be limited to respect the scoping of internal names for components. For example, a value specification cannot be permuted to precede a type specification on which it depends.) For example, according to this definition the signature

```
signature I = sig {
  type T = Int
  type U = T×T
  type V = Int
}
```

matches the signature

```
signature J = sig {
  type T = Int
  type U = Int×T
}.
```

8.2.1 EXERCISE [★★★★]: How much of the development in the rest of the chapter can be carried out in a nominal setting? □

Principal Signatures

The *principal signature* of a module, when it exists, is the most precise signature that the module implements. If a module M has a principal signature I_M, then M implements another signature I exactly when I_M matches I. Checking whether a module implements a signature is thus reduced to checking the subtyping relation between this signature and the module's principal signature. Naturally, this reduction is possible only if every module expression has a principal signature; otherwise there is some module expression M and a signature I such that M implements I, yet there is no way to express this fact as a subtyping relationship.

Unfortunately few module languages have principal signatures for all module expressions. One reason is that the language of signatures may be too weak to permit a precise description of the properties of a module. For example, if subtyping for signatures is nominal, then the inferred signature for a module is not, in general, its smallest signature in the declared subtyping hierarchy. A work-around for weak signatures is to draw a distinction between a signature expression and its internal representation in a type checker. Every well-formed signature has an internal representation, but some modules may have an internal representation that is not denotable by a signature of the language itself. This creates an unnatural separation between what a particular type checking algorithm knows about a module and what a programmer may state about it in a signature. An alternative solution is to require that the programmer specify a signature for every module, which is then deemed to be the smallest signature for that module, even if it is larger (i.e., weaker) than necessary. This avoids the need for principal signatures, at the expense of some verbosity as well as some loss of flexibility when the specified signature precludes uses of the module that would otherwise be permissible.

Evaluation

Complete programs (those with no free variables) are executed by evaluating each of the module bindings in the order given. A basic module is evaluated by evaluating each of its component bindings in turn according to the rules of the core language, resulting in a *module value*. We insist on a "call by value" binding discipline for module variables: a module variable is bound to the value of its binding. The motivation for this requirement is explained in §8.5.

The notion of an *initializer* for a module arises here as a value binding whose right-hand side has a side-effect (initializing the module's internal state) when evaluated. For example, evaluating the right-hand side of the binding of `f` in

```
module p = mod {
  val f =
    let r = ref 0 in
    λx:Nat. r := plus x (!r)
}
```

allocates a storage cell and then returns a function whose body uses this cell. This example also illustrates the need to distinguish between module expressions and module values. Each time the expression `mod { val f = ... }` is evaluated, a new cell is allocated and a different module value results.

8.3 Compilation and Linking

The process of evaluating a program may be decomposed into two steps: compilation and execution. For present purposes, the most important aspect of compilation is type checking, and the most important aspect of execution is linking. We shall not concern ourselves with code generation or the execution of compiled code. A key distinction between compilation and execution is that the former may be performed on a module-by-module basis, provided only that we are given the signatures of the free module variables occurring in a module, whereas the latter is performed on a complete program in which we have at hand the bindings of all of its free module variables. We follow Cardelli (1997) in modelling linking as a process of binding modules to module variables.

Compilation

To support code re-use and team development, it is important to compile modules independently from one another. To compile a module, it is necessary to have an assignment of a signature to each of its free module variables (external references) provided by the typing context. There are two main methods of obtaining this context: *separate* and *incremental* compilation.[2]

2. We caution the reader that this terminology is not standard; these and related phrases are used with a variety of loosely related meanings in the literature.

The difference is whether the signatures of free module variables are explicitly given by the programmer (separate compilation) or are inferred by the compiler from the source code of the referenced module (incremental compilation). Both separate and incremental compilation may be supported in the same language. Furthermore, both mechanisms are compatible with *cut-off compilation* (Adams, Tichy, and Weinert, 1994): if the source code of a module has changed, but its signature has not, then there is no need to recompile modules that depend on it—recompilation may be "cut off" at that point.

In a *separate* compilation system, the programmer states signature assumptions for each of the external references in a module. This is typically achieved by "import" declarations that state such assumptions. The module is compiled relative to these assumptions, independently of whether the implementation of the externally referenced modules is available. This affords maximal flexibility in the order of development of the modules in a program and permits re-use of libraries of previously compiled modules whose source may not be available at all. Separate compilation places a burden on the linker to ensure that the binding of a module variable implements the presumed signature. A subtle point is that two different modules may import the same module, but with a different assumed signature. The linker must ensure that each such assumption is satisfied to ensure safety, or else insist that all imports specify equivalent signatures. Since most conventional linkers are incapable of verifying typing constraints, it is usually necessary to devise language-specific linkers or to introduce post-linking checks (similar to Java bytecode verification) to ensure type safety.

In an *incremental* compilation system, it is not necessary to specify the signatures of externally referenced modules. Instead, the compiler consults the implementation of a module to determine its signature, which is used for compiling any module that depends on it. This implies that the implementation of any externally referenced module must be present in order to compile the referring module. This impedes independent development, but avoids the need to ensure that the binding of a module implements the presumed signature, since it does so by explicit construction. A module system that lacks principal signatures cannot properly support incremental compilation.

Linking

A linker assembles a complete program from a collection of module bindings, called the *linking context*.[3] This is achieved by tracing the external

3. We are talking here about conventional *static linking*. Languages that support *dynamic linking* permit name resolution during execution.

references occurring in the collection of program fragments (starting with a specified root module), and building a sequence of module bindings that is consistent with the occurrences of these references. Whenever an external reference is encountered, its binding is determined by consulting the linking context, and emitted as part of the resulting fully linked program. The external reference is thereby said to be *resolved*. The occurrence of external references constrains the order of the bindings in the fully linked program, but it does not completely determine it. Further constraints on the order of bindings are imposed by initialization code whose side effects constitute an implicit dependency of one module on another.

This motivates the definition of a *dependency relation* among a set of modules, consisting of its *reference dependencies* together with its *initialization dependencies*. Reference dependencies are determined by inspection of the code of a module. If a module N contains an external reference m to a module M, then N is said to contain a reference dependency on M. Signatures may also contain reference dependencies on modules, for if a signature I contains a reference m to a module M, then I depends on M and hence m must be bound before I can be used. (At this point such dependencies are inessential, because they can only arise in type selections of the form m.X, which may be replaced by their definitions. However, once abstract types are introduced in §8.5, such references are not in general eliminable in this way.) Initialization dependencies arise when the evaluation of one module is materially affected by the evaluation of another, even though no reference dependency need exist between them. Initialization dependencies cannot always be determined by inspection; for example, one module may read a file that another writes without either sharing a common reference. Therefore, initialization dependencies must be explicitly specified (by some means not detailed here) to ensure that they are respected by the linker.

Ordinarily, the dependency relation among a collection of modules is required to be *acyclic*, precluding circular dependencies of a module on itself (whether via intermediate modules or not). This is enough to ensure that it is always possible to find a linear ordering of modules consistent with the dependency relation. It is possible to permit circular dependencies, at the expense of considerable complications in the general case; see §8.9.

It is worth noticing that, in the simple setting we are describing at the moment, all the external references to a given module m, everywhere in a given set of modules, are guaranteed to be resolved to the *same* module value at link time—that is, external references are *definite*. These definite references are to be contrasted with the *indefinite* references that arise with parameterized modules and signatures (see §8.8). Indefinite references raise difficulties related to aliasing, called coherence problems.

8.4 Phase Distinction

Most modern programming languages are *statically typed*, meaning that type checking may be performed prior to, and independently of, execution. Statically typed languages maintain a clear separation between the *static (type checking)* and *dynamic (execution)* phases of processing, and are therefore said to respect the *phase distinction*.[4] This can be made precise by considering the forms of reasoning required during type checking to test type equivalence. If type checking may be performed without testing equivalence of run-time expressions, then the phase distinction is respected, and the language is said to be *statically typed*. If, however, type checking requires testing equivalence of run-time expressions (sometimes called "symbolic execution"), then the phase distinction is violated, and the language is said to be *dependently typed*.[5] Examples of dependently typed programming languages include Russell (Donahue and Demers, 1985), Pebble (Burstall and Lampson, 1984), and Cayenne (Augustsson, 1998). See Chapter 2 for further information on dependently typed languages.

Since modules contain bindings for types, testing type equivalence involves reasoning about the identity of the type components of modules. But since modules also contain bindings for values, we are at risk of violating the phase distinction. For example, a type expression of the form `m.X` appears superficially to be dependent on the entire module `m`, including its dynamic components. Consequently, checking equality of `m.X` with another type threatens to require comparison of modules for equality, in violation of the phase distinction. We take it as a fundamental design principle that a module system should preserve the phase distinction in the sense that a module system should be statically typed if the underlying core language is. The type theory of modularity developed in this chapter is carefully designed to ensure that the phase distinction is preserved.

The phase distinction is related to the distinction between first- and second-class modules. Informally, a *first-class* module expression is one whose type

4. This terminology was introduced by Cardelli (1988a) in an attempt to relate phases to a universe distinction in type theory. The present formulation is derived from Harper, Mitchell, and Moggi's definition (1990).

5. The natural contrasting phrase is "dynamically typed," but this conflicts with the term's established usage to refer to languages (such as Java or Scheme) with run-time dispatch on tagged data. Our use of the phase "dependently typed" stresses the core semantic issue, rather than focusing on purely syntactic features such as the occurrence of terms in types. The module language of this chapter will exhibit superficial syntactic dependencies that do not, in fact, amount to semantic dependencies in the sense used here. Technically this is achieved by restricting type selection to *separable* modules—those with a fully transparent interface; see Dreyer, Crary, and Harper (2003) for further details.

components are not determined until run-time; otherwise it is *second-class.* The essential difference between a first- and a second-class module expression is whether or not its type components are determined statically (during type checking) or dynamically (during execution). A rough-and-ready criterion for a module expression to be first-class is that the bindings of its type components depend on the outcome of a run-time test. If so, then the identity of its type components cannot be determined statically, rendering the module first-class; if not, it is second-class. (Consequently, a module expression with *no* type components is vacuously second-class, even though its evaluation may involve arbitrary run-time computation.)

All basic module expressions, including module values, are second-class because they explicitly specify their type components. For example, the following module expression is second-class:

```
mod {
  type X = Nat
  val f = λx:X. x
  type Y = Bool
}
```

On the other hand, consider the following module expression, M

```
if ...moon is full... then m₁ else m₂
```

where m_1 and m_2 are bound by the following declarations:

```
module m₁ = mod {
  type X = Int
  type Y = X→X
  val x = 3
  val f = succ
}
module m₂ = mod {
  type X = Bool
  type Y = X→X
  val x = false
  val f = not
}
```

The expression M is chosen so that the definitions of its type components X and Y are dependent on a run-time test whose outcome cannot be predicted at typechecking time. Consequently, it is first-class.

If, instead, m_1 were defined as follows, then the bindings of X and Y would not be dependent on a run-time condition:

```
module m2 = mod {
  type X = Bool
  type Y = Bool→Bool
  val x = true
  val f = not
}
```

In this case M is second-class, despite its syntactic form. The distinction between first- and second-class module is a matter of evaluation behavior.

Up to this point, the type system for modules we have developed so far is too weak to permit any first-class module expressions to be well-typed. For example, the conditional M given above does not implement any signature in the language of signatures developed thus far, for the simple reason that signatures must reveal the definitions of their type components. To assign a signature to M it is necessary to suppress the identity of its type component, X. To do so, we require a richer language of signatures.

8.5 Abstract Type Components

So far in our development signatures are *transparent*—a signature I for a module M must reveal the definitions of the type components of M. As we have just mentioned, a first-class module expression cannot implement a transparent signature. Worse, limiting ourselves to transparent signatures impedes modular programming by creating tight dependencies of one module on another. A transparent signature for a module M must expose the representations of its type components, and modules that makes use of M may be sensitive to that choice. Consequently, any change to M has a knock-on effect on all modules that make use of it. In many cases such a close coupling is unnecessary, and therefore undesirable.

The solution to both of these shortcomings is to permit not only *concrete* (or *transparent*) type declarations in signatures, as we have until now, but also *abstract* (or *opaque*) type declaration revealing the existence, but not the definition, of a type component. An abstract type declaration is said to "hold its type abstract," or to "hide its representation." Signatures in which type declarations may be either concrete and abstract are said to be *translucent*, because they partially reveal their type components. Transparent signatures, which reveal all of their type components, and *opaque* signatures, which hold all of their type components abstract, are two important limiting cases.

Signatures with abstract type declarations are similar to existential types (see Mitchell and Plotkin (1988) and *TAPL*, Chapter 24). Just as with existential types, translucent signatures permit changing the type definitions within

```
CD ::=                        component declarations:
        type X[>X]                        opaque type
        type X[>X] = T               transparent type
```

Figure 8-2: Translucent signature syntax

a module without fear of disrupting the type correctness of any module that makes use of it. In short, translucency supports representation independence in much the same manner as do existential types. However, the relationship to existentials is more analogical than technically accurate. In particular, existentials do not support *dot notation for existential types* (i.e., given an existential package p with an abstract type component X, one cannot just refer to p.X; instead, p must first be "opened" in some particular lexical scope), and so do not offer a fully satisfactory foundation for module systems. In particular, dot notation is required to give adequately expressive types for hierarchical and parameterized modules, as explained in §8.6 and §8.8. This point is discussed in detail by Cardelli and Leroy (1990) and Lillibridge (1997).

The passage to translucent signatures has surprisingly far-reaching consequences. Most immediately, translucent signatures support a flexible form of data abstraction and permit formation of first-class module expressions. Translucent types are crucial for permitting fine-grained control over the propagation of type definitions in hierarchical and parameterized modules while maintaining static typing. Less obviously, they make possible a number of significant enrichments of the module language with a minimum of additional machinery. In particular, translucent signatures provide type-indexed families of signatures "for free" and support a direct and natural way of ensuring type compatibility among the arguments of a parameterized module. (See §8.7, §8.6 and §8.8 for further discussion of these points.) It is remarkable that a single mechanism, translucent signatures, not only affords flexible type abstraction, but also provides all of the supporting apparatus required for several important extensions to the basic formalism. As might be expected, this increase in expressiveness goes hand-in-hand with some significant meta-theoretic challenges. Thus, in terms of both power and cost, the extension to translucent signatures is the most significant step in the chapter.

Translucent Signatures

To support translucency we extend the syntax of our language to permit two forms of type declaration—one that reveals the definition, and one that suppresses it, as detailed in Figure 8-2. For example, the signature

```
signature I = sig {
  type X
  type Y = X→Nat
  val c : X
  val f : Y
}
```

specifies the existence of type components named X and Y, revealing the definition of Y, but hiding the definition of X.

The signature matching relation is generalized to permit "forgetting" of type definitions: an abstract type declaration `type X` in a super-signature may be matched by either an abstract or a concrete type declaration in the sub-signature. For example, the signature

```
signature J = sig {
  type X = Nat
  type Y = X→Nat
  val c : X
  val f : Y
}
```

matches the signature I.

As we noted on page 300, the definitions of type components of a signature are propagated forward when checking whether one signature matches another. So, for example, the signature

```
signature K = sig {
  type X = Nat
  type Y = X→Nat
  val c : Nat
  val f : Nat→X
}
```

matches the signature J, and so, perhaps surprisingly, it also matches the signature I.

8.5.1 EXERCISE [★, ↛]: Check in detail that K matches J and I. □

A module implements a translucent signature if it provides the type components specified in the signature with, where given, bindings equivalent to the specified definitions. During type checking, the definitions of type components of a module are again propagated forward while checking the remainder of the components against the specified signature. For example, the module M declared by the binding

```
module m =
  mod {
    type X = Nat
    type Y = X→Nat
    val c = 5
    val f = λx:X. succ x
  }
```

implements the translucent signature I given above.

8.5.2 EXERCISE [★, ↛]: Check in detail that M implements I. □

Sealing

To limit the visibility of the type components of a module M to the degree specified in the signature I, it is necessary to *seal* M with I, written M:>I. (Note the similarity to the term-level *ascription* operator described in *TAPL*, Chapter 11.) A sealed module expression M:>I is well-formed only if M implements I; the sealed module is considered to implement I (and, by subsumption, the supertypes of I). A sealed module is evaluated by stripping off the seal and evaluating the underlying module. This reflects the informal idea that data abstraction is relevant only during type checking and has no significance at run time.

For example, consider the signature, I, given in the preceding subsection, and the following module expression, M:

```
mod {
  type X = Nat
  type Y = X→Nat
  val c = 5
  val f = λx:X. succ x
}
```

It is easy to check that M implements I, so that M:>I is a well-formed module expression with signature I. Since X is held abstract by I, no use of the sealed module may rely on its identity.

A "decorated" module binding of the form module m : I = M may be seen as syntactic sugar for the "bare" binding module m = (M:>I)—that is, the module M is implicitly sealed with signature I by the binding. For example, if M and I are as in the preceding example, then the module binding

```
module m = M:>I
```

assigns to m the signature I. Since I holds X abstract, m.X is opaque, whereas m.Y is equivalent to m.X→Int.

`M,N ::= ...`	*modules:*	`T,U ::= ...`	*type:*
`M :> I`	*sealing*	`M.X`	*type selection*
		`t,u ::= ...`	*term:*
		`M.x`	*value selection*

Figure 8-3: Mechanisms for abstraction

The formalization of abstract types considered here differs from conventional existential types (as described in *TAPL*, Chapter 24) by separating the imposition of abstraction on a module from any means of binding that module or its components to variables. In the existential framework abstraction is imposed through a binding construct that holds the representation type of the abstract type abstract within a specified scope, which is a single core language expression. For this reason existential types are sometimes said to impose a *closed scope* abstraction discipline. However, in the presence of translucent sums, it is also necessary to make direct reference to abstract types within types, as well as terms. Achieving this using existential types requires that the abstract type binding be "extruded" to encompass essentially the region of a program in which it is used. In practice this means that the lowest-level, and most widely used, abstract types must be given the largest scope, thereby everting the natural structure of the program. In contrast the present framework is based on an *open scope* mechanism in which abstraction is imposed without specifying the scope in which it may be used. This avoids the complex re-structuring required in the pure existential framework, and, moreover, scales naturally to support later extensions to the language. To support open-scope abstraction we extend the grammar of module expressions to permit sealing, remove signatures from module bindings, and permit type and value selection from an arbitrary module expression. (See Figure 8-3 for the revised grammar.)

One consequence of sealing modules with abstract type components is that signatures may now contain unavoidable dependencies on modules. For example, consider the following bindings:

```
signature I = sig {
  type X
  val c : X
  val f : X→X
}
```

```
module m : I = mod {
  type X = Int
  val c = 0
  val f = succ
}
signature J = sig {
  type Y
  val d : m.X
}
module n : J = mod {
  type Y = m.X
  val d = m.f(m.f(m.c))
}.
```

Since J contains a reference to m.X, which is opaque, the signature J is only sensible within the scope of the binding for m. The meaning of the signature J is tied to the binding of the module variable m. In particular, any module implementing J must define the type of d to be equivalent to m.X.

Determinacy and Abstraction

Any adequate abstraction mechanism must ensure *representation independence*, which ensures that the behavior of clients are insulated from the details of the implementation of an abstraction. We will not attempt to give a precise definition of independence here (but see work by Reynolds (1974) and Mitchell (1986)). At a minimum, though, it should ensure that if the modules M and N implement the interface I, then replacing M:>I by N:>I should not disturb the type correctness of a program. In particular, if the type X is abstract in I, then the definition of X must not "leak" from M:>I so as to affect the type correctness of client code. For if it did, then we could choose N to conflict with M on the definition of X and violate even this minimum requirement for abstraction.

This suggests that representation independence is closely tied up with type equivalence—when is one abstract type equivalent to another? In particular, when is (M:>I).X equivalent to (N:>I).X? To ensure that type equality is reflexive (as surely it ought to be), we must ensure that this equivalence hold whenever M and N are equivalent. But module equivalence is, in general, undecidable and, moreover, conflicts with the phase distinction, both undesirable. To avoid this, we simply *prohibit* type selection from sealed modules so that embarrassing questions such as these never arise.

Another strong reason to limit type selection is to ensure type safety in the presence of first-class modules. Since type expressions may be compared for equality with other types during type checking, it is important to ensure that every type expression stand for a fixed type at compile time. Surprisingly, first-class modules violate this seemingly innocent requirement. For example, if M is the conditional module expression

```
if ... moon-is-full ...
  then mod { type X = Int }
  else mod { type X = Bool }
```

then M.X might turn out to be either Int or Bool, but we cannot tell which at compile time. Consequently, it makes no sense to compare M.X for equality with another type. The following exercise shows that permitting such type expressions is, in fact, unsound.

8.5.3 EXERCISE [★★★]: Devise an expression t involving unrestricted selection from the first-class module expression M that incurs a type error at run time. □

Now a first-class module expression such as this can only be well-formed if we seal it with an interface that hides the identity of the type component X. This establishes a close connection between first-class modules and sealing that provides further support for the prohibition of type selection from sealed modules. More generally, since a sealed module may, in fact, be first-class, its abstract type components may or may not be statically well-determined. Consequently, we must "assume the worst" of it, and prohibit type selection.

At the present stage of development, only sealing poses any problems for type selection, but, as we enrich the language, further constructs (such as application of a generative functor) raise similar concerns. It is therefore useful to isolate a subset of module expressions, the *determinate* ones, whose type components are statically known and can be selected without fear of violating safety or representation independence. The remaining module expressions are said to be *indeterminate*; they do not permit type selection.

Basic module expressions, including module values, are determinate because they provide explicit definitions for their type components. For example, the module expression (call it M)

```
mod {
  type X = Bool
  type Y = X→X
  val x = false
  val f = not
}
```

is determinate because we can see immediately that M.X is equivalent to Bool and M.Y is equivalent to Bool→Bool.

By forcing evaluation of its right-hand side, a module binding resolves any indeterminacy before the module variable is bound to the resulting value. Consequently, module variables are also determinate. For example, consider the following module binding:

```
module m = if ... moon-is-full ...
           then mod { type X = Int }
           else mod { type X = Bool }
```

Even though the conditional is indeterminate, the variable `m` is determinate. In fact, the *only* way (so far) to make use of an indeterminate module expression is to bind it to a variable and refer to that variable to access its components.

This sheds light on the informal idea that abstract types are "new" in the sense of being distinct from all other types in a program, regardless of any coincidences of representation. By α-conversion the name of a bound variable is automatically changed so as to avoid clashes with any other module variable in scope at that point in the program, thereby ensuring that its abstract type components are "new."

8.5.4 EXERCISE [★]: What would go wrong if we changed the evaluation of module bindings to call-by-name? □

For the time being, module values and variables are the *only* determinate module expressions. Sealed modules are indeterminate, for the reasons outlined above.

8.5.5 EXERCISE [★]: Show that if sealed modules were determinate, then representation independence could be violated. That is, find a well-typed term `t` whose type correctness is destroyed by replacing one implementation of an abstract type with another. □

8.5.6 EXERCISE [★]: Why would it be bad for two copies of `M:>I` to induce interchangeable abstract type components? □

This same observation also accounts for the informal idea that data abstraction ties a type to a particular set of operations that interpret it: any non-trivial computation with a value of that type must be through these operations. This greatly facilitates maintaining a representation invariant on the data structure, since those, and only those, operations may potentially violate it. Moreover, by insisting that sealed modules are indeterminate, we ensure that the operations from two different abstract types are not interchangeable, even if the underlying representations of values of those types are the same.

8.5.7 **Exercise [Recommended, ★★]:** Devise an example of two implementations of an abstract signature that share a common representation type but differ in the operations used to interpret it. Assuming that these two implementations give rise to the same (but hidden) abstract type, give a program (using sealing as a determinate construct) that incurs an error that would otherwise be avoided. □

An important special case of this arises when the implementation of an abstraction involves private state. In that case two instances of the abstract type must be kept distinct, even though both the representation type and the code of the associated operations are identical! The following exercise explores one example of what can go wrong.

8.5.8 **Exercise [Recommended, ★★]:** Devise an implementation of a hash table involving state, and show that, if two instances of the hash table were to determine equivalent abstract types, then errors could arise that would otherwise be avoided. □

The Avoidance Problem

Consider a local module binding construct of the form

```
let module m = M in M'.
```

This expression implements the signature I′ provided that (1) M implements some signature I, and (2) M′ implements some signature I′ under the assumption that m implements I.

At first glance, it would seem reasonable to say that the principal signature for a `let` expression would simply be the principal signature (I′) of its body. But what if the principal signature of the body involves an abstract type component from M? For example, consider the following the module expression:

```
let
   module m = M :> I
in
   mod { val z = m.y }
```

where I is the signature

```
sig {
  type X
  val y : X
}.
```

Clearly, the principal signature of the body of the `let` is `sig { val z : m.X }`. But this signature cannot be the type of `N`, because it involves an essential reference to the locally bound module variable `m`. (An analogous observation for the `unpack` form for existential types motivates the scoping restrictions discussed in *TAPL*, §28.7.)

It is tempting to consider `N` to be ill-formed, since it attempts to export the type `m.X` outside of its scope. But this neglects the possibility that `N` has *some* signature that does not involve `m.X`. For example, if the core language subtype relation has a maximal type `Top`, then another possible signature for the body of the `let` is `sig { val z : Top }`. Indeed, this may even be the principal signature for `N`. In general, the principal signature of a `let` expression of the form `let module m = M in M'` is the least signature for `M'` that does not involve the bound module variable `m`.

The problem of finding such a signature is called the *avoidance problem*. First reported by Ghelli and Pierce (1992) in the context of System $F_{\leq}$, the avoidance problem is a central design issue for module systems that support data abstraction. Unfortunately, it does not appear to admit a completely satisfactory solution. In some languages (including ML), there exists a signature I involving a module variable `m` with more than one minimal super-signature avoiding `m`, none of which is least. In such cases the occurrence of `m` cannot be avoided without losing valuable type information.

8.5.9 EXERCISE [★★★]: Consider a signature I

```
sig {
  type X = λW:*. m.Z
  type Y = m.Z
}
```

containing a free module variable `m` whose signature has an abstract type component Z. Show that I has infinitely many super-signatures that avoid `m`, but none that is a sub-signature of all the others Assume, for this exercise, that the core language is just F^{ω}, with no subtyping between core-language types. (For substantial extra credit, find a similar example where the core language is full $F_{\leq}$.) □

What to do? A fallback position is to admit as well formed those `let` expressions for which there is a principal signature avoiding the bound module variable, and to reject all others. The trouble is that there is no simple characterization of which modules admit principal signatures and which do not. Reliance on a particular algorithm for detecting cases for which a principal signature exists ruins the declarative nature of the type system. An al-

`CB`	::=	...	*component bindings:*	`M` ::= ...	*modules:*
		`module m [> m] = M`	*module binding*	`M.m`	*module selection*
`CD`	::=	...	*component declarations:*		
		`module m [> m] : I`	*module declaration*		

Figure 8-4: Mechanisms for hierarchy

ternative is to require the programmer to specify the signatures of all `let` expressions. Rather than solving the problem, this approach simply shifts the burden to the programmer. Another possibility is to prohibit leaving the scope of a module variable whose signature has an abstract type component. This means that all abstract types must be global, rather than local. To soften the blow we may rename locally declared abstract types with special names that indicate that they are "hidden," relying on a programming convention to avoid using types with such names. Such a convention may be systematically imposed by "name mangling" during elaboration of the source language program into internal form. Using this approach, hiding abstract types can be handled in much the same manner as type inference, pattern compilation, and overloading resolution (Dreyer, Crary, and Harper, 2003).

8.6 Module Hierarchies

To avoid name clashes, it is useful to organize a collection of module bindings into "clusters" of closely related bindings with more limited cross-cluster dependencies. This may be achieved by permitting module bindings to occur as components of other modules (with the usual distinction between its internal and external names). Correspondingly, we introduce a new form of module expression, the selection of a module component from another module. The additional syntax to support module hierarchies is given in Figure 8-4.

A module that is bound within another is called a *submodule* of the surrounding module. Most of the properties and relations associated with modules are extended recursively to sub-modules. For example, if all of the submodules of a module are determinate, then so is the module itself. Equivalently, if any sub-module is indeterminate (in particular, if it is sealed), then the module itself is indeterminate. The implementation relation between modules and signatures is extended recursively to submodules so that the module

```
module q = mod {
  module m = mod {
    val x = 5
    val y = 6
  }
  module n = mod {
    val z = 7
  }
}
```

implements this signature:

```
signature Q = sig {
  module m : sig { val x:Nat val y:Nat }
  module n : sig { val z:Nat }
}
```

The signature matching relation is extended covariantly to submodules. For example, the signature Q above matches the signature

```
signature Q' = sig {
  module m : sig { val y:Nat }
}
```

(among others).

Besides simple namespace management, hierarchical modularity is also useful in representing compound abstractions. A familiar example is the dictionary abstraction, which builds on the concept of a linearly ordered type of keys. The layering of dictionaries atop keys is naturally expressed using a module hierarchy.

```
signature Ordered = sig {
  type X
  val leq : X × X → Bool
}

signature Dict = sig {
  module key : Ordered
  type Dict : *→*
  val new : ∀V. Dict V
  val add : ∀V. Dict V → key.X → V → Dict V
  val member : ∀V. Dict V → key.X → Bool
  val lookup : ∀V. Dict V → key.X → V
}
```

The Ordered signature specifies a type equipped with a binary operation that is intended to be a total ordering of that type. The Dict signature specifies a sub-module key implementing an ordered type.

The types of the operations declared in the signature `Dict` make reference to the type `key.X`, the type of keys. This illustrates the *dependence* of the "rest" of a signature on (the type components of) a preceding sub-module declaration. Strictly speaking, the type selections `key.X` occurring within the signature `Dict` refer to the *internal name* of the sub-module `key`, whereas any selections from a module implementing `Dict` refer to the *external name*, or *label*, of that sub-module. To distinguish these two aspects of the sub-module declaration we may write the `Dict` signature as follows:

```
signature Dict = sig {
  module key > k : Ordered
  type Dict : *→*
  val new : ∀V. Dict V
  val add : ∀V. Dict V → k.X → V → Dict V
  val member : ∀V. Dict V → k.X → Bool
  val lookup : ∀V. Dict V → k.X → V
}
```

In most cases it is not necessary to make explicit the distinction between the internal and external name of a sub-module, and we rarely do. However, there are situations in which the distinction is critical, as in the following example. Consider the following module expression (call it `M`):

```
mod {
  type X = Int
  module m =  mod {
    type X = Bool
    val f = λa:X. 3
  }
}
```

We wish to assign a signature to `M` that specifies `M.m.f` to be a function of type `M.m.X→M.X`. Without distinguishing internal from external names, there is no way to write such a signature while holding `M.m.X` and `M.X` abstract. The only possible attempt

```
sig {
  type X
  module m : sig { type X  val f : X → X }
},
```

fails because of shadowing of the outer declaration of `X` by the inner one. However, by distinguishing the internal from the external name, we may write the desired signature as follows:

```
sig {
  type X > X'
  module m : sig { type X > X"  val f : X" → X' }
}.
```

Since the internal name is a bound variable, it may be renamed at will, thereby avoiding problems of shadowing.

Returning to the Dict signature, the declaration of the sub-module key indicates that any module implementing Dict comes equipped with its own ordered type of keys. At first glance this may seem unnatural, since we do not ordinarily expect a dictionary abstraction to *provide* an ordered type of keys, but rather to *require* one. The distinction is largely a matter of perspective. Even though the key sub-module is a component of an implementation of Dict, it would ordinarily be obtained "off the shelf" by reference to another module such as the type of integers ordered by magnitude, or the type of strings ordered lexicographically. However, nothing precludes defining the key module "in place," for example in the case that there is precisely one dictionary in use in an entire program. Conversely, we would ordinarily expect the type constructor Dict to be constructed as part of the implementation of Dict, but this need not be the case. We might, in fact, copy this type from another module, say a generic implementation of balanced binary search trees. Or we may choose to construct a suitable data structure "on the spot." Thus, the components of a module may sometimes play the role of an "argument" to that module, yet at other times play the role of a "result." This flexibility is of particular importance when considering families of signatures and modules, to which we now turn.

8.7 Signature Families

To support code re-use, it is important to isolate repeated patterns in both modules and signatures so that we may consolidate what is common to many instances, allowing only the essential differences to vary. This is achieved by introducing *families* of signatures and modules that isolate the pattern and that may be specialized to recover a specific instance of the pattern. In this section we consider families of signatures; families of modules are discussed in §8.8.

A good example of the need for signature families is provided by the Dict abstraction in the preceding section. An implementation of the Dict signature for an ordered type of keys takes the following form:

```
module dict1 = mod {
  module key = key1
  type Dict = λX:* . ...
  ...
}
```

Here key_1 is some module implementing the signature `Ordered`. The principal signature for $dict_1$ specifies the type of keys:

```
signature Dict1 = sig {
  module key : sig {
    type X = key1.X
    val leq : X × X → Bool
  }
  type Dict : *→*
  ...
}
```

We may seal the module $dict_1$ with the signature $Dict_1$ to ensure that the type constructor `Dict` is held abstract. Note that it would *not* make sense to seal $dict_1$ with the signature `Dict`.

8.7.1 EXERCISE [★]: Why? □

Now suppose that we wish to implement a second dictionary whose keys are drawn from the module key_2. As matters stand, we have no choice but to replicate the same text, replacing key_1 by key_2 wherever it occurs.

```
signature Dict2 = sig {
  module key : sig {
    type X = key2.X
    val leq : X × X → Bool
  }
  type Dict : *→*
  ...
}

module dict2 :> Dict2 = mod {
  module key = key2
  type Dict : *→* = ...
  ...
}
```

Doing this makes the code unnecessarily difficult to modify—any change to the signature `Dict` must be replicated for $dict_1$ and $dict_2$.

Clearly, what is needed is some means of isolating the common pattern as a *family of modules* implementing a corresponding *family of signatures*, both indexed by the type of keys. That way we may obtain each dictionary signature and module as an instance of the family for the corresponding ordered type of keys. We turn first to the representation of families of signatures; families of modules are considered in the next section.

Representing Families

There are two main ways of representing families, *parameterization* and *fibration*.[6] Using parameterization, we explicitly abstract the type of keys from the Dict signature using a form of λ-abstraction.

```
signature DictP = λY:*.
  sig {
    module key : sig {
      type X = Y
      val leq : X×X → Bool
    }
    type Dict : *→*
    ...
}
```

Instances are obtained by application, writing

```
signature Dict₁ = DictP(key₁.X)
signature Dict₂ = DictP(key₂.X)
```

to obtain the signatures $\texttt{Dict}_1$ and $\texttt{Dict}_2$ that we wrote out explicitly above.

Using fibration, on the other hand, we simply specify the type of keys by "patching" the generic Dict signature using a "where clause" as follows:

```
signature Dict₁ = Dict where key.X = key₁.X
signature Dict₂ = Dict where key.X = key₂.X
```

As with parameterization, the result of these declarations is the same as the explicit definitions of $\texttt{Dict}_1$ and $\texttt{Dict}_2$ given earlier. Observe that $\texttt{Dict}_1$ and $\texttt{Dict}_2$ both match Dict.[7]

6. This terminology is borrowed from category theory, which considers two methods for representing families of categories F indexed by a category I. An *indexed category* is a functor $\mathbf{Ind}_F : I^{op} \to \mathbf{Cat}$ mapping I into the "category of categories"—roughly, a function from I to categories. A *fibration* is a functor (satisfying some conditions) $\mathbf{Fib}_F : F \to I$ assigning to each family in F its index in I. Our use of this terminology is analogical, not technically precise.

7. These where clauses can be thought of as a form of "signature inheritance," analogous to the "code inheritance" found in object-oriented languages. The fact that where clauses give rise to subtypes is a natural corollary.

In both representations, the family of signatures is indexed by a type. While theoretically sufficient, it is pragmatically unfortunate that, in both representations, the indexing type is separated from its interpretation in terms of operations. For example, since a type can be ordered in several different ways—for example, strings might be ordered lexicographically or by the prefix ordering—it is preferable to maintain the association of a type with its ordering operation. This may be achieved by generalizing type-indexed families to module-indexed families. In the present case this would amount to parameterization or fibration over a module implementing the signature `Ordered`. In parameterized form this would be written

```
signature DictP' = λkey : Ordered.
  sig {
    module key = key
    type Dict = ...
    ...
  }
```

with instances

```
signature Dict1 = DictP'(key1)
signature Dict2 = DictP'(key2).
```

In fibered form we would write

```
signature Dict1 = Dict where key = key1
signature Dict2 = Dict where key = key2.
```

In either case, instantiation of a signature family by a module may be viewed as a convenient form of type indexing, since it is only the type components of the instantiating module that affect the result. This is particularly useful in situations where the indexing module contains several type components, possibly nested within sub-modules.

8.7.2 EXERCISE [★★★]: Give a formal definition of the operation `I where m = M`, making explicit any restrictions that must be made for this operation to be sensible. □

Parameterization vs. Fibration

The chief advantage of parameterization over fibration is familiarity. It is natural (especially for functional programmers) to consider a family of signatures indexed over implementations of a signature `I` as a "function" mapping implementations of `I` to signatures. Representing signature families by parameterization requires a modest enrichment of the syntax to permit λ-abstractions and applications of signatures, an extension of signature equivalence to account for instantiation by substitution, and an extension of the type system to classify parameterized signatures as a kind of function. Fibering, on the other hand, avoids the need for a new form of signature family by exploiting submodule declarations, which are useful for other reasons.

A more important difference is that the parameterized approach requires the programmer to anticipate the patterns of abstraction and instantiation that may arise in any future use of a given signature. When several (type or module) components are involved, it can be difficult to anticipate which are to be thought of as parameters and which are to be thought of as constructed components of the module. Indeed, the context may dictate one choice in one situation, and another in another. The fibered approach avoids the need to anticipate the future, because it affords a kind of "after the fact" parameterization—any module or abstract type component may be considered to be the "argument" in a given situation without prior arrangement.

Taken in isolation, one may argue the advantages and disadvantages of either representation as compared to the other, with neither coming out a clear winner. However, when examined in the larger context of modular programming, a distinct advantage for fibration over parameterization emerges. To explain why this is the case, we must first consider families of modules.

8.8 Module Families

Needless to say, the justifications for introducing families of signatures apply just as well to implementations. Continuing with the example from §8.7, we might well require, in the same program, several different dictionary modules, differing only in the choice of key type. We would then like to abstract the common pattern by forming a *family of modules* indexed by modules satisfying a particular signature (`Ordered`).

A natural representation of a family of modules is as a λ-abstraction of a module expression over a module variable of a specified signature. Such an abstraction is called a *parameterized module*, or *functor*.[8] Instances of the family are obtained by functor application.[9]

The syntax required to support functors is given in Figure 8-5. (This grammar permits higher-order functors, but for now we concentrate on the first-

8. Rod Burstall once remarked that if we do not call the factorial function a "parameterized integer," then we should not call a functor a "parameterized module"!

9. We adopt here an indexed approach to module families, but it is worth noticing that a fibered approach also makes sense and has been explored under the name *mixin modules*; we discuss these briefly on page 343 below.

M, F ::= ...	*modules:*	Π (m:I_1)I_2	*functor signature*
λ(m:I) N	*functor*	λm:I_1.I_2	*parameterized signature*
F(M)	*application*	I_1 I_2	*application*
I ::= ...	*signatures:*	I where X=T	where *signature*

Figure 8-5: Mechanisms for functors

order case, in which only basic modules may be provided as functor arguments. See §8.9 for a discussion of the higher-order case.) The metavariables F and G range over functors.

In §8.7 we noted that it would be useful to define a family of dictionary modules indexed by the type of keys. Using the notation of Figure 8-5, a dictionary functor might be written

```
module dictFun = λkey:Ordered. mod { ... }
```

where ... represents some implementation of the dictionary type and operations. The dictionary module $\texttt{dict}_1$ (with signature $\texttt{Dict}_1$, defined on page 320) would then be obtained by applying dictFun to the key module $\texttt{key}_1$:

```
module dict₁ = dictFun(key₁)
```

If a functor is a kind of function, then its signature should be like a function type—for example, the signature of the dictFun functor should be something like this:

```
signature DictFun =
  Ordered →
    sig {
      type Dict : *→*
      val new : ∀V. Dict V
      val add : ∀V. Dict V → key.X → V → Dict V
      val member : ∀V. Dict V → key.X → Bool
      val lookup : ∀V. Dict V → key.X → V
    }
```

However, the arrow notation does not quite give us what we need because it does not express the dependency between the argument and the result of the dictionary functor—i.e., the fact that the module key appearing in the result signature is precisely the functor's argument. To capture this dependency, we need an additional form of signature, called a *functor signature*, of the form Πm:I.J. Such a signature binds the module variable m in the signature J, permitting the dependency of the result signature on the argument to be expressed. The signature I is the called the *domain*, and J is called the *range*. (The signature Πm:I.J is a form of *dependent function type*; see Chapter 2 for background.) The type of the dictionary functor given above may now be written as follows:

```
signature DictFun =
  Πkey:Ordered.
    sig {
      type Dict : *→*
      val new : ∀V. Dict V
      val add : ∀V. Dict V → key.X → V → Dict V
      val member : ∀V. Dict V → key.X → Bool
      val lookup : ∀V. Dict V → key.X → V
    }
```

Instantiating DictFun by a module M implementing the domain signature Ordered yields a module whose type is the instance of the range signature obtained by replacing key by M throughout.

8.8.1 EXERCISE [★]: One might guess that a family of modules would have a family of signatures, but, instead of this, we introduced a new notion of functor signatures. Why? □

8.8.2 EXERCISE [★]: Note that DictFun can be written more concisely in terms of the parameterized signature family DictP, as Πkey:Ordered. DictP(key). Can DictFun also be expressed using the fibered signature family Dict? □

Functor arguments are required to be determinate because the range signature may involve type selections from the domain parameter (as in the example above). Substitution of the argument for the parameter results in a specialization of the range signature. Rather than use substitution, we may also formulate the typing rule for functor application using subsumption. Just as for ordinary function types, functor signatures are *contravariant* in the domain and *covariant* in the range. This implies that we may weaken a functor signature by strengthening its domain type. In particular, if F is a functor with signature Πm:I.J, and M is a determinate module with transparent signature I′<:I, then F also implements the signature Πm:I′.J. Since I′ is transparent, any type selection of the form m.X in J may be replaced by its definition in I′, thereby eliminating the dependence of the range signature on the functor argument. This results in a signature of the form I′→J′, where J′<:J. By covariance F implements I′→J′, and hence F(M) implements J′. In effect we've performed the substitution of `M` for `m` in `J` using the types of `F` and `M` alone, rather than by inspecting `M` itself.

8.8.3 EXERCISE [★, ↛]: Work out the type checking of the application `dictFun(M)`, where `M` is a determinate implementation of the key signature `Ordered` of your choosing, using the rules just described. □

Coherence

Since families of modules are just functions from modules to modules, one might guess that the language design issues they raise would be just the ones familiar from higher-order functional programming languages. However, a closer look reveals a significant difficulty, called the *coherence problem*, that must be overcome in any practical language with module families.

Suppose we have defined modules `ab` and `bc`, each providing a function `f` that maps between some input type `In` and some output type `Out`. For `ab`, the input and output types are `A` and `B`; for `bc` they are `B` and `C`:

```
module ab = mod {
  type In = A
  type Out = B
  val f : In → Out =  /* ... some function from A to B */
}

module bc = mod {
  type In = B
  type Out = C
  val f : In → Out = /* ... some function from B to C */
}
```

Since the output type of `ab` is the same as the input type of `bc`, we can write a third module of the same form that uses the `f` functions of `ab` and `bc` to construct its own `f` mapping from `A` to `C`.

```
module ac = mod {
  type In = A
  type Out = C
  val f = λx:In. bc.f (ab.f x)
}
```

The point to notice here is that the well-typedness of `ac.f` depends on the fact that the result type of `ab.f` is the same as the argument type of `bc.f`.

Now, suppose that we have a *lot* of modules of the same form as `ab` and `bc`, and we want to write many modules like `ac` that "compose" the transformations provided by a pair of existing modules.[10] We would like to write a composition functor that encapsulates, once and for all, the boilerplate involved in building these composite modules. To do this, we first define a generic signature for "transformers"; this is the type of the inputs and the output of the composition functor.

```
signature Tr =
  sig {
    type In
    type Out
    val f : In → Out
  }
```

Both ab and bc implement Tr.

A naive first attempt at writing the composition functor itself would be this:

```
module compose =
  λm:Tr. λn:Tr.
    mod {
      type In = m.In
      type Out = n.Out
      val f = λx:In. n.f (m.f x)
    }
```

However, this is not well typed: the type expected by `n.f` is `n.In`, while the type returned by `m.f` is `m.Out`, and we have no reason to believe that these are the same. That is, we have failed to express the fact that, for composition to make sense, the argument modules `m` and `n` must be *coherent* in the sense that they *share* this type.

There are two well-known techniques for ensuring coherence, called *sharing by construction* (also *sharing by parameterization* or *Pebble-style sharing*) and *sharing by specification* (or *ML-style sharing*). Sharing by construction was invented by Burstall and Lampson (1984) in their Pebble language and has been explored by many people, famously Jones (1996). Sharing by specification was originated by MacQueen (1984) and is used in the ML module system.

10. One real-world domain where this sort of situation arises is in networking protocol toolkits such as FoxNet (Biagioni, Haines, Harper, Lee, Milnes, and Moss, 1994) and Ensemble (van Renesse, Birman, Hayden, Vaysburd, and Karr, 1998): the modules ab and bc in the example correspond to individual protocol layers or "micro protocols," the functions f correspond to the processing performed by each protocol layer, and the input and output types correspond to different packet or message formats. Composite modules like ac correspond to protocol stacks such as TCP/IP.

Sharing by specification relies on the technique of fibered signature families introduced in §8.7: the required coherence between the module parameters `m` and `n` is expressed by refining the signature of `n` so that the only modules to which `compose` can legally be applied are those whose `Out` component coincides with the `In` component of `m`:

```
module compose =
  λm:Tr. λn:(Tr where In = m.Out).
    mod {
      type In = m.In
      type Out = n.Out
      val f = λx:In. n.f (m.f x)
    }
```

The type of this functor is

```
Π(m:Tr) Π(n:Tr where In = m.Out)
  Tr where In=m.In and Out=m.Out
```

(writing `and` as a more readable synonym for `where`).

Before we go on, a short digression on notation is in order. The definition of `compose` that we have just given is a little hard to read: since we have defined functors to take just one parameter at a time and used currying to write multiple-argument functors, the inherently symmetric sharing relation between `m.Out` and `n.In` has to be de-symmetrized. We can recover the symmetry in two steps. We begin by *un*-currying `compose`—i.e., we rewrite `compose` into a one-argument functor whose parameter is a module with two sub-modules `m` and `n`:

```
signature TrPair = sig {
  module m : Tr
  module n : Tr where In = m.Out
}

module compose =
  λp:TrPair.
    mod {
      type In = p.m.In
      type Out = p.n.Out
      val f = λx:In. p.n.f (p.m.f x)
    }
```

Second, we rewrite the signature `TrPair` in a symmetric way using a new keyword `sharing`:

```
signature TrPair = sig {
  module m : Tr
  module n : Tr
  sharing n.In = m.Out
}
```

The signature of compose now becomes:

```
Π(p:TrPair) Tr where In=p.m.In where Out=p.m.Out
```

Fortunately, `sharing` declarations add no foundational complexity to the language: they are simple syntactic sugar. The `sharing` form just desugars into the primitive `where` form—i.e., the compiler can straightforwardly expand the second definition of `TrPair` into the first. This syntax clarifies the essential intuition that the argument to `compose` is not simply a pair of transformer modules, but a *coherent* pair of modules.[11]

The sharing-by-construction style expresses the coherence required by the `compose` functor in a different way: by "factoring out" the shared type as another parameter to `compose`. To achieve this, we first replace the signature `Tr` by a signature family, indexed by the types `In` and `Out`:

```
signature Tr = λIn:*. λOut:*.
                 sig {
                   val f : In → Out
                 }

module ab = mod { val f : A → B = ... }
            : Tr A B

module cb = mod { val f : B → C = ... }
            : Tr B C
```

Similarly, the signature of composable pairs, `TrPair` is parameterized on three types:

```
signature TrPair = λIn:*. λMid:*. λOut:*.
                     sig {
                       module m : Tr In Mid
                       module n : Tr Mid Out
                     }
```

The coherence between `m` and `n` is expressed here by the fact that their signatures both mention the same type `Mid`. Now we can write a `compose` functor

11. That is, in category-theoretic terms, not just a product but a pullback.

```
module compose =
  λIn:*. λMid:*. λOut:*.
    λp : TrPair In Mid Out.
      mod {
        val f = λx:In. p.n.f (p.m.f x)
      }
```

of type:

```
ΠIn:*. ΠMid:*. ΠOut:*.
  Πp:(TrPair In Mid Out).
    Tr In Out
```

We are using a little syntactic sugar here to make the example easier to read: `compose` takes three types and a module as parameters, whereas, strictly speaking, functors can only take modules as parameters. What we've written can be regarded as an abbreviation for a heavier notation where each "bare type" parameter is wrapped in a little module.

Sharing by construction has an appealing directness, especially for programmers trained in the mental habits of higher-order functional languages. Moreover, since it relies only on abstraction and application for defining signature families, it can be carried out even in rudimentary module systems lacking the translucency required to express fibered signatures. Unfortunately, it suffers from a defect that makes it difficult to use in practice: it does not scale to deep hierarchies of functors.

To see why, note how the parameterized form of the `compose` functor has to take the "middle type" `Mid` as an explicit parameter. This is not so bad in the present example, where the hierarchy is shallow. But suppose that, for some reason, we want to write a functor that composes together *four* transformations.

In the fibered style, we can write another signature that packages together two `TrPairs` with an appropriate `sharing` declaration relating the final output of the first with the initial input of the second:

```
signature TrQuad = sig {
  module xy : TrPair
  module zw : TrPair
  sharing zw.m.In = xy.n.Out
}
```

Note how the coherence between the first and second transformations and between the third and fourth is expressed by the two uses of the `TrPair` signature—all that needs to be stated explicitly in `TrQuad` is the coherence of the second and third. The `compose4` functor is equally straightforward to write, using three applications of the original `compose`:

```
module compose4 =
  λq:TrQuad.
    let xtheny = compose q.xy in
    let zthenw = compose q.zw in
    let p = mod { module m = xtheny, module n = zthenw } in
    compose p
```

In the parameterized style, on the other hand, the TrQuad signature is much more awkward:

```
signature TrQuad = λT1:*. λT2:*. λT3:*. λT4:*. λT5:*.
                     sig {
                       module xy : TrPair T1 T2 T3
                       module zw : TrPair T3 T4 T5
                     }
```

Note how the "internal" coherence constraints on xy and zw have "come to the outside" as parameters to TrQuad. Now compose4 looks like this:

```
module compose4 =
  λT1:*. λT2:*. λT3:*. λT4:*. λT5:*.
    λq : TrQuad T1 T2 T3 T4 T5.
      let xtheny = compose T1 T2 T3 q.xy in
      let zthenw = compose T3 T4 T5 q.zw in
      let p = mod { module m = xtheny, module n = zthenw } in
      compose T1 T3 T5 p
```

The type parameters to compose4 are *nuisance parameters*: they are present solely to express the required type sharing relationships among the "real" arguments to the functor.

8.8.4 EXERCISE [★]: Suppose we extended this pattern to write compose8 (using two applications of compose4 and one of compose). How many type parameters would compose8 need to take in the parameterized style? What about compose16? □

This example shows how sharing by parameterization forces the "plumbing" required to ensure coherence of a functor low in the dependency hierarchy to be recapitulated by every higher-level functor that uses it, by yet higher level functors that use these, etc. Setting up this plumbing (and worse, maintaining it as the program evolves), quickly becomes impractical except for shallow hierarchies. This failure of scalability was observed early on by MacQueen (1984), but has not been widely recognized.

It is important to emphasize that the representation of signature families bears strongly on the method of expressing sharing relationships. If signature families are represented in parameterized form, then sharing by construction is the only available method of ensuring coherence. We must instantiate two families by application to the common types or modules to ensure compatibility. On the other hand, if signature families are represented in fibered form, then either method of ensuring coherence is available, since we may either specialize two or more signatures with the common component using the `where` construct, or we may specify that they cohere on the common components using `sharing`. The crucial reason for this is that a fibered signature *is a signature*—it can be instantiated, or not, as a given situation demands. This allows decisions about parameterization and sharing to be performed in a natural "post-hoc" manner. Since each module internally recapitulates the whole module dependency graph, coherence requirements can be satisfied simply by adding a few equations tying together subgraphs as appropriate.

The Pragmatics of Functors

Since relatively few present-day languages support families of modules, it is worth surveying the practical motivations for including them in a module system. These fall into several categories:

1. Many abstractions are naturally parametric in a type and its associated operations. For example, we illustrated in §8.8 that a dictionary abstraction is naturally parametric in both the type of its keys and the interpretation of that type as pre-ordered. Thus, *functors arise naturally in shared libraries.*

2. Many programs are naturally functorial in nature. For example, the architecture of the FoxNet implementation of TCP/IP (Biagioni et al., 1994) and related networking protocols is based on treating each "layer" of a protocol stack as a functor that is parametric in the layers that occur "above" and "below" it in the protocol hierarchy. To take another example, the SML/NJ compiler for Standard ML implements cross-compilation by defining the central code generation module to be parametric in the target architecture module, so that several code generators can be simultaneously active and share the bulk of the code. Thus, *some program architectures are naturally functorial.*

3. A variety of link-time techniques—based on mechanisms such as "path hacking," class loaders, and various tools provided by the programming environment—are commonly used to achieve effects similar to those expressible using functors. For example, partial linking of several object files into a single, further-linkable object file (using `ld -r` in Unix, for example) is nothing but a means of defining a functor whose parameters are the

unresolved modules and whose result is the partially linked module constructed by the linker. Because such devices are extra-linguistic in nature, they can be unsafe because the external tools are not aware of typing restrictions. In particular, when used for languages with abstract types, such devices may violate coherence constraints, leading to unsafe code. Thus, *functors codify and formalize certain extra-linguistic programming practices.*

Some of the problems addressed by functors are also amenable to treatment by more primitive modularity mechanisms. (This helps explain why the software industry has not yet ground to a halt due to the lack of functors in mainstream languages!) These mechanisms are often more convenient for specific purposes, even if they may be subsumed or explained by the more general mechanism of functors.

For example, Haskell encourages the use of type classes to define interpretations of types by operations. One may, for instance, introduce a class of ordered types as those that come equipped with a binary relation on them. Instances of this class are introduced by specifying the (sole) interpretation of a type by a given binary relation. Instances are often conditional on other instance requirements. For example, one may declare the type `Int` to be pre-ordered by the standard magnitude comparison function, and one may declare the product type `(A,B)` to be pre-ordered lexicographically (say), provided that `A` and `B` are also ordered. In the terminology of this chapter, type classes are simply signatures and instance declarations are functors mapping zero or more instances of some classes to an instance of a designated class. (This use of functors is limited in that a given type may implement the class of ordered types in at most one way, whereas in general a type may admit many orderings. A benefit of this limitation is that the "functor applications" required to calculate appropriate instances of classes may be performed automatically by the compiler.)

Another case where a more primitive mechanism may suffice concerns a parameterized abstraction, such as dictionaries (parameterized on keys), provided by a library. If we happen to know that any given program using this abstraction instantiates it *just once*, then the abstraction itself need not be functorized. Instead, the dictionary library can simply be a module containing an unresolved external reference to a key module that must be resolved in the linking context of each program that uses it. Specifying the instance is generally achieved by extra-linguistic mechanisms such as modifying a search path or installing a special-purpose loader, but such mechanisms could also be internalized as a part of the module language.

Another important special case is found in object-oriented languages. The nearest analogs of modules in these languages are classes and objects. Objects may be viewed as first-class modules with one abstract type, which specifies the types of the instance variables of the object. (This correspondence between objects and modules is explored in depth in *TAPL*, Chapter 24.) While sufficient to capture some common cases, this idiom makes it awkward to manage a collection of inter-related abstract types. (One example is the mathematical notion of a vector space, which involves an abstract type of vectors together with a related type of scalars, each with its own set of associated operations.) Another issue is that these languages offer no analog of sharing (by parameterization or specification) of representations, which is the core issue underlying the well-known difficulties with binary methods (Bruce et al., 1996).

Classes provide a limited form of modularity by serving as the locus of code sharing for all instances of the class. But inheritance is, by its very nature, anti-modular in that it couples the code of a sub-class to the code of its super-class. In particular, there is no notion of signature for a class, nor—in most object-oriented languages[12]—any means of inheriting from an unknown (abstract) super-class. Moreover, if a sub-class determines a subtype of the super-class type, it is impossible to determine anything about the behavior of an instance of a class from its type alone. For knowing that `o` is an object of a (non-`final`) class `C` means only that `o` is an instance of some sub-class of `C`, whose behavior may be totally unrelated to instances of `C` itself. For these reasons classes provide only a weak form of modularity, and cannot be considered to replace it. Fisher and Reppy have examined these issues in the design of the Moby language (1999).

An often-repeated argument for functors is that they may be used as a replacement for a linking mechanism. The idea is that all inter-module references are to be mediated by a functor—the so-called *fully functorized* style of programming—so as to improve program readability by making explicit all cross-module references. But adopting a fully functorized style amounts to replacing each definite reference in a module by an indefinite reference—the free module variable is λ-abstracted in the functor. A central "linking module" then applies these functors in dependency order to construct the complete system; i.e., the behavior of the linker itself is internalized and made explicit as a module-level program. Experience has shown this to be a bad idea: all this parameterization—most of it unnecessary—gives rise to spurious coherence issues, which must be dealt with by explicitly (and tediously) decorating

12. Languages with *mixin modules* are, in this respect, closer to the module systems we are discussing.

`I ::= ...`		*signatures:*
	Π_G `(m:I1):I2`	*generative functor*
	Π_A `(m:I1):I2`	*applicative functor*

Figure 8-6: Mechanisms for applicative and generative functors

module code with numerous sharing declarations, resulting in a net decrease in clarity and readability for most programs.

Functors and Determinacy

When is a functor application determinate? There are two possibilities, depending on whether we take the functor to be *generative* or *applicative*. If generative, each instance of a functor that yields an abstract type "generates" a new abstract type at the point of instantiation. If applicative, there is one abstract type covering all instances of the functor with equivalent arguments. The difference between these two forms of functor is that the application of a generative functor is indeterminate, whereas the application of an applicative functor is determinate. To model both forms of functor we introduce two forms of functor signature, as described in Figure 8-6.

Needless to say, the classification of functors into applicative and generative is not arbitrary. If the body of a functor is indeterminate, then the functor can only be regarded as generative. Otherwise, an application of such a functor would be determinate, even though it is essentially a substitution instance of its indeterminate body. Thus a functor may be deemed applicative only if its body is determinate, but we may regard any functor as generative, by neglecting the possible determinacy of its body. Therefore, it is natural to posit that the applicative functor type is a subtype of the corresponding generative functor type.

8.8.5 EXERCISE [★★★]: Show that it is unsound to consider the generative functor type to match the applicative. (Hint: Adapt the solution to Exercise 8.5.6.) □

Assuming we have both applicative and generative functors at our disposal, when is it appropriate to use one or the other? Let us consider several examples.

If a functor implements an abstract type using per-instance state, it should be generative. For example, consider the implementation of a type of symbols using a hash table. (Here and elsewhere, we omit the result signature on functors for the sake of brevity.)

```
signature ST = sig {
  type Symbol
  val str2sym : String → Symbol
  val sym2str : Symbol → String
  val eq : Symbol × Symbol → Bool
}

module stFun :> Π_G m:(sig{}).ST =
  λ_G m:(sig{}). mod {
    type Symbol = Int
    val table : string array = Array.new (100, NONE)
    val str2sym = λs:String. ...
    val sym2str = λs:Symbol.
                        case Array.sub (table, n) of
                          SOME x ⇒ x | NONE ⇒ ...
    val eq = λ(n1,n2) = (n1 = n2)
  }

module stOne = stFun (mod{})
module stTwo = stFun (mod{})
```

The two instances, stOne and stTwo, of stFun generate distinct abstract Symbol types, and stOne.Symbol is distinct from stTwo.Symbol. Were these types confused, symbols from one table could be intermixed with symbols from another, leading to incorrect results and run-time exceptions that could be avoided by keeping them apart. In particular, the NONE clause in the body of stFun can safely be omitted if the functor is generative, but must be included (or we run the risk of a match failure) if it is applicative.

A natural example of an applicative functor is one whose argument consists solely of types and whose result does not involve any effects. For in such a case there is no reason to distinguish abstract types in different instances of the functor. For example, consider a functor setFun that takes a type of elements as argument and yields an abstract type of sets of these elements.

```
signature setFunInt =
  Π_A m:(sig { type X }).
    sig {
      type Set
      val insert : m.X × Set → Set
      ... }

module setFun :> setFunInt =
  λ_A m : sig { type X }.
    mod {
      type Set = ...
      val insert = ... }
```

Notice that the functor itself is sealed with an applicative functor type to ensure that the Set type in the result is abstract.

One consequence of restricting an applicative functor to have a determinate body is that neither its body nor any of its sub-modules may be sealed. (Were we to do so, the body would be indeterminate, forcing the functor to be generative.) This explains why we sealed the setFun functor itself, rather than writing it in the form

```
module setFun =
  λm:sig { type X }.
    (mod {
       type Set = ...
       val insert = ...
     } :>
     sig {
       type Set
       val insert : m.X * Set → Set
       ...
     }).
```

While sealing the functor itself can be used to impose abstraction on its instances, it cannot be used to impose abstraction within the body of the functor. One way to remedy this deficiency is to distinguish two forms of sealing, *static sealing* and *dynamic sealing*, and two associated forms of indeterminacy, *static indeterminacy* and *dynamic indeterminacy*. The dynamic forms of sealing and indeterminacy are just those considered up to now. The static forms are added solely to enrich the class of applicative functors. A statically sealed module is statically indeterminate, which ensures representation independence. An applicative functor body is permitted to be statically indeterminate, but not dynamically indeterminate (which would force generativity). The terminology stems from considering that, for an applicative functor, abstraction is imposed *once* when the functor is type-checked, rather than *each time* the functor is applied; the abstraction effect is "static," rather than "dynamic."

8.9 Advanced Topics

First-Class Modules

The framework developed here is compatible with treating *modules as first-class values*, by which we mean that we may readily enrich the language to permit modules to be manipulated as ordinary values in the core language. For example, we may store a module in a data structure, then retrieve it and reconstitute it as a module-level expression, without violating representation independence or type safety. We need only ensure that any means of creating a module from a core language computation is considered indeterminate so as to preserve safety and representation independence.

Why not just do away with the distinction between the core and module languages entirely? While this would seem to simplify matters by collapsing a distinction, it complicates the type theory significantly, requiring that the core language be enriched with the mechanisms required to support modularity. These include types for submodules and functors, a subtyping relation, and the means to ensure static type checking in their presence. These complications are not insurmountable. One such formalism was developed by Harper and Lillibridge (1994), who also showed that the type checking problem for this language is undecidable, due to complex interactions between subtyping, impredicative polymorphism, and type sharing specifications. Dreyer, Crary, and Harper's formalism (Dreyer, Crary, and Harper, 2003), on the other hand, achieves adequate expressiveness, including support for first-class modules, without incurring undecidability.

Finally, even if we were to attempt to consolidate the module and core levels, we would find ourselves facing the same questions at a higher level. For, as the development of this chapter makes clear, once we introduce separate compilation (as surely we must), we once again face the same questions of modularity, at the level of compilation units. Module arise even when you try to avoid them!

Higher-Order Modules

Higher-order modules—i.e., functors taking functors as parameters—present some interesting further difficulties. The classic (if somewhat contrived) motivating example is the `apply` functor, defined as follows:

```
module apply =
  λf:(Πi:I.J).
    λi:I.
      f(i)
module m :> I = ...
module f :> Πi:I.J = ...
module n = f(m)
module p = apply(f)(m)
```

One might expect that `n` and `p` are equivalent, since both apply `f` to `m`. But this need not be so, at least if we wish to give a *single* type for `apply` that governs *all* of its uses. For then we must specify whether the argument, `f`, to `apply` is applicative or generative. If it is required to be applicative, we may ascribe the following type to `apply`:

```
ΠA f:(ΠA i:I.J). ΠA i:I. (J where X=f(i).X).
```

This expresses the dependence of the result type `X` on the two arguments consistent with the definition of `apply`. Indeed, `apply(f)(a).X` is equivalent to `f(a).X`, as desired.

On the other hand the functor argument to `apply` might be taken to be generative, in which case the best typing for `apply` is

```
ΠG f:(ΠG i:I.J). ΠG i:I. J
```

Since `f` is taken to be generative, we lose type sharing information in the result, because the application `f(a)` is indeterminate, and hence the "type" `f(a).X` is ill-formed. Consequently, the abstract type `X` in `n` and `p` are not known by the type checker to be the same.

It has been suggested that there should only be *one* apply functor that covers both cases illustrated above. To do so requires that we employ a form of intersection type (at the level of signatures) that captures the two forms of behavior just described. An alternative, suggested by MacQueen and Tofte (1994), is to refrain from assigning types to functors, in effect re-type-checking the body on each use. This means that the *code*, and not just the *type*, of the functor must be available to all clients, which precludes separate compilation.

Static and Dynamic Equivalence

There are two main choices for module equivalence: *static equivalence* and *dynamic equivalence.* Static equivalence deems two modules to be equivalent whenever their static parts are equivalent. This is the coarsest equivalence between modules that conservatively extends core language type equivalence, and is therefore the most permissive choice. The alternative, dynamic equivalence, considers both the static and dynamic parts of modules in the definition of equivalence. Dynamic equivalence is, in general, undecidable, so some conservative approximation must be used in practice.

However, dynamic equivalence makes it possible to distinguish two different interpretations of the same type without generativity. For example, if `f` is a module variable of functor type, and `M` and `N` are determinate modules of its domain type, then `f(M).X` is equivalent to `f(N).X` iff `M` and `N` are equivalent modules. Static equivalence ignores the dynamic part of these two modules, whereas dynamic equivalence would distinguish these types if `M` and `N` differ only in their dynamic components.

Recursive Modules

The model of linking discussed in §8.1 requires that the dependency relation among modules be acyclic—that there be a linear ordering of the modules consistent with their dependencies. It is natural to consider whether this restriction might be lifted to permit a more general form of "cross-linking" of modules. Since cyclic dependencies amount to (direct or indirect) self-reference, one approach to modelling such a generalization is via *recursive modules* (Crary, Harper, and Puri, 1999; Russo, 2001). Another approach is to devise a linking formalism that permits cyclic dependencies (Ancona and Zucca, 1998; Hirschowitz and Leroy, 2002; Flatt and Felleisen, 1998).

Cyclic dependencies raise some significant problems that must be addressed in any satisfactory solution. Most importantly, permitting recursive modules should not disrupt the semantics of the underlying language. Without restriction, cyclic dependencies among modules can introduce a type A satisfying the equation $A = A \to \texttt{Int}$, or a value v of type `Int` satisfying the equation v=v+1. In most languages such equations have no solution, and should not be permitted. Another issue is the interaction with effects. Permitting cyclic dependencies conflicts with the need for a linear initialization order consistent with dependencies. Care must be taken to ensure that values are not referenced before they are defined (or, at a minimum, that such references are caught at run time). Finally, for maximum flexibility, mutually recursive modules should be separately compilable. This requires some form of "forward" declaration to cut cycles in the dependency graph. It also requires a linking formalism that can support mutually cross-referencing modules, even in the presence of type declarations.

8.10 Relation to Some Existing Languages

The design issues discussed in this chapter are largely motivated by the ML module system. There are two closely related realizations of the ML module system, the Standard ML module system and the Objective Caml module system. Basic modules are called structures, signatures are called signatures, and functors are so-called in both cases. Both designs provide for hierarchy and parameterization using essential the same mechanisms as described here, and both adopt the approach to sharing by specification described in §8.8. The designs differ significantly in their treatment of separate compilation, the avoidance problem, and higher-order modularity. The two languages are based on rather different foundations. Standard ML is defined by an elaboration relation that constitutes an algorithmic specification of the well-formed programs. Objective Caml lacks a formal definition, but the design follows quite closely a type theory of the general kind considered here.

Standard ML, as officially defined (Milner, Tofte, Harper, and MacQueen, 1997), permits only first-order, generative functors, provides no support for separate or incremental compilation, and handles the avoidance problem by a technical device that sacrifices principality. To amplify the last point first, the elaboration relation that defines the static semantics of Standard ML relies on an internal notion of "type names" that are generated during elaboration. Hidden abstract types are represented by type names that cannot be designated by any Standard ML type expression, and hence internal "signatures" are not expressible by any signature in the language. Consequently, the Standard ML module system does not in general admit principal (source language) signatures. As to separate compilation, the formal definition of Standard ML does not address it, so each implementation provides its own mechanisms. The most widely used implementation, Standard ML of New Jersey (SML/NJ), has a well-developed compilation manager (Blume and Appel, 1999; Blume, 2002) that supports incremental and cut-off compilation. SML/NJ also provides extensions to permit higher-order modularity that rely on elaborate internal representations of functors that cannot be written in any source language signature, and is therefore incompatible with separate compilation. Moscow/ML (Sestoft, 2003; Russo, 1998) is an implementation of Standard ML based on a type-theoretic interpretation of the language. It provides recursive and first-class structures, and both applicative and generative functors.

Objective Caml permits higher-order, applicative functors, supports separate and incremental compilation, and handles the avoidance problem by sacrificing principality. Again taking the last point first, Objective Caml rejects certain well-formed programs (in the sense of the underlying type theory of the language) when the implementation does not succeed in weakening a signature to avoid the occurrence of an abstract type (Dreyer, Crary, and Harper, 2003). The commitment to applicative functors stems from a desire to permit type selections of the form `f(m).X` in sharing specifications.

The Haskell (Peyton Jones, 2003) module system is rather weak, providing only rudimentary namespace management. This deficiency is ameliorated by type classes. Viewed in terms of the framework of this chapter, the Haskell type class system amounts to a stylized use of modules. Polymorphic abstraction is generalized to functor abstraction—expressions take not only types, but associated operations, as arguments. The functor arguments are generated automatically during type inference based on a significant methodological restriction: no type may admit more than one interpretation by a given set of operations. (For example, in conjunction with type classes no type may be partially ordered in more than one way in a given program.) These interpretations are specified by type class declarations that amount to functor definitions. The type checker implicitly instantiates these functors (through a process of backchaining) to determine the required implicit arguments. Experimental designs for richer modularity mechanisms have been proposed in the literature. For example, Jones (1996) regards modules as polymorphic records, which forces the programmer to manage explicitly the separation of the static from the dynamic parts of a module.

Flatt and Felleisen's *units* (1998) provide a form of modularity for Scheme programs (and other languages) that emphasizes separate compilation and recursive linking. Their language does not consider type abstraction or the associated problems of type sharing. In their realization, units are first-class values, amounting to records in the underlying language. In other formulations, units are used to structure existing C code to provide namespace management and a flexible linking formalism (Reid et al., 2000).

Ancona and Zucca's *mixin modules* (1998; 2002) isolate a variety of combinators for combining modules into programs. As suggested by Bracha and Cook (1990), mixins provide a basis for modelling inheritance, as well as supporting cyclic dependency relationships among modules. Mixins may be seen as fibered representations of families of modules in which instantiation is represented by "mixing in" one module with another.

8.10.1 EXERCISE [★★★]: The C language lacks an internal notion of module, preferring instead to exploit the ambient file system to provide most of the requisite mechanisms. Discuss. □

8.10.2 EXERCISE [★★★]: The Java language also lacks direct analogs of most of the mechanisms we have introduced. However, Java does offer a rich collection of program structuring mechanisms, some of which can be used to achieve effects similar to the ones illustrated here. Discuss. □

8.11 History and Further Reading

The development of the linguistic and methodological foundations of data abstraction and modularity dates back to the earliest days of academic computer science (Parnas, 1972). Seminal work by Wirth (1973) and Hoare (1972) (among many others) was influential on the development of languages in the Algol family such as Pascal (Jensen and Wirth, 1975), Modula-2 (Wirth, 1983), CLU (Liskov, 1993), and Modula-3 (Cardelli, Donahue, Jordan, Kalsow, and Nelson, 1989). The Lisp family of languages (Steele, 1990) influenced the design of ML (Gordon, Milner, and Wadsworth, 1979), which introduced type inference, polymorphism, and abstract types. This sparked the development of several languages, such as Hope (Burstall, MacQueen, and Sannella, 1980), Standard ML (Milner, Tofte, Harper, and MacQueen, 1997), Objective Caml

(Leroy, 2000), and Haskell (Peyton Jones, 2003), founded on these ideas. The ML module system, originally proposed by MacQueen (1984), further developed in the design of Standard ML and Objective Caml, forms the conceptual basis for much of the material presented in this chapter.

The theoretical framework employed in this chapter (and in *TAPL*) is the typed λ-calculus. One important topic was to develop type systems to support data abstraction. A fundamental first step was taken by Mitchell and Plotkin (1988) who related abstract types to second-order existential quantification, extending the connection between type polymorphism and second-order universal quantification discovered by Girard (1972) and Reynolds (1974). MacQueen (1986) pointed out that existential types are not adequate for expressing modular structure, suggesting instead a formalism based on dependent types. These initial steps provided the impetus for further research into type systems for modularity with the overall goal of providing the abstraction guarantees afforded by existential types and the flexible modular programming mechanisms afforded by dependent types.

One strand of research focused on enriching the existential framework to support controlled propagation of type sharing information in a program. Three important developments were Harper and Lillibridge's translucent sum types (1994; Lillibridge, 1997), Cardelli and Leroy's "dot notation" (1990) and Leroy's manifest types (1994; 1996), and Stone and Harper's singleton kinds (2000; Stone, 2000). These type systems support hierarchy and parameterization with control over the propagation of type sharing relationships, even in the presence of first-class modules.

Another strand focused on developing the mechanisms of dependent types to support higher-order modules. Building on MacQueen's suggestions, Harper and Mitchell proposed a calculus of dependent types suitable for modelling many aspects of the ML module system (1993). This framework was further refined by Harper, Mitchell, and Moggi (1990) to ensure respect for the phase distinction in a fully expressive higher-order module system. Further work by Russo (1999) further underscored the point that the apparent dependencies are not really dependencies at all, by performing a "manual" form of phase-splitting during elaboration in the setting of a type-theoretic semantics for Standard ML. This formalism also provided the foundation for compiling modules into typed intermédiate languages (Shao, League, and Monnier, 1998). Shao (1999) considered a type system that ensures the existence of principal signatures, at the expense of ruling out some programs that are expressible in ML.

The abstract-type formalisms provided only weak support for higher-order modules, and the dependent-type formalisms provided no support for abstraction. Leroy introduced applicative functors (1995) in an effort to enrich the abstract type formalism with richer higher-order constructs, but in the process sacrificed generative type abstraction. A fully comprehensive formalism was introduced by Dreyer, Crary, and Harper (2003), based on interpreting type abstraction as a *pro forma* computational effect.

A rather different approach to the semantics of modularity is the elaboration framework of The Definition of Standard ML (Milner, Tofte, Harper, and MacQueen, 1997). The type checking rules for modular programming are given by an algorithm (expressed in inference rule format) for computing an internal representation of the signature of a module. A weakness of this approach is that it lacks any connection with the typed λ-calculus formalisms that form the foundation for the semantics and implementation of programming languages. This deficiency was addressed by Russo (1998), who re-formulated The Definition using constructs from type theory. Harper and Stone (2000) provided an alternative definition for Standard ML based on a separation between elaboration, which included type inference, overloading resolution, pattern compilation, and semantics, which was based on a foundational type theory for modularity.

Garcia et al. (2003) make an interesting comparison of the modularity mechanisms found in several popular languages, from the point of view of supporting a particular style of "generic programming."

9 *Type Definitions*

Christopher A. Stone

Practical uses of interesting type systems often involve large and complex types, and it is useful to have methods for abbreviating these types. The simplest idea is to treat these definitions purely as meta-level constructs (derived forms), an approach with few theoretical complications. For example, in a language with recursive and variant types (e.g., $\lambda\mu$ in *TAPL*, Chapter 20), we could define

$$\begin{array}{lcl} \texttt{Nat} & \stackrel{\text{def}}{=} & \mu\texttt{Y.<zero:Unit, succ:Y>} \\ \texttt{NatList} & \stackrel{\text{def}}{=} & \mu\texttt{X. <nil:Unit, cons:Nat}\times\texttt{X>} \end{array}$$

after which the `cons` function for lists could be described as having the type `Nat → NatList → NatList` rather than the much larger type

```
(μY. <zero:Unit, succ:Y>) →
  (μX. <nil:Unit, cons:(μY.<zero:Unit, succ:Y>)×X>)  →
     (μX. <nil:Unit, cons:(μY.<zero:Unit, succ:Y>)×X>).
```

As long as these definitions are non-circular, they are convenient but inessential syntactic sugar. In principle the symbolic names can all be replaced by their definitions, and so we can ignore them when reasoning about the language itself: we may write types such as `Nat → NatList → NatList` informally, but "officially" we always mean the corresponding expanded type.

It is not always possible or practical, however, to omit type definitions from the language being studied. In some instances type definitions are explicitly part of the language itself. For example, the ML language permits type definitions by the user using the `type` keyword. C and C++ allow similar definitions with the `typedef` keyword.

Alternatively, a language implementation might preserve definitions rather than substituting them away; expanding all definitions can lead to significantly larger types. Techniques such as DAG representations and hash consing (Shao, League, and Monnier, 1998) can ameliorate this problem but the results can be significantly less readable: if a type is originally written using abbreviations, it is often desirable to retain them for displaying the type (e.g., when reporting errors during type checking, as discussed in *TAPL*, §11.4).

If type definitions are included in the language or its implementation, we would still like to know that properties such as type safety continue to hold, and that our algorithms (e.g., for type checking or code transformations) are correct. However, the addition of definitional mechanisms can change the properties of type systems in ways that are not immediately obvious. For example, suppose X is an operator mapping types to types. In F^ω, the type equivalence $X\,T_1 \equiv X\,T_2$ holds if and only if $T_1 \equiv T_2$. But if X is defined as the constant operator λY::*.Int, then suddenly $X\,T_1 \equiv X\,T_2$ holds for arbitrary T_1 and T_2.

As definitional mechanisms become more sophisticated, ensuring a proper implementation can be more difficult. For example, after the module definition (using roughly the syntax of Chapter 8)

```
module n = mod
             type t = Nat
             val  x : t = 3
           end
```

we can use n.t as a synonym for Nat. In this case we have a definition not for the simple name t, but for the entire projection n.t. Moreover, module components can be referenced indirectly; we cannot eliminate the type definition just by replacing n.t by Nat. For example, the further definitions

```
module n' = n

module diag = λ(p : sig
                      type t
                      val x : t
                    end).
                 mod
                   type u = p.t × p.t
                   val  y : u = {p.x, p.x}
                 end

module nn = diag(n')
```

nowhere mention the projection n.t, yet a correct type checker must nevertheless conclude both that n'.t is a synonym for int (by definition the components of n' are the same as the components of n) and that nn.u is equal to the type int × int (guaranteed by the definition of diag). Additionally, the definition for u in the functor's result, which depends on the specific functor argument, must be retained in order to type check further uses of diag.

It is therefore useful to study type definitions as primitive concepts. The focus here is definitions for types because these have the most significant effect on type equivalence and type checking and hence on language properties such as safety. Very similar approaches are used, however, to study term-level definitions and their effects upon term equivalence.

We look at three approaches to adding type definitions to a language. Section 9.1 defines the language $\lambda^{\mathtt{let}}$, which adds *primitive definitions* of type variables to the typing context. The context can record X::K if X is an unknown type variable of kind K, and can record X::K=T if X is known to be equal to the type T of kind K. This mechanism directly allows definitions analogous to NatList above.

Section 9.2 formalizes parts of Chapter 8 by considering a calculus $\lambda^{\llparenthesis\rrparenthesis}$ of second-class modules based on *translucent sums.* Again we have the choice between specifying either just a kind or both a kind and a definition, but now here all type definitions appear in module interfaces. This requires specifying a language of modules and interfaces, and also introduces a limited form of dependent type (since modules, which contain terms, can appear in types).

Finally, Section 9.3 defines λ^{S}, a generalization of $\lambda^{\mathtt{let}}$ that incorporates definitions into the kind system itself. The kind * classifies all ordinary types, while the new, more-precise *singleton kind* S(T) classifies only those ordinary types equivalent to T. This allows definitions at any point where a kind is specified. We then relate $\lambda^{\llparenthesis\rrparenthesis}$ to λ^{S} by showing that modules can be translated away using a *phase-splitting* transformation.

All three systems are described as variants of $F^{\omega}_{\times\eta}$, the higher-order polymorphic lambda calculus extended with product types and with extensionality (eta). The types and kinds of this base language are shown in Figure 9-1, and the terms are shown in Figure 9-2. Although not formally part of the system, many examples will assume the existence of familiar base types (e.g., Nat or Bool) and terms (e.g., numeric constants and addition).

The least usual aspect of the formulation of $F^{\omega}_{\times\eta}$ is the use of the judgment $\Gamma \vdash \diamond$, which formalizes the notion of Γ being a well-formed context (see *TAPL*, 30.3.18). A typing context is well-formed if all bound variables are distinct, and if each type within the context is well-formed with respect to the preceding portion of the context. For convenience in working with the system, all judgments are designed to require (directly or indirectly) that their typing context be well-formed.

The evaluation rules for terms are standard and have been omitted.

$F^{\omega}_{\times\eta}$

T ::=		*types:*
	X	*type variable*
	T→T	*type of functions*
	T×T	*type of pairs*
	∀X::K.T	*universal type*
	λX::K.T	*type operator abstraction*
	T T	*type operator application*
K ::=		*kinds:*
	*	*kind of proper types*
	K⇒K	*kind of type operators*

Context Validity $\boxed{\Gamma \vdash \diamond}$

$$\cdot \vdash \diamond \qquad \text{(CTX-EMPTY)}$$

$$\frac{\Gamma \vdash \mathsf{T} :: * \qquad x \notin dom(\Gamma)}{\Gamma, x{:}\mathsf{T} \vdash \diamond} \qquad \text{(CTX-TYPE)}$$

$$\frac{\Gamma \vdash \diamond \qquad \mathsf{X} \notin dom(\Gamma)}{\Gamma, \mathsf{X}{::}\mathsf{K} \vdash \diamond} \qquad \text{(CTX-KIND)}$$

Kinding $\boxed{\Gamma \vdash \mathsf{T} :: \mathsf{K}}$

$$\frac{\mathsf{X}{::}\mathsf{K} \in \Gamma \qquad \Gamma \vdash \diamond}{\Gamma \vdash \mathsf{X} :: \mathsf{K}} \qquad \text{(K-VAR)}$$

$$\frac{\Gamma, \mathsf{X}{::}\mathsf{K}_1 \vdash \mathsf{T}_2 :: \mathsf{K}_2}{\Gamma \vdash \lambda\mathsf{X}{::}\mathsf{K}_1.\mathsf{T}_2 :: \mathsf{K}_1 \Rightarrow \mathsf{K}_2} \qquad \text{(K-ABS)}$$

$$\frac{\Gamma \vdash \mathsf{T}_1 :: \mathsf{K}_{11} \Rightarrow \mathsf{K}_{12} \qquad \Gamma \vdash \mathsf{T}_2 :: \mathsf{K}_{11}}{\Gamma \vdash \mathsf{T}_1\ \mathsf{T}_2 :: \mathsf{K}_{12}} \qquad \text{(K-APP)}$$

$$\frac{\Gamma \vdash \mathsf{T}_1 :: * \qquad \Gamma \vdash \mathsf{T}_2 :: *}{\Gamma \vdash \mathsf{T}_1 \to \mathsf{T}_2 :: *} \qquad \text{(K-ARROW)}$$

$$\frac{\Gamma \vdash \mathsf{T}_1 :: * \qquad \Gamma \vdash \mathsf{T}_2 :: *}{\Gamma \vdash \mathsf{T}_1 \times \mathsf{T}_2 :: *} \qquad \text{(K-TIMES)}$$

$$\frac{\Gamma, \mathsf{X}{::}\mathsf{K}_1 \vdash \mathsf{T}_2 :: *}{\Gamma \vdash \forall\mathsf{X}{::}\mathsf{K}_1.\mathsf{T}_2 :: *} \qquad \text{(K-ALL)}$$

Type Equivalence $\boxed{\Gamma \vdash \mathsf{S} \equiv \mathsf{T} :: \mathsf{K}}$

$$\frac{\Gamma \vdash \mathsf{T} :: \mathsf{K}}{\Gamma \vdash \mathsf{T} \equiv \mathsf{T} :: \mathsf{K}} \qquad \text{(Q-REFL)}$$

$$\frac{\Gamma \vdash \mathsf{T} \equiv \mathsf{S} :: \mathsf{K}}{\Gamma \vdash \mathsf{S} \equiv \mathsf{T} :: \mathsf{K}} \qquad \text{(Q-SYM)}$$

$$\frac{\Gamma \vdash \mathsf{S} \equiv \mathsf{U} :: \mathsf{K} \qquad \Gamma \vdash \mathsf{U} \equiv \mathsf{T} :: \mathsf{K}}{\Gamma \vdash \mathsf{S} \equiv \mathsf{T} :: \mathsf{K}} \qquad \text{(Q-TRANS)}$$

$$\frac{\Gamma \vdash \mathsf{S}_1 \equiv \mathsf{T}_1 :: * \qquad \Gamma \vdash \mathsf{S}_2 \equiv \mathsf{T}_2 :: *}{\Gamma \vdash \mathsf{S}_1 \to \mathsf{S}_2 \equiv \mathsf{T}_1 \to \mathsf{T}_2 :: *} \qquad \text{(Q-ARROW)}$$

$$\frac{\Gamma \vdash \mathsf{S}_1 \equiv \mathsf{T}_1 :: * \qquad \Gamma \vdash \mathsf{S}_2 \equiv \mathsf{T}_2 :: *}{\Gamma \vdash \mathsf{S}_1 \times \mathsf{S}_2 \equiv \mathsf{T}_1 \times \mathsf{T}_2 :: *} \qquad \text{(Q-TIMES)}$$

$$\frac{\Gamma, \mathsf{X}{::}\mathsf{K}_1 \vdash \mathsf{S}_2 \equiv \mathsf{T}_2 :: *}{\Gamma \vdash \forall\mathsf{X}{::}\mathsf{K}_1.\mathsf{S}_2 \equiv \forall\mathsf{X}{::}\mathsf{K}_1.\mathsf{T}_2 :: *} \qquad \text{(Q-ALL)}$$

$$\frac{\Gamma, \mathsf{X}{::}\mathsf{K}_1 \vdash \mathsf{S}_2 \equiv \mathsf{T}_2 :: \mathsf{K}_2}{\Gamma \vdash \lambda\mathsf{X}{::}\mathsf{K}_1.\mathsf{S}_2 \equiv \lambda\mathsf{X}{::}\mathsf{K}_1.\mathsf{T}_2 :: \mathsf{K}_1 \Rightarrow \mathsf{K}_2} \qquad \text{(Q-ABS)}$$

$$\frac{\Gamma \vdash \mathsf{S}_1 \equiv \mathsf{T}_1 :: \mathsf{K}_{11} \Rightarrow \mathsf{K}_{12} \qquad \Gamma \vdash \mathsf{S}_2 \equiv \mathsf{T}_2 :: \mathsf{K}_{11}}{\Gamma \vdash \mathsf{S}_1\ \mathsf{S}_2 \equiv \mathsf{T}_1\ \mathsf{T}_2 :: \mathsf{K}_{12}} \qquad \text{(Q-APP)}$$

$$\frac{\Gamma, \mathsf{X}{::}\mathsf{K}_{11} \vdash \mathsf{S}_{12} \equiv \mathsf{T}_{12} :: \mathsf{K}_{12} \qquad \Gamma \vdash \mathsf{S}_2 \equiv \mathsf{T}_2 :: \mathsf{K}_{11}}{\Gamma \vdash (\lambda\mathsf{X}{::}\mathsf{K}_{11}.\mathsf{S}_{12})\mathsf{S}_2 \equiv [\mathsf{X} \mapsto \mathsf{T}_2]\mathsf{T}_{12} :: \mathsf{K}_{12}} \qquad \text{(Q-BETA)}$$

$$\frac{\Gamma, \mathsf{X}{::}\mathsf{K}_1 \vdash \mathsf{S}\ \mathsf{X} \equiv \mathsf{T}\ \mathsf{X} : \mathsf{K}_2}{\Gamma \vdash \mathsf{S} \equiv \mathsf{T} : \mathsf{K}_1 \to \mathsf{K}_2} \qquad \text{(Q-EXT)}$$

Figure 9-1: Types and kinds of $F^{\omega}_{\times\eta}$

t ::=	*terms:*
x	*variable*
λx:T.t	*abstraction*
t t	*application*
λX::K.t	*type abstraction*
t [T]	*type application*
{t,t}	*pair*
t.1	*first projection*
t.2	*second projection*

Typing $\boxed{\Gamma \vdash t : T}$

$$\frac{x{:}T \in \Gamma \qquad \Gamma \vdash \diamond}{\Gamma \vdash x : T} \quad \text{(T-VAR)}$$

$$\frac{\Gamma, x{:}T_1 \vdash t_2 :: T_2}{\Gamma \vdash \lambda x{:}T_1.t_2 :: T_1 \to T_2} \quad \text{(T-ABS)}$$

$$\frac{\Gamma \vdash t_1 : T_{11} \Rightarrow T_{12} \qquad \Gamma \vdash t_2 : T_{11}}{\Gamma \vdash t_1\ t_2 : T_{12}} \quad \text{(T-APP)}$$

$$\frac{\Gamma, X{::}K_1 \vdash t_2 : T_2}{\Gamma \vdash \lambda X{::}K_1.t_2 : \forall X{::}K_1.T_2} \quad \text{(T-TABS)}$$

$$\frac{\Gamma \vdash t_1 : \forall X{::}K_{11}.T_{12} \qquad \Gamma \vdash T_2 :: K_{11}}{\Gamma \vdash t_1\ [T_2] : [X \mapsto T_2]K_{12}} \quad \text{(T-TAPP)}$$

$$\frac{\Gamma \vdash t_1 : T_1 \qquad \Gamma \vdash t_2 : T_2}{\Gamma \vdash \{t_1,t_2\} : T_1 \times T_2} \quad \text{(T-PAIR)}$$

$$\frac{\Gamma \vdash t_1 : T_{11} \times T_{12}}{\Gamma \vdash t_1.1 : T_{11}} \quad \text{(T-PROJ1)}$$

$$\frac{\Gamma \vdash t_1 : T_{11} \times T_{12}}{\Gamma \vdash t_1.2 : T_{12}} \quad \text{(T-PROJ2)}$$

$$\frac{\Gamma \vdash t : S \qquad \Gamma \vdash S \equiv T :: *}{\Gamma \vdash t : T} \quad \text{(T-EQ)}$$

Figure 9-2: Terms of $F^{\omega}_{\times\eta}$

9.1 Definitions in the Typing Context

In a language with eager evaluation, side-effects prevent us from eliminating term-level definitions by replacing variables by their definitions. As an alternative, therefore, closed-scope term-level definitions are often treated as derived forms involving applications, namely

$$\texttt{let}\ x{=}t_1\ \texttt{in}\ t_2 \stackrel{\text{def}}{=} (\lambda x{:}T_1.t_2)\ t_1$$

where T_1 is the type of t_1. In languages with type operators a similar approach can be used at the level of types, putting

$$\texttt{let}\ X{=}T_1\ \texttt{in}\ T_2 \stackrel{\text{def}}{=} (\lambda X{::}K_1.T_2)\ T_1$$

where K_1 is the kind of the type T_1.

However, a type definition used within a term does not correspond to an instantiation of a polymorphic abstraction as one might expect. Although

```
let X=Nat in (λx:X.x+1)(4)
```

is semantically reasonable, the polymorphic instantiation

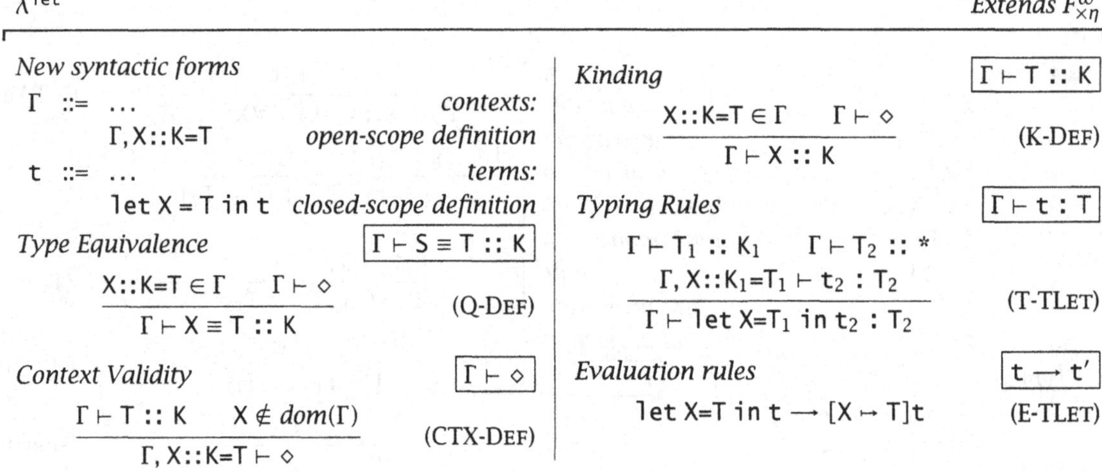

Figure 9-3: Adding definitions to the context

```
(λX::*. (λx:X.x+1)(4))[Nat]
```

is ill-typed because its sub-term `λX::*. (λx:X.x+1)(4)` is ill-typed.

We therefore extend $F^{\omega}_{\times\eta}$ by making definitions of type variables into a primitive notion, resulting in the language $\lambda^{\mathtt{let}}$ shown in Figure 9-3. The syntax of contexts is broadened to permit defined type variables, and the new rule Q-DEF equates type variables with their definitions. Equivalence of well-formed types therefore depends upon definitions in the typing context. In $\lambda^{\mathtt{let}}$ we can prove

```
X::*=Int ⊢ Int→X ≡ X→Int :: *
```

but not

```
X::*=Bool ⊢ Int→X ≡ X→Int :: *
```

or

```
X::* ⊢ Int→X ≡ X→Int :: *.
```

This is an immediate difference from ordinary $F^{\omega}_{\times\eta}$, where type equivalence can be determined by looking only at the two types involved (in this case, `Int→X` and `X→Int`, which are never equal in $F^{\omega}_{\times\eta}$).

Context validity is extended by the rule CTX-DEF, which requires that definitions make sense in the preceding context. Consequently, type definitions

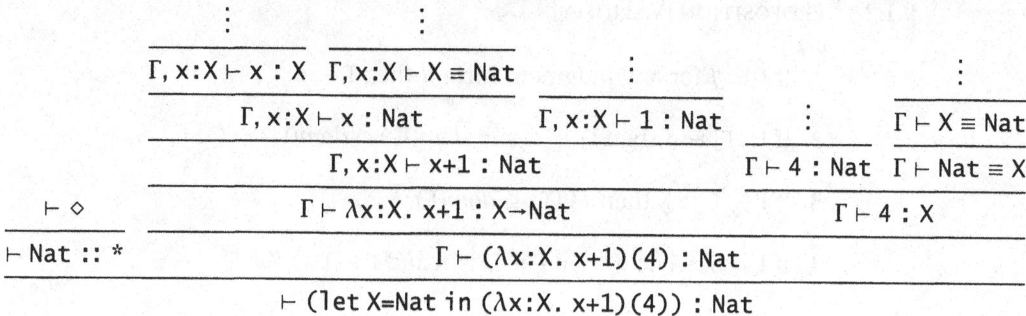

Figure 9-4: Typing of `let X=Nat in (λx:X.x+1)(4)`, using $\Gamma \stackrel{\text{def}}{=}$ `X::*=Nat`

in well-formed contexts are never circular, which will ensure that all definitions can in principle be substituted away.[1]

The new kinding rule K-DEF looks up the kind of a defined type variable, paralleling the $F^{\omega}_{\times\eta}$ rule K-VAR for type variables without definitions.

Definitions in the context are open-scope; they can be considered ambient and usable anywhere. We can also use this mechanism to describe the typing of primitive closed-scope (local) type definitions; the type checking rule T-TLET puts the definition into the context for use while type checking a specific term. Thus, for example, the code `let X=Nat in (λx:X.x+1)(4)` would be well-typed in the presence of natural numbers and addition; a proof appears in Figure 9-4, where the omitted leaf proofs are uninteresting context-validity checks.

The following propositions collect a number of useful properties of λ^{let}. They are all provable via induction on derivations.

9.1.1 PROPOSITION [WEAKENING]:

1. If $\Gamma_1,\Gamma_3 \vdash \mathsf{T} :: \mathsf{K}$ and $\Gamma_1,\Gamma_2,\Gamma_3 \vdash \diamond$ then $\Gamma_1,\Gamma_2,\Gamma_3 \vdash \mathsf{T} :: \mathsf{K}$.

2. If $\Gamma_1,\Gamma_3 \vdash \mathsf{S} \equiv \mathsf{T} :: \mathsf{K}$ and $\Gamma_1,\Gamma_2,\Gamma_3 \vdash \diamond$ then $\Gamma_1,\Gamma_2,\Gamma_2 \vdash \mathsf{S} \equiv \mathsf{T} :: \mathsf{K}$. □

1. The non-circularity requirement for context validity would not prevent T itself from being a recursive type, as in the Nat and NatList examples, assuming recursive types were added to the language.

9.1.2 **Proposition [Validity]:**

1. If $\Gamma \vdash \mathcal{J}$ for any judgment form $\mathcal{J}$ then $\Gamma \vdash \diamond$.

2. If $\Gamma_1, \Gamma_2 \vdash \diamond$ then $\Gamma_1 \vdash \diamond$ and $dom(\Gamma_1) \cap dom(\Gamma_2) = \emptyset$.

3. If $\Gamma \vdash \mathsf{T} :: \mathsf{K}$ then $FV(\mathsf{T}) \subseteq dom(\Gamma)$.

4. If $\Gamma \vdash \mathsf{S} \equiv \mathsf{T} :: \mathsf{K}$ then $\Gamma \vdash \mathsf{S} :: \mathsf{K}$ and $\Gamma \vdash \mathsf{T} :: \mathsf{K}$. □

9.1.3 **Proposition [Substitution]:**

1. If $\Gamma_1, \mathsf{X}{::}\mathsf{K}, \Gamma_2 \vdash \mathcal{J}$ for any judgment form $\mathcal{J}$ and $\Gamma_1 \vdash \mathsf{T} :: \mathsf{K}$ then $\Gamma_1, [\mathsf{X} \mapsto \mathsf{T}]\Gamma_2 \vdash [\mathsf{X} \mapsto \mathsf{T}]\mathcal{J}$.

2. If $\Gamma_1, \mathsf{X}{::}\mathsf{K}{=}\mathsf{S}, \Gamma_2 \vdash \mathcal{J}$ for any judgment form $\mathcal{J}$ and $\Gamma_1 \vdash \mathsf{S} \equiv \mathsf{T} :: \mathsf{K}$ then $\Gamma_1, [\mathsf{X} \mapsto \mathsf{T}]\Gamma_2 \vdash [\mathsf{X} \mapsto \mathsf{T}]\mathcal{J}$.

3. If $\Gamma_1, \mathsf{X}{::}\mathsf{K}, \Gamma_2 \vdash \mathsf{S} :: \mathsf{L}$ and $\Gamma_1 \vdash \mathsf{T} \equiv \mathsf{T}' :: \mathsf{K}$ then $\Gamma_1, [\mathsf{X} \mapsto \mathsf{T}]\Gamma_2 \vdash [\mathsf{X} \mapsto \mathsf{T}]\mathsf{S} \equiv [\mathsf{X} \mapsto \mathsf{T}']\mathsf{S} :: \mathsf{L}$. □

9.1.4 **Exercise [★★, Recommended]:** Explain why the type system would be unsound if the premise $\Gamma \vdash \mathsf{T}_2 :: *$ were omitted from T-TLet. □

9.1.5 **Exercise [★★, Recommended]:** Suppose we wanted to add primitive type definitions to the simply-typed calculus $\lambda_{\to}$. What changes to that language would be appropriate? □

Deciding Equivalence

The hardest part of type checking in λ^{let}, as in F^{ω}, is deciding type equivalence. There are multiple ways to approach this. For example, we could define a notion of reduction (and/or parallel reduction) that allows beta-reduction and allows a variable to be replaced by its definition, a step known as *delta-reduction.*[2] Such notions of reduction can be shown to be confluent and normalizing (Severi and Poll, 1994), which provides a method for determining type equivalence: compute normal forms and check for equality up to bound variables.

2. Some authors (e.g., Barendregt, 1984) instead use the name delta-reduction to refer to the slightly different process of executing built-in primitive operators, e.g., replacing 3+4 by 7 in a language where addition and integer constants are taken as primitive.

If explicit definitions are being used to keep the representation small, however, then computing normal forms can be an expensive way to determine type equivalence. For example, if we had definitions such as

$$\texttt{Pair} \overset{\text{def}}{=} \lambda\texttt{Y::*.(Y}\times\texttt{Y)}$$
$$\texttt{List} \overset{\text{def}}{=} \lambda\texttt{Y::*. (}\mu\texttt{X. <nil:Unit, cons:\{Nat,X\}>)}$$

we would like to be able to determine that `List(List(Pair(Nat)))` and `List(List(Nat × Nat))` are equivalent without expanding them to their common (but noticeably larger) normal form. Although for arbitrary types we might not be able to do any better, in practice code reuses the same defined names and so simple short-circuiting heuristics can help.

One approach to avoiding explicit construction of normal forms involves simultaneous reduction and comparison of the types using weak head reduction, as discussed in Chapter 6. Instead of fully normalizing the types, only the "outermost" applications or definitions are reduced. If the resulting types turn out to have the same shape, then corresponding sub-components of the types can be recursively compared. Conversely, if the two types are weak head normalized but fail to have the same structure then the types are not equivalent and the algorithm can short-circuit and report inequivalence.

Figure 9-5 presents an algorithmic version of equivalence in this fashion. The weak head normalization relation $\Gamma \vdash \mathsf{T}_1 \Downarrow \mathsf{T}_n$ specifies that there is a finite sequence of types $\mathsf{T}_1,\ldots,\mathsf{T}_n$ with $n \geq 1$ such that each weak head reduces to the next, and such that T_n is weak head normal. Given Γ and S there is at most one T such that $\Gamma \vdash \mathsf{S} \Downarrow \mathsf{T}$.

The algorithmic type equivalence judgment $\Gamma \vdash \mathsf{S} \Leftrightarrow \mathsf{T} :: \mathsf{K}$ holds if the weak head normal forms of T_1 and T_2 are structurally equivalent; this is the algorithmic equivalent to type equivalence for well-formed types. As in Chapter 6, extensional equivalence is implemented here for types with arrow kinds by applying both sides to a fresh variable and checking for equivalent results.

Finally, the structural equivalence judgment $\Gamma \vdash \mathsf{T}_1 \leftrightarrow \mathsf{T}_2 \uparrow \mathsf{K}$ implements equivalence for weak head-normal types only; T_1 and T_2 must have the same shape and their subcomponents must be algorithmically equivalent. Then K will be the common kind of T_1 and T_2. Given Γ, S, and T, there is at most one rule that can apply.

Conveniently, the correctness of this comparison algorithm can be shown using the same logical relations proof as in Chapter 6 with only minor modifications. We here are interested in equivalence of types that are classified by kinds, but this corresponds exactly to the problem considered in Chapter 6 of equivalence of terms classified by types. In particular, the kind * here corresponds to the base type b from Chapter 6. Rewriting the logical equivalence

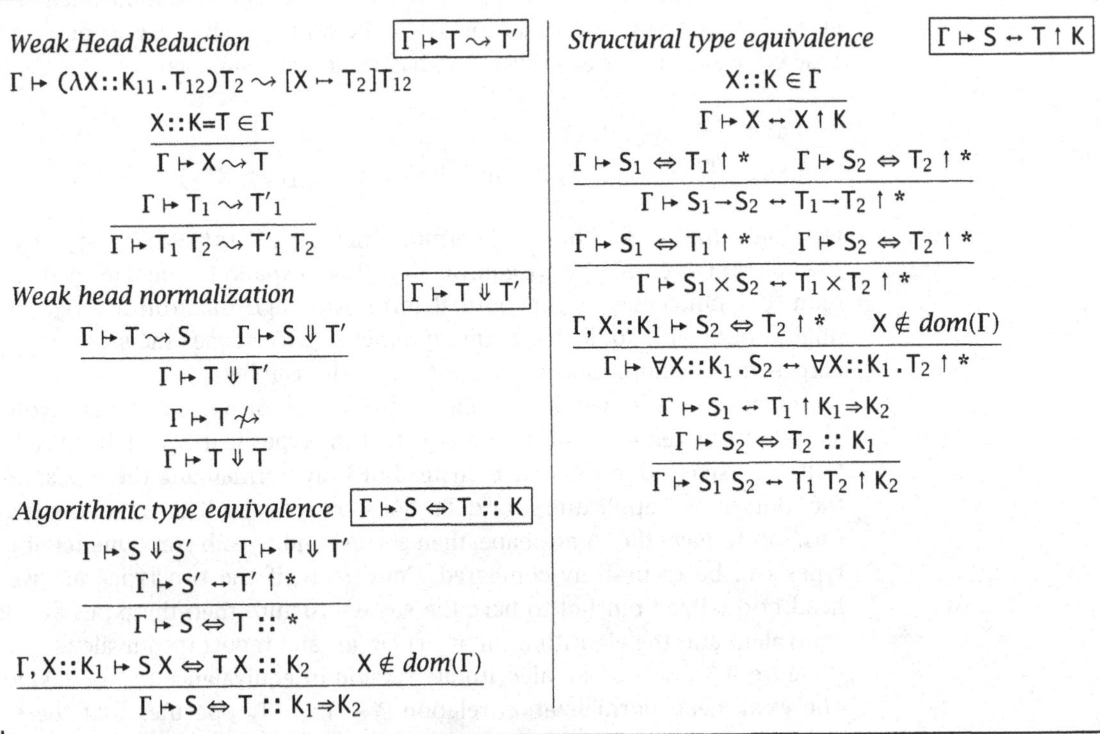

Figure 9-5: Algorithmic equivalence with definitions

relation to refer to types and kinds (and simplifying it a bit, as we have no "unit kind") yields:

9.1.6 DEFINITION [LOGICAL EQUIVALENCE]: Logical equivalence is defined as follows:

$\Gamma \vdash S$ **is** $T :: K$ if and only if either:
$K{=}*$ and $\Gamma \vdash S \Leftrightarrow T :: *$,
or $K{=}K_1{\Rightarrow}K_2$ and for all S', T', and for all $\Gamma' \supseteq \Gamma$,
if $\Gamma' \vdash S'$ **is** $T' :: K_1$
then $\Gamma' \vdash S\,S'$ **is** $T\,T' :: K_2$. □

Similarly, γ or δ will now represent a substitutions mapping *type variables* to *types*. Recall that $\gamma[X \mapsto T]$ is the substitution that agrees with γ except that it maps X to the type T.

The biggest difference from Chapter 6 is that we must be more careful about substitutions. The proof of the Fundamental Theorem of Logical Relations will not go through if we allow substitutions that replace a defined type variable by an unrelated type. (Specifically, the Q-DEF case would fail.) The following definition builds in this restriction, while still being easy to show symmetric and transitive:

9.1.7 DEFINITION: $\Gamma' \vdash \gamma$ **is** δ :: Γ if and only if

- For every $X{::}K \in \Gamma$ we have $\Gamma' \vdash \gamma(X)$ **is** $\delta(X)$ :: K.
- For every $X{::}K{=}T \in \Gamma$ we have $\Gamma' \vdash \gamma(X)$ **is** $\delta(X)$ :: K, $\Gamma' \vdash \gamma(X)$ **is** $\delta(T)$ :: K, and $\Gamma' \vdash \gamma(T)$ **is** $\delta(X)$ :: K. □

9.1.8 EXERCISE [★★★, RECOMMENDED]: Show how to adapt the methods of Chapter 6 to prove that if $\Gamma \vdash S :: K$ and $\Gamma \vdash T :: K$ then it is decidable whether $\Gamma \vdash S \equiv T :: K$ in λ^{let}. □

A major advantage of this variant algorithm is that it allows further refinements. For example, an implementation might check for alpha-equivalence of corresponding components before reducing. Thus, a request to compare `List(T₁)` with `List(T₂)` could directly check whether T_1 and T_2 are equivalent without expanding the definition of `List`.

One must be careful in trying to optimize, though, since the addition of definitions alters usual properties of type equivalence. In $F^{\omega}_{\times\eta}$ the equivalence $X\,T_1 \equiv X\,T_2$ holds if and only if $T_1 \equiv T_2$. In a λ^{let}-style language, however, we can prove

$$X{::}(*{\Rightarrow}*){=}(\lambda Y{::}*.\text{Nat}) \vdash X\ \text{Nat} \equiv X\ \text{Bool}$$

even though `Nat` and `Bool` are not equivalent—both applications are provably equal to `Nat`. Therefore, although comparing $X\,T_1$ with $X\,T_2$ by showing that T_1 and T_2 are equivalent may often be faster than expanding out a definition for X, if the arguments are inequivalent we may need to consider the expansion anyway.[3]

One might think to special-case variables like X above whose definitions completely ignore their arguments, but similar behavior can arise more generally.

9.1.9 EXERCISE [RECOMMENDED, ★★]: Find a typing context and pairwise inequivalent T_1, T_2, and T_3 such that $X\,T_1 \equiv X\,T_2$ but $X\,T_2 \not\equiv X\,T_3$ (and so X cannot completely ignore its argument). □

3. The presence of definitions has consequences for unification as well (e.g., in implementations of ML type inference): the most general substitution making $X\,T_1$ and $X\,T_2$ equal might not make T_1 and T_2 unify.

If the simultaneous comparison process finds no short-cuts, it will do work equivalent to entirely normalizing and comparing the two types. It may still be more memory-efficient, however, than separate normalizations. Full normal forms are not explicitly computed and stored; when two subcomponents of the types are found to be equal their reduced forms can be immediately discarded, freeing up memory for the rest of the comparison.

9.1.10 EXERCISE [★★★, ↛]: Extend the `fullomega` checker to include definitions, and make type equivalence checking as efficient as possible. □

9.2 Definitions in Module Interfaces

In the presence of modules, type definitions are often permitted to appear within interfaces. The most interesting aspect of the theory of ML-style module systems involves tracking information about the types involved, given that type components in modules may have definitions that are not syntactically apparent.

One line of research in formalizing the type theory of ML-like module systems (as discussed in Chapter 8) led to the calculi known as *translucent sums* (Harper and Lillibridge, 1994) and *manifest types* (Leroy, 1994). These similar systems largely correspond to the module systems of Revised Standard ML (Milner, Tofte, Harper, and MacQueen, 1997) and (with some extensions—see Leroy [1995]) of Objective Caml.

The Language $\lambda^{\llparenthesis\rrparenthesis}$

Figure 9-6 defines a minimalist language $\lambda^{\llparenthesis\rrparenthesis}$ with second-class modules, based on the calculus of Lillibridge (1997). Modules are not first-class values able to be passed to term-level functions, and similarly interfaces are not types. Though simpler than any module system usable in practice, $\lambda^{\llparenthesis\rrparenthesis}$ is still complex enough to demonstrate many issues discussed in Chapter 8.

In ML, modules can contain any combination of named value, type, and sub-module components in any order. $\lambda^{\llparenthesis\rrparenthesis}$ instead builds up modules starting with two primitives: modules that contain a single unnamed term, written $\llparenthesis\mathsf{t}\rrparenthesis$, and modules that contain a single unnamed type, written $\llparenthesis\mathsf{T}::\mathsf{K}\rrparenthesis$. The contents of primitive modules can be extracted by using the ! operator.

For each sort of module, there are corresponding interfaces. The interface $\llparenthesis\mathsf{T}\rrparenthesis$ classifies primitive modules containing a value of type T, while the *opaque* interface $\llparenthesis\mathsf{K}\rrparenthesis$ classifies modules containing a type of kind K. Modules containing types may also have a *transparent* interface $\llparenthesis\mathsf{K}{=}\mathsf{T}\rrparenthesis$ if they contain just the type T (or a provably equivalent type) of kind K.

$\lambda^{(\!|\,|\!)}$ — *extends* $F^{\omega}_{\times\eta}$

Syntax

Γ	::=	...	*contexts:*
		m:I	*module variable*
W	::=		*determinate modules:*
		m	*variable*
		(|v|)	*term module*
		(|T::K|)	*type module*
		(|W,W|)	*pairing*
		W.1	*first projection*
		W.2	*second projection*
		λm:I.M	*functor*
W_v	::=		*module values:*
		(|v|)	*term module*
		(|T::K|)	*type module*
		(|W_v,W_v|)	*pairing*
		λm:I.M	*functor*
M	::=		*modules:*
		W	*determinates*
		(|t|)	*term module*
		(|M,M|)	*pairing*
		M.1	*first projection*
		M.2	*second projection*
		M M	*application*
		M :> I	*generative sealing*
I	::=		*interfaces:*
		(|T|)	*term interface*
		(|K|)	*opaque interface*
		(|K=T|)	*transparent interface*
		Σm:I.I	*pair interface*
		Πm:I.I	*functor interface*
t	::=	...	*terms:*
		!M	*module projection*
T	::=	...	*types:*
		!W	*module projection*

Derived Forms

$I_1 \times I_2 \stackrel{\text{def}}{=} \Sigma m{:}I_1.I_2 \qquad (m \notin FV(I_2))$

$I_1 \to I_2 \stackrel{\text{def}}{=} \Pi m{:}I_1.I_2 \qquad (m \notin FV(I_2))$

Context Validity $\boxed{\Gamma \vdash \diamond}$

$$\frac{\Gamma \vdash I \qquad m \notin dom(\Gamma)}{\Gamma, m{:}I \vdash \diamond} \quad \text{(CTX-MOD)}$$

Well-Formed Interface $\boxed{\Gamma \vdash I}$

$$\frac{\Gamma \vdash T :: *}{\Gamma \vdash (\!|T|\!)} \quad \text{(I-TERM)}$$

$$\frac{\Gamma \vdash \diamond}{\Gamma \vdash (\!|K|\!)} \quad \text{(I-OPAQUE)}$$

$$\frac{\Gamma \vdash T :: K}{\Gamma \vdash (\!|K{=}T|\!)} \quad \text{(I-TRANSP)}$$

$$\frac{\Gamma, m{:}I_1 \vdash I_2}{\Gamma \vdash \Sigma m{:}I_1.I_2} \quad \text{(I-SIGMA)}$$

$$\frac{\Gamma, m{:}I_1 \vdash I_2}{\Gamma \vdash \Pi m{:}I_1.I_2} \quad \text{(I-PI)}$$

Subinterface $\boxed{\Gamma \vdash I <: I'}$

$$\frac{\Gamma \vdash T \equiv T' :: *}{\Gamma \vdash (\!|T|\!) <: (\!|T'|\!)} \quad \text{(SI-TERM)}$$

$$\Gamma \vdash (\!|K|\!) <: (\!|K|\!) \quad \text{(SI-OPAQUE)}$$

$$\frac{\Gamma \vdash T \equiv T' :: K}{\Gamma \vdash (\!|K{=}T|\!) <: (\!|K{=}T'|\!)} \quad \text{(SI-TRANSP)}$$

$$\frac{\Gamma \vdash T :: K}{\Gamma \vdash (\!|K{=}T|\!) <: (\!|K|\!)} \quad \text{(SI-FORGET)}$$

Figure 9-6: Syntax, typing, and semantics for $\lambda^{(\!|\,|\!)}$

Subinterface (continued) $\boxed{\Gamma \vdash I <: I'}$

$$\frac{\Gamma \vdash \Pi m{:}I_{11}.I_{12} \qquad \Gamma \vdash I_{21} \equiv I_{11} \qquad \Gamma, m{:}I_{21} \vdash I_{12} <: I_{22}}{\Gamma \vdash \Pi m{:}I_{11}.I_{12} <: \Pi m{:}I_{21}.I_{22}} \quad \text{(SI-Pi)}$$

$$\frac{\Gamma \vdash \Sigma m{:}I_{21}.I_{22} \qquad \Gamma \vdash I_{11} <: I_{21} \qquad \Gamma, m{:}I_{11} \vdash I_{12} <: I_{22}}{\Gamma \vdash \Sigma m{:}I_{11}.I_{12} <: \Sigma m{:}I_{21}.I_{22}} \quad \text{(SI-Sigma)}$$

Interface Equivalence $\boxed{\Gamma \vdash I <: I'}$

$$\frac{\Gamma \vdash I <: I' \qquad \Gamma \vdash I' <: I}{\Gamma \vdash I \equiv I'} \quad \text{(QI-Eqv)}$$

Kinding $\boxed{\Gamma \vdash T :: K}$

$$\frac{\Gamma \vdash W : (\!|K|\!)}{\Gamma \vdash \,!W :: K} \quad \text{(K-MProj)}$$

Type Equivalence $\boxed{\Gamma \vdash S \equiv T :: K}$

$$\frac{\Gamma \vdash T :: K \qquad \Gamma \vdash W : (\!|K{=}T|\!)}{\Gamma \vdash \,!W \equiv T :: K} \quad \text{(Q-MProj)}$$

Well-Formed Modules $\boxed{\Gamma \vdash M : I}$

$$\frac{\Gamma \vdash t : T}{\Gamma \vdash (\!|t|\!) : (\!|T|\!)} \quad \text{(M-Term)}$$

$$\frac{\Gamma \vdash T :: K}{\Gamma \vdash (\!|T{::}K|\!) : (\!|K{=}T|\!)} \quad \text{(M-Type)}$$

$$\frac{\Gamma \vdash M : I' \qquad \Gamma \vdash I' <: I}{\Gamma \vdash M : I} \quad \text{(M-Sub)}$$

$$\frac{\Gamma \vdash \diamond \qquad m{:}I \in \Gamma}{\Gamma \vdash m : I} \quad \text{(M-Var)}$$

$$\frac{\Gamma, m{:}I_1 \vdash M_2 : I_2}{\Gamma \vdash \lambda m{:}I_1.M_2 : \Pi m{:}I_1.I_2} \quad \text{(M-Abs)}$$

$$\frac{\Gamma \vdash M_1 : I_1 \qquad \Gamma \vdash M_2 : I_2}{\Gamma \vdash (\!|M_1,M_2|\!) : I_1 \times I_2} \quad \text{(M-Pair)}$$

$$\frac{\Gamma \vdash M : \Sigma m{:}I_1.I_2}{\Gamma \vdash M.1 : I_1} \quad \text{(M-Fst)}$$

$$\frac{\Gamma \vdash M : I_1 \times I_2}{\Gamma \vdash M.2 : I_2} \quad \text{(M-Snd)}$$

$$\frac{\Gamma \vdash M_1 : I_1 \to I_2 \qquad \Gamma \vdash M_2 : I_1}{\Gamma \vdash M_1\, M_2 : I_2} \quad \text{(M-Apply)}$$

$$\frac{\Gamma \vdash W : (\!|K|\!)}{\Gamma \vdash W : (\!|K{=}!W|\!)} \quad \text{(M-Self)}$$

$$\frac{\Gamma \vdash \Sigma m{:}I_1.I_2 \qquad \Gamma \vdash W : \Sigma m{:}I'_1.I_2 \qquad \Gamma \vdash W.1 : I_I}{\Gamma \vdash W : \Sigma m{:}I_1.I_2} \quad \text{(M-Self1)}$$

$$\frac{\Gamma \vdash W : \Sigma m{:}I_1.I'_2 \qquad \Gamma \vdash W.2 : I_2}{\Gamma \vdash W : I_1 \times I_2} \quad \text{(M-Self2)}$$

$$\frac{\Gamma \vdash M : I}{\Gamma \vdash (M :> I) : I} \quad \text{(M-Seal)}$$

Typing $\boxed{\Gamma \vdash t : T}$

$$\frac{\Gamma \vdash M : (\!|T|\!)}{\Gamma \vdash \,!M : T} \quad \text{(T-Mod-Proj)}$$

Figure 9-6: Syntax, typing, and semantics for $\lambda^{(\!|\,|\!)}$, continued

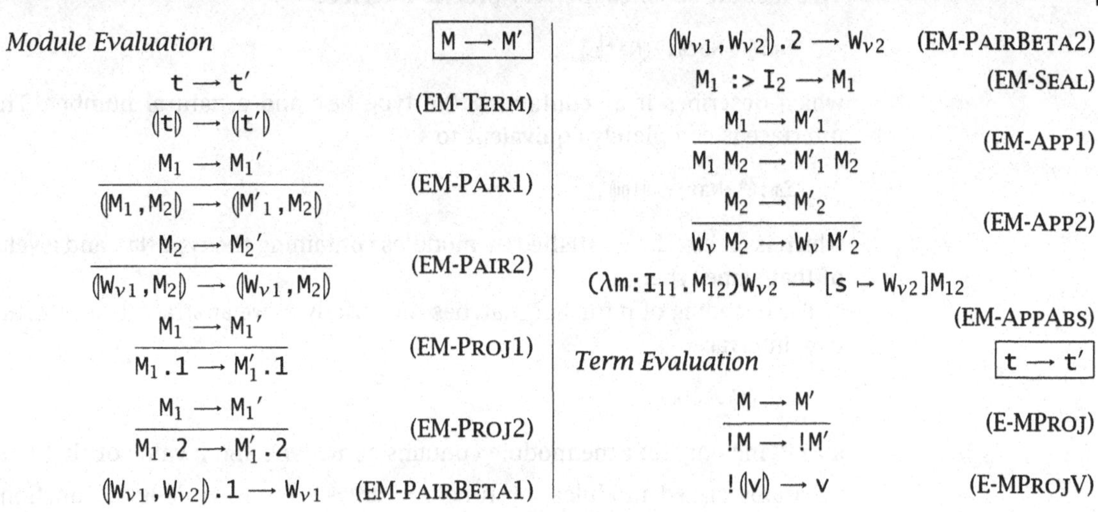

Figure 9-6: Syntax, typing, and semantics for $\lambda^{(\!|\,|\!)}$, continued

More complex modules can be created by using the module-level pairing operator $(\!| \cdot , \cdot |\!)$. The projection operators .1 and .2 then access the submodules within such a pair.

Interfaces of module-pairs are given by specifying the interfaces of the two submodules. However, in order to permit specifications such as "a module containing an abstract type and a term of that type," these interfaces are allowed to be dependent. The interface $\Sigma m{:}I_1.I_2$ classifies module pairs whose first component satisfies the interface I_1 and whose second component satisfies I_2, where the latter interface may refer to the contents of the first component by the name m. (In the vocabulary of Chapter 8, m is an internal name for the first component of the module pair, while the external names of the two components are always 1 and 2.)

For example, consider again the module n, defined by

```
module n = mod
              type t = Nat
              val  x : t = 3
           end
```

This is in essence a module containing a single type and a single term, and hence can be encoded into $\lambda^{(\!|\,|\!)}$ as

$$(\!|\ (\!|\texttt{Nat::*}|\!),\ (\!|3|\!)\ |\!).$$

This module satisfies the very precise interface

```
Σm:(|*=Nat|). (|Nat|),
```

which describes it as containing the type Nat and a natural number. This interface is completely equivalent to

```
Σm:(|*=Nat|). (|!m|),
```

which is an interface satisfied by modules containing the type Nat and a value of that same type.

The encoding of n further matches the strictly more abstract (less informative) interface

```
Σm:(|*|). (|!m|)
```

specifying only that the module contains some type and a value of that type.

Parameterized modules, or functors, are simply module-level functions. Thus, for example, the diag functor defined above can be encoded as

```
λm:(Σm':(|*|). (|!m'|)).
                (| (|!m.1×!m.1::*|), (|{!m.2,!m.2}|) |)
```

The argument of this functor is required to be a module pair containing a type and a value of that type (in sub-modules); it then returns a module pair containing a pair type and a pair value (in sub-modules). By convention, first and second projections bind most tightly, followed by applications, !, and finally the binary operators such as ×. Thus the type being returned by this functor is (!(m.1))×(!(m.1)).

Interfaces for functors are also dependent, because the types in the functor's result may depend upon the types contained in the functor's argument value. The interface Πm:I_1.I_2 classifies functors that require an argument satisfying I_1 and which return a result satisfying I_2, where I_2 can involve the argument value m. Thus, one possible most-precise interface describing the encoded diag functor would be

```
Πm:(Σm':(|*|). (|!m'|)).
           (Σm":(|*=!m.1×!m.1|). (|!m"|)).
```

In both Σm:I_1.I_2 and Πm:I_1.I_2 the variable m is bound in I_2. In those cases where m does not appear in I_2 we can omit mention of the dependent variable, writing non-dependent pair interfaces as $I_1 \times I_2$, and non-dependent functor interfaces as $I_1 \rightarrow I_2$.

The remaining module expression is the sealing operation M :> I. This is the generative sealing operation of Chapter 8, taking a module M and hiding all information about that module except what is explicitly mentioned in the interface I. This is used for information-hiding purposes, in order to create abstract (opaque) types.

The syntax separates out a syntactic set of modules which are *determinate* (have type components that are predictable at compile-time) in the terminology of Chapter 8. Only determinate modules are allowed in types. Some non-values (e.g., `⦇⦇Nat::*⦈, ⦇Bool::*⦈⦈.1`) are syntactically determinate and so can appear within types. This design results from the fact that we must allow module projections such as `!m.1` within types, yet it is desirable for the syntax of types to be closed under replacements of variables by values (e.g., replacing `m` by `⦇⦇Nat::*⦈, ⦇Bool::*⦈⦈`).[4]

Typing and Evaluation Rules

The static semantics of $\lambda^{\llparenthesis\rrparenthesis}$ appears in Figure 9-6. The judgment $\Gamma \vdash$ I defines the well-formedness of interfaces, which requires all types in the interface to be well-formed. More interesting is the subinterface relation $\Gamma \vdash$ I <: I′, which is nontrivial even though $\lambda^{\llparenthesis\rrparenthesis}$ has no subtyping relation. The key rule here is SI-FORGET, which specifies that a module with a transparent interface can be used as if it had the corresponding opaque interface; type definitions in interfaces may be neglected when not relevant. Subtyping for other base interfaces coincides with equivalence. For simplicity SI-PI specifies that interfaces for functors are invariant in their domain (contravariance would be a reasonable alternative), but otherwise the dependent interfaces are covariant.

9.2.1 EXERCISE [★]: Find a syntactically different (but equivalent) precise interface for the `diag` functor above, and a strictly less-precise interface also satisfied by `diag`. □

9.2.2 EXERCISE [★, RECOMMENDED]: The language $\lambda^{\llparenthesis\rrparenthesis}$ has a sub-interface relation, but no subtyping. Suppose we added this, e.g., with `Nat <: Top`. How should the interfaces `⦇Nat⦈` and `⦇Top⦈` be related? How about `⦇*=Nat⦈` and `⦇*=Top⦈`? □

Interface equivalence could be defined directly, but it is shorter as in rule QI-EQV to define equivalent interfaces as being mutual subinterfaces.

$\lambda^{\llparenthesis\rrparenthesis}$ adds the single kinding rule K-MPROJ, stating that we can project from a syntactically determinate module `W` to obtain a type as long as `W` is a module whose interface guarantees that it contains a type. In this rule we need only

4. An alternative is to redefine substitution so that it reduces any new projections-from-pair-values introduced (Lillibridge, 1997).

check that W has an opaque interface of the form ⦇K⦈ because by subsumption and SI-FORGET, any module with a transparent interface also has an opaque interface.

Type equivalence is extended as in λ^{let}, but the new rule Q-MPROJ looks for type definitions that occur in transparent interfaces rather than for type definitions directly in the context.

The rules M-TERM and M-TYPE give precise interfaces to the two sorts of primitive modules; transparent interfaces can be weakened by subsumption as specified in M-SUB.

The rules M-VAR through M-APPLY are similar to those in other systems with dependent types. The only surprise might be the requirement of non-dependent interfaces in the rules M-SND and M-APPLY. In many systems applications of (or projections from) items whose classifier has dependencies can be handled using substitution, but substitution of general modules may lead to ill-formed types, as only syntactically determinate modules may appear in types.

The rule M-SELF is justified by the following observation: assume a determinate module W satisfies the interface ⦇K⦈. Now consider the interface ⦇K=!W⦈; this is the interface of a module containing a single type, specifically the type contained in W. Clearly W itself satisfies this description and hence ought to have this latter interface. M-SELF ensures that this is always provable. The rules M-SELF1 and M-SELF2 are similar, and allow the M-SELF rule to be applied to submodules of a larger module. For example, by using all three rules we can conclude

$$\mathtt{m} : (\!|{*}|\!) \times (\!|{*}|\!) \vdash \mathtt{m} : (\!|{*}{=}!\mathtt{m.1}|\!) \times (\!|{*}{=}!\mathtt{m.2}|\!),$$

i.e., that if m is a module containing two types, then it satisfies an interface requiring a pair containing the two types in m.

In the presence of the SELF rules, the more usual dependent typing rules are admissible for determinate modules (Lillibridge, 1997):

$$\frac{\Gamma \vdash \mathtt{W} : \Sigma \mathtt{m}{:}\mathtt{I}_1.\mathtt{I}_2}{\Gamma \vdash \mathtt{W.2} : [\mathtt{m} \mapsto \mathtt{W.1}]\mathtt{I}_2} \qquad \text{(M-SNDW)}$$

$$\frac{\Gamma \vdash \mathtt{M}_1 : \Pi \mathtt{m}{:}\mathtt{I}_1.\mathtt{I}_2 \qquad \Gamma \vdash \mathtt{W}_2 : \mathtt{I}_1}{\Gamma \vdash \mathtt{M}_1\ \mathtt{W}_2 : [\mathtt{m} \mapsto \mathtt{W}_2]\mathtt{I}_2} \qquad \text{(M-APPLYW)}$$

For example, suppose that we had $\mathtt{M}_1 : \Pi\mathtt{m}{:}(\!|{*}|\!).\,(\!|{*}{=}!\mathtt{m} \times !\mathtt{m}|\!)$ and $\mathtt{W}_2 : (\!|{*}|\!)$. The interface of if $\mathtt{M}_1$ is dependent so we cannot directly use M-APPLY to type check the application $\mathtt{M}_1\ \mathtt{W}_2$, but we can show, using SI-PI, SI-FORGET, SI-OPAQUE, and M-SUB, that $\mathtt{M}_1$ satisfies the strictly less precise interface

Πm:(*=!W$_2$). (*=!m × !m) and hence that M$_1$ satisfies the equivalent interface Πm:(*=!W$_2$). (*=!W$_2$ × !W$_2$), i.e., we have that M$_1$: (*=!W$_2$) → (*=!W$_2$ × !W$_2$). Now by M-SELF we have W$_2$: (*=!W$_2$), so the premises of M-APPLY are satisfied and we obtain M$_1$ W$_2$: (*=!W$_2$ × !W$_2$), exactly as the admissible rule M-APPLYW predicts.

Finally, the M-SEAL rule is an explicit form of subsumption hiding all information not mentioned in the specified interface. The module

```
((Nat::*),(3))
```

has the very precise interface (*=Nat) × (Nat), allowing the contents of its second projection to be used as a natural number. In contrast, the sealed module

```
((Nat::*),(3))  :>  Σm':(*).(!m')
```

must be checked as having only the more abstract interface Σm':(*).(!m'). This enforces abstraction; we know that we could change this line to

```
((Bool::*),(true))  :>  Σm':(*).(!m')
```

and any code using the module would continue to type check.

The evaluation relation for modules looks very much like the evaluation relation for any lambda calculus with pairs. The one completely new rule is EM-SEAL. This sealing operation is *generative* and affects type checking by mimicking the creation of a fresh abstract type whenever the sealing operation is performed, but once we have checked that abstraction is being respected we can ignore the sealing; when the program begins running it has no observable effect.

Type Equivalence and Type Checking

The translucent sums calculus suffers from the avoidance problem discussed in Chapter 8, and hence fails to have most-specific interfaces.

9.2.3 EXERCISE [★★★]: Find a $\lambda^{()}$ module that (even up to equivalence) does not have a most-precise interface. □

This makes type checking difficult, though in practice programs can often be restricted to subsets guaranteed to have principal interfaces. Leroy (1996), for example, considers modules restricted to *named form* where every subexpression has a name. Thus, instead of writing

```
(λm::(*). m) ( ((Nat::*), (Bool::*)).2 )
```

Natural interface $\boxed{\Gamma \mapsto W \uparrow I}$	*Weak head reduction* $\boxed{\Gamma \mapsto T \rightsquigarrow T'}$
$\dfrac{m:I \in \Gamma}{\Gamma \mapsto m \uparrow I}$	$\dfrac{\Gamma \mapsto\ !W \uparrow (\!\lvert K{=}T\rvert\!)}{\Gamma \mapsto\ !W \rightsquigarrow T}$
$\Gamma \mapsto (\!\lvert T::K\rvert\!) \uparrow (\!\lvert K{=}T\rvert\!)$	$\Gamma \mapsto\ !((\!\lvert W_1, W_2\rvert\!).1) \rightsquigarrow\ !W_1$
$\dfrac{\Gamma \mapsto W_1 \uparrow \Sigma m{:}I_1.I_2}{\Gamma \mapsto W_1.1 \uparrow I_1}$	$\Gamma \mapsto\ !((\!\lvert W_1, W_2\rvert\!).2) \rightsquigarrow\ !W_2$
$\dfrac{\Gamma \mapsto W_1 \uparrow \Sigma m{:}I_1.I_2}{\Gamma \mapsto W_1.2 \uparrow [m \mapsto W_1.1]I_1}$	$\Gamma \mapsto (\lambda X{::}K_{11}.T_{12})T_2 \rightsquigarrow [X \mapsto T_2]T_{12}$
	$\dfrac{\Gamma \mapsto T_1 \rightsquigarrow T'_1}{\Gamma \mapsto T_1\ T_2 \rightsquigarrow T'_1\ T_2}$

Figure 9-7: Algorithmic equivalence for $\lambda^{(\!\lvert\,\rvert\!)}$

we must assign names to all intermediate module computations, e.g.:

```
let m1 = λm::(|*|). m
in let m2 =  (|Nat::*|)
   in let m3 = (|Bool::*|)
      in let m4 = (|m2, m3|)
         in let m5 = m4.2
            in let m = m1 m5
               in ...
```

Given these restrictions, every module has a most-specific interface.

Even in the absence of most-specific interface, however, type *equivalence* remains decidable. A similar comparison algorithm to that for λ^{let} will work, except that now it is module projections of the form !W that may have definitions. For example, if m : $(\!\lvert * \rvert\!) \times (\!\lvert *{=}\text{Nat}\rvert\!)$ then !m.2 is known to be equivalent to Nat.

When does !W have a definition? A necessary, though not sufficient, condition is that W have a transparent interface. For example, starting from the bare assumptions that $m_1 : (\!\lvert * \rvert\!)$ and $m_2 : (\!\lvert *{=}!m_1\rvert\!)$ (which would be the case if m_1 were a module containing an abstract type, and m_2 were defined as being m_1), then intuitively $!m_2$ has as its definition the abstract type $!m_1$, while $!m_1$ itself has no definition. Using M-SELF, though, we can further show that $m_1 : (\!\lvert *{=}!m_1\rvert\!)$. For the purposes of an algorithm, it is not useful to say that $!m_1$ has itself as a definition.

In general, the M-SELF rule allows more equations to be added to the interfaces of determinate modules, but never introduces any "new" information. It therefore is irrelevant when trying to detect definitions, and this leads to the notion of the *natural interface* of a module. The natural interface is the most-precise interface that can be computed without using the rule M-SELF. We say that the type $\texttt{!W}$ has the definition $\texttt{T}$ if its natural interface is a transparent interface $(\!|\texttt{K=T}|\!)$. Figure 9-7 defines an algorithmic judgment $\Gamma \mapsto \texttt{W} \uparrow \texttt{I}$ for computing the natural interface $\texttt{I}$ given Γ and $\texttt{W}$. Figure 9-7 then extends weak head reduction to reduce type projections from determinate modules.

Algorithmic and structural type equivalence are not shown, as they are very similar to the definition for $\lambda^{\texttt{let}}$; the only difference would be that structural type equivalence must be extended to equate $\texttt{!W}$ (where $\texttt{!W}$ is weak head normal) with itself.

9.2.4 EXERCISE [$\star$, $\twoheadrightarrow$]: Verify that according to the definition of weak head reduction shown in Figure 9-7 we have $\texttt{m} : (\Sigma\texttt{m'}:(\!|\texttt{*}|\!).(\!|\texttt{*=!m'}|\!)) \mapsto \texttt{!m.2} \Downarrow \texttt{!m.1}$. □

Proofs of properties of module languages such as $\lambda^{(\!|\,|\!)}$ can quickly become difficult, however, because the type equivalence relation now is defined in terms of all the other judgments of the static semantics, including well-formedness of modules (via Q-MPROJ) and hence on well-formedness of terms. However, soundness and decidability results have been shown for systems closely related to $\lambda^{(\!|\,|\!)}$(Lillibridge, 1997; Dreyer, Crary, and Harper, 2003).

9.3 Singleton Kinds

In $\lambda^{\texttt{let}}$, definitions were recorded with a new sort of context entry. Instead of just listing the kinds of type variables, contexts could additionally specify definitions. Definitions in $\lambda^{(\!|\,|\!)}$ were similar, but the choice between kind and kind-with-definition was in module interfaces.

In general, wherever a language normally requires a kind, we could allow either the kind or the kind and a specific type. For example, we could extend $F^{\omega}_{\times\eta}$ with a new sort of polymorphic abstraction, written, $\lambda\texttt{X::K}_1\texttt{=T}_1\texttt{.t}_2$, that is allowed to be instantiated only with the argument $\texttt{T}_1$ (or an equivalent type).

With this mechanism, we could now express type definitions in terms of polymorphic instantiation. The derived form becomes

$$\texttt{let X=T}_1\texttt{ in t}_2 \stackrel{\text{def}}{=} (\lambda\texttt{X::K}_1\texttt{=T}_1\texttt{.t}_2)\ [\texttt{T}_1]$$

where $\texttt{K}_1$ is the kind of $\texttt{T}_1$. The constraint on the function argument—namely that the value passed in for $\texttt{X}$ will be $\texttt{T}_1$—is enough to type check the function body. This definition repeats the type $\texttt{T}_1$, but the result still can be significantly smaller than $[\texttt{X} \mapsto \texttt{T}_1]\texttt{t}_2$.

Minamide, Morrisett, and Harper (1996) used this idea for the purposes of polymorphic closure conversion. The goal was to turn both free term variables and free type variables of functions into arguments; this was useful in the context of a type-passing interpretation of polymorphism (Tarditi et al., 1996) where types are computed and analyzed at run time. By using restricted polymorphic abstractions, they were able to preserve well-formedness when pulling types out of function bodies.

The cases where this sort of construct is genuinely useful are probably rare, but rather than trying to predict exactly where definitions will and will not be needed, the more general approach is to permit definitions at all points where type variables appear. One natural formulation of this idea augments the kinds themselves to include definitions.

The *singleton kind* S(T::K) classifies exactly those types of kind K provably equivalent to T. For example, the kind S(int × int :: *) classifies all types that are provably equivalent to the type of pairs of integers; up to equivalence there is exactly one such type. Then instead of choosing between a kind specification Y::* or a kind-and-definition specification Y::*=Nat, we specify either Y::* or Y::S(Nat :: *).

Figure 9-8 defines λ^S, an alternate variant of $F^{\omega}_{\times\eta}$ including singleton kinds. Because the changes are pervasive, the type and kind judgments are shown in full rather than just listing additions to $F^{\omega}_{\times\eta}$.

The built-in singleton kinds in λ^S are of the form S(T) where T is restricted to be an ordinary type of kind *. We will show later, however, that more general singleton kinds of the form S(T::K) are nevertheless expressible.

The types of λ^S include ordinary types, type operators, and (to permit expressiveness similar to that of $\lambda^{(|)}$) pairs of types. The addition of singletons allows kinds to refer to types, and thus it is natural to permit the kinds classifying type operators or pairs of types to be dependent. The kind ΣX::K_1.K_2 classifies pairs whose first component has kind K_1 and second component has kind K_2, where K_2 can use the type variable X to refer to the value of the first component. In the case where K_2 does not mention X, we can abbreviate this to $K_1 \times K_2$. Thus, for example, we give the pair of types (a collection of two types, not the single type for a pair of values) {Nat,Nat} the kind * × * stating simply that it is a pair of types, or give it the very precise kind S(Nat) × S(Nat), i.e., that we have a pair of types whose components are both equal to Nat, or an in-between kind such as ΣX::*. S(X), i.e., that we have a pair of types whose first component has kind *, and whose second component is the same as the first, or S(Nat) × *, i.e., that the first type is Nat and the second is some proper type, and so on.

Similarly, the kind ΠX::K_1.K_2 classifies type operators that take an argument X of kind K_1 and return a result of kind K_2, where K_2 can depend on the argument X. If K_2 does not mention X then the kind can be written $K_1 \Rightarrow K_2$.

Thus, possible kinds for the identity function λX::*.X on types will include the familiar *⇒* as well as the very precise kind ΠX::*. S(X), stating that,

λ^S *extends* $F^{\omega}_{\times\eta}$

Syntax

K ::=		*kinds:*
	$*$	*kind of proper types*
	$S(T)$	*singleton kind*
	$\Pi X::K.K$	*kind of type operators*
	$\Sigma X::K.K$	*kind of pairs of types*
T ::=		*types:*
	X	*type variable*
	$T\to T$	*type of functions*
	$T\times T$	*type of pairs of terms*
	$\forall X::K.T$	*universal type*
	$\lambda X::K.T$	*type operator abstraction*
	$T\ T$	*type operator application*
	$\{T,T\}$	*pair of types*
	$\pi_1\ T$	*first projection*
	$\pi_2\ T$	*second projection*

Derived Forms

$K_1 \times K_2 \stackrel{\text{def}}{=} \Sigma X::K_1.K_2 \qquad (X \notin FV(K_2))$

$K_1 \Rightarrow K_2 \stackrel{\text{def}}{=} \Pi X::K_1.K_2 \qquad (X \notin FV(K_2))$

Kind validity $\boxed{\Gamma \vdash K}$

$$\frac{\Gamma \vdash \diamond}{\Gamma \vdash *} \quad \text{(WK-*)}$$

$$\frac{\Gamma \vdash T :: *}{\Gamma \vdash S(T)} \quad \text{(WK-SING)}$$

$$\frac{\Gamma, X::K_1 \vdash K_2}{\Gamma \vdash \Pi X::K_1.K_2} \quad \text{(WK-PI)}$$

$$\frac{\Gamma, X::K_1 \vdash K_2}{\Gamma \vdash \Sigma X::K_1.K_2} \quad \text{(WK-SIGMA)}$$

Subkinding $\boxed{\Gamma \vdash K <: L}$

$$\frac{\Gamma \vdash \diamond}{\Gamma \vdash * <: *} \quad \text{(SK-*)}$$

$$\frac{\Gamma \vdash S \equiv T :: *}{\Gamma \vdash S(S) <: S(T)} \quad \text{(SK-SING)}$$

$$\frac{\Gamma \vdash T :: *}{\Gamma \vdash S(T) <: *} \quad \text{(SK-FORGET)}$$

$$\frac{\begin{array}{c}\Gamma \vdash L_1 <: K_1 \\ \Gamma, X::L_1 \vdash K_2 <: L_2 \\ \Gamma \vdash \Pi X::K_1.K_2\end{array}}{\Gamma \vdash \Pi X::K_1.K_2 <: \Pi X::L_1.L_2} \quad \text{(SK-PI)}$$

$$\frac{\begin{array}{c}\Gamma \vdash K_1 <: L_1 \\ \Gamma, X::K_1 \vdash K_2 <: L_2 \\ \Gamma \vdash \Sigma X::L_1.L_2\end{array}}{\Gamma \vdash \Sigma X::K_1.K_2 <: \Sigma X::L_1.L_2} \quad \text{(SK-SIGMA)}$$

Kind Equivalence $\boxed{\Gamma \vdash K \equiv L}$

$$\frac{\Gamma \vdash K <: L \qquad \Gamma \vdash L <: K}{\Gamma \vdash K \equiv L} \quad \text{(QK-EQV)}$$

Kinding rules $\boxed{\Gamma \vdash T :: K}$

$$\frac{X::K \in \Gamma \qquad \Gamma \vdash \diamond}{\Gamma \vdash X :: K} \quad \text{(K-VAR)}$$

$$\frac{\Gamma \vdash T :: *}{\Gamma \vdash T :: S(T)} \quad \text{(K-SINTRO)}$$

$$\frac{\Gamma, X::K_1 \vdash T_2 :: K_2}{\Gamma \vdash \lambda X::K_1.T_2 :: \Pi X::K_1.K_2} \quad \text{(K-ABS)}$$

$$\frac{\Gamma \vdash T_1 :: \Pi X::K_1.K_2 \qquad \Gamma \vdash T_2 :: K_1}{\Gamma \vdash T_1\ T_2 :: [X \mapsto T_2]K_2} \quad \text{(K-APP)}$$

Figure 9-8: Singleton kinds

Kinding rules (continued) $\boxed{\Gamma \vdash T :: K}$

$$\frac{\Gamma \vdash T_1 :: * \qquad \Gamma \vdash T_2 :: *}{\Gamma \vdash T_1 \to T_2 :: *} \quad \text{(K-ARROW)}$$

$$\frac{\Gamma \vdash T_1 :: * \qquad \Gamma \vdash T_2 :: *}{\Gamma \vdash T_1 \times T_2 :: *} \quad \text{(K-TIMES)}$$

$$\frac{\Gamma, X{::}K_1 \vdash T_2 :: *}{\Gamma \vdash \forall X{::}K_1 . T_2 :: *} \quad \text{(K-ALL)}$$

$$\frac{\Gamma \vdash \Sigma X{::}K_1 . K_2 \qquad \Gamma \vdash T_1 :: K_1 \qquad \Gamma \vdash T_2 :: [X \mapsto T_1]K_2}{\Gamma \vdash \{T_1 , T_2\} :: \Sigma X{::}K_1 . K_2} \quad \text{(K-PAIR)}$$

$$\frac{\Gamma \vdash T :: \Sigma X{::}K_1 . K_2}{\Gamma \vdash \pi_1 \, T :: K_1} \quad \text{(K-FST)}$$

$$\frac{\Gamma \vdash T :: \Sigma X{::}K_1 . K_2}{\Gamma \vdash \pi_2 \, T :: [X \mapsto \pi_1 \, T]K_2} \quad \text{(K-SND)}$$

$$\frac{\Gamma \vdash T :: \Pi X{::}K_1 . L \qquad \Gamma, X :: K_1 \vdash T(X) :: K_2 \qquad X \notin FV(T)}{\Gamma \vdash T :: \Pi X{::}K_1 . K_2} \quad \text{(K-ABSSELF)}$$

$$\frac{\Gamma \vdash T :: \Sigma X{::}K'_1 . K_2 \qquad \Gamma \vdash \pi_1 \, T :: K_1}{\Gamma \vdash T :: \Sigma X{::}K_1 . K_2} \quad \text{(K-SELF1)}$$

$$\frac{\Gamma \vdash T :: \Sigma X{::}K_1 . K'_2 \qquad \Gamma \vdash \pi_2 \, T :: K_2}{\Gamma \vdash T :: K_1 \times K_2} \quad \text{(K-SELF2)}$$

$$\frac{\Gamma \vdash T :: K_1 \qquad \Gamma \vdash K_1 <: K_2}{\Gamma \vdash T :: K_2} \quad \text{(K-SUB)}$$

Equivalence rules $\boxed{\Gamma \vdash S \equiv T :: K}$

$$\frac{\Gamma \vdash T :: K}{\Gamma \vdash T \equiv T :: K} \quad \text{(Q-REFL)}$$

$$\frac{\Gamma \vdash T \equiv S :: K}{\Gamma \vdash S \equiv T :: K} \quad \text{(Q-SYM)}$$

$$\frac{\Gamma \vdash S \equiv U :: K \qquad \Gamma \vdash U \equiv T :: K}{\Gamma \vdash S \equiv T :: K} \quad \text{(Q-TRANS)}$$

$$\frac{\Gamma \vdash S_1 \equiv T_1 :: \Pi X{::}K_1 . K_2 \qquad \Gamma \vdash S_2 \equiv T_2 :: K_1}{\Gamma \vdash S_1 \, S_2 \equiv T_1 \, T_2 :: [X \mapsto S_1]K_2} \quad \text{(Q-APP)}$$

$$\frac{\Gamma \vdash S \equiv T :: \Sigma X{::}K_1 . K_2}{\Gamma \vdash \pi_1 \, S \equiv \pi_1 \, T :: K_1} \quad \text{(Q-FST)}$$

$$\frac{\Gamma \vdash S \equiv T :: \Sigma X{::}K_1 . K_2}{\Gamma \vdash \pi_2 \, S \equiv \pi_2 \, T :: [X \mapsto \pi_1 \, S]K_2} \quad \text{(Q-SND)}$$

$$\frac{\Gamma \vdash \Sigma X{::}K_1 . K_2 \qquad \Gamma \vdash S_1 \equiv T_1 :: K_1 \qquad \Gamma \vdash S_2 \equiv T_2 :: [X \mapsto S_1]K_2}{\Gamma \vdash \{S_1 , S_2\} \equiv \{T_1 , T_2\} :: \Sigma X{::}K_1 . K_2} \quad \text{(Q-PAIR)}$$

$$\frac{\Gamma \vdash K_1 \equiv K_2 \qquad \Gamma, X :: K_1 \vdash S_2 \equiv T_2 :: K_2}{\Gamma \vdash \lambda X{::}K_1 . S_2 \equiv \lambda X{::}K_2 . T_2 :: \Pi X{::}K_1 . K_2} \quad \text{(Q-ABS)}$$

$$\frac{\Gamma \vdash K_1 \equiv K_2 \qquad \Gamma, X :: K_1 \vdash T_1 \equiv T_2 :: *}{\Gamma \vdash \forall X{::}K_1 . T_1 \equiv \forall X{::}K_2 . T_2 :: *} \quad \text{(Q-ALL)}$$

$$\frac{\Gamma \vdash S :: \mathcal{S}(T)}{\Gamma \vdash S \equiv T :: \mathcal{S}(S)} \quad \text{(Q-SELIM)}$$

$$\frac{\Gamma \vdash \Sigma X{::}K_1 . K_2 \qquad \Gamma \vdash \pi_1 S \equiv \pi_1 T :: K_1 \qquad \Gamma \vdash \pi_2 S \equiv \pi_2 T :: [X \mapsto \pi_1 \, S]K_2}{\Gamma \vdash S \equiv T :: \Sigma X{::}K_1 . K_2} \quad \text{(Q-PAIR-EXT)}$$

$$\frac{\Gamma \vdash S :: \Pi X{::}K_1 . L_1 \qquad \Gamma \vdash T :: \Pi X{::}K_1 . L_2 \qquad \Gamma, X :: K_1 \vdash S \, X \equiv T \, X :: K_2}{\Gamma \vdash S \equiv T :: \Pi X{::}K_1 . K_2} \quad \text{(Q-EXT)}$$

$$\frac{\Gamma \vdash S \equiv T :: L \qquad \Gamma \vdash L <: K}{\Gamma \vdash S \equiv T :: K} \quad \text{(Q-SUB)}$$

Figure 9-8: Singleton kinds, continued

given any type X of kind *, the function returns a result equal to X. There are infinitely many other possibilities as well, including S(Nat)⇒S(Nat), which states that the function can be applied to the type Nat and will return the same type Nat.

Every type of kind S(T) is, by the definition of λ^S, also a proper type of kind *. This induces a *subkinding* relation with S(T) <: * for any type T. Subkinding between singleton kinds coincides with equivalence, and subkinding is lifted to the kinds of functions and of pairs in the normal way; e.g., function kinds are contravariant in their argument and covariant in their result.

9.3.1 EXERCISE [★]: The language λ^S has subkinding but not subtyping. If subtyping were added, with Nat <: Top, then how should the kinds S(Nat) and S(Top) be related? □

The well-formedness rules for types are mostly the familiar rules for a dependently-typed (or, in this case, dependently-kinded) lambda calculus with functions and pairs. Five rules stand out for special consideration, however. Rule K-SUB is a subsumption rule that makes use of the subkinding rule; a type with a more-precise kind can also be used as a type with a less-precise kind. Rule K-SINTRO is the introduction rule for singleton kinds. This rule allows a well-formed type T of kind * to be given the more precise singleton kind S(T).

Rules K-SELF1 and K-SELF2 serve the same purpose as M-SELF1 and M-SELF2 in the translucent sum calculus, while K-ABSSELF serves a similar purpose for kinds of type operator abstractions. In most type systems all three rules would be admissible, but here they allow more precise typings. For example, suppose Y is a pair of types, that is, Y::* × *. Now consider the kind $S(\pi_1\ \mathsf{Y}) \times S(\pi_2\ \mathsf{Y})$, i.e., the kind of pairs of types whose first component is equal to the first component of Y, and whose second component is equal to the second component of Y. Regardless of whether the language includes eta-equivalence for types (λ^S does), Y itself should satisfy this latter kind. Rules K-SELF1 and K-SINTRO allow us to conclude that Y : $S(\pi_1\ \mathsf{Y}) \times *$, and then K-SELF2 and K-SINTRO allow us to further prove Y : $S(\pi_1\ \mathsf{Y}) \times S(\pi_2\ \mathsf{Y})$.

Similarly, assume Z :: *⇒*. The kind ΠX::*. S(Z X) classifies all type operators that, when given a type argument X, yield the same result as Z does when given X. Again, Z itself has this property and rule K-ABSSELF is used to prove it.

Collectively, the three SELF rules ensure that types have every kind that their eta-expansions do.

Rules Q-REFL through Q-ALL are standard for a lambda calculus with dependencies; they insure that definitional equivalence is a congruence on well-formed types. Rule Q-SELIM is the elimination rule for singleton kinds, letting us make use of the fact that a type has a singleton kind. Rules Q-PAIR-EXT and Q-EXT yield extensionality: componentwise-equivalent pairs are equivalent and pointwise-equivalent functions are equivalent. Finally, we have a subsumption rule for equivalence, Q-SUB, corresponding to the subsumption rule for typing.

The addition of singleton kinds has more consequences for equivalence than might appear at first. An attentive reader may have noticed that the definition of type equivalence omits the beta-reduction rule for function applications and the two standard rules for reducing projections from pairs. A surprising fact about languages with singletons, noticed by Aspinall (1994), is that other elimination rules can become admissible (i.e., if the premises are provable using the above rules then so is the conclusion):

$$\frac{\Gamma \vdash \mathtt{T}_1 :: \mathtt{K}_1 \qquad \Gamma \vdash \mathtt{T}_2 :: \mathtt{K}_2}{\Gamma \vdash \pi_1\ \{\mathtt{T}_1, \mathtt{T}_2\} \equiv \mathtt{T}_1 :: \mathtt{K}_1} \qquad \text{(Q-BETA-FST)}$$

$$\frac{\Gamma \vdash \mathtt{T}_1 :: \mathtt{K}_1 \qquad \Gamma \vdash \mathtt{T}_2 :: \mathtt{K}_2}{\Gamma \vdash \pi_2\ \{\mathtt{T}_1, \mathtt{T}_2\} \equiv \mathtt{T}_2 :: \mathtt{K}_2} \qquad \text{(Q-BETA-SND)}$$

$$\frac{\Gamma,\ \mathtt{X}::\mathtt{K}_1 \vdash \mathtt{T}_{12} :: \mathtt{K}_{12} \qquad \Gamma \vdash \mathtt{T}_2 :: \mathtt{K}_{12}}{\Gamma \vdash (\lambda \mathtt{X}::\mathtt{K}_{11}.\mathtt{T}_{12})\mathtt{T}_2 \equiv [\mathtt{X} \mapsto \mathtt{T}_2]\mathtt{T}_{12} :: [\mathtt{X} \mapsto \mathtt{T}_2]\mathtt{K}_{12}} \qquad \text{(Q-APPABS)}$$

More importantly (since we would have added beta-equivalence had it not been admissible), the kind at which two types are compared can determine whether or not they are equivalent. Types do not have unique kinds, and a pair of types can be equivalent at one kind but not another.

For example, consider the identity function on types, λX::*.X, and the constant function λX::*.Nat. There is no way to prove the judgment

$$(\lambda \mathtt{X}::*.\mathtt{X}) \equiv (\lambda \mathtt{X}::*.\mathtt{Nat}) :: (*\Rightarrow *).$$

However, by subsumption both functions also have the kind $S(\mathtt{Nat})\Rightarrow *$, and at this kind we can prove

$$\vdash (\lambda \mathtt{X}::*.\mathtt{X}) \equiv (\lambda \mathtt{X}::*.\mathtt{Nat}) :: (S(\mathtt{Nat})\Rightarrow *).$$

Viewed as functions that will only be applied to the argument Nat, the two functions do return the same result Nat. By extensionality, then, the two functions are equivalent at kind $S(\mathtt{Nat})\Rightarrow *$.

Using this result and Rule Q-APP we can further show that

$$\mathtt{Y} :: (S(\mathtt{Nat})\Rightarrow *)\Rightarrow * \ \vdash\ \mathtt{Y}(\lambda \mathtt{X}::*.\mathtt{X}) \equiv \mathtt{Y}(\lambda \mathtt{X}::*.\mathtt{Nat}) :: *.$$

In this equivalence judgment, both sides are normal with respect to beta and eta-reduction. Y itself has no obvious definition that can be expanded away. Nevertheless, equivalence remains decidable; one algorithm appears below.

$$
\begin{aligned}
S(\mathsf{T} :: *) &\stackrel{\text{def}}{=} S(\mathsf{T}) \\
S(\mathsf{T} :: S(\mathsf{T}')) &\stackrel{\text{def}}{=} S(\mathsf{T}) \\
S(\mathsf{T} :: \Pi \mathsf{X}::\mathsf{K}_1.\mathsf{K}_2) &\stackrel{\text{def}}{=} \Pi \mathsf{X}::\mathsf{K}_1.S(\mathsf{T}\,\mathsf{X} :: \mathsf{K}_2) \qquad \text{where } \mathsf{X} \notin FV(\mathsf{T}) \\
S(\mathsf{T} :: \Sigma \mathsf{X}::\mathsf{K}_1.\mathsf{K}_2) &\stackrel{\text{def}}{=} S(\pi_1\,\mathsf{T} :: \mathsf{K}_1) \times S(\pi_2\,\mathsf{T} :: [\mathsf{X} \mapsto \pi_1\,\mathsf{T}]\mathsf{K}_2)
\end{aligned}
$$

Figure 9-9: Labeled singleton kinds

Singletons at Higher Kinds

In λ^{let} the context could contain definitions for type operators, for example $\mathsf{Y} :: (*\Rightarrow*) = (\lambda\mathsf{X}::*.\mathsf{X}\to\mathsf{X})$. We cannot directly represent this definition as $\mathsf{Y} :: S(\lambda\mathsf{X}::*.\mathsf{X}\to\mathsf{X})$ because the kind $S(\mathsf{T})$ is well-formed only for types T of kind $*$.

Using extensionality, however, more general singletons are definable. For example, one can show that the kind

$$\Pi\mathsf{X}::*.S(\mathsf{X}\to\mathsf{X})$$

classifies all type operators that are equivalent to $\lambda\mathsf{X}::*.\mathsf{X}\to\mathsf{X}$ at kind $*\Rightarrow*$.

More generally, whenever $\mathsf{T} :: \mathsf{K}$ holds we can define the kind of types equivalent to T at kind K as a derived form, written $S(\mathsf{T} :: \mathsf{K})$. Again the kind classifier is crucial, since the function $\lambda\mathsf{X}::*.\mathsf{X}$ should have kind

$$S((\lambda\mathsf{X}::*.\mathsf{Nat}) :: S(\mathsf{Nat})\Rightarrow*)$$

but not kind

$$S((\lambda\mathsf{X}::*.\mathsf{Nat}) :: *\Rightarrow*).$$

Figure 9-9 defines labeled singleton kinds $S(\mathsf{T}::\mathsf{K})$ by induction on the size of the classifying kind K. The sizes of kinds are defined as follows:

$$
\begin{aligned}
size(*) &\stackrel{\text{def}}{=} 1 \\
size(S(\mathsf{T})) &\stackrel{\text{def}}{=} 2 \\
size(\Sigma\mathsf{X}::\mathsf{K}_1.\mathsf{K}_2) &\stackrel{\text{def}}{=} 1 + size(\mathsf{K}_1) + size(\mathsf{K}_2) \\
size(\Pi\mathsf{X}::\mathsf{K}_1.\mathsf{K}_2) &\stackrel{\text{def}}{=} 1 + size(\mathsf{K}_1) + size(\mathsf{K}_2)
\end{aligned}
$$

An easy inductive proof shows that substitutions have no effect on the size of kinds, and hence the labeled singleton kinds in Figure 9-9 are well-defined.

These labeled singletons behave exactly as one would expect. To show this, we start with some basic facts about λ^{S}.

9.3.2 PROPOSITION [WEAKENING]: 1. If $\Gamma_1, \Gamma_3 \vdash \mathcal{J}$ for any λ^S judgment form $\mathcal{J}$ and $\Gamma_1, \Gamma_2, \Gamma_3 \vdash \diamond$ then $\Gamma_1, \Gamma_2, \Gamma_3 \vdash \mathcal{J}$.

2. If Γ_1, X::K, $\Gamma_2 \vdash \mathcal{J}$ and $\Gamma_1 \vdash$ L <: K then Γ_1, X::L, $\Gamma_2 \vdash \mathcal{J}$. □

9.3.3 PROPOSITION [SUBSTITUTION]:

1. If Γ_1, X::K, $\Gamma_2 \vdash \mathcal{J}$ for any judgment form $\mathcal{J}$ and $\Gamma_1 \vdash$ T :: K then Γ_1, [X ↦ T]$\Gamma_2 \vdash$ [X ↦ T]$\mathcal{J}$.

2. If Γ_1, X::K, $\Gamma_2 \vdash$ S :: L and $\Gamma_1 \vdash$ T ≡ T′ :: K then Γ_1, [X ↦ T]$\Gamma_2 \vdash$ [X ↦ T]S ≡ [X ↦ T′]S :: [X ↦ T]L. □

9.3.4 PROPOSITION [VALIDITY]:

1. If Γ ⊢ T :: K then *FV*(T) ∪ *FV*(K) ⊆ *dom*(Γ).

2. If $\Gamma_1, \Gamma_2 \vdash \diamond$ then $\Gamma_1 \vdash \diamond$ and $dom(\Gamma_1) \cap dom(\Gamma_2) = \emptyset$.

3. If Γ ⊢ K then Γ ⊢ ◇.

4. If Γ ⊢ T :: K then Γ ⊢ K.

5. If Γ ⊢ S ≡ T :: K then Γ ⊢ S :: K and Γ ⊢ T :: K. □

At this point we can consider properties of the labeled singletons themselves.

9.3.5 PROPOSITION: [X ↦ S](*S*(T :: K)) = *S*([X ↦ S]T :: [X ↦ S]K). □

Proof: By induction on the size of K. □

9.3.6 PROPOSITION [LABELED SINGLETONS]: 1. If Γ ⊢ T :: K then Γ ⊢ T :: *S*(T::K).

2. If Γ ⊢ S :: *S*(T :: K) and Γ ⊢ T :: K then Γ ⊢ S ≡ T :: K.

3. If Γ ⊢ S ≡ T :: K and Γ ⊢ K <: L then Γ ⊢ *S*(S::K) <: *S*(T::L).

4. If Γ ⊢ T :: K then Γ ⊢ *S*(T::K) <: *S*(T::*S*(T::K)). □

Proof: We show the proof of just the first part, which follows by induction on the size of K. Assume Γ ⊢ T :: K.

Case: K = *, so *S*(T::K) = *S*(T).

Then Γ ⊢ S :: *S*(T) by Rule K-SINTRO.

Case: $K = S(S)$, so $S(T::K) = S(T)$.

By Proposition 9.3.4(5) we have $\Gamma \vdash S(S)$, so by inversion of Rule WK-SING we have $\Gamma \vdash S :: *$. Therefore $\Gamma \vdash S(S) <: *$, and so by K-SUB we have $\Gamma \vdash T :: *$ and hence $\Gamma \vdash T :: S(T)$ by K-SINTRO.

Case: $K = \Pi X::K_1.K_2$, so $S(T::K) = \Pi X::K_1.S(T\,X :: K_2)$.

By Proposition 9.3.4(5) and inversion we have $\Gamma, X::K_1 \vdash \diamond$, so by Proposition 9.3.2(1) and K-APP, $\Gamma, X::K_1 \vdash T\,X :: K_2$. By the inductive hypothesis, $\Gamma, X::K_1 \vdash T\,X :: S(T\,X :: K_2)$. Thus by Rule K-ABSSELF we have $\Gamma \vdash T :: \Pi X::K_1.S(T\,X :: K_2)$ as desired.

Case: $K = \Sigma X::K_1.K_2$, so $S(T::K) = S(\pi_1\,T :: K_1) \times S(\pi_2\,T :: [X \mapsto \pi_1\,T]K_2)$

By K-FST and K-SND and the inductive hypothesis, we have $\Gamma \vdash \pi_1\,T :: S(\pi_1\,T :: K_1)$ and $\Gamma \vdash \pi_2\,T :: S(\pi_2\,T :: [X \mapsto \pi_1\,T]K_2)$. Therefore, by Rules K-SELF1 and K-SELF2 the desired result follows. □

9.3.7 EXERCISE [★★]: Prove Part 2 of Proposition 9.3.6. Why do we need the extra assumption $\Gamma \vdash T :: K$? □

At this point, it is not too hard to show that the BETA rules are admissible, as there is a natural proof involving labeled singletons.

9.3.8 EXERCISE [★★, RECOMMENDED]: Prove that rules Q-BETA-FST, Q-BETA-SND, and Q-APPABS are admissible. □

Aspinall (1994) took a slightly different approach to formalizing a language with singletons. His language $\lambda_{\leq\{\}}$ included only a very restricted form of extensionality. The encoding of labeled singletons used here was thus unavailable, and labeled singletons were therefore made primitive language constructs.[5] The properties of Proposition 9.3.6 are then axioms describing the behavior of these primitive singletons. In this formulation, Proposition 9.3.6(4) is necessary to have principal kinds; otherwise

$$
\begin{aligned}
* \quad & :> \quad S(\text{Nat}::*) \\
& :> \quad S(\text{Nat}::S(\text{Nat}::*)) \\
& :> \quad S(\text{Nat}::S(\text{Nat}::S(\text{Nat}::*))) \\
& :> \quad \cdots
\end{aligned}
$$

would be an infinite sequence of increasingly more-precise kinds for Nat.

An interesting consequence of making labeled singletons primitive is that Aspinall was able to *define* the equivalence judgment $\Gamma \vdash S \equiv T :: K$ as syntactic sugar for the judgment $\Gamma \vdash S :: S(T :: K)$; there was not a separate collection of rules defining the equivalence judgment.

5. More precisely, Aspinall studied term equivalence in a language with singleton types, but the ideas apply just as well for type equivalence with singleton kinds.

A disadvantage of making labeled singletons primitive rather than relying on extensionality is that most-precise classifiers can be large. For example, in an Aspinall-style system the most-precise kind of λX::*.λY::*.X would be

$$S((\lambda X::*.\lambda Y::*.X) :: \Pi X::*.S((\lambda Y::*.X) :: (\Pi Y::*.S(X :: *))))$$

rather than

$$\Pi X::*.\ \Pi Y::*.\ S(X)$$

as in λ^S. The advantages are not entirely one-sided; $S(Z :: *\Rightarrow*\Rightarrow*)$ seems simpler than the λ^S kind $\Pi Y_1::*.\Pi Y_2::*.S(Z\ Y_1\ Y_2)$.

Algorithmic Type Equivalence

Figure 9-10 shows an algorithmic version of equivalence for well-kinded λ^S types. The general framework is very similar to that for λ^{let} and $\lambda^{()}$.

First of all, there is a judgment for computing "natural kinds" in analogy with the natural interfaces for modules in Figure 9-7. These are the most-precise kind available without using singleton introduction rules, and a type has a definition T if its natural kind is a singleton $S(T)$.

The algorithmic equivalence relation is defined by induction on the classifying kind: type operators are compared by applying both sides to a fresh variable (to determine if they are pointwise equivalent), while pairs of types are compared componentwise. Types of kind * are head-normalized and compared structurally very much as before. Finally, types with singleton kinds are easy to compare because of the precondition that the two types actually have the kind at which they are being compared; any two types of kind $S(T)$ are equivalent to T and hence equivalent to each other.

Viewed as an algorithm with inputs Γ, S, and T, the structural equivalence judgment both compares S and T and determines the natural kind of S. This kind is used only to determine the kind at which to compare arguments of two irreducible applications.

Finally, there is a kind equivalence algorithm, necessary since kinds can contain types, and hence can be equivalent without being identical.

9.3.9 **Exercise** [★★, Recommended]: Show that

$$Y::(S(Nat)\Rightarrow*)\Rightarrow* \mapsto Y(\lambda X::*.X) \Leftrightarrow Y(\lambda X::*.Nat) :: *$$

is provable, but

$$Y::(*\Rightarrow*)\Rightarrow* \mapsto Y(\lambda X::*.X) \Leftrightarrow Y(\lambda X::*.Nat) :: *$$

is not. □

Natural kind $\boxed{\Gamma \mapsto T \uparrow K}$

$$\frac{X{::}K \in \Gamma}{\Gamma \mapsto X \uparrow K}$$

$$\frac{\Gamma \mapsto T_1 \uparrow \Pi X{::}K_1.K_2}{\Gamma \mapsto T_1\, T_2 \uparrow [X \mapsto T_2]K_2}$$

$$\frac{\Gamma \mapsto T_1 \uparrow \Sigma X{::}K_1.K_2}{\Gamma \mapsto \pi_1\, T_1 \uparrow K_1}$$

$$\frac{\Gamma \mapsto T_1 \uparrow \Sigma X{::}K_1.K_2}{\Gamma \mapsto \pi_2\, T_2 \uparrow [X \mapsto \pi_1\, T_1]K_2}$$

Weak head reduction $\boxed{\Gamma \mapsto T \rightsquigarrow T'}$

$$\frac{\Gamma \mapsto T \uparrow S(T')}{\Gamma \mapsto T \rightsquigarrow T'}$$

$$\Gamma \mapsto (\lambda X{::}K_{11}.T_{12})T_2 \rightsquigarrow [X \mapsto T_2]T_{12}$$

$$\Gamma \mapsto \pi_1\, \{T_1,T_2\} \rightsquigarrow T_1$$

$$\Gamma \mapsto \pi_2\, \{T_1,T_2\} \rightsquigarrow T_2$$

$$\frac{\Gamma \mapsto T_1 \rightsquigarrow T'_1}{\Gamma \mapsto T_1\, T_2 \rightsquigarrow T'_1\, T_2}$$

$$\frac{\Gamma \mapsto T_1 \rightsquigarrow T'_1}{\Gamma \mapsto \pi_1\, T_1 \rightsquigarrow \pi_1\, T'_1}$$

$$\frac{\Gamma \mapsto T_1 \rightsquigarrow T'_1}{\Gamma \mapsto \pi_2\, T_1 \rightsquigarrow \pi_2\, T'_1}$$

Head Normalization $\boxed{\Gamma \mapsto S \Downarrow T}$

$$\frac{\Gamma \mapsto S \rightsquigarrow S' \qquad \Gamma \mapsto S' \Downarrow T}{\Gamma \mapsto S \Downarrow T}$$

$$\frac{\Gamma \mapsto S \not\rightsquigarrow}{\Gamma \mapsto S \Downarrow S}$$

Type Equivalence $\boxed{\Gamma \mapsto S \leftrightarrow T :: K}$

$$\frac{\Gamma \mapsto S \Downarrow S' \qquad \Gamma \mapsto T \Downarrow T' \qquad \Gamma \mapsto S' \leftrightarrow T' \uparrow *}{\Gamma \mapsto S \Leftrightarrow T :: *}$$

$$\Gamma \mapsto S \Leftrightarrow T :: S(T')$$

$$\frac{X \notin dom(\Gamma) \qquad \Gamma, X{::}K_1 \mapsto S\, X \Leftrightarrow T\, X :: K_2}{\Gamma \mapsto S \Leftrightarrow T :: \Pi X{::}K_1.K_2}$$

$$\frac{\Gamma \mapsto \pi_1\, S \Leftrightarrow \pi_1\, T :: K_1 \qquad \Gamma \mapsto \pi_2\, S \Leftrightarrow \pi_2\, T :: [X \mapsto \pi_1\, S]K_2}{\Gamma \mapsto S \Leftrightarrow T :: \Sigma X{::}K_1.K_2}$$

Structural Type Equivalence $\boxed{\Gamma \mapsto S \leftrightarrow T \uparrow K}$

$$\frac{X{::}K \in \Gamma}{\Gamma \mapsto X \leftrightarrow X \uparrow K}$$

$$\frac{\Gamma \mapsto S_1 \Leftrightarrow T_1 :: * \qquad \Gamma \mapsto S_2 \Leftrightarrow T_2 :: *}{\Gamma \mapsto S_1 {\to} S_2 \leftrightarrow T_1 {\to} T_2 \uparrow *}$$

$$\frac{\Gamma \mapsto S_1 \Leftrightarrow T_1 :: * \qquad \Gamma \mapsto S_2 \Leftrightarrow T_2 :: *}{\Gamma \mapsto S_1 \times S_2 \leftrightarrow T_1 \times T_2 \uparrow *}$$

$$\frac{\Gamma \mapsto K_1 \Leftrightarrow L_1 \qquad X \notin dom(\Gamma) \qquad \Gamma, X{::}K_1 \mapsto S_2 \Leftrightarrow T_2 :: *}{\Gamma \mapsto \forall X{::}K_1.S_2 \leftrightarrow \forall X{::}L_1.T_2 \uparrow *}$$

$$\frac{\Gamma \mapsto S_1 \leftrightarrow T_1 \uparrow \Pi X{::}K_1.K_2 \qquad \Gamma \mapsto S_2 \Leftrightarrow T_2 :: K_1}{\Gamma \mapsto S_1\, S_2 \leftrightarrow T_1\, T_2 \uparrow [X \mapsto S_2]K_2}$$

$$\frac{\Gamma \mapsto S_1 \leftrightarrow T_1 \uparrow \Sigma X{::}K_1.K_2}{\Gamma \mapsto \pi_1\, S_1 \leftrightarrow \pi_1\, T_1 \uparrow K_1}$$

$$\frac{\Gamma \mapsto S_1 \leftrightarrow T_1 \uparrow \Sigma X{::}K_1.K_2}{\Gamma \mapsto \pi_2\, S_1 \leftrightarrow \pi_2\, T_1 \uparrow [X \mapsto \pi_1\, S_1]K_2}$$

Kind Equivalence $\boxed{\Gamma \mapsto K \Leftrightarrow L}$

$$\Gamma \mapsto * \Leftrightarrow *$$

$$\frac{\Gamma \mapsto S \Leftrightarrow T :: *}{\Gamma \mapsto S(S) \Leftrightarrow S(T)}$$

$$\frac{\Gamma \mapsto K_1 \Leftrightarrow K_2 \qquad X \notin dom(\Gamma) \qquad \Gamma, X{::}K_1 \mapsto K_2 \Leftrightarrow L_2}{\Gamma \mapsto \Pi X{::}K_1.K_2 \Leftrightarrow \Pi X{::}L_1.L_2}$$

$$\frac{\Gamma \mapsto K_1 \Leftrightarrow K_2 \qquad X \notin dom(\Gamma) \qquad \Gamma, X{::}K_1 \mapsto K_2 \Leftrightarrow L_2}{\Gamma \mapsto \Sigma X{::}K_1.K_2 \Leftrightarrow \Sigma X{::}L_1.L_2}$$

Figure 9-10: Algorithmic equivalence for λ^S

The equivalence algorithm is correct and terminating for well-formed types:

9.3.10 FACT: Assume $\Gamma \vdash S :: K$ and $\Gamma \vdash T :: K$. Then $\Gamma \mapsto S \Leftrightarrow T :: K$ if and only if $\Gamma \vdash S \equiv T :: K$. Furthermore, the judgment $\Gamma \mapsto S \Leftrightarrow T :: K$ is always decidable (i.e, proof search will terminate whether or not S and T are equivalent). □

The correctness of this equivalence algorithm is nontrivial. The approach suggested in Chapter 6 does not directly apply because there is no a priori reason to believe that algorithmic equivalence is symmetric and transitive. The problem is in the "asymmetry" of the rules. The structural equivalence judgment $\Gamma \mapsto S \leftrightarrow T \uparrow K$ computes the natural kind K of S as it goes along, but might have just as well computed the natural kind of T instead. Although we the two natural kinds turn out to be provably equivalent, this does not guarantee that the algorithm is unaffected—kinds in the classifier end up in the context, which can affect how later weak head normalizations proceed, which could a priori result in a different answer or affect termination.

If the algorithm cannot be shown directly to be symmetric or transitive, then a logical equivalence relation defined as for $\lambda^{\mathtt{let}}$ cannot directly be shown to be symmetric or transitive. Stone and Harper (2000; 2005) showed, however, that variants of Kripke logical relations can be used to prove the correctness of closely-related algorithms, from which the correctness of the above algorithm can be derived.

Phase-Splitting

$\lambda^{\langle\rangle}$ added second-class modules to a language and in so doing increased the number of sorts of entities in the language: modules and interfaces, in addition to the pre-existing terms, types, and kinds. Interestingly, modules and interfaces can sometimes be decomposed into uses of terms, types, and kinds. Some compilers for Standard ML (Petersen, Cheng, Harper, and Stone, 2000; Shao, 1997, 1998) even implement modules using this technique.

The translation is possible if the module system has a phase distinction, as discussed in Chapter 8: types in modules must depend only on other types. $\lambda^{\langle\rangle}$ appears to violate this requirement, as the type !W may involve term values. Similarly, a functor application $M_1\ M_2$ can yield a module containing types, and the result syntactically appears to depend on all of M_2, which can contain terms.

As observed by Harper, Mitchell, and Moggi (1990), however, the dependency of types on the terms in modules is illusory. References to modules in types really involve only the type components of that module; all else is irrelevant. Similarly, in a functor application $M_1\ M_2$ the types returned to depend only on types defined in M_1 and types defined in M_2; there is no way that the terms in these modules can affect the resulting types.

It is therefore possible to split every module into a type part and a term part, referred to here as the *static* and *dynamic* parts of the module; the former can be represented as a type (perhaps of a higher kind), and the latter as a term (potentially polymorphic).

A module containing many types and many values would split into a collection of types (not to be confused with the type of a tuple of terms) and a collection of values. In parallel, a functor application can be split into an application of types (the type part of the functor applied to the type part of the argument) and an application of a polymorphic term (the term part of the functor applied to both the type part of the argument and the term part of the argument). For example, the functor

```
module diag = λ(p : sig
                      type t
                      val x : t
                    end).
                mod
                  type u = p.t × p.t
                  val  y : u = {p.x, p.x}
                end
```

which we encoded in $\lambda^{(\!|\,|\!)}$ as

```
λm:(Σm':⦇*⦈. ⦇!m'⦈).  ⦇ ⦇!m.1× !m.1⦈, ⦇{!m.2,!m.2}⦈ ⦈
```

could have its behavior with respect to producing types modeled by the type operator `λX::*. X×X`, since `diag` takes a type in its argument and returns a corresponding pair type in its result. Similarly, the behavior of `diag` in producing terms can be modeled as the polymorphic abstraction `λX::*. λx:X. {x,x}`, representing that it takes a type and a term of that type in the argument, and that it returns a pair value.

Interfaces can be split correspondingly into a kind classifying the static portion of the module, and a type classifying the dynamic portion of the module. For example, a specification

```
diag : (Πm:(Σm':⦇*⦈. ⦇!m'⦈). (Σm":⦇*=!m.1× !m.1⦈. ⦇!m"⦈))
```

could be split into two specifications for the static and dynamic parts of `diag`:

$$\texttt{diag}_s :: \Pi\texttt{X::*}.\ S(\texttt{X}\times\texttt{X})$$

and

$$\texttt{diag}_d : \forall\texttt{X::*}.\ \texttt{X} \to \texttt{diag}_s\texttt{(X)}.$$

Equations in $\lambda^{(\!|\,|\!)}$ interfaces become singleton kinds after phase-splitting.

Figure 9-11 specifies a formal translation from $\lambda^{(\!|\,|\!)}$ into λ^{S}. For simplicity, the translation maintains the invariant that every module and every interface

Modules

$$
\begin{array}{lll@{\qquad}lll}
\lvert m\rvert_s & := & X_m & \lvert m\rvert_d & := & x_m \\
\lvert \llparenthesis t\rrparenthesis\rvert_s & := & S_0 & \lvert \llparenthesis t\rrparenthesis\rvert_d & := & v \\
\lvert \llparenthesis T::K\rrparenthesis\rvert_s & := & \lvert T\rvert & \lvert \llparenthesis T::K\rrparenthesis\rvert_d & := & t_0 \\
\lvert \llparenthesis M_1,M_2\rrparenthesis\rvert_s & := & \{\ \lvert M_1\rvert_s,\ \lvert M_2\rvert_s\ \} & \lvert \llparenthesis M_1,M_2\rrparenthesis\rvert_d & := & \{\ \lvert M_1\rvert_d,\ \lvert M_2\rvert_d\ \} \\
\lvert M.1\rvert_s & := & \pi_1(\lvert M\rvert_s) & \lvert M.1\rvert_d & := & \pi_1(\lvert M\rvert_d) \\
\lvert M.2\rvert_s & := & \pi_2(\lvert M\rvert_s) & \lvert M.2\rvert_d & := & \pi_2(\lvert M\rvert_d) \\
\lvert \lambda m:I.M\rvert_s & := & \lambda X_m:\lvert I\rvert_s.\lvert M\rvert_s & \lvert \lambda m:I.M\rvert_d & := & \lambda X_m:\lvert I\rvert_s. \\
 & & & & & \quad \lambda x_m:\lvert I\rvert_d(X_m). \\
 & & & & & \qquad \lvert M\rvert_d \\
\lvert M_1\ M_2\rvert_s & := & \lvert M_1\rvert_s\ \lvert M_2\rvert_s & \lvert M_1\ M_2\rvert_d & := & (\lvert M_1\rvert_d\ [\lvert M_2\rvert_s])\ \lvert M_2\rvert_d \\
\lvert M :> I\rvert_s & := & \lvert M\rvert_s & \lvert M :> I\rvert_d & := & \lvert M\rvert_d
\end{array}
$$

Interfaces

$$
\begin{array}{lll@{\qquad}lll}
\lvert \llparenthesis T\rrparenthesis\rvert_s & := & K_0 & \lvert \llparenthesis T\rrparenthesis\rvert_d(T_s) & := & \lvert T\rvert \\
\lvert \llparenthesis K\rrparenthesis\rvert_s & := & K & \lvert \llparenthesis K\rrparenthesis\rvert_d(T_s) & := & T_0 \\
\lvert \llparenthesis K{=}T\rrparenthesis\rvert_s & := & S(\lvert T\rvert :: K) & \lvert \llparenthesis K{=}T\rrparenthesis\rvert_d(T_s) & := & T_0 \\
\lvert \Pi m:I_1.I_2\rvert_s & := & \Pi X_m::\lvert I_1\rvert_s. & \lvert \Pi m:I_1.I_2\rvert_d(T_s) & := & \forall X_m::\lvert I_1\rvert_s. \\
 & & \quad \lvert I_2\rvert_s & \quad [\text{if } X_m \notin FV(T_s)] & & \quad \lvert I_1\rvert_d(X_m) \to \\
 & & & & & \qquad (\lvert I_2\rvert_d(T_s\ X_m)) \\
\lvert \Sigma m:I_1.I_2\rvert_s & := & \Sigma X_m::\lvert I_1\rvert_s. & \lvert \Sigma m:I_1.I_2\rvert_d(T_s) & := & \lvert I_1\rvert_d(\pi_1\ T_s)\ \times \\
 & & \quad \lvert I_2\rvert_s & & & \quad ([X_m \mapsto \pi_1\ T_s]\lvert I_2\rvert_d(\pi_2\ T_s))
\end{array}
$$

Types and Contexts

$$
\begin{array}{lll@{\qquad}lll}
\lvert X\rvert & := & X & \lvert \cdot\rvert & := & \cdot \\
\lvert T_1 \to T_2\rvert & := & \lvert T_1\rvert \to \lvert T_2\rvert & \lvert \Gamma, X::K\rvert & := & \lvert \Gamma\rvert, X::K \\
\lvert T_1 \times T_2\rvert & := & \lvert T_1\rvert \times \lvert T_2\rvert & \lvert \Gamma, x:T\rvert & := & \lvert \Gamma\rvert, x:\lvert T\rvert \\
\lvert \forall X::K_1.T_2\rvert & := & \forall X::K_1.\lvert T_2\rvert & \lvert \Gamma, m:I\rvert & := & \lvert \Gamma\rvert, X_m::\lvert I\rvert_s, \\
\lvert \lambda X::K_1.T_2\rvert & := & \lambda X::K_1.\lvert T_2\rvert & & & \quad x_m:\lvert I\rvert_d(X_m) \\
\lvert T_1\ T_2\rvert & := & \lvert T_1\rvert\ \lvert T_2\rvert & & & \\
\lvert\, !W\rvert & := & \lvert W\rvert_s & & &
\end{array}
$$

Terms

$$
\begin{array}{lll@{\qquad}lll}
\lvert x\rvert & := & x & \lvert \{t_1,t_2\}\rvert & := & \{\ \lvert t_1\rvert,\ \lvert t_2\rvert\ \} \\
\lvert \lambda x:T.t\rvert & := & \lambda x:\lvert T\rvert.\lvert t\rvert & \lvert t.1\rvert & := & \lvert t\rvert.1 \\
\lvert t_1\ [t_2]\rvert & := & \lvert t_1\rvert\ [\ \lvert t_2\rvert\ ] & \lvert t.2\rvert & := & \lvert t\rvert.2 \\
\lvert \lambda X::K.t\rvert & := & \lambda X::K.\lvert t\rvert & \lvert\, !M\rvert & := & \lvert M\rvert_d \\
\lvert t_1\ T_2\rvert & := & \lvert t_1\rvert\ \lvert T_2\rvert & & &
\end{array}
$$

Figure 9-11: Phase-splitting translation

has static and dynamic parts. Since $\lambda^{(\!|\,|\!)}$ contains primitive modules that contain only terms or only types, the translation uses an arbitrary term $\mathtt{t}_0$ of some type T_0 to represent the dynamic part of a module containing only a type (an obvious choice for $\mathtt{t}_0$ would be the value of type `Unit`), and uses an arbitrary type S_0 of kind K_0 representing the static part of a module containing only a term.

Also, for every module variable `m` we assume there exists a type variable $\mathsf{X}_\mathtt{m}$ and a term variable $\mathtt{x}_\mathtt{m}$. These will be bound to the static and dynamic parts respectively of whatever `m` would have been bound to in the original code.

Figure 9-11 begins by defining $|\mathsf{M}|_s$, which is a type expression containing all the types in the module M. In most cases this is straightforward. The static part of a module variable `m` is the corresponding type variable $\mathsf{X}_\mathtt{m}$; the static part of a module containing the type T is T itself, or more precisely, the translation of T, which eliminates occurrences of modules (see below). The static part of the first or second projection from a module pair is the first or second projection the pair's static part. The static part of an application is the application of its static parts.

The static part of a sealed module is defined to be the static part of the underlying module; generative sealing is the one construct in $\lambda^{(\!|\,|\!)}$ with no direct equivalent in λ^S. The λ^S language has no abstraction mechanism, and there is no easy way to add a generative construct to its equational theory of types. However, since sealing has no dynamic effect it is possible to take a well-formed $\lambda^{(\!|\,|\!)}$ term and erase all occurrence of sealing, yielding a well-typed and behaviorally-equivalent term. Implementations of $\lambda^{(\!|\,|\!)}$ based on phase-splitting typically first do type checking in $\lambda^{(\!|\,|\!)}$ to ensure that abstraction is being respected, and then erase the sealing as they perform phase-splitting.

The definition $|\mathsf{M}|_d$ of the dynamic part of a module M is similar. The dynamic part of a functor is parameterized both by the static part of the argument and the dynamic part, since values returned by a functor can depend both on the types in the argument and the values in the argument. Module applications then turn into the corresponding polymorphic instantiation followed by an application.

The static part $|\mathtt{I}|_s$ of a module interface I is a kind describing the types in any module satisfying I. Singleton kinds are used to describe equations found in transparent interfaces.

The dynamic part of a module interface is more interesting. The values in a module may be describable only in terms of the types in the module. For example, after phase-splitting the dynamic part of a module of interface $\Sigma\mathtt{m}{:}(\!|{*}|\!).(\!|{!}\mathtt{m}|\!)$ (a module containing an abstract type and a value of that type) can only be described as containing a value whose type is contained in the static part of that same module. The definition of the dynamic part of an interface, $|\mathtt{I}|_d(\mathtt{T}_s)$, is therefore defined in terms of both the interface I and the static part $\mathtt{T}_s$ of a module satisfying I. Such a static part is available wherever the dynamic part of an interface is needed. For example, the definition of the dynamic part of a functor module with argument interface I is a polymorphic function requiring in succession both $\mathtt{X_m}$ (the static part of the functor's argument) and a valid dynamic part for a module with that static part, i.e., a value of type $|\mathtt{I}|_d(\mathtt{X_m})$.

Recall that the static part of a module application is the application of the static parts. Therefore, when computing the dynamic part of an interface $\Pi\mathtt{m}:\mathtt{I}_1.\mathtt{I}_2$, we know that the module being returned satisfies the interface $\mathtt{I}_2$ and that the static part of the module being returned is the static part of this functor applied to the static part of the functor argument. Thus, the type of the value returned by the dynamic part is $|\mathtt{I}_2|_d(\mathtt{T}_s\ \mathtt{X_m})$, where $\mathtt{T}_s$ is the static part of the functor as a whole.

Similarly, if we have a module pair with interface $\Sigma\mathtt{m}:\mathtt{I}_1.\mathtt{I}_2$ having static part $\mathtt{T}_s$, then the static parts of the components are $\pi_1\ \mathtt{T}_s$ and $\pi_2\ \mathtt{T}_s$ respectively. Further, since $\mathtt{I}_2$ may contain free-occurrences of m, its dynamic part may refer to $\mathtt{X_m}$. $\mathtt{X_m}$ stands for the static part of (i.e., the types in) in the module's first component, so we can replace it by $\pi_1\ \mathtt{T}_s$, the static part of the module's first component. No similar substitution is needed for $\mathtt{x_m}$; the dynamic part of $\mathtt{I}_2$ is still a type and cannot contain term variables.

The translation of |T| of a type is very simple. Phase-splitting is possible because references to modules in types just involve the types in these modules. We can therefore replace all module projections of the form !W by the static part $|\mathtt{W}|_s$ of W. Similarly, the translation of a term goes through and translates all types, and replaces every projection !M of a value from a module by the dynamic part of M.

The translation of a context translates types, leaves kinds alone (since $\lambda^{()}$ kinds do not contain types, terms, or variables), and replaces every assumption of a module variable m with assumptions for the two corresponding variables $\mathtt{X_m}$ and $\mathtt{x_m}$.

9.3.11 EXERCISE [★★, RECOMMENDED]: Compute the static and dynamic parts for the $\lambda^{()}$ definition of the diag functor. How do these differ from the intuitive translations given above? □

We can show that this transformation turns well-formed $\lambda^{()}$ code into well-formed λ^S code. We distinguish proofs in the two languages $\lambda^{()}$ and λ^S by writing $\vdash^{()}$ and $\vdash^S$ respectively.

9.3.12 LEMMA: If $\mathtt{Y} \notin FV(\mathtt{I})$ then $|\mathtt{I}|_d(\mathtt{T}_s) = [\mathtt{Y} \mapsto \mathtt{T}_s]|\mathtt{I}_d|(\mathtt{Y})$. □

9.3.13 **Theorem [Phase-Splitting]:**

1. If $\Gamma \vdash^{(|)} \diamond$ then $|\Gamma| \vdash^{S} \diamond$.
2. If $\Gamma \vdash^{(|)} \mathtt{T} :: \mathtt{K}$ then $|\Gamma| \vdash^{S} |\mathtt{T}| :: \mathtt{K}$.
3. If $\Gamma \vdash^{(|)} \mathtt{S} \equiv \mathtt{T} :: \mathtt{K}$ then $|\Gamma| \vdash^{S} |\mathtt{S}| \equiv |\mathtt{T}| :: \mathtt{K}$.
4. If $\Gamma \vdash^{(|)} \mathtt{t} : \mathtt{T}$ then $|\Gamma| \vdash^{S} |\mathtt{t}| : |\mathtt{T}|$.
5. If $\Gamma \vdash^{(|)} \mathtt{I}$ then $|\Gamma| \vdash^{S} |\mathtt{I}|_s$, and if further $\mathtt{Y} \notin dom(\Gamma)$ and $\mathtt{Y} \neq \mathtt{X_m}$ for every $\mathtt{m}$ then $|\Gamma|, \mathtt{Y}{::}\,|\mathtt{I}|_s \vdash^{S} |\mathtt{I}|_d(\mathtt{Y}) :: *$.
6. If $\Gamma \vdash^{(|)} \mathtt{I_1} <: \mathtt{I_2}$ then $|\Gamma| \vdash^{S} |\mathtt{I_1}|_s <: |\mathtt{I_2}|_s$ and if further $\mathtt{Y} \notin dom(\Gamma)$ and $\mathtt{Y} \neq \mathtt{X_m}$ for every $\mathtt{m}$ then $|\Gamma|, \mathtt{Y}{::}\,|\mathtt{I_1}|_s \vdash^{S} |\mathtt{I_1}|_d(\mathtt{Y}) \equiv |\mathtt{I_2}|_d(\mathtt{Y}) :: *$.
7. If $\Gamma \vdash^{(|)} \mathtt{I_1} \equiv \mathtt{I_2}$ then $|\Gamma| \vdash^{S} |\mathtt{I_1}|_s <: |\mathtt{I_2}|_s$ and if further $\mathtt{Y} \notin dom(\Gamma)$ and $\mathtt{Y} \neq \mathtt{X_m}$ for every $\mathtt{m}$ then $|\Gamma|, \mathtt{Y}{::}\,|\mathtt{I_1}|_s \vdash^{S} |\mathtt{I_1}|_d(\mathtt{Y}) \equiv |\mathtt{I_2}|_d(\mathtt{Y}) :: *$.
8. If $\Gamma \vdash^{(|)} \mathtt{M} : \mathtt{I}$ then $|\Gamma| \vdash^{S} |\mathtt{M}|_s :: |\mathtt{I}|_s$ and $|\Gamma| \vdash^{S} |\mathtt{M}|_d : |\mathtt{I}|_d(|\mathtt{M}|_s)$. □

Proof: By induction on derivations and cases on the last rule used. Two representative cases are sketched here.

Case I-Sigma: $\Gamma \vdash^{(|)} \Sigma\mathtt{m}{:}\mathtt{I_1}.\mathtt{I_2}$ because $\Gamma, \mathtt{m}{:}\mathtt{I_1} \vdash^{(|)} \mathtt{I_2}$.

By the inductive hypothesis, $|\Gamma|, \mathtt{X_m}{::}\,|\mathtt{I_1}|_s, \mathtt{x_m}{:}\,|\mathtt{I_1}|_d(\mathtt{X_m}) \vdash^{S} |\mathtt{I_2}|_s$. Inspection of λ^S shows that terms variables have no effect on the well-formedness of kinds, so we have $|\Gamma|, \mathtt{X_m}{::}\,|\mathtt{I_1}|_s \vdash^{S} |\mathtt{I_2}|_s$ and hence $|\Gamma| \vdash^{S} \Sigma\mathtt{X_m}{::}\,|\mathtt{I_1}|_s.|\mathtt{I_2}|_s$. That is, $|\Gamma| \vdash^{S} |\Sigma\mathtt{m}{:}\mathtt{I_1}.\mathtt{I_2}|$.

Also by the inductive hypothesis $|\Gamma|, \mathtt{X_m}{::}\,|\mathtt{I_1}|_s, \mathtt{x_m}{:}\,|\mathtt{I_1}|_d(\mathtt{X_m}), \mathtt{Y_2}{:}\,|\mathtt{I_2}|_s \vdash^{S} |\mathtt{I_2}|_d(\mathtt{Y_2}) :: *$ where $\mathtt{Y_2}$ is fresh. By Proposition 9.3.2(1) and the observation that term variables have no effect on the well-formedness of types, we have $|\Gamma|, \mathtt{Y}{::}\,(\Sigma\mathtt{X_m}{::}\,|\mathtt{I_1}|_s.|\mathtt{I_2}|_s), \mathtt{X_m}{::}\,|\mathtt{I_1}|_s, \mathtt{Y_2}{:}\,|\mathtt{I_2}|_s \vdash^{S} |\mathtt{I_2}|_d(\mathtt{Y_2}) :: *$. By Proposition 9.3.3(1), $|\Gamma|, \mathtt{Y}{::}\,(\Sigma\mathtt{X_m}{::}\,|\mathtt{I_1}|_s.|\mathtt{I_2}|_s), \mathtt{Y_2}{:}[\mathtt{X_m} \mapsto \pi_1\,\mathtt{Y}]|\mathtt{I_2}|_s \vdash^{S} [\mathtt{X_m} \mapsto \pi_1\,\mathtt{Y}]|\mathtt{I_2}|_d(\mathtt{Y_2}) :: *$. By Lemma 9.3.12 and Proposition 9.3.3(1), $|\Gamma|, \mathtt{Y}{::}\,(\Sigma\mathtt{X_m}{::}\,|\mathtt{I_1}|_s.|\mathtt{I_2}|_s) \vdash^{S} [\mathtt{X_m} \mapsto \pi_1\,\mathtt{Y}]|\mathtt{I_2}|_d(\pi_2\,\mathtt{Y}) :: *$. That is, $|\Gamma|, \mathtt{Y}{::}\,(\Sigma\mathtt{X_m}{::}\,|\mathtt{I_1}|_s.|\mathtt{I_2}|_s) \vdash^{S} |\Sigma\mathtt{m}{:}\mathtt{I_1}.\mathtt{I_2}|_d(\mathtt{Y}) :: *$.

Case M-Self2: $\Gamma \vdash^{(|)} \mathtt{W} : \mathtt{I_1} \times \mathtt{I_2}$ because $\Gamma \vdash^{(|)} \mathtt{W} : \Sigma\mathtt{m}{:}\mathtt{I_1}.\mathtt{I'_2}$ and $\Gamma \vdash^{(|)} \mathtt{W.2} : \mathtt{I_2}$.

By the inductive hypothesis, $|\Gamma| \vdash^{S} |\mathtt{W}|_s :: \Sigma\mathtt{X_m}{::}\,|\mathtt{I_1}|_s.|\mathtt{I'_2}|_s$ and $|\Gamma| \vdash^{S} \pi_2\,|\mathtt{W}|_s :: |\mathtt{I_2}|_s$. By Rule K-Self2, then, $|\Gamma| \vdash^{S} |\mathtt{W}|_s :: |\mathtt{I_1}|_s \times |\mathtt{I_2}|_s$. That is, $|\Gamma| \vdash^{S} |\mathtt{W}|_s :: |\mathtt{I_1} \times \mathtt{I_2}|_s$. Similarly, by the inductive hypothesis we have $|\Gamma| \vdash^{S} |\mathtt{W}|_d : |\mathtt{I_1}|_d(\pi_1\,|\mathtt{W}|_s) \times \ldots$ and $|\Gamma| \vdash^{S} \pi_2\,|\mathtt{W}|_d : |\mathtt{I_2}|_d(\pi_2\,|\mathtt{W}|_s)$. Since λ^S has no subtyping and terms can be shown to have unique types up to equivalence, it follows that $|\Gamma| \vdash^{S} |\mathtt{W}|_d : |\mathtt{I_1}|_d(\pi_1\,|\mathtt{W}|_s) \times |\mathtt{I_2}|_d(\pi_2\,|\mathtt{W}|_s)$. That is, $|\Gamma| \vdash^{S} |\mathtt{W}|_d : |\mathtt{I_1} \times \mathtt{I_2}|_d(|\mathtt{W}|_s)$. □

Many variations on the phase-splitting transformation are possible. Also, instead of relying on singleton kinds, type definitions can be eliminated during phase-splitting. This approach is taken by the FLINT compiler for Standard ML (Shao, 1998).

If the source language $\lambda^{()}$is modified to make Π interfaces contravariant in their domains, then to type check the result we either need to add a limited form of subtyping in λ^S (in addition to the subkinding that already exists), or to insert explicit type coercions (Breazu-Tannen, Coquand, Gunter, and Scedrov, 1991) This last approach is taken by the TILT compiler for Standard ML (Petersen, Cheng, Harper, and Stone, 2000).

9.3.14 EXERCISE [★★, RECOMMENDED]:

1. Suppose we add terms of the form `let m=M in t` to $\lambda^{()}$, allowing modules to be defined locally within terms. Can the phase-splitting algorithm be extended to handle such terms?

2. Suppose we added a conditional expression at the module level to $\lambda^{()}$, `if t then M else M'`. Can the phase-splitting algorithm be extended to handle these modules? □

9.3.15 EXERCISE [★★★★, ↛]: Formally specify a method for obtaining more optimized λ^S code corresponding to $\lambda^{()}$ inputs. For example, the `diag` functor encoded in $\lambda^{()}$ might split into `λX::*. X×X` and `λX::*. λx:X. {x,x}` as originally suggested. Verify that your optimization preserves well-formedness of code, in analogy with Theorem 9.3.13. □

9.4 Notes

Primitive definitions are permitted in most implementations of λ-calculus-based systems. The AUTOMATH system (de Bruijn, 1980; van Daalen, 1980), for example, relied vitally on definitions, as do modern systems such as Coq (Barras et al., 1997). Most directly related to the system $\lambda^{\texttt{let}}$ is the work of Severi and Poll (1994), who studied a pure type system supporting primitive definitions at all levels. They observed that one might wish to permit primitive definitions for items (e.g., kinds) even if the language does not include operators parameterized by such items. Their decidability proof is not based on logical relations, but instead defines a rewrite rule implementing beta-delta reduction, which they show to be confluent and strongly normalizing.

For many references on the theory of module systems, see Chapter 8; the presentation of $\lambda^{()}$ is most similar to that of Lillibridge (1997) and Dreyer, Crary, and Harper (2003).

Aspinall (1994) suggested that if types are viewed as program specifications, then singleton *types* would allow very specific specifications (e.g., requiring that a particular function not only map natural numbers to natural numbers, but that it compute factorials; the function could be specified as begin a member of a singleton type, namely the type of all terms equivalent to a reference implementation for factorial). He presented a system of labeled singleton types with beta-equivalence and a limited form of extensionality for lambda abstractions. Stone and Harper (2000) proved decidability of a system essentially equivalent to λ^S, and later simplified their proof (Stone and Harper, 2005). Coquand, Pollack, and Takeyama (2003) took a different approach to deciding equivalence in the presence of singletons and extensionality; their algorithm is based on eta-expanding and expanding definitions, followed by a comparison for beta-equivalence.

Courant (2002) has studied a system with labeled singleton types but no extensionality principles at all; then equivalence depends on the typing context but not the classifier at which the comparison is taking place, and so it was possible to use a more traditional approach to equivalence by proving confluence and strong-normalization of a rewrite relation similar to that used by Severi and Poll.

Part V

Type Inference

10 The Essence of ML Type Inference

François Pottier and Didier Rémy

10.1 What Is ML?

The name ML appeared during the late seventies. It then referred to a general-purpose programming language that was used as a meta-language (whence its name) within the theorem prover LCF (Gordon, Milner, and Wadsworth, 1979). Since then, several new programming languages, each of which offers several different implementations, have drawn inspiration from it. So, what does ML stand for today?

For a semanticist, ML might stand for a programming language featuring first-class functions, data structures built out of products and sums, mutable memory cells called *references*, exception handling, automatic memory management, and a call-by-value semantics. This view encompasses the Standard ML (Milner, Tofte, and Harper, 1990) and Caml (Leroy, 2000) families of programming languages. We refer to it as *ML-the-programming-language.*

For a type theorist, ML might stand for a particular breed of type systems, based on the simply-typed λ-calculus, but extended with a simple form of polymorphism introduced by `let` declarations. These type systems have decidable type inference; their type inference algorithms strongly rely on first-order unification and can be made efficient in practice. Besides Standard ML and Caml, this view encompasses programming languages such as Haskell (Peyton Jones, 2003) and Clean (Brus, van Eekelen, van Leer, and Plasmeijer, 1987), whose semantics is rather different—indeed, it is nonstrict and pure (Sabry, 1998)—but whose type system fits this description. We refer to it as *ML-the-type-system.* It is also referred to as the *Hindley-Milner type discipline* in the literature.

Code for this chapter may be found on the book's web site.

For us, ML might also stand for the particular programming language whose formal definition is given and studied in this chapter. It is a core calculus featuring first-class functions, local definitions, and constants. It is equipped with a call-by-value semantics. By customizing constants and their semantics, one may recover data structures, references, and more. We refer to this particular calculus as *ML-the-calculus.*

Why study ML-the-type-system today, such a long time after its initial discovery? One may think of at least two reasons.

First, its treatment in the literature is often cursory, because it is considered either as a simple extension of the simply-typed λ-calculus (*TAPL*, Chapter 9) or as a subset of Girard and Reynolds' System F (*TAPL*, Chapter 23). The former view is supported by the claim that local (`let`) definitions, which distinguish ML-the-type-system from the simply-typed λ-calculus, may be understood as a simple textual expansion facility. However, this view tells only part of the story, because it fails to give an account of the *principal types* property enjoyed by ML-the-type-system, leads to a naive type inference algorithm whose time complexity is exponential not only in the worst case but in the common case, and breaks down when the language is extended with side effects, such as state or exceptions. The latter view is supported by the fact that every type derivation within ML-the-type-system is also a valid type derivation within an implicitly-typed variant of System F. Such a view is correct but again fails to give an account of type inference for ML-the-type-system, since type inference for System F is undecidable (Wells, 1999).

Second, existing accounts of type inference for ML-the-type-system (Milner, 1978; Damas and Milner, 1982; Tofte, 1988; Leroy, 1992; Lee and Yi, 1998; Jones, 1999) often involve heavy manipulations of type substitutions. Such a ubiquitous use of type substitutions is often quite obscure. Furthermore, actual implementations of the type inference algorithm do *not* explicitly manipulate substitutions; instead, they extend a standard first-order unification algorithm, where terms are updated in place as new equations are discovered (Huet, 1976; Martelli and Montanari, 1982). Thus, it is hard to tell, from these accounts, how to write an efficient type inference algorithm for ML-the-type-system. Yet, in spite of the increasing speed of computers, efficiency remains crucial when ML-the-type-system is extended with expensive features, such as Objective Caml's object types (Rémy and Vouillon, 1998), variant types (Garrigue, 1998), or polymorphic methods (Garrigue and Rémy, 1999).

Our emphasis on efficiency might come as a surprise, since type inference for ML-the-type-system is known to be DEXPTIME-complete (Kfoury, Tiuryn, and Urzyczyn, 1990; Mairson, Kanellakis, and Mitchell, 1991). In practice, however, most implementations of it behave well. This apparent contradiction may be explained by observing that types usually remain small and that `let` constructs are never deeply nested towards the left. Indeed, under the assumption that types have bounded size and that programs have bounded "scheme depth," type inference may be performed in quasi-linear time (McAllester, 2003). In ML-the-programming-language, algebraic data type definitions allow complex data structures to be described by concise expressions, such as "list X," which helps achieve the bounded-type-size property.

In fact, in such favorable circumstances, even an inefficient algorithm may behave well. For instance, some deployed implementations of type inference for ML-the-type-system contain sources of inefficiency (see remark 10.1.21 on page 404) and do not operate in quasi-linear time under the bounded-type-size assumption. However, such implementations are put under greater stress when types become larger, a situation that occurs in some programs (Saha, Heintze, and Oliva, 1998) and also arises when large, transparent type expressions are used instead of algebraic data types, as in Objective Caml's object-oriented fragment (Rémy and Vouillon, 1998).

For these reasons, we believe it is worth giving an account of ML-the-type-system that focuses on *type inference* and strives to be at once elegant and faithful to an efficient implementation, such as Rémy's (1992a). In this presentation, we forego type substitutions and instead put emphasis on constraints, which offer a number of advantages.

First, constraints allow a modular presentation of type inference as the combination of a constraint generator and a constraint solver, allowing separate reasoning about *when* a program is correct and *how* to check whether it is correct. This perspective has long been standard in the setting of the simply-typed λ-calculus: see, for example, Wand (1987b) and *TAPL*, Chapter 22. In the setting of ML-the-type-system, such a decomposition is provided by the reduction of typability problems to acyclic semi-unification problems (Henglein, 1993; Kfoury, Tiuryn, and Urzyczyn, 1994). This approach, however, was apparently never used in production implementations of ML-the-programming-language. An experimental extension of SML/NJ with polymorphic recursion (Emms and LeiSS, 1996) did reduce type inference to a semi-unification problem. Semi-unification found applications in the closely related area of program analysis; see, for example, Fähndrich, Rehof, and Das (2000) and Birkedal and Tofte (2001). In this chapter, we give a constraint-based description of a "classic" implementation of ML-the-type-system, which is based on first-order unification and a mechanism for creating and instantiating principal *type schemes.*

Second, it is often natural to define and implement the solver as a constraint rewriting system. The constraint language allows reasoning not only about correctness—is every rewriting step meaning-preserving?—but also about low-level implementation details, since constraints are the data struc-

$\mathtt{x,y}$ ::=		*Identifiers:*	m	*Memory location*
	$\mathtt{z}$	*Variable*	$\lambda\mathtt{z.t}$	*Function*
	m	*Memory location*	$\mathtt{c}\ \mathtt{v}_1 \ldots \mathtt{v}_k$	*Data*
	$\mathtt{c}$	*Constant*		$\mathtt{c} \in \mathcal{Q}^+ \wedge k \le a(\mathtt{c})$
$\mathtt{t}$ ::=		*Expressions:*	$\mathtt{c}\ \mathtt{v}_1 \ldots \mathtt{v}_k$	*Partial application*
	$\mathtt{x}$	*Identifier*		$\mathtt{c} \in \mathcal{Q}^- \wedge k < a(\mathtt{c})$
	$\lambda\mathtt{z.t}$	*Function*	$\mathcal{E}$ ::=	*Evaluation Contexts:*
	$\mathtt{t\ t}$	*Application*	$[]$	*Empty context*
	$\mathtt{let\ z = t\ in\ t}$	*Local definition*	$\mathcal{E}\ \mathtt{t}$	*Left side of an application*
$\mathtt{v,w}$ ::=		*Values:*	$\mathtt{v}\ \mathcal{E}$	*Right side of an application*
	$\mathtt{z}$	*Variable*	$\mathtt{let\ z} = \mathcal{E}\ \mathtt{in\ t}$	*Local definition*

Figure 10-1: Syntax of ML-the-calculus

tures manipulated throughout the type inference process. For instance, describing unification in terms of *multi-equations* allows reasoning about the sharing of nodes in memory, which a substitution-based approach cannot account for. Last, constraints are more general than type substitutions, and allow smooth extensions of ML-the-type-system with recursive types, rows, subtyping, and more. These arguments are developed, for example, in Jouannaud and Kirchner (1991).

Before delving into the details of this new presentation of ML-the-type-system, it is worth recalling its standard definition. Thus, in what follows, we first define the syntax and operational semantics of ML-the-calculus, and equip it with a type system, known as *Damas and Milner's type system.*

ML-the-Calculus

The syntax of ML-the-calculus is defined in Figure 10-1. It is made up of several syntactic categories.

Identifiers group several kinds of names that may be referenced in a program: variables, memory locations, and constants. We let x and y range over identifiers. *Variables*—also called *program variables*, to avoid ambiguity—are names that may be bound to values using λ or `let` binding forms; in other words, they are names for function parameters or local definitions. We let z and f range over program variables. We sometimes write _ for a program variable that does not occur free within its scope: for instance, λ_.t stands for λz.t, provided z is fresh for t. (We say that z is *fresh for* t when z does not occur free in $\mathtt{t}$.) *Memory locations* are names that represent memory addresses. They are used to model references (see Example 10.1.9 below). Memory locations never appear in *source programs*, that is, programs that are submitted to a compiler. They only appear during execution, when new memory blocks are allocated. *Constants* are fixed names for primitive values and operations, such as integer literals and integer arithmetic operations. Constants are elements of a finite or infinite set $\mathcal{Q}$. They are never subject to α-conversion, in contrast to variables and memory locations. Program variables, memory locations, and constants belong to distinct syntactic classes and may never be confused.

The set of constants $\mathcal{Q}$ is kept abstract, so most of our development is independent of its concrete definition. We assume that every constant $\mathtt{c}$ has a nonnegative integer *arity* $a(\mathtt{c})$. We further assume that $\mathcal{Q}$ is partitioned into subsets of *constructors* $\mathcal{Q}^+$ and *destructors* $\mathcal{Q}^-$. Constructors and destructors differ in that the former are used to *form* values, while the latter are used to *operate* on values.

10.1.1 EXAMPLE [INTEGERS]: For every integer n, one may introduce a nullary constructor $\hat{n}$. In addition, one may introduce a binary destructor $\hat{+}$, whose applications are written infix, so $\mathtt{t}_1 \,\hat{+}\, \mathtt{t}_2$ stands for the double application $\hat{+}\ \mathtt{t}_1\ \mathtt{t}_2$ of the destructor $\hat{+}$ to the expressions $\mathtt{t}_1$ and $\mathtt{t}_2$. □

Expressions—also known as *terms* or *programs*—are the main syntactic category. Indeed, unlike procedural languages such as C and Java, functional languages, including ML-the-programming-language, suppress the distinction between expressions and statements. Expressions consist of identifiers, *λ-abstractions, applications*, and local definitions. The λ-abstraction $\lambda\mathtt{z.t}$ represents the function of one parameter named $\mathtt{z}$ whose result is the expression $\mathtt{t}$, or, in other words, the function that maps $\mathtt{z}$ to $\mathtt{t}$. Note that the variable $\mathtt{z}$ is bound within the term $\mathtt{t}$, so (for instance) the notations $\lambda\mathtt{z}_1.\mathtt{z}_1$ and $\lambda\mathtt{z}_2.\mathtt{z}_2$ denote the same entity. The application $\mathtt{t}_1\ \mathtt{t}_2$ represents the result of calling the function $\mathtt{t}_1$ with actual parameter $\mathtt{t}_2$, or, in other words, the result of applying $\mathtt{t}_1$ to $\mathtt{t}_2$. Application is left-associative, that is, $\mathtt{t}_1\ \mathtt{t}_2\ \mathtt{t}_3$ stands for $(\mathtt{t}_1\ \mathtt{t}_2)\ \mathtt{t}_3$. The construct $\mathtt{let}\ \mathtt{z} = \mathtt{t}_1\ \mathtt{in}\ \mathtt{t}_2$ represents the result of evaluating $\mathtt{t}_2$ after binding the variable $\mathtt{z}$ to $\mathtt{t}_1$. Note that the variable $\mathtt{z}$ is bound within $\mathtt{t}_2$, but not within $\mathtt{t}_1$, so for instance $\mathtt{let}\ \mathtt{z}_1 = \mathtt{z}_1\ \mathtt{in}\ \mathtt{z}_1$ and $\mathtt{let}\ \mathtt{z}_2 = \mathtt{z}_1\ \mathtt{in}\ \mathtt{z}_2$ are the same object. The construct $\mathtt{let}\ \mathtt{z} = \mathtt{t}_1\ \mathtt{in}\ \mathtt{t}_2$ has the same meaning as $(\lambda\mathtt{z.t}_2)\ \mathtt{t}_1$, but is dealt with in a more flexible way by ML-the-type-system. To sum up, the syntax of ML-the-calculus is that of the pure λ-calculus, extended with memory locations, constants, and the `let` construct.

Values form a subset of expressions. They are expressions whose evaluation is completed. Values include identifiers, λ-abstractions, and applications of constants, of the form $\mathtt{c}\ \mathtt{v}_1\ \ldots\ \mathtt{v}_k$, where k does not exceed c's arity if c is a constructor, and k is smaller than c's arity if c is a destructor. In what follows, we are often interested in closed values—ones that do not contain any free program variables. We use the meta-variables v and w for values.

10.1.2 EXAMPLE: The integer literals $\ldots, \widehat{-1}, \hat{0}, \hat{1}, \ldots$ are nullary constructors, so they are values. Integer addition $\hat{+}$ is a binary destructor, so it is a value, and so is every partial application $\hat{+}\ \mathtt{v}$. Thus, both $\hat{+}\ \hat{1}$ and $\hat{+}\ \hat{+}$ are values. An application of $\hat{+}$ to two values, such as $\hat{2}\hat{+}\hat{2}$, is not a value. □

10.1.3 EXAMPLE [PAIRS]: Let $(\cdot,\cdot)$ be a binary constructor. If $\mathtt{t}_1$ are $\mathtt{t}_2$ are expressions, then the double application $(\cdot,\cdot)\ \mathtt{t}_1\ \mathtt{t}_2$ may be called the *pair* of $\mathtt{t}_1$ and $\mathtt{t}_2$, and may be written $(\mathtt{t}_1, \mathtt{t}_2)$. By the definition above, $(\mathtt{t}_1, \mathtt{t}_2)$ is a value if and only if $\mathtt{t}_1$ and $\mathtt{t}_2$ are both values. □

Stores are finite mappings from memory locations to closed values. A store μ represents what is usually called a heap, that is, a collection of values, each of which is allocated at a particular address in memory and may contain pointers to other elements of the heap. ML-the-programming-language allows overwriting the contents of an existing memory block—an operation sometimes referred to as a *side effect*. In the operational semantics, this effect is achieved by mapping an existing memory location to a new value. We write $\emptyset$ for the empty store. We write $\mu[m \mapsto \mathtt{v}]$ for the store that maps m to v and otherwise coincides with μ. When μ and μ' have disjoint domains, we write $\mu\mu'$ for their union. We write $dom(\mu)$ for the domain of μ and $range(\mu)$ for the set of memory locations that appear in its codomain.

The operational semantics of a pure language like the λ-calculus may be defined as a rewriting system on expressions. Because ML-the-calculus has side effects, however, we define its operational semantics as a rewriting system on *configurations*. A configuration $\mathtt{t}/\mu$ is a pair of an expression t and a store μ. The memory locations in the domain of μ are *not* considered bound within $\mathtt{t}/\mu$, so, for instance, $m_1/(m_1 \mapsto \hat{0})$ and $m_2/(m_2 \mapsto \hat{0})$ denote distinct entities. (In the literature, memory locations are often considered bound inside configurations. This offers the advantage of making memory allocation a deterministic operation. However, there is still a need for non-α-convertible configurations: rules R-EXTEND and R-CONTEXT in Figure 10-2 cannot otherwise be correctly stated! Quite a few papers run into this pitfall.)

A configuration $\mathtt{t}/\mu$ is *closed* if and only if t has no free program variables and every memory location that appears within t or within the range of μ is in the domain of μ. If t is a closed source program, its evaluation begins within an empty store—that is, with the configuration $\mathtt{t}/\emptyset$. Because source programs do not contain memory locations, this configuration is closed. Furthermore, we shall see that closed configurations are preserved by reduction.

$$(\lambda z.t)\ v \longrightarrow [z \mapsto v]t \qquad \text{(R-BETA)}$$

$$\text{let } z = v \text{ in } t \longrightarrow [z \mapsto v]t \qquad \text{(R-LET)}$$

$$\frac{t/\mu \xrightarrow{\delta} t'/\mu'}{t/\mu \longrightarrow t'/\mu'} \qquad \text{(R-DELTA)}$$

$$\frac{t/\mu \longrightarrow t'/\mu' \quad dom(\mu'') \# dom(\mu') \quad range(\mu'') \# dom(\mu' \setminus \mu)}{t/\mu\mu'' \longrightarrow t'/\mu'\mu''} \qquad \text{(R-EXTEND)}$$

$$\frac{t/\mu \longrightarrow t'/\mu'}{\mathcal{E}[t]/\mu \twoheadrightarrow \mathcal{E}[t']/\mu'} \qquad \text{(R-CONTEXT)}$$

Figure 10-2: Semantics of ML-the-calculus

Note that, instead of separating expressions and stores, it is possible to make store fragments part of the syntax of expressions; this idea, proposed in Crank and Felleisen (1991), has also been used for the encoding of reference cells in process calculi.

A *context* is an expression where a single subexpression has been replaced with a *hole*, written []. *Evaluation contexts* form a strict subset of contexts. In an evaluation context, the hole is meant to highlight a point in the program where it is valid to apply a reduction rule. Thus, the definition of evaluation contexts determines a reduction strategy: it tells where and in what order reduction steps may occur. For instance, the fact that λz.[] is not an evaluation context means that the body of a function is never evaluated—that is, not until the function is applied. The fact that t $\mathcal{E}$ is an evaluation context only if t is a value means that, to evaluate an application $t_1\ t_2$, one should fully evaluate t_1 before attempting to evaluate t_2. More generally, in the case of a multiple application, it means that arguments should be evaluated from left to right. Of course, other choices could be made: for instance, defining $\mathcal{E}$ ::= ... | t $\mathcal{E}$ | $\mathcal{E}$ v | ... would enforce a right-to-left evaluation order, while defining $\mathcal{E}$ ::= ... | t $\mathcal{E}$ | $\mathcal{E}$ t | ... would leave the evaluation order unspecified, effectively allowing reduction to alternate between both subexpressions, and making evaluation nondeterministic (because side effects could occur in different order). The fact that let z = v in $\mathcal{E}$ is not an evaluation context means that the body of a local definition is never evaluated—that is, not until the definition itself is reduced. We write $\mathcal{E}$[t] for the expression obtained by replacing the hole in $\mathcal{E}$ with the expression t.

Figure 10-2 defines first a relation $\longrightarrow$ between arbitrary configurations, then a relation $\twoheadrightarrow$ between closed configurations. If $t/\mu \longrightarrow t'/\mu$ holds for every store μ, then we write $t \longrightarrow t'$ and say that the reduction is *pure*.

The semantics need not be deterministic. That is, a configuration may reduce to two different configurations. In fact, our semantics is deterministic only if the relation $\xrightarrow{\delta}$, which is a parameter to our semantics, is itself deterministic. In practice, $\xrightarrow{\delta}$ is usually deterministic, up to α-conversion of memory locations. As explained above, the semantics could also be made nondeterministic by a different choice in the definition of evaluation contexts.

The key reduction rule is R-BETA, which states that a function application $(\lambda z.t)\ v$ reduces to the function body, namely t, where every occurrence of the formal argument z has been replaced with the actual argument v. The λ construct, which prevented the function body t from being evaluated, disappears, so the new term may (in general) be further reduced. Because ML-the-calculus adopts a *call-by-value* strategy, rule R-BETA is applicable only if the actual argument is a value v. In other words, a function cannot be invoked until its actual argument has been fully evaluated. Rule R-LET is very similar to R-BETA. Indeed, it specifies that `let z = v in t` has the same behavior, with respect to reduction, as $(\lambda z.t)\ v$. Substitution of a value for a program variable throughout a term is expensive, so R-BETA and R-LET are never implemented literally: they are only a simple specification. Actual implementations usually employ *runtime environments*, which may be understood as a form of *explicit substitutions* (Abadi, Cardelli, Curien, and Lévy, 1991; Hardin, Maranget, and Pagano, 1998). Note that our choice of a call-by-value reduction strategy has essentially no impact on the type system; the programming language Haskell, whose reduction strategy is known as *lazy* or *call-by-need*, also relies on the Hindley-Milner type discipline.

Rule R-DELTA describes the semantics of constants. It states that a certain relation $\xrightarrow{\delta}$ is a subset of $\longrightarrow$. Of course, since the set of constants is unspecified, the relation $\xrightarrow{\delta}$ must be kept abstract as well. We require that, if $t/\mu \xrightarrow{\delta} t'/\mu'$ holds, then

(i) t is of the form $c\ v_1\ \ldots\ v_n$, where c is a destructor of arity n; and

(ii) $dom(\mu)$ is a subset of $dom(\mu')$.

Condition (i) ensures that δ-reduction concerns full applications of destructors only, and that these are evaluated in accordance with the call-by-value strategy. Condition (ii) ensures that δ-reduction may allocate new memory locations, but not deallocate existing locations. In particular, a "garbage collection" operator, which destroys unreachable memory cells, cannot be made available as a constant. Doing so would not make much sense anyway in the presence of R-EXTEND. Condition (ii) allows proving that, if t/μ reduces (by $\longrightarrow$) to t'/μ', then $dom(\mu)$ is also a subset of $dom(\mu')$; checking this is left as an exercise to the reader.

Rule R-EXTEND states that any valid reduction is also valid in a larger store. The initial and final stores μ and μ' in the original reduction are both extended with a new store fragment μ''. The rule's second premise requires that the domain of μ'' be disjoint with that of μ' (and consequently, also with that of μ), so that the new memory locations are indeed undefined in the original reduction. (They may, however, appear in the image of μ.) The last premise ensures that the new memory locations in μ'' do not accidentally carry the same names as the locations allocated during the original reduction step, that is, the locations in $dom(\mu' \setminus \mu)$. The notation $A \# B$ stands for $A \cap B = \emptyset$.

Rule R-CONTEXT completes the definition of the operational semantics by defining $\longrightarrow\!\!\!\!\blacktriangleright$, a relation between closed configurations, in terms of $\longrightarrow$. The rule states that reduction may take place not only at the term's root, but also deep inside it, provided the path from the root to the point where reduction occurs forms an evaluation context. This is how evaluation contexts determine an evaluation strategy. As a purely technical point, because $\longrightarrow\!\!\!\!\blacktriangleright$ relates closed configurations only, we do not need to require that the memory locations in $dom(\mu' \setminus \mu)$ be fresh for $\mathcal{E}$; indeed, every memory location that appears within $\mathcal{E}$ must be a member of $dom(\mu)$.

10.1.4 EXAMPLE [INTEGERS, CONTINUED]: The operational semantics of integer addition may be defined as follows:

$$\hat{k}_1 \mathbin{\hat{+}} \hat{k}_2 \xrightarrow{\delta} \widehat{k_1 + k_2} \qquad \text{(R-ADD)}$$

The left-hand term is the double application $\hat{+}\ \hat{k}_1\ \hat{k}_2$, while the right-hand term is the integer literal $\hat{k}$, where k is the sum of k_1 and k_2. The distinction between object level and meta level (that is, between $\hat{k}$ and k) is needed here to avoid ambiguity. □

10.1.5 EXAMPLE [PAIRS, CONTINUED]: In addition to the pair constructor defined in Example 10.1.3, we may introduce two destructors π_1 and π_2 of arity 1. We may define their operational semantics as follows, for $i \in \{1,2\}$:

$$\pi_i\ (\mathtt{v}_1, \mathtt{v}_2) \xrightarrow{\delta} \mathtt{v}_i \qquad \text{(R-PROJ)}$$

Thus, our treatment of constants is general enough to account for pair construction and destruction; we need not build these features explicitly into the language. □

10.1.6 EXERCISE [BOOLEANS, RECOMMENDED, ★★, ↛]: Let `true` and `false` be nullary constructors. Let `if` be a ternary destructor. Extend the semantics with

$$\mathtt{if}\ \mathtt{true}\ \mathtt{v}_1\ \mathtt{v}_2 \xrightarrow{\delta} \mathtt{v}_1 \qquad \text{(R-TRUE)}$$

$$\mathtt{if}\ \mathtt{false}\ \mathtt{v}_1\ \mathtt{v}_2 \xrightarrow{\delta} \mathtt{v}_2 \qquad \text{(R-FALSE)}$$

Let us use the syntactic sugar $\mathtt{if}\ \mathtt{t}_0\ \mathtt{then}\ \mathtt{t}_1\ \mathtt{else}\ \mathtt{t}_2$ for the triple application of $\mathtt{if}\ \mathtt{t}_0\ \mathtt{t}_1\ \mathtt{t}_2$. Explain why these definitions do not quite provide the expected behavior. Without modifying the semantics of `if`, suggest a new definition of the syntactic sugar `if` t_0 `then` t_1 `else` t_2 that corrects the problem. □

10.1.7 EXAMPLE [SUMS]: Booleans may in fact be viewed as a special case of the more general concept of *sum.* Let $\mathtt{inj}_1$ and $\mathtt{inj}_2$ be unary constructors, called respectively *left* and *right injections.* Let `case` be a ternary destructor, whose semantics is defined as follows, for $i \in \{1, 2\}$:

$$\mathtt{case}\ (\mathtt{inj}_i\ \mathsf{v})\ \mathsf{v}_1\ \mathsf{v}_2 \xrightarrow{\delta} \mathsf{v}_i\ \mathsf{v} \qquad \text{(R-CASE)}$$

Here, the value $\mathtt{inj}_i\ \mathsf{v}$ is being scrutinized, while the values v_1 and v_2, which are typically functions, represent the two arms of a standard `case` construct. The rule selects an appropriate arm (here, v_i) based on whether the value under scrutiny was formed using a left or right injection. The arm v_i is executed and given access to the data carried by the injection (here, v). □

10.1.8 EXERCISE [★, ↛]: Explain how to encode `true`, `false`, and the `if` construct in terms of sums. Check that the behavior of R-TRUE and R-FALSE is properly emulated. □

10.1.9 EXAMPLE [REFERENCES]: Let `ref` and ! be unary destructors. Let := be a binary destructor. We write $\mathsf{t}_1 := \mathsf{t}_2$ for the double application $:=\ \mathsf{t}_1\ \mathsf{t}_2$. Define the operational semantics of these three destructors as follows:

$$\mathtt{ref}\ \mathsf{v}/\emptyset \xrightarrow{\delta} m/(m \mapsto \mathsf{v}) \quad \text{if } m \text{ is fresh for } \mathsf{v} \qquad \text{(R-REF)}$$

$$!m/(m \mapsto \mathsf{v}) \xrightarrow{\delta} \mathsf{v}/(m \mapsto \mathsf{v}) \qquad \text{(R-DEREF)}$$

$$m := \mathsf{v}/(m \mapsto \mathsf{v}_0) \xrightarrow{\delta} \mathsf{v}/(m \mapsto \mathsf{v}) \qquad \text{(R-ASSIGN)}$$

According to R-REF, evaluating `ref` v allocates a fresh memory location m and binds v to it. The name m must be chosen fresh for v to prevent inadvertent capture of the memory locations that appear free within v. By R-DEREF, evaluating $!m$ returns the value bound to the memory location m within the current store. By R-ASSIGN, evaluating $m := \mathsf{v}$ discards the value v_0 currently bound to m and produces a new store where m is bound to v. Here, the value returned by the assignment $m := \mathsf{v}$ is v itself; in ML-the-programming-language, it is usually a nullary constructor (), pronounced *unit.* □

10.1.10 EXAMPLE [RECURSION]: Let `fix` be a binary destructor, whose operational semantics is:

$$\mathtt{fix}\ \mathsf{v}_1\ \mathsf{v}_2 \xrightarrow{\delta} \mathsf{v}_1\ (\mathtt{fix}\ \mathsf{v}_1)\ \mathsf{v}_2 \qquad \text{(R-FIX)}$$

`fix` is a fixpoint combinator: it effectively allows recursive definitions of functions. Indeed, the construct `letrec f =` λ`z.`t_1 `in` t_2 provided by ML-the-programming-language may be viewed as syntactic sugar for `let f = fix (`λ`f.`λ`z.`t_1`) in` t_2. □

10.1.11 **Exercise [Recommended, ★★, ↛]:** Assuming the availability of Booleans and conditionals, integer literals, subtraction, multiplication, integer comparison, and a fixpoint combinator, most of which were defined in previous examples, define a function that computes the factorial of its integer argument, and apply it to $\hat{3}$. Determine, step by step, how this expression reduces to a value. □

It is straightforward to check that, if $\mathtt{t}/\mu$ reduces to $\mathtt{t}'/\mu'$, then $\mathtt{t}$ is not a value. In other words, values are irreducible: they represent completed computations. The proof is left as an exercise to the reader. The converse, however, does not hold: if the closed configuration $\mathtt{t}/\mu$ is irreducible with respect to $\longrightarrow$, then $\mathtt{t}$ is not necessarily a value. In that case, the configuration $\mathtt{t}/\mu$ is said to be *stuck*. It represents a *runtime error*, that is, a situation that does not allow computation to proceed, yet is not considered a valid outcome. A closed source program $\mathtt{t}$ is said to *go wrong* if and only if the initial configuration $\mathtt{t}/\emptyset$ reduces to a stuck configuration.

10.1.12 **Example:** Runtime errors typically arise when destructors are applied to arguments of an unexpected nature. For instance, the expressions $\hat{+}\ \hat{1}\ m$ and $\pi_1\ \hat{2}$ and $!\hat{3}$ are stuck, regardless of the current store. The program $\mathtt{let\ z} = \hat{+}\ \hat{+}\ \mathtt{in\ z}\ 1$ is not stuck, because $\hat{+}\ \hat{+}$ is a value. However, its reduct through R-Let is $\hat{+}\ \hat{+}\ 1$, which is stuck, so this program goes wrong. The primary purpose of type systems is to prevent such situations from arising. □

10.1.13 **Remark:** The configuration $!m/\mu$ is stuck if m is not in the domain of μ. In that case, however, $!m/\mu$ is not closed. Because we consider $\longrightarrow$ as a relation between closed configurations only, this situation cannot arise. In other words, the semantics of ML-the-calculus never allows the creation of *dangling pointers*. As a result, no particular precautions need be taken to guard against them. Several strongly typed programming languages do nevertheless allow dangling pointers in a controlled fashion (Tofte and Talpin, 1997; Walker, Crary, and Morrisett, 2000; DeLine and Fähndrich, 2001; Grossman, Morrisett, Jim, Hicks, Wang, and Cheney, 2002). □

Damas and Milner's Type System

ML-the-type-system was originally defined by Milner (1978). Here, we reproduce the definition given a few years later by Damas and Milner (1982), which is written in a more standard style: typing judgments are defined inductively by a collection of typing rules. We refer to this type system as DM.

We must first define *types*. In DM, types are terms built out of *type constructors* and *type variables*. Furthermore, they are *first-order* terms: that is, in the grammar of types, none of the productions *binds* a type variable. This situation is identical to that of the simply-typed λ-calculus.

We begin with several considerations concerning the specification of type constructors.

First, we do not wish to fix the set of type constructors. Certainly, since ML-the-calculus has functions, we need to be able to form an arrow type $\mathsf{T} \to \mathsf{T}'$ out of arbitrary types T and T'; that is, we need a binary type constructor $\to$. However, because ML-the-calculus includes an unspecified set of constants, we cannot say much else in general. If constants include integer literals and integer operations, as in Example 10.1.1, then a nullary type constructor int is needed; if they include pair construction and destruction, as in Examples 10.1.3 and 10.1.5, then a binary type constructor $\times$ is needed; etc.

Second, it is common to refer to the parameters of a type constructor by position, that is, by numeric index. For instance, when one writes $\mathsf{T} \to \mathsf{T}'$, it is understood that the type constructor $\to$ has arity 2, that T is its first parameter, known as its *domain*, and that T' is its second parameter, known as its *codomain*. Here, however, we refer to parameters by names, known as *directions*. For instance, we define two directions *domain* and *codomain* and let the type constructor $\to$ have arity $\{\mathit{domain}, \mathit{codomain}\}$. The extra generality afforded by directions is exploited in the definition of nonstructural subtyping (Example 10.2.9) and in the definition of rows (§10.8).

Last, we allow types to be classified using *kinds*. As a result, every type constructor must come not only with an arity, but with a richer *signature*, which describes the kinds of the types to which it is applicable and the kind of the type that it produces. A distinguished kind $\star$ is associated with "normal" types, that is, types that are directly ascribed to expressions and values. For instance, the signature of the type constructor $\to$ is $\{\mathit{domain} \mapsto \star, \mathit{codomain} \mapsto \star\} \Rightarrow \star$, because it is applicable to two normal types and produces a normal type. Introducing kinds other than $\star$ allows viewing some types as ill-formed: this is illustrated, for instance, in §10.8. In the simplest case, however, $\star$ is really the only kind, so the signature of a type constructor is nothing but its arity (a set of directions), and every term is a well-formed type, provided every application of a type constructor respects its arity.

10.1.14 **Definition:** Let d range over a finite or denumerable set of *directions* and κ over a finite or denumerable set of *kinds*. Let $\star$ be a distinguished kind. Let K range over partial mappings from directions to kinds. Let F range over a finite or denumerable set of *type constructors*, each of which has a *signature* of the form $K \Rightarrow \kappa$. The domain of K is called the *arity* of F, while κ is referred to as its *image kind*. We write κ instead of $K \Rightarrow \kappa$ when K is empty. Let $\to$ be a type constructor of signature $\{\mathit{domain} \mapsto \star, \mathit{codomain} \mapsto \star\} \Rightarrow \star$. □

The type constructors and their signatures collectively form a *signature* S. In the following, we assume that a fixed signature S is given and that every type constructor in it has *finite* arity, so as to ensure that types are machine representable. However, in §10.8, we shall explicitly work with several distinct signatures, one of which involves type constructors of denumerable arity.

A *type variable* is a name that is used to stand for a type. For simplicity, we assume that every type variable is branded with a kind, or in other words, that type variables of distinct kinds are drawn from disjoint sets. Each of these sets of type variables is individually subject to α-conversion: that is, renamings must preserve kinds. Attaching kinds to type variables is only a technical convenience; in practice, every operation performed during type inference preserves the property that every type is well-kinded, so it is not necessary to keep track of the kind of every type variable. It is only necessary to check that all types supplied by the programmer, within type declarations, type annotations, or module interfaces, are well-kinded.

10.1.15 Definition: For every kind κ, let $\mathcal{V}_\kappa$ be a disjoint, denumerable set of *type variables*. Let X, Y, and Z range over the set $\mathcal{V}$ of all type variables. Let $\bar{\mathsf{X}}$ and $\bar{\mathsf{Y}}$ range over finite sets of type variables. We write $\bar{\mathsf{X}}\bar{\mathsf{Y}}$ for the set $\bar{\mathsf{X}} \cup \bar{\mathsf{Y}}$ and often write X for the singleton set $\{\mathsf{X}\}$. We write $ftv(o)$ for the set of *free type variables* of an object o. □

The set of types, ranged over by T, is the free many-kinded term algebra that arises out of the type constructors and type variables. Types are given by the following inductive definition:

10.1.16 Definition: A *type* of kind κ is either a member of $\mathcal{V}_\kappa$, or a term of the form $F\,\{d_1 \mapsto \mathsf{T}_1, \ldots, d_n \mapsto \mathsf{T}_n\}$, where F has signature $\{d_1 \mapsto \kappa_1, \ldots, d_n \mapsto \kappa_n\} \Rightarrow \kappa$ and $\mathsf{T}_1, \ldots, \mathsf{T}_n$ are types of kind $\kappa_1, \ldots, \kappa_n$, respectively. □

As a notational convention, we assume that, for every type constructor F, the directions that form the arity of F are implicitly ordered, so that we may say that F has signature $\kappa_1 \otimes \ldots \otimes \kappa_n \Rightarrow \kappa$ and employ the syntax $F\,\mathsf{T}_1 \ldots \mathsf{T}_n$ for applications of F. Applications of the type constructor $\rightarrow$ are written infix and associate to the right, so $\mathsf{T} \rightarrow \mathsf{T}' \rightarrow \mathsf{T}''$ stands for $\mathsf{T} \rightarrow (\mathsf{T}' \rightarrow \mathsf{T}'')$.

In order to give meaning to the free type variables of a type, or more generally, of a typing judgment, traditional presentations of ML-the-type-system, including Damas and Milner's, employ *type substitutions.* Most of our presentation avoids substitutions and uses constraints instead. However, we do need substitutions on a few occasions, especially when relating our presentation to Damas and Milner's.

10.1.17 Definition: A *type substitution* θ is a total, kind-preserving mapping of type variables to types that is the identity everywhere but on a finite subset of $\mathcal{V}$, which we call the *domain* of θ and write $dom(\theta)$. The *range* of θ, which we write $range(\theta)$, is the set $ftv(\theta(dom(\theta)))$. A type substitution may naturally be viewed as a total, kind-preserving mapping of types to types. □

If $\vec{X}$ and $\vec{T}$ are respectively a vector of distinct type variables and a vector of types of the same (finite) length such that, for every index i, X_i and T_i have the same kind, then $[\vec{X} \mapsto \vec{T}]$ denotes the substitution that maps X_i to T_i for every index i and is the identity elsewhere. The domain of $[\vec{X} \mapsto \vec{T}]$ is a subset of $\bar{X}$, the set underlying the vector $\vec{X}$. Its range is a subset of $ftv(\bar{T})$, where $\bar{T}$ is the set underlying the vector $\vec{T}$. (These may be strict subsets; for instance, the domain of $[X \mapsto X]$ is the empty set, since this substitution is the identity.) Every substitution θ may be written under the form $[\vec{X} \mapsto \vec{T}]$, where $\bar{X} = dom(\theta)$. Then, θ is *idempotent* if and only if $\bar{X} \# ftv(\bar{T})$ holds.

As pointed out earlier, types are first-order terms. As a result, every type variable that appears within a type T appears *free* within T. Things become more interesting when we introduce *type schemes.* As its name implies, a type scheme may describe an entire family of types; this effect is achieved via *universal quantification* over a set of type variables.

10.1.18 **Definition:** A type scheme S is an object of the form $\forall\bar{X}.T$, where T is a type of kind $\star$ and the type variables $\bar{X}$ are considered bound within T. Any type of the form $[\vec{X} \mapsto \vec{T}]T$ is called an *instance* of the type scheme $\forall\bar{X}.T$. □

One may view the type T as the trivial type scheme $\forall\emptyset.T$, where no type variables are universally quantified, so types of kind $\star$ may be viewed as a subset of type schemes. The type scheme $\forall\bar{X}.T$ may be viewed as a finite way of describing the possibly infinite family of its instances. Note that, throughout most of this chapter, we work with *constrained type schemes*, a generalization of DM type schemes (Definition 10.2.2).

Typing environments, or *environments* for short, are used to collect assumptions about an expression's free identifiers.

10.1.19 **Definition:** An *environment* Γ is a finite ordered sequence of pairs of a program identifier and a type scheme. We write $\emptyset$ for the empty environment and ";" for the concatenation of environments. An environment may be viewed as a finite mapping from program identifiers to type schemes by letting $\Gamma(\mathtt{x}) = S$ if and only if Γ is of the form $\Gamma_1;\mathtt{x} : S;\Gamma_2$, where Γ_2 contains no assumption about x. The set of *defined program identifiers* of an environment Γ, written $dpi(\Gamma)$, is defined by $dpi(\emptyset) = \emptyset$ and $dpi(\Gamma;\mathtt{x} : S) = dpi(\Gamma) \cup \{\mathtt{x}\}$. □

To complete the definition of Damas and Milner's type system, there remains to define *typing judgments.* A typing judgment takes the form $\Gamma \vdash \mathtt{t} : S$, where t is an expression of interest, Γ is an environment, which typically contains assumptions about t's free program identifiers, and S is a type scheme.

$$\frac{\Gamma(\mathtt{x}) = \mathsf{S}}{\Gamma \vdash \mathtt{x} : \mathsf{S}} \quad (\text{DM-VAR})$$

$$\frac{\Gamma; \mathtt{z} : \mathsf{T} \vdash \mathtt{t} : \mathsf{T}'}{\Gamma \vdash \lambda \mathtt{z}.\mathtt{t} : \mathsf{T} \to \mathsf{T}'} \quad (\text{DM-ABS})$$

$$\frac{\Gamma \vdash \mathtt{t}_1 : \mathsf{T} \to \mathsf{T}' \qquad \Gamma \vdash \mathtt{t}_2 : \mathsf{T}}{\Gamma \vdash \mathtt{t}_1\ \mathtt{t}_2 : \mathsf{T}'} \quad (\text{DM-APP})$$

$$\frac{\Gamma \vdash \mathtt{t}_1 : \mathsf{S} \qquad \Gamma; \mathtt{z} : \mathsf{S} \vdash \mathtt{t}_2 : \mathsf{T}}{\Gamma \vdash \mathtt{let}\ \mathtt{z} = \mathtt{t}_1\ \mathtt{in}\ \mathtt{t}_2 : \mathsf{T}} \quad (\text{DM-LET})$$

$$\frac{\Gamma \vdash \mathtt{t} : \mathsf{T} \qquad \bar{\mathsf{X}} \# \mathit{ftv}(\Gamma)}{\Gamma \vdash \mathtt{t} : \forall \bar{\mathsf{X}}.\mathsf{T}} \quad (\text{DM-GEN})$$

$$\frac{\Gamma \vdash \mathtt{t} : \forall \bar{\mathsf{X}}.\mathsf{T}}{\Gamma \vdash \mathtt{t} : [\vec{\mathsf{X}} \mapsto \vec{\mathsf{T}}]\mathsf{T}} \quad (\text{DM-INST})$$

Figure 10-3: Typing rules for DM

Such a judgment may be read: *under assumptions* Γ, *the expression* t *has the type scheme* S. By abuse of language, it is sometimes said that t *has type* S. A typing judgment is *valid* (or *holds*) if and only if it may be derived using the rules that appear in Figure 10-3. An expression t is *well-typed* within the environment Γ if and only if there exists some type scheme S such that the judgment $\Gamma \vdash \mathtt{t} : \mathsf{S}$ holds; it is *ill-typed* within Γ otherwise.

Rule DM-VAR allows fetching a type scheme for an identifier x from the environment. It is equally applicable to program variables, memory locations, and constants. If no assumption concerning x appears in the environment Γ, then the rule isn't applicable. In that case, the expression x is ill-typed within Γ. Assumptions about constants are usually collected in a so-called *initial environment* Γ_0. It is the environment under which closed programs are typechecked, so every subexpression is typechecked under some extension Γ of Γ_0. Of course, the type schemes assigned by Γ_0 to constants must be consistent with their operational semantics; we say more about this later (§10.5). Rule DM-ABS specifies how to typecheck a λ-abstraction $\lambda \mathtt{z}.\mathtt{t}$. Its premise requires the body of the function, t, to be well-typed under an extra assumption that causes all free occurrences of z within t to receive a common type T. Its conclusion forms the arrow type $\mathsf{T} \to \mathsf{T}'$ out of the types of the function's formal parameter, T, and result, T'. It is worth noting that this rule always augments the environment with a type T—recall that, by convention, types form a subset of type schemes—but never with a nontrivial type scheme. Rule DM-APP states that the type of a function application is the codomain of the function's type, provided that the domain of the function's type is a valid type for the actual argument. Rule DM-LET closely mirrors the operational semantics: whereas the semantics of the local definition $\mathtt{let}\ \mathtt{z} = \mathtt{t}_1\ \mathtt{in}\ \mathtt{t}_2$ is to augment the runtime environment by binding z to the value of $\mathtt{t}_1$ prior to evaluating $\mathtt{t}_2$, the effect of DM-LET is to augment the typing environment by binding $\mathtt{z}$ to a type scheme for $\mathtt{t}_1$ prior to typechecking $\mathtt{t}_2$. Rule DM-GEN turns a type into a type scheme by universally quantifying over a set of type variables that do not appear free in the environment; this restriction is discussed in Example 10.1.20 below. Rule DM-INST, on the contrary, turns a type scheme into one of its instances, which may be chosen arbitrarily. These two operations are referred to as *generalization* and *instantiation*. The notion of type scheme and the rules DM-GEN and DM-INST are characteristic of ML-the-type-system: they distinguish it from the simply-typed λ-calculus.

10.1.20 EXAMPLE: It is unsound to allow generalizing type variables that appear free in the environment. For instance, consider the typing judgment $\mathtt{z} : \mathsf{X} \vdash \mathtt{z} : \mathsf{X}$ **(1)**, which, according to DM-VAR, is valid. Applying an unrestricted version of DM-GEN to it, we obtain $\mathtt{z} : \mathsf{X} \vdash \mathtt{z} : \forall \mathsf{X}.\mathsf{X}$ **(2)**, whence, by DM-INST, $\mathtt{z} : \mathsf{X} \vdash \mathtt{z} : \mathsf{Y}$ **(3)**. By DM-ABS and DM-GEN, we then have $\emptyset \vdash \lambda \mathtt{z}.\mathtt{z} : \forall \mathsf{XY}.\mathsf{X} \rightarrow \mathsf{Y}$. In other words, the identity function has unrelated argument and result types! Then, the expression $(\lambda \mathtt{z}.\mathtt{z})\ \hat{0}\ \hat{0}$, which reduces to the stuck expression $\hat{0}\ \hat{0}$, has type scheme $\forall \mathsf{Z}.\mathsf{Z}$. So, well-typed programs may cause runtime errors: the type system is unsound.

What happened? It is clear that the judgment (1) is correct only because the type assigned to $\mathtt{z}$ is the *same* in its assumption and in its right-hand side. For the same reason, the judgments (2) and (3)—the former of which may be written $\mathtt{z} : \mathsf{X} \vdash \mathtt{z} : \forall \mathsf{Y}.\mathsf{Y}$—are incorrect. Indeed, such judgments defeat the very purpose of environments, since they disregard their assumption. By universally quantifying over X in the right-hand side only, we break the connection between occurrences of X in the assumption, which remain free, and occurrences in the right-hand side, which become bound. This is correct only if there are in fact no free occurrences of X in the assumption. □

10.1.21 REMARK: A naive implementation of DM-GEN would traverse the environment Γ in order to compute the set of its free type variables. However, the number of entries in Γ may be linear in the program size, so, even if types have bounded size, the time required by this computation may be linear in the program size. Since it is performed at every `let` node, this naive approach gives type inference *quadratic* time complexity. To avoid this pitfall, our constraint solver annotates every type variable with an integer rank, which allows telling, in constant time, whether it appears free in Γ (page 444). □

It is a key feature of ML-the-type-system that DM-ABS may only introduce a type T, rather than a type scheme, into the environment. Indeed, this allows the rule's conclusion to form the arrow type $\mathsf{T} \rightarrow \mathsf{T}'$. If instead the rule were to introduce the assumption $\mathtt{z} : \mathsf{S}$ into the environment, then its conclusion would have to form $\mathsf{S} \rightarrow \mathsf{T}'$, which is not a well-formed type. In other words, this restriction is necessary to preserve the stratification between types and type schemes. If we were to remove this stratification, thus allowing universal quantifiers to appear deep inside types, we would obtain an implicitly-typed version of System F (*TAPL*, Chapter 23). Type inference for System F is undecidable (Wells, 1999), while type inference for ML-the-type-system is decidable, as we show later, so this design choice has a rather drastic impact.

10.1.22 **Exercise [Recommended, ★]:** Build a type derivation for the expression $\lambda z_1.\ \mathtt{let}\ z_2 = z_1\ \mathtt{in}\ z_2$. □

10.1.23 **Exercise [Recommended, ★]:** Let int be a nullary type constructor of signature ★. Let Γ_0 consist of the bindings $\hat{+} : \mathsf{int} \to \mathsf{int} \to \mathsf{int}$ and $\hat{k} : \mathsf{int}$, for every integer k. Can you find derivations of the following valid typing judgments? Which of these judgments are valid in the simply-typed λ-calculus, where $\mathtt{let}\ z = t_1\ \mathtt{in}\ t_2$ is syntactic sugar for $(\lambda z.t_2)\ t_1$?

$$\Gamma_0 \vdash \lambda z.z : \mathsf{int} \to \mathsf{int}$$
$$\Gamma_0 \vdash \lambda z.z : \forall X.X \to X$$
$$\Gamma_0 \vdash \mathtt{let}\ f = \lambda z.z \hat{+} \hat{1}\ \mathtt{in}\ f\ \hat{2} : \mathsf{int}$$
$$\Gamma_0 \vdash \mathtt{let}\ f = \lambda z.z\ \mathtt{in}\ f\ f\ \hat{2} : \mathsf{int}$$

Show that the expressions $\hat{1}\ \hat{2}$ and $\lambda f.(f\ f)$ are ill-typed within Γ_0. Could these expressions be well-typed in a more powerful type system? □

DM enjoys a number of nice theoretical properties, which have practical implications.

First, it is sound: that is, well-typed programs do not go wrong. This essential property ensures that programs that are accepted by the typechecker may be compiled without runtime checks. Establishing this property requires (i) suitable hypotheses about the semantics of constants and the type schemes assigned to constants in the initial environment, and (ii) in the presence of side effects, a slight restriction of the syntax of `let` constructs, known as the *value restriction.*

Furthermore, there exists an algorithm that, given a (closed) environment Γ and a program t, tells whether t is well-typed with respect to Γ, and if so, produces a *principal* type scheme S. A principal type scheme is such that (i) it is valid, that is, $\Gamma \vdash t : S$ holds, and (ii) it is most general, that is, every judgment of the form $\Gamma \vdash t : S'$ follows from $\Gamma \vdash t : S$ by DM-Inst and DM-Gen. (For the sake of simplicity, we have stated the properties of the type inference algorithm only in the case of a closed environment Γ; the specification is slightly heavier in the general case.) This implies that type inference is decidable: the compiler need not require expressions to be annotated with types. The fact that, under a fixed environment Γ, all of the type information associated with an expression t may be summarized in the form of a single, principal type scheme is also key to modular programming. Indeed, exporting a value out of a module requires explicitly assigning a type scheme to it as part of the module's signature. If the chosen type scheme is not principal, then part of the value's (hence, of the module's) potential for reuse is lost.

Road Map

Before proving the above claims, we first generalize our presentation by moving to a *constraint-based* setting. The necessary tools—the constraint language, its interpretation, and a number of constraint equivalence laws—are introduced in §10.2. In §10.3, we describe the standard constraint-based type system HM(X) (Odersky, Sulzmann, and Wehr, 1999). We prove that, when constraints are made up of equations between free, finite terms, HM(X) is a reformulation of DM. In the presence of a more powerful constraint language, HM(X) is an extension of DM. In §10.4, we show that type inference may be viewed as a combination of constraint generation and constraint solving, as promised earlier. Then, in §10.5, we give a type soundness theorem. It is stated purely in terms of constraints, but—thanks to the results developed in the previous sections—applies equally to HM(X) and DM.

Throughout this core material, the syntax and interpretation of constraints are left partly unspecified. Thus, the development is *parameterized* with respect to them—hence the unknown X in the name HM(X). We really describe a family of constraint-based type systems, all of which share a common constraint generator and a common type soundness proof. Constraint solving, however, cannot be independent of X: on the contrary, the design of an efficient solver is heavily dependent on the syntax and interpretation of constraints. In §10.6, we consider constraint solving in the particular case where constraints are made up of equations interpreted in a free tree model, and define a constraint solver on top of a standard first-order unification algorithm.

The remainder of this chapter deals with extensions of the framework. In §10.7, we explain how to extend ML-the-calculus with a number of features, including products, sums, references, recursion, algebraic data types, and recursive types. Last, in §10.8, we extend the type language with *rows* and use them to assign polymorphic type schemes to operations on records and variants.

σ ::=		*type scheme:*
	$\forall\bar{X}[C].T$	
C, D ::=		*constraint:*
	true	*truth*
	false	*falsity*
	$P\,T_1 \ldots T_n$	*predicate application*
	$C \wedge C$	*conjunction*
	$\exists\bar{X}.C$	*existential quantification*
	def $x : \sigma$ in C	*type scheme introduction*
	$x \preceq T$	*type scheme instantiation*

C, D ::=		*Syntactic sugar for constraints:*
	...	*As before*
	$\sigma \preceq T$	*Definition 10.2.3*
	let $x : \sigma$ in C	*Definition 10.2.3*
	$\exists\sigma$	*Definition 10.2.3*
	def Γ in C	*Definition 10.2.4*
	let Γ in C	*Definition 10.2.4*
	$\exists\Gamma$	*Definition 10.2.4*

Figure 10-4: Syntax of type schemes and constraints

10.2 Constraints

In this section, we define the syntax and logical meaning of constraints. Both are partly unspecified. Indeed, the set of *type constructors* (Definition 10.1.14) must contain at least the binary type constructor $\rightarrow$, but might contain more. Similarly, the syntax of constraints involves a set of so-called *predicates* on types, which we require to contain at least a binary *subtyping* predicate $\leq$, but might contain more. (The introduction of subtyping, which is absent in DM, has little impact on the complexity of our proofs, yet increases the framework's expressive power. When subtyping is not desired, we interpret the predicate $\leq$ as equality.) The logical interpretation of type constructors and of predicates is left almost entirely unspecified. This freedom allows reasoning not only about Damas and Milner's type system, but also about a family of constraint-based extensions of it.

Syntax of Constraints

We now define the syntax of constrained type schemes and of constraints and introduce some extra constraint forms as syntactic sugar.

10.2.1 **Definition:** Let P range over a finite or denumerable set of *predicates*, each of which has a *signature* of the form $\kappa_1 \otimes \ldots \otimes \kappa_n \Rightarrow \cdot$, where $n \geq 0$. For every kind κ, let $=_\kappa$ and $\leq_\kappa$ be distinguished predicates of signature $\kappa \otimes \kappa \Rightarrow \cdot$. □

10.2.2 **Definition:** The syntax of *type schemes* and *constraints* is given in Figure 10-4. It is further restricted by the following requirements. In the type scheme $\forall\bar{X}[C].T$ and in the constraint $x \preceq T$, the type T must have kind $\star$. In the constraint $P\,\mathsf{T}_1 \ldots \mathsf{T}_n$, the types $\mathsf{T}_1, \ldots, \mathsf{T}_n$ must have kind $\kappa_1, \ldots, \kappa_n$, respectively, if P has signature $\kappa_1 \otimes \ldots \otimes \kappa_n \Rightarrow \cdot$. We write $\forall\bar{\mathsf{X}}.\mathsf{T}$ for $\forall\bar{\mathsf{X}}[\mathsf{true}].\mathsf{T}$, which allows viewing DM type schemes as a subset of constrained type schemes. □

We write $\mathsf{T}_1 =_\kappa \mathsf{T}_2$ and $\mathsf{T}_1 \leq_\kappa \mathsf{T}_2$ for the binary predicate applications $=_\kappa \mathsf{T}_1\,\mathsf{T}_2$ and $\leq_\kappa \mathsf{T}_1\,\mathsf{T}_2$, and refer to them as equality and subtyping constraints, respectively. We often omit the subscript κ, so $\mathsf{T}_1 = \mathsf{T}_2$ and $\mathsf{T}_1 \leq \mathsf{T}_2$ are well-formed constraints whenever T_1 and T_2 have the same kind. By convention, $\exists$ and def bind tighter than $\wedge$; that is, $\exists\bar{\mathsf{X}}.C \wedge D$ is $(\exists\bar{\mathsf{X}}.C) \wedge D$ and $\mathsf{def}\ \mathsf{x} : \sigma\ \mathsf{in}\ C \wedge D$ is $(\mathsf{def}\ \mathsf{x} : \sigma\ \mathsf{in}\ C) \wedge D$. In $\forall\bar{\mathsf{X}}[C].\mathsf{T}$, the type variables $\bar{\mathsf{X}}$ are bound within C and T. In $\exists\bar{\mathsf{X}}.C$, the type variables $\bar{\mathsf{X}}$ are bound within C. The sets of free type variables of a type scheme σ and of a constraint C, written $ftv(\sigma)$ and $ftv(C)$, respectively, are defined accordingly. In $\mathsf{def}\ \mathsf{x} : \sigma\ \mathsf{in}\ C$, the identifier x is bound within C. The sets of free program identifiers of a type scheme σ and of a constraint C, written $fpi(\sigma)$ and $fpi(C)$, respectively, are defined accordingly. Note that x occurs free in the constraint $\mathsf{x} \preceq \mathsf{T}$.

The constraint true, which is always satisfied, mainly serves to indicate the absence of a nontrivial constraint, while false, which has no solution, may be understood as the indication of a type error. Composite constraints include conjunction and existential quantification, which have their standard meaning, as well as *type scheme introduction* and *type scheme instantiation* constraints, which are similar to Gustavsson and Svenningsson's constraint abstractions (2001). In order to be able to explain these last two forms, we must first introduce a number of derived constraint forms:

10.2.3 **Definition:** Let σ be $\forall\bar{\mathsf{X}}[D].\mathsf{T}$. If $\bar{\mathsf{X}} \# ftv(\mathsf{T}')$ holds, then $\sigma \preceq \mathsf{T}'$ (read: T' *is an instance of* σ) stands for the constraint $\exists\bar{\mathsf{X}}.(D \wedge \mathsf{T} \leq \mathsf{T}')$. We write $\exists\sigma$ (read: σ *has an instance*) for $\exists\bar{\mathsf{X}}.D$ and $\mathsf{let}\ \mathsf{x} : \sigma\ \mathsf{in}\ C$ for $\exists\sigma \wedge \mathsf{def}\ \mathsf{x} : \sigma\ \mathsf{in}\ C$. □

Constrained type schemes generalize Damas and Milner's type schemes, while this definition of instantiation constraints generalizes Damas and Milner's notion of instance (Definition 10.1.18). Let us draw a comparison. First, Damas and Milner's instance relation is binary (given a type scheme S and a type T, either T is an instance of S, or it isn't), and is purely syntactic. For instance, the type $\mathsf{Y} \to \mathsf{Z}$ is *not* an instance of $\forall\mathsf{X}.\mathsf{X} \to \mathsf{X}$ in Damas and Milner's sense, because Y and Z are distinct type variables. In our presentation, on the other hand, $\forall\mathsf{X}.\mathsf{X} \to \mathsf{X} \preceq \mathsf{Y} \to \mathsf{Z}$ is not an assertion; rather, it is a constraint, which by definition is $\exists\mathsf{X}.(\mathsf{true} \wedge \mathsf{X} \to \mathsf{X} \leq \mathsf{Y} \to \mathsf{Z})$. We later prove that it is equivalent to $\exists\mathsf{X}.(\mathsf{Y} \leq \mathsf{X} \wedge \mathsf{X} \leq \mathsf{Z})$ and to $\mathsf{Y} \leq \mathsf{Z}$, and, if subtyping is interpreted as equality, to $\mathsf{Y} = \mathsf{Z}$. That is, $\sigma \preceq \mathsf{T}'$ represents a condition on (the ground types denoted by) the type variables in $ftv(\sigma, \mathsf{T}')$ for T' to be an instance of σ, in a logical, rather than purely syntactic, sense. Second, the definition of instantiation constraints involves subtyping, to ensure that any supertype of an instance of σ is again an instance of σ (see rule C-ExTrans on page 418). This is consistent with the purpose of subtyping: to allow a subtype where a supertype is expected (*TAPL*, Chapter 15). Third and last, every type scheme σ is now of the form $\forall\bar{X}[C].T$. The constraint C, whose free type variables may or may not be members of $\bar{X}$, is meant to restrict the set of instances of the type scheme $\forall\bar{X}[C].T$. This is evident in the instantiation constraint $\forall\bar{X}[C].T \preceq T'$, which by Definition 10.2.3 stands for $\exists\bar{X}.(C \wedge T \leq T')$: the values that $\bar{X}$ may assume are restricted by the demand that C be satisfied. This requirement vanishes in the case of DM type schemes, where C is true. Our notions of constrained type scheme and of instantiation constraint are standard, coinciding with those of HM(X) (Odersky, Sulzmann, and Wehr, 1999).

Let us now come back to an explanation of type scheme introduction and instantiation constraints. In brief, the construct def x : σ in C binds the name x to the type scheme σ within the constraint C. If C contains a subconstraint of the form x $\preceq$ T, where this occurrence of x is free in C, then this subconstraint acquires the meaning $\sigma \preceq T$. Thus, the constraint x $\preceq$ T is indeed an instantiation constraint, where the type scheme that is being instantiated is referred to by name. The constraint def x : σ in C may be viewed as an *explicit substitution* of the type scheme σ for the name x within C. Later (§10.4), we use such explicit substitutions to supplant typing environments. That is, where Damas and Milner's type system augments the current typing environment (DM-Abs, DM-Let), we introduce a new def binding in the current constraint; where it looks up the current typing environment (DM-Var), we employ an instantiation constraint. (The reader may wish to look ahead at Figure 10-9 on page 431.) The point is that it is then up to a constraint solver to choose a strategy for reducing explicit substitutions—for instance, one might wish to simplify σ before substituting it for x within C—whereas the use of environments in standard type systems such as DM and HM(X) imposes an eager substitution strategy, which is inefficient and thus never literally implemented. The use of type scheme introduction and instantiation constraints allows separating constraint generation and constraint solving without compromising efficiency, or, in other words, without introducing a gap between the description of the type inference algorithm and its actual implementation. Although the algorithm that we plan to describe is not new (Rémy, 1992a), its description in terms of constraints is: to the best of our knowledge, the only close relative of our def constraints is to be found in Gustavsson and Svenningsson (2001). An earlier work that contains similar ideas is Müller (1994). Approaches based on semi-unification (Henglein, 1989, 1993) achieve a similar separation between constraint generation and constraint solving, but are based on a rather different constraint language.

In the type system of Damas and Milner, every type scheme S has a fixed, nonempty set of instances. In a constraint-based setting, things are more complex: given a type scheme σ and a type T, whether T is an instance of σ (that is, whether the constraint $\sigma \preceq \mathsf{T}$ is satisfied) depends on the meaning assigned to the type variables in $ftv(\sigma, \mathsf{T})$. Similarly, given a type scheme, whether *some* type is an instance of σ (that is, whether the constraint $\exists \mathsf{Z}.\sigma \preceq \mathsf{Z}$, where Z is fresh for σ, is satisfied) depends on the meaning assigned to the type variables in $ftv(\sigma)$. Because we do not wish to allow forming type schemes that have no instances, we often use the constraint $\exists \mathsf{Z}.\sigma \preceq \mathsf{Z}$. In fact, we later prove that it is equivalent to $\exists \sigma$, as defined above. We also use the constraint form $\mathsf{let}\ \mathsf{x} : \sigma\ \mathsf{in}\ C$, which requires σ to have an instance and at the same time associates it with the name x. Because the def form is more primitive, it is easier to work with at a low level, but it is no longer explicitly used after §10.2; we always use let instead.

10.2.4 **Definition:** Environments Γ remain as in Definition 10.1.19, except DM type schemes S are replaced with constrained type schemes σ. The set of *free program identifiers* of an environment Γ, written $fpi(\Gamma)$, is defined by $fpi(\emptyset) = \emptyset$ and $fpi(\Gamma; \mathsf{x} : \sigma) = fpi(\Gamma) \cup fpi(\sigma)$. We write $dfpi(\Gamma)$ for $dpi(\Gamma) \cup fpi(\Gamma)$. We define $\mathsf{def}\ \emptyset\ \mathsf{in}\ C$ as C and $\mathsf{def}\ \Gamma; \mathsf{x} : \sigma\ \mathsf{in}\ C$ as $\mathsf{def}\ \Gamma\ \mathsf{in}\ \mathsf{def}\ \mathsf{x} : \sigma\ \mathsf{in}\ C$. Similarly, we define $\mathsf{let}\ \emptyset\ \mathsf{in}\ C$ as C and $\mathsf{let}\ \Gamma; \mathsf{x} : \sigma\ \mathsf{in}\ C$ as $\mathsf{let}\ \Gamma\ \mathsf{in}\ \mathsf{let}\ \mathsf{x} : \sigma\ \mathsf{in}\ C$. We define $\exists \emptyset$ as true and $\exists(\Gamma; \mathsf{x} : \sigma)$ as $\exists \Gamma \wedge \mathsf{def}\ \Gamma\ \mathsf{in}\ \exists \sigma$. □

In order to establish or express certain laws of equivalence between constraints, we need *constraint contexts*. A constraint context is a constraint with zero, one, or several *holes*, written []. The syntax of contexts is as follows:

$$\mathbb{C} ::= [\,] \mid C \mid \mathbb{C} \wedge \mathbb{C} \mid \exists \bar{\mathsf{X}}.\mathbb{C} \mid \mathsf{def}\ \mathsf{x} : \sigma\ \mathsf{in}\ \mathbb{C} \mid \mathsf{def}\ \mathsf{x} : \forall \bar{\mathsf{X}}[\mathbb{C}].\mathsf{T}\ \mathsf{in}\ C$$

The application of a constraint context $\mathbb{C}$ to a constraint C, written $\mathbb{C}[C]$, is defined in the usual way. Because a constraint context may have any number of holes, C may disappear or be duplicated in the process. Because a hole may appear in the scope of a binder, some of C's free type variables and free program identifiers may become bound in $\mathbb{C}[C]$. We write $dtv(\mathbb{C})$ and $dpi(\mathbb{C})$ for the sets of type variables and program identifiers, respectively, that $\mathbb{C}$ may thus capture. We write $\mathsf{let}\ \mathsf{x} : \forall \bar{\mathsf{X}}[\mathbb{C}].\mathsf{T}\ \mathsf{in}\ C$ for $\exists \bar{\mathsf{X}}.\mathbb{C} \wedge \mathsf{def}\ \mathsf{x} : \forall \bar{\mathsf{X}}[\mathbb{C}].\mathsf{T}\ \mathsf{in}\ C$. (Being able to state such a definition is why we require multi-hole contexts.) We let $\mathcal{X}$ range over *existential constraint contexts*, defined by $\mathcal{X} ::= \exists \bar{\mathsf{X}}.[\,]$.

Meaning of Constraints

We have defined the syntax of constraints and given an informal description of their meaning. We now give a formal definition of the interpretation of constraints. We begin with the definition of a *model*:

10.2.5 **Definition:** For every kind κ, let $\mathcal{M}_\kappa$ be a nonempty set, whose elements are called the *ground types* of kind κ. In the following, t ranges over $\mathcal{M}_\kappa$, for some κ that may be determined from the context. For every type constructor F of signature $K \Rightarrow \kappa$, let F denote a total function from $\mathcal{M}_K$ into $\mathcal{M}_\kappa$, where the indexed product $\mathcal{M}_K$ is the set of all mappings T of domain $dom(K)$ that map every $d \in dom(K)$ to an element of $\mathcal{M}_{K(d)}$. For every predicate symbol P of signature $\kappa_1 \otimes \ldots \otimes \kappa_n \Rightarrow \cdot$, let P denote a predicate on $\mathcal{M}_{\kappa_1} \times \ldots \times \mathcal{M}_{\kappa_n}$. For every kind κ, we require the predicate $=_\kappa$ to be equality on $\mathcal{M}_\kappa$ and the predicate $\leq_\kappa$ to be a partial order on $\mathcal{M}_\kappa$. □

For the sake of convenience, we abuse notation and write F for both the type constructor and its interpretation, and similarly for predicates.

By varying the set of type constructors, the set of predicates, the set of ground types, and the interpretation of type constructors and predicates, one may define an entire family of related type systems. We refer to the collection of these choices as X. Thus, the type system HM(X), described in §10.3, is *parameterized* by X.

The following examples give standard ways of defining the set of ground types and the interpretation of type constructors.

10.2.6 **Example [Syntactic models]:** For every kind κ, let $\mathcal{M}_\kappa$ consist of the *closed* types of kind κ. Then, ground types are types that do not have any free type variables, and form the so-called *Herbrand universe.* Let every type constructor F be interpreted as itself. Models that define ground types and interpret type constructors in this manner are referred to as *syntactic.* □

10.2.7 **Example [Tree models]:** Let a *path* π be a finite sequence of directions. The empty path is written ϵ and the concatenation of the paths π and π' is written $\pi \cdot \pi'$. Let a *tree* be a partial function t from paths to type constructors whose domain is nonempty and prefix-closed and such that, for every path π in the domain of t, if the type constructor $t(\pi)$ has signature $K \Rightarrow \kappa$, then $\pi \cdot d \in dom(t)$ is equivalent to $d \in dom(K)$ and, furthermore, for every $d \in dom(K)$, the type constructor $t(\pi \cdot d)$ has image kind $K(d)$. If π is in the domain of t, then the *subtree* of t rooted at π, written t/π, is the partial function $\pi' \mapsto t(\pi \cdot \pi')$. A tree is *finite* if and only if it has finite domain. A tree is *regular* if and only if it has a finite number of distinct subtrees. Every finite tree is thus regular. Let $\mathcal{M}_\kappa$ consist of the *finite* (respectively *regular*) trees t such that $t(\epsilon)$ has image kind κ: then, we have a *finite* (respectively *regular*) *tree model.*

If F has signature $K \Rightarrow \kappa$, one may interpret F as the function that maps $T \in \mathcal{M}_K$ to the ground type $t \in \mathcal{M}_\kappa$ defined by $t(\epsilon) = F$ and $t/d = T(d)$ for $d \in dom(T)$, that is, the unique ground type whose head symbol is F and whose subtree rooted at d is $T(d)$. Then, we have a *free* tree model. Note that free finite tree models coincide with syntactic models, as defined in the previous example. □

Rows (§10.8) are interpreted in a tree model, albeit not a free one. The following examples suggest different ways of interpreting the subtyping predicate.

10.2.8 EXAMPLE [EQUALITY MODELS]: The simplest way of interpreting the subtyping predicate is to let $\leq$ denote equality on every $\mathcal{M}_\kappa$. Models that do so are referred to as *equality models.* When no predicate other than equality is available, we say that the model is *equality-only.* □

10.2.9 EXAMPLE [STRUCTURAL, NONSTRUCTURAL SUBTYPING]: Let a *variance* ν be a nonempty subset of $\{-,+\}$, written $-$ (*contravariant*), $+$ (*covariant*), or $\pm$ (*invariant*) for short. Define the *composition* of two variances as an associative, commutative operation with $+$ as neutral element, $\pm$ as absorbing element (that is, $\pm- = \pm+ = \pm\pm = \pm$), and such that $-- = +$. Now, consider a free (finite or regular) tree model, where every direction d comes with a fixed variance $\nu(d)$. Define the variance $\nu(\pi)$ of a path π as the composition of the variances of its elements. Let $\leqslant$ be a partial order on type constructors such that (i) if $F_1 \leqslant F_2$ holds and F_1 and F_2 have signature $K_1 \Rightarrow \kappa_1$ and $K_2 \Rightarrow \kappa_2$, respectively, then K_1 and K_2 agree on the intersection of their domains and κ_1 and κ_2 coincide; and (ii) $F_0 \leqslant F_1 \leqslant F_2$ implies $dom(F_0) \cap dom(F_2) \subseteq dom(F_1)$. Let $\leqslant^+$, $\leqslant^-$, and $\leqslant^\pm$ stand for $\leqslant$, $\geqslant$, and $=$, respectively. Then, define the interpretation of subtyping as follows: if $t_1, t_2 \in \mathcal{M}_\kappa$, let $t_1 \leq t_2$ hold if and only if, for every path $\pi \in dom(t_1) \cap dom(t_2)$, $t_1(\pi) \leqslant^{\nu(\pi)} t_2(\pi)$ holds. It is not difficult to check that $\leq$ is a partial order on every $\mathcal{M}_\kappa$. The reader is referred to Amadio and Cardelli (1993), Kozen, Palsberg, and Schwartzbach (1995), and Brandt and Henglein (1997) for more details about this construction. Models that define subtyping in this manner are referred to as *nonstructural subtyping models.*

A simple nonstructural subtyping model is obtained by: letting the directions *domain* and *codomain* be contra- and covariant, respectively; introducing, in addition to the type constructor $\rightarrow$, two type constructors $\bot$ and $\top$ of signature $\star$; and letting $\bot \leqslant \rightarrow \leqslant \top$. This gives rise to a model where $\bot$ is the least ground type, $\top$ is the greatest ground type, and the arrow type constructor is, as usual, contravariant in its domain and covariant in its codomain. This form of subtyping is called *nonstructural* because comparable ground types may have different shapes: consider, for instance, $\bot$ and $\bot \rightarrow \top$.

A typical use of nonstructural subtyping is in type systems for records. One may, for instance, introduce a covariant direction *content* of kind $\star$, a kind

$\circ$, a type constructor abs of signature $\circ$, a type constructor pre of signature $\{content \mapsto \star\} \Rightarrow \circ$, and let pre $\leqslant$ abs. This gives rise to a model where pre $t \leq$ abs holds for every $t \in \mathcal{M}_\star$. Again, comparable ground types may have different shapes: consider, for instance, pre $\top$ and abs. §10.8 says more about typechecking operations on records.

Nonstructural subtyping has been studied, for example, in Kozen, Palsberg, and Schwartzbach (1995), Palsberg, Wand, and O'Keefe (1997), Jim and Palsberg (1999), Pottier (2001b), Su et al. (2002), and Niehren and Priesnitz (2003).

An important particular case arises when any two type constructors related by $\leqslant$ have the same arity (and thus also the same signatures). In that case, it is not difficult to show that any two ground types related by subtyping must have the same shape, that is, if $t_1 \leq t_2$ holds, then $dom(t_1)$ and $dom(t_2)$ must coincide. For this reason, such an interpretation of subtyping is usually referred to as *atomic* or *structural* subtyping. It has been studied in the finite (Mitchell, 1984, 1991b; Tiuryn, 1992; Pratt and Tiuryn, 1996; Frey, 1997; Rehof, 1997; Kuncak and Rinard, 2003; Simonet, 2003) and regular (Tiuryn and Wand, 1993) cases. Structural subtyping is often used in automated program analyses that enrich standard types with atomic annotations without altering their shape. □

Many other kinds of constraints exist, which we lack space to list; see Comon (1994) for a short survey.

Throughout this chapter, we assume (unless otherwise stated) that the set of type constructors, the set of predicates, and the model—which, together, form the parameter X—are arbitrary, but fixed.

As usual, the meaning of a constraint is a function of the meaning of its free type variables and of its free program identifiers, which are respectively given by a *ground assignment* and a *ground environment.*

10.2.10 Definition: A *ground assignment* ϕ is a total, kind-preserving mapping from $\mathcal{V}$ into $\mathcal{M}$. Ground assignments are extended to types by $\phi(F\,\mathsf{T}_1 \ldots \mathsf{T}_n) = F(\phi(\mathsf{T}_1), \ldots, \phi(\mathsf{T}_n))$. Then, for every type T of kind κ, $\phi(\mathsf{T})$ is a ground type of kind κ.

A *ground type scheme* s is a set of ground types, which we require to be *upward-closed* with respect to subtyping: that is, $t \in s$ and $t \leq t'$ must imply $t' \in s$. A *ground environment* ψ is a partial mapping from identifiers to ground type schemes.

Because the syntax of type schemes and constraints is mutually recursive, so is their interpretation. The interpretation of a type scheme σ under a ground assignment ϕ and a ground environment ψ is a ground type scheme, written $(\phi, \psi)\sigma$. It is defined in Figure 10-5. The $\uparrow$ is the upward closure

Interpretation of type schemes:

$$(\phi, \psi)(\forall \bar{X}[C].T) = \uparrow\{\phi[\vec{X} \mapsto \vec{t}](T)\ ;\ \phi[\vec{X} \mapsto \vec{t}], \psi \models C\}$$

Interpretation of constraints:

$$\phi, \psi \models \text{true} \quad \text{(CM-TRUE)}$$

$$\frac{P(\phi(T_1), \ldots, \phi(T_n))}{\phi, \psi \models P\, T_1 \ldots T_n} \quad \text{(CM-PREDICATE)}$$

$$\frac{\phi, \psi \models C_1 \qquad \phi, \psi \models C_2}{\phi, \psi \models C_1 \wedge C_2} \quad \text{(CM-AND)}$$

$$\frac{\phi[\vec{X} \mapsto \vec{t}], \psi \models C}{\phi, \psi \models \exists \bar{X}.C} \quad \text{(CM-EXISTS)}$$

$$\frac{\phi, \psi[x \mapsto (\phi, \psi)\sigma] \models C}{\phi, \psi \models \text{def } x : \sigma \text{ in } C} \quad \text{(CM-DEF)}$$

$$\frac{\phi(T) \in \psi(x)}{\phi, \psi \models x \preceq T} \quad \text{(CM-INSTANCE)}$$

Figure 10-5: Meaning of constraints

operator and $\models$ is the constraint satisfaction predicate, defined next. The interpretation of a constraint C under a ground assignment ϕ and a ground environment ψ is a truth value, written $\phi, \psi \models C$ (read: ϕ and ψ *satisfy* C). The three-place predicate $\models$ is defined by the rules in Figure 10-5. A constraint C is *satisfiable* if and only if $\phi, \psi \models C$ holds for some ϕ and ψ. It is *false* (or *unsatisfiable*) otherwise. □

Let us now explain these definitions. The interpretation of the type scheme $\forall \bar{X}[C].T$ is a set of ground types, which we may refer to as the type scheme's *ground instances*. It contains the images of T under extensions of ϕ with new values for the universally quantified variables $\bar{X}$; these values may be arbitrary, but must be such that the constraint C is satisfied. We implicitly require $\vec{X}$ and $\vec{t}$ to have matching kinds, so that $\phi[\vec{X} \mapsto \vec{t}]$ remains a kind-preserving ground assignment. This set is upward closed, so any ground type that lies above a ground instance of σ is also a ground instance of σ. This interpretation is standard; see, for example, Pottier (2001a).

The rules that define $\models$ (Figure 10-5) are syntax-directed. CM-TRUE states that the constraint true is a tautology, that is, holds in every context. No rule matches the constraint false, which means that it holds in no context. CM-PREDICATE states that the meaning of a predicate application is given by the predicate's interpretation within the model. More specifically, if P's signature is $\kappa_1 \otimes \ldots \otimes \kappa_n \Rightarrow \cdot$, then, by well-formedness of the constraint, every T_i is of kind κ_i, so $\phi(T_i)$ is a ground type in $\mathcal{M}_{\kappa_i}$. By Definition 10.2.5, P denotes a predicate on $\mathcal{M}_{\kappa_1} \times \ldots \times \mathcal{M}_{\kappa_n}$, so the rule's premise is mathematically well-formed. It is independent of ψ, which is natural, since a predicate application has no free program identifiers. CM-AND requires each of the conjuncts to be valid in isolation. CM-EXISTS allows the type variables $\vec{X}$ to denote arbitrary ground types $\vec{t}$ within C, independently of their image through ϕ. CM-DEF deals with type scheme introduction constraints, of the form def $x : \sigma$ in C. It binds x, within C, to the ground type scheme currently denoted by σ. Last, CM-INSTANCE concerns type scheme instantiation constraints of the form $x \preceq T$. Such a constraint is valid if and only if the ground type denoted by T is a member of the ground type scheme denoted by x.

It is possible to prove that the constraints def $x : \sigma$ in C and $[x \mapsto \sigma]C$ have the same meaning, where the latter denotes the capture-avoiding substitution of σ for x throughout C. As a matter of fact, it would have been possible to use this equivalence as a definition of the meaning of def constraints, but the present style is pleasant as well. This confirms our claim that the def form is an explicit substitution form.

Because constraints lie at the heart of our treatment of ML-the-type-system, most of our proofs involve establishing logical properties of constraints. These properties are usually not stated in terms of the satisfaction predicate $\models$, which is too low-level. Instead, we reason in terms of *entailment* or *equivalence* assertions. Let us first define these notions.

10.2.11 DEFINITION: We write $C_1 \Vdash C_2$, and say that C_1 *entails* C_2, if and only if, for every ground assignment ϕ and for every ground environment ψ, the assertion $\phi, \psi \models C_1$ implies $\phi, \psi \models C_2$. We write $C_1 \equiv C_2$, and say that C_1 and C_2 are *equivalent*, if and only if $C_1 \Vdash C_2$ and $C_2 \Vdash C_1$ hold. □

In other words, C_1 entails C_2 when C_1 imposes stricter requirements on its free type variables and program identifiers than C_2 does. Note that C is unsatisfiable if and only if $C \equiv$ false holds. It is straightforward to check that entailment is reflexive and transitive and that $\equiv$ is indeed an equivalence relation.

We immediately exploit the notion of constraint equivalence to define what it means for a type constructor to be *covariant*, *contravariant*, or *invariant* with respect to one of its parameters. Let F be a type constructor of signature $\kappa_1 \otimes \ldots \otimes \kappa_n \Rightarrow \kappa$. Let $i \in \{1, \ldots, n\}$. F is covariant (respectively contravariant, invariant) with respect to its ith parameter if and only if, for all types $T_1, \ldots, T_n$ and T_i' of appropriate kinds, the constraint $F\,T_1 \ldots T_i \ldots T_n \leq F\,T_1 \ldots T_i' \ldots T_n$ is equivalent to $T_i \leq T_i'$ (respectively $T_i' \leq T_i$, $T_i = T_i'$).

10.2.12 EXERCISE [★, ↛]: Check the following facts: (i) in an equality model, covariance, contravariance, and invariance coincide; (ii) in an equality free tree model, every type constructor is invariant with respect to each of its parameters; and (iii) in a nonstructural subtyping model, if the direction d has been declared covariant (respectively contravariant, invariant), then every type constructor whose arity includes d is covariant (respectively contravariant, invariant) with respect to d. □

In the following, we require the type constructor $\rightarrow$ to be contravariant with respect to its domain and covariant with respect to its codomain—a standard requirement in type systems with subtyping (*TAPL*, Chapter 15). This requirement is summed up by the following equivalence law:

$$\mathsf{T}_1 \rightarrow \mathsf{T}_2 \leq \mathsf{T}_1' \rightarrow \mathsf{T}_2' \equiv \mathsf{T}_1' \leq \mathsf{T}_1 \wedge \mathsf{T}_2 \leq \mathsf{T}_2' \qquad \text{(C-ARROW)}$$

Note that this requirement bears on the interpretation of types and of the subtyping predicate. In an equality free tree model, by (i) and (ii) in the exercise above, it is always satisfied. In a nonstructural subtyping model, it boils down to requiring that the directions *domain* and *codomain* be declared contravariant and covariant, respectively. In the general case, we do not have any knowledge of the model and cannot formulate a more precise requirement. Thus, it is up to the designer of the model to ensure that C-ARROW holds.

We also exploit the notion of constraint equivalence to define what it means for two type constructors to be *incompatible*. Two type constructors F_1 and F_2 with the same image kind are incompatible if and only if all constraints of the form $F_1\,\vec{\mathsf{T}}_1 \leq F_2\,\vec{\mathsf{T}}_2$ and $F_2\,\vec{\mathsf{T}}_2 \leq F_1\,\vec{\mathsf{T}}_1$ are false. Note that in an equality free tree model, any two distinct type constructors are incompatible. In the following, we often indicate that a newly introduced type constructor must be *isolated*. We implicitly require that, whenever both F_1 and F_2 are isolated, F_1 and F_2 be incompatible. Thus, the notion of isolation provides a concise and modular way of stating a collection of incompatibility requirements. We require the type constructor $\rightarrow$ to be isolated.

Reasoning with Constraints

In this section, we give a number of equivalence laws that are often useful and help understand the meaning of constraints. To begin, we note that entailment is preserved by arbitrary constraint contexts, as stated by the theorem below. As a result, constraint equivalence is a congruence. Throughout this chapter, these facts are often used implicitly.

10.2.13 THEOREM [CONGRUENCE]: $C_1 \Vdash C_2$ implies $\mathbb{C}[C_1] \Vdash \mathbb{C}[C_2]$. □

Next, we define what it means for a constraint to determine a set of type variables. In brief, C determines $\bar{\mathsf{Y}}$ if and only if, given a ground assignment for $ftv(C) \setminus \bar{\mathsf{Y}}$ and given that C holds, it is possible to reconstruct, in a unique way, a ground assignment for $\bar{\mathsf{Y}}$. Determinacy appears in the equivalence law C-LETALL on page 418 and is exploited by the constraint solver in §10.6.

10.2.14 DEFINITION: *C determines* $\bar{Y}$ if and only if, for every environment Γ, two ground assignments that satisfy $\mathsf{def}\ \Gamma\ \mathsf{in}\ C$ and that coincide outside $\bar{Y}$ must coincide on $\bar{Y}$ as well. □

We now give a toolbox of constraint equivalence laws. It is worth noting that they do not form a complete axiomatization of constraint equivalence; in fact, they cannot, since the syntax and meaning of constraints is partly unspecified.

10.2.15 THEOREM: All equivalence laws in Figure 10-6 hold. □

Let us explain. C-And and C-AndAnd state that conjunction is commutative and associative. C-Dup states that redundant conjuncts may be freely added or removed, where a conjunct is redundant if and only if it is entailed by another conjunct. Throughout this chapter, these three laws are often used implicitly. C-ExEx and C-Ex* allow grouping consecutive existential quantifiers and suppressing redundant ones, where a quantifier is redundant if and only if the variables bound by it do not occur free within its scope. C-ExAnd allows conjunction and existential quantification to commute, provided no capture occurs; it is known as a *scope extrusion* law. When the rule is oriented from left to right, its side-condition may always be satisfied by suitable α-conversion. C-ExTrans states that it is equivalent for a type T to be an instance of σ or to be a supertype of some instance of σ. We note that the instances of a monotype are its supertypes, that is, by Definition 10.2.3, $\mathsf{T}' \preceq \mathsf{T}$ and $\mathsf{T}' \leq \mathsf{T}$ are equivalent. As a result, specializing C-ExTrans to the case where σ is a monotype, we find that $\mathsf{T}' \leq \mathsf{T}$ is equivalent to $\exists \mathsf{Z}.(\mathsf{T}' \leq \mathsf{Z} \wedge \mathsf{Z} \leq \mathsf{T})$, for fresh Z, a standard equivalence law. When oriented from left to right, it becomes an interesting simplification law: in a chain of subtyping constraints, an intermediate variable such as Z may be suppressed, provided it is local, as witnessed by the existential quantifier $\exists \mathsf{Z}$. C-InId states that, within the scope of the binding $\mathsf{x} : \sigma$, every free occurrence of x may be safely replaced with σ. The restriction to free occurrences stems from the side-condition $\mathsf{x} \notin dpi(\mathbb{C})$. When the rule is oriented from left to right, its other side-conditions, which require the context $\mathsf{let}\ \mathsf{x} : \sigma\ \mathsf{in}\ \mathbb{C}$ not to capture σ's free type variables or free program identifiers, may always be satisfied by suitable α-conversion. C-In* complements the previous rule by allowing redundant let bindings to be simplified. We note that C-InId and C-In* provide a simple procedure for eliminating let forms. C-InAnd states that the let form commutes with conjunction; C-InAnd* spells out a common particular case. C-InEx states that it commutes with existential quantification. When the rule is oriented from left to right, its side-condition may always be satisfied by suitable α-conversion. C-LetLet states that let forms may commute, provided they bind distinct

$$C_1 \wedge C_2 \equiv C_2 \wedge C_1 \qquad \text{(C-And)}$$

$$(C_1 \wedge C_2) \wedge C_3 \equiv C_1 \wedge (C_2 \wedge C_3) \qquad \text{(C-AndAnd)}$$

$$C_1 \wedge C_2 \equiv C_1 \quad \text{if } C_1 \Vdash C_2 \qquad \text{(C-Dup)}$$

$$\exists\bar{X}.\exists\bar{Y}.C \equiv \exists\bar{X}\bar{Y}.C \qquad \text{(C-ExEx)}$$

$$\exists\bar{X}.C \equiv C \quad \text{if } \bar{X} \# ftv(C) \qquad \text{(C-Ex*)}$$

$$(\exists\bar{X}.C_1) \wedge C_2 \equiv \exists\bar{X}.(C_1 \wedge C_2) \quad \text{if } \bar{X} \# ftv(C_2) \qquad \text{(C-ExAnd)}$$

$$\exists Z.(\sigma \preceq Z \wedge Z \leq T) \equiv \sigma \preceq T \quad \text{if } Z \notin ftv(\sigma, T) \qquad \text{(C-ExTrans)}$$

$$\text{let } x : \sigma \text{ in } \mathbb{C}[x \preceq T] \equiv \text{let } x : \sigma \text{ in } \mathbb{C}[\sigma \preceq T] \qquad \text{(C-InId)}$$
$$\text{if } x \notin dpi(\mathbb{C}) \text{ and } dtv(\mathbb{C}) \# ftv(\sigma) \text{ and } \{x\} \cup dpi(\mathbb{C}) \# fpi(\sigma)$$

$$\text{let } \Gamma \text{ in } C \equiv \exists\Gamma \wedge C \quad \text{if } dpi(\Gamma) \# fpi(C) \qquad \text{(C-In*)}$$

$$\text{let } \Gamma \text{ in } (C_1 \wedge C_2) \equiv (\text{let } \Gamma \text{ in } C_1) \wedge (\text{let } \Gamma \text{ in } C_2) \qquad \text{(C-InAnd)}$$

$$\text{let } \Gamma \text{ in } (C_1 \wedge C_2) \equiv (\text{let } \Gamma \text{ in } C_1) \wedge C_2 \quad \text{if } dpi(\Gamma) \# fpi(C_2) \qquad \text{(C-InAnd*)}$$

$$\text{let } \Gamma \text{ in } \exists\bar{X}.C \equiv \exists\bar{X}.\text{let } \Gamma \text{ in } C \quad \text{if } \bar{X} \# ftv(\Gamma) \qquad \text{(C-InEx)}$$

$$\text{let } \Gamma_1; \Gamma_2 \text{ in } C \equiv \text{let } \Gamma_2; \Gamma_1 \text{ in } C \qquad \text{(C-LetLet)}$$
$$\text{if } dpi(\Gamma_1) \# dpi(\Gamma_2) \text{ and } dpi(\Gamma_2) \# fpi(\Gamma_1) \text{ and } dpi(\Gamma_1) \# fpi(\Gamma_2)$$

$$\text{let } x : \forall\bar{X}[C_1 \wedge C_2].T \text{ in } C_3 \equiv C_1 \wedge \text{let } x : \forall\bar{X}[C_2].T \text{ in } C_3 \quad \text{if } \bar{X} \# ftv(C_1) \qquad \text{(C-LetAnd)}$$

$$\text{let } \Gamma; x : \forall\bar{X}[C_1].T \text{ in } C_2 \equiv \text{let } \Gamma; x : \forall\bar{X}[\text{let } \Gamma \text{ in } C_1].T \text{ in } C_2 \qquad \text{(C-LetDup)}$$
$$\text{if } \bar{X} \# ftv(\Gamma) \text{ and } dpi(\Gamma) \# fpi(\Gamma)$$

$$\text{let } x : \forall\bar{X}[\exists\bar{Y}.C_1].T \text{ in } C_2 \equiv \text{let } x : \forall\bar{X}\bar{Y}[C_1].T \text{ in } C_2 \quad \text{if } \bar{Y} \# ftv(T) \qquad \text{(C-LetEx)}$$

$$\text{let } x : \forall\bar{X}\bar{Y}[C_1].T \text{ in } C_2 \equiv \exists\bar{Y}.\text{let } x : \forall\bar{X}[C_1].T \text{ in } C_2 \qquad \text{(C-LetAll)}$$
$$\text{if } \bar{Y} \# ftv(C_2) \text{ and } \exists\bar{X}.C_1 \text{ determines } \bar{Y}$$

$$\exists X.(T \leq X \wedge \text{let } x : X \text{ in } C) \equiv \text{let } x : T \text{ in } C \quad \text{if } X \notin ftv(T, C) \qquad \text{(C-LetSub)}$$

$$\vec{X} = \vec{T} \wedge [\vec{X} \mapsto \vec{T}]C \equiv \vec{X} = \vec{T} \wedge C \qquad \text{(C-Eq)}$$

$$\text{true} \equiv \exists\bar{X}.(\vec{X} = \vec{T}) \quad \text{if } \bar{X} \# ftv(\vec{T}) \qquad \text{(C-Name)}$$

$$[\vec{X} \mapsto \vec{T}]C \equiv \exists\bar{X}.(\vec{X} = \vec{T} \wedge C) \quad \text{if } \bar{X} \# ftv(\vec{T}) \qquad \text{(C-NameEq)}$$

Figure 10-6: Constraint equivalence laws

program identifiers and provided no free program identifiers are captured in the process. C-LetAnd allows the conjunct C_1 to be moved outside of the constrained type scheme $\forall\bar{X}[C_1 \wedge C_2].T$, provided it does not involve any of the universally quantified type variables $\bar{X}$. When oriented from left to right, the rule yields an important simplification law: indeed, taking an instance of $\forall\bar{X}[C_2].T$ is less expensive than taking an instance of $\forall\bar{X}[C_1 \wedge C_2].T$, since the latter involves creating a copy of C_1, while the former does not. C-LetDup allows pushing a series of let bindings into a constrained type scheme, provided no capture occurs in the process. It is not used as a simplification law but as a tool in some proofs. C-LetEx states that it does not make any difference for a set of type variables $\bar{Y}$ to be existentially quantified inside a constrained type scheme or part of the type scheme's universal quantifiers. Indeed, in either case, taking an instance of the type scheme means producing a constraint where $\bar{Y}$ is existentially quantified. C-LetAll states that it is equivalent for a set of type variables $\bar{Y}$ to be part of a type scheme's universal quantifiers or existentially bound outside the let form, provided these type variables are determined. In other words, when a type variable is sufficiently constrained, it does not matter whether it is polymorphic or monomorphic. Together, C-LetEx and C-LetAll allow, in some situations, hoisting existential quantifiers out of the left-hand side of a let form.

10.2.16 Example: C-LetAll would be invalid without the condition that $\exists\bar{X}.C_1$ determines $\bar{Y}$. Consider, for instance, the constraint $\mathsf{let}\ x : \forall Y.Y \to Y\ \mathsf{in}\ (x \preceq \mathsf{int} \to \mathsf{int} \wedge x \preceq \mathsf{bool} \to \mathsf{bool})$ **(1)**, where int and bool are incompatible nullary type constructors. By C-InId and C-In*, it is equivalent to $\forall Y.Y \to Y \leq \mathsf{int} \to \mathsf{int} \wedge \forall Y.Y \to Y \leq \mathsf{bool} \to \mathsf{bool}$ which, by Definition 10.2.3, means $\exists Y.(Y \to Y \leq \mathsf{int} \to \mathsf{int}) \wedge \exists Y.(Y \to Y \leq \mathsf{bool} \to \mathsf{bool})$, that is, true. Now, if C-LetAll was valid without its side-condition, then (1) would also be equivalent to $\exists Y.\mathsf{let}\ x : Y \to Y\ \mathsf{in}\ (x \preceq \mathsf{int} \to \mathsf{int} \wedge x \preceq \mathsf{bool} \to \mathsf{bool})$, which by C-InId and C-In* is $\exists Y.(Y \to Y \leq \mathsf{int} \to \mathsf{int} \wedge Y \to Y \leq \mathsf{bool} \to \mathsf{bool})$. By C-Arrow and C-ExTrans, this is $\mathsf{int} = \mathsf{bool}$, that is, false. Thus, the law is invalid in this case. It is easy to see why: when the type scheme σ contains a $\forall Y$ quantifier, every instance of σ receives its own $\exists Y$ quantifier, making Y a distinct (local) type variable; but when Y is not universally quantified, all instances of σ share references to a single (global) type variable Y. This corresponds to the intuition that, in the former case, σ is polymorphic in Y, while in the latter case, it is monomorphic in Y. It is possible to prove that, when deprived of its side-condition, C-LetAll is only an entailment law, that is, its right-hand side entails its left-hand side. Similarly, it is in general invalid to hoist an existential quantifier out of the left-hand side of a let form. To see this, one may study the (equivalent) constraint $\mathsf{let}\ x : \forall X[\exists Y.X = Y \to Y].X\ \mathsf{in}\ (x \preceq \mathsf{int} \to \mathsf{int} \wedge x \preceq \mathsf{bool} \to \mathsf{bool})$. Naturally, in the above examples, the side-condition "true determines Y" does not hold: by Definition 10.2.14, it is equivalent to "two ground assignments that coincide outside Y must coincide on Y as well," which is false when $\mathcal{M}_\star$ contains two distinct elements, such as int and bool here.

There are cases, however, where the side-condition does hold. For instance, we later prove that $\exists$X.Y = int determines Y; see Lemma 10.6.7. As a result, C-LETALL states that let x : $\forall$XY[Y = int].Y $\rightarrow$ X in C **(1)** is equivalent to $\exists$Y.let x : $\forall$X[Y = int].Y $\rightarrow$ X in C **(2)**, provided Y $\notin$ $ftv(C)$. The intuition is simple: because Y is forced to assume the value int by the equation Y = int, it makes no difference whether Y is or isn't universally quantified. By C-LETAND, (2) is equivalent to $\exists$Y.(Y = int $\wedge$ let x : $\forall$X.Y $\rightarrow$ X in C) **(3)**. In an efficient constraint solver, simplifying (1) into (3) before using C-INID to eliminate the let form is worthwhile, since doing so obviates the need for copying the type variable Y and the equation Y = int at every free occurrence of x inside C. □

C-LETSUB is the analog of an environment strengthening lemma: roughly speaking, it states that, if a constraint holds under the assumption that x has type X, where X is some supertype of T, then it also holds under the assumption that x has type T. The last three rules deal with the equality predicate. C-EQ states that it is valid to replace equals with equals; note the absence of a side-condition. When oriented from left to right, C-NAME allows introducing fresh names $\vec{X}$ for the types $\vec{T}$. As always, $\vec{X}$ stands for a vector of distinct type variables; $\vec{T}$ stands for a vector of the same length of types of appropriate kind. Of course, this makes sense only if the definition is not circular, that is, if the type variables $\bar{X}$ do not occur free within the terms $\bar{T}$. When oriented from right to left, C-NAME may be viewed as a simplification law: it allows eliminating type variables whose value has been determined. C-NAMEEQ is a combination of C-EQ and C-NAME. It shows that applying an idempotent substitution to a constraint C amounts to placing C within a certain context.

So far, we have considered def a primitive constraint form and defined the let form in terms of def, conjunction, and existential quantification. The motivation for this approach was to simplify the (omitted) proofs of several constraint equivalence laws. However, in the remainder of this chapter, we work with let forms exclusively and never employ the def construct. This offers us an extra property: every constraint that contains a false subconstraint must be false.

10.2.17 LEMMA: $\mathbb{C}$[false] ≡ false. □

Reasoning with Constraints in an Equality-Only Syntactic Model

We have given a number of equivalence laws that are valid with respect to any interpretation of constraints, that is, within any model. However, an important special case is that of *equality-only syntactic models.* Indeed, in that specific setting, our constraint-based type systems are in close correspondence with DM. In brief, we aim to prove that every satisfiable constraint C such that $fpi(C) = \emptyset$ admits a *canonical solved form* and to show that this notion corresponds to the standard concept of a *most general unifier.* These results are exploited when we relate HM(X) with Damas and Milner's system (p. 428).

Thus, let us now assume that constraints are interpreted in an equality-only syntactic model. Let us further assume that, for every kind κ, (i) there are at least *two* type constructors of image kind κ and (ii) for every type constructor F of image kind κ, there exists $t \in \mathcal{M}_\kappa$ such that $t(\epsilon) = F$. We refer to models that violate (i) or (ii) as *degenerate*; one may argue that such models are of little interest. The assumption that the model is nondegenerate is used in the proof of Theorem 10.3.7. Last, throughout the present subsection we manipulate only constraints that have *no free program identifiers.*

A *solved form* is a conjunction of equations, where the left-hand sides are distinct type variables that do not appear in the right-hand sides, possibly surrounded by a number of existential quantifiers. Our definition is identical to Lassez, Maher, and Marriott's solved forms (1988) and to Jouannaud and Kirchner's tree solved forms (1991), except we allow for prenex existential quantifiers, which are made necessary by our richer constraint language. Jouannaud and Kirchner also define *dag* solved forms, which may be exponentially smaller. Because we define solved forms only for proof purposes, we need not take performance into account at this point. The efficient constraint solver presented in §10.6 does manipulate graphs, rather than trees. Type scheme introduction and instantiation constructs cannot appear within solved forms; indeed, provided the constraint at hand has no free program identifiers, they can be expanded away. For this reason, their presence in the constraint language has no impact on the results contained in this section.

10.2.18 DEFINITION: A *solved form* is of the form $\exists \bar{Y}.(\vec{X} = \vec{T})$, where $\bar{X} \# ftv(\vec{T})$. □

Solved forms offer a convenient way of reasoning about constraints because every satisfiable constraint is equivalent to one. This property is established by the following lemma.

10.2.19 LEMMA: Every constraint is equivalent to either a solved form or $\mathtt{false}$. □

It is possible to impose further restrictions on solved forms. A solved form $\exists \bar{Y}.(\vec{X} = \vec{T})$ is *canonical* if and only if its free type variables are exactly $\bar{X}$. This is stated, in an equivalent way, by the following definition.

10.2.20 DEFINITION: A *canonical solved form* is a constraint of the form $\exists \bar{Y}.(\vec{X} = \vec{T})$, where $ftv(\vec{T}) \subseteq \bar{Y}$ and $\bar{X} \# \bar{Y}$. □

10.2.21 LEMMA: Every solved form is equivalent to a canonical solved form. □

It is easy to describe the solutions of a canonical solved form: they are the ground refinements of the substitution $[\vec{X} \mapsto \vec{T}]$. Hence, every canonical solved form is satisfiable.

The following definition allows entertaining a dual view of canonical solved forms, either as constraints or as idempotent type substitutions. The latter view is commonly found in standard treatments of unification (Lassez, Maher, and Marriott, 1988; Jouannaud and Kirchner, 1991) and in classic presentations of ML-the-type-system.

10.2.22 DEFINITION: If $[\vec{X} \mapsto \vec{T}]$ is an idempotent substitution of domain $\bar{X}$, let $\exists[\vec{X} \mapsto \vec{T}]$ denote the canonical solved form $\exists\bar{Y}.(\vec{X} = \vec{T})$, where $\bar{Y} = ftv(\vec{T})$. An idempotent substitution θ is a *most general unifier* of the constraint C if and only if $\exists\theta$ and C are equivalent. □

By definition, equivalent constraints admit the same most general unifiers. Many properties of canonical solved forms may be reformulated in terms of most general unifiers. By Lemmas 10.2.19 and 10.2.21, every satisfiable constraint admits a most general unifier.

10.3 HM(X)

Constraint-based type systems appeared during the 1980s (Mitchell, 1984; Fuh and Mishra, 1988) and were widely studied during the following decade (Curtis, 1990; Aiken and Wimmers, 1993; Jones, 1994; Smith, 1994; Palsberg, 1995; Trifonov and Smith, 1996; Fähndrich, 1999; Pottier, 2001b). We now present one such system, baptized HM(X) because it is a *parameterized* extension of Hindley and Milner's type discipline; the meaning of the parameter X was explained on page 411. Its original description is due to Odersky, Sulzmann, and Wehr (1999). Since then, it has been completed in a number of works including Müller (1998), Sulzmann, Müller, and Zenger (1999), Sulzmann (2000), Pottier (2001a), and Skalka and Pottier (2002). Each of these presentations introduces minor variations. Here, we follow Pottier (2001a), which is itself inspired by Sulzmann, Müller, and Zenger (1999).

Definition

Our presentation of HM(X) relies on the constraint language introduced in §10.2. Technically, our approach to constraints is less abstract than that of Odersky, Sulzmann, and Wehr (1999). We interpret constraints within a model, give conjunction and existential quantification their standard mean-

$$\frac{\Gamma(\mathtt{x}) = \sigma \qquad C \Vdash \exists\sigma}{C, \Gamma \vdash \mathtt{x} : \sigma} \quad \text{(HMX-VAR)}$$

$$\frac{C, (\Gamma; \mathtt{z} : \mathsf{T}) \vdash \mathtt{t} : \mathsf{T}'}{C, \Gamma \vdash \lambda\mathtt{z}.\mathtt{t} : \mathsf{T} \rightarrow \mathsf{T}'} \quad \text{(HMX-ABS)}$$

$$\frac{C, \Gamma \vdash \mathtt{t}_1 : \mathsf{T} \rightarrow \mathsf{T}' \qquad C, \Gamma \vdash \mathtt{t}_2 : \mathsf{T}}{C, \Gamma \vdash \mathtt{t}_1\ \mathtt{t}_2 : \mathsf{T}'} \quad \text{(HMX-APP)}$$

$$\frac{C, \Gamma \vdash \mathtt{t}_1 : \sigma \qquad C, (\Gamma; \mathtt{z} : \sigma) \vdash \mathtt{t}_2 : \mathsf{T}}{C, \Gamma \vdash \mathtt{let}\ \mathtt{z} = \mathtt{t}_1\ \mathtt{in}\ \mathtt{t}_2 : \mathsf{T}} \quad \text{(HMX-LET)}$$

$$\frac{C \wedge D, \Gamma \vdash \mathtt{t} : \mathsf{T} \qquad \bar{\mathsf{X}} \# \mathit{ftv}(C, \Gamma)}{C \wedge \exists\bar{\mathsf{X}}.D, \Gamma \vdash \mathtt{t} : \forall\bar{\mathsf{X}}[D].\mathsf{T}} \quad \text{(HMX-GEN)}$$

$$\frac{C, \Gamma \vdash \mathtt{t} : \forall\bar{\mathsf{X}}[D].\mathsf{T}}{C \wedge D, \Gamma \vdash \mathtt{t} : \mathsf{T}} \quad \text{(HMX-INST)}$$

$$\frac{C, \Gamma \vdash \mathtt{t} : \mathsf{T} \qquad C \Vdash \mathsf{T} \leq \mathsf{T}'}{C, \Gamma \vdash \mathtt{t} : \mathsf{T}'} \quad \text{(HMX-SUB)}$$

$$\frac{C, \Gamma \vdash \mathtt{t} : \sigma \qquad \bar{\mathsf{X}} \# \mathit{ftv}(\Gamma, \sigma)}{\exists\bar{\mathsf{X}}.C, \Gamma \vdash \mathtt{t} : \sigma} \quad \text{(HMX-EXISTS)}$$

Figure 10-7: Typing rules for HM(X)

ing, and derive a number of equivalence laws (§10.2). Odersky et al., on the other hand, do not explicitly rely on a logical interpretation; instead, they axiomatize constraint equivalence, that is, they consider a number of equivalence laws as axioms. Thus, they ensure that their high-level proofs, such as type soundness and correctness and completeness of type inference, are independent of the low-level details of the logical interpretation of constraints. Their approach is also more general, since it allows dealing with other logical interpretations, such as "open-world" interpretations, where constraints are interpreted not within a fixed model, but within a family of extensions of a "current" model. In this chapter, we have avoided this extra layer of abstraction and given fixed meaning to constraints, making things somewhat simpler. However, the changes required to adopt Odersky et al.'s approach would not be extensive, since the forthcoming proofs do indeed rely mostly on constraint equivalence laws, rather than on low-level details of the logical interpretation of constraints.

Another slight departure from Odersky et al.'s work lies in the fact that we have enriched the constraint language with type scheme introduction and instantiation forms, which were absent in the original presentation of HM(X). To prevent this addition from affecting HM(X), we require the constraints that appear in HM(X) typing judgments to have no free program identifiers. Note that this does not prevent them from containing let forms.

The type system HM(X) consists of a four-place judgment whose parameters are a constraint C, an environment Γ, an expression $\mathtt{t}$, and a type scheme σ. A judgment is written $C, \Gamma \vdash \mathtt{t} : \sigma$ and is read: *under the assumptions C and Γ, the expression $\mathtt{t}$ has type σ*. One may view C as an assumption about the judgment's free type variables and Γ as an assumption about $\mathtt{t}$'s free program identifiers. Recall that Γ now contains constrained type schemes, and that σ is a constrained type scheme.

We would like the validity of a typing judgment to depend not on the syntax, but only on the meaning of its constraint assumption. We enforce this point of view by considering judgments equal modulo equivalence of their constraint assumptions. In other words, the typing judgments $C, \Gamma \vdash \mathtt{t} : \sigma$ and $D, \Gamma \vdash \mathtt{t} : \sigma$ are considered identical when $C \equiv D$ holds. A judgment is *valid*, or *holds*, if and only if it is derivable via the rules given in Figure 10-7. Note that a valid judgment may involve an arbitrary constraint. A (closed) program $\mathtt{t}$ is *well-typed* within the (closed) environment Γ if and only if a judgment of the form $C, \Gamma \vdash \mathtt{t} : \sigma$ holds for some satisfiable constraint C. One might wonder why we do not make the apparently stronger requirement that $C \wedge \exists\sigma$ be satisfiable; however, by inspection of the typing rules, the reader may check that, if the above judgment is derivable, then $C \Vdash \exists\sigma$ holds, hence the two requirements are equivalent.

Let us now explain the rules. Like DM-VAR, HMX-VAR looks up the environment to determine the type scheme associated with the program identifier $\mathtt{x}$. Its second premise plays a minor technical role: as noted in the previous paragraph, its presence helps simplify the definition of well-typedness. HMX-ABS, HMX-APP, and HMX-LET are identical to DM-ABS, DM-APP, and DM-LET, respectively, except that the assumption C is made available to every subderivation. We recall that the type T may be viewed as the type scheme $\forall\emptyset[\mathtt{true}].\mathsf{T}$ (Definitions 10.1.18 and 10.2.2). As a result, types form a subset of type schemes, which implies that $\Gamma; \mathtt{z} : \mathsf{T}$ is a well-formed environment and $C, \Gamma \vdash \mathtt{t} : \mathsf{T}$ a well-formed typing judgment. To understand HMX-GEN, it is best to first consider the particular case where C is $\mathtt{true}$. This yields the following, simpler rule:

$$\frac{D, \Gamma \vdash \mathtt{t} : \mathsf{T} \qquad \bar{\mathsf{X}} \,\#\, ftv(\Gamma)}{\exists\bar{\mathsf{X}}.D, \Gamma \vdash \mathtt{t} : \forall\bar{\mathsf{X}}[D].\mathsf{T}} \qquad \text{(HMX-GEN')}$$

The second premise is identical to that of DM-GEN: the type variables that are generalized must not occur free within the environment. The conclusion forms the type scheme $\forall\bar{\mathsf{X}}[D].\mathsf{T}$, where the type variables $\bar{\mathsf{X}}$ have become universally quantified, but are still subject to the constraint D. Note that the type variables that occur free in D may include not only $\bar{\mathsf{X}}$, but also other type variables, typically free in Γ. HMX-GEN may be viewed as a more liberal version of HMX-GEN', whereby part of the current constraint, namely C, need not be copied if it does not concern the type variables that are being generalized, namely $\bar{\mathsf{X}}$. This optimization is important in practice, because C may be very large. An intuitive explanation for its correctness is given by the constraint equivalence law C-LETAND, which expresses the same optimization in terms of let constraints. Because HM(X) does not use let constraints, the optimization is hard-wired into the typing rule. As a last technical remark, let us point out that replacing $C \wedge \exists \bar{X}.D$ with $C \wedge D$ in HMX-GEN's conclusion would not affect the set of derivable judgments; this fact may be established using HMX-EXISTS and Lemma 10.3.1. HMX-INST allows taking an instance of a type scheme. The reader may be surprised to find that, contrary to DM-INST, it does not involve a type substitution. Instead, the rule merely drops the universal quantifier, which amounts to applying the identity substitution $\vec{X} \mapsto \vec{X}$. One should recall, however, that type schemes are considered equal modulo α-conversion, so it is possible to rename the type scheme's universal quantifiers prior to using HMX-INST. The reason why this provides sufficient expressive power appears in Exercise 10.3.2 below. The constraint D carried by the type scheme is recorded as part of the current constraint in HMX-INST's conclusion. The *subsumption* rule HMX-SUB allows a type T to be replaced at any time with an arbitrary supertype T'. Because both T and T' may have free type variables, whether $\mathsf{T} \leq \mathsf{T}'$ holds depends on the current assumption C, which is why the rule's second premise is an entailment assertion. An operational explanation of HMX-SUB is that it requires all uses of subsumption to be explicitly recorded in the current constraint. Note that HMX-SUB remains a useful and necessary rule even when subtyping is interpreted as equality: then, it allows exploiting the type equations found in C. Last, HMX-EXISTS allows the type variables that occur only within the current constraint to become existentially quantified. As a result, these type variables no longer occur free in the rule's conclusion; in other words, they have become local to the subderivation rooted at the premise. One may prove that the presence of HMX-EXISTS in the type system does not augment the set of well-typed programs, but does augment the set of valid typing judgments; it is a pleasant technical convenience. Indeed, because judgments are considered equal modulo constraint equivalence, constraints may be transparently simplified at any time. (By simplifying a constraint, we mean replacing it with an equivalent constraint whose syntactic representation is considered simpler.) Bearing this fact in mind, one finds that an effect of rule HMX-EXISTS is to enable more simplifications: because constraint equivalence is a congruence, $C \equiv D$ implies $\exists \bar{X}.C \equiv \exists \bar{X}.D$, but the converse does not hold in general. For instance, there is in general no way of simplifying the judgment $\mathsf{X} \leq \mathsf{Y} \leq \mathsf{Z}, \Gamma \vdash \mathtt{t} : \sigma$, but if it is known that Y does not appear free in Γ or σ, then HMX-EXISTS allows deriving $\exists \mathsf{Y}.(\mathsf{X} \leq \mathsf{Y} \leq \mathsf{Z}), \Gamma \vdash \mathtt{t} : \sigma$, which is the same judgment as $\mathsf{X} \leq \mathsf{Z}, \Gamma \vdash \mathtt{t} : \sigma$. Thus, an interesting simplification has been enabled. Note that $\mathsf{X} \leq \mathsf{Y} \leq \mathsf{Z} \equiv \mathsf{X} \leq \mathsf{Z}$ does not hold, while, according to C-EXTRANS, $\exists \mathsf{Y}.(\mathsf{X} \leq \mathsf{Y} \leq \mathsf{Z}) \equiv \mathsf{X} \leq \mathsf{Z}$ does.

A pleasant property of HM(X) is that strengthening a judgment's constraint assumption (that is, weakening the judgment itself) preserves its validity. It is worth noting that in traditional presentations, which rely more heavily on type substitutions, the analog of this result is a *type substitution* lemma; see for instance Tofte (1988), Lemma 2.7; Rémy (1992a), Lemma 1; Leroy (1992), Proposition 1.2; and Skalka and Pottier (2002), Lemma 3.4. Here, the lemma further states that weakening a judgment does not alter the shape of its derivation, a useful property when reasoning by induction on type derivations.

10.3.1 LEMMA [WEAKENING]: If $C' \Vdash C$, then every derivation of $C, \Gamma \vdash \mathtt{t} : \sigma$ may be turned into a derivation of $C', \Gamma \vdash \mathtt{t} : \sigma$ with the same shape. □

10.3.2 EXERCISE [RECOMMENDED, ★★]: In some presentations of HM(X), HMX-INST is replaced with the following variant:

$$\frac{C, \Gamma \vdash \mathtt{t} : \forall \bar{\mathsf{X}}[D].\mathsf{T} \qquad C \Vdash [\vec{\mathsf{X}} \mapsto \vec{\mathsf{T}}]D}{C, \Gamma \vdash \mathtt{t} : [\vec{\mathsf{X}} \mapsto \vec{\mathsf{T}}]\mathsf{T}} \quad \text{(HMX-INST')}$$

Show that HMX-INST' is admissible in our presentation of HM(X)—that is, if its premise is derivable according to the rules of Figure 10-7, then so is its conclusion. Thus, the choice between HMX-INST and HMX-INST' is only stylistic: it makes no difference in the system's expressive power. Because HMX-INST is more elementary, choosing it simplifies some proofs. □

10.3.3 EXERCISE [★]: Give a derivation of $\mathsf{true}, \emptyset \vdash \lambda \mathtt{z}.\mathtt{z} : \mathsf{int} \to \mathsf{int}$. Give a derivation of $\mathsf{true}, \emptyset \vdash \lambda \mathtt{z}.\mathtt{z} : \forall \mathsf{X}.\mathsf{X} \to \mathsf{X}$. Check that the former judgment also follows from the latter via HMX-INST' (Exercise 10.3.2), and determine which derivation of $\mathsf{true}, \emptyset \vdash \lambda \mathtt{z}.\mathtt{z} : \mathsf{int} \to \mathsf{int}$ this path gives rise to. □

We do not give a direct type soundness proof for HM(X). Instead, in the forthcoming sections, we prove that well-typedness in HM(X) is equivalent to the satisfiability of a certain constraint and use that characterization as a basis for our type soundness proof. A direct type soundness result, based on a denotational semantics, may be found in Odersky, Sulzmann, and Wehr (1999). Another type soundness proof, which follows Wright and Felleisen's syntactic approach (1994), appears in Skalka and Pottier (2002). Last, a hybrid approach, which combines some of the advantages of the previous two, is given in Pottier (2001a).

An Alternate Presentation of HM(X)

The presentation of HM(X) given in Figure 10-7 has only four syntax-directed rules out of eight. It is a good specification of the type system, but it is far

$$\frac{\Gamma(\mathtt{x}) = \forall\bar{X}[D].\mathsf{T}}{C \wedge D, \Gamma \vdash \mathtt{x} : \mathsf{T}} \quad \text{(HMD-VARINST)}$$

$$\frac{C, (\Gamma; \mathtt{z} : \mathsf{T}) \vdash \mathtt{t} : \mathsf{T}'}{C, \Gamma \vdash \lambda \mathtt{z}.\mathtt{t} : \mathsf{T} \to \mathsf{T}'} \quad \text{(HMD-ABS)}$$

$$\frac{C, \Gamma \vdash \mathtt{t}_1 : \mathsf{T} \to \mathsf{T}' \qquad C, \Gamma \vdash \mathtt{t}_2 : \mathsf{T}}{C, \Gamma \vdash \mathtt{t}_1\ \mathtt{t}_2 : \mathsf{T}'} \quad \text{(HMD-APP)}$$

$$\frac{C \wedge D, \Gamma \vdash \mathtt{t}_1 : \mathsf{T}_1 \qquad \bar{X} \# \mathit{ftv}(C, \Gamma) \qquad C \wedge \exists\bar{X}.D, (\Gamma; \mathtt{z} : \forall\bar{X}[D].\mathsf{T}_1) \vdash \mathtt{t}_2 : \mathsf{T}_2}{C \wedge \exists\bar{X}.D, \Gamma \vdash \mathtt{let}\ \mathtt{z} = \mathtt{t}_1\ \mathtt{in}\ \mathtt{t}_2 : \mathsf{T}_2} \quad \text{(HMD-LETGEN)}$$

$$\frac{C, \Gamma \vdash \mathtt{t} : \mathsf{T} \qquad C \Vdash \mathsf{T} \leq \mathsf{T}'}{C, \Gamma \vdash \mathtt{t} : \mathsf{T}'} \quad \text{(HMD-SUB)}$$

$$\frac{C, \Gamma \vdash \mathtt{t} : \mathsf{T} \qquad \bar{X} \# \mathit{ftv}(\Gamma, \mathsf{T})}{\exists\bar{X}.C, \Gamma \vdash \mathtt{t} : \mathsf{T}} \quad \text{(HMD-EXISTS)}$$

Figure 10-8: An alternate presentation of HM(X)

from an algorithmic description. As a first step towards such a description, we provide an alternate presentation of HM(X), where generalization is performed only at `let` expressions and instantiation takes place only at references to program identifiers (Figure 10-8). This presentation only has two non-syntax-directed rules, making it sometimes easier to reason about. It has the property that all judgments are of the form $C, \Gamma \vdash \mathtt{t} : \mathsf{T}$, rather than $C, \Gamma \vdash \mathtt{t} : \sigma$. The following theorem states that the two presentations are indeed equivalent.

10.3.4 THEOREM: $C, \Gamma \vdash \mathtt{t} : \mathsf{T}$ is derivable via the rules of Figure 10-8 if and only if it is a valid HM(X) judgment. □

This theorem shows that the rule sets of Figures 10-7 and 10-8 derive the same monomorphic judgments, that is, the same judgments of the form $C, \Gamma \vdash \mathtt{t} : \mathsf{T}$. The fact that judgments of the form $C, \Gamma \vdash \mathtt{t} : \sigma$, where σ is a not a monotype, cannot be derived using the new rule set is a technical simplification, without deep significance.

10.3.5 EXERCISE [★★★, ↛]: Show that it is possible to simplify the presentation of Damas and Milner's type system in an analogous manner. That is, define an alternate set of typing rules for DM, which allows deriving judgments of the form $\Gamma \vdash \mathtt{t} : \mathsf{T}$; then, show that this new rule set is equivalent to the previous one, in the same sense as above. Which auxiliary properties of DM does your proof require? A solution is given by Clement, Despeyroux, Despeyroux, and Kahn (1986). □

Relating HM(X) with Damas and Milner's Type System

In order to explain our interest in HM(X), we wish to show that it is more general than Damas and Milner's type system. Since HM(X) really is a family of type systems, we must make this statement more precise. First, every member of the HM(X) family contains DM. Conversely, DM contains HM(=), the constraint-based type system obtained by specializing HM(X) to the setting of an equality-only syntactic model.

The first of these assertions is easy to prove because the mapping from DM judgments to HM(X) judgments is essentially the identity: every valid DM judgment may be viewed as a valid HM(X) judgment under the trivial assumption true. This statement relies on the fact that the DM type scheme $\forall\bar{\mathsf{X}}.\mathsf{T}$ is identified with the constrained type scheme $\forall\bar{\mathsf{X}}[\mathsf{true}].\mathsf{T}$, so DM type schemes (respectively environments) form a subset of HM(X) type schemes (respectively environments). Its proof is easy and relies on Exercise 10.3.2.

10.3.6 THEOREM: If $\Gamma \vdash \mathsf{t} : \mathsf{S}$ holds in DM, then $\mathsf{true}, \Gamma \vdash \mathsf{t} : \mathsf{S}$ holds in HM(X). □

We are now interested in proving that HM(=), as defined above, is contained within DM. To this end, we must translate every HM(=) judgment to a DM judgment. It turns out that this is possible if the original judgment's constraint assumption is satisfiable. The translation relies on the fact that the definition of HM(=) assumes an equality-only syntactic model. Indeed, in that setting, every satisfiable constraint admits a most general unifier (Definition 10.2.22), whose properties we make essential use of.

Unfortunately, due to lack of space, we cannot give the details of this translation, which are fairly involved. Let us merely say that, given a type scheme σ and an idempotent type substitution θ such that $ftv(\sigma) \subseteq dom(\theta)$ and $\exists\theta \Vdash \exists\sigma$ hold, the translation of σ under θ is a DM type scheme, written $[\![\sigma]\!]_\theta$. Its meaning is intended to be the same as that of the HM(X) type scheme $\theta(\sigma)$. For instance, under the identity substitution, the translation of the HM(X) type scheme $\forall\mathsf{XY}[\mathsf{X} = \mathsf{Y} \rightarrow \mathsf{Y}].\mathsf{X}$ is the DM type scheme $\forall\mathsf{Z}.\mathsf{Z} \rightarrow \mathsf{Z}$. The translation is extended to environments in such a way that $[\![\Gamma]\!]_\theta$ is defined when $ftv(\Gamma) \subseteq dom(\theta)$ holds. We are now ready to state the main theorem.

10.3.7 THEOREM: Let $C, \Gamma \vdash \mathsf{t} : \sigma$ hold in HM(=). Let θ be a most general unifier of C such that $ftv(\Gamma, \sigma) \subseteq dom(\theta)$. Then, $[\![\Gamma]\!]_\theta \vdash \mathsf{t} : [\![\sigma]\!]_\theta$ holds in DM. □

Note that, by requiring θ to be a most general unifier of C, we also require C to be satisfiable. Judgments that carry an unsatisfiable constraint cannot be translated.

Together, Theorems 10.3.6 and 10.3.7 yield a precise correspondence between DM and HM(=): there exists a compositional translation from each to the other. In other words, they may be viewed as two equivalent formulations of a single type system. One might also say that HM(=) is a constraint-based formulation of DM. Furthermore, Theorem 10.3.6 states that every member of the HM(X) family is an extension of DM. This explains our double interest in HM(X), as an alternate formulation of DM, which we believe is more pleasant for reasons already discussed, and as a more expressive framework.

10.4 Constraint Generation

We now explain how to reduce type inference problems for HM(X) to constraint solving problems. A type inference problem consists of a type environment Γ, an expression $\mathtt{t}$, and a type T of kind $\star$. The problem is to determine whether there exists a satisfiable constraint C such that $C, \Gamma \vdash \mathtt{t} : \mathsf{T}$ holds. A constraint solving problem consists of a constraint C. The problem is to determine whether C is satisfiable. To reduce a type inference problem $(\Gamma, \mathtt{t}, \mathsf{T})$ to a constraint solving problem, we must produce a constraint C that is both *sufficient* and *necessary* for $C, \Gamma \vdash \mathtt{t} : \mathsf{T}$ to hold. Below, we explain how to compute such a constraint, which we write $[\![\Gamma \vdash \mathtt{t} : \mathsf{T}]\!]$. We check that it is indeed *sufficient* by proving $[\![\Gamma \vdash \mathtt{t} : \mathsf{T}]\!], \Gamma \vdash \mathtt{t} : \mathsf{T}$. That is, the constraint $[\![\Gamma \vdash \mathtt{t} : \mathsf{T}]\!]$ is specific enough to guarantee that $\mathtt{t}$ has type T under environment Γ. We say that constraint generation is *sound.* We check that it is indeed *necessary* by proving that, for every constraint C, the validity of $C, \Gamma \vdash \mathtt{t} : \mathsf{T}$ implies $C \Vdash [\![\Gamma \vdash \mathtt{t} : \mathsf{T}]\!]$. That is, every constraint that guarantees that $\mathtt{t}$ has type T under environment Γ is at least as specific as $[\![\Gamma \vdash \mathtt{t} : \mathsf{T}]\!]$. We say that constraint generation is *complete.* Together, these properties mean that $[\![\Gamma \vdash \mathtt{t} : \mathsf{T}]\!]$ is the *least specific* constraint that guarantees that $\mathtt{t}$ has type T under environment Γ.

We now see how to reduce a type inference problem to a constraint solving problem. Indeed, if there exists a satisfiable constraint C such that $C, \Gamma \vdash \mathtt{t} : \mathsf{T}$ holds, then, by the completeness property, $C \Vdash [\![\Gamma \vdash \mathtt{t} : \mathsf{T}]\!]$ holds, so $[\![\Gamma \vdash \mathtt{t} : \mathsf{T}]\!]$ is satisfiable. Conversely, by the soundness property, if $[\![\Gamma \vdash \mathtt{t} : \mathsf{T}]\!]$ is satisfiable, then we have a satisfiable constraint C such that $C, \Gamma \vdash \mathtt{t} : \mathsf{T}$ holds. In other words, $\mathtt{t}$ is well-typed with type T under environment Γ if and only if $[\![\Gamma \vdash \mathtt{t} : \mathsf{T}]\!]$ is satisfiable.

The reader may be somewhat puzzled by the fact that our formulation of the type inference problem requires an appropriate type T to be known in advance, whereas the very purpose of type inference seems to consist in *discovering* the type of $\mathtt{t}$! In other words, we have made T an *input* of the constraint generation algorithm, instead of an *output.* Fortunately, this causes no loss of generality, because it is possible to let T be a type variable X, chosen fresh for Γ. Then, the constraint produced by the algorithm will contain information about X. This is the point of the following exercise.

10.4.1 EXERCISE [RECOMMENDED, ★]: Let $\mathsf{X} \notin ftv(\Gamma)$. Show that, if there exist a satisfiable constraint C and a type T such that $C, \Gamma \vdash \mathtt{t} : \mathsf{T}$ holds, then there exists a satisfiable constraint C' such that $C', \Gamma \vdash \mathtt{t} : \mathsf{X}$ holds. Conclude that, given a closed environment Γ and an arbitrary type variable X, the term t is well-typed within Γ if and only if $[\![\Gamma \vdash \mathtt{t} : \mathsf{X}]\!]$ is satisfiable. □

This shows that providing T as an input to the constraint generation procedure is not essential. We adopt this style because it is convenient. A somewhat naive alternative would be to provide Γ and t only, and to have the procedure return both a constraint C and a type T (Sulzmann, Müller, and Zenger, 1999). It turns out that this does not quite work, because C and T may mention "fresh" variables, which we must be able to quantify over, if we are to avoid an informal treatment of "freshness." Thus, the true alternative is to provide Γ and t only and to have the procedure return a *type scheme* σ (Bourdoncle and Merz, 1997; Bonniot, 2002).

The existence of a sound and complete constraint generation procedure is the analog of the existence of *principal type schemes* in classic presentations of ML-the-type-system (Damas and Milner, 1982). Indeed, a principal type scheme is least specific in the sense that all valid types are substitution instances of it. Here, the constraint $[\![\Gamma \vdash \mathtt{t} : \mathsf{T}]\!]$ is least specific in the sense that all valid constraints entail it. More about principal types and principal typings may be found in Jim (1996) and Wells (2002).

How do we perform constraint generation? A standard approach (Sulzmann, Müller, and Zenger, 1999; Bonniot, 2002) is to define $[\![\Gamma \vdash \mathtt{t} : \mathsf{T}]\!]$ by induction on the structure of t. At every `let` node, following HMD-LETGEN, part of the current constraint, namely D, is turned into a type scheme, namely $\forall \bar{\mathsf{X}}[D].\mathsf{T}$, which is used to extend the environment. Then, at every occurrence of the program variable that was bound at this `let` node, following HMD-VARINST, this type scheme is retrieved from the environment, and a copy of D is added back to the current constraint. If such an approach is adopted, it is important to simplify the type scheme $\forall \bar{\mathsf{X}}[D].\mathsf{T}$ before it is stored in the environment, because it would be inefficient to copy an unsimplified constraint. In other words, in an efficient implementation of this standard approach, constraint generation and constraint simplification cannot be separated.

Type scheme introduction and elimination constraints, which we introduced in §10.2 but did not use in the specification of HM(X), are intended as a means of solving this problem. By extending our vocabulary, we are able to achieve the desired separation between constraint generation, on the one hand, and constraint solving and simplification, on the other hand, without

$$
\begin{aligned}
[\![x : T]\!] &= x \preceq T \\
[\![\lambda z.t : T]\!] &= \exists X_1X_2.(\text{let } z : X_1 \text{ in } [\![t : X_2]\!] \wedge X_1 \rightarrow X_2 \leq T) \\
[\![t_1\ t_2 : T]\!] &= \exists X_2.([\![t_1 : X_2 \rightarrow T]\!] \wedge [\![t_2 : X_2]\!]) \\
[\![\mathtt{let}\ z = t_1\ \mathtt{in}\ t_2 : T]\!] &= \text{let } z : \forall X[[\![t_1 : X]\!]].X \text{ in } [\![t_2 : T]\!]
\end{aligned}
$$

Figure 10-9: Constraint generation

compromising efficiency. Indeed, by exploiting these new constraint forms, we may define a constraint generation procedure whose time and space complexity is linear, because it no longer involves copying subconstraints back and forth between the environment and the constraint that is being generated. (It is then up to the constraint solver to perform simplification and copying, if and when necessary.) In fact, the environment is suppressed altogether: we define $[\![t : T]\!]$ by induction on the structure of t—notice the absence of the parameter Γ. Then, the constraint $[\![\Gamma \vdash t : T]\!]$ discussed above becomes syntactic sugar for let Γ in $[\![t : T]\!]$. We now employ the full constraint language: the program identifiers that appear free in t may also appear free in $[\![t : T]\!]$, as part of instantiation constraints. They become bound when $[\![t : T]\!]$ is placed within the context let Γ in []. A similar approach to constraint generation appears in Müller (1994).

The defining equations for $[\![t : T]\!]$ appear in Figure 10-9. We refer to them as the *constraint generation rules.* The definition is quite terse and certainly simpler than the declarative specification of HM(X) given in Figure 10-7; yet, we prove below that the two are equivalent.

Before explaining the definition, we state the requirements that bear on the type variables X_1, X_2, and X, which appear bound in the right-hand sides of the second, third, and fourth equations. These type variables must have kind $\star$. They must be chosen distinct (that is, $X_1 \neq X_2$ in the second equation) and fresh for the objects that appear on the left-hand side—that is, the type variables that appear bound in an equation's right-hand side must not occur free in the term and type that appear in the equation's left-hand side. Provided this restriction is obeyed, different choices of X_1, X_2, and X lead to α-equivalent constraints—that is, to the same constraint, since we identify objects up to α-conversion—which guarantees that the above equations make sense. Since expressions do not have free type variables, the freshness requirement may be simplified to: type variables that appear bound in an equation's right-hand side must not appear free in T. However, this simplification would be rendered invalid by the introduction of open type annotations within expressions. Note that we are able to state a precise (as opposed to informal) freshness requirement. This is made possible by the fact that $[\![t : T]\!]$ has no free type variables other than those of T, which in turn depends on our explicit use of existential quantification to limit the scope of auxiliary variables.

Let us now review the four equations. The first equation may be read: x *has type* T *if and only if* T *is an instance of the type scheme associated with* x. Note that we no longer consult the type scheme associated with x in the environment—indeed, there is no environment. Instead, we merely generate an instantiation constraint, where x appears free. (For this reason, every program identifier that occurs free within t typically also occurs free within $[\![t : T]\!]$.) This constraint acquires its full meaning when it is later placed within a context of the form let x : σ in []. This equation roughly corresponds to HMD-VARINST. The second equation may be read: λz.t *has type* T *if and only if, for some* X_1 *and* X_2*, (i) under the assumption that* z *has type* X_1, t *has type* X_2*, and (ii)* T *is a supertype of* $X_1 \to X_2$. Here, the types associated with z and t must be fresh type variables, namely X_1 and X_2, because we cannot in general guess them. These type variables are *bound* so as to guarantee that the generated constraint is unique up to α-conversion. They are *existentially* bound because we intend the constraint solver to discover their value. Condition (i) is expressed by the subconstraint let z : X_1 in $[\![t : X_2]\!]$. This makes sense as follows. The constraint $[\![t : X_2]\!]$ typically contains a number of instantiation constraints bearing on z, of the form $z \preceq T_i$. By wrapping it within the context let z : X_1 in [], we effectively require every T_i to be a supertype of X_1. Note that z does not occur free in the constraint let z : X_1 in $[\![t : X_2]\!]$, which is necessary for well-formedness of the definition, since it does not occur free in λz.t. This equation roughly corresponds to HMD-EXISTS, HMD-ABS, and HMD-SUB. The third equation may be read: t_1 t_2 *has type* T *if and only if, for some* X_2, t_1 *has type* $X_2 \to T$ *and* t_2 *has type* X_2. Here, the fresh type variable X_2 stands for the unknown type of t_2. This equation roughly corresponds to HMD-APP. The last equation, which roughly corresponds to HMD-LETGEN, may be read: `let` z = t_1 `in` t_2 *has type* T *if and only if, under the assumption that* z *has every type* X *such that* $[\![t_1 : X]\!]$ *holds,* t_2 *has type* T. As in the case of λ-abstractions, the instantiation constraints bearing on z that appear within $[\![t_2 : T]\!]$ are given a meaning via a let prefix. The difference is that z may now be assigned a type scheme, as opposed to a monotype. An appropriate type scheme is built as follows. The constraint $[\![t_1 : X]\!]$ is the least specific constraint that must be imposed on the fresh type variable X so as to make it a valid type for t_1. In other words, t_1 has every type X such that $[\![t_1 : X]\!]$ holds, and none other. That is, the type scheme $\forall X[[\![t_1 : X]\!]].X$, abbreviated σ in the following, is a *principal* type scheme for t_1. It is interesting to note that there is no question of which type variables to generalize. Indeed, by construction, no type variables other than X may appear free in $[\![t_1 : X]\!]$, so we cannot generalize more variables. On the other hand, it is valid to generalize X, since it does not appear free anywhere else. This interesting simplification is inspired by Sulzmann, Müller, and Zenger (1999), where a similar technique is used. Now, what happens when $[\![t_2 : T]\!]$ is placed inside the context let $z : \sigma$ in []? When placed inside this context, an instantiation constraint of the form $z \preceq T'$ acquires the meaning $\sigma \preceq T'$, which by definition of σ and by Lemma 10.4.6 (see below) is equivalent to $[\![t_1 : T']\!]$. Thus, the constraint produced by the fourth equation simulates a textual expansion of the `let` construct, where every occurrence of z would be replaced with t_1. Thanks to type scheme introduction and instantiation constraints, however, this effect is achieved without duplication of source code or constraints. In other words, constraint generation has linear time and space complexity.

10.4.2 EXERCISE [★, ↛]: Define the *size* of an expression, of a type, and of a constraint, viewed as abstract syntax trees. Check that the size of $[\![t : T]\!]$ is linear in the sum of the sizes of t and T. □

10.4.3 EXERCISE [RECOMMENDED, ★, ↛]: Compute and simplify, as best as you can, the constraint $[\![\texttt{let } f = \lambda z.z \texttt{ in } f\ f : T]\!]$. □

We now state several properties of constraint generation. We begin with soundness, whose statement was explained above.

10.4.4 THEOREM [SOUNDNESS]: let Γ in $[\![t : T]\!], \Gamma \vdash t : T$. □

The following lemmas are used in the proof of the completeness property and in a number of other occasions. The first two state that $[\![t : T]\!]$ is *covariant* with respect to T. Roughly speaking, this means that enough subtyping constraints are generated to achieve completeness with respect to HMD-SUB.

10.4.5 LEMMA: $[\![t : T]\!] \wedge T \leq T' \Vdash [\![t : T']\!]$. □

10.4.6 LEMMA: $X \notin ftv(T)$ implies $\exists X.([\![t : X]\!] \wedge X \leq T) \equiv [\![t : T]\!]$. □

The next lemma gives a simplified version of the second constraint generation rule, in the specific case where the expected type is an arrow type. Thus, fresh type variables need not be generated; one may directly use the arrow's domain and codomain instead.

10.4.7 LEMMA: $[\![\lambda z.t : T_1 \rightarrow T_2]\!]$ is equivalent to let $z : T_1$ in $[\![t : T_2]\!]$. □

We conclude with the completeness property. The theorem states that if, within HM(X), t has type T under assumptions C and Γ, then C must be at least as specific as $\text{let}\ \Gamma\ \text{in}\ [\![\mathtt{t} : \mathsf{T}]\!]$. The statement requires C and Γ to have no free program identifiers, which is natural, since they are part of an HM(X) judgment. The hypothesis $C \Vdash \exists\Gamma$ excludes the somewhat pathological situation where Γ contains constraints not apparent in C. This hypothesis vanishes when Γ is the initial environment; see Definition 10.5.2.

10.4.8 **Theorem [Completeness]:** Let $C \Vdash \exists\Gamma$. Assume $fpi(C,\Gamma) = \emptyset$. If $C, \Gamma \vdash \mathtt{t} : \mathsf{T}$ holds in HM(X), then C entails $\text{let}\ \Gamma\ \text{in}\ [\![\mathtt{t} : \mathsf{T}]\!]$. □

10.5 Type Soundness

We are now ready to establish type soundness for our type system. The statement that we wish to prove is sometimes known as *Milner's slogan*: "Well-typed programs do not go wrong" (Milner, 1978). Below, we define well-typedness in terms of our constraint generation rules, for the sake of convenience, and establish type soundness with respect to that particular definition. Theorems 10.3.6 and 10.4.8 imply that type soundness also holds when well-typedness is defined with respect to the typing judgments of DM or HM(X). We establish type soundness by following Wright and Felleisen's so-called *syntactic approach* (1994). The approach consists of isolating two independent properties. *Subject reduction*, whose exact statement will be given below, implies that well-typedness is preserved by reduction. *Progress* states that no stuck configuration is well-typed. It is immediate to check that, if both properties hold, then no well-typed program can reduce to a stuck configuration. Subject reduction itself depends on a key lemma, usually known as a (term) *substitution lemma*. Here is a version of this lemma, stated in terms of the constraint generation rules.

10.5.1 **Lemma:** $\text{let}\ \mathtt{z} : \forall\bar{\mathsf{X}}[[\![\mathtt{t}_2 : \mathsf{T}_2]\!]].\mathsf{T}_2\ \text{in}\ [\![\mathtt{t}_1 : \mathsf{T}_1]\!]$ entails $[\![[\mathtt{z} \mapsto \mathtt{t}_2]\mathtt{t}_1 : \mathsf{T}_1]\!]$. □

Before going on, let us give a few definitions and formulate several requirements. First, we must define an initial environment Γ_0, which assigns a type scheme to every constant. A couple of requirements must be established to ensure that Γ_0 is consistent with the semantics of constants, as specified by $\xrightarrow{\delta}$. Second, we must extend constraint generation and well-typedness to configurations, as opposed to programs, since reduction operates on configurations. Last, we must formulate a restriction to tame the interaction between side effects and `let`-polymorphism, which is unsound if unrestricted.

10.5.2 **Definition:** Let Γ_0 be an environment whose domain is the set of constants $\mathcal{Q}$. We require $ftv(\Gamma_0) = \emptyset$, $fpi(\Gamma_0) = \emptyset$, and $\exists\Gamma_0 \equiv \text{true}$. We refer to Γ_0 as the *initial* typing environment. □

10.5.3 **Definition:** Let ref be an isolated, invariant type constructor of signature $\star \Rightarrow \star$. A *store type* M is a finite mapping from memory locations to types. We write ref M for the environment that maps every $m \in dom(M)$ to ref $M(m)$. Assuming $dom(\mu)$ and $dom(M)$ coincide, the constraint $[\![\mu : M]\!]$ is defined as the conjunction of the constraints $[\![\mu(m) : M(m)]\!]$, where m ranges over $dom(\mu)$. Under the same assumption, the constraint $[\![\mathtt{t}/\mu : \mathsf{T}/M]\!]$ is defined as $[\![\mathtt{t} : \mathsf{T}]\!] \wedge [\![\mu : M]\!]$. A closed configuration $\mathtt{t}/\mu$ is *well-typed* if and only if there exist a type T and a store type M such that $dom(\mu) = dom(M)$ and the constraint let Γ_0; ref M in $[\![\mathtt{t}/\mu : \mathsf{T}/M]\!]$ is satisfiable. □

The type ref T is the type of references (that is, memory locations) that store data of type T (*TAPL*, Chapter 13). It must be *invariant* in its parameter, reflecting the fact that references may be both read and written.

A store is a complex object: it may contain values that indirectly refer to each other via memory locations. In fact, it is a representation of the graph formed by objects and pointers in memory, which may contain cycles. We rely on store types to deal with such cycles. In the definition of well-typedness, the store type M imposes a constraint on the contents of the store—the value $\mu(m)$ must have type $M(m)$—but also plays the role of a hypothesis: by placing the constraint $[\![\mathtt{t}/\mu : \mathsf{T}/M]\!]$ within the context let ref M in [], we give meaning to free occurrences of memory locations within $[\![\mathtt{t}/\mu : \mathsf{T}/M]\!]$, and stipulate that it is valid to assume that m has type $M(m)$. In other words, we essentially view the store as a large, mutually recursive binding of locations to values. The context let Γ_0 in [] gives meaning to occurrences of constants within $[\![\mathtt{t}/\mu : \mathsf{T}/M]\!]$.

We now define a relation between configurations that plays a key role in the statement of the subject reduction property. The point of subject reduction is to guarantee that well-typedness is preserved by reduction. However, such a simple statement is too weak to be amenable to inductive proof. Thus, for the purposes of the proof, we must be more specific. To begin, let us consider the simpler case of a pure semantics, that is, a semantics without stores. Then, we must state that if an expression t has type T under a certain constraint, then its reduct t′ has type T under the same constraint. In terms of generated constraints, this statement becomes: let Γ_0 in $[\![\mathtt{t} : \mathsf{T}]\!]$ entails let Γ_0 in $[\![\mathtt{t}' : \mathsf{T}]\!]$. Let us now return to the general case, where a store is present. The statement of well-typedness for a configuration $\mathtt{t}/\mu$ now involves a store type M whose domain is that of μ. So, the statement of well-typedness for its reduct $\mathtt{t}'/\mu'$ must involve a store type M' whose domain is that of μ', which is larger if allocation occurred. The types of existing memory locations must not change: we must request that M and M' agree on $dom(M)$, that is, M' must extend M. Furthermore, the types assigned to new memory locations in

$dom(M') \setminus dom(M)$ might involve new type variables, that is, variables that do not appear free in M or T. We must allow these variables to be hidden—that is, existentially quantified—otherwise the entailment assertion cannot hold. These considerations lead us to the following definition:

10.5.4 **Definition:** $\mathtt{t}/\mu \sqsubseteq \mathtt{t}'/\mu'$ holds if and only if, for every type T and for every store type M such that $dom(\mu) = dom(M)$, there exist a set of type variables $\bar{\mathsf{Y}}$ and a store type M' such that $\bar{\mathsf{Y}} \# ftv(\mathsf{T}, M)$ and $ftv(M') \subseteq \bar{\mathsf{Y}} \cup ftv(M)$ and $dom(M') = dom(\mu')$ and M' extends M and

$$\begin{array}{l} \mathsf{let}\ \Gamma_0; \mathsf{ref}\ M\ \ \mathsf{in}\ [\![\mathtt{t}\ /\mu\ \ : \mathsf{T}/M\ ]\!] \\ \Vdash \exists \bar{\mathsf{Y}}.\mathsf{let}\ \Gamma_0; \mathsf{ref}\ M'\ \mathsf{in}\ [\![\mathtt{t}'/\mu' : \mathsf{T}/M']\!]. \end{array}$$

The relation $\sqsubseteq$ is intended to express a connection between a configuration and its reduct. Thus, subject reduction may be stated as: $(\longrightarrow) \subseteq (\sqsubseteq)$, that is, $\sqsubseteq$ is indeed a conservative description of reduction. □

We have introduced an initial environment Γ_0 and used it in the definition of well-typedness, but we haven't yet ensured that the type schemes assigned to constants are an adequate description of their semantics. We now formulate two requirements that relate Γ_0 with $\xrightarrow{\delta}$. They are specializations of the subject reduction and progress properties to configurations that involve an application of a constant. They represent proof obligations that must be discharged when concrete definitions of $\mathcal{Q}$, $\xrightarrow{\delta}$, and Γ_0 are given.

10.5.5 **Definition:** We require (i) $(\xrightarrow{\delta}) \subseteq (\sqsubseteq)$; and (ii) if the configuration $\mathtt{c}\ \mathtt{v}_1\ \ldots\ \mathtt{v}_k/\mu$ (where $k \geq 0$) is well-typed, then either it is reducible, or $\mathtt{c}\ \mathtt{v}_1\ \ldots\ \mathtt{v}_k$ is a value. □

The last point that remains to be settled before proving type soundness is the interaction between side effects and `let`-polymorphism. The following example illustrates the problem:

$$\mathtt{let}\ \mathtt{r} = \mathtt{ref}\ \lambda\mathtt{z}.\mathtt{z}\ \mathtt{in}\ \mathtt{let}\ _ = (\mathtt{r} := \lambda\mathtt{z}.(\mathtt{z}\ \hat{+}\ \hat{1}))\ \mathtt{in}\ !\mathtt{r}\ \mathtt{true}$$

This expression reduces to $\mathtt{true}\ \hat{+}\ \hat{1}$, so it must not be well-typed. Yet, if natural type schemes are assigned to `ref`, !, and := (see Example 10.7.5), then it is well-typed with respect to the rules given so far, because r receives the polymorphic type scheme $\forall \mathsf{X}.\mathsf{ref}\ (\mathsf{X} \to \mathsf{X})$, which allows writing a function of type $\mathsf{int} \to \mathsf{int}$ into r and reading it back with type $\mathsf{bool} \to \mathsf{bool}$. The problem is that `let`-polymorphism simulates a textual duplication of the `let`-bound expression `ref` λz.z, while the semantics first reduces it to a value m, causing a new binding $m \mapsto \lambda\mathtt{z}.\mathtt{z}$ to appear in the store, then duplicates the address m.

The new store binding is not duplicated: both copies of m refer to the same memory cell. For this reason, generalization is unsound in this case, and must be restricted. Many authors have attempted to come up with a sound type system that accepts all pure programs and remains flexible enough in the presence of side effects (Tofte, 1988; Leroy, 1992). These proposals are often complex, which is why they have been abandoned in favor of an extremely simple syntactic restriction, known as the *value restriction* (Wright, 1995).

10.5.6 DEFINITION: A program satisfies the *value restriction* if and only if all subexpressions of the form `let z =` t_1 `in` t_2 are in fact of the form `let z =` v_1 `in` t_2. In the following, we assume that either all constants have pure semantics, or all programs satisfy the value restriction. □

Put slightly differently, the value restriction states that only values may be generalized. This eliminates the problem altogether, since duplicating values does not affect a program's semantics. Note that any program that does not satisfy the value restriction can be turned into one that does and has the same semantics: it suffices to change `let z =` t_1 `in` t_2 into $(\lambda z.t_2)\ t_1$ when t_1 is not a value. Of course, such a transformation may cause the program to become ill-typed. In other words, the value restriction causes some perfectly safe programs to be rejected. In particular, in its above form, it prevents generalizing applications of the form $c\ v_1\ \ldots\ v_k$, where c is a destructor of arity k. This is excessive, because many destructors have pure semantics; only a few, such as `ref`, allocate new mutable storage. Furthermore, we use pure destructors to encode numerous language features (§10.7). Fortunately, it is easy to relax the restriction to allow generalizing not only values, but also a more general class of *nonexpansive* expressions, whose syntax guarantees that such expressions cannot allocate new mutable storage (that is, expand the domain of the store). The term nonexpansive was coined by Tofte (1988). Nonexpansive expressions may include applications of the form $c\ t_1\ \ldots\ t_k$, where c is a pure destructor of arity k and $t_1, \ldots, t_k$ are nonexpansive. Experience shows that this slightly relaxed restriction is acceptable in practice. Some limitations remain: for instance, *constructor functions* (that is, functions that do not allocate mutable storage and build a value) are regarded as ordinary functions, so their applications are considered potentially expansive, even though a naked constructor application would be a value and thus considered nonexpansive. For instance, in the expression `let f = c v in let z = f w in t`, where `c` is a constructor of arity 2, the partial application `c v`, to which the name `f` is bound, is a constructor function (of arity 1). The program variable `z` cannot receive a polymorphic type scheme, because `f w` is not a value, even though it has the same semantic meaning as `c v w`, which is a value. A recent improvement to the value restriction (Garrigue, 2004) provides a partial remedy. Technically, the effect of the value restriction (as stated in Definition 10.5.6) is summarized by the following result.

10.5.7 LEMMA: Under the value restriction, the production $\mathcal{E} ::=$ `let z =` $\mathcal{E}$ `in t` may be suppressed from the grammar of evaluation contexts (Figure 10-1) without altering the operational semantics. □

We are finished with definitions and requirements. Let us now turn to the type soundness results.

10.5.8 THEOREM [SUBJECT REDUCTION]: $(\longrightarrow) \subseteq (\sqsubseteq)$. □

Subject reduction ensures that well-typedness is preserved by reduction.

10.5.9 COROLLARY: Let $\mathtt{t}/\mu \longrightarrow \mathtt{t}'/\mu'$. If $\mathtt{t}/\mu$ is well-typed, then so is $\mathtt{t}'/\mu'$. □

Let us now state the progress property.

10.5.10 THEOREM [PROGRESS]: If $\mathtt{t}/\mu$ is well-typed, then either it is reducible, or `t` is a value. □

We may now conclude:

10.5.11 THEOREM [TYPE SOUNDNESS]: Well-typed source programs do not go wrong. □

Recall that this result holds only if the requirements of Definition 10.5.5 are met. In other words, some proof obligations remain to be discharged when concrete definitions of $\mathcal{Q}$, $\xrightarrow{\delta}$, and Γ_0 are given. This is illustrated by several examples in §10.7 and §10.8.

10.6 Constraint Solving

We have introduced a parameterized constraint language, given equivalence laws describing the interaction between its logical connectives, and exploited them to prove theorems about type inference and type soundness, which are valid independently of the nature of primitive constraints—the so-called predicate applications. However, there would be little point in proposing a parameterized constraint solver, because much of the difficulty of designing an efficient constraint solver lies precisely in the treatment of primitive constraints and in its interaction with `let`-polymorphism. In this section, we focus on constraint solving in the setting of an *equality-only free tree model.* Thus, the constraint solver developed here allows performing type inference for HM(=) (that is, for Damas and Milner's type system) and for its extension with recursive types. Of course, some of its mechanisms may be useful in other settings. The program analysis and type inference literature abounds with constraint-based systems of all kinds; a short list of papers that put particular emphasis on constraint solving is Aiken and Wimmers (1992), Henglein (1993), Niehren, Müller, and Podelski (1997), Fähndrich (1999), Melski and Reps (2000), Müller, Niehren, and Treinen (2001), Pottier (2001b), Nielson, Nielson, and Seidl (2002), McAllester (2002; 2003), and Simonet (2003).

We begin with a rule-based presentation of a standard, efficient first-order unification algorithm. This yields a constraint solver for a subset of the constraint language, except for the type scheme introduction and instantiation forms. On top of it, we build a full constraint solver, which corresponds to the code that accompanies this chapter.

Unification

Unification is the process of solving equations between terms. It was first introduced by Robinson (1971), but his original algorithm could be very inefficient. Efficient algorithms, which perform unification in quasi-linear time, were independently proposed by Martelli and Montanari (1976; 1982) and by Huet (1976, Chapter 5). Both algorithms rely on a data structure that efficiently solves the *union-find* problem (Tarjan, 1975). Martelli and Montanari's algorithm performs unification in topological (top-down) order, and is thus restricted to the acyclic case, that is, to the case where equations are interpreted in a syntactic model. In this specific case, unification may actually be performed in truly linear time (Paterson and Wegman, 1978). On the other hand, Huet's algorithm is able to deal with cyclic structures. The acyclicity check is postponed until the very end of the solving process if equations are interpreted within a syntactic model, or omitted altogether if working within a regular tree model. Except for the final acyclicity check, Huet's algorithm is incremental. Furthermore, it is simple; we present a version of it here. Knight (1989) and Baader and Siekmann (1994) also describe Huet's algorithm, and provide further historical background and references.

Following Jouannaud and Kirchner (1991), we specify the algorithm as a (nondeterministic) system of constraint rewriting rules. As suggested above, it is almost the same for finite and regular tree models; only one rule, which implements the *occurs check*, must be removed in the latter case. In other words, the algorithm works with possibly cyclic data structures and does not rely in an essential way on the occurs check. In order to more closely reflect the behavior of the actual algorithm, and in particular the union-find data structure, we modify the syntax of constraints by replacing equations with multi-equations—equations involving an arbitrary number of types, as opposed to exactly two.

10.6.1 DEFINITION: Let there be, for every kind κ and for every $n \geq 1$, a predicate $=^n_\kappa$, of signature $\kappa^n \Rightarrow \cdot$, whose interpretation is (n-ary) equality. The predicate constraint $=^n_\kappa \mathsf{T}_1 \ldots \mathsf{T}_n$ is written $\mathsf{T}_1 = \ldots = \mathsf{T}_n$, and called a *multi-equation*. We consider the constraint true as a multi-equation of length 0 and let ϵ range over all multi-equations. In the following, we identify multi-equations up to permutations of their members, so a multi-equation ϵ of kind κ may be viewed as a finite *multiset* of types of kind κ. We write $\epsilon = \epsilon'$ for the multi-equation obtained by concatenating ϵ and ϵ'. □

Thus, we are interested in the following subset of the constraint language:

$$U ::= \mathsf{true} \mid \mathsf{false} \mid \epsilon \mid U \wedge U \mid \exists\bar{\mathsf{X}}.U$$

Equations are replaced with multi-equations; no other predicates are available. Type scheme introduction and instantiation forms are absent.

10.6.2 DEFINITION: A multi-equation is *standard* if and only if its variable members are distinct and it has at most one nonvariable member. A constraint U is *standard* if and only if every multi-equation inside U is standard and every variable that occurs (free or bound) in U is a member of at most one multi-equation inside U. (Note that to be a member of ϵ implies, but is not equivalent to, to occur free in ϵ.) □

A union-find algorithm maintains equivalence classes (that is, disjoint sets) of variables, and associates with each class a *descriptor*, which in our case is either absent or a nonvariable term. Thus, a *standard* constraint represents a state of the union-find algorithm. A constraint that is not standard may be viewed as a superposition of a state of the union-find algorithm, on the one hand, and of control information, on the other hand. For instance, a multi-equation of the form $\epsilon = \mathsf{T}_1 = \mathsf{T}_2$, where ϵ is made up of distinct variables and T_1 and T_2 are nonvariable terms, may be viewed, roughly speaking, as the equivalence class $\epsilon = \mathsf{T}_1$, together with a pending request to solve $\mathsf{T}_1 = \mathsf{T}_2$ and to update the class's descriptor accordingly. Because multi-equations encode both state and control, our specification of the unification algorithm remains rather abstract. It would be possible to give a lower-level description, where state (standard conjunctions of multi-equations) and control (pending binary equations) are distinguished.

10.6.3 DEFINITION: Let U be a conjunction of multi-equations. Y is *dominated* by X with respect to U (written: $\mathsf{Y} \prec_U \mathsf{X}$) if and only if U contains a conjunct of the form $\mathsf{X} = F\vec{\mathsf{T}} = \epsilon$, where $\mathsf{Y} \in ftv(\vec{\mathsf{T}})$. U is *cyclic* if and only if the graph of $\prec_U$ exhibits a cycle. □

$(\exists \bar{X}.U_1) \wedge U_2$	$\rightarrow$	$\exists \bar{X}.(U_1 \wedge U_2)$ if $\bar{X} \# \mathit{ftv}(U_2)$	(S-ExAnd)
$X = \epsilon \wedge X = \epsilon'$	$\rightarrow$	$X = \epsilon = \epsilon'$	(S-Fuse)
$X = X = \epsilon$	$\rightarrow$	$X = \epsilon$	(S-Stutter)
$F\vec{X} = F\vec{T} = \epsilon$	$\rightarrow$	$\vec{X} = \vec{T} \wedge F\vec{X} = \epsilon$	(S-Decompose)
$F\,T_1 \ldots T_i \ldots T_n = \epsilon$	$\rightarrow$	$\exists X.(X = T_i \wedge F\,T_1 \ldots X \ldots T_n = \epsilon)$ if $T_i \notin \mathcal{V} \wedge X \notin \mathit{ftv}(T_1, \ldots, T_n, \epsilon)$	(S-Name-1)
$F\vec{T} = F'\vec{T}' = \epsilon$	$\rightarrow$	false if $F \neq F'$	(S-Clash)
T	$\rightarrow$	true	(S-Single)
$U \wedge \text{true}$	$\rightarrow$	U	(S-True)
U	$\rightarrow$	false if the model is syntactic and U is cyclic	(S-Cycle)
$\mathcal{U}[\text{false}]$	$\rightarrow$	false if $\mathcal{U} \neq []$	(S-Fail)

Figure 10-10: Unification

The specification of the unification algorithm consists of a set of constraint rewriting rules, given in Figure 10-10. Rewriting is performed modulo α-conversion, modulo permutations of the members of a multi-equation, modulo commutativity and associativity of conjunction, and under an arbitrary context. The specification is nondeterministic: several rule instances may be simultaneously applicable.

S-ExAnd is a directed version of C-ExAnd, whose effect is to float up all existential quantifiers. In the process, all multi-equations become part of a single conjunction, possibly causing rules whose left-hand side is a conjunction of multi-equations, namely S-Fuse and S-Cycle, to become applicable. S-Fuse identifies two multi-equations that share a common variable X, and fuses them. The new multi-equation is not necessarily standard, even if the two original multi-equations were. Indeed, it may have repeated variables or contain two nonvariable terms. The purpose of the next few rules, whose left-hand side consists of a single multi-equation, is to deal with these situations. S-Stutter eliminates redundant variables. It only deals with variables, as opposed to terms of arbitrary size, so as to have constant time cost. The comparison of nonvariable terms is implemented by S-DECOMPOSE and S-CLASH. S-DECOMPOSE decomposes an equation between two terms whose head symbols match. It produces a conjunction of equations between their subterms, namely $\vec{X} = \vec{T}$. Only one of the two terms remains in the original multi-equation, which may thus become standard. The terms $\vec{X}$ are copied: there are two occurrences of $\vec{X}$ on the right-hand side. For this reason, we require them to be type variables, as opposed to terms of arbitrary size. (We slightly abuse notation by using $\vec{X}$ to denote a vector of type variables whose elements are not necessarily distinct.) By doing so, we allow explicit reasoning about sharing: since a variable represents a pointer to an equivalence class, we explicitly specify that only pointers, not whole terms, are copied. As a result of this decision, S-DECOMPOSE is not applicable when both terms at hand have a nonvariable subterm. S-NAME-1 remedies this problem by introducing a fresh variable that stands for one such subterm. When repeatedly applied, S-NAME-1 yields a unification problem composed of so-called *small terms* only—that is, where sharing has been made fully explicit. S-CLASH complements S-DECOMPOSE by dealing with the case where two terms with different head symbols are equated; in a free tree model, such an equation is false, so failure is signaled. S-SINGLE and S-TRUE suppress multi-equations of size 1 and 0, respectively, which are tautologies. S-CYCLE is the occurs check: it signals failure if the constraint is cyclic. It is applicable only in the case of syntactic unification, that is, when ground types are finite trees. It is a global check: its left-hand side is an entire conjunction of multi-equations. S-FAIL propagates failure; $\mathcal{U}$ ranges over unification constraint contexts.

The constraint rewriting system in Figure 10-10 enjoys the following properties. First, rewriting is strongly normalizing, so the rules define a (nondeterministic) algorithm. Second, rewriting is meaning-preserving. Third, every normal form is either false or of the form $\exists\vec{X}.U$, where U is satisfiable. The latter two properties indicate that the algorithm is indeed a constraint solver.

10.6.4 LEMMA: The rewriting system $\rightarrow$ is strongly normalizing. □

10.6.5 LEMMA: $U_1 \rightarrow U_2$ implies $U_1 \equiv U_2$. □

10.6.6 LEMMA: Every normal form is either false or of the form $\mathcal{X}[U]$, where $\mathcal{X}$ is an existential constraint context, U is a standard conjunction of multi-equations and, if the model is syntactic, U is acyclic. These conditions imply that U is satisfiable. □

A Constraint Solver

On top of the unification algorithm, we now define a constraint solver. Its specification is independent of the rules and strategy employed by the unification algorithm. However, the structure of the unification algorithm's normal forms as well as the logical properties of multi-equations are exploited when performing generalization, that is, when creating and simplifying type schemes. Like the unification algorithm, the constraint solver is specified in terms of a reduction system. However, the objects that are subject to rewriting are not just constraints: they have more complex structure. Working with such richer states allows distinguishing the solver's external language—namely, the full constraint language, which is used to express the problem that one wishes to solve—and an internal language, introduced below, which is used to describe the solver's private data structures. In the following, C and D range over external constraints, that is, constraints that were part of the solver's input. External constraints are to be viewed as abstract syntax trees, subject to no implicit laws other than α-conversion. As a simplifying assumption, we require external constraints not to contain any occurrence of false—otherwise the problem at hand is clearly false. *Internal* data structures include unification constraints U, as previously studied, and *stacks*, whose syntax is as follows:

$$S ::= [] \mid S[[] \wedge C] \mid S[\exists \bar{X}.[]] \mid S[\text{let } x : \forall \bar{X}[[]].T \text{ in } C] \mid S[\text{let } x : \sigma \text{ in } []]$$

In the second and fourth productions, C is an external constraint. In the last production, we require σ to be of the form $\forall \bar{X}[U].X$, and we demand $\exists \sigma \equiv$ true. Every stack may be viewed as a one-hole constraint context (page 410); indeed, one may interpret $[]$ as the empty context and $\cdot[\cdot]$ as context composition, which replaces the hole of its first context argument with its second context argument. A stack may also be viewed, literally, as a list of *frames.* Frames may be added and deleted at the inner end of a stack, that is, near the hole of the constraint context that it represents. We refer to the four kinds of frames as *conjunction, existential,* let, and *environment* frames, respectively. A *state* of the constraint solver is a triple $S; U; C$ where S is a stack, U is a unification constraint, and C is an external constraint. The state $S; U; C$ is to be understood as a representation of the constraint $S[U \wedge C]$, that is, the constraint obtained by placing both U and C within the hole of the constraint context S. The notion of α-equivalence between states is defined accordingly. In particular, one may rename type variables in $dtv(S)$, provided U and C are renamed as well. In brief, the three components of a state play the following roles. C is an external constraint that the solver intends to examine next. U

is the internal state of the underlying unification algorithm; one might think of it as the knowledge that has been obtained so far. S tells where the type variables that occur free in U and C are bound, associates type schemes with the program variables that occur free in C, and records what should be done after C is solved. The solver's initial state is usually of the form $[];\mathsf{true};C$, where C is the external constraint that one wishes to solve, that is, whose satisfiability one wishes to determine. If the constraint to be solved is of the form $\mathsf{let}\ \Gamma_0\ \mathsf{in}\ C$, and if the type schemes that appear within Γ_0 meet the requirements that bear on environment frames, as defined above, then it is possible to pick $\mathsf{let}\ \Gamma_0\ \mathsf{in}\ [];\mathsf{true};C$ as an initial state. For simplicity, we make the (unessential) assumption that states have no free type variables.

The solver consists of a (nondeterministic) state rewriting system, given in Figure 10-11. Rewriting is performed modulo α-conversion. S-UNIFY makes the unification algorithm a component of the constraint solver, and allows the current unification problem U to be solved at any time. Rules S-EX-1 to S-EX-4 float existential quantifiers out of the unification problem into the stack and through the stack up to the nearest enclosing let frame, if there is any, or to the outermost level, otherwise. Their side-conditions prevent capture of type variables, and can always be satisfied by suitable α-conversion of the left-hand state. If $S;U;C$ is a normal form with respect to these five rules, then U must be either false or a conjunction of standard multi-equations, and every type variable in $dtv(S)$ must be either universally quantified at a let frame or existentially bound at the outermost level. (Recall that, by assumption, states have no free type variables.) In other words, provided these rules are applied in an eager fashion, there is no need for existential frames to appear in the machine representation of stacks. Instead, it suffices to maintain, at every let frame and at the outermost level, a list of the type variables that are bound at this point and, conversely, to annotate every type variable in $dtv(S)$ with an integer *rank*, which allows telling, in constant time, where the variable is bound: type variables of rank 0 are bound at the outermost level, and type variables of rank $k \geq 1$ are bound at the kth let frame down in the stack S. The code that accompanies this chapter adopts this convention. Ranks were initially described in Rémy (1992a) and have also been studied by McAllester (2003).

Rules S-SOLVE-EQ to S-SOLVE-LET encode an analysis of the structure of the third component of the current state. There is one rule for each possible case, except false, which by assumption cannot arise, and true, which is dealt with further on. S-SOLVE-EQ discovers an equation and makes it available to the unification algorithm. S-SOLVE-ID discovers an instantiation constraint $\mathsf{x} \preceq \mathsf{T}$ and replaces it with $\sigma \preceq \mathsf{T}$, where the type scheme $\sigma = S(\mathsf{x})$ is the type

$$S;U;C \;\rightarrow\; S;U';C \quad \text{if } U \rightarrow U' \qquad \text{(S-UNIFY)}$$

$$S;\exists\bar{X}.U;C \;\rightarrow\; S[\exists\bar{X}.[\,]];U;C \quad \text{if } \bar{X} \# ftv(C) \qquad \text{(S-EX-1)}$$

$$S[(\exists\bar{X}.S') \wedge D];U;C \;\rightarrow\; S[\exists\bar{X}.(S' \wedge D)];U;C \quad \text{if } \bar{X} \# ftv(D) \qquad \text{(S-EX-2)}$$

$$S[\mathsf{let}\ \mathsf{x} : \forall\bar{X}[\exists\bar{Y}.S'].\mathsf{T}\ \mathsf{in}\ D];U;C \;\rightarrow\; S[\mathsf{let}\ \mathsf{x} : \forall\bar{X}\bar{Y}[S].'\mathsf{T}\ \mathsf{in}\ D];U;C \quad \text{if } \bar{Y} \# ftv(\mathsf{T}) \qquad \text{(S-EX-3)}$$

$$S[\mathsf{let}\ \mathsf{x} : \sigma\ \mathsf{in}\ \exists\bar{X}.S'];U;C \;\rightarrow\; S[\exists\bar{X}.\mathsf{let}\ \mathsf{x} : \sigma\ \mathsf{in}\ S'];U;C \quad \text{if } \bar{X} \# ftv(\sigma) \qquad \text{(S-EX-4)}$$

$$S;U;\mathsf{T}_1 = \mathsf{T}_2 \;\rightarrow\; S;U \wedge \mathsf{T}_1 = \mathsf{T}_2;\mathsf{true} \qquad \text{(S-SOLVE-EQ)}$$

$$S;U;\mathsf{x} \preceq \mathsf{T} \;\rightarrow\; S;U;S(\mathsf{x}) \preceq \mathsf{T} \qquad \text{(S-SOLVE-ID)}$$

$$S;U;C_1 \wedge C_2 \;\rightarrow\; S[[\,] \wedge C_2];U;C_1 \qquad \text{(S-SOLVE-AND)}$$

$$S;U;\exists\bar{X}.C \;\rightarrow\; S[\exists\bar{X}.[\,]];U;C \quad \text{if } \bar{X} \# ftv(U) \qquad \text{(S-SOLVE-EX)}$$

$$S;U;\mathsf{let}\ \mathsf{x} : \forall\bar{X}[D].\mathsf{T}\ \mathsf{in}\ C \;\rightarrow\; S[\mathsf{let}\ \mathsf{x} : \forall\bar{X}[[\,]].\mathsf{T}\ \mathsf{in}\ C];U;D \quad \text{if } \bar{X} \# ftv(U) \qquad \text{(S-SOLVE-LET)}$$

$$S[[\,] \wedge C];U;\mathsf{true} \;\rightarrow\; S;U;C \qquad \text{(S-POP-AND)}$$

$$S[\mathsf{let}\ \mathsf{x} : \forall\bar{X}[[\,]].\mathsf{T}\ \mathsf{in}\ C];U;\mathsf{true} \;\rightarrow\; S[\mathsf{let}\ \mathsf{x} : \forall\bar{X}\mathsf{X}[[\,]].\mathsf{X}\ \mathsf{in}\ C];\ U \wedge \mathsf{X} = \mathsf{T};\mathsf{true} \quad \text{if } \mathsf{X} \notin ftv(U,\mathsf{T}) \wedge \mathsf{T} \notin \mathcal{V} \qquad \text{(S-NAME-2)}$$

$$S[\mathsf{let}\ \mathsf{x} : \forall\bar{X}\mathsf{Y}[[\,]].\mathsf{X}\ \mathsf{in}\ C];\mathsf{Y} = \mathsf{Z} = \epsilon \wedge U;\mathsf{true} \;\rightarrow\; S[\mathsf{let}\ \mathsf{x} : \forall\bar{X}\mathsf{Y}[[\,]].\theta(\mathsf{X})\ \mathsf{in}\ C];\ \mathsf{Y} \wedge \mathsf{Z} = \theta(\epsilon) \wedge \theta(U);\mathsf{true} \quad \text{if } \mathsf{Y} \neq \mathsf{Z} \wedge \theta = [\mathsf{Y} \mapsto \mathsf{Z}] \qquad \text{(S-COMPRESS)}$$

$$S[\mathsf{let}\ \mathsf{x} : \forall\bar{X}\mathsf{Y}[[\,]].\mathsf{X}\ \mathsf{in}\ C];\mathsf{Y} = \epsilon \wedge U;\mathsf{true} \;\rightarrow\; S[\mathsf{let}\ \mathsf{x} : \forall\bar{X}[[\,]].\mathsf{X}\ \mathsf{in}\ C];\epsilon \wedge U;\mathsf{true} \quad \text{if } \mathsf{Y} \notin \mathsf{X} \cup ftv(\epsilon, U) \qquad \text{(S-UNNAME)}$$

$$S[\mathsf{let}\ \mathsf{x} : \forall\bar{X}\bar{Y}[[\,]].\mathsf{X}\ \mathsf{in}\ C];U;\mathsf{true} \;\rightarrow\; S[\exists\bar{Y}.\mathsf{let}\ \mathsf{x} : \forall\bar{X}[[\,]].\mathsf{X}\ \mathsf{in}\ C];U;\mathsf{true} \quad \text{if } \bar{Y} \# ftv(C) \wedge \exists\bar{X}.U \text{ determines } \bar{Y} \qquad \text{(S-LETALL)}$$

$$S[\mathsf{let}\ \mathsf{x} : \forall\bar{X}[[\,]].\mathsf{X}\ \mathsf{in}\ C];U_1 \wedge U_2;\mathsf{true} \;\rightarrow\; S[\mathsf{let}\ \mathsf{x} : \forall\bar{X}[U_2].\mathsf{X}\ \mathsf{in}\ [\,]];U_1;C \quad \text{if } \bar{X} \# ftv(U_1) \wedge \exists\bar{X}.U_2 \equiv \mathsf{true} \qquad \text{(S-POP-LET)}$$

$$S[\mathsf{let}\ \mathsf{x} : \sigma\ \mathsf{in}\ [\,]];U;\mathsf{true} \;\rightarrow\; S;U;\mathsf{true} \qquad \text{(S-POP-ENV)}$$

Figure 10-11: A constraint solver

scheme carried by the nearest environment frame that defines x in the stack S. It is defined as follows:

$$\begin{array}{rcll} S[[] \wedge C](\mathsf{x}) & = & S(\mathsf{x}) & \\ S[\exists\bar{\mathsf{X}}.[]](\mathsf{x}) & = & S(\mathsf{x}) & \text{if } \bar{\mathsf{X}} \# \mathit{ftv}(S(\mathsf{x})) \\ S[\mathsf{let}\ \mathsf{y} : \forall\bar{\mathsf{X}}[[]].\mathsf{T}\ \mathsf{in}\ C](\mathsf{x}) & = & S(\mathsf{x}) & \text{if } \bar{\mathsf{X}} \# \mathit{ftv}(S(\mathsf{x})) \\ S[\mathsf{let}\ \mathsf{y} : \sigma\ \mathsf{in}\ []](\mathsf{x}) & = & S(\mathsf{x}) & \text{if } \mathsf{x} \neq \mathsf{y} \\ S[\mathsf{let}\ \mathsf{x} : \sigma\ \mathsf{in}\ []](\mathsf{x}) & = & \sigma & \end{array}$$

If $\mathsf{x} \in \mathit{dpi}(S)$ does not hold, then $S(\mathsf{x})$ is undefined and the rule is not applicable. If it does hold, then the rule may always be made applicable by suitable α-conversion of the left-hand state. Recall that, if σ is of the form $\forall\bar{\mathsf{X}}[U].\mathsf{X}$, where $\bar{\mathsf{X}} \# \mathit{ftv}(\mathsf{T})$, then $\sigma \preceq \mathsf{T}$ stands for $\exists\bar{\mathsf{X}}.(U \wedge \mathsf{X} = \mathsf{T})$. The process of constructing this constraint is informally referred to as "taking an instance of σ." In the worst case, it is just as inefficient as textually expanding the corresponding `let` construct in the program's source code, and leads to exponential time complexity. In practice, however, the unification constraint U is often compact because it was simplified before the environment frame $\mathsf{let}\ \mathsf{x} : \sigma\ \mathsf{in}\ []$ was created, which explains why the solver usually performs well. (The creation of environment frames, performed by S-POP-LET, is discussed below.) S-SOLVE-AND discovers a conjunction. It arbitrarily chooses to explore the left branch first, and pushes a conjunction frame onto the stack, so as to record that the right branch should be explored afterwards. S-SOLVE-EX discovers an existential quantifier and enters it, creating a new existential frame to record its existence. Similarly, S-SOLVE-LET discovers a let form and enters its left-hand side, creating a new let frame to record its existence. The choice of examining the left-hand side first is not arbitrary. Indeed, examining the right-hand side first would require creating an environment frame—but environment frames must contain simplified type schemes of the form $\forall\bar{\mathsf{X}}[U].\mathsf{X}$, whereas the type scheme $\forall\bar{\mathsf{X}}[D].\mathsf{T}$ is arbitrary. In other words, our strategy is to simplify type schemes prior to allowing them to be copied by S-SOLVE-ID, so as to avoid any duplication of effort. The side-conditions of S-SOLVE-EX and S-SOLVE-LET may always be satisfied by suitable α-conversion of the left-hand state.

Rules S-SOLVE-EQ to S-SOLVE-LET may be referred to as *forward* rules, because they "move down into" the external constraint, causing the stack to grow. This process stops when the external constraint at hand becomes true. Then part of the work has been finished, and the solver must examine the stack in order to determine what to do next. This task is performed by the last series of rules, which may be referred to as *backward* rules, because they "move back out," causing the stack to shrink and possibly scheduling new external constraints for examination. These rules encode an analysis of the structure of the innermost stack frame. There are three cases, corresponding to conjunction, let, and environment frames. The case of existential stack frames need not be considered, because rules S-Ex-2 to S-Ex-4 allow either fusing them with let frames or floating them up to the outermost level, where they shall remain inert. S-Pop-And deals with conjunction frames. The frame is popped, and the external constraint that it carries is scheduled for examination. S-Pop-Env deals with environment frames. Because the right-hand side of the let construct at hand has been solved—that is, turned into a unification constraint U—it cannot contain an occurrence of x. Furthermore, by assumption, $\exists\sigma$ is true. Thus, this environment frame is no longer useful: it is destroyed. The remaining rules deal with let frames. Roughly speaking, their purpose is to change the state $S[\mathsf{let}\ \mathsf{x} : \forall\bar{\mathsf{X}}[[]].\mathsf{T}\ \mathsf{in}\ C]; U; \mathsf{true}$ into $S[\mathsf{let}\ \mathsf{x} : \forall\bar{\mathsf{X}}[U].\mathsf{T}\ \mathsf{in}\ []]; \mathsf{true}; C$, that is, to turn the current unification constraint U into a type scheme, turn the let frame into an environment frame, and schedule the right-hand side of the let construct (that is, the external constraint C) for examination. In fact, the process is more complex, because the type scheme $\forall\bar{\mathsf{X}}[U].\mathsf{T}$ must be *simplified* before becoming part of an environment frame. The simplification process is described by rules S-Name-2 to S-Pop-Let. In the following, we refer to type variables in $\bar{\mathsf{X}}$ as *young* and to type variables in $dtv(S) \setminus \bar{\mathsf{X}}$ as *old*. The former are the universal quantifiers of the type scheme that is being created; the latter contain its free type variables.

S-Name-2 ensures that the body T of the type scheme that is being created is a type variable, as opposed to an arbitrary term. If it isn't, then it is replaced with a fresh variable X, and the equation $\mathsf{X} = \mathsf{T}$ is added so as to recall that X stands for T. Thus, the rule moves the term T into the current unification problem, where it potentially becomes subject to S-Name-1. This ensures that sharing is made explicit everywhere. S-Compress determines that the (young) type variable Y is an alias for the type variable Z. Then, every free occurrence of Y other than its defining occurrence is replaced with Z. In an actual implementation, this occurs transparently when the union-find algorithm performs *path compression* (Tarjan, 1975, 1979). We note that the rule does not allow substituting a younger type variable for an older one; indeed, that would make no sense, since the younger variable could then possibly escape its scope. In other words, in implementation terms, the union-find algorithm must be slightly modified so that, in each equivalence class, the representative element is always a type variable with minimum rank. S-UnName determines that the (young) type variable Y has no occurrences other than its defining occurrence in the current type scheme. (This occurs, in particular, when S-Compress has just been applied.) Then, Y is suppressed altogether. In the particular case where the remaining multi-equation ϵ has cardinal 1, it may then be suppressed by S-SINGLE. In other words, the combination of S-UNNAME and S-SINGLE is able to suppress young unused type variables as well as the term that they stand for. This may, in turn, cause new type variables to become eligible for elimination by S-UNNAME. In fact, assuming the current unification constraint is acyclic, an inductive argument shows that every young type variable may be suppressed unless it is dominated either by X or by an old type variable. (In the setting of a regular tree model, it is possible to extend the rule so that young cycles that are not dominated either by X or by an old type variable are suppressed as well.) S-LETALL is a directed version of C-LETALL. It turns the young type variables $\bar{Y}$ into old variables. How to tell whether $\exists\bar{X}.U$ determines $\bar{Y}$ is discussed later (see Lemma 10.6.7). Why S-LETALL is an interesting and important rule will be explained shortly. S-POP-LET is meant to be applied when the current state has become a normal form with respect to S-UNIFY, S-NAME-2, S-COMPRESS, S-UNNAME, and S-LETALL, that is, when the type scheme that is about to be created is fully simplified. It splits the current unification constraint into two components U_1 and U_2, where U_1 is made up entirely of *old* variables, as expressed by the side-condition $\bar{X} \# \mathit{ftv}(U_1)$, and U_2 constrains *young* variables only, as expressed by the side-condition $\exists\bar{X}.U_2 \equiv \mathsf{true}$. Note that U_2 may still contain free occurrences of old type variables, so the type scheme $\forall\bar{X}[U_2].\mathsf{X}$ that appears on the right-hand side is not necessarily closed. It is not obvious why such a decomposition must exist; Lemma 10.6.10 proves that it does. Let us say for now that S-LETALL plays a role in guaranteeing its existence, whence comes part of its importance. Once the decomposition $U_1 \wedge U_2$ is obtained, the behavior of S-POP-LET is simple. The unification constraint U_1 concerns old variables only, that is, variables that are not quantified in the current let frame; thus, it need not become part of the new type scheme and may instead remain part of the current unification constraint. This is justified by C-LETAND and C-INAND* and corresponds to the difference between HMX-GEN' and HMX-GEN discussed in §10.3. The unification constraint U_2, on the other hand, becomes part of the newly built type scheme $\forall\bar{X}[U_2].\mathsf{X}$. The property $\exists\bar{X}.U_2 \equiv \mathsf{true}$ guarantees that the newly created environment frame meets the requirements imposed on such frames. Note that the more type variables are considered old, the larger U_1 may become, and the smaller U_2. This is another reason why S-LETALL is interesting: by allowing more variables to be considered old, it decreases the size of the type scheme $\forall\bar{X}[U_2].\mathsf{X}$, making it cheaper to instantiate.

To complete our description of the constraint solver, there remains to explain how to decide when $\exists\bar{X}.U$ determines $\bar{Y}$, since this predicate occurs in the side-condition of S-LETALL. The following lemma describes two important situations where, by examining the structure of an equation, it is possible to discover that a constraint C determines some of its free type variables $\bar{Y}$ (Definition 10.2.14). In the first situation, the type variables $\bar{Y}$ are equated with or dominated by a distinct type variable X that occurs free in C. In that case, because the model is a free tree model, the values of the type variables $\bar{Y}$ are determined by the value of X: they are subtrees of it at specific positions. For instance, $X = Y_1 \to Y_2$ determines Y_1Y_2, while $\exists Y_1.(X = Y_1 \to Y_2)$ determines Y_2. In the second situation, the type variables $\bar{Y}$ are equated with a term T, all of whose type variables are free in C. Again, the value of the type variables $\bar{Y}$ is then determined by the values of the type variables $ftv(\mathsf{T})$. For instance, $X = Y_1 \to Y_2$ determines X, while $\exists Y_1.(X = Y_1 \to Y_2)$ does not. In the second situation, no assumption is in fact made about the model. (Note that $X = Y_1 \to Y_2$ determines Y_1Y_2 and determines X, but does not simultaneously determine XY_1Y_2.)

10.6.7 LEMMA: Let $\bar{X} \# \bar{Y}$. Assume either ϵ is $X = \epsilon'$, where $X \notin \bar{X}\bar{Y}$ and $\bar{Y} \subseteq ftv(\epsilon')$, or ϵ is $\bar{Y} = \mathsf{T} = \epsilon'$, where $ftv(\mathsf{T}) \# \bar{X}\bar{Y}$. Then, $\exists\bar{X}.(C \wedge \epsilon)$ determines $\bar{Y}$. □

Thanks to Lemma 10.6.7, an efficient implementation of S-LETALL comes to mind. The problem is, given a constraint $\exists\bar{X}.U$, where U is a standard conjunction of multi-equations, to determine the greatest subset $\bar{Y}$ of $\bar{X}$ such that $\exists(\bar{X} \setminus \bar{Y}).U$ determines $\bar{Y}$. By the first part of the lemma, it is safe for $\bar{Y}$ to include all members of $\bar{X}$ that are directly or indirectly dominated (with respect to U) by some free variable of $\exists\bar{X}.U$. Those can be found, in time linear in the size of U, by a top-down traversal of the graph of $\prec_U$. By the second part of the lemma, it is safe to close $\bar{Y}$ under the closure law $X \in \bar{X} \wedge (\forall Y \quad Y \prec_U X \Rightarrow Y \in \bar{Y}) \Rightarrow X \in \bar{Y}$. That is, it is safe to also include all members of $\bar{X}$ whose descendants (with respect to U) have already been found to be members of $\bar{Y}$. This closure computation may be performed, again in linear time, by a bottom-up traversal of the graph of $\prec_U$. When U is acyclic, it is possible to show that this procedure is complete, that is, does compute the greatest subset $\bar{Y}$ that meets our requirement.

The above discussion has shown that when Y and Z are equated, if Y is young and Z is old, then S-LETALL allows making Y old as well. If binding information is encoded in terms of integer ranks, as suggested earlier, then this remark may be formulated as follows: when Y and Z are equated, if the rank of Y exceeds that of Z, then it may be decreased so that both ranks match. As a result, it is possible to attach ranks with multi-equations, rather than with variables. When two multi-equations are fused, the smaller rank is kept. This treatment of ranks is inspired by Rémy (1992a); see the resolution rule FUSE, as well as the simplification rules PROPAGATE and REALIZE, in that paper.

Let us now state the properties of the constraint solver. First, the reduction system is terminating, so it defines an algorithm.

10.6.8 LEMMA: The reduction system $\rightarrow$ is strongly normalizing. □

Second, every rewriting step preserves the meaning of the constraint that the current state represents. We recall that the state $S; U; C$ is meant to represent the constraint $S[U \wedge C]$.

10.6.9 LEMMA: $S; U; C \rightarrow S'; U'; C'$ implies $S[U \wedge C] \equiv S'[U' \wedge C']$. □

Last, we classify the normal forms of the reduction system:

10.6.10 LEMMA: A normal form for the reduction system $\rightarrow$ is one of (i) $S; U; \mathsf{x} \preceq \mathsf{T}$, where $\mathsf{x} \notin dpi(S)$; (ii) $S; \mathsf{false}; \mathsf{true}$; or (iii) $\mathcal{X}; U; \mathsf{true}$, where $\mathcal{X}$ is an existential constraint context and U a satisfiable conjunction of multi-equations. □

In case (i), the constraint $S[U \wedge C]$ has a free program identifier x. In other words, the source program contains an unbound program identifier. Such an error could of course be detected prior to constraint solving, if desired. In case (ii), the unification algorithm failed. By Lemma 10.2.17, the constraint $S[U \wedge C]$ is then false. In case (iii), the constraint $S[U \wedge C]$ is equivalent to $\mathcal{X}[U]$, where U is satisfiable, so it is satisfiable as well. If the initial constraint is closed, case (i) cannot arise, while cases (ii) and (iii) respectively denote failure and success. Thus, Lemmas 10.6.9 and 10.6.10 indeed prove that the algorithm is a constraint solver.

10.6.11 REMARK: Type inference for ML-the-calculus is DEXPTIME-complete (Kfoury, Tiuryn, and Urzyczyn, 1990; Mairson, Kanellakis, and Mitchell, 1991). Thus, our constraint solver cannot run any faster, asymptotically. This cost is essentially due to `let`-polymorphism, which requires a constraint to be duplicated at every occurrence of a `let`-bound variable (S-SOLVE-ID). In order to limit the amount of duplication to a bare minimum, it is important that rule S-LETALL be applied before S-POP-LET, allowing variables and constraints that need not be duplicated to be shared. We have observed that algorithms based on this strategy behave remarkably well in practice (Rémy, 1992a). In fact, McAllester (2003) has proved that they have linear time complexity, provided the size of type schemes and the (left-) nesting depth of `let` constructs are bounded. Unfortunately, many implementations of type inference for ML-the-programming-language do not behave as efficiently as the algorithm presented here. Some spend an excessive amount of time in computing the set of nongeneralizable type variables; some do not treat types as dags, thus losing precious sharing information; others perform the expensive occurs check after every unification step, rather than only once at every `let` construct, as suggested here (S-POP-LET). □

10.7 From ML-the-Calculus to ML-the-Language

In this section, we explain how to extend the framework developed so far to accommodate operations on values of base type (such as integers), pairs, sums, references, and recursive function definitions. Then, we describe algebraic data type definitions. Last, the issues associated with recursive types are briefly discussed. For space reasons, exceptions are not discussed; the reader is referred to (*TAPL*, Chapter 14).

Simple Extensions

Introducing new constants and extending $\xrightarrow{\delta}$ and Γ_0 appropriately allows adding many features of ML-the-programming-language to ML-the-calculus. In each case, it is necessary to check that the requirements of Definition 10.5.5 are met, that is, to ensure that the new initial environment faithfully reflects the nature of the new constants as well as the behavior of the new reduction rules. Below, we describe several such extensions in isolation. The first exercise establishes a technical result that is useful in the next exercises.

10.7.1 EXERCISE [RECOMMENDED, ★]: Let Γ_0 contain the binding $\mathsf{c} : \forall \bar{\mathsf{X}}.\mathsf{T}_1 \to \ldots \to \mathsf{T}_n \to \mathsf{T}$. Prove $\mathsf{let}\ \Gamma_0\ \mathsf{in}\ [\![\mathsf{c}\ \mathsf{t}_1\ \ldots\ \mathsf{t}_n : \mathsf{T}']\!]$ equivalent to $\mathsf{let}\ \Gamma_0\ \mathsf{in}\ \exists \bar{\mathsf{X}}.(\bigwedge_{i=1}^{n} [\![\mathsf{t}_i : \mathsf{T}_i]\!] \wedge \mathsf{T} \leq \mathsf{T}')$. □

10.7.2 EXERCISE [INTEGERS, RECOMMENDED, ★★]: Integer literals and integer addition have been introduced and given an operational semantics in Examples 10.1.1, 10.1.2, and 10.1.4. Let us now introduce an isolated type constructor int of signature ⋆ and extend the initial environment Γ_0 with the bindings $\hat{n} : \mathsf{int}$, for every integer n, and $\hat{+} : \mathsf{int} \to \mathsf{int} \to \mathsf{int}$. Check that these definitions meet the requirements of Definition 10.5.5. □

10.7.3 EXERCISE [PAIRS, ★★, ↛]: Pairs and pair projections have been introduced and given an operational semantics in Examples 10.1.3 and 10.1.5. Let us now introduce an isolated type constructor × of signature $\star \otimes \star \Rightarrow \star$, covariant in both of its parameters, and extend the initial environment Γ_0 with the following bindings:

$$\begin{aligned}(\cdot,\cdot) &: \forall \mathsf{XY}.\mathsf{X} \to \mathsf{Y} \to \mathsf{X} \times \mathsf{Y}\\ \pi_1 &: \forall \mathsf{XY}.\mathsf{X} \times \mathsf{Y} \to \mathsf{X}\\ \pi_2 &: \forall \mathsf{XY}.\mathsf{X} \times \mathsf{Y} \to \mathsf{Y}\end{aligned}$$

Check that these definitions meet the requirements of Definition 10.5.5. □

10.7.4 EXERCISE [SUMS, ★★, ↛]: Sums have been introduced and given an operational semantics in Example 10.1.7. Let us now introduce an isolated type constructor + of signature $\star \otimes \star \Rightarrow \star$, covariant in both of its parameters, and extend the initial environment Γ_0 with the following bindings:

$$\begin{array}{rl} \mathtt{inj}_1 : & \forall XY.X \to X + Y \\ \mathtt{inj}_2 : & \forall XY.Y \to X + Y \\ \mathtt{case} : & \forall XYZ.(X + Y) \to (X \to Z) \to (Y \to Z) \to Z \end{array}$$

Check that these definitions meet the requirements of Definition 10.5.5. □

10.7.5 EXERCISE [REFERENCES, ★★★]: References have been introduced and given an operational semantics in Example 10.1.9. The type constructor `ref` has been introduced in Definition 10.5.3. Let us now extend the initial environment Γ_0 with the following bindings:

$$\begin{array}{rl} \mathtt{ref} : & \forall X.X \to \mathrm{ref}\,X \\ ! : & \forall X.\mathrm{ref}\,X \to X \\ := : & \forall X.\mathrm{ref}\,X \to X \to X \end{array}$$

Check that these definitions meet the requirements of Definition 10.5.5. □

10.7.6 EXERCISE [RECURSION, RECOMMENDED, ★★★, ↛]: The fixpoint combinator `fix` has been introduced and given an operational semantics in Example 10.1.10. Let us now extend the initial environment Γ_0 with the following binding:

$$\mathtt{fix} : \quad \forall XY.((X \to Y) \to (X \to Y)) \to X \to Y$$

Check that these definitions meet the requirements of Definition 10.5.5. Recall how the `letrec` syntactic sugar was defined in Example 10.1.10, and check that this gives rise to the following constraint generation rule:

$$\begin{array}{rl} & \mathrm{let}\ \Gamma_0\ \mathrm{in}\ [\![\mathtt{letrec}\ f = \lambda z.t_1\ \mathtt{in}\ t_2 : T]\!] \\ \equiv & \mathrm{let}\ \Gamma_0\ \mathrm{in}\ \mathrm{let}\ f : \forall XY[\mathrm{let}\ f : X \to Y; z : X\ \mathrm{in}\ [\![t_1 : Y]\!]].X \to Y\ \mathrm{in}\ [\![t_2 : T]\!] \end{array}$$

Note the somewhat peculiar structure of this constraint: the program variable `f` is bound twice in it, with different type schemes. The constraint requires all occurrences of `f` within t_1 to be assigned the monomorphic type $X \to Y$. This type is generalized and turned into a type scheme before inspecting t_2, however, so every occurrence of `f` within t_2 may receive a different type, as usual with `let`-polymorphism. A more powerful way of typechecking recursive function definitions, proposed by (Mycroft, 1984) and known as *polymorphic recursion*, allows the types of occurrences of `f` within t_1 to be possibly distinct instances of a single type scheme. However, type inference for this extension is equivalent to semi-unification (Henglein, 1993), which has been proved undecidable (Kfoury, Tiuryn, and Urzyczyn, 1993). Hence, type inference must either require type annotations or rely on a semi-algorithm. □

In the exercises above, we have considered a number of extensions (integers, booleans, pairs, etc.) in isolation. We have checked that each of them preserves type soundness. Unfortunately, this does not in general imply that their combination preserves type soundness. In fact, it is possible to prove that these extensions are independent in a suitable sense and that independent extensions may be safely combined. Unfortunately, we lack space to further explain these notions.

Algebraic Data Types

Exercises 10.7.3 and 10.7.4 have shown how to extend the language with binary, anonymous products and sums. These constructs are quite general but still have several shortcomings. First, they are only binary, while we would like to have k-ary products and sums, for arbitrary $k \geq 0$. Such a generalization is of course straightforward. Second, more interestingly, their components must be referred to by numeric index (as in "extract the second component of the pair"), rather than by name ("extract the component named y"). In practice, it is crucial to use names, because they make programs more readable and more robust in the face of changes. One could introduce a mechanism that allows defining names as syntactic sugar for numeric indices. That would help a little, but not much, because these names would not appear in types, which would still be made of anonymous products and sums. Third, in the absence of recursive types, products and sums do not have sufficient expressiveness to allow defining unbounded data structures, such as lists. Indeed, it is easy to see that every value whose type T is composed of base types (int, bool, etc.), products, and sums must have bounded size, where the bound $|\mathsf{T}|$ is a function of T. More precisely, up to a constant factor, we have $|\mathsf{int}| = |\mathsf{bool}| = 1$, $|\mathsf{T}_1 \times \mathsf{T}_2| = 1 + |\mathsf{T}_1| + |\mathsf{T}_2|$, and $|\mathsf{T}_1 + \mathsf{T}_2| = 1 + \max(|\mathsf{T}_1|, |\mathsf{T}_2|)$. The following example describes another facet of the same problem.

10.7.7 EXAMPLE: A list is either empty, or a pair of an element and another list. So, it seems natural to try and encode the type of lists as a sum of some arbitrary type (say, unit) on the one hand, and of a product of some element type and of the type of lists itself on the other hand. With this encoding in mind, we can go ahead and write code—for instance, a function that computes the length of a list:

$$\texttt{letrec length} = \lambda \texttt{l.case l} \; (\lambda_.\hat{0}) \; (\lambda \texttt{z}.\hat{1} \,\hat{+}\, \texttt{length} \; (\pi_2 \; \texttt{z}))$$

We have used integers, pairs, sums, and the `letrec` construct introduced in the previous section. The code analyzes the list `l` using a `case` construct.

If the left branch is taken, the list is empty, so 0 is returned. If the right branch is taken, then z becomes bound to a pair of some element and the tail of the list. The latter is obtained using the projection operator π_2. Its length is computed using a recursive call to `length` and incremented by 1. This code makes perfect sense. However, applying the constraint generation and constraint solving algorithms eventually leads to an equation of the form $X = Y + (Z \times X)$, where X stands for the type of `l`. This equation accurately reflects our encoding of the type of lists. However, in a syntactic model, it has no solution, so our definition of `length` is ill-typed. It is possible to adopt a free regular tree model, thus introducing *equirecursive* types into the system (*TAPL*, Chapter 20); however, there are good reasons not to do so (see the section on Recursive Types on p. 459). □

To work around this problem, ML-the-programming-language offers *algebraic data type* definitions, whose elegance lies in the fact that, while representing only a modest theoretical extension, they do solve the three problems mentioned above. An algebraic data type may be viewed as an *abstract type* that is declared to be *isomorphic* to a (k-ary) product or sum type with named components. The type of each component is declared, as well, and may refer to the algebraic data type that is being defined: thus, algebraic data types are *isorecursive* (*TAPL*, Chapter 20). In order to allow sufficient flexibility when declaring the type of each component, algebraic data type definitions may be parameterized by a number of type variables. Last, in order to allow the description of complex data structures, it is necessary to allow several algebraic data types to be defined at once; the definitions may then be mutually recursive. In fact, in order to simplify this formal presentation, we assume that all algebraic data types are defined at once at the beginning of the program. This decision is, of course, at odds with modular programming but will not otherwise be a problem.

In the following, D ranges over a set of *data types*. We assume that data types form a subset of type constructors. We require each of them to be isolated and to have image kind $\star$. Furthermore, ℓ ranges over a set $\mathcal{L}$ of *labels*, which we use both as data constructors and as record labels. An *algebraic data type definition* is either a *variant type* definition or a *record type* definition, whose respective forms are

$$D\vec{X} \approx \sum_{i=1}^{k} \ell_i : T_i \qquad \text{and} \qquad D\vec{X} \approx \prod_{i=1}^{k} \ell_i : T_i.$$

In either case, k must be nonnegative. If D has signature $\vec{\kappa} \Rightarrow \star$, then the type variables $\vec{X}$ must have kind $\vec{\kappa}$. Every T_i must have kind $\star$. We refer to $\vec{X}$ as the *parameters* and to $\vec{T}$ (the vector formed by $T_1, \ldots, T_k$) as the *components* of the definition. The parameters are bound within the components, and the definition must be closed, that is, $ftv(\vec{\mathsf{T}}) \subseteq \bar{\mathsf{X}}$ must hold. Last, for an algebraic data type definition to be valid, the behavior of the type constructor D with respect to subtyping must match its definition. This requirement is clarified below.

10.7.8 DEFINITION: Consider an algebraic data type definition whose parameters and components are respectively $\vec{\mathsf{X}}$ and $\vec{\mathsf{T}}$. Let $\vec{\mathsf{X}}'$ and $\vec{\mathsf{T}}'$ be their images under an arbitrary renaming. Then, $\mathsf{D}\,\vec{\mathsf{X}} \leq \mathsf{D}\,\vec{\mathsf{X}}' \Vdash \vec{\mathsf{T}} \leq \vec{\mathsf{T}}'$ must hold. □

Because it is stated in terms of an entailment assertion, the above requirement bears on the interpretation of subtyping. The idea is, since $\mathsf{D}\,\vec{\mathsf{X}}$ is declared to be isomorphic to (a sum or a product of) $\vec{\mathsf{T}}$, whenever two types built with D are comparable, their unfoldings should be comparable as well. The reverse entailment assertion is not required for type soundness, and it is sometimes useful to declare algebraic data types that do not validate it—so-called *phantom types* (Fluet and Pucella, 2002). Note that the requirement may always be satisfied by making the type constructor D invariant in all of its parameters. Indeed, in that case, $\mathsf{D}\,\vec{\mathsf{X}} \leq \mathsf{D}\,\vec{\mathsf{X}}'$ entails $\vec{\mathsf{X}} = \vec{\mathsf{X}}'$, which must entail $\vec{\mathsf{T}} = \vec{\mathsf{T}}'$ since $\vec{\mathsf{T}}'$ is precisely $[\vec{\mathsf{X}} \mapsto \vec{\mathsf{X}}']\vec{\mathsf{T}}$. In an equality free tree model, every type constructor is naturally invariant, so the requirement is trivially satisfied. In other settings, however, it is often possible to satisfy the requirement of Definition 10.7.8 while assigning D a less restrictive variance. The following example illustrates such a case.

10.7.9 EXAMPLE: Let list be a data type of signature $\star \Rightarrow \star$. Let $\mathtt{Nil}$ and $\mathtt{Cons}$ be data constructors. Then, the following is a definition of list as a variant type:

$$\mathsf{list}\,\mathsf{X} \approx \Sigma\,(\mathtt{Nil} : \mathsf{unit}; \mathsf{Cons} : \mathsf{X} \times \mathsf{list}\,\mathsf{X})$$

Because data types form a subset of type constructors, it is valid to form the type $\mathsf{list}\,\mathsf{X}$ in the right-hand side of the definition, even though we are still in the process of defining the meaning of list. In other words, data type definitions may be recursive. However, because $\approx$ is not interpreted as equality, the type $\mathsf{list}\,\mathsf{X}$ is not a recursive type: it is nothing but an application of the unary type constructor list to the type variable X. To check that the definition of list satisfies the requirement of Definition 10.7.8, we must ensure that

$$\mathsf{list}\,\mathsf{X} \leq \mathsf{list}\,\mathsf{X}' \Vdash \mathsf{unit} \leq \mathsf{unit} \wedge \mathsf{X} \times \mathsf{list}\,\mathsf{X} \leq \mathsf{X}' \times \mathsf{list}\,\mathsf{X}'$$

holds. This assertion is equivalent to $\mathsf{list}\,\mathsf{X} \leq \mathsf{list}\,\mathsf{X}' \Vdash \mathsf{X} \leq \mathsf{X}'$. To satisfy the requirement, it is sufficient to make list a covariant type constructor, that is, to define subtyping in the model so that $\mathsf{list}\,\mathsf{X} \leq \mathsf{list}\,\mathsf{X}' \equiv \mathsf{X} \leq \mathsf{X}'$ holds.

Let tree be a data type of signature $\star \Rightarrow \star$. Let root and sons be record labels. Then, the following is a definition of tree as a record type:

$$\mathsf{tree}\,\mathsf{X} \approx \Pi\,(\mathsf{root} : \mathsf{X}; \mathsf{sons} : \mathsf{list}\,(\mathsf{tree}\,\mathsf{X}))$$

This definition is again recursive, and relies on the previous definition. Because list is covariant, it is straightforward to check that the definition of tree is valid if tree is made a covariant type constructor as well. □

A *prologue* is a set of algebraic data type definitions, where each data type is defined at most once and where each data constructor or record label appears at most once. A *program* is a pair of a prologue and an expression. The effect of a prologue is to enrich the programming language with new constants. That is, a variant type definition extends the operational semantics with several injections and a case construct, as in Example 10.1.7. A record type definition extends it with a record formation construct and several projections, as in Examples 10.1.3 and 10.1.5. In either case, the initial typing environment Γ_0 is extended with information about these new constants. Thus, algebraic data type definitions might be viewed as a simple configuration language that allows specifying in which instance of ML-the-calculus the expression that follows the prologue should be typechecked and interpreted. Let us now give a precise account of this phenomenon.

To begin, suppose the prologue contains the definition $\mathsf{D}\,\vec{\mathsf{X}} \approx \sum_{i=1}^{k} \ell_i : \mathsf{T}_i$. Then, for each $i \in \{1, \ldots, k\}$, a constructor of arity 1, named ℓ_i, is introduced. Furthermore, a destructor of arity $k+1$, named case_D, is introduced. When $k > 0$, it is common to write $\mathsf{case}\ \mathsf{t}\ [\ell_i : \mathsf{t}_i]_{i=1}^{k}$ for the application $\mathsf{case}_\mathsf{D}\ \mathsf{t}\ \mathsf{t}_1 \ldots \mathsf{t}_n$. The operational semantics is extended with the following reduction rules, for $i \in \{1, \ldots, k\}$:

$$\mathsf{case}\ (\ell_i\ \mathsf{v})\ [\ell_j : \mathsf{v}_j]_{j=1}^{k} \xrightarrow{\delta} \mathsf{v}_i\ \mathsf{v} \qquad \text{(R-ALG-CASE)}$$

For each $i \in \{1, \ldots, k\}$, the initial environment is extended with the binding $\ell_i : \forall \vec{\mathsf{X}}.\mathsf{T}_i \to \mathsf{D}\,\vec{\mathsf{X}}$. It is further extended with the binding $\mathsf{case}_\mathsf{D} : \forall \vec{\mathsf{X}}\mathsf{Z}.\mathsf{D}\,\vec{\mathsf{X}} \to (\mathsf{T}_1 \to \mathsf{Z}) \to \ldots (\mathsf{T}_k \to \mathsf{Z}) \to \mathsf{Z}$.

Now, suppose the prologue contains the definition $\mathsf{D}\,\vec{\mathsf{X}} \approx \prod_{i=1}^{k} \ell_i : \mathsf{T}_i$. Then, for each $i \in \{1, \ldots, k\}$, a destructor of arity 1, named ℓ_i, is introduced. Furthermore, a constructor of arity k, named make_D, is introduced. It is common to write $\mathsf{t}.\ell$ for the application $\ell\ \mathsf{t}$ and, when $k > 0$, to write $\{\ell_i = \mathsf{t}_i\}_{i=1}^{k}$ for the application $\mathsf{make}_\mathsf{D}\ \mathsf{t}_1 \ldots \mathsf{t}_k$. The operational semantics is extended with the following reduction rules, for $i \in \{1, \ldots, k\}$:

$$(\{\ell_j = \mathsf{v}_j\}_{j=1}^{k}).\ell_i \xrightarrow{\delta} \mathsf{v}_i \qquad \text{(R-ALG-PROJ)}$$

For each $i \in \{1, \ldots, k\}$, the initial environment is extended with the binding $\ell_i : \forall \vec{\mathsf{X}}.\mathsf{D}\,\vec{\mathsf{X}} \to \mathsf{T}_i$. It is further extended with the binding $\mathsf{make}_\mathsf{D} : \forall \vec{\mathsf{X}}.\mathsf{T}_1 \to \ldots \to \mathsf{T}_k \to \mathsf{D}\,\vec{\mathsf{X}}$.

10.7.10 **Example:** The effect of defining list (Example 10.7.9) is to make Nil and Cons data constructors of arity 1 and to introduce a binary destructor $\mathtt{case}_{\mathsf{list}}$. The definition also extends the initial environment as follows:

$$\begin{array}{rl} \mathtt{Nil}: & \forall X.\mathsf{unit} \to \mathsf{list}\,X \\ \mathtt{Cons}: & \forall X.X \times \mathsf{list}\,X \to \mathsf{list}\,X \\ \mathtt{case}_{\mathsf{list}}: & \forall XZ.\mathsf{list}\,X \to (\mathsf{unit} \to Z) \to (X \times \mathsf{list}\,X \to Z) \to Z \end{array}$$

Thus, the value $\mathtt{Cons}(\hat{0}, \mathtt{Nil}())$, an integer list of length 1, has type list int. A function that computes the length of a list may now be written as follows:

$$\mathtt{letrec\ length} = \lambda \mathtt{l}.\mathtt{case\ l}\ [\ \mathtt{Nil} : \lambda_.\hat{0} \mid \mathtt{Cons} : \lambda \mathtt{z}.\hat{1} \mathbin{\hat{+}} \mathtt{length}\ (\pi_2\ \mathtt{z})\ ]$$

Recall that this notation is syntactic sugar for

$$\mathtt{letrec\ length} = \lambda \mathtt{l}.\mathtt{case}_{\mathsf{list}}\ \mathtt{l}\ (\lambda_.\hat{0})\ (\lambda \mathtt{z}.\hat{1} \mathbin{\hat{+}} \mathtt{length}\ (\pi_2\ \mathtt{z}))$$

The difference with the code in Example 10.7.7 appears minimal: the case construct is now annotated with the data type list. As a result, the type inference algorithm employs the type scheme assigned to $\mathtt{case}_{\mathsf{list}}$, which is derived from the definition of list, instead of the type scheme assigned to the anonymous case construct, given in Exercise 10.7.4. This is good for a couple of reasons. First, the former is more informative than the latter, because it contains the type T_i associated with the data constructor ℓ_i. Here, for instance, the generated constraint requires the type of z to be $X \times \mathsf{list}\,X$ for some X, so a good error message would be given if a mistake was made in the second branch, such as omitting the use of π_2. Second, and more fundamentally, the code is now well-typed, even in the absence of recursive types. In Example 10.7.7, a cyclic equation was produced because case required the type of l to be a sum type and because a sum type carries the types of its left and right branches as subterms. Here, $\mathtt{case}_{\mathsf{list}}$ requires l to have type list X for some X. This is an abstract type: it does not explicitly contain the types of the branches. As a result, the generated constraint no longer involves a cyclic equation. It is, in fact, satisfiable; the reader may check that length has type $\forall X.\mathsf{list}\,X \to \mathsf{int}$, as expected. □

Example 10.7.10 stresses the importance of using declared, abstract types, as opposed to anonymous, concrete sum or product types, in order to obviate the need for recursive types. The essence of the trick lies in the fact that the type schemes associated with operations on algebraic data types implicitly fold and unfold the data type's definition. More precisely, let us recall the type scheme assigned to the ith injection in the setting of (k-ary) anonymous sums: it is $\forall X_1 \ldots X_k.X_i \to X_1 + \ldots + X_k$, or, more concisely, $\forall X_1 \ldots X_k.X_i \to \sum_{i=1}^{k} X_i$.

By instantiating each X_i with T_i and generalizing again, we find that a more specific type scheme is $\forall\bar{X}.T_i \rightarrow \sum_{i=1}^{k} T_i$. Perhaps this could have been the type scheme assigned to ℓ_i? Instead, however, it is $\forall\bar{X}.T_i \rightarrow D\vec{X}$. We now realize that the latter type scheme not only reflects the operational behavior of the ith injection but also folds the definition of the algebraic data type D by turning the anonymous sum $\sum_{i=1}^{k} T_i$—which forms the definition's right-hand side—into the parameterized abstract type $D\vec{X}$—which is the definition's left-hand side. Conversely, the type scheme assigned to $\texttt{case}_D$ unfolds the definition. The situation is identical in the case of record types: in either case, constructors fold, destructors unfold. In other words, occurrences of data constructors and record labels in the code may be viewed as explicit instructions for the typechecker to fold or unfold an algebraic data type definition. This mechanism is characteristic of isorecursive types.

10.7.11 **Exercise** [★, ↛]: For a fixed k, check that all of the machinery associated with k-ary anonymous products—that is, constructors, destructors, reduction rules, and extensions to the initial typing environment—may be viewed as the result of a single algebraic data type definition. Conduct a similar check in the case of k-ary anonymous sums. □

10.7.12 **Exercise** [★★★, ↛]: Check that the above definitions meet the requirements of Definition 10.5.5. □

10.7.13 **Exercise** [★★★, ↛]: For the sake of simplicity, we have assumed that all data constructors have arity one. If desired, it is possible to accept variant data type definitions of the form $D\vec{X} \approx \sum_{i=1}^{k} \ell_i : \vec{T}_i$, where the arity of the data constructor ℓ_i is the length of the vector $\vec{T}_i$, and may be an arbitrary nonnegative integer. This allows, for instance, altering the definition of list so that the data constructors `Nil` and `Cons` are respectively nullary and binary. Make the necessary changes in the above definitions and check that the requirements of Definition 10.5.5 are still met. □

One significant drawback of algebraic data type definitions resides in the fact that a label ℓ cannot be *shared* by two distinct variant or record type definitions. Indeed, every algebraic data type definition extends the calculus with new constants. Strictly speaking, our presentation does not allow a single constant c to be associated with two distinct definitions. Even if we did allow such a collision, the initial environment would contain two bindings for c, one of which would then hide the other. This phenomenon arises in actual implementations of ML-the-programming-language, where a new algebraic data type definition may hide some of the data constructors or record labels introduced by a previous definition. An elegant solution to this lack of expressiveness is discussed in §10.8.

Recursive Types

We have shown that specializing HM(X) with an equality-only syntactic model yields HM($=$), a constraint-based formulation of Damas and Milner's type system. Similarly, it is possible to specialize HM(X) with an equality-only free regular tree model, yielding a constraint-based type system that may be viewed as an extension of Damas and Milner's type discipline with recursive types. This flavor of recursive types is sometimes known as *equirecursive*, since cyclic *equations*, such as $\mathsf{X} = \mathsf{X} \rightarrow \mathsf{X}$, are then satisfiable. Our theorems about type inference and type soundness, which are independent of the model, remain valid. The constraint solver described in §10.6 may be used in the setting of an equality-only free regular tree model; the only difference with the syntactic case is that the occurs check is no longer performed.

Note that, although ground types are regular, types remain finite objects: their syntax is unchanged. The μ notation commonly employed to describe recursive types may be emulated using type equations: for instance, the notation $\mu\mathsf{X}.\mathsf{X} \rightarrow \mathsf{X}$ corresponds, in our constraint-based approach, to the type scheme $\forall\mathsf{X}[\mathsf{X} = \mathsf{X} \rightarrow \mathsf{X}].\mathsf{X}$.

Although recursive types come for free, as explained above, they have not been adopted in mainstream programming languages based on ML-the-type-system. The reason is pragmatic: experience shows that many nonsensical expressions are well-typed in the presence of recursive types, whereas they are not in their absence. Thus, the gain in expressiveness is offset by the fact that many programming mistakes are detected later than otherwise possible. Consider, for instance, the following OCaml session:

```
ocaml -rectypes
# let rec map f = function
    | [] → []
    | x :: l → (map f x) :: (map f l);;
val map : 'a → ('b list as 'b) → ('c list as 'c) = <fun>
```

This nonsensical version of map is essentially useless, yet well-typed. Its principal type scheme, in our notation, is $\forall\mathsf{XYZ}[\mathsf{Y} = \mathsf{list}\,\mathsf{Y} \wedge \mathsf{Z} = \mathsf{list}\,\mathsf{Z}].\mathsf{X} \rightarrow \mathsf{Y} \rightarrow \mathsf{Z}$. In the absence of recursive types, it is ill-typed, since the constraint $\mathsf{Y} = \mathsf{list}\,\mathsf{Y} \wedge \mathsf{Z} = \mathsf{list}\,\mathsf{Z}$ is then false.

The need for equirecursive types is usually suppressed by the presence of algebraic data types, which offer isorecursive types, in the language. Yet, they are still necessary in some situations, such as in Objective Caml's extensions with objects (Rémy and Vouillon, 1998) or polymorphic variants (Garrigue, 1998, 2000, 2002), where recursive object or variant types are commonly inferred. In order to allow recursive object or variant types while still rejecting the above version of map, Objective Caml's constraint solver implements a selective occurs check, which forbids cycles unless they involve the type constructors $\langle\cdot\rangle$ or $[\cdot]$ respectively associated with objects and variants. The corresponding model is a tree model where every infinite path down a tree must encounter the type constructor $\langle\cdot\rangle$ or $[\cdot]$ infinitely often.

10.8 Rows

In §10.7, we have shown how to extend ML-the-programming-language with algebraic data types, that is, variant and record type definitions, which we now refer to as *simple*. This mechanism has a severe limitation: two distinct definitions must define incompatible types. As a result, one cannot hope to write code that uniformly operates over variants or records of different shapes, because the type of such code is not even expressible.

For instance, it is impossible to express the type of the *polymorphic record access* operation, which retrieves the value stored at a particular field ℓ inside a record, regardless of which other fields are present. Indeed, if the label ℓ appears with type T in the definition of the simple record type $\mathsf{D}\vec{\mathsf{X}}$, then the associated record access operation has type $\forall\vec{\mathsf{X}}.\mathsf{D}\vec{\mathsf{X}} \to \mathsf{T}$. If ℓ appears with type T' in the definition of another simple record type, say $\mathsf{D}'\vec{\mathsf{X}}'$, then the associated record access operation has type $\forall\vec{\mathsf{X}}'.\mathsf{D}'\vec{\mathsf{X}}' \to \mathsf{T}'$; and so on. The most precise type scheme that subsumes all of these incomparable type schemes is $\forall\mathsf{XY}.\mathsf{X} \to \mathsf{Y}$. It is, however, not a sound type scheme for the record access operation. Another powerful operation whose type is currently not expressible is *polymorphic record extension*, which copies a record and stores a value at field ℓ in the copy, possibly creating the field if it did not previously exist, again regardless of which other fields are present. (If ℓ was known to previously exist, the operation is known as *polymorphic record update*.)

In order to assign types to polymorphic record operations, we must do away with record type definitions: we must replace named record types, such as $\mathsf{D}\vec{\mathsf{X}}$, with structural record types that provide a direct description of the record's domain and contents. (Following the analogy between a record and a partial function from labels to values, we use the word *domain* to refer to the set of fields that are defined in a record.) For instance, a product type is structural: the type $\mathsf{T}_1 \times \mathsf{T}_2$ is the (undeclared) type of pairs whose first component has type T_1 and whose second component has type T_2. Thus, we wish to design record types that behave very much like product types. In doing so, we face two orthogonal difficulties. First, as opposed to pairs, records may have different domains. Because the type system must statically ensure that no undefined field is accessed, information about a record's domain must be made part of its type. Second, because we suppress record type definitions, labels must now be predefined. However, for efficiency and modularity reasons, it is impossible to explicitly list every label in existence in every record type.

In what follows, we explain how to address the first difficulty in the simple setting of a finite set of labels. Then we introduce *rows*, which allow dealing with an infinite set of labels, and address the second difficulty. We define the syntax and logical interpretation of rows, study the new constraint equivalence laws that arise in their presence, and extend the first-order unification algorithm with support for rows. Then we review several applications of rows, including polymorphic operations on records, variants, and objects, and discuss alternatives to rows.

Because our interest is in typechecking and type inference issues, we do not address the compilation issue: how does one efficiently compile polymorphic records or polymorphic variants? A few relevant papers are Pugh and Weddell (1990), Ohori (1995), and Garrigue (1998). The problem of optimizing message dispatch in object-oriented languages, which has received considerable attention in the literature, is related.

Records with Finite Carrier

Let us temporarily assume that $\mathcal{L}$ is finite. In fact, for the sake of definiteness, let us assume that $\mathcal{L}$ is the three-element set $\{\ell_a, \ell_b, \ell_c\}$.

To begin, let us consider only *full* records, whose domain is exactly $\mathcal{L}$—in other words, tuples indexed by $\mathcal{L}$. To describe them, it is natural to introduce a type constructor Π of signature $\star \otimes \star \otimes \star \Rightarrow \star$. The type $\Pi\ \mathsf{T}_a\ \mathsf{T}_b\ \mathsf{T}_c$ represents all records where the field ℓ_a (respectively ℓ_b, ℓ_c) contains a value of type T_a (respectively T_b, T_c). Note that Π is nothing but a product type constructor of arity 3. The basic operations on records, namely *creation* of a record out of a default value, which is stored into every field, *update* of a particular field (say, ℓ_b), and *access* to a particular field (say, ℓ_b), may be assigned the following type schemes:

$$\begin{aligned} \{\cdot\} &: \forall \mathsf{X}.\mathsf{X} \rightarrow \Pi\ \mathsf{X}\ \mathsf{X}\ \mathsf{X} \\ \{\cdot \text{ with } \ell_b = \cdot\} &: \forall \mathsf{X}_a \mathsf{X}_b \mathsf{X}'_b \mathsf{X}_c.\Pi\ \mathsf{X}_a\ \mathsf{X}_b\ \mathsf{X}_c \rightarrow \mathsf{X}'_b \rightarrow \Pi\ \mathsf{X}_a\ \mathsf{X}'_b\ \mathsf{X}_c \\ \cdot.\{\ell_b\} &: \forall \mathsf{X}_a \mathsf{X}_b \mathsf{X}_c.\Pi\ \mathsf{X}_a\ \mathsf{X}_b\ \mathsf{X}_c \rightarrow \mathsf{X}_b \end{aligned}$$

Here, polymorphism allows updating or accessing a field without knowledge of the types of the other fields. This flexibility stems from the key property that all record types are formed using a single Π type constructor.

This is fine, but in general, the domain of a record is not necessarily $\mathcal{L}$: it may be a subset of $\mathcal{L}$. How may we deal with this fact while maintaining the above key property? A naive approach consists of encoding arbitrary records in terms of full records, using the standard algebraic data type option, whose definition is option X $\approx$ pre X + abs. We use pre for present and abs for absent: indeed, a field that is defined with value v is encoded as a field with value pre v, while an undefined field is encoded as a field with value abs. Thus, an arbitrary record whose fields, if present, have types T_a, T_b, and T_c, respectively, may be encoded as a full record of type Π (option T_a) (option T_b) (option T_c). This naive approach suffers from a serious drawback: record types still contain no domain information. As a result, field access must involve a dynamic check, so as to determine whether the desired field is present; in our encoding, this corresponds to the use of $\text{case}_{\text{option}}$.

To avoid this overhead and increase programming safety, we must move this check from runtime to compile time. In other words, we must make the type system aware of the difference between pre and abs. To do so, we replace the definition of option by two separate algebraic data type definitions, namely pre X $\approx$ pre X and abs $\approx$ abs. In other words, we introduce a unary type constructor pre, whose only associated data constructor is pre, and a nullary type constructor abs, whose only associated data constructor is abs. Record types now contain domain information; for instance, a record of type Π abs (pre T_b) (pre T_c) must have domain $\{\ell_b, \ell_c\}$. Thus, the type of a field tells whether it is defined. Since the type pre has no data constructors other than pre, the accessor pre^{-1}, whose type is $\forall X.\text{pre } X \to X$, and which allows retrieving the value stored in a field, cannot fail. Thus, the dynamic check has been eliminated.

To complete the definition of our encoding, we now define operations on arbitrary records in terms of operations on full records. To distinguish between the two, we write the former with angle braces, instead of curly braces. The *empty record* $\langle\rangle$, where all fields are undefined, may be defined as $\{\text{abs}\}$. *Extension* at a particular field (say, ℓ_b) $\langle \cdot \text{ with } \ell_b = \cdot\rangle$ is defined as $\lambda r.\lambda z.\{r \text{ with } \ell_b = \text{pre } z\}$. *Access* at a particular field (say, ℓ_b) $\cdot.\langle \ell_b\rangle$ is defined as $\lambda z.\text{pre}^{-1} z.\{\ell_b\}$. It is straightforward to check that these operations have the following principal type schemes:

$$\begin{aligned}
\langle\rangle &: \Pi \text{ abs abs abs} \\
\langle \cdot \text{ with } \ell_b = \cdot\rangle &: \forall X_a X_b X'_b X_c.\Pi\, X_a\, X_b\, X_c \to X'_b \to \Pi\, X_a\, (\text{pre } X'_b)\, X_c \\
\cdot.\langle \ell_b\rangle &: \forall X_a X_b X_c.\Pi\, X_a\, (\text{pre } X_b)\, X_c \to X_b
\end{aligned}$$

It is important to notice that the type schemes associated with extension and access at ℓ_b are polymorphic in X_a and X_c, which now means that these operations are insensitive, not only to the type, but also to the presence or absence of the fields ℓ_a and ℓ_c. Furthermore, extension is polymorphic in X_b, which means that it is insensitive to the presence or absence of the field ℓ_b in its argument. The subterm pre X'_b in its result type reflects the fact that

ℓ_b is defined in the extended record. Conversely, the subterm pre X_b in the type of the access operation reflects the requirement that ℓ_b be defined in its argument.

Our encoding of arbitrary records in terms of full records was carried out for pedagogical purposes. In practice, no such encoding is necessary: the *data* constructors pre and abs have no machine representation, and the compiler is free to lay out records in memory in an efficient manner. The encoding is interesting, however, because it provides a natural way of introducing the *type* constructors pre and abs, which play an important role in our treatment of polymorphic record operations.

Once we forget about the encoding, the arguments of the type constructor Π are expected to be either type variables or formed with pre or abs, while, conversely, the type constructors pre and abs are not intended to appear anywhere else. It is possible to enforce this invariant using kinds. In addition to $\star$, let us introduce the kind $\circ$ of *field types.* Then, let us adopt the following signatures: pre: $\star \Rightarrow \circ$, abs : $\circ$, and $\Pi : \circ \otimes \circ \otimes \circ \Rightarrow \star$.

10.8.1 EXERCISE [RECOMMENDED, $\star$, $\nrightarrow$]: Check that the three type schemes given above are well-kinded. What is the kind of each type variable? □

10.8.2 EXERCISE [RECOMMENDED, $\star\star$]: Our Π types contain information about every field, regardless of whether it is defined: we encode definedness information within the type of each field, using the type constructors pre and abs. A perhaps more natural approach would be to introduce a family of record type constructors, indexed by the subsets of $\mathcal{L}$, so that the types of records with different domains are formed with different constructors. For instance, the empty record would have type $\{\}$; a record that defines the field ℓ_a only would have a type of the form $\{\ell_a : \mathsf{T}_a\}$; a record that defines the fields ℓ_b and ℓ_c only would have a type of the form $\{\ell_b : \mathsf{T}_b; \ell_c : \mathsf{T}_c\}$; and so on. Assuming that the type discipline is Damas and Milner's (that is, assuming an equality-only syntactic model), would it be possible to assign satisfactory type schemes to polymorphic record access and extension? Would it help to equip record types with a nontrivial subtyping relation? □

Records with Infinite Carrier

The treatment of records described above is not quite satisfactory, from practical and theoretical points of view. First, in practice, the set $\mathcal{L}$ of all record labels that appear within a program could be very large. Because every record type is just as large as $\mathcal{L}$ itself, even if the record that it describes only has a few fields, this is unpleasant. Furthermore, in a modular setting, the set of all record labels that appear within a program cannot be determined until link time, so it is still unknown at compile time, when each compilation unit is separately typechecked. As a result, it may only be assumed to be a subset of the infinite set of all syntactically valid record labels. Resolving these issues requires coming up with a treatment of records that does not become more costly as $\mathcal{L}$ grows and that, in fact, allows $\mathcal{L}$ to be infinite. Thus, from here on, let us assume that $\mathcal{L}$ is infinite.

As in the previous section, we first concentrate on full records, whose domain is exactly $\mathcal{L}$. The case of arbitrary records, whose domain is a subset of $\mathcal{L}$, will then follow in the same manner, by using the type constructors pre and abs to encode domain information.

Of course, even though we have assumed that $\mathcal{L}$ is infinite, we must ensure that every record has a finite representation. We choose to restrict our attention to records that are *almost constant*, that is, records where all fields but a finite number contain the same value. Every such record may be defined in terms of two primitive operations, namely (i) *creation* of a constant record out of a value; for instance, {false} is the record where every field contains the value false; and (ii) *update* of a record at a particular field; for instance, {{false} with ℓ = 1} carries the value 1 at field ℓ and the value false at every other field. As usual, an *access* operation allows retrieving the contents of a field. Thus, the three primitive operations are the same as in the previous subsection, only in the setting of an infinite number of fields.

If we were to continue as before, we would now introduce a type constructor Π, equipped with an infinite family of type parameters. Because types must remain finite objects, we cannot do so. Instead, we must find a finite (and economical) representation of such an infinite family of types. This is precisely the role played by *rows*.

A row is a type that denotes a function from labels to types or, equivalently, a family of types indexed by labels. Its domain is $\mathcal{L}$—the row is then *complete*—or a cofinite subset of $\mathcal{L}$—the row is then *incomplete*. (A subset of $\mathcal{L}$ is cofinite if and only if its complement is finite. Incomplete rows are used only as building blocks for complete rows.) Because rows must admit a finite representation, we build them out of two syntactic constructions, namely (i) construction of a *constant row* out of a type; for instance, the notation ∂bool denotes a row that maps every label in its domain to bool; and (ii) strict *extension* of an incomplete row; for instance, (ℓ : int ; ∂bool) denotes a row that maps ℓ to int and every other field in its domain to bool. Formally, ∂ is a unary type constructor, while, for every label ℓ, $(\ell : \cdot \ ; \cdot)$ is a binary type constructor. These two constructions are reminiscent of the two operations used above to build records. There are, however, a couple of subtle but important differences. First, ∂T may be a complete or incomplete row. Second, (ℓ : T ; T′) is defined only if ℓ is not in the domain of the row T′, so this construction is strict extension, not update. These aspects are made clear by a *kinding discipline*, to be introduced later on.

It is possible for two syntactically distinct rows to denote the same function from labels to types. For instance, according to the intuitive interpretation of rows given above, the three complete rows $(\ell : \mathsf{int} \,;\, \partial\mathsf{bool})$, $(\ell : \mathsf{int} \,;\, (\ell' : \mathsf{bool} \,;\, \partial\mathsf{bool}))$, and $(\ell' : \mathsf{bool} \,;\, (\ell : \mathsf{int} \,;\, \partial\mathsf{bool}))$ denote the same total function from labels to types. In the following, we define the logical interpretation of types in such a way that the interpretations of these three rows in the model are indeed equal.

We may now make the record type constructor Π a unary type constructor, whose parameter is a row. Then, (say) $\Pi\ (\ell : \mathsf{int} \,;\, \partial\mathsf{bool})$ is a record type, and we intend it to be a valid type for the record `{{false} with ℓ = 1}`. The basic operations on records may be assigned the following type schemes:

$$\begin{aligned} \{\cdot\} :&\quad \forall \mathsf{X}.\mathsf{X} \to \Pi\ (\partial\mathsf{X}) \\ \{\cdot\ \mathsf{with}\ \ell = \cdot\} :&\quad \forall \mathsf{X}\mathsf{X}'\mathsf{Y}.\Pi\ (\ell : \mathsf{X} \,;\, \mathsf{Y}) \to \mathsf{X}' \to \Pi\ (\ell : \mathsf{X}' \,;\, \mathsf{Y}) \\ \cdot.\{\ell\} :&\quad \forall \mathsf{X}\mathsf{Y}.\Pi\ (\ell : \mathsf{X} \,;\, \mathsf{Y}) \to \mathsf{X} \end{aligned}$$

These type schemes are reminiscent of those given above. However, in the previous section, the size of the type schemes was linear in the cardinal of $\mathcal{L}$, whereas here it is constant, even though $\mathcal{L}$ is infinite. This is made possible by the fact that record types no longer list all labels in existence; instead, they use rows. In the type scheme assigned to record creation, the constant row $\partial\mathsf{X}$ is used to indicate that all fields have the same type in the newly created record. In the next two type schemes, the row $(\ell : \mathsf{X}_\ell \,;\, \mathsf{X})$ is used to separate the type X_ℓ, which describes the contents of the field ℓ, and the row X, which collectively describes the contents of all other fields. Here, the type variable X stands for an arbitrary row; it is often referred to as a *row variable*. The ability of quantifying over row and type variables alike confers great expressiveness to the type system.

We have explained, in an informal manner, how rows allow typechecking operations on full records, in the setting of an infinite set of labels. We return to this issue in Example 10.8.25. To deal with the case of arbitrary records, whose domain is finite, we rely on the field type constructors pre and abs, as explained previously. We return to this point in Example 10.8.30. In the following, we give a formal exposition of rows. We begin with their syntax and logical interpretation. Then we give some new constraint equivalence laws, which characterize rows, and allow extending our first-order unification algorithm with support for rows. We conclude with several illustrations of the use of rows and some pointers to related work.

Syntax of Rows

In the following, the set of labels $\mathcal{L}$ is considered denumerable. We let L range over finite subsets of $\mathcal{L}$. When $\ell \notin L$ holds, we write $\ell.L$ for $\{\ell\} \uplus L$. Before explaining how the syntax of types is enriched with rows, we introduce *row kinds*, whose grammar is as follows:

$$s ::= \mathit{Type} \mid \mathit{Row}(L)$$

Row kinds help distinguish between three kinds of types, namely ordinary types, complete rows, and incomplete rows. While ordinary types are used to describe expressions, complete or incomplete rows are used only as building blocks for ordinary types. For instance, the record type $\Pi\ (\ell : \mathsf{int}\ ;\ \partial\mathsf{bool})$, which was informally introduced above, is intended to be an ordinary type, that is, a type of row kind *Type*. Its subterm $(\ell : \mathsf{int}\ ;\ \partial\mathsf{bool})$ is a complete row, that is, a type of row kind $\mathit{Row}(\emptyset)$. Its subterm $\partial\mathsf{bool}$ is an incomplete row, whose row kind is $\mathit{Row}(\{\ell\})$. Intuitively, a row of kind $\mathit{Row}(L)$ denotes a family of types whose domain is $\mathcal{L} \setminus L$. In other words, L is the set of labels that the row does not define. The purpose of row kinds is to outlaw meaningless types, such as $\Pi\ (\mathsf{int})$, which makes no sense because the argument to the record type constructor Π should be a (complete) row, or $(\ell : \mathsf{T}_1\ ;\ \ell : \mathsf{T}_2\ ;\ \partial\mathsf{bool})$, which makes no sense because no label may occur twice within a row.

Let us now define the syntax of types in the presence of rows. As usual, it is given by a signature S (Definition 10.1.14), which lists all type constructors together with their signatures. Here, for the sake of generality, we do not wish to give a fixed signature S. Instead, we give a procedure that builds S out of two simpler signatures, referred to as S_0 and S_1. The input signature S_0 lists the type constructors that have nothing to do with rows, such as $\rightarrow$, $\times$, int, etc. The input signature S_1 lists the type constructors that allow a row to be a subterm of an ordinary type, such as the record type constructor Π. In a type system equipped with extensible variant types or with object types, there might be several such type constructors; see the sections on Polymorphic Variants (p. 483) and Other Applications of Rows (p. 486). Without loss of generality, we assume that all type constructors in S_1 are unary. The point of parameterizing the definition of S over S_0 and S_1 is to make the construction more general: instead of defining a fixed type grammar featuring rows, we wish to explain how to enrich an arbitrary type grammar with rows.

In the following, we let G (respectively H) range over the type constructors in S_0 (respectively S_1). We let κ range over the kinds involved in the definition of S_0 and S_1, and refer to them as *basic kinds*. We let F range over the type constructors in S. The kinds involved in the definition of S are *composite kinds*, that is, pairs of a basic kind κ and a row kind s, written $\kappa.s$.

This allows the kind discipline enforced by S to reflect that enforced by S_0 and S_1 and also to impose restrictions on the structure and use of rows, as suggested above. For the sake of conciseness, we write $K.s$ for the mapping $(d \mapsto K(d).s)^{d \in dom(K)}$ and $(K \Rightarrow \kappa).s$ for the (composite) kind signature $K.s \Rightarrow \kappa.s$. (In other words, we let $.s$ distribute over basic signatures.) We use symmetric notations to build a composite kind signature out of a basic kind and a row kind signature.

10.8.3 **Definition:** The signature S is defined as follows:

$F \in dom(S)$	Signature	Conditions
G^s	$(K \Rightarrow \kappa).s$	$(G : K \Rightarrow \kappa) \in S_0$
H	$K.Row(\emptyset) \Rightarrow \kappa.Type$	$(H : K \Rightarrow \kappa) \in S_1$
$\partial^{\kappa,L}$	$\kappa.(Type \Rightarrow Row(L))$	
$\ell^{\kappa,L}$	$\kappa.(Type \otimes Row(\ell.L) \Rightarrow Row(L))$	$\ell \notin L$

We sometimes refer to S as the *row extension of* S_0 *with* S_1. □

Examples 10.8.7 and 10.8.8 suggest common choices of S_0 and S_1 and give a perhaps more concrete-looking definition of the grammar of types that they determine. First, however, let us explain the definition. The type constructors that populate S come in four varieties: they may be (i) taken from S_0, (ii) taken from S_1, (iii) a unary row constructor ∂, or (iv) a binary row constructor $(\ell : \cdot\, ; \cdot)$. Let us review and explain each case.

Let us first consider case (i) and assume, for the time being, that s is *Type*. Then, for every type constructor G in S_0, there is a corresponding type constructor G^{Type} in S. For instance, S_0 must contain an arrow type constructor $\rightarrow$, whose signature is $\{domain \mapsto \star, codomain \mapsto \star\} \Rightarrow \star$. Then, S contains a type constructor $\rightarrow^{Type}$, whose signature is $\{domain \mapsto \star.Type, codomain \mapsto \star.Type\} \Rightarrow \star.Type$. Thus, $\rightarrow^{Type}$ is a binary type constructor whose parameters and result must have basic kind $\star$ and must have row kind *Type*; in other words, they must be ordinary types, as opposed to complete or incomplete rows. The family of all type constructors of the form G^{Type}, where G ranges over S_0, forms a copy of S_0 at row kind *Type*: one might say, roughly speaking, that S contains S_0. This is not surprising, since our purpose is to enrich the existing signature S_0 with syntax for rows.

Perhaps more surprising is the existence of the type constructor G^s, for every G in S_0, and for every row kind s. For instance, for every L, S contains a type constructor $\rightarrow^{Row(L)}$, whose signature is $\{domain \mapsto \star.Row(L), codomain \mapsto \star.Row(L)\} \Rightarrow \star.Row(L)$. Thus, $\rightarrow^{Row(L)}$ is a binary type constructor whose parameters and result must have basic kind $\star$ and must have row kind $Row(L)$. In other words, this type constructor maps a pair of rows that have a common domain to a row with the same domain. Recall that a row is to be interpreted as a family of types. Our intention is that $\rightarrow^{Row(L)}$ maps two families of types to a family of arrow types. This is made precise in the next subsection. One should point out that the type constructors G^s, with $s \neq Type$, are required only in some advanced applications of rows; Examples 10.8.28 and 10.8.39 provide illustrations. They are not used when assigning types to the usual primitive operations on records, namely creation, update, and access (Examples 10.8.25 and 10.8.30).

Case (ii) is simple: it simply means that S *contains* S_1. It is only worth noting that every type constructor H maps a parameter of row kind $Row(\emptyset)$ to a result of row kind *Type*, that is, a complete row to an ordinary type. Thanks to this design choice, the type $\Pi\ (\mathsf{int}^{Type})$ is invalid: indeed, int^{Type} has row kind *Type*, while Π expects a parameter of row kind $Row(\emptyset)$.

Cases (iii) and (iv) introduce new type constructors that were not present in S_0 or S_1 and allow forming rows. They were informally described in the previous subsection. First, for every κ and L, there is a *constant row constructor* $\partial^{\kappa,L}$. Its parameter must have row kind *Type*, while its result has row kind $Row(L)$; in other words, this type constructor maps an ordinary type to a row. It is worth noting that the row thus built may be complete or incomplete; for instance, $\partial^{\star,\emptyset}\ \mathsf{bool}$ is a complete row, and may be used, for example, to build the type $\Pi\ (\partial^{\star,\emptyset}\ \mathsf{bool})$, while $\partial^{\star,\{\ell\}}\ \mathsf{bool}$ is an incomplete row, and may be used, for example, to build the type $\Pi\ (\ell : \mathsf{int}\ ;\ \partial^{\star,\{\ell\}}\ \mathsf{bool})$. Second, for every κ, L, and $\ell \notin L$, there is a *row extension constructor* $\ell^{\kappa,L}$. We usually write $\ell^{\kappa,L} : \mathsf{T}_1\ ;\ \mathsf{T}_2$ for $\ell^{\kappa,L}\ \mathsf{T}_1\ \mathsf{T}_2$ and let this symbol be right associative so as to recover the familiar list notation for rows. According to the definition of S, if T_2 has row kind $Row(\ell.L)$, then $\ell^{\kappa,L} : \mathsf{T}_1\ ;\ \mathsf{T}_2$ has row kind $Row(L)$. Thanks to this design choice, the type $(\ell^{\star,L} : \mathsf{T}_1\ ;\ \ell^{\star,L} : \mathsf{T}_2\ ;\ \partial^{\star,\ell.L}\ \mathsf{bool})$ is invalid; indeed, the outer ℓ expects a parameter of row kind $Row(\ell.L)$, while the inner ℓ produces a type of row kind $Row(L)$.

The superscripts carried by the type constructors G, ℓ, and ∂ in the signature S make all kind information explicit, obviating the need for assigning several kinds to a single type constructor. In practice, however, we often drop the superscripts and use *unannotated* types. No ambiguity arises because, given a type expression T of known kind, it is possible to reconstruct all superscripts in a unique manner. This is the topic of the next example and exercises.

10.8.4 EXAMPLE [ILL-KINDED TYPES]: Assume that S_0 contains type constructors int and $\rightarrow$, whose signatures are respectively $\star$ and $\star \otimes \star \Rightarrow \star$, and that S_1 contains a type constructor Π, whose signature is $\star \Rightarrow \star$.

The unannotated type $\mathsf{X} \rightarrow \Pi(\mathsf{X})$ is invalid. Indeed, because Π's image row kind is *Type*, the arrow must be $\rightarrow^{Type}$. Thus, the leftmost occurrence of X

must have row kind *Type*. On the other hand, because Π expects a parameter of row kind $Row(\emptyset)$, its rightmost occurrence must have row kind $Row(\emptyset)$—a contradiction. The unannotated type $\mathsf{X} \to \Pi(\partial \mathsf{X})$ is, however, valid, provided X has kind $\star.Type$. In fact, it is the type of the primitive record creation operation.

The unannotated type $(\ell : \mathsf{T}\ ;\ \ell : \mathsf{T} ; \mathsf{T}'')$ is also invalid: there is no way of reconstructing the missing superscripts so as to make it valid. Indeed, the row $(\ell : \mathsf{T}'\ ;\ \mathsf{T}'')$ must have row kind $Row(L)$ for some L that does not contain ℓ. However, the context where it occurs requires it to also have row kind $Row(L)$ for some L that does contain ℓ. This makes it impossible to reconstruct consistent superscripts.

Any type of the form $\Pi(\Pi(\mathsf{T}))$ is invalid, because the outer Π expects a parameter of row kind $Row(\emptyset)$, while the inner Π constructs a type of row kind *Type*. This is an intentional limitation: unlike those of S_0, the type constructors of S_1 are not lifted to every row kind s. (If they were, we would be led to work not only with rows of ordinary types, but also with rows of rows, rows of rows of rows, and so on. Rémy (1990) explores this avenue.) □

10.8.5 **Exercise [Recommended, ★]:** Consider the unannotated type

$$\mathsf{X} \to \Pi(\ell : \mathsf{int}\ ;\ (\mathsf{Y} \to \partial \mathsf{X})).$$

Can you guess the kind of the type variables X and Y, as well as the missing superscripts, so as to ensure that this type has kind $\star.Type$? □

10.8.6 **Exercise [★★★, ↛]:** Propose a kind checking algorithm that, given an unannotated type T, given the kind of T, and given the kind of all type variables that appear within T, ensures that T is well-kinded, and reconstructs the missing superscripts within T. Next, propose a kind inference algorithm that, given an unannotated type T, discovers the kind of T and the kind of all type variables that appear within T so as to ensure that T is well-kinded. □

We have given a very general definition of the syntax of types. In this view, types, ranged over by the meta-variable T, encompass both "ordinary" types and rows: the distinction between the two is established only via the kind system. In the literature, however, it is common to establish this distinction by letting distinct meta-variables, say T and R, range over ordinary types and rows, respectively, so as to give the syntax a more concrete aspect. The next two examples illustrate this style and suggest common choices for S_0 and S_1.

10.8.7 **Example:** Assume that there is a single basic kind $\star$, that S_0 consists of the arrow type constructor $\to$, whose signature is $\star \otimes \star \Rightarrow \star$, and that S_1 consists of the record type constructor Π, whose signature is $\star \Rightarrow \star$. Then, the composite kinds are $\star.\mathit{Type}$ and $\star.\mathit{Row}(L)$, where L ranges over the finite subsets of $\mathcal{L}$. Let us employ T (respectively R) to range over types of the former (respectively latter) kind, and refer to them as ordinary types (respectively rows). Then, the syntax of types, as defined by the signature S, may be presented under the following form:

$$\begin{array}{rcl} \mathsf{T} & ::= & \mathsf{X} \mid \mathsf{T} \to \mathsf{T} \mid \Pi\,\mathsf{R} \\ \mathsf{R} & ::= & \mathsf{X} \mid \mathsf{R} \to \mathsf{R} \mid (\ell : \mathsf{T}\,;\, \mathsf{R}) \mid \partial \mathsf{T} \end{array}$$

Ordinary types T include ordinary type variables (that is, type variables of kind $\star.\mathit{Type}$), arrow types (where the type constructor $\to$ is really $\to^{\mathit{Type}}$), and record types, which are formed by applying the record type constructor Π to a row. Rows R include row variables (that is, type variables of kind $\star.\mathit{Row}(L)$ for some L), arrow rows (where the row constructor $\to$ is really $\to^{\mathit{Row}(L)}$ for some L), row extension (whereby a row R is extended with an ordinary type T at a certain label ℓ), and constant rows (formed out of an ordinary type T). It would be possible to also introduce a syntactic distinction between ordinary type variables and row variables, if desired.

Such a presentation is rather pleasant, because the syntactic segregation between ordinary types and rows makes the syntax less ambiguous. It does not allow getting rid of the kind system, however: (row) kinds are still necessary to keep track of the domain of every row. □

10.8.8 EXAMPLE: Assume that there are two basic kinds $\star$ and $\circ$, that S_0 consists of the type constructors $\to$, abs, and pre, whose respective signatures are $\star \otimes \star \Rightarrow \star$, $\circ$, and $\star \Rightarrow \circ$, and that S_1 consists of the record type constructor Π, whose signature is $\circ \Rightarrow \star$. Then, the composite kinds are $\star.\mathit{Type}$, $\star.\mathit{Row}(L)$, $\circ.\mathit{Type}$, and $\circ.\mathit{Row}(L)$, where L ranges over the finite subsets of $\mathcal{L}$. Let us employ $\mathsf{T}^\star$, $\mathsf{R}^\star$, T°, and R°, respectively, to range over types of these four kinds. Then, the syntax of types, as defined by the signature S, may be presented under the following form:

$$\begin{array}{rcl} \mathsf{T}^\star & ::= & \mathsf{X} \mid \mathsf{T}^\star \to \mathsf{T}^\star \mid \Pi\,\mathsf{R}^\circ \\ \mathsf{R}^\star & ::= & \mathsf{X} \mid \mathsf{R}^\star \to \mathsf{R}^\star \mid (\ell : \mathsf{T}^\star\,;\, \mathsf{R}^\star) \mid \partial \mathsf{T}^\star \\ \mathsf{T}^\circ & ::= & \mathsf{X} \mid \mathsf{abs} \mid \mathsf{pre}\;\mathsf{T}^\star \\ \mathsf{R}^\circ & ::= & \mathsf{X} \mid \mathsf{abs} \mid \mathsf{pre}\;\mathsf{R}^\star \mid (\ell : \mathsf{T}^\circ\,;\, \mathsf{R}^\circ) \mid \partial \mathsf{T}^\circ \end{array}$$

Ordinary types $\mathsf{T}^\star$ are as in the previous example, except the record type constructor Π must now be applied to a row of field types R°. Rows $\mathsf{R}^\star$ are unchanged. Field types T° include field type variables (that is, type variables of kind $\circ.\mathit{Type}$) and applications of the type constructors abs and pre (which are really $\mathsf{abs}^{\mathit{Type}}$ and $\mathsf{pre}^{\mathit{Type}}$). Field rows R° include field row variables (that is, type variables of kind $\circ.Row(L)$ for some L), applications of the row constructors abs and pre (which are really $\mathsf{abs}^{Row(L)}$ and $\mathsf{pre}^{Row(L)}$ for some L), row extension, and constant rows, where row components are field types T°.

In many basic applications of rows, $\mathsf{abs}^{Row(L)}$ and $\mathsf{pre}^{Row(L)}$ are never required: that is, they do not appear in the type schemes that populate the initial environment. (Applications where they are required appear in Pottier [2000].) In that case, they may be removed from the syntax. Then, the nonterminal $\mathsf{R}^\star$ becomes unreachable from the nonterminal $\mathsf{T}^\star$, which is the grammar's natural entry point, so it may be removed as well. In that simplified setting, the syntax of types and rows becomes:

$$\begin{array}{rcl} \mathsf{T}^\star & ::= & \mathsf{X} \mid \mathsf{T}^\star \to \mathsf{T}^\star \mid \Pi\, \mathsf{R}^\circ \\ \mathsf{T}^\circ & ::= & \mathsf{X} \mid \mathsf{abs} \mid \mathsf{pre}\ \mathsf{T}^\star \\ \mathsf{R}^\circ & ::= & \mathsf{X} \mid (\ell : \mathsf{T}^\circ \,;\, \mathsf{R}^\circ) \mid \partial \mathsf{T}^\circ \end{array}$$

This is the syntax found in some introductory accounts of rows (Rémy, 1989; Pottier, 2000). □

Meaning of Rows

We now give meaning to the type grammar defined in the previous section by interpreting it within a model. We choose to define a regular tree model, but alternatives exist; see Remark 10.8.12 below. In this model, every type constructor whose image row kind is *Type* (that is, every type constructor of the form G^{Type} or H) is interpreted as itself, as in a free tree model. However, every application of a type constructor whose image row kind is $Row(L)$ for some L receives special treatment: it is interpreted as a family of types indexed by $\mathcal{L} \setminus L$, which we encode as an infinitely branching tree. To serve as the root label of this tree, we introduce, for every κ and for every L, a symbol L^κ, whose arity is $\mathcal{L} \setminus L$. More precisely,

10.8.9 **Definition:** The model, which consists of a set $\mathcal{M}_{\kappa.s}$ for every κ and s, is the regular tree algebra that arises out the following signature:

Symbol	Signature	Conditions
G	$(K \Rightarrow \kappa).Type$	$(G : K \Rightarrow \kappa) \in S_0$
H	$K.Row(\emptyset) \Rightarrow \kappa.Type$	$(H : K \Rightarrow \kappa) \in S_1$
L^κ	$\kappa.(Type^{\mathcal{L}\setminus L} \Rightarrow Row(L))$	

The first two lines in this signature coincide with the definitions of G^{Type} and H in the signature S. Indeed, as stated above, we intend to interpret these type constructors in a syntactic manner, so each of them must have a counterpart in the model. The third line introduces the symbols L^κ hinted at above.

According to this signature, if t is a ground type of kind $\kappa.\mathit{Type}$ (that is, an element of $\mathcal{M}_{\kappa.\mathit{Type}}$), then its head symbol $t(\epsilon)$ must be of the form G or H. If t is a ground type of kind $\kappa.\mathit{Row}(L)$, then its head symbol must be L^κ, and its immediate subtrees, which are indexed by $\mathcal{L} \setminus L$, are ground types of kind $\kappa.\mathit{Type}$; in other words, the ground row t is effectively a family of ordinary ground types indexed by $\mathcal{L} \setminus L$. Thus, our intuition that rows denote infinite families of types is made literally true.

We have defined the model; there remains to explain how types are mapped to elements of the model.

10.8.10 **Definition**: The interpretation of the type constructors that populate S is defined as follows.

1. Let $(G : K \Rightarrow \kappa) \in S_0$. Then, G^{Type} is interpreted as the function that maps $T \in \mathcal{M}_{K.\mathit{Type}}$ to the ground type $t \in \mathcal{M}_{\kappa.\mathit{Type}}$ defined by $t(\epsilon) = G$ and $t/d = T(d)$ for every $d \in \mathit{dom}(K)$. This is a syntactic interpretation.

2. Let $(H : K \Rightarrow \kappa) \in S_1$. Then, H is interpreted as the function that maps $T \in \mathcal{M}_{K.\mathit{Row}(\emptyset)}$ to the ground type $t \in \mathcal{M}_{\kappa.\mathit{Type}}$ defined by $t(\epsilon) = H$ and $t/d = T(d)$ for every $d \in \mathit{dom}(K)$. (Because H is unary, there is exactly one such d.) This is also a syntactic interpretation.

3. Let $(G : K \Rightarrow \kappa) \in S_0$. Then, $G^{\mathit{Row}(L)}$ is interpreted as the function that maps $T \in \mathcal{M}_{K.\mathit{Row}(L)}$ to the ground type $t \in \mathcal{M}_{\kappa.\mathit{Row}(L)}$ defined by $t(\epsilon) = L^\kappa$ and $t(\ell) = G$ and $t/(\ell \cdot d) = T(d)/\ell$ for every $\ell \in \mathcal{L} \setminus L$ and $d \in \mathit{dom}(K)$. Thus, when applied to a family of rows, the type constructor $G^{\mathit{Row}(L)}$ produces a row where every component has head symbol G. This definition may sound quite technical; its effect is summed up in a simpler fashion by the equations C-Row-GD and C-Row-GL in the next section.

4. Interpret $\partial^{\kappa,L}$ as the function that maps $t_1 \in \mathcal{M}_{\kappa.\mathit{Type}}$ to the ground type $t \in \mathcal{M}_{\kappa.\mathit{Row}(L)}$ defined by $t(\epsilon) = L^\kappa$ and $t/\ell = t_1$ for every $\ell \in \mathcal{L} \setminus L$. Note that t/ℓ does not depend on ℓ: t is a constant ground row.

5. Let $\ell \notin L$. Then, $\ell^{\kappa,L}$ is interpreted as the function that maps $(t_1, t_2) \in \mathcal{M}_{\kappa.\mathit{Type}} \times \mathcal{M}_{\kappa.\mathit{Row}(\ell.L)}$ to the ground type $t \in \mathcal{M}_{\kappa.\mathit{Row}(L)}$ defined by $t(\epsilon) = L^\kappa$ and $t/\ell = t_1$ and $t/\ell' = t_2(\ell')$ for every $\ell' \in \mathcal{L} \setminus \ell.L$. This definition is precisely row extension; indeed, the ground row t maps ℓ to t_1 and coincides with the ground row t_2 at every other label ℓ'. □

Defining a model and an interpretation allows our presentation of rows to fit within the formalism proposed earlier in this chapter (§10.2). It also provides a basis for the intuition that rows denote infinite families of types. From a formal point of view, the model and its interpretation allow proving several constraint equivalence laws concerning rows, which are given and discussed in the next subsection. Of course, it is also possible to accept these equivalence laws as axioms and give a purely syntactic account of rows without relying on a model; this is how rows were historically dealt with (Rémy, 1993).

10.8.11 REMARK: We have not defined the interpretation of the subtyping predicate, because much of the material that follows is independent of it. One common approach is to adopt a nonstructural definition of subtyping (Example 10.2.9), where every L^{κ} is considered covariant in every direction, and where the variances and relative ordering of all other symbols (G and H) are chosen at will, subject to the restrictions associated with nonstructural subtyping and to the conditions necessary to ensure type soundness.

Recall that the arrow type constructor $\rightarrow$ is contravariant in its domain and covariant in its codomain. The record type constructor Π is usually covariant. These properties are exploited in proofs of the subject reduction theorem. The type constructors $\rightarrow$ and Π are usually incompatible. This property is exploited in proofs of the progress theorem. In the case of Example 10.8.7, because no type constructors other than $\rightarrow$ and Π are present, these conditions imply that there is no sensible way of interpreting subtyping other than equality. In the case of Example 10.8.8, two sensible interpretations of subtyping exist: one is equality, while the other is the nonstructural subtyping order obtained by letting $\mathsf{pre} \leqslant \mathsf{abs}$. In the former interpretation, abs means "definitely absent," while in the latter, it means "possibly absent." □

10.8.12 REMARK: The model proposed above is a regular tree model. Of course, it is possible to adopt a finite tree model instead. Furthermore, other interpretations of rows are possible: for instance, Fähndrich (1999) extends the set constraints formalism with rows. In his model, an ordinary type is interpreted as a set of values, while a row is interpreted as a set of functions from labels to values. While the definition of the model may vary, the key point is that the characteristic laws of rows, which we discuss next, hold in the model. □

Reasoning with Rows

The interpretation presented in the previous section was designed to support the intuition that a row denotes an infinite family of types, indexed by labels, that the row constructor $\ell : \cdot\ ;\ \cdot$ denotes row extension, and that the row constructor ∂ denotes the creation of a constant row. From a formal point of

$$(\ell_1 : T_1 \,;\, \ell_2 : T_2 \,;\, T_3) = (\ell_2 : T_2 \,;\, \ell_1 : T_1 \,;\, T_3) \quad \text{(C-Row-LL)}$$
$$\partial T = (\ell : T \,;\, \partial T) \quad \text{(C-Row-DL)}$$
$$G\, \partial T_1 \,\ldots\, \partial T_n = \partial(G\, T_1 \,\ldots\, T_n) \quad \text{(C-Row-GD)}$$
$$G\,(\ell : T_1 \,;\, T_1') \,\ldots\, (\ell : T_n \,;\, T_n') = (\ell : G\, T_1 \,\ldots\, T_n \,;\, G\, T_1' \,\ldots\, T_n') \quad \text{(C-Row-GL)}$$

Figure 10-12: Equational reasoning with rows

view, the definition of the model and interpretation may be exploited to establish some reasoning principles concerning rows. These principles take the form of equations between types (Figure 10-12) and constraint equivalence laws (Figure 10-13), which we now explain and prove.

10.8.13 Remark: As stated earlier, we omit the superscripts of row constructors. We also omit the side conditions that concern the kind of the type variables (X) and type meta-variables (T) involved. Thus, each equation in Figure 10-12 really stands for the (infinite) family of equations obtained by reconstructing the missing kind information in a consistent way. For instance, the second equation may be read $\partial^{\ell.L}T = (\ell^{\kappa,L} : T \,;\, \partial^{L}T)$, where $\ell \notin L$ and T has kind $\kappa.Type$. □

10.8.14 Exercise [Recommended, ★, ↛]: Reconstruct all of the missing kind information in the equations of Figure 10-12. □

10.8.15 Remark: There is a slight catch with the unannotated version of the second equation in Figure 10-12: its left-hand side admits strictly more kinds than its right-hand side, because the former has row kind *Row*(L) for every L, while the latter has row kind *Row*(L) for every L such that $\ell \notin L$ holds. As a result, while replacing the unannotated term $(\ell : T \,;\, \partial T)$ with ∂T is always valid, the converse is not: replacing the unannotated term ∂T with $(\ell : T \,;\, \partial T)$ is valid only if it does not result in an ill-kinded term. □

The first equation in Figure 10-12 states that rows are equal up to commutation of labels. For the equation to be well-kinded, the labels ℓ_1 and ℓ_2 must be distinct. The equation holds under our interpretation because extension of a ground row at ℓ_1 and extension of a ground row at ℓ_2 commute. The second equation states that ∂T maps every label within its domain to T, that is, $\partial^L T$ maps every label $\ell \notin L$ to T. This equation holds because ∂T is interpreted as a constant row. The last two equations deal with the relationship between the row constructors G and the ordinary type constructor G. Indeed, notice that their left-hand sides involve $G^{Row(L)}$ for some L, while their right-hand sides involve G^{Type}. Both equations state that it is equivalent to apply

$$(\ell_1 : T_1 ; T_1') = (\ell_2 : T_2 ; T_2') \quad \equiv \quad \exists X.(T_1' = (\ell_2 : T_2 ; X) \wedge T_2' = (\ell_1 : T_1 ; X)) \quad \text{if } X \# ftv(T_1, T_1', T_2, T_2') \wedge \ell_1 \neq \ell_2 \qquad \text{(C-MUTATE-LL)}$$

$$\partial T = (\ell : T' ; T'') \quad \equiv \quad T = T' \wedge \partial T = T'' \qquad \text{(C-MUTATE-DL)}$$

$$G\,T_1 \,\ldots\, T_n = \partial T \quad \equiv \quad \exists X_1 \ldots X_n.(G\,X_1 \,\ldots\, X_n = T \wedge \textstyle\bigwedge_{i=1}^{n}(T_i = \partial X_i)) \quad \text{if } X_1 \ldots X_n \# ftv(T_1, \ldots, T_n, T) \qquad \text{(C-MUTATE-GD)}$$

$$G\,T_1 \,\ldots\, T_n = (\ell : T ; T') \quad \equiv \quad \exists X_1 \ldots X_n, X_1' \ldots X_n'.(G\,X_1 \,\ldots\, X_n = T \wedge G\,X_1' \,\ldots\, X_n' = T' \wedge \textstyle\bigwedge_{i=1}^{n}(T_i = (\ell : X_i ; X_i'))) \quad \text{if } X_1 \ldots X_n, X_1' \ldots X_n' \# ftv(T_1, \ldots, T_n, T, T') \qquad \text{(C-MUTATE-GL)}$$

Figure 10-13: Constraint equivalence laws involving rows

$G^{Row(L)}$ at the level of rows or to apply G^{Type} at the level of types. Our interpretation of $G^{Row(L)}$ was designed to give rise to these equations; indeed, the application of $G^{Row(L)}$ to n ground rows (where n is the arity of G) is interpreted as a pointwise application of G^{Type} to the rows' components (item 3 of Definition 10.8.10). Their use is illustrated in Examples 10.8.28 and 10.8.39.

10.8.16 LEMMA: Each of the equations in Figure 10-12 is equivalent to true. □

The four equations in Figure 10-12 show that two types with distinct head symbols may denote the same element of the model. In other words, in the presence of rows, the interpretation of types is no longer free: an equation of the form $T_1 = T_2$, where T_1 and T_2 have distinct head symbols, is not necessarily equivalent to false. In Figure 10-13, we give several constraint equivalence laws, known as *mutation* laws, that concern such "heterogeneous" equations, and, when viewed as rewriting rules, allow solving them. To each equation in Figure 10-12 corresponds a mutation law. The soundness of the mutation law, that is, the fact that its right-hand side entails its left-hand side, follows from the corresponding equation. The completeness of the mutation law, that is, the fact that its left-hand side entails its right-hand side, holds by design of the model.

10.8.17 EXERCISE [RECOMMENDED, ★, ↛]: Reconstruct all of the missing kind information in the laws of Figure 10-13. □

Let us now review the four mutation laws. For the sake of brevity, in the following informal explanation, we assume that a ground assignment ϕ that satisfies the left-hand equation is fixed, and write "the ground type T" for "the ground type $\phi(\mathsf{T})$." C-MUTATE-LL concerns an equation between two rows, which are both given by extension but exhibit distinct head labels ℓ_1 and ℓ_2. When this equation is satisfied, both of its members must denote the same ground row. Thus, the ground row T'_1 must map ℓ_2 to the ground type T_2, while, symmetrically, the ground row T'_2 must map ℓ_1 to the ground type T_1. This may be expressed by two equations of the form $\mathsf{T}'_1 = (\ell_2 : \mathsf{T}_2 \ ; \ldots)$ and $\mathsf{T}'_2 = (\ell_1 : \mathsf{T}_1 \ ; \ldots)$. Furthermore, because the ground rows T'_1 and T'_2 must agree on their common labels, the ellipses in these two equations must denote the same ground row. This is expressed by letting the two equations share a fresh, existentially quantified row variable X. C-MUTATE-DL concerns an equation between two rows, one of which is given as a constant row, the other of which is given by extension. Then, because the ground row $\partial\mathsf{T}$ maps every label to the ground type T, the ground type T' must coincide with the ground type T, while the ground row T'' must map every label in its domain to the ground type T. This is expressed by the equations $\mathsf{T} = \mathsf{T}'$ and $\partial\mathsf{T} = \mathsf{T}''$. C-MUTATE-GD and C-MUTATE-GL concern an equation between two rows, one of which is given as an application of a row constructor G, the other of which is given either as a constant row or by extension. Again, the laws exploit the fact that the ground row $G\ \mathsf{T}_1 \ldots \mathsf{T}_n$ is obtained by applying the type constructor G, pointwise, to the ground rows $\mathsf{T}_1, \ldots, \mathsf{T}_n$. If, as in C-MUTATE-GD, it coincides with the constant ground row $\partial\mathsf{T}$, then every T_i must itself be a constant ground row, of the form $\partial\mathsf{X}_i$, and T must coincide with $G\ \mathsf{X}_1 \ldots \mathsf{X}_n$. C-MUTATE-GL is obtained in a similar manner.

10.8.18 **Lemma:** Each of the equivalence laws in Figure 10-13 holds. □

Solving Equality Constraints in the Presence of Rows

We now extend the unification algorithm given in §10.6 with support for rows. The extended algorithm is intended to solve unification problems where the syntax and interpretation of types are as defined in the discussions above of the syntax (p. 466) and meaning (p. 471) of rows. Its specification consists of the original rewriting rules of Figure 10-10, minus S-CLASH, which is removed and replaced with the rules given in Figure 10-14. Indeed, S-CLASH is no longer valid in the presence of rows: not all distinct type constructors are incompatible.

The extended algorithm features four mutation rules, which are in direct correspondence with the mutation laws of Figure 10-13, as well as a weakened version of S-CLASH, dubbed S-CLASH', which applies when neither S-DECOMPOSE nor the mutation rules are applicable. (Let us point out that, in

$$
\begin{array}{rcll}
(\ell_1 : X_1 ; X_1') = (\ell_2 : T_2 ; T_2') = \epsilon & \rightarrow & \exists X.(X_1' = (\ell_2 : T_2 ; X) \wedge T_2' = (\ell_1 : X_1 ; X)) & \\
& & \wedge\ (\ell_1 : X_1 ; X_1') = \epsilon & \text{(S-MUTATE-LL)} \\
& & \text{if } \ell_1 \neq \ell_2 & \\
\partial X = (\ell : T ; T') = \epsilon & \rightarrow & X = T \wedge \partial X = T' \wedge \partial X = \epsilon & \text{(S-MUTATE-DL)} \\
G\, T_1 \ldots T_n = \partial X = \epsilon & \rightarrow & \exists X_1 \ldots X_n.(G\, X_1 \ldots X_n = X \wedge \bigwedge_{i=1}^{n}(T_i = \partial X_i)) & \\
& & \wedge\ \partial X = \epsilon & \text{(S-MUTATE-GD)} \\
G\, T_1 \ldots T_n = (\ell : X ; X') = \epsilon & \rightarrow & \exists X_1 \ldots X_n, X_1' \ldots X_n'.(G\, X_1 \ldots X_n = X \wedge & \\
& & \quad G\, X_1' \ldots X_n' = X' \wedge & \\
& & \quad \bigwedge_{i=1}^{n}(T_i = (\ell : X_i ; X_i'))) & \\
& & \wedge\ (\ell : X ; X') = \epsilon & \text{(S-MUTATE-GL)} \\
F\vec{T} = F'\vec{T}' = \epsilon & \rightarrow & \mathsf{false} & \text{(S-CLASH')} \\
& & \text{if } F \neq F' \text{ and none of the four rules above applies} &
\end{array}
$$

Figure 10-14: Row unification (changes to Figure 10-10)

S-DECOMPOSE, the meta-variable F ranges over all type constructors in the signature S, so that S-DECOMPOSE is applicable to multi-equations of the form $\partial X = \partial T = \epsilon$ or $(\ell : X ; X') = (\ell : T ; T') = \epsilon$.) Three of the mutation rules may allocate fresh type variables, which must be chosen fresh for the rule's left-hand side. The four mutation rules paraphrase the four mutation laws very closely. Two minor differences are (i) the mutation rules deal with multi-equations, as opposed to equations; and (ii) any subterm that appears more than once on the right-hand side of a rule is required to be a type variable, as opposed to an arbitrary type. Neither of these features is specific to rows: both may be found in the definition of the standard unification algorithm (Figure 10-10), where they help reason about sharing.

10.8.19 EXERCISE [★, ↛]: Check that the rewriting rules in Figure 10-14 preserve well-kindedness. Conclude that, provided its input constraint is well-kinded, the unification algorithm needs not keep track of kinds. □

The properties of the unification algorithm are preserved by this extension, as witnessed by the next three lemmas. Note that the termination of reduction is ensured only when the initial unification problem is well-kinded. The ill-kinded unification problem $X = (\ell_1 : T ; Y) \wedge X = (\ell_2 : T ; Y)$, where ℓ_1 and ℓ_2 are distinct, illustrates this point.

10.8.20 LEMMA: The rewriting system $\rightarrow$ is strongly normalizing. □

10.8.21 LEMMA: $U_1 \rightarrow U_2$ implies $U_1 \equiv U_2$. □

10.8.22 LEMMA: Every normal form is either false or of the form $\mathcal{X}[U]$, where $\mathcal{X}$ is an existential constraint context, U is a standard conjunction of multi-equations and, if the model is syntactic, U is acyclic. These conditions imply that U is satisfiable. □

The time complexity of standard first-order unification is quasi-linear. What is, then, the time complexity of row unification? Only a partial answer is known. In practice, the algorithm given in this chapter is extremely efficient and appears to behave just as well as standard unification. In theory, the complexity of row unification remains unexplored and forms an interesting open issue.

10.8.23 EXERCISE [★★★, ↛]: The unification algorithm presented above, although very efficient in practice, does *not* have linear or quasi-linear time complexity. Find a family of unification problems U_n such that the size of U_n is linear with respect to n and the number of steps required to reach its normal form is quadratic with respect to n. □

10.8.24 REMARK: Mutation is a common technique for solving equations in a large class of non-free algebras that are described by *syntactic theories* (Kirchner and Klay, 1990). The equations of Figure 10-12 happen to form a syntactic presentation of an equational theory. Thus, it is possible to derive a unification algorithm out of these equations in a systematic way (Rémy, 1993). Here, we have presented the same algorithm in a direct manner, without relying on the apparatus of syntactic theories. □

Operations on Records

We now illustrate the use of rows for typechecking operations on records. We begin with full records; our treatment follows Rémy (1992b).

10.8.25 EXAMPLE [FULL RECORDS]: As before, let us begin with full records, whose domain is exactly $\mathcal{L}$. The primitive operations are record creation $\{\cdot\}$, update $\{\cdot \text{ with } \ell = \cdot\}$, and access $\cdot.\{\ell\}$.

Let $<$ denote a fixed strict total order on row labels. For every set of labels L of cardinal n, let us introduce a $(n+1)$-ary constructor $\{\}_L$. We use the following syntactic sugar: we write $\{\ell_1 = \mathtt{t}_1; \ldots; \ell_n = \mathtt{t}_n; \mathtt{t}\}$ for the application $\{\}_L\ \mathtt{t}_{i_1}\ \ldots\ \mathtt{t}_{i_n}\ \mathtt{t}$, where $L = \{\ell_1, \ldots, \ell_n\} = \{\ell_{i_1}, \ldots, \ell_{i_n}\}$ and $\ell_{i_1} < \ldots < \ell_{i_n}$ holds. The use of the total order $<$ makes the meaning of record expressions independent of the order in which fields are defined; in particular, it allows fixing the order in which $\mathtt{t}_1, \ldots, \mathtt{t}_n$ are evaluated. We abbreviate the record value $\{\ell_1 = \mathsf{v}_1; \ldots; \ell_n = \mathsf{v}_n; \mathsf{v}\}$ as $\{\mathsf{V}; \mathsf{v}\}$, where V is the finite function that maps ℓ_i to v_i for every $i \in \{1, \ldots, n\}$.

The operational semantics of the above three operations may now be defined in the following straightforward manner. First, record creation $\{\cdot\}$ is precisely the unary constructor $\{\}_\emptyset$. Second, for every $\ell \in \mathcal{L}$, let update $\{\cdot \text{ with } \ell = \cdot\}$ and access $\cdot.\{\ell\}$ be destructors of arity 1 and 2, respectively, equipped with the following reduction rules:

$$\begin{array}{rcllr} \{\{\mathsf{V};\mathsf{v}\} \text{ with } \ell = \mathsf{v}'\} & \xrightarrow{\delta} & \{\mathsf{V}[\ell \mapsto \mathsf{v}'];\mathsf{v}\} & & \text{(R-UPDATE)} \\ \{\mathsf{V};\mathsf{v}\}.\{\ell\} & \xrightarrow{\delta} & \mathsf{V}(\ell) & (\ell \in dom(\mathsf{V})) & \text{(R-ACCESS-1)} \\ \{\mathsf{V};\mathsf{v}\}.\{\ell\} & \xrightarrow{\delta} & \mathsf{v} & (\ell \notin dom(\mathsf{V})) & \text{(R-ACCESS-2)} \end{array}$$

In these rules, $\mathsf{V}[\ell \mapsto \mathsf{v}]$ stands for the function that maps ℓ to v and coincides with V at every other label, while $\mathsf{V}(\ell)$ stands for the image of ℓ through V. Because these rules make use of the syntactic sugar defined above, they are, strictly speaking, rule schemes: each of them really stands for the infinite family of rules that would be obtained if the syntactic sugar was eliminated.

Let us now define the syntax of types as in Example 10.8.7. Let the initial environment Γ_0 contain the following bindings:

$$\begin{array}{rl} \{\}_{\{\ell_1,\ldots,\ell_n\}}: & \forall \mathsf{X}_1 \ldots \mathsf{X}_n \mathsf{X}.\mathsf{X}_1 \to \ldots \to \mathsf{X}_n \to \mathsf{X} \to \Pi\ (\ell_1 : \mathsf{X}_1; \ldots; \ell_n : \mathsf{X}_n; \partial \mathsf{X}) \\ & \text{where } \ell_1 < \ldots < \ell_n \\ \{\cdot \text{ with } \ell = \cdot\}: & \forall \mathsf{X}\mathsf{X}'\mathsf{Y}.\Pi\ (\ell : \mathsf{X}\,;\,\mathsf{Y}) \to \mathsf{X}' \to \Pi\ (\ell : \mathsf{X}'\,;\,\mathsf{Y}) \\ \cdot.\{\ell\}: & \forall \mathsf{X}\mathsf{Y}.\Pi\ (\ell : \mathsf{X}\,;\,\mathsf{Y}) \to \mathsf{X} \end{array}$$

Note that, in particular, the type scheme assigned to record creation $\{\cdot\}$ is $\forall \mathsf{X}.\mathsf{X} \to \Pi\ (\partial \mathsf{X})$. As a result, these bindings are exactly as stated in the discussion of records with infinite carrier (p. 463).

To illustrate how these definitions work together, let us consider the program $\{\{0\} \text{ with } \ell_1 = \texttt{true}\}.\{\ell_2\}$, which builds a record, extends it at ℓ_1, then accesses it at ℓ_2. Can we build an HM(X) type derivation for it, under the constraint true and the initial environment Γ_0? To begin, by looking up Γ_0 and using HMX-INST, we find that $\{\cdot\}$ has type $\mathsf{int} \to \Pi\ (\partial\mathsf{int})$. Thus, assuming that 0 has type int, the expression $\{0\}$ has type $\Pi\ (\partial\mathsf{int})$. Indeed, this expression denotes a record all of whose fields hold an integer value. Then, by looking up Γ_0 and using HMX-INST, we find that $\{\cdot \text{ with } \ell_1 = \cdot\}$ has type $\Pi\ (\ell_1 : \mathsf{int}\,;\,\partial\mathsf{int}) \to \mathsf{bool} \to \Pi\ (\ell_1 : \mathsf{bool}\,;\,\partial\mathsf{int})$. May we immediately use HMX-APP to typecheck the application of $\{\cdot \text{ with } \ell_1 = \cdot\}$ to $\{0\}$? Unfortunately, no, because there is an apparent mismatch between the expected type $\Pi\ (\ell_1 : \mathsf{int}\,;\,\partial\mathsf{int})$ and the effective type $\Pi\ (\partial\mathsf{int})$. To work around this problem, let us recall that, by C-ROW-DL, the equation $\Pi\ (\partial\mathsf{int}) = \Pi\ (\ell_1 : \mathsf{int}\,;\,\partial\mathsf{int})$ is equivalent to true. Thus, HMX-SUB allows proving that $\{0\}$ has type $\Pi\ (\ell_1 : \mathsf{int}\,;\,\partial\mathsf{int})$.

Assuming that `true` has type bool, we may now apply HMX-APP and deduce

$$\texttt{true}, \Gamma_0 \vdash \{\{0\}\ \texttt{with}\ \ell_1 = \texttt{true}\} : \Pi\,(\ell_1 : \mathsf{bool}\,;\, \partial\mathsf{int}).$$

We let the reader check that, in a similar manner involving C-ROW-DL, C-ROW-LL, and HMX-SUB, one may prove that $\{\{0\}\ \texttt{with}\ \ell_1 = \texttt{true}\}.\{\ell_2\}$ has type int, provided ℓ_1 and ℓ_2 are distinct. □

10.8.26 EXERCISE [★★, ↛]: Unfold the definition of the constraint $\texttt{let}\ \Gamma_0\ \texttt{in}\ [\![\{\{0\}\ \texttt{with}\ \ell_1 = \texttt{true}\}.\{\ell_2\} : \mathsf{X}]\!]$, which states that X is a valid type for the above program. Assuming that subtyping is interpreted as equality, simulate a run of the constraint solver (§10.6), extended with support for rows, so as to solve this constraint. Check that the solved form is equivalent to X = int. □

10.8.27 EXERCISE [★★★]: Check that the definitions of Example 10.8.25 meet the requirements of Definition 10.5.5. □

10.8.28 EXAMPLE [RECORD APPLICATION]: Let us now introduce a more unusual primitive operation on full records. This operation accepts two records, the first of which is expected to hold a function in every field and produces a new record, whose contents are obtained by applying, pointwise, the functions in the first record to the values in the second record. In other words, this new primitive operation lifts the standard application combinator (which may be defined as λf.λz.f z), pointwise, to the level of records. For this reason, we refer to it as `rapply`. Its operational semantics is defined by making it a binary destructor and equipping it with the following reduction rules:

$$\texttt{rapply}\ \{\mathsf{V};\mathsf{v}\}\ \{\mathsf{V}';\mathsf{v}'\} \xrightarrow{\delta} \{\mathsf{V}\,\mathsf{V}';\mathsf{v}\ \mathsf{v}'\} \qquad \text{(R-APPLY-1)}$$

$$\texttt{rapply}\ \{\mathsf{V};\mathsf{v}\}\ \{\mathsf{V}';\mathsf{v}'\} \xrightarrow{\delta} \texttt{rapply}\ \{\mathsf{V};\mathsf{v}\}\ \{\mathsf{V}'[\ell \mapsto \mathsf{v}'];\mathsf{v}'\} \quad \text{if } \ell \in dom(\mathsf{V}) \setminus dom(\mathsf{V}') \qquad \text{(R-APPLY-2)}$$

$$\texttt{rapply}\ \{\mathsf{V};\mathsf{v}\}\ \{\mathsf{V}';\mathsf{v}'\} \xrightarrow{\delta} \texttt{rapply}\ \{\mathsf{V}[\ell' \mapsto \mathsf{v}];\mathsf{v}\}\ \{\mathsf{V}';\mathsf{v}'\} \quad \text{if } \ell' \in dom(\mathsf{V}') \setminus dom(\mathsf{V}) \qquad \text{(R-APPLY-3)}$$

In the first rule, V V′ is defined only if V and V′ have a common domain; it is then defined as the function that maps ℓ to the expression V(ℓ) V′(ℓ). The second and third rules, which are symmetric, deal with the case where some field is explicitly defined in one input record but not in the other; in that case, the field is made explicit by creating a copy of the record's default value.

The syntax of types remains as in Example 10.8.25. We extend the initial environment Γ_0 with the following binding:

$$\texttt{rapply}: \quad \forall \mathsf{XY}.\Pi\,(\mathsf{X} \to \mathsf{Y}) \to \Pi\,\mathsf{X} \to \Pi\,\mathsf{Y}$$

To understand this type scheme, recall that the principal type scheme of the standard application combinator (which may be defined as λf.λz.f z) is $\forall$XY.(X → Y) → X → Y. The type scheme assigned to `rapply` is very similar; the most visible difference is that both arguments, as well as the result, are now wrapped within the record type constructor Π. A more subtle, yet essential change is that X and Y are now row variables: their kind is $\star.Row(\emptyset)$. As a result, the leftmost occurrence of the arrow constructor is really $\to^{Row(\emptyset)}$. Thus, we are exploiting the presence of type constructors of the form G^s, with $s \neq Type$, in the signature S.

To illustrate how these definitions work together, let us consider the program `rapply` {ℓ = `not`; `succ`} {ℓ = `true`; 0}, where the terms `not` and `succ` are assumed to have types bool → bool and int → int, respectively. Can we build an HM(X) type derivation for it, under the constraint true and the initial environment Γ_0? To begin, it is straightforward to derive that the record {ℓ = `not`; `succ`} has type Π (ℓ : bool → bool ; ∂(int → int)) **(1)**. In order to use `rapply`, however, we must prove that this record has a type of the form Π (R_1 → R_2), where R_1 and R_2 are rows. This is where C-Row-GD and C-Row-GL (Figure 10-12) come into play. Indeed, by C-Row-GD, the type ∂(int → int) may be written ∂int → ∂int. So, (1) may be written Π (ℓ : bool → bool ; ∂int → ∂int) **(2)**, which by C-Row-GL may be written Π ((ℓ : bool ; ∂int) → (ℓ : bool ; ∂int)) **(3)**. Thus, HMX-Sub allows deriving that the record {ℓ = `not`; `succ`} has type (3). We let the reader continue and conclude that the program has type Π (ℓ : bool ; ∂int) under the constraint true and the initial environment Γ_0.

This example illustrates a very important use of rows, namely to lift an operation on ordinary values so as to turn it into a pointwise operation on records. Here, we have chosen to lift the standard application combinator, giving rise to `rapply` on records. The point is that, thanks to the expressive power of rows, we were also able to lift the standard combinator's type scheme in the most straightforward manner, giving rise to a suitable type scheme for `rapply`. □

10.8.29 Exercise [★★★, ↛]: Check that the definitions of Example 10.8.28 meet the requirements of Definition 10.5.5. □

The previous examples have illustrated the use of rows to typecheck operations on full records. Let us now move to records with finite domain. As explained in the discussion above of records with finite carrier (p. 461), they may be either encoded in terms of full records, or given a direct definition. The latter approach is illustrated below.

10.8.30 Example [Finite records]: For every set of labels L of cardinal n, let us introduce a n-ary constructor $\langle\rangle_L$. We define the notations $\langle \ell_1 = t_1; \ldots; \ell_n = t_n \rangle$

and $\langle V \rangle$, where V is a finite mapping of labels to values, in a manner similar to that of Example 10.8.25.

The three primitive operations on finite records, namely the empty record $\langle\rangle$, extension $\langle \cdot \text{ with } \ell = \cdot \rangle$, and access $\cdot.\langle \ell \rangle$, may be defined as follows. First, the empty record $\langle\rangle$ is precisely the nullary constructor $\langle\rangle_\emptyset$. Second, for every $\ell \in \mathcal{L}$, let extension $\langle \cdot \text{ with } \ell = \cdot \rangle$ and access $\cdot.\langle \ell \rangle$ be destructors of arity 1 and 2, respectively, equipped with the following reduction rules:

$$\langle \langle V \rangle \text{ with } \ell = v \rangle \xrightarrow{\delta} \langle V[\ell \mapsto v] \rangle \qquad \text{(R-EXTEND)}$$
$$\langle V \rangle.\langle \ell \rangle \xrightarrow{\delta} V(\ell) \qquad (\ell \in dom(V)) \qquad \text{(R-ACCESS)}$$

Let us now define the syntax of types as in Example 10.8.8. Let the initial environment Γ_0 contain the following bindings:

$$\langle\rangle_{\{\ell_1,\ldots,\ell_n\}} : \forall X_1 \ldots X_n . X_1 \to \ldots \to X_n \to \Pi\ (\ell_1 : \text{pre } X_1 ; \ldots ; \ell_n : \text{pre } X_n ; \partial\text{abs})$$
$$\text{where } \ell_1 < \ldots < \ell_n$$
$$\langle \cdot \text{ with } \ell = \cdot \rangle : \forall XX'Y . \Pi\ (\ell : X ; Y) \to X' \to \Pi\ (\ell : \text{pre } X' ; Y)$$
$$\cdot.\langle \ell \rangle : \forall XY . \Pi(\ell : \text{pre } X ; Y) \to X$$

Note that, in particular, the type scheme assigned to the empty record $\langle\rangle$ is $\Pi\ (\partial\text{abs})$. □

10.8.31 EXERCISE [RECOMMENDED, ★, ↛]: Reconstruct all of the missing kind information in the type schemes given in Example 10.8.30. □

10.8.32 EXERCISE [RECOMMENDED, ★★, ↛]: Give an encoding of finite records in terms of full records, along the lines of the discussion of records with finite carrier (p. 461). Check that the principal type schemes associated, via the encoding, with the three operations on finite records are precisely those given in Example 10.8.30. □

10.8.33 EXERCISE [RECOMMENDED, ★]: The extension operation, as defined above, may either change the value of an existing field or create a new field, depending on whether the field ℓ is or isn't present in the input record. This flavor is known as free extension. Can you define a strict flavor of extension that is not applicable when the field ℓ already exists? Can you define (free and strict flavors of) a restriction operation that removes a field from a record? □

10.8.34 EXERCISE [RECOMMENDED, ★]: Explain why, when $\text{pre} \leq \text{abs}$ holds, subsumption allows a record with more fields to be supplied in a context where a record with fewer fields is expected. This phenomenon is often known as *width subtyping*. Explain why such is not the case when subtyping is interpreted as equality. □

10.8.35 EXERCISE [★★★, ↛]: Check that the definitions of Example 10.8.30 meet the requirements of Definition 10.5.5. □

Polymorphic Variants

So far, we have emphasized the use of rows for flexible typechecking of operations on records. The record type constructor Π expects one parameter, which is a row; informally speaking, one might say that it is a product constructor of infinite arity. It appears natural to also define sums of infinite arity. This may be done by introducing a new unary type constructor Σ, whose parameter is a row.

As in the case of records, we use a nullary type constructor abs and a unary type constructor pre in order to associate information with every row label. Thus, for instance, the type $\Sigma\ (\ell_1 : \mathsf{pre}\ \mathsf{T}_1\ ;\ \ell_2 : \mathsf{pre}\ \mathsf{T}_2\ ;\ \partial\mathsf{abs})$ is intended to contain values of the form $\ell_1\ \mathsf{v}_1$, where v_1 has type T_1, or of the form $\ell_2\ \mathsf{v}_2$, where v_2 has type T_2. The type constructors abs and pre are not the same type constructors as in the case of records. In particular, their subtyping relationship, if there is one, is reversed. Indeed, the type $\Sigma\ (\ell_1 : \mathsf{pre}\ \mathsf{T}_1\ ;\ \ell_2 : \mathsf{abs}\ ;\ \partial\mathsf{abs})$ is intended to contain only values of the form $\ell_1\ \mathsf{v}_1$, where v_1 has type T_1, so it is safe to make it a subtype of the above type; in other words, it is safe to allow $\mathsf{abs} \le \mathsf{pre}\ \mathsf{T}_2$. In spite of this, we keep the names abs and pre by tradition.

The advantages of this approach over algebraic data types are the same as in the case of records. The namespace of data constructors becomes global, so it becomes possible for two distinct sum types to share data constructors. Also, the expressiveness afforded by rows allows assigning types to new operations, such as *filtering* (see below), which allows functions that perform case analysis to be incrementally extended with new cases. One disadvantage is that it becomes more difficult to understand what it means for a function defined by pattern matching to be exhaustive; this issue is, however, out of the scope of this chapter.

10.8.36 EXAMPLE [POLYMORPHIC VARIANTS]: For every label $\ell \in \mathcal{L}$, let us introduce a unary constructor ℓ and a ternary destructor $[\,\ell : \cdot \mid \cdot\,]\ \cdot$. We refer to the former as a *data constructor*, and to the latter as a *filter*. Let us also introduce a unary destructor $[\,]$. We equip these destructors with the following reduction rules:

$$[\,\ell : \mathsf{v} \mid \mathsf{v}'\,]\ (\ell\ \mathsf{w}) \xrightarrow{\delta} \mathsf{v}\ \mathsf{w} \qquad \text{(R-FILTER-1)}$$

$$[\,\ell : \mathsf{v} \mid \mathsf{v}'\,]\ (\ell'\ \mathsf{w}) \xrightarrow{\delta} \mathsf{v}'\ (\ell'\ \mathsf{w}) \quad \text{if } \ell \neq \ell' \qquad \text{(R-FILTER-2)}$$

Let us define the syntax of types as follows. Let there be two basic kinds $\star$ and $\bullet$. Let $\mathcal{S}_0$ consist of the type constructors $\rightarrow$, abs, and pre, whose respective signatures are $\star \otimes \star \Rightarrow \star$, $\bullet$, and $\star \Rightarrow \bullet$. Let $\mathcal{S}_1$ consist of the record type constructor Σ, whose signature is $\bullet \Rightarrow \star$. Note the similarity with the case of records (Example 10.8.8).

Subtyping is typically interpreted in one of two ways. One is equality. The other is the nonstructural subtyping order obtained by letting $\rightarrow$ be contravariant in its domain and covariant in its codomain, Σ be covariant, $\rightarrow$ and Σ be incompatible, and letting $\mathsf{abs} \leqslant \mathsf{pre}$. Compare this definition with the case of records (Remark 10.8.11).

To complete the setup, let the initial environment Γ_0 contain the following bindings:

$$\begin{aligned} \ell\,\cdot : &\quad \forall \mathsf{XY}.\mathsf{X} \rightarrow \Sigma\,(\ell : \mathsf{pre}\,\mathsf{X}\,;\mathsf{Y}) \\ [\,\ell : \cdot \mid \cdot\,]\,\cdot : &\quad \forall \mathsf{XX'YY'}.(\mathsf{X} \rightarrow \mathsf{Y}) \rightarrow (\Sigma\,(\ell : \mathsf{X'}\,;\mathsf{Y'}) \rightarrow \mathsf{Y}) \rightarrow \Sigma\,(\ell : \mathsf{pre}\,\mathsf{X}\,;\mathsf{Y'}) \rightarrow \mathsf{Y} \\ [\,] : &\quad \forall \mathsf{X}.\Sigma\,(\partial \mathsf{abs}) \rightarrow \mathsf{X} \end{aligned}$$

The first binding means, in particular, that if v has type T, then a value of the form ℓ v has type $\Sigma\,(\ell : \mathsf{pre}\,\mathsf{T}\,;\partial\mathsf{abs})$. This is a sum type with only one branch labeled ℓ, hence a very precise type for this value. However, it is possible to instantiate the row variable Y with rows other than $\partial\mathsf{abs}$. For instance, the value ℓ v also has type $\Sigma\,(\ell : \mathsf{pre}\,\mathsf{T}\,;\ell' : \mathsf{pre}\,\mathsf{T'}\,;\partial\mathsf{abs})$. This is a sum type with two branches, hence a somewhat less precise type, but still a valid one for this value. It is clear that, through this mechanism, the value ℓ v admits an infinite number of types. The point is that, if v has type T and v′ has type T′, then both ℓ v and ℓ' v′ have type $\Sigma\,(\ell : \mathsf{pre}\,\mathsf{T}\,;\ell' : \mathsf{pre}\,\mathsf{T'}\,;\partial\mathsf{abs})$, so they may be stored together in a homogeneous data structure, such as a list.

Filters are used to perform case analysis on variants, that is, on values of a sum type. According to R-Filter-1 and R-Filter-2, a filter $[\,\ell : \mathsf{v} \mid \mathsf{v'}\,]$ is a function that expects an argument of the form ℓ' w and reduces to v w if ℓ' is ℓ and to v′ (ℓ' w) otherwise. Thus, a filter defines a two-way branch, where the label of the data constructor at hand determines which branch is taken. The expressive power of filters stems from the fact that they may be organized in a sequence, so as to define a multi-way branch. The inert filter [], which does not have a reduction rule, serves as a terminator for such sequences. For instance, the composite filter $[\,\ell : \mathsf{v} \mid [\,\ell' : \mathsf{v'} \mid [\,]\,]\,]$, which may be abbreviated as $[\,\ell : \mathsf{v} \mid \ell' : \mathsf{v'}\,]$, may be applied either to a value of the form ℓ w, yielding v w, or to a value of the form ℓ' w′, yielding v′ w′. Applying it to a value w whose head symbol is not ℓ or ℓ' would lead to the term [] w, which is stuck, since [] does not have a reduction rule.

For the type system to be sound, we must ensure that every application of the form [] w is ill-typed. This is achieved by the third binding above: the domain type of [] is $\Sigma\,(\partial\mathsf{abs})$, a sum type with zero branches, which contains no values. The return type of [] may be chosen at will, which is fine; since it can never be invoked, it can never return. The second binding above means that, if v accepts values of type T and v′ accepts values of type $\Sigma\,(\ell : \mathsf{T''}\,;\mathsf{T'})$, then the filter $[\,\ell : \mathsf{v} \mid \mathsf{v'}\,]$ accepts values of type $\Sigma\,(\ell : \mathsf{pre}\,\mathsf{T}\,;\mathsf{T'})$. Note that any choice of T'' will do, including, in particular, abs. In other words, it is okay if v' does not accept values of the form ℓ w. Indeed, by definition of the semantics of filters, it will never be passed such a value. □

10.8.37 EXERCISE [★★★, ↛]: Check that the definitions of Example 10.8.36 meet the requirements of Definition 10.5.5. □

10.8.38 REMARK: It is interesting to study the similarity between the type schemes assigned to the primitive operations on polymorphic variants and those assigned to the primitive operations on records (Example 10.8.30). The type of [] involves the complete row ∂abs, just like the empty record ⟨⟩. The type of [ℓ : · | ·] · is pretty much identical to the type of record extension ⟨· with ℓ = ·⟩, provided the three continuation arrows → Y are dropped. Last, the type of the data constructor ℓ is strongly reminiscent of the type of record access ·.⟨ℓ⟩. With some thought, this is hardly a surprise. Indeed, records and variants are *dual*: it is possible to encode the latter in terms of the former and vice-versa. For instance, in the encoding of variants in terms of records, a function defined by cases is encoded as a record of ordinary functions, in continuation-passing style. Thus, the encoding of [] is λf.f ⟨⟩, the encoding of [ℓ : v | v′] is λf.f ⟨v′ with ℓ = v⟩, and the encoding of ℓ v is λr.r.⟨ℓ⟩ v. The reader is encouraged to study the type schemes that arise out of this encoding and how they relate to the type schemes given in Example 10.8.36. □

10.8.39 EXAMPLE [FIRST-CLASS MESSAGES]: In a programming language equipped with both records and variants, it is possible to make the duality between these two forms of data explicit by extending the language with a primitive operation # that turns a record of ordinary functions into a single function, defined by cases. More precisely, # may be introduced as a binary destructor, whose reduction rule is

$$\#\, v\ (\ell\ w) \quad \xrightarrow{\delta} \quad v.\langle \ell \rangle\ w \qquad \text{(R-SEND)}$$

What type may we assign to such an operation? In order to simplify the answer, let us assume that we are dealing with full records (Example 10.8.25) and full variants; that is, we have a single basic kind ★, and do not employ abs and pre. Then, a suitable type scheme would be

$$\forall XY.\Pi\ (X \to \partial Y) \to \Sigma\ X \to Y$$

In other words, this operation accepts a record of functions, all of which have the same return type Y, but may have arbitrary domain types, which are given by the row X. It produces a function that accepts a parameter of sum type Σ X and returns a result of type Y. The fact that the row X appears both in the Σ type and in the Π type reflects the operational semantics. Indeed, according to R-SEND, the label ℓ carried by the value ℓ w is used to extract, out of the record v, a function, which is then applied to w. Thus, the domain type of the function stored at ℓ within the record v should match the type of w. In other words, at every label, the domain of the contents of the record and the contents of the sum should be type compatible. This is encoded by letting a single row variable X stand for both of these rows. Note that the arrow in $X \to \partial Y$ is really $\to^{Row(\emptyset)}$; once again, we are exploiting the presence of type constructors of the form G^s, with $s \neq Type$, in the signature S.

If the record of functions v is viewed as an *object*, and if the variant ℓ w is viewed as a *message* ℓ carrying a parameter w, then R-SEND may be understood as *(first-class) message dispatch*, a common feature of object-oriented languages. (The *first-class* qualifier refers to the fact that the message name ℓ is not statically fixed, but is discovered at runtime.) The issue of type inference in the presence of such a feature has been studied by Nishimura (1998), Müller and Nishimura (1998), and Pottier (2000). These papers address two issues that are not dealt with in the above example, namely (i) accommodating finite (as opposed to full) record and variants and (ii) allowing distinct methods to have distinct result types. This is achieved via the use of subtyping and of some form of conditional constraints. □

10.8.40 EXERCISE [★★★, ↛]: Check that the definitions of Example 10.8.39 meet the requirements of Definition 10.5.5. □

The name *polymorphic variants* stems from the highly polymorphic type schemes assigned to the operations on variants (Example 10.8.36). A row-based type system for polymorphic variants was first proposed by Rémy (1989). A somewhat similar, constraint-based type system for polymorphic variants was then studied by Garrigue (1998; 2000; 2002) and implemented by him as part of the programming language Objective Caml.

Other Applications of Rows

Typechecking records and variants is the best-known application of rows. Many variations of it are conceivable, some of which we have illustrated, such as the choice between full and finite records and variants. However, rows may also be put to other uses, of which we now list a few.

First, since objects may be viewed as records of functions, at least from a typechecking point of view, rows may be used to typecheck object-oriented languages in a structural style (Wand, 1994; Rémy, 1994). This is, in particular, the route followed in Objective Caml (Rémy and Vouillon, 1998). There, an object type consists of a row of method types, and gives the object's interface. Such a style is considered structural, as opposed to the style adopted by many popular object-oriented languages, such as C++, Java, and C#, where an object type consists of the name of its class. Thanks to rows, method invocation may be assigned a polymorphic type scheme, similar to that of record access (Example 10.8.30), making it possible to invoke a specific method (say, ℓ) without knowing which class the receiver object belongs to.

Rows may also be used to encode sets of properties within types or to encode type refinements, with applications in type-based program analysis. Some instances worth mentioning are soft typing (Cartwright and Fagan, 1991; Wright and Cartwright, 1994), exception analysis (Leroy and Pessaux, 2000; Pottier and Simonet, 2003), and static enforcement of an access control policy (Pottier, Skalka, and Smith, 2001). BANE (Fähndrich, 1999), a versatile program analysis toolkit, also implements a form of rows.

Variations on Rows

A type system may be said to have rows, in a broad sense, if mappings from labels to types may be (i) defined incrementally, via some syntax for extending an existing mapping with information about a new label and (ii) abstracted by a type variable. In this chapter, which follows Rémy's ideas (1993; 1992a; 1992b), the former feature is provided by the row constructors $(\ell : \cdot\ ;\ \cdot)$, while the latter is provided by the existence of row variables, that is, type variables of row kind $Row(L)$ for some L. There are, however, type systems that provide (i) and (ii) while departing significantly from the one presented here. These systems differ mainly in how they settle some important design choices:

1. Does a row denote a finite or an infinite mapping from labels to types?

2. Is a row with duplicate labels considered well-formed? If not, by which mechanism is it ruled out?

In Rémy's approach, every row denotes an infinite (in fact, cofinite) mapping from labels to types. The type constructors abs and pre are used to encode domain information within field types. A row with duplicate labels, such as $(\ell : \mathsf{T}_1\ ;\ \ell : \mathsf{T}_2\ ; \mathsf{T}_3)$, is ruled out by the kind system. Below, we mention a number of type systems that make different design choices.

The first use of rows for typechecking operations on records, including record extension, is due to Wand (1987a; 1988). In Wand's approach, rows denote finite mappings. Furthermore, rows with duplicate labels are considered legal; row extension is interpreted as function extension, so that, if a label occurs twice, the later occurrence takes precedence. This leads to a difficulty in the constraint solving process: the constraint $(\ell : T_1 ; R_1) = (\ell : T_2 ; R_2)$ entails $T_1 = T_2$, but does not entail $R_1 = R_2$, because R_1 and R_2 may have different domains—indeed, their domains may differ at ℓ. Wand's proposed solution (1988) introduces a four-way disjunction, because each of R_1 and R_2 may or may not define ℓ. This gives type inference exponential time complexity.

Later work (Berthomieu, 1993; Berthomieu and le Moniès de Sagazan, 1995) interprets rows as infinite mappings but sticks with Wand's interpretation of row extension as function extension, so that duplicate labels are allowed. The constraint solving algorithm rewrites the problematic constraint $(\ell : T_1 ; R_1) = (\ell : T_2 ; R_2)$ to $(T_1 = T_2) \wedge (R_1 =_{\{\ell\}} R_2)$, where the new predicate $=_L$ is interpreted as row equality *outside* L. Of course, the entire constraint solver must then be extended to deal with constraints of the form $T_1 =_L T_2$. The advantage of this approach over Wand's lies in the fact that no disjunctions are ever introduced, so that the time complexity of constraint solving apparently remains polynomial.

Several other works make opposite choices, sticking with Wand's interpretation of rows as finite mappings but forbidding duplicate labels. No kind discipline is imposed: some other mechanism is used to ensure that duplicate labels do not arise. In Jategaonkar and Mitchell (1988) and Jategaonkar (1989), somewhat ad hoc steps are taken to ensure that, if the row $(\ell : T ; X)$ appears anywhere within a type derivation, then X is never instantiated with a row that defines ℓ. In Gaster and Jones (1996), Gaster (1998), and Jones and Peyton Jones (1999), explicit constraints prevent duplicate labels from arising. This line of work uses *qualified types* (Jones, 1994), a constraint-based type system that bears strong similarity with HM(X). For every label ℓ, a unary predicate $\cdot$ lacks ℓ is introduced; roughly speaking, the constraint R lacks ℓ is considered to hold if the (finite) row R does not define the label ℓ. The constrained type scheme assigned to record access is

$$\cdot.\langle\ell\rangle : \forall XY[Y \text{ lacks } \ell].\Pi\,(\ell : X ; Y) \to X.$$

The constraint Y lacks ℓ ensures that the row $(\ell : X ; Y)$ is well-formed. Although interesting, this approach is not as expressive as that described in this chapter. For instance, although it accommodates record update (where the field being modified is known to exist in the initial record) and strict record extension (where the field is known not to initially exist), it cannot express a suitable type scheme for free record extension, where it is not known whether the field initially exists. This approach has been implemented as the "Trex" extension to Hugs (Jones and Peterson, 1999).

It is worth mentioning a line of type systems (Ohori and Buneman, 1988, 1989; Ohori, 1995) that do not have rows, because they lack feature (i) above, but are still able to assign a polymorphic type scheme to record access. One might explain their approach as follows. First, these systems are equipped with ordinary, structural record types, of the form $\{\ell_1 : \mathsf{T}_1; \ldots ; \ell_n : \mathsf{T}_n\}$. Second, for every label ℓ, a binary predicate $\cdot$ has $\ell : \cdot$ is available. The idea is that the constraint T has ℓ : T′ holds if and only if T is a record type that contains the field $\ell : \mathsf{T}'$. Then, record access may be assigned the constrained type scheme

$$\cdot.\langle \ell \rangle : \forall \mathsf{XY}[\mathsf{X} \text{ has } \ell : \mathsf{Y}].\mathsf{X} \to \mathsf{Y}.$$

This technique also accommodates a restricted form of record update, where the field being written must initially exist and must keep its initial type; it does not, however, accommodate any form of record extension, because of the absence of row extension in the syntax of types. Although the papers cited above employ different terminology, we believe it is fair to view them as constraint-based type systems. In fact, Odersky, Sulzmann, and Wehr (1999) prove that Ohori's system (1995) may be viewed as an instance of HM(X). Sulzmann (2000) proposes several extensions of it, also presented as instances of HM(X), which accommodate record extension and concatenation using new, ad hoc constraint forms in addition to $\cdot$ has ℓ.

In the *label-selective λ-calculus* (Garrigue and Aït-Kaci, 1994; Furuse and Garrigue, 1995), the arrow type constructor carries a label, and arrows that carry distinct labels may commute, so as to allow labeled function arguments to be supplied in any order. Some of the ideas that underlie this type system are closely related to rows.

Pottier (2003) describes an instance of HM(X) where rows are not part of the syntax of types: equivalent expressive power is obtained via an extension of the constraint language. The idea is to work with constraints of the form $\mathsf{R}_1 \leq_L \mathsf{R}_2$, where L may be finite or cofinite, and to interpret such a constraint as row subtyping *inside L*. In this approach, no new type variables need be allocated during constraint solving; contrast this with S-MUTATE-LL, S-MUTATE-GD, and S-MUTATE-GL in Figure 10-14. One benefit is to simplify the complexity analysis; another is to yield insights that lead to generalizations of rows.

Even though rows were originally invented with type inference in mind, they are useful in explicitly typed languages as well; indeed, other approaches to typechecking operations on records appear quite complex (Cardelli and Mitchell, 1991).

A Solutions to Selected Exercises

1.1.4 SOLUTION: The proof of each lemma proceeds by induction on the typing derivation. Almost all cases follow directly from the induction hypothesis. The base cases are straightforward as well, but some slight amount of work is involved. For instance, in the base case for weakening we are given the judgment $\Gamma_1, \mathtt{x}{:}\mathtt{T}, \Gamma_2 \vdash \mathtt{x} : \mathtt{T}$. and must prove that for arbitrary Γ_3, $\Gamma_1, \mathtt{x}{:}\mathtt{T}, \Gamma_2, \Gamma_3 \vdash \mathtt{x} : \mathtt{T}$. The latter judgment follows directly from the variable rule as the rule schema allows the context $\Gamma_1, \mathtt{x}{:}\mathtt{T}, \Gamma_2, \Gamma_3$. Notice, however, that if we were not careful in the definition of the variable rule and had omitted Γ_2 from the context in the rule schema, we would be unable to prove this weakening lemma. Hence, while simple, the rules for the variables and constants play an integral role in defining the structural properties of a type system.

1.2.1 SOLUTION: Since the variable may only appear on the extreme right-hand side of the context, we will be unable to prove the exchange lemma. In the literature, you will see this formulation of the variable rule all the time because authors often treat contexts as finite partial maps. In other words, contexts that differ only in the order in which we write down their elements are treated equally and are never distinguished from one another. In this chapter, we choose not to take this perspective so that we may study the complete set of structure rules directly.

1.2.13 SOLUTION: No: the lemma is false. Fortunately, the preservation theorem for our language only depends upon a substitution lemma involving variables: LEMMA [LINEAR VARIABLE SUBSTITUTION]: Let $\Gamma_3 = \Gamma_1 \circ \Gamma_2$. If $\Gamma_1, \mathtt{x}{:}\mathtt{T} \vdash \mathtt{t}_1 : \mathtt{T}_1$ and $\Gamma_2 \vdash \mathtt{y} : \mathtt{T}$ then $\Gamma_3 \vdash [\mathtt{x} \mapsto \mathtt{y}]\mathtt{t}_1 : \mathtt{T}_1$.

1.3.1 SOLUTION: The type of linear trees with elements of type T follows.

```
type T tree = rec a.lin (unit + lin (T * a * a))
```

It will be convenient to define some constructors for trees of type T as well.

```
fun nilT (nil:unit) : T tree =
  roll (lin inl nil)

fun nodeT (arg : lin (T * T tree * T tree)) : TL =
  roll (lin inr arg)
```

As we recurse into the tree structure, we must create a list of subtrees that have yet to be processed. This list will be constructed from parts of the tree itself. In ML, we could define the appropriate sort of list using the following datatype.

```
datatype (T1,T2) TL =
  done
| right of T2 * T1 tree * TL
| left of T2 * T2 tree * TL
```

Let us assume that our recursive tree map procedure takes a tree `t` and a TL-list `l` as an argument. If `l` is the first constructor `done`, then all we have to do is process `t`. If `l` is the second constructor (say `right(elem,tr,l')`) then when we finish processing `t`, we have finished processing a left subtree, but we still need to process the right subtree (`tr`) and glue the processed tree element (`elem`) together with the results. We also need to recursively process the rest of the list `l'`. If `l` is the last constructor (say `left(elem,tl,l')`) then when we finish processing `t`, we have just finished processing a right subtree and we need to assemble the tree element (`elem`), the left subtree (`tl`) and the recently finished right subtree, and recursively process the rest of the list.

In our linear lambda calculus, the ML type definition given above and its associated constructors will be defined as follows. We will use $\mathtt{in}_0$, $\mathtt{in}_1$,... $\mathtt{in}_{n-1}$ to inject into a n-ary sum when n is greater than two.

```
type TL =
  mu a.
    lin (unit + lin (T2 * T1 tree * a)
              + lin (T2 * T2 tree * a))

fun done (nil:unit) : TL = roll (lin in0 nil)

fun right (arg : lin (T2 * T1 tree * TL)) : TL =
  roll (lin in2 arg)

fun left (arg : lin (T2 * T2 tree * TL)) : TL =
  roll (lin in1 arg)
```

The algorithm is factored into a top-level function `treeMap` and two helpers. The first processes a subtree we have not seen yet. The second determines what to do next by looking at the TL stack.

```
type FT = T1 → T2

fun treeMap(f:FT,t:T1 tree) : T2 tree =
   procTree (f,t,done())

and procTree(f:FT,t:T1 tree,tl:TL) : T2 tree =
   case unroll t (
     inl nil ⇒ procTL (f,nilT2(),tl)
   | inr tree ⇒
      split tree as elem,t1,t2 in
      procTree (f,t1,right lin <f elem,t2,tl>)

and procTL(f:FT,t:T2 tree,tl:TL): T2 tree =
   case unroll tl (
     in0 nil  ⇒ t
   | in1 arg ⇒
       split arg as elem,t2,tl in
       procTree (f,t2,left lin <elem,t,tl>)
   | in2 arg ⇒
       split arg as elem,t1,tl in
       procTL (f,nodeT2 lin <elem,t1,t2>,tl)
```

1.3.4 SOLUTION: If an unrestricted array can contain a linear object, the linear object might never be used because the programmer might forget to use the entire array. Due to our swapping operational semantics for arrays, even though an unrestricted array (containing linear objects) can be used many times, the linear objects themselves can never be used more than once. In short, the supposedly linear objects would actually be *affine*.

1.4.1 SOLUTION: Consider the following expression. If we generalized the syntax to allow nested sub expressions but made no change to the typing rules, it would type check despite the fact that booleans are confused with integers.

```
let x = ord <true,true> in
let y = ord <ord <3,2>,x> in
split y as z1,z2 in
split z2 as b1,b2 in
if b1 then ...   (* using an int as if it was a bool *)
```

Can we change the typing rules in some way to solve the soundness problem?

1.4.2 SOLUTION: Consider the following well-typed expression.

```
let x1 = ord true in
let f = ord λy:ord bool.ord <x1,y> in
let x2 = ord false in
f x2
```

At the point of execution just before the function call, the stack will be organized with x1, which belongs to f's closure, at the bottom of the stack, f allocated immediately on top of x1, and x2 allocated immediately on top of f.

When the function f is called, f should be deallocated, since ordered objects are always deallocated when they are used. However, f is in the middle of the stack rather than on top, so the ordered abstract machine gets stuck. The main problem centers around checking ordered functions with ordered arguments.

1.4.3 SOLUTION: The previous problem demonstrates that the difficulty with ordered functions is that when the function has an ordered argument, the function will appear in the middle of the stack when it is called. We cannot deallocate the function at that point, but one thing we can do is substitute a placeholder with type junk for the used function pointer. The only thing that can be done with an object of type junk is to pop it off the stack. When the code in the function body has used up the ordered function argument, the junk item will appear at the top of the stack. At this point, programmer will explicitly pop it off the stack and move on to using objects in the function's closure.

The typing rule for the specialized ordered abstraction with ordered argument appears below. We also give the typing rule for the command pop x; t, which pops its argument (x) off the top of the stack and continues execution with t below. It is up to you to define their operational rules.

$$\frac{\Gamma, \mathtt{f{:}ord\ junk}, \mathtt{x{:}ord}\ P_1 \vdash t_2 : T_2}{\Gamma \vdash \mathtt{ord}\ \lambda_f\, \mathtt{x{:}(ord}\ P_1\mathtt{)}.t_2 : \mathtt{ord\ (ord}\ P_1\mathtt{)}{\to}T_2} \quad \text{(T-ABS)}$$

$$\frac{\Gamma_2 \vdash \mathtt{x} : \mathtt{ord\ junk} \qquad \Gamma_1 \vdash \mathtt{t} : \mathtt{T}}{\Gamma_1 \circ \Gamma_2 \vdash \mathtt{pop\ x;\ t} : \mathtt{T}} \quad \text{(T-POP)}$$

2.1.1 SOLUTION: We can introduce a type family for rectangular matrices thus:

```
Matrix      :: Nat → Nat → *
idmatrix    : Πn:Nat. Matrix n n
multmatrix : Πl:Nat. Πm:Nat. Πn:Nat.
                        Matrix l m → Matrix m n → Matrix l n
```

Suppose we have a dependent type for ranges of integers: {n...m} denotes the type of integers between n and m inclusive, either n or m may be omitted. A possible typing for dates is given by:

```
Year  =  {2003..} :: *
Month =  {1..12}  :: *
Day    :: Month → *
```

where

```
Day(n)  =  {1..31}  if n ∈ {1,3,5,7,8,10,12}
Day(n)  =  {1..30}  if n ∈ {4,6,9,11}
Day(2) =  {1..29}
```

A date is then given by an element of the Σ-type (see page 48):

```
Date :: Σy:Year. Σm:Month. Day(m)
```

Of course, we could gain more accuracy by making the type of days also depend on the year.

2.1.2 SOLUTION: A type representing the constructive axiom of choice for a predicate P is `(Πa:A.Σb:B. P(a,b)) → (Σf:A→B. Πx:A. P(x, f x))`. It can be shown in Martin-Löf's type theory that this type is inhabited (Martin-Löf, 1984).

2.1.3 SOLUTION: `Σa:A.Σb:B.Id(f a, g b)`

2.1.4 SOLUTION: Here are some terms representing β-reduction and its closure on lambda terms:

```
Eval      :: ΠA:Ty. Tm A → Tm A → *
evalAppAbs : ΠA:Ty. ΠB:Ty.
               Πt1:(Tm A → Tm B).
               Πt2:(Tm A) → Eval (app (lam t1) t2) (t1 t2)
evalLam   :  ΠA:Ty. ΠB:Ty.
              Πft1,ft1':(Tm A → Tm B).
               (Πx: Tm A. Eval (ft1 x) (ft1' x))
                  → Eval (lam ft1) (lam ft1')
evalApp1 :  ΠA:Ty. ΠB:Ty.
              Πt1,t1':(Tm (arrow A B)).
               Πt2: Tm B. Eval t1 t1'
                         → Eval (app t1 t2) (app t1' t2)
evalApp2 :  ΠA:Ty. ΠB:Ty.
              Πt1: (Tm (arrow A B)).
               Πt2,t2': Tm B. Eval t2 t2'
                              → Eval (app t1 t2) (app t1 t2')
```

2.6.4 SOLUTION: We give the solution in the syntax of the implementation.

```
eqSucc =
   λx:Prf(nat).λy:Prf(nat).λh:Prf(eq nat x y).
     h(λz:Prf(nat).eq nat (succ x) (succ z)) (eqRefl nat (succ x))
 : Πx:Prf(nat).Πy:Prf(nat).Prf(eq nat x y) →
                                Prf(eq nat (succ x) (succ y));
```

```
addAssoc = λx:Prf(nat).λy:Prf(nat).λz:Prf(nat).
                eq nat (add x (add y z)) (add (add x y) z);

proofOfAddAssoc = λx:Prf(nat).λy:Prf(nat).λz:Prf(nat).
        natInd (λx1:Prf(nat).addAssoc x1 y z)
                (eqRefl nat (add y z))
                (λx1:Prf(nat).λp:Prf(addAssoc x1 y z).
                        eqSucc (add x1 (add y z)) (add (add x1 y) z) p)
                x
  : Πx:Prf(nat).Πy:Prf(nat).Πz:Prf(nat).Prf(addAssoc x y z);
```

2.7.1 SOLUTION: Let i : *Syntax*(λLF) → *Syntax*(λP) be the obvious mapping between the syntaxes, which collapses each λLF λ-construct to the single λP λ-operator, etc. (Except that type and term variables have disoint images). Then we would hope to show:

1. $\Gamma \vdash_{\lambda LF} \mathtt{t} : \mathtt{T} \iff i(\Gamma) \vdash_{\lambda P} i(\mathtt{t}) : i(\mathtt{T})$

2. $\Gamma \vdash_{\lambda LF} \mathtt{T} :: \mathtt{K} \iff i(\Gamma) \vdash_{\lambda P} i(\mathtt{T}) : i(\mathtt{K})$

3. $\Gamma \vdash_{\lambda LF} \mathtt{K} \iff i(\Gamma) \vdash_{\lambda P} i(\mathtt{K}) : \square$

There are two difficulties in establishing this equivalence. First, the presentation of λLF includes Q-ETA, but η equalities are not included in the definition of PTS we gave. If Q-ETA is removed from λLF, the left to right direction is straightforward. The right to left direction raises the second difficulty: we must show that the untyped conversion relation of PTS can be simulated by the declarative equality in λLF. This requires showing the Church-Rosser property for the PTS conversion.

2.8.1 SOLUTION: To complete the definition, we must give a simultaneous definition of the interpretation of index sorts, $[\![\mathtt{I}]\!]_\eta \subseteq \mathbb{Z}$, index terms, $[\![\mathtt{i}]\!]_\eta \in \mathbb{Z}$, and satisfaction between environments and contexts, $\eta \models \Gamma$ and environments and propositions, $\eta \models \mathtt{P}$. The definitions are given below.

$$\begin{array}{lll} \eta \models \varnothing & & \\ \eta \models \Gamma, x : I & \text{if } \eta \models \Gamma \text{ and } \eta(x) \in [\![I]\!]_\eta \\ \eta \models \Gamma, P & \text{if } \eta \models \Gamma \text{ and } \eta \models P \end{array} \qquad \begin{array}{ll} \eta \models \mathtt{P}_1 \wedge \mathtt{P}_2 & \text{if } \eta \models \mathtt{P}_1,\ \eta \models \mathtt{P}_2 \\ \eta \models \mathtt{i}_1 \mathtt{<=} \mathtt{i}_2 & \text{if } [\![\mathtt{i}_1]\!]_\eta \leq [\![\mathtt{i}_2]\!]_\eta \end{array}$$

$$\begin{array}{lll} [\![\mathtt{x}]\!]_\eta & = & \eta(x) \\ [\![q]\!]_\eta & = & q \\ [\![q\mathtt{i}]\!]_\eta & = & q \times [\![\mathtt{i}]\!]_\eta \\ [\![\mathtt{i}_1 + \mathtt{i}_2]\!]_\eta & = & [\![\mathtt{i}_1]\!]_\eta + [\![\mathtt{i}_2]\!]_\eta \end{array} \qquad \begin{array}{ll} [\![\mathtt{int}]\!]_\eta & = \mathbb{Z} \\ [\![\{\mathtt{x}:\mathtt{I} \mid \mathtt{P}\}]\!]_\eta & = \\ \quad \{ z \in [\![I]\!]_\eta \mid \eta[\mathtt{x} \mapsto z] \models \mathtt{P} \} & \end{array}$$

Finally, $\Gamma \models i : I$ is defined as $\forall \eta.\ \eta \models \Gamma \implies [\![i]\!]_\eta \in [\![I]\!]_\eta$.

3.2.7 SOLUTION: All TL-typing rules are closed under arbitrary substitutions. Consequently all substitutions of TL-typable closed terms yield typable terms. In particular, $S(\texttt{t}_1)$ is TL-typable.

3.2.18 SOLUTION:

1. That $\texttt{t} \uparrow$ implies $\|\texttt{t}\| \uparrow$ follows directly from the Conditional Correctness Theorem, part 2. Assume now $\texttt{t} \downarrow$, that is $\texttt{t}$ terminates. By the Soundness Theorem $\texttt{t}$ cannot terminate with a stuck state, so $\texttt{t} \xrightarrow{\texttt{T}}{}^{*} \texttt{v}$ for some value $\texttt{v}$. By Conditional Correctness, part 1, this implies that $\|\texttt{t}\| \longrightarrow^{*} \|\texttt{v}\|$. By Lemma 3.2.9, part 1, $\|\texttt{v}\|$ is also a value. Since all values are final (easy), this shows that $\|\texttt{t}\| \downarrow$.

2. The implication from right to left follows directly from Conditional Correctness, part 1. As for the converse direction, assume $\|\texttt{t}\| \longrightarrow^{*} \|\texttt{v}\|$. By Soundness evaluation of $\texttt{t}$ does not get stuck and by part 1 of the corollary there exists a TL-value $\texttt{v}'$ such that $\texttt{t} \xrightarrow{\texttt{T}}{}^{*} \texttt{v}'$. By Conditional Correctness, part 1, we have $\|\texttt{t}\| \longrightarrow^{*} \|\texttt{v}'\|$. Since $\longrightarrow$ is deterministic and we also have $\|\texttt{t}\| \longrightarrow^{*} \|\texttt{v}\|$ by assumption, we can conclude that $\|\texttt{v}'\| = \|\texttt{v}\|$, and we are done.

3.2.19 SOLUTION: (Sketch) There is a better completion. The two occurrences of `tt` can be given distinct labels.

3.4.2 SOLUTION: Both of the two recursive calls would have to specify ρ_i, ρ_o as actual parameters, and so all intermediate arguments and results would end up in the same two regions; namely the two argument regions supplied to the function at the outermost level.

3.4.3 SOLUTION: An n-ary region abstraction can be converted into a stack of unary ones, but one must decide where the intermediate region closures that the semantics require are allocated. The following solution takes care not to cause any net heap allocation in the translation of an n-ary application:

$$(\lambda\rho_1,\ldots,\rho_n.\texttt{t})\ \texttt{at}\ \rho \Rightarrow (\lambda\rho'.(\lambda\rho_1.\cdots(\lambda\rho_n.\texttt{t})\ \texttt{at}\ \rho'\cdots)\ \texttt{at}\ \rho')\ \texttt{at}\ \rho$$
$$\texttt{f}\ [[\rho_1,\ldots,\rho_n]] \Rightarrow \texttt{new}\,\rho'.\texttt{f}\ [[\rho']]\ [[\rho_1]]\cdots[[\rho_n]]$$

3.4.4 SOLUTION: When the region abstraction is applied (i.e., each time `f` is mentioned), a closure must be allocated to contain the region parameters and the free variables of the function body, because the ordinary BL parameter may not be supplied right away. The parameter ρ' selects the region in which this closure will be allocated. It is not part of the TT syntax for `letrec` because this closure allocation is implicit in the `letrec` construct; instead the original syntax for applying the region abstraction is

$$\mathtt{t} ::= \mathtt{f}[\rho_1, \ldots, \rho_k] \ \mathtt{at}\ \rho'$$

which can be expressed as $\mathtt{f}\ [[\rho_1, \ldots, \rho_k, \rho']]$ in RAL.

3.4.5 SOLUTION: ρ is the region where a closure for the region abstraction is allocated. This closure contains the values of the free variables of the lambda expression. The intention in TT was that this closure would be consulted when the region abstraction is applied, such that the variables could be moved to the final closure in ρ'. However, due to the syntactic requirement that the region abstraction is applied whenever `f` is mentioned in $\mathtt{t}_1$ or $\mathtt{t}_2$, the free variables will actually still be in scope at the application point. Since the body of the region abstraction is also statically known, nothing actually needs to be allocated in ρ, and indeed the ML Kit, a practical realization of TT (refer to Section 3.8), does not allocate this closure. But this was not realized when TT was first formulated.

3.4.6 SOLUTION: By a simple induction over the derivation of the evaluation relation, we may prove that if $\mathtt{t}_\bullet \xrightarrow{\text{RAL}} \mathtt{t}'_\bullet$ and $\mathtt{t}_\bullet \preceq \mathtt{t}$, then there is a $\mathtt{t}'$ such that $\mathtt{t} \xrightarrow{\text{RAL}} \mathtt{t}'$ and $\mathtt{t}'_\bullet \preceq \mathtt{t}'$.

Apply this lemma to each step of the reduction of the original $\mathtt{t}_\bullet$. In the case $Y = \mathsf{bv}$, note that $\mathsf{bv} \preceq \mathtt{t}$ implies $\mathsf{bv} = \mathtt{t}$.

3.5.2 SOLUTION: The only interesting issue in the proof is that the substitutions substitute from sets of variables to another syntactic class (from region variables to places, for example). Observe, however, that everywhere in the typing rules something is required to be a type, region, or effect variable (rather than, say, a place or effect), it occurs in a binding context and so is unaffected by substitution.

3.5.13 SOLUTION: The reference operations would need a formal semantics, so we would have to extend the evaluation and typing judgments with stores and store typings as in Chapter 13 of *TAPL*. But that would break the lexical scoping of region variables, on which the correct operation of rule (RE-DEALLOC) depends critically. So the entire semantic treatment of region allocation and deallocation needs to be reworked. How to do this can be seen in Calcagno, Helsen, and Thiemann (2002).

3.6.1 SOLUTION: No. It is typable (if and) only if the input program satisfies our syntactic restriction on the use of the `fix` operator, and is typable in (region-free) *F* with recursion, such that the type of the entire program is either `bool` or a type variable. If the input program is ill-typed, it can never be region annotated; a derivation of $\emptyset \vdash \mathtt{t} :^{\varphi} \mathtt{T}$ can be converted into a derivation of $\emptyset \vdash \|\mathtt{t}\| : \|\mathtt{T}\|$ in System *F* with recursion simply by erasing all of the region-related syntax. ($\|\mathtt{T}\|$, is of course, T with the region annotations removed, in a way similar to $\|\mathtt{t}\|$.) Such an erasure transforms each RTL type rule into either a well-known *F* rule or the identity rule that concludes any judgment from itself.

3.6.3 SOLUTION: The constraints collected during the analysis of that subexpression did not entail ρ_5 being in φ at all. It was only when the two sides of the `m` application were combined that ρ_5 entered the picture. (The point here is that construction of `new` must necessarily happen *while* each subterm is analyzed; the raw type tree plus constraints does not immediately show where it is useful to insert `new` except at the root.)

3.6.4 SOLUTION: Effect polymorphism serves to enforce relations between the effect parts of different arrow constructions in the polymorphic variant of a type. In a first-order program, there is at most one arrow in each type, so there is no need for explicit effect polymorphism.

5.2.1 SOLUTION: The assertion that x has type singleton for value v can be written simply as $x = v$. The singleton type for the value v can be written as $\{x \mid x = v\}$ and correspondingly the assertion can also be written as $x : \{x \mid x = v\}$

5.2.2 SOLUTION: $\{x \mid x : \mathtt{ptr}\ \{\{y \mid y = 0\}\,;\mathtt{int}\} \vee x : \mathtt{ptr}\ \{\{y \mid y = 1\}\,;\mathtt{int};\mathtt{int}\}\}$.

5.2.3 SOLUTION: We assume that the same `listinv` formula constructor is used to specify that the contents of the memory is well-typed. The function specification is then:

$$\begin{array}{lcl} \mathtt{Pre} & = & \mathtt{r}_1 : \mathtt{ptr}\ \{\mathtt{int};\mathtt{int}\} \wedge \mathtt{r}_2 : \mathtt{list\ int} \wedge \mathtt{listinv}\ \mathtt{r}_M \\ \mathtt{Post} & = & \mathtt{r}_R : \mathtt{list\ int} \wedge \mathtt{listinv}\ \mathtt{r}_M \end{array}$$

5.2.4 SOLUTION: The challenge here is to express the sequence property. We can do that either by adding a new type constructor or simply by using a universal quantifier.

$$\begin{array}{lcl} \mathtt{Pre} & = & \mathtt{listinv}\ \mathtt{r}_M \wedge \forall i.(0 \le i \wedge i < \mathtt{r}_2) \Rightarrow (\mathtt{r}_1 + 4 * i) : \mathtt{ptr}\ \{\mathtt{list\ int}\} \\ \mathtt{Post} & = & \mathtt{listinv}\ \mathtt{r}_M \end{array}$$

5.2.5 SOLUTION: We show the solution for the more complicated case when the array elements are structures. We must add the `array` *S* type constructor, where S is a structure type. We also add the (sizeof S N) formula to state that the size of the structure S is N bytes.

In order to handle the sizeof formula constructor we add the following two rules:

$$\texttt{sizeof}\ W\ 4$$

$$\frac{\texttt{sizeof}\ S\ N}{\texttt{sizeof}\ (W;S)\ (N+4)}$$

By indexing into an array we can obtain pointers to elements, provided that the index is in the bounds of the array. For the purpose of bounds checking we must fetch the length of the array from memory and hence we must add a requirement that the memory contents is well-typed.

$$\frac{A : \texttt{array}\ S \qquad (\texttt{sizeof}\ S\ N) \qquad 0 \le I \qquad I < (\texttt{sel}\ M\ A) \qquad \texttt{listinv}\ M}{(A + 4 + I * N) : \texttt{ptr}\ \{S\}}$$

5.3.1 SOLUTION: For the first program fragment the symbolic state at the end is $\sigma = \{\texttt{r}_a = b+1, \texttt{r}_b = b, \texttt{r}_c = (b+1)+2, \texttt{r}_d = b+1\}$. For the second program fragment the resulting symbolic state is $\sigma = \{\texttt{r}_1 = b+1, \texttt{r}_2 = b, \texttt{r}_c = (b+1)+2, \texttt{r}_d = b+1\}$. Notice that the symbolic state is the same, considering the renaming of registers once we consider the

5.3.2 SOLUTION: With the addition of the new instruction in the first code fragment, the symbolic state at the end of the block becomes $\sigma = \{\texttt{r}_a = 3, \texttt{r}_b = b, \texttt{r}_c = (b+1)+2, \texttt{r}_d = b+1\}$. The symbolic state of register $\texttt{r}_a$ is different from the symbolic state of the corresponding register ($\texttt{r}_1$) in the second code fragment.

5.3.4 SOLUTION: The key observation is that the symbolic evaluator carries precise information about the result of the load in line 6 in Figure 5-2. Everytime this value is used, we have to prove that it has the right type. We have to ensure that VCGen "forgets" the precise description of the result of the load, and maintains only the fact that it is a value of type ptr {int}. We do this by adding an invariant annotation immediately after the load:

```
          ...
6 LCons:  rt := Mem[rx]                                  ; Load the first data
7         INV rt : ptr {int} ∧ rx : ptr {maybepair;mp_list} ∧ listinv rM
8         ...
```

When encountering this invariant, the VCGen assumes fresh values for all registers and assumes that the invariant holds for these values. This effectively means that the fact sel m_1 $\texttt{x}_1$: ptr {int} is proved only once, when the invariant is first encountered. Notice also that the invariant must preserve all useful information about the live registers. For the $\texttt{r}_x$ register we know that it is not equal to zero and has type mp_list, hence it is a pointer to a list cell.

5.3.5 SOLUTION: We assume that for each function staring at address L in the agent we have a precondition Pre_{L} and a postcondition $Post_{\mathsf{L}}$. These can be specified by the agent producer using annotations. For example, in JVML they are specified as types in a special table in the `.class` file that contains the agent.

Assume also that the set of registers is $\mathsf{r}_1, \ldots, \mathsf{r}_n$ and that the callee-save registers are $\mathsf{r}_1, \ldots, \mathsf{r}_{CS}$. Unlike in the original symbolic evaluator we must identify for each `return` instruction to which function it belongs, and thus what postcondition to use. This can be done by carrying an additional parameter in the symbolic evaluator to specify the postcondition to use for the `return` instructions. Instead, we are going to assume that return instructions are annotated with the starting address of the function to which they belong. We also assume that each start of a function contains an invariant corresponding to the precondition. Now we can extend the symbolic evaluator as follows:

$$SE(i, \sigma) = \begin{cases} \ldots & \\ (\sigma\ Post_{\mathsf{L}}) & \text{if } \Pi_i = \mathtt{return}_{\mathsf{L}} \\ (\sigma\ Pre_{\mathsf{L}}) \wedge & \text{if } \Pi_i = \mathtt{call\ L} \\ \forall x_{CS+1}.\ldots.x_n.(\sigma'\ Post_{\mathsf{L}}) \Rightarrow SE(i+1, \sigma') & \end{cases}$$

where $\sigma' = \sigma[\mathsf{r}_{CS+1} = x_{CS+1}, \ldots, \mathsf{r}_n = x_n]$. Thus a function call first asserts that the precondition holds, then modifies the symbolic state so that the non callee-save registers are modified to have arbitrary values. The state σ' models the state after the call. In this state the postcondition is assumed to hold and the symbolic evaluation continues.

5.3.6 SOLUTION: We extend the symbolic evaluator as follows:

$$SE(i, \sigma) = \begin{cases} \ldots \\ \mathtt{false} \quad \text{if } \Pi_i = \mathsf{UNREACHABLE} \end{cases}$$

Notice that indeed we stop the evaluation at that point, but we require that the agent producer proves that this context is never reachable. The agent producer can actually produce a proof of `false` if this program point follows a function call to a function that never returns and whose postcondition is `false`, as is the case with the `myexit` function in the problem statement. It is also possible to prove `false` at a program point following a conditional branch that can be proved to be always taken.

5.3.7 SOLUTION: We shall consider that each label in the program also acts as a nullary constructor in the logic, denoting the program counter where it is placed. We extend the symbolic evaluator to read the annotation that follows an indirect jump and to require a proof that the address being jumped to is equal to one of the declared destinations. Otherwise, the indirect jump is handled as a conditional branch.

$$SE(i,\sigma) = \begin{cases} \ldots & \\ ((\sigma\ e) = \mathtt{L1} \lor (\sigma\ e) = \mathtt{L2}) \land & \text{if } \Pi_i = \mathtt{jump\ at}\ e \\ ((\sigma\ e) = \mathtt{L1} \Rightarrow SE(L1,\sigma)) \land & \text{and } \Pi_{i+1} = \mathtt{JUMPDEST(L1,L2)} \\ ((\sigma\ e) = \mathtt{L2} \Rightarrow SE(L2,\sigma)) & \end{cases}$$

5.4.1 SOLUTION: We prove here only the soundness of the CONS rule. We must prove the following statement: $\models_{\mathcal{M}} \forall E.\forall W.(E : \mathtt{list}\ W) \land (E \neq 0) \Rightarrow E : \mathtt{ptr}\ \{W;\mathtt{list}\ W\}$. Assuming that the left-hand side of the implication holds, and using the definition of $\models_{\mathcal{M}}$ (see page 200), we derive that $(\mathcal{M}(E) = W \land \mathcal{M}(E{+}4) = \mathtt{list}\ W)$. Now we can verify the right-hand side of the implication: $\models_{\mathcal{M}} E : \mathtt{ptr}\ \{W;\mathtt{list}\ W\}$.

5.4.6 SOLUTION: Let ρ_1 be a state such that $\models_{\mathcal{M}} \rho_1\ Pre$. We assume that $Dom(\mathcal{M}) \subseteq \mathcal{A}ddr$ and $\models_{\mathcal{M}} VC$. By convention the first instruction in the program (at program counter 1) is an invariant INV *Pre*. Let $\sigma_1 = \{\mathtt{r}_1 = x_1, \ldots, \mathtt{r}_n = x_n\}$ and $\tau_1 = \{x_1 = \rho_1\ \mathtt{r}_1, \ldots, x_n = \rho_1\ \mathtt{r}_n\}$. This means that $\rho_1 = \tau_1 \circ \sigma_1$. We also know that $SE(1,\sigma_1) = \sigma_1\ Pre$ and therefore we know that $\models_{\mathcal{M}} \tau_1\ SE(1,\sigma_1)$. This allows us to establish that the induction hypothesis holds for the first instruction: $IH(1,\rho_1,\sigma_1,\tau_1)$.

We can prove by induction on the number of transition steps, that for any (i,ρ) reachable from the initial state $(1,\rho_1)$, there exist σ and τ such that $IH(i,\rho,\sigma,\tau)$. Furthermore, either i points to a `return` instruction or else we can make further progress. The base case follows from the argument above and the inductive step is proved using Theorem 5.4.4.

5.5.1 SOLUTION:

```
all (λa : ι.
      (imp (hastype a (ptr (seq1 int)))
           (addr a)))
```

5.5.2 SOLUTION: The proof of the predicate $\forall a.a : \mathtt{ptr}\ \{\mathtt{int}\} \Rightarrow \mathtt{addr}\ a$ is:

$$\dfrac{\dfrac{\dfrac{\overline{a : \mathtt{ptr}\ \{\mathtt{int}\}}\ u}{\mathtt{addr}\ a}\ \text{PTRADDR}}{a : \mathtt{ptr}\ \{\mathtt{int}\} \Rightarrow \mathtt{addr}\ a}\ \text{IMPI}^u}{\forall a.a : \mathtt{ptr}\ \{\mathtt{int}\} \Rightarrow \mathtt{addr}\ a}\ \text{ALLI}^a$$

The LF representation of this proof is shown below. Notice how the parameter a and the hypothesis u are properly scoped by using higher-order representation.

```
alli (λa : ι.(imp (hastype a (ptr (seq1 int)))
                  (addr a)))
        (impi (hastype a (ptr (seq1 int)))
              (addr a)
              (λu : pf (hastype a (ptr (seq1 int)))
                    (ptraddr a (seq1 int) u)))
```

In the above representation we used LF constants declared in Figure 5-11 along with the following declaration for ptraddr:

$$\texttt{ptraddr} \quad : \quad \Pi A : \iota.\Pi S : s.\texttt{pf (hastype } A \texttt{ (ptr } S\texttt{))} \to \texttt{pf (addr } A\texttt{)}$$

6.2.1 SOLUTION: The if direction (s′ = t′ implies s⇔*t) follows directly from symmetry and transitivity. For the only-if direction, suppose s⇔*t. We claim that s and t have a common reduct (that is, there exists u such that s⇒*u and t⇒*u):

Proof: The proof is by induction on s ⇔* t.

Base step:

Suppose s⇔*t holds because s⇒t. Then let u be t.

Induction step: (Symmetry)

Suppose s⇔*t holds because t⇔*s. By induction, t and s have a common reduct u.

Induction step: (Transitivity)

Suppose s⇔*t holds because s⇔*u′ and u′⇔*t. By induction, s and u′ have a common reduct s″, and u′ and t have a common reduct t″. Thus u′⇒*s″ and u′⇒*t″, so by confluence there exists u such that s″⇒*u and t″⇒*u. Therefore u is a common reduct of s and t. □

We have shown that s and t have a common reduct u. Observe that s⇒*s′ and s⇒*u. By confluence, there exists r such that s′⇒*r and u⇒*r. But s′ is a normal form, so r = s′. Hence u⇒*s′. Similarly u⇒*t′. Then, by confluence, s′ and t′ must have a common reduct, but again they are normal forms so they must be equal.

6.2.2 SOLUTION: By induction on derivations. We show the case for Q-EXT; the others are straightforward. For Q-EXT, choose x so as not to be free in s or t. By induction, s x ⇔* t x. It is easy to show by induction that λx:T_1.s x ⇔* λx:T_1.t x (by repeatedly using QR-ABS). By QR-ETA, λx:T_1.s x ⇒ s and λx:T_1.t x ⇒ t. Therefore s ⇔* t by symmetry and transitivity.

6.2.3 SOLUTION: Let T and T′ be any two distinct types. Let t be λx:T.(λy:T′.y)x. By QR-ABS and QR-BETA, t reduces to λx:T.x, and by QR-ETA, t reduces to

λy:T'.y. These two terms are distinct normal forms, so they have no common reduct.

6.3.1 SOLUTION: s is λx:Unit.x and t is λx:Unit.unit.

6.6.3 SOLUTION: The logical equivalence x:b $\vdash$ x is x : b holds but $\vdash$ x is x : b does not.

6.6.4 SOLUTION: The logical equivalence $\vdash$ λx:b.x is λx:b.k : b$\to$b holds, but y:b $\vdash$ λx:b.x is λx:b.k : b$\to$b does not.

Proof: We begin by showing the former logical equivalence holds. Suppose $\vdash$ s is t : b. We wish to show that $\vdash$ (λx:b.x) s is (λx:b.k) t : b. It is sufficient to show that: $\vdash$ (λx:b.x) s $\Leftrightarrow$ (λx:b.k) t : b. Since $\vdash$ s is t : b, we have that $\vdash$ s $\Leftrightarrow$ t : b. By inversion s $\Downarrow$ s', t $\Downarrow$ t', and $\vdash$ s' $\leftrightarrow$ t' : b. Since the context is empty, and there exists only one constant, it is easy to verify that s' = t' = k. Therefore ((λx:b.x) s) $\Downarrow$ k and ((λx:b.k) t) $\Downarrow$ k. The desired conclusion follows.

Now we show that the latter logical equivalence does not hold. Let s = t = y. Then certainly y:b $\vdash$ s is t : b. However, ((λx:b.x) s) $\Downarrow$ y and ((λx:b.k) t) $\Downarrow$ k, and y and k are not path equivalent. Therefore (λx:b.x) s and (λx:b.k) t are not algorithmically equivalent and hence not logically equivalent at b. □

6.9.2 SOLUTION: By induction on T. The case T = Unit is trivial, and the case T = b follows from algorithmic transitivity (Lemma 6.5.4).

Suppose T = $T_1 \to T_2$. Then $\Gamma \vdash$ s is t : $T_1 \to T_2$ and $\Gamma \vdash$ t is u : $T_1 \to T_2$. We wish to show that $\Gamma \vdash$ s is u : $T_1 \to T_2$. Suppose $\Gamma' \supseteq \Gamma$ and $\Gamma' \vdash$ s' is u' : T_1. Then we wish to show that $\Gamma' \vdash$ s s' is u u' : T_2.

By logical symmetry (Lemma 6.9.1), $\Gamma' \vdash$ u' is s' : T_1, and then by induction, $\Gamma' \vdash$ u' is u' : T_1. By the definition of logical equivalence, we may deduce $\Gamma' \vdash$ s s' is t u' : T_2 and also $\Gamma' \vdash$ t u' is u u' : T_2. By induction, $\Gamma' \vdash$ s s' is u u' : T_2.

6.9.10 SOLUTION:

Case T-CONST: t = k
T = b

By the Main Lemma, $\Gamma' \vdash$ k is k : b. Therefore $\Gamma' \vdash \gamma$(k) is δ(k) : b, since k contains no free variables.

Case Q-REFL:

Immediate by the first clause of the induction hypothesis.

Case Q-SYMM:

Immediate from the induction hypothesis and logical symmetry.

Case Q-TRANS:

By logical symmetry, $\Gamma' \vdash \delta$ is $\gamma : \Gamma$, so by logical transitivity, $\Gamma' \vdash \delta$ is $\delta : \Gamma$. Therefore, by induction (using γ and δ), $\Gamma' \vdash \gamma(s)$ is $\delta(t) : T$, and also by induction (using δ and δ), $\Gamma' \vdash \delta(t)$ is $\delta(u) : T$. By logical transitivity, $\Gamma' \vdash \gamma(s)$ is $\delta(u) : T$.

Case Q-ABS: $s = \lambda x{:}T_1.s_2$
$t = \lambda x{:}T_1.t_2$
$T = T_1 \to T_2$

We wish to show that $\Gamma' \vdash \gamma(\lambda x{:}T_1.s_2)$ is $\delta(\lambda x{:}T_1.t_2) : T_1 \to T_2$. Suppose $\Gamma'' \supseteq \Gamma'$ and $\Gamma'' \vdash s'$ is $t' : T_1$. We wish to show that $\Gamma'' \vdash (\lambda x{:}T_1.\gamma(s_2))s'$ is $(\lambda x{:}T_1.\delta(t_2))t' : T_2$. By logical weak head closure, it is sufficient to show that $\Gamma'' \vdash [x \mapsto s']\gamma(s_2)$ is $[x \mapsto t']\delta(t_2) : T_2$.

By logical monotonicity, $\Gamma'' \vdash \gamma$ is $\delta : \Gamma$. Thus, $\Gamma'' \vdash \gamma[x \mapsto s']$ is $\delta[x \mapsto t'] : (\Gamma, x{:}T_1)$. Therefore, by induction, $\Gamma'' \vdash \gamma[x \mapsto s'](s_2)$ is $\delta[x \mapsto t'](t_2) : T_2$, which is equivalent to the desired conclusion.

Case Q-APP: $s = s_1\ s_2$
$t = t_1\ t_2$
$T = T_{12}$

By induction, $\Gamma' \vdash \gamma(s_1)$ is $\delta(t_1) : T_1 \to T_2$ and $\Gamma' \vdash \gamma(s_2)$ is $\delta(t_2) : T_1$. By the definition of the logical relation, since $\Gamma' \supseteq \Gamma$, we may conclude $\Gamma' \vdash \gamma(s_1)\gamma(s_2)$ is $\delta(t_1)\delta(t_2) : T_2$. That is, $\Gamma' \vdash \gamma(s_1\ s_2)$ is $\delta(t_1\ t_2) : T_2$.

Case Q-EXT: $s = s$
$t = t$
$T = T_1 \to T_2$

We wish to show that $\Gamma' \vdash \gamma(s)$ is $\delta(t) : T_1 \to T_2$. Suppose $\Gamma'' \supseteq \Gamma'$ and $\Gamma'' \vdash s'$ is $t' : T_1$. We wish to show that $\Gamma'' \vdash \gamma(s)\ s'$ is $\delta(t)\ t' : T_2$.

By logical monotonicity, $\Gamma'' \vdash \gamma$ is $\delta : \Gamma$. Thus, $\Gamma'' \vdash \gamma[x \mapsto s']$ is $\delta[x \mapsto t'] : (\Gamma, x{:}T_1)$. Therefore, by induction, $\Gamma'' \vdash \gamma[x \mapsto s'](s\ x)$ is $\delta[x \mapsto t'](t\ x) : T_2$. That is, $\Gamma'' \vdash \gamma(s)\ s'$ is $\delta(t)\ t' : T_2$, as desired.

6.9.12 SOLUTION: By soundness, $\Gamma \vdash s_1 \equiv t_1 : T_1 \to T_2$ and $\Gamma \vdash s_2 \equiv t_2 : T_1$. By Q-APP, $\Gamma \vdash s_1\ s_2 \equiv t_1\ t_2 : T_2$. By completeness, $\Gamma \vdash s_1\ s_2 \Leftrightarrow t_1\ t_2 : T_2$.

6.9.13 SOLUTION: The key observation is that the left- and right-hand sides of the algorithm do not interact, except insofar as a failure to match in path equivalence allows the algorithm to quit early. That is, except for early termination, one can trace the execution of the algorithm ignoring the terms either to the left or to the right of the arrows. Therefore we can devise a termination metric that takes each side into account independently.

Therefore, define the metric $M(\Gamma \vdash \mathtt{s} \Leftrightarrow \mathtt{t} : \mathsf{T})$ to be the size of the derivation (if it exists) of $\Gamma \vdash \mathtt{s} \Leftrightarrow \mathtt{s} : \mathsf{T}$ plus the size of the derivation (if it exists) of $\Gamma \vdash \mathtt{t} \Leftrightarrow \mathtt{t} : \mathsf{T}$. Define the metric $M(\Gamma \vdash \mathtt{p} \leftrightarrow \mathtt{q} : \mathsf{T})$ similarly. It is straightforward to show that the metric decreases in each recursive call of the algorithm. It is also straightforward to show that all normalizations terminate, since the normalization derivations being sought already exist within the derivations measured by the metric.

Thus, it remains to show only that the metric is actually defined, that is, that there exist derivations of $\Gamma \vdash \mathtt{s} \Leftrightarrow \mathtt{s} : \mathsf{T}$ and $\Gamma \vdash \mathtt{t} \Leftrightarrow \mathtt{t} : \mathsf{T}$. This follows by the completeness of the algorithm from our assumptions that $\Gamma \vdash \mathtt{s} : \mathsf{T}$ and $\Gamma \vdash \mathtt{t} : \mathsf{T}$.

This strategy works precisely because the two sides of the algorithm do not interact. It fails when the two sides do interact, such as in the algorithm for full $F_{\leq}$ (*TAPL*, Chapter 28), wherein bounded universal types on the right-hand side affect the context, which in turn affects the promotion of variables on the left-hand side. On the other hand, in the algorithm for kernel $F_{\leq}$, the bounds on the left- and right-hand sides are required to be the same, so the two sides do act independently (although the side being considered does switch back and forth because of contravariance).

6.9.14 SOLUTION: First, we extend the proofs of the basic algorithmic properties (symmetry, transitivity, weak head closure, and monotonicity) to deal with the new algorithm. These proofs are straightforward.

Second, we define logical equivalence as follows:

$\Gamma \vdash \mathtt{s}$ is $\mathtt{t} : \mathsf{T}$ if and only if either:
- T=Unit,
- or T=b and $\Gamma \vdash \mathtt{s} \Leftrightarrow \mathtt{t} : \mathsf{b}$,
- or $\mathsf{T}=\mathsf{T}_1 \to \mathsf{T}_2$ and, for all $\mathtt{s}'$, $\mathtt{t}'$ and all $\Gamma' \supseteq \Gamma$,
  if $\Gamma' \vdash \mathtt{s}'$ is $\mathtt{t}' : \mathsf{T}_1$
  then $\Gamma' \vdash \mathtt{s}\ \mathtt{s}'$ is $\mathtt{t}\ \mathtt{t}' : \mathsf{T}_2$,
- or $\mathsf{T}=\mathsf{T}_1 \times \mathsf{T}_2$ and $\Gamma \vdash \mathtt{s.1}$ is $\mathtt{t.1} : \mathsf{T}_1$ and
  $\Gamma \vdash \mathtt{s.2}$ is $\mathtt{t.2} : \mathsf{T}_2$.

Third, we extend the proofs of the basic logical properties (symmetry, transitivity, weak head closure, and monotonicity) to deal with the new definition of logical equivalence. These proofs are also straightforward.

Fourth, we extend the Main Lemma to account for product types (the other cases are unchanged):

Case: $\mathtt{T} = \mathtt{T}_1 \times \mathtt{T}_2$

1. Suppose $\Gamma \vdash \mathtt{s}$ is $\mathtt{t} : \mathtt{T}_1 \times \mathtt{T}_2$. We wish to show that $\Gamma \vdash \mathtt{s} \Leftrightarrow \mathtt{t} : \mathtt{T}_1 \times \mathtt{T}_2$. The definition of logical equivalence provides that $\Gamma \vdash \mathtt{s.1}$ is $\mathtt{t.1} : \mathtt{T}_1$, and so $\Gamma \vdash \mathtt{s.1} \Leftrightarrow \mathtt{t.1} : \mathtt{T}_1$ follows by induction. Similarly, $\Gamma \vdash \mathtt{s.2} \Leftrightarrow \mathtt{t.2} : \mathtt{T}_2$. Therefore, $\Gamma \vdash \mathtt{s} \Leftrightarrow \mathtt{t} : \mathtt{T}_1 \times \mathtt{T}_2$.

2. Suppose $\Gamma \vdash \mathtt{p} \leftrightarrow \mathtt{q} : \mathtt{T}_1 \times \mathtt{T}_2$. We wish to show that $\Gamma \vdash \mathtt{p}$ is $\mathtt{q} : \mathtt{T}_1 \times \mathtt{T}_2$. The algorithm provides that $\Gamma \vdash \mathtt{p.1} \leftrightarrow \mathtt{q.1} : \mathtt{T}_1$, so $\Gamma \vdash \mathtt{p.1}$ is $\mathtt{q.1} : \mathtt{T}_1$ follows by induction. Similarly, $\Gamma \vdash \mathtt{p.2}$ is $\mathtt{q.2} : \mathtt{T}_2$. Therefore $\Gamma \vdash \mathtt{p}$ is $\mathtt{q} : \mathtt{T}_1 \times \mathtt{T}_2$.

Finally, we extend the proof of the Fundamental Theorem to cover the new typing and equivalence cases:

Case T-PAIR: $\mathtt{t} = \langle \mathtt{t}_1, \mathtt{t}_2 \rangle$
$\mathtt{T} = \mathtt{T}_1 \times \mathtt{T}_2$

By induction, $\Gamma' \vdash \gamma(\mathtt{t}_1)$ is $\delta(\mathtt{t}_1) : \mathtt{T}_1$, so by logical weak head closure, $\Gamma' \vdash \gamma(\langle \mathtt{t}_1, \mathtt{t}_2 \rangle)\mathtt{.1}$ is $\delta(\langle \mathtt{t}_1, \mathtt{t}_2 \rangle)\mathtt{.1} : \mathtt{T}_1$. Similarly, $\Gamma' \vdash \gamma(\langle \mathtt{t}_1, \mathtt{t}_2 \rangle)\mathtt{.2}$ is $\delta(\langle \mathtt{t}_1, \mathtt{t}_2 \rangle)\mathtt{.2} : \mathtt{T}_2$. Therefore $\Gamma' \vdash \gamma(\langle \mathtt{t}_1, \mathtt{t}_2 \rangle)$ is $\delta(\langle \mathtt{t}_1, \mathtt{t}_2 \rangle) : \mathtt{T}_1 \times \mathtt{T}_2$.

Case T-PROJ1: $\mathtt{t} = \mathtt{t}_1\mathtt{.1}$
$\mathtt{T} = \mathtt{T}_1$

We wish to show that $\Gamma' \vdash \gamma(\mathtt{t}_1\mathtt{.1})$ is $\delta(\mathtt{t}_1\mathtt{.1}) : \mathtt{T}_1$. By induction, $\Gamma' \vdash \gamma(\mathtt{t}_1)$ is $\delta(\mathtt{t}_1) : \mathtt{T}_1 \times \mathtt{T}_2$, and the desired follows by the definition of logical equivalence.

Case T-PROJ2:

Similar to the case for T-PROJ1.

Case Q-PAIR: $\mathtt{s} = \langle \mathtt{s}_1, \mathtt{s}_2 \rangle$
$\mathtt{t} = \langle \mathtt{t}_1, \mathtt{t}_2 \rangle$
$\mathtt{T} = \mathtt{T}_1 \times \mathtt{T}_2$

By induction, $\Gamma' \vdash \gamma(\mathtt{s}_1)$ is $\delta(\mathtt{t}_1) : \mathtt{T}_1$, so by logical weak head closure, $\Gamma' \vdash \gamma(\langle \mathtt{s}_1, \mathtt{s}_2 \rangle)\mathtt{.1}$ is $\delta(\langle \mathtt{t}_1, \mathtt{t}_2 \rangle)\mathtt{.1} : \mathtt{T}_1$. Similarly, $\Gamma' \vdash \gamma(\langle \mathtt{s}_1, \mathtt{s}_2 \rangle)\mathtt{.2}$ is $\delta(\langle \mathtt{t}_1, \mathtt{t}_2 \rangle)\mathtt{.2} : \mathtt{T}_2$. Therefore $\Gamma' \vdash \gamma(\langle \mathtt{s}_1, \mathtt{s}_2 \rangle)$ is $\delta(\langle \mathtt{t}_1, \mathtt{t}_2 \rangle) : \mathtt{T}_1 \times \mathtt{T}_2$.

Case Q-PROJ1: $\mathtt{s} = \mathtt{s}_1\mathtt{.1}$
$\mathtt{t} = \mathtt{t}_1\mathtt{.1}$
$\mathtt{T} = \mathtt{T}_1$

We wish to show that $\Gamma' \vdash \gamma(\mathtt{s}_1\mathtt{.1})$ is $\delta(\mathtt{t}_1\mathtt{.1}) : \mathtt{T}_1$. By induction, $\Gamma' \vdash \gamma(\mathtt{s}_1)$ is $\delta(\mathtt{t}_1) : \mathtt{T}_1 \times \mathtt{T}_2$, and the desired follows by the definition of logical equivalence.

Case Q-PROJ2:

Similar to the case for Q-PROJ1.

Case Q-BETA-PROD1: $\texttt{s} = \langle \texttt{s}_1, \texttt{s}_2 \rangle\texttt{.1}$
$\texttt{t} = \texttt{t}$
$\texttt{T} = \texttt{T}_1$

By induction, $\Gamma' \vdash \gamma(\texttt{s}_1)$ is $\delta(\texttt{t}) : \texttt{T}_1$. Therefore, by logical weak head closure, $\Gamma' \vdash \gamma(\langle \texttt{s}_1, \texttt{s}_2 \rangle\texttt{.1})$ is $\delta(\texttt{t}) : \texttt{T}_1$.

Case Q-BETA-PROD2: $\texttt{s} = \langle \texttt{s}_1, \texttt{s}_2 \rangle\texttt{.2}$
$\texttt{t} = \texttt{t}$
$\texttt{T} = \texttt{T}_2$

By induction, $\Gamma' \vdash \gamma(\texttt{s}_2)$ is $\delta(\texttt{t}) : \texttt{T}_2$. Therefore, by logical weak head closure, $\Gamma' \vdash \gamma(\langle \texttt{s}_1, \texttt{s}_2 \rangle\texttt{.2})$ is $\delta(\texttt{t}) : \texttt{T}_2$.

Case Q-EXT-PROD: $\texttt{s} = \texttt{s}$
$\texttt{t} = \texttt{t}$
$\texttt{T} = \texttt{T}_1 \times \texttt{T}_2$

We wish to show that $\Gamma' \vdash \gamma(\texttt{s})$ is $\delta(\texttt{t}) : \texttt{T}_1 \times \texttt{T}_2$. It suffices to show that $\Gamma' \vdash \gamma(\texttt{s.1})$ is $\delta(\texttt{t.1}) : \texttt{T}_1$ and $\Gamma' \vdash \gamma(\texttt{s.2})$ is $\delta(\texttt{t.2}) : \texttt{T}_2$, each of which follows immediately by induction.

6.9.15 SOLUTION: We must add a case for universal types to the definition of logical equivalence. The most obvious definition is to quantify over all type arguments and compare the type applications at the corresponding instantiated type:

$\Gamma \vdash \texttt{s}$ is $\texttt{t} : \forall\texttt{X.T}$ if and only if
for all closed types $\texttt{T}'$, $\Gamma \vdash \texttt{s [T']}$ is $\texttt{t [T']} : [\texttt{X} \mapsto \texttt{T}']\texttt{T}$

Unfortunately, this is an invalid definition, because logical equivalence is defined by induction on types, and there is no guarantee that the type $[\texttt{X} \mapsto \texttt{T}']\texttt{T}$ is smaller than $\forall\texttt{X.T}$.

The problem is tied to the issue of *impredicativity* (*TAPL*, §23.10). In both $\forall\texttt{X.T}$, the domain of the quantified type variable X includes the very type being defined. This prevents the obvious definition from being well-founded.

For the simple definition attempt given above, the impredicativity problem is fatal. Sometimes we can save the simple definition by changing the language to be predicative. However, for an impredicative language, a more sophisticated definition is required.

The solution to the problem is Girard's method of candidates (Girard, Lafont, and Taylor, 1989). An explanation of Girard's method is beyond the scope of this discussion, but informally the method works as follows: Instead of quantifying over types, the definition of logical equivalence quantifies over possible interpretations of types called *candidates*. Importantly, candidates come equipped with their own notion of logical equivalence that can be defined independently (*i.e.*, without reference to the general definition of logical equivalence). Thus, the definition of logical equivalence may refer to arbitrary candidates and remain well-founded.

7.4.2 HINT: First prove

$$\langle S_1, \mathtt{t}_1\rangle \longrightarrow \langle S_2, \mathtt{t}_2\rangle \Rightarrow (\forall S)(\langle S@S_2, \mathtt{t}_2\rangle \downarrow \Rightarrow \langle S@S_1, \mathtt{t}_1\rangle \downarrow)$$

by considering the different cases for $\longrightarrow$. Deduce the 'if' part of (7.7) from this. For the 'only if' part, show that

$$\{(S, \mathtt{t}) \mid (\exists S_1, S_2, \mathtt{v})\ S = S_1@S_2\ \&\ \langle S_2, \mathtt{t}\rangle \longrightarrow^* \langle Id, \mathtt{v}\rangle\ \&\ \langle S_1, \mathtt{v}\rangle \downarrow\}$$

is closed under the axiom and rules in Figure 7-2 inductively defining the termination relation.

7.5.4 SOLUTION: For property (iii), assuming R is compatible, argue by induction on the derivation of $\Gamma \vdash \mathtt{t} : \mathtt{T}$ that this typing judgment implies that $\Gamma \vdash \mathtt{t}\ R\ \mathtt{t} : \mathtt{T}$ holds. For property (v), if $R = \bigcup_{i \in I} R_i$ with $I \neq \emptyset$ and each R_i compatible, first note that by (iii), R is reflexive since it contains at least one relation R_i. For each of the compatibility properties in Figure 7-4 with a *single* hypothesis, it is clear that R has this property because each of the R_i does. For compatibility properties with multiple hypotheses, we can break them down into a chain of single-hypothesis compatibilities and appeal to the transitivity of R (which we are assuming). For example consider the compatibility property for function application. It suffices to show that R satisfies

$$\frac{\Gamma \vdash \mathtt{v}_1\ R\ \mathtt{v}_1' : \mathtt{T}_1 \to \mathtt{T}_2 \qquad \Gamma \vdash \mathtt{v}_2 : \mathtt{T}_1}{\Gamma \vdash \mathtt{v}_1\ \mathtt{v}_2\ R\ \mathtt{v}_1'\ \mathtt{v}_2 : \mathtt{T}_2} \tag{A.1}$$

and

$$\frac{\Gamma \vdash \mathtt{v}_1 : \mathtt{T}_1 \to \mathtt{T}_2 \qquad \Gamma \vdash \mathtt{v}_2\ R\ \mathtt{v}_2' : \mathtt{T}_1}{\Gamma \vdash \mathtt{v}_1\ \mathtt{v}_2\ R\ \mathtt{v}_1\ \mathtt{v}_2' : \mathtt{T}_2}. \tag{A.2}$$

For then if $\Gamma \vdash \mathtt{v}_1\ R\ \mathtt{v}_1' : \mathtt{T}_1 \to \mathtt{T}_2$ and $\Gamma \vdash \mathtt{v}_2\ R\ \mathtt{v}_2' : \mathtt{T}_1$, we get

$$\begin{array}{ll} \Gamma \vdash \mathtt{v}_1\ \mathtt{v}_2\ R\ \mathtt{v}_1'\ \mathtt{v}_2 : \mathtt{T}_2 & \text{by (A.1), since } \Gamma \vdash \mathtt{v}_2 : \mathtt{T}_1 \\ \Gamma \vdash \mathtt{v}_1'\ \mathtt{v}_2\ R\ \mathtt{v}_1'\ \mathtt{v}_2' : \mathtt{T}_2 & \text{by (A.2), since } \Gamma \vdash \mathtt{v}_1' : \mathtt{T}_1 \to \mathtt{T}_2. \end{array}$$

and hence $\Gamma \vdash \mathtt{v}_1\ \mathtt{v}_2\ R\ \mathtt{v}_1'\ \mathtt{v}_2' : \mathtt{T}_2$ by transitivity. Each of the single-hypothesis properties (A.1) and (A.2) holds of R because they hold for each R_i: each is a special case of the compatibility property for function application because each R_i, being compatible, is also reflexive by (iii).

7.5.10 SOLUTION: Consider the frame stacks

$$S \stackrel{\text{def}}{=} Id \circ (\texttt{x.(fun f(x':Bool) = if x' then true else f x')x})$$

$$S_{\mathsf{T}} \stackrel{\text{def}}{=} Id \circ (\texttt{x.(fun f(x':T) = true)x})$$

Note that $\emptyset \vdash S : \texttt{Bool} \multimap \texttt{Bool}$ and $\emptyset \vdash S_{\mathsf{T}} : \mathsf{T} \multimap \texttt{Bool}$. It is not hard to see for all $\emptyset \vdash \mathtt{b} : \texttt{Bool}$ that

$$S[\mathtt{b}]\downarrow \text{ iff } \langle Id, \mathtt{b}\rangle \longrightarrow^* \langle Id, \texttt{true}\rangle \tag{A.3}$$

and for all $\emptyset \vdash \mathtt{t} : \mathsf{T}$ that

$$\mathtt{t}\downarrow \text{ iff } \langle Id, S_{\mathsf{T}}[\mathtt{t}]\rangle \longrightarrow^* \langle Id, \texttt{true}\rangle \tag{A.4}$$

From (A.3) and the fact that $=_{\text{ctx}}$ is a congruence (so that $\emptyset \vdash \mathtt{b} =_{\text{ctx}} \mathtt{b}' : \texttt{Bool}$ implies $\emptyset \vdash S[\mathtt{b}] =_{\text{ctx}} S[\mathtt{b}'] : \texttt{Bool}$) it follows that $=_{\text{ctx}}$ is $\texttt{true}$-adequate; hence it is contained in $=^{\texttt{true}}_{\text{ctx}}$. Similarly, (A.4) and the fact that $=^{\texttt{true}}_{\text{ctx}}$ is a congruence implies that it is adequate and hence contained in $=_{\text{ctx}}$.

7.6.7 SOLUTION: Since $(-)^{st}$ is inflationary we have $r \subseteq r^{st}$; and since r only relates values, this implies $r \subseteq r^{stv}$. Then since $(-)^{st}$ is monotone, we have $r^{st} \subseteq r^{stvst}$. Conversely, since $(r')^{v} \subseteq r'$ for any r', we have $r^{stv} \subseteq r^{st}$; and then since $(-)^{st}$ is monotone and idempotent, $r^{stvst} \subseteq r^{stst} = r^{st}$.

7.6.14 HINT: The proof of (7.26) is just like the proof of (7.21), using the following property of the termination relation:

$$(\langle S, \mathtt{v.1}\rangle\downarrow \Leftrightarrow \langle S', \mathtt{v'.1}\rangle\downarrow) \text{ iff } (\langle S \circ (\mathtt{x.x.1}), \mathtt{v}\rangle\downarrow \Leftrightarrow \langle S' \circ (\mathtt{x.x.1}), \mathtt{v'}\rangle\downarrow).$$

Similarly, the proof of (7.27) follows from:

$$(\langle S, \mathtt{v\ T}\rangle\downarrow \Leftrightarrow \langle S', \mathtt{v'\ T'}\rangle\downarrow) \text{ iff } (\langle S \circ (\mathtt{x.x\ T}), \mathtt{v}\rangle\downarrow \Leftrightarrow \langle S' \circ (\mathtt{x.x\ T'}), \mathtt{v'}\rangle\downarrow).$$

7.6.18 SOLUTION: It suffices to show

$$(\forall n = 0, 1, \ldots)\ (\mathsf{F}_n, \mathsf{F}'_n) \in \mathsf{fun}(r_1, r_2) \tag{A.5}$$

where F_n and F'_n are the unwindings associated with F and F' respectively, as in Theorem 7.4.4. For if (A.5) holds, then using the fact that $(-)^{st}$ is inflationary

$$(\mathsf{F}_n, \mathsf{F}'_n) \in \mathsf{fun}(r_1, r_2) \subseteq \mathsf{fun}(r_1, r_2)^{st}$$

for each n; so by the *Admissibility* property in Lemma 7.6.8 we have $(\mathsf{F}, \mathsf{F}') \in \mathsf{fun}(r_1, r_2)^{st}$. Thus $(\mathsf{F}, \mathsf{F}') \in \mathsf{fun}(r_1, r_2)^{stv} = \mathsf{fun}(r_1, r_2)$ by Lemma 7.6.13, since $(r_2)^{st} = r_2$. (A.5) is proved by induction on n:

Base case $n = 0$: By definition of F_0, $\langle S, \mathsf{F}_0\ \mathsf{v}_1\rangle \downarrow$ does not hold for any $S \in \mathit{Stack}(\mathsf{T}_2)$ and $\mathsf{v}_1 \in \mathit{Val}(\mathsf{T}_1)$; similarly for F'_0. Hence for all $(\mathsf{v}_1, \mathsf{v}'_1) \in (r_1)^v$, $(\mathsf{F}_0\ \mathsf{v}_1, \mathsf{F}'_0\ \mathsf{v}'_1) \in s^t$ for any $s \in \mathit{SRel}(\mathsf{T}_2, \mathsf{T}'_2)$ and hence in particular for $s = (r_2)^s$. So $(\mathsf{F}_0\ \mathsf{v}_1, \mathsf{F}'_0\ \mathsf{v}'_1) \in (r_2)^{st} = r_2$ for all $(\mathsf{v}_1, \mathsf{v}'_1) \in (r_1)^v$. Therefore $(\mathsf{F}_0, \mathsf{F}'_0) \in \mathtt{fun}(r_1, r_2)$.

Induction step: Suppose $(\mathsf{F}_n, \mathsf{F}'_n) \in \mathtt{fun}(r_1, r_2)$. Then for any $(\mathsf{v}_1, \mathsf{v}'_1) \in (r_1)^v$, from (7.29) we have

$$([\mathtt{f} \mapsto \mathsf{F}_n][\mathtt{x} \mapsto \mathsf{v}_1]\mathtt{t}, [\mathtt{f} \mapsto \mathsf{F}'_n][\mathtt{x} \mapsto \mathsf{v}'_1]\mathtt{t}') \in r_2.$$

By definition of F_{n+1} and Corollary 7.5.8 we have $\varnothing \vdash \mathsf{F}_{n+1}\mathsf{v}_1 =_{\text{ctx}} [\mathtt{f} \mapsto \mathsf{F}_n][\mathtt{x} \mapsto \mathsf{v}_1]\mathtt{t}$; and similarly, $\varnothing \vdash \mathsf{F}'_{n+1}\mathsf{v}'_1 =_{\text{ctx}} [\mathtt{f} \mapsto \mathsf{F}'_n][\mathtt{x} \mapsto \mathsf{v}'_1]\mathtt{t}'$. So since r_2 is closed, we can apply the *Equivalence-respecting* property in Lemma 7.6.8 to conclude that $(\mathsf{F}_{n+1}\mathsf{v}_1, \mathsf{F}'_{n+1}\mathsf{v}'_1) \in r_2$. Since this holds for any $(\mathsf{v}_1, \mathsf{v}'_1) \in (r_1)^v$, we have $(\mathsf{F}_{n+1}, \mathsf{F}'_{n+1}) \in \mathtt{fun}(r_1, r_2)$.

7.6.19 SOLUTION: To show $(\mathsf{v}, \mathsf{v}') \in \{\mathtt{l}_i{=}r_i\ ^{i \in 1..n}\}$ we must show $(\mathsf{v}.\mathtt{l}_i, \mathsf{v}'.\mathtt{l}_i) \in r_i$ for each $i \in 1..n$. Since each r_i is closed, this is equivalent to showing $(\mathsf{v}.\mathtt{l}_i, \mathsf{v}'.\mathtt{l}_i) \in (r_i)^{st}$, i.e. that $\langle S, \mathsf{v}.\mathtt{l}_i\rangle \downarrow \Leftrightarrow \langle S', \mathsf{v}'.\mathtt{l}_i\rangle \downarrow$ holds for all (S, S') in $(r_i)^s$. But by definition of v, $\langle S, \mathsf{v}.\mathtt{l}_i\rangle \downarrow \Leftrightarrow \langle S, \mathsf{v}_i\rangle \downarrow$; and similarly for v'. So it suffices to show $\langle S, \mathsf{v}_i\rangle \downarrow \Leftrightarrow \langle S', \mathsf{v}'_i\rangle$; and this holds because by assumption $(\mathsf{v}_i, \mathsf{v}'_i) \in r_i$ and $(S, S') \in (r_i)^s$.

7.6.20 SOLUTION: To show $(\lambda\mathsf{X}.\mathsf{v}, \lambda\mathsf{X}.\mathsf{v}') \in \lambda r.R(r)$ we have to show for each $\mathsf{T}_1, \mathsf{T}'_1 \in \mathit{Typ}$ and $r \in \mathit{TRel}(\mathsf{T}_1, \mathsf{T}'_1)$ that $((\lambda\mathsf{X}.\mathsf{v})\mathsf{T}, (\lambda\mathsf{X}.\mathsf{v}')\mathsf{T}') \in R(r)$. Since each $R(r)$ is closed, this is equivalent to showing $((\lambda\mathsf{X}.\mathsf{v})\mathsf{T}, (\lambda\mathsf{X}.\mathsf{v}')\mathsf{T}') \in R(r)^{st}$, i.e. that $\langle S, (\lambda\mathsf{X}.\mathsf{v})\mathsf{T}\rangle \downarrow \Leftrightarrow \langle S', (\lambda\mathsf{X}.\mathsf{v}')\mathsf{T}'\rangle \downarrow$ holds for all $(S, S') \in R(r)^s$. But $\langle S, (\lambda\mathsf{X}.\mathsf{v})\mathsf{T}\rangle \downarrow \Leftrightarrow \langle S, [\mathsf{X} \mapsto \mathsf{T}_1]\mathsf{v}\rangle \downarrow$; and similarly for v'. So it suffices to show $\langle S, [\mathsf{X} \mapsto \mathsf{T}_1]\mathsf{v}\rangle \downarrow \Leftrightarrow \langle S, [\mathsf{X} \mapsto \mathsf{T}'_1]\mathsf{v}'\rangle \downarrow$; and this holds because by assumption $([\mathsf{X} \mapsto \mathsf{T}_1]\mathsf{v}, [\mathsf{X} \mapsto \mathsf{T}_1]\mathsf{v}) \in R(r)$ and $(S, S') \in R(r)^s$.

7.6.21 HINT: To show $(\mathtt{if}\ \mathsf{v}\ \mathtt{then}\ \mathtt{t}_1\ \mathtt{else}\ \mathtt{t}_2, \mathtt{if}\ \mathsf{v}'\ \mathtt{then}\ \mathtt{t}'_1\ \mathtt{else}\ \mathtt{t}'_2) \in r = (r)^{st}$ it suffices to show for all $(S, S') \in (r)^s$ that

$$\langle S, \mathtt{if}\ \mathsf{v}\ \mathtt{then}\ \mathtt{t}_1\ \mathtt{else}\ \mathtt{t}_2\rangle \downarrow \Leftrightarrow \langle S', \mathtt{if}\ \mathsf{v}'\ \mathtt{then}\ \mathtt{t}'_1\ \mathtt{else}\ \mathtt{t}'_2\rangle \downarrow$$

or equivalently that

$$\langle S \circ (\mathtt{x}.\mathtt{if}\ \mathtt{x}\ \mathtt{then}\ \mathtt{t}_1\ \mathtt{else}\ \mathtt{t}_2), \mathsf{v}\rangle \downarrow \Leftrightarrow \langle S' \circ (\mathtt{x}.\mathtt{if}\ \mathtt{x}\ \mathtt{then}\ \mathtt{t}'_1\ \mathtt{else}\ \mathtt{t}'_2), \mathsf{v}'\rangle \downarrow.$$

Do this by proving that

$$(S \circ (\mathtt{x}.\mathtt{if}\ \mathtt{x}\ \mathtt{then}\ \mathtt{t}_1\ \mathtt{else}\ \mathtt{t}_2), S' \circ (\mathtt{x}.\mathtt{if}\ \mathtt{x}\ \mathtt{then}\ \mathtt{t}'_1\ \mathtt{else}\ \mathtt{t}'_2) \in (\mathit{Id}_{\mathtt{Bool}})^s.$$

7.6.22 SOLUTION: For any $(S, S') \in (r_2)^s$ it follows from the assumptions on t, t′ and the definition of $\{\exists r_1, R(r_1)\}$ (Figure 7-5) that

$$(S \circ (\texttt{y.let \{*X,x\}=y in t}), S' \circ (\texttt{y.let \{*X,x\}=y in t'}))$$

is in $\{\exists r_1, R(r_1)\}^s$. Hence if $(\texttt{v}, \texttt{v}') \in \{\exists r_1, R(r_1)\}^{stv} \subseteq (\{\exists r_1, R(r_1)\}^s)^t$, then

$$\langle S \circ (\texttt{y.let \{*X,x\}=y in t}), \texttt{v}\rangle\downarrow \;\Leftrightarrow\; \langle S' \circ (\texttt{y.let \{*X,x\}=y in t'}), \texttt{v}'\rangle\downarrow$$

and so $\langle S, \texttt{let \{*X,x\}=v in t}\rangle\downarrow \Leftrightarrow \langle S, \texttt{let \{*X,x\}=v' in t'}\rangle\downarrow$. Since this is true for all $(S, S') \in (r_2)^s$, we deduce that

$$(\texttt{let \{*X,x\}=v in t}, \texttt{let \{*X,x\}=v in t}) \in (r_2)^{st} = r_2.$$

7.6.23 SOLUTION: For any $(S, S') \in (r_2)^s$ it follows from the assumptions on t, t′ that $(S \circ (\texttt{x.t}_2), S' \circ (\texttt{x.t}'_2)) \in (r_1)^{vs}$. Since $((r_1)^{vs})^t = r_1$, if $(\texttt{t}_1, \texttt{t}'_1) \in r_1$ then we get $\langle S \circ (\texttt{x.t}_2), \texttt{t}_1\rangle\downarrow \Leftrightarrow \langle S' \circ (\texttt{x.t}'_2), \texttt{t}'_1\rangle\downarrow$, and hence that

$$\langle S, \texttt{let x=t}_1\texttt{ in t}_2\rangle\downarrow \;\Leftrightarrow\; \langle S', \texttt{let x=t}'_1\texttt{ in t}'_2\rangle\downarrow.$$

Since this holds for all $(S, S') \in (r_2)^s$, we deduce that

$$(\texttt{let x=t}_1\texttt{ in t}_2, \texttt{let x=t}'_1\texttt{ in t}'_2) \in (r_2)^{st} = r_2.$$

7.7.10 SOLUTION: Since N has no closed values, neither does {∃X,N}. On the other hand

```
val v = λY.fun f(x:∀X.N→Y) = (f x):Y
```

is a closed value of type ∀Y.(∀X.N→Y)→Y. If i and j were to exist with the stated properties we could use them to construct from v a closed value of type {∃X,N}, which is impossible. (For i(j v) and v are ciu-equivalent (Theorem 7.5.7); so since v↓, we also have i(j v)↓. Hence by Exercise 7.4.2, $\langle Id, \texttt{j v}\rangle \longrightarrow^* \langle Id, \texttt{v}'\rangle$ for some v′, which is a closed value of type {∃X,N}, by Exercise 7.4.3.)

8.2.1 SOLUTION: As of this writing, the question of how far nominal module systems can be pushed is wide open. A step in this direction was recently taken by Odersky, Cremet, Rockl, and Zenger (2003).

8.5.3 SOLUTION: Define $\texttt{m}_1$ to be the module

```
module m₁ = mod {
  type X = Int
  val c = 0
  val f = succ
}
```

and define m_2 to be the module

```
module m₂ = mod {
  type X = Bool
  val c = true
  val f = not
}.
```

Define `M` to be the expression `if flip() then m₁ else m₂`, where the function `flip:unit→bool` alternates between `true` and `false` on each call. Now consider the term `t = M.f(M.c)`. This is well-typed, because `M.f : M.X→M.X` and `M.c : M.X`. But evaluation of `t` goes wrong by applying either `succ` to a value of type `Bool` or `not` to a value of type `Int`.

8.5.4 SOLUTION: In a call-by-name setting, variables may no longer be considered determinate, because they stand for unevaluated module expressions. Therefore we cannot "determinize" an indeterminate module expression by binding it to a variable, with the result that there is no way to use its type components.

8.5.5 SOLUTION: Consider the following declarations:

```
signature I = sig { type X  val x : X }
module m = mod { type X = Int  val x = 5 }
module n = mod { type X = Bool  val x = true }
```

Then the term `(λx : (m:>I).X ...)((m:>I).x)` is well typed, but the term `(λx : (n:>I).X ...)((m:>I).x)` is not.

8.5.6 SOLUTION: For example, we might hash the same value in the two different hash tables, producing two hash codes that, because they have the same type, could be compared and (surprisingly) found to be different. Conversely, we could get unlucky and hash two *different* values to the same hash code.

8.5.7 SOLUTION: Consider the signature

```
signature INT_DICT =
  sig {
    type T
    val insert : T × Int → T
    val lookup : T × Int → Bool
  }
```

If `M` and `N` both implement INT_{DICT} as a list of integers, but `M` requires that the list be sorted while `N` does not, then interchanging `N.lookup` with `M.lookup` could cause an inserted key not to be found.

8.5.9 SOLUTION: The signature

```
signature J = sig {
  type X : *→*
  type Y : * }
```

is a super-signature of I that avoids m. For each type A the signature

```
signature K_A = sig {
  type X : *→*
  type Y = X(A) }
```

is also a super-signature of I that avoids m. But the signature J is a proper super-signature of every signature K_A, so it cannot be principal, and yet the signatures K_A and K_B are incomparable whenever A and B are inequivalent types.

For an example in System $F_{\leq}$, see Ghelli and Pierce (1992).

8.7.1 SOLUTION: Because there would be no way to obtain instances of the completely abstract type $(\mathtt{dict_1}\!:\!>\mathtt{Dict}).\mathtt{X}$, and hence no way to ever put anything into a dictionary.

8.7.2 SOLUTION:

$$\begin{aligned}
\mathtt{sig}\,\{\,\mathtt{CD_1},\ \ldots,\ \mathtt{CD}_n\,\}\ \mathtt{where\ m = M} \quad &= \\
&\mathtt{sig}\,\{\,\mathtt{CD_1\ where\ m{=}M},\ \ldots,\ \mathtt{CD}_n\ \mathtt{where\ m{=}M}\,\}
\end{aligned}$$

$$\begin{aligned}
\mathtt{type\ X\ where\ m = M} &= \mathtt{type\ X} \\
\mathtt{type\ X = T\ where\ m = M} &= \mathtt{type\ X = T} \\
\mathtt{val\ x : T\ where\ m = M} &= \mathtt{val\ x : T} \\
\mathtt{module\ m : I\ where\ m = M} &= \mathtt{module\ m : (I\ is\ M)} \\
\mathtt{module\ n : I\ where\ m = M} &= \mathtt{module\ n : I} \quad (\textit{if}\ \mathtt{m} \neq \mathtt{n})
\end{aligned}$$

$$\begin{aligned}
\mathtt{sig}\,\{\,\mathtt{CD_1},\ \ldots,\ \mathtt{CD}_n\,\}\ \mathtt{is\ M} &= \mathtt{sig}\,\{\,\mathtt{CD_1\ is\ M},\ \ldots,\ \mathtt{CD}_n\ \mathtt{is\ M}\,\} \\
\mathtt{type\ X\ is\ M} &= \mathtt{type\ X = M.X} \\
\mathtt{type\ X = T\ is\ M} &= \mathtt{type\ X = T} \\
\mathtt{val\ x : T\ is\ M} &= \mathtt{val\ x : T} \\
\mathtt{module\ m : I\ is\ M} &= \mathtt{module\ m : (I\ is\ M.m)}
\end{aligned}$$

8.8.1 SOLUTION: A functor signature is an signature *describing* module-level functions; a family of signatures *is itself* a function from modules to signatures. The body of a functor signature is a family of signatures indexed by the functor parameter. Or, in the slogan coined by Sannella, Sokolowski, and Tarlecki (1992), *parameterized (program specification)* ≠ *(parameterized program) specification.*

In a sense, in the case of first-order module systems, there is no real need for functor signatures *per se*, because there are no variable functors. We could just say that a family of modules has a family of signatures, each module instance determining a corresponding signature instance. But for higher-order or separate compilation purposes we need a notation meaning "F is a functor implementing signature I."

8.8.2 SOLUTION: Yes, but we need to make sure that the dictFun functor includes its parameter as a submodule of its result:

```
module dictFun =
  λk:ordered.
    mod {
      module key = k
      ... (as before) ...
    }

signature DictFun =
  Πk:Ordered.
     sig {
       module key = k
       type Dict : *→*
       val new : ∀V. Dict V
       val add : ∀V. Dict V → key.X → V → Dict V
       val member : ∀V. Dict V → key.X → Bool
       val lookup : ∀V. Dict V → key.X → V
     }
```

Or, more concisely, DictFun = Πm:K. (D where k = m).

8.8.4 SOLUTION: The compose8 functor will require 9 type parameters; compose16 will require 17. Note that, in this series of examples, the part of each functor that is doing useful work is the same size as as its predecessor, while the amount of "nuisance parameterization" increases exponentially.

8.8.5 SOLUTION: Let HashFun be a generative hash table functor. If, by subsumption, HashFun could be regarded as applicative, then two instances would determine the *same* abstract type, permitting confusion of distinct hash tables.

8.10.1 SOLUTION: A module in our sense corresponds to a ".c" file, which contains procedure and function definitions, type definitions, and declarations of global variables. Procedures, functions, and variables may be made private by declaring them static; otherwise they are presumed to be exported. An signature in our sense corresponds to a "`.h`" file, which contains procedure and function headers, type definitions, and declarations of global variables. The compiled versions of modules correspond to "`.o`" files, which are linked (e.g., using the `ld` command in Unix) into complete executable programs.

8.10.2 SOLUTION: A rigorous comparison of Java's modularity features with the ones described in this chapter is actually quite difficult. Here are some observations, however.

A class in Java is a medium-scale program structuring device, and is often a unit of abstraction, maintaining interesting invariants among its fields and allowing access to the fields only through its own methods. In these ways, a class is like a module. However, Java classes do not have type components. Conversely, class instantiation (in the sense of saying `new` to a class to get an object) is something that we don't do with modules. Also, classes in Java are not units of compilation—it is not generally possible to compile a class separately from other classes that it refers to (e.g., because mutually recursive references are allowed).

An object in Java is also something like a module, providing a collection of named components; like classes, however, objects do not contain type components[1]—just methods (functions) and fields (reference cells holding pointers to objects).

Both Java signatures and abstract classes (all of whose methods are virtual) are something like signatures in the sense of this chapter, since they describe the components of an object without providing implementations.

Signatures and abstract classes can be used to achieve separate compilation in Java, but in a somewhat different style from the separate compilation discussed here. One defines an signature `I`, then defines one class that implements `I` and, separately, another that expects to be given an object implementing `I`. These two classes can be compiled separately from each other.

Java's *packages* are also useful in structuring and decomposing the namespaces of large software systems, but they do not have many of the characteristics of modules in our sense: packages are not units of separate compilation, and there is no notion of an "signature of a package." This suggests that packages could be turned into something more like real modules by equipping them with signatures. This extension has been explored by Bauer, Appel, and Felten (1999).

9.1.4 SOLUTION: The premise $\Gamma \vdash T_2 :: *$ in T-TLET ensures that the local variable X appears only within the scope where it is defined and not in T_2. Omitting the

1. ...except in experimental extensions with *virtual types* (Thorup, 1997; Torgersen, 1998; Igarashi and Pierce, 1999, etc.).

side condition would allow not just ⊢ `(let X=Nat in λy:X.y+1) : Nat→Nat` but also ⊢ `(let X=Nat in λy:X.y+1) : X→Nat`. Thus, code such as

```
(let X=Nat in λy:X.y+1) (let X=Nat×Nat in {5,4})
```

would type check because the function could be given type `X→Nat` and the argument could be given type `X`. At run-time, however, this code would try to increment a pair, and hence ought to be rejected.

9.1.5 SOLUTION: If primitive definitions were added to the simply-typed lambda calculus, we would probably want to allow type variables to appear in types (requiring an extension of the syntax of types) and to allow type definitions to appear in the context. In contrast to λ^{let}, though, every type variable would have a definition (and be of kind *, since the language lacks type operators). These definitions would induce a context-sensitive type equivalence relation based purely on definition expansion; thus adding the F^{ω} rule T-EQ would be appropriate.

Given the lack of type operators, a further extension might be to allow parameterized type definitions with fixed arity, i.e., to allow definitions such as $\mathsf{X(Y_1,Y_2) = Y_1 \to Y_2}$ in the context and then to allow fully-applied uses of `X` such as `X(Nat,Bool→Bool)` to appear in types. This leads to the possibility of ill-formed types supplying the wrong number of arguments (e.g., `X` by itself or `X(Nat)`) and so might require a type well-formedness judgment.

9.1.8 SOLUTION: This logical relation satisfies the same properties as that in Chapter 6 (being a monotone partial equivalence relation and closed under weak head-expansion), for the same reasons.

A.1 LEMMA:

1. If $\Gamma \vdash \mathsf{S}$ **is** $\mathsf{T} :: \mathsf{K}$ and $\Gamma' \supseteq \Gamma$ then $\Gamma' \vdash \mathsf{S}$ **is** $\mathsf{T} :: \mathsf{K}$
2. If $\Gamma \vdash \mathsf{S}$ **is** $\mathsf{T} :: \mathsf{K}$ then $\Gamma \vdash \mathsf{T}$ **is** $\mathsf{S} :: \mathsf{K}$.
3. If $\Gamma \vdash \mathsf{S}$ **is** $\mathsf{T} :: \mathsf{K}$ and $\Gamma \vdash \mathsf{T}$ **is** $\mathsf{U} :: \mathsf{K}$ then $\Gamma \vdash \mathsf{S}$ **is** $\mathsf{U} :: \mathsf{K}$.
4. If $\Gamma \vdash \mathsf{S}$ **is** $\mathsf{T} :: \mathsf{K}$ and $\Gamma \mapsto \mathsf{S}' \leadsto^* \mathsf{S}$ and $\Gamma \mapsto \mathsf{T}' \leadsto^* \mathsf{T}$ then $\Gamma \vdash \mathsf{S}'$ **is** $\mathsf{T}' :: \mathsf{K}$.

A corresponding version of the Main Lemma holds as well. It is no longer true that all paths are weak head-normal, so we make this an explicit requirement in part 2:

A.2 LEMMA [MAIN LEMMA]: 1. If $\Gamma \vdash \mathsf{S}$ **is** $\mathsf{T} :: \mathsf{K}$ then $\Gamma \mapsto \mathsf{S} \Leftrightarrow \mathsf{T} :: \mathsf{K}$.

2. If $\Gamma \mapsto \mathsf{S} \leftrightarrow \mathsf{T} :: \mathsf{K}$ where S and T are paths (a variable applied zero or more times) with $\Gamma \mapsto \mathsf{S} \Downarrow \mathsf{S}$ and $\Gamma \mapsto \mathsf{T} \Downarrow \mathsf{T}$, then $\Gamma \vdash \mathsf{S}$ **is** $\mathsf{T} :: \mathsf{K}$. □

Proof: By simultaneous induction on K. □

Because the definition of logical equivalence of substitutions has changed, we need to recheck that it is an equivalence relation.

A.3 **Lemma:**

1. If $\Gamma' \vdash \gamma$ **is** δ :: Γ then $\Gamma' \vdash \delta$ **is** γ :: Γ.

2. If $\Gamma' \vdash \gamma$ **is** γ' :: Γ and $\Gamma' \vdash \gamma'$ **is** γ'' :: Γ then $\Gamma' \vdash \gamma$ **is** γ'' :: Γ. □

Proof: 1. Follows from Lemma A.1(2).

2. Assume X::K $\in \Gamma$. Then by Lemma A.1(3) $\Gamma' \vdash \gamma(\mathsf{X})$ **is** $\gamma''(\mathsf{X})$ :: K just as before.

   Alternatively, assume X::K=T $\in \Gamma$. Then among other consequences we know that $\Gamma' \vdash \gamma(\mathsf{X})$ **is** $\gamma'(\mathsf{X})$ :: K, $\Gamma' \vdash \gamma(\mathsf{T})$ **is** $\gamma'(\mathsf{X})$ :: K, $\Gamma' \vdash \gamma'(\mathsf{X})$ **is** $\gamma''(\mathsf{X})$ :: K, and $\Gamma' \vdash \gamma'(\mathsf{X})$ **is** $\gamma''(\mathsf{T})$ :: K. By Lemma A.1(2,3), then, $\Gamma' \vdash \gamma(\mathsf{X})$ **is** $\gamma''(\mathsf{X})$ :: K, $\Gamma' \vdash \gamma(\mathsf{T})$ **is** $\gamma''(\mathsf{X})$ :: K and $\Gamma' \vdash \gamma(\mathsf{X})$ **is** $\gamma''(\mathsf{T})$ :: K as required. □

Finally, we have the Fundamental Theorem:

A.4 **Theorem [Fundamental Theorem]:**

1. If $\Gamma \vdash$ T :: K and $\Gamma' \vdash \gamma$ **is** δ :: Γ then $\Gamma' \vdash \gamma(\mathsf{T})$ **is** $\delta(\mathsf{T})$: K.

2. If $\Gamma \vdash \mathsf{S} \equiv \mathsf{T}$ :: K and $\Gamma' \vdash \gamma$ **is** δ :: Γ then $\Gamma' \vdash \gamma(\mathsf{S})$ **is** $\delta(\mathsf{T})$: K. □

Proof: We proceed by induction on derivations. Most of the cases are exactly the same (modulo the transition from a lambda-calculus of terms to a lambda-calculus of types) as the corresponding proof in Chapter 6. The cases for the new rules Q-Def and K-Def follow directly from our assumptions for γ and δ. The cases for K-All and Q-All are similar to each other; we sketch just the former.

Case Q-All: $\Gamma \vdash \forall$X::K$_1$.T$_2$ :: * because Γ,X::K$_1 \vdash T_2$ :: *.

Using the Main Lemma we have that Γ',X::K$_1 \vdash \gamma[\mathsf{X}{\mapsto}\mathsf{X}]$ **is** $\delta[\mathsf{X}{\mapsto}\mathsf{X}]$: Γ,X::K$_1$. By the inductive hypothesis we have Γ',X::K$_1 \vdash (\gamma[\mathsf{X}{\mapsto}\mathsf{X}])\mathsf{T}_2$ **is** $(\delta[\mathsf{X}{\mapsto}\mathsf{X}])\mathsf{T}_2$: *. By the Main Lemma, Γ',X::K$_1 \vdash (\gamma[\mathsf{X}{\mapsto}\mathsf{X}])\mathsf{T}_2 \Leftrightarrow (\delta[\mathsf{X}{\mapsto}\mathsf{X}])\mathsf{T}_2$: *. Thus $\Gamma' \vdash \gamma(\forall\mathsf{X}{::}\mathsf{K}_1.\mathsf{T}_2) \leftrightarrow \delta(\forall\mathsf{X}{::}\mathsf{K}_1.\mathsf{T}_2)$: *. Universally-quantified types are weak head normal, so by the Main Lemma one last time, $\Gamma' \vdash \gamma(\forall\mathsf{X}{::}\mathsf{K}_1.\mathsf{T}_2)$ **is** $\delta(\forall\mathsf{X}{::}\mathsf{K}_1.\mathsf{T}_2)$: *. □

Because the definition for logical equivalence of substitutions has become more involved, the fact that the identity substitution is logically related to itself is no longer an immediate corollary of the Main Lemma.

A.5 LEMMA: Let γ be the identity substitution. If $\Gamma \vdash \diamond$ then $\Gamma \vdash \gamma$ **is** $\gamma :: \Gamma$. □

Proof: By induction on the proof of $\Gamma \vdash \diamond$.

Case CTX-TYPE: $\Gamma = \Gamma', \mathtt{x{:}T}$ with $\Gamma' \vdash \diamond$.

By the inductive hypothesis.

Case CTX-KIND: $\Gamma = \Gamma', \mathtt{X{::}K}$ with $\Gamma' \vdash \diamond$.

By the inductive hypothesis we have that $\Gamma' \vdash \gamma$ **is** $\gamma :: \Gamma'$. By monotonicity, $\Gamma \vdash \gamma$ **is** $\gamma :: \Gamma'$. Finally, by the Main Lemma we have $\Gamma \vdash \mathtt{X}$ **is** $\mathtt{X} :: \mathtt{K}$, so $\Gamma \vdash \gamma$ **is** $\gamma :: \Gamma$.

Case CTX-DEF: $\Gamma = \Gamma', \mathtt{X{::}K{=}T}$ with $\Gamma' \vdash \mathtt{T} :: \mathtt{K}$.

By the inductive hypothesis and monotonicity we again have $\Gamma \vdash \gamma$ **is** $\gamma :: \Gamma'$. By the Fundamental Theorem, $\Gamma \vdash \mathtt{T}$ **is** $\mathtt{T} :: \mathtt{K}$. By weak head expansion, then, $\Gamma \vdash \mathtt{X}$ **is** $\mathtt{T} :: \mathtt{K}$, $\Gamma \vdash \mathtt{T}$ **is** $\mathtt{X} :: \mathtt{K}$, and $\Gamma \vdash \mathtt{X}$ **is** $\mathtt{X} :: \mathtt{K}$. Therefore, $\Gamma \vdash \gamma$ **is** $\gamma :: \Gamma$. □

A.6 COROLLARY [COMPLETENESS]: If $\Gamma \vdash \mathtt{S} :: \mathtt{K}$ and $\Gamma \vdash \mathtt{T} :: \mathtt{K}$ and $\Gamma \vdash \mathtt{S} \equiv \mathtt{T} :: \mathtt{K}$ then $\Gamma \mapsto \mathtt{S} \Leftrightarrow \mathtt{T} :: \mathtt{K}$. □

Proof: Apply the Fundamental Theorem with the identity substitution. □

A.7 COROLLARY [TERMINATION]: If $\Gamma \vdash \mathtt{S} :: \mathtt{K}$ and $\Gamma \vdash \mathtt{T} :: \mathtt{K}$ then $\Gamma \mapsto \mathtt{S} \Leftrightarrow \mathtt{T} :: \mathtt{K}$ is decidable (i.e., deterministic proof search must always terminate with success or failure). □

Proof: By completeness we know that $\Gamma \mapsto \mathtt{S} \Leftrightarrow \mathtt{S} :: \mathtt{K}$ and that $\Gamma \mapsto \mathtt{T} \Leftrightarrow \mathtt{T} :: \mathtt{K}$. We can show by induction on the former algorithm that the comparison of S and T must terminate. □

9.1.9 SOLUTION: As one example, the equivalence

$$\mathtt{X :: (*{\Rightarrow}*{\Rightarrow}*) = (\lambda Y{::}(*{\Rightarrow}*).\ Y\ Nat)} \vdash \mathtt{X(\lambda Z{::}*.Z)} \equiv \mathtt{X(\lambda Z{::}*.Nat)}$$

is provable, because both sides are provably equivalent to Nat. However, given the same definition for X we have $\mathtt{X(\lambda Z{::}*.Nat)} \not\equiv \mathtt{X(\lambda Z{::}*.Bool)}$.

Pfenning and Schürmann (1998) give a syntactic criterion for detecting a collection of *injective* type operators that yield equivalent results only when given equivalent arguments, and hence can be treated specially by an implementation.

9.2.1 SOLUTION: An equivalent most-precise interface would be

```
Πm:(Σm':⦇*⦈. ⦇!m'⦈).
            (Σm":⦇*=!m.1×!m.1⦈. ⦇!m.1×!m.1⦈),
```

which is a subinterface of infinitely many interfaces, including

```
Πm:(Σm':⦇*⦈. ⦇!m'⦈). (Σm":⦇*⦈. ⦇!m"⦈)
```

and

```
Πm:(Σm':⦇*=Nat⦈. ⦇Nat⦈). (Σm":⦇*=Nat×Nat⦈. ⦇Nat×Nat⦈).
```

9.2.2 SOLUTION: If Nat <: Top then we could allow ⦇Nat⦈ <: ⦇Top⦈ in analogy with depth subtyping for records. In contrast, the interfaces ⦇*=Nat⦈ and ⦇*=Top⦈ must be unrelated, because a module containing the type Nat is not a module containing the type Top nor vice versa. To see what goes wrong, assume that ⦇*=Nat⦈ <: ⦇*=Top⦈ and let M be the module ⦇Nat⦈. Then M : ⦇*=Nat⦈, which by subsumption would further yield M : ⦇*=Top⦈. At this point, we could then show that !M ≡ Nat and !M ≡ Top and hence that Nat ≡ Top.

9.2.3 SOLUTION: The module defined by

```
(λm : Σm:⦇*⦈.⦇!m⦈). ⦇ ⦇ λX::*.(!m.1)::*⇒*⦈, !m.2 ⦈
(⦇ ⦇Nat::*⦈, ⦇3::Nat⦈ ⦈ :> Σm:⦇*⦈.⦇!m⦈)
```

or, using syntactic sugar,

```
let m = ⦇ ⦇Nat::*⦈, ⦇3::Nat⦈ ⦈ :> Σm:⦇*⦈.⦇!m⦈
in
    ⦇ ⦇ λX::*.(!m.1)::*⇒*⦈, !m.2 ⦈
```

satisfies the interface Σm′:⦇*⇒*⦈. ⦇(!m′)(Nat)⦈ and more generally the interface Σm′:⦇*⇒*⦈. ⦇(!m′)(T)⦈ for any type T, but it satisfies no interface that is a subinterface of all of these.

9.3.1 SOLUTION: If Nat <: Top then we should expect *S*(Nat) and *S*(Top) to be kinds unrelated in the subkinding hierarchy. All types of kind *S*(Nat) are provably equivalent to Nat, and hence should not be provably equivalent to Top. See also Exercise A.

9.3.7 SOLUTION: We again proceed by induction on the size of K. Assume Γ ⊢ S :: *S*(T :: K) and Γ ⊢ T :: K.

Case: K = *, so *S*(T::K) = *S*(T).

Then Γ ⊢ S ≡ T :: *S*(T) by Rule Q-SELIM, and Γ ⊢ *S*(T) <: * by SK-FORGET, so Γ ⊢ S ≡ T :: * by Rule Q-SUB.

Case: $\mathsf{K} = S(\mathsf{U})$, so $S(\mathsf{T}::\mathsf{K}) = S(\mathsf{T})$.

By Rule Q-SELIM we have $\Gamma \vdash \mathsf{S} \equiv \mathsf{T} :: S(\mathsf{S})$. By Proposition 9.3.4(5), inversion of K-SING, and SK-FORGET we have $\Gamma \vdash S(\mathsf{S}) <: *$, so $\Gamma \vdash \mathsf{S} \equiv \mathsf{T} :: *$ by Q-SUB. Since $\Gamma \vdash \mathsf{T} :: S(\mathsf{U})$, by similar arguments we have $\Gamma \vdash \mathsf{T} \equiv \mathsf{U} :: *$ and so $\Gamma \vdash \mathsf{S} \equiv \mathsf{U} :: *$ and $\Gamma \vdash S(\mathsf{S}) <: S(\mathsf{U})$. Therefore by Q-SUB we have $\Gamma \vdash \mathsf{S} \equiv \mathsf{T} :: S(\mathsf{U})$ as required.

Case: $\mathsf{K} = \Pi \mathsf{X}::\mathsf{K}_1.\mathsf{K}_2$, so $S(\mathsf{T}::\mathsf{K}) = \Pi \mathsf{X}::\mathsf{K}_1.S(\mathsf{T}\,\mathsf{X} :: \mathsf{K}_2)$.

By Proposition 9.3.4(5) and inversion we have $\Gamma, \mathsf{X}::\mathsf{K}_1 \vdash \diamond$, so by Proposition 9.3.2(1) and K-APP, $\Gamma, \mathsf{X}::\mathsf{K}_1 \vdash \mathsf{S}\,\mathsf{X} :: S(\mathsf{T}\,\mathsf{X} :: \mathsf{K}_2)$. By the same reasoning we have $\Gamma, \mathsf{X}::\mathsf{K}_1 \vdash \mathsf{T}\,\mathsf{X} :: \mathsf{K}_2$. By the inductive hypothesis, $\Gamma, \mathsf{X}::\mathsf{K}_1 \vdash \mathsf{S}\,\mathsf{X} \equiv \mathsf{T}\,\mathsf{X} :: \mathsf{K}_2$. Therefore, by Rule Q-EXT we have $\Gamma \vdash \mathsf{S} \equiv \mathsf{T} :: \Pi \mathsf{X}::\mathsf{K}_1.\mathsf{K}_2$.

Case: $\mathsf{K} = \Sigma \mathsf{X}::\mathsf{K}_1.\mathsf{K}_2$, so $S(\mathsf{T}::\mathsf{K}) = S(\pi_1\,\mathsf{T} :: \mathsf{K}_1) \times S(\pi_2\,\mathsf{T} :: [\mathsf{X} \mapsto \pi_1\,\mathsf{T}]\mathsf{K}_2)$

By K-FST and K-SND we have $\Gamma \vdash \pi_1\,\mathsf{S} :: S(\pi_1\,\mathsf{T} :: \mathsf{K}_1)$ and $\Gamma \vdash \pi_2\,\mathsf{S} :: S(\pi_2\,\mathsf{T} :: [\mathsf{X} \mapsto \pi_1\,\mathsf{T}]\mathsf{K}_2)$. Again by K-FST and K-SND we have $\Gamma \vdash \pi_1\,\mathsf{T} :: \mathsf{K}_1$ and $\Gamma \vdash \pi_2\,\mathsf{T} :: [\mathsf{X} \mapsto \pi_1\,\mathsf{T}]\mathsf{K}_2$, so by the inductive hypothesis we have we have $\Gamma \vdash \pi_1\,\mathsf{S} \equiv \pi_1\,\mathsf{T} :: \mathsf{K}_1$ and and $\Gamma \vdash \pi_1\,\mathsf{S} \equiv \pi_2\,\mathsf{T} :: [\mathsf{X} \mapsto \pi_1\,\mathsf{T}]\mathsf{K}_2)$. By Rule Q-PAIR-EXT, therefore, we have $\Gamma \vdash \mathsf{S} \equiv \mathsf{T} :: \Sigma \mathsf{X}::\mathsf{K}_1.\mathsf{K}_2$ as desired.

By the definitions in Figure 9-9 it is possible for $S(\mathsf{T}::\mathsf{K})$ to be a well-formed kind even if T does not satisfy kind K; for example, take $\mathsf{T} = \mathtt{Nat}$ and $\mathsf{K} = S(\mathtt{Nat}{\to}\mathtt{Nat})$. Then we have $\Gamma \vdash \mathtt{Nat} :: S(\mathtt{Nat}::S(\mathtt{Nat}{\to}\mathtt{Nat}))$ but not $\Gamma \vdash \mathtt{Nat} \equiv \mathtt{Nat} :: S(\mathtt{Nat}{\to}\mathtt{Nat})$.

9.3.8 SOLUTION: Using the properties of Fact 9.3.6, we can show the admissibility of Q-BETA-FST.

$$\dfrac{\dfrac{\dfrac{\dfrac{\Gamma \vdash \mathsf{T}_1 :: \mathsf{K}_1}{\Gamma \vdash \mathsf{T}_1 :: S(\mathsf{T}_1 :: \mathsf{K}_1)} \quad \Gamma \vdash \mathsf{T}_2 :: S(\mathsf{T}_1 :: \mathsf{K}_2)}{\Gamma \vdash \{\mathsf{T}_1,\mathsf{T}_2\} :: S(\mathsf{T}_1 :: \mathsf{K}_1) \times \mathsf{K}_2}}{\Gamma \vdash \pi_1\,\{\mathsf{T}_1,\mathsf{T}_2\} :: S(\mathsf{T}_1 :: \mathsf{K}_1)}}{\Gamma \vdash \pi_1\,\{\mathsf{T}_1,\mathsf{T}_2\} \equiv \mathsf{T}_1 :: \mathsf{K}_1}$$

The proof for Q-BETA-SND is exactly analogous, and a similar idea works for Q-APPABS:

$$\dfrac{\dfrac{\dfrac{\dfrac{\Gamma, \mathsf{X}::\mathsf{K}_{11} \vdash \mathsf{T}_{12} :: \mathsf{K}_{12}}{\Gamma, \mathsf{X}::\mathsf{K}_{11} \vdash \mathsf{T}_{12} :: S(\mathsf{T}_{12} :: \mathsf{K}_{12})}}{\Gamma \vdash (\lambda \mathsf{X}::\mathsf{K}_{11}.\mathsf{T}_{12}) :: (\Pi \mathsf{X}::\mathsf{K}_{11}.S(\mathsf{T}_{12} :: \mathsf{K}_{12}))} \quad \Gamma \vdash \mathsf{T}_2 :: \mathsf{K}_{12}}{\Gamma \vdash (\lambda \mathsf{X}::\mathsf{K}_{11}.\mathsf{T}_{12})\mathsf{T}_2 :: S([\mathsf{X} \mapsto \mathsf{T}_2]\mathsf{T}_{12} :: [\mathsf{X} \mapsto \mathsf{T}_2]\mathsf{K}_{12})}}{\Gamma \vdash (\lambda \mathsf{X}::\mathsf{K}_{11}.\mathsf{T}_{12})\mathsf{T}_2 \equiv [\mathsf{X} \mapsto \mathsf{T}_2]\mathsf{T}_{12} :: [\mathsf{X} \mapsto \mathsf{T}_2]\mathsf{K}_{12}}$$

9.3.9 SOLUTION: Let $\Gamma_1 \stackrel{\text{def}}{=} \mathtt{Y}::(\mathcal{S}(\mathtt{Nat})\Rightarrow *)\Rightarrow *$. Then

$$\mathtt{Y}::(\mathcal{S}(\mathtt{Nat})\Rightarrow *)\Rightarrow * \;\Vdash\; \mathtt{Y}(\lambda\mathtt{X}::*.\mathtt{X}) \Leftrightarrow \mathtt{Y}(\lambda\mathtt{X}::*.\mathtt{Nat}) :: *$$

because

- $\Gamma_1 \Vdash \mathtt{Y}(\lambda\mathtt{X}::*.\mathtt{X}) \Downarrow \mathtt{Y}(\lambda\mathtt{X}::*.\mathtt{X})$
- $\Gamma_1 \Vdash \mathtt{Y}(\lambda\mathtt{X}::*.\mathtt{Nat}) \Downarrow \mathtt{Y}(\lambda\mathtt{X}::*.\mathtt{Nat})$
- $\Gamma_1 \Vdash \mathtt{Y}(\lambda\mathtt{X}::*.\mathtt{X}) \leftrightarrow \mathtt{Y}(\lambda\mathtt{X}::*.\mathtt{X}) \uparrow *$, because
  - $\Gamma_1 \Vdash \mathtt{Y} \leftrightarrow \mathtt{Y} \uparrow (\mathcal{S}(\mathtt{Nat})\Rightarrow *)\Rightarrow *$, and
  - $\Gamma_1 \Vdash \lambda\mathtt{X}::*.\mathtt{X} \Leftrightarrow \lambda\mathtt{X}::*.\mathtt{Nat} : \mathcal{S}(\mathtt{Nat})\Rightarrow *$, because
    - $\Gamma_1,\mathtt{Z}::\mathtt{S}(\mathtt{Nat}) \Vdash (\lambda\mathtt{X}::*.\mathtt{X})\mathtt{Z} \Leftrightarrow (\lambda\mathtt{X}::*.\mathtt{Nat})\mathtt{Z} :: *$, because
      - $\Gamma_1,\mathtt{Z}::\mathtt{S}(\mathtt{Nat}) \Vdash (\lambda\mathtt{X}::*.\mathtt{X})\mathtt{Z} \Downarrow \mathtt{Nat}$
      - $\Gamma_1,\mathtt{Z}::\mathtt{S}(\mathtt{Nat}) \Vdash (\lambda\mathtt{X}::*.\mathtt{Nat})\mathtt{Z} \Downarrow \mathtt{Nat}$
      - $\Gamma_1,\mathtt{Z}::\mathtt{S}(\mathtt{Nat}) \Vdash \mathtt{Nat} \leftrightarrow \mathtt{Nat} \uparrow *$.

The analogous proof for $\mathtt{Y}::(*\Rightarrow *)\Rightarrow * \Vdash \mathtt{Y}(\lambda\mathtt{X}::*.\mathtt{X}) \Leftrightarrow \mathtt{Y}(\lambda\mathtt{X}::*.\mathtt{Nat}) :: *$ fails because it requires proving $\mathtt{Y}::(*\Rightarrow *)\Rightarrow *,\ \mathtt{Z}::* \Vdash (\lambda\mathtt{X}::*.\mathtt{X})\mathtt{Z} \Leftrightarrow (\lambda\mathtt{X}::*.\mathtt{Nat})\mathtt{Z} :: *$ and hence that $\mathtt{Y}::(*\Rightarrow *)\Rightarrow *,\ \mathtt{Z}::* \Vdash \mathtt{Z} \leftrightarrow \mathtt{Nat} \uparrow *$.

9.3.11 SOLUTION: The compile-time part is

$$\lambda\mathtt{X}_m::*\times\mathtt{K}_0.\ \{(\pi_1\,\mathtt{X}_m)\times(\pi_1\,\mathtt{X}_m),\ \mathtt{S}_0\}$$

and the run-time part is

$$\lambda\mathtt{X}_m::*\times\mathtt{K}_0.\ \lambda\mathtt{x}_m:\mathtt{T}_0\times(\pi_1\,\mathtt{X}_m).\ \{\mathtt{t}_0,\ \{\mathtt{x}_m.2,\ \mathtt{x}_m.2\}\}.$$

These perform the same computations as the intuitive phase-splittings, but take some useless arguments (e.g., the second argument of the type pair $\mathtt{X}_m$ and the first argument of the pair $\mathtt{x}_m$) and return some useless results ($\mathtt{S}_0$ and $\mathtt{t}_0$).

9.3.14 SOLUTION:

1. Terms containing local modules can be translated as

$$|\mathtt{let\ m{=}M\ in\ t}| \;:=\; \begin{array}{l}\mathtt{let}\ \mathtt{X}_m = |\mathtt{M}|_c\ \mathtt{in}\\ \quad\mathtt{let}\ \mathtt{x}_m = |\mathtt{M}|_r\ \mathtt{in}\\ \quad\quad|\mathtt{t}|.\end{array}$$

   Both `let` forms can be expressed as derived forms in $\lambda^{\mathcal{S}}$, or one could extend the language to make them primitive.

2. Adding a conditional module expression destroys the phase distinction, because the types in a conditional module, e.g.

   ```
   if ... then (|Nat::*|) else (|Unit::*|),
   ```

   depends on the run-time value of the test.

10.1.22 SOLUTION: Within Damas and Milner's type system, we have:

$$\text{DM-ABS}\ \dfrac{\text{DM-LET}\ \dfrac{\text{DM-VAR}\ \dfrac{}{z_1 : X \vdash z_1 : X} \qquad \dfrac{}{z_1 : X; z_2 : X \vdash z_2 : X}\ \text{DM-VAR}}{z_1 : X \vdash \texttt{let}\ z_2 = z_1\ \texttt{in}\ z_2 : X}}{\emptyset \vdash \lambda z_1.\texttt{let}\ z_2 = z_1\ \texttt{in}\ z_2 : X \rightarrow X}$$

Note that, because X occurs free within the environment $z_1 : X$, it is impossible to apply DM-GEN to the judgment $z_1 : X \vdash z_1 : X$ in a nontrivial way. For this reason, z_2 cannot receive the type scheme $\forall X.X$, and the whole expression cannot receive type $X \rightarrow Y$, where X and Y are distinct.

10.1.23 SOLUTION: It is straightforward to prove that the identity function has type $\text{int} \rightarrow \text{int}$:

$$\dfrac{\dfrac{}{\Gamma_0; z : \text{int} \vdash z : \text{int}}\ \text{DM-VAR}}{\Gamma_0 \vdash \lambda z.z : \text{int} \rightarrow \text{int}}\ \text{DM-ABS}$$

In fact, nothing in this type derivation depends on the choice of int as the type of z. Thus, we may just as well use a type variable X instead. Furthermore, after forming the arrow type $X \rightarrow X$, we may employ DM-GEN to quantify universally over X, since X no longer appears in the environment.

$$\text{DM-GEN}\ \dfrac{\text{DM-ABS}\ \dfrac{\text{DM-VAR}\ \dfrac{}{\Gamma_0; z : X \vdash z : X}}{\Gamma_0 \vdash \lambda z.z : X \rightarrow X} \qquad X \notin ftv(\Gamma_0)}{\Gamma_0 \vdash \lambda z.z : \forall X.X \rightarrow X}$$

It is worth noting that, although the type derivation employs an arbitrary type variable X, the final typing judgment has no free type variables. It is thus independent of the choice of X. In the following, we refer to the above type derivation as Δ_0.

Next, we prove that the successor function has type $\text{int} \rightarrow \text{int}$ under the initial environment Γ_0. We write Γ_1 for $\Gamma_0; z : \text{int}$, and make uses of DM-VAR implicit.

$$\text{DM-ABS}\ \dfrac{\text{DM-APP}\ \dfrac{\text{DM-APP}\ \dfrac{\Gamma_1 \vdash \hat{+} : \text{int} \rightarrow \text{int} \rightarrow \text{int} \qquad \Gamma_1 \vdash z : \text{int}}{\Gamma_1 \vdash \hat{+}\ z : \text{int} \rightarrow \text{int}} \qquad \Gamma_1 \vdash \hat{1} : \text{int}}{\Gamma_1 \vdash z\ \hat{+}\ \hat{1} : \text{int}}}{\Gamma_0 \vdash \lambda z.z\ \hat{+}\ \hat{1} : \text{int} \rightarrow \text{int}}$$

In the following, we refer to the above type derivation as Δ_1. We may now build a derivation for the third typing judgment. We write Γ_2 for $\Gamma_0; \mathtt{f} : \mathtt{int} \to \mathtt{int}$.

$$\dfrac{\Delta_1 \qquad \dfrac{\Gamma_2 \vdash \mathtt{f} : \mathtt{int} \to \mathtt{int} \qquad \Gamma_2 \vdash \hat{2} : \mathtt{int}}{\Gamma_2 \vdash \mathtt{f}\ \hat{2} : \mathtt{int}}\ \text{DM-APP}}{\Gamma_0 \vdash \mathtt{let\ f} = \lambda \mathtt{z.z} \mathbin{\hat{+}} \hat{1}\ \mathtt{in\ f}\ \hat{2} : \mathtt{int}}\ \text{DM-LET}$$

To derive the fourth typing judgment, we re-use Δ_0, which proves that the identity function has polymorphic type $\forall \mathtt{X.X} \to \mathtt{X}$. We write Γ_3 for $\Gamma_0; \mathtt{f} : \forall \mathtt{X.X} \to \mathtt{X}$. By DM-VAR and DM-INST, we have both $\Gamma_3 \vdash \mathtt{f} : (\mathtt{int} \to \mathtt{int}) \to (\mathtt{int} \to \mathtt{int})$ and $\Gamma_3 \vdash \mathtt{f} : \mathtt{int} \to \mathtt{int}$. Thus, we may build the following derivation:

$$\dfrac{\Delta_0 \qquad \text{DM-APP}\ \dfrac{\text{DM-APP}\ \dfrac{\Gamma_3 \vdash \mathtt{f} : (\mathtt{int} \to \mathtt{int}) \to (\mathtt{int} \to \mathtt{int}) \qquad \Gamma_3 \vdash \mathtt{f} : \mathtt{int} \to \mathtt{int}}{\Gamma_3 \vdash \mathtt{f\ f} : \mathtt{int} \to \mathtt{int}} \qquad \Gamma_3 \vdash \hat{2} : \mathtt{int}}{\Gamma_3 \vdash \mathtt{f\ f}\ \hat{2} : \mathtt{int}}}{\Gamma_0 \vdash \mathtt{let\ f} = \lambda \mathtt{z.z\ in\ f\ f}\ \hat{2} : \mathtt{int}}\ \text{DM-LET}$$

The first and third judgments are valid in the simply-typed λ-calculus, because they use neither DM-GEN nor DM-INST, and use DM-LET only to introduce the *monomorphic* binding $\mathtt{f} : \mathtt{int} \to \mathtt{int}$ into the environment. The second judgment, of course, is not: because it involves a nontrivial type scheme, it is not even a well-formed judgment in the simply-typed λ-calculus. The fourth judgment is well-formed, but *not* derivable, in the simply-typed λ-calculus. This is because $\mathtt{f}$ is used at two incompatible types, namely $(\mathtt{int} \to \mathtt{int}) \to (\mathtt{int} \to \mathtt{int})$ and $\mathtt{int} \to \mathtt{int}$, inside the expression $\mathtt{f\ f}\ \hat{2}$. Both of these types are *instances* of $\forall \mathtt{X.X} \to \mathtt{X}$, the type scheme assigned to $\mathtt{f}$ in the environment Γ_3.

By inspection of the rules, a derivation of $\Gamma_0 \vdash \hat{1} : \mathtt{T}$ must begin with an instance of DM-VAR, of the form $\Gamma_0 \vdash \hat{1} : \mathtt{int}$. It may be followed by an arbitrary number of instances of the sequence (DM-GEN; DM-INST), turning $\mathtt{int}$ into a type scheme of the form $\forall \bar{\mathtt{X}}.\mathtt{int}$, then back to $\mathtt{int}$. Thus, $\mathtt{T}$ must be $\mathtt{int}$. Because $\mathtt{int}$ is not an arrow type, there follows that the application $\hat{1}\ \hat{2}$ cannot be well-typed under Γ_0. In fact, because this expression is stuck, it cannot be well-typed in a sound type system.

The expression $\lambda \mathtt{f.(f\ f)}$ is ill-typed in the simply-typed λ-calculus, because no type $\mathtt{T}$ may coincide with a type of the form $\mathtt{T} \to \mathtt{T}'$: indeed, $\mathtt{T}$ would be a subterm of itself. In DM, this expression is ill-typed as well, but the proof of this fact is slightly more complex. One must point out that, because $\mathtt{f}$ is λ-bound, it must be assigned a type $\mathtt{T}$ (as opposed to a type scheme) in the environment. Furthermore, one must note that DM-GEN is not applicable (except in a trivial way) to the judgment $\Gamma_0; \mathtt{f} : \mathtt{T} \vdash \mathtt{f} : \mathtt{T}$, because all of the type variables in the type T appear free in the environment $\Gamma_0; \mathtt{f} : \mathsf{T}$. Once these points are made, the proof is the same as in the simply-typed λ-calculus.

It is important to note that the above argument crucially relies on the fact that f is λ-bound and must be assigned a *type*, as opposed to a type scheme. Indeed, we have proved earlier in this exercise that the self-application f f is well-typed when f is let-bound and is assigned the type scheme $\forall \mathsf{X}.\mathsf{X} \to \mathsf{X}$. For the same reason, $\lambda \mathtt{f}.(\mathtt{f}\ \mathtt{f})$ is well-typed in an implicitly-typed variant of System F. It also relies on the fact that types are *finite*: indeed, $\lambda \mathtt{f}.(\mathtt{f}\ \mathtt{f})$ is well-typed in an extension of the simply-typed λ-calculus with recursive types, where the equation $\mathsf{T} = \mathsf{T} \to \mathsf{T}'$ has a solution.

Later, we will develop a type inference algorithm for ML-the-type-system and prove that it is correct and complete. Then, to prove that a term is ill-typed, it will be sufficient to simulate a run of the algorithm and to check that it reports a failure.

10.3.2 SOLUTION: Our hypotheses are $C, \Gamma \vdash \mathtt{t} : \forall \bar{\mathsf{X}}[D].\mathsf{T}$ **(1)** and $C \Vdash [\vec{\mathsf{X}} \mapsto \vec{\mathsf{T}}]D$ **(2)**. We may also assume, *w.l.o.g.*, $\bar{\mathsf{X}} \# ftv(C, \Gamma, \vec{\mathsf{T}})$ **(3)**. By HMX-INST and (1), we have $C \wedge D, \Gamma \vdash \mathtt{t} : \mathsf{T}$, which by Lemma 10.3.1 yields $C \wedge D \wedge \vec{\mathsf{X}} = \vec{\mathsf{T}}, \Gamma \vdash \mathtt{t} : \mathsf{T}$ **(4)**. Now, we claim that $\vec{\mathsf{X}} = \vec{\mathsf{T}} \Vdash \mathsf{T} \leq [\vec{\mathsf{X}} \mapsto \vec{\mathsf{T}}]\mathsf{T}$ **(5)** holds; the proof appears in the next paragraph. Applying HMX-SUB to (4) and to (5), we obtain $C \wedge D \wedge \vec{\mathsf{X}} = \vec{\mathsf{T}}, \Gamma \vdash \mathtt{t} : [\vec{\mathsf{X}} \mapsto \vec{\mathsf{T}}]\mathsf{T}$ **(6)**. By C-EQ and by (2), we have $C \wedge \vec{\mathsf{X}} = \vec{\mathsf{T}} \Vdash D$, so (6) may be written $C \wedge \vec{\mathsf{X}} = \vec{\mathsf{T}}, \Gamma \vdash \mathtt{t} : [\vec{\mathsf{X}} \mapsto \vec{\mathsf{T}}]\mathsf{T}$ **(7)**. Last, (3) implies $\bar{\mathsf{X}} \# ftv(\Gamma, [\vec{\mathsf{X}} \mapsto \vec{\mathsf{T}}]\mathsf{T})$ **(8)**. Applying rule HMX-EXISTS to (7) and (8), we get $\exists \bar{\mathsf{X}}.(C \wedge \vec{\mathsf{X}} = \vec{\mathsf{T}}), \Gamma \vdash \mathtt{t} : [\vec{\mathsf{X}} \mapsto \vec{\mathsf{T}}]\mathsf{T}$ **(9)**. By C-NAMEEQ and by (3), $\exists \bar{\mathsf{X}}.(C \wedge \vec{\mathsf{X}} = \vec{\mathsf{T}})$ is equivalent to C, hence (9) is the goal $C, \Gamma \vdash \mathtt{t} : [\vec{\mathsf{X}} \mapsto \vec{\mathsf{T}}]\mathsf{T}$.

There now remains to establish (5). One possible proof method is to unfold the definition of $\Vdash$ and reason by structural induction on T. Here is another, axiomatic approach. Let Z be fresh for T, $\vec{\mathsf{X}}$, and $\vec{\mathsf{T}}$. By reflexivity of subtyping and by C-EXTRANS, we have $\mathsf{true} \equiv \mathsf{T} \leq \mathsf{T} \equiv \exists \mathsf{Z}.(\mathsf{T} \leq \mathsf{Z} \wedge \mathsf{Z} \leq \mathsf{T})$, which by congruence of $\equiv$ and by C-EXAND implies $\vec{\mathsf{X}} = \vec{\mathsf{T}} \equiv \exists \mathsf{Z}.(\mathsf{T} \leq \mathsf{Z} \wedge \vec{\mathsf{X}} = \vec{\mathsf{T}} \wedge \mathsf{Z} \leq \mathsf{T})$ **(10)**. Furthermore, by C-EQ, we have $(\vec{\mathsf{X}} = \vec{\mathsf{T}} \wedge \mathsf{Z} \leq \mathsf{T}) \equiv (\vec{\mathsf{X}} = \vec{\mathsf{T}} \wedge \mathsf{Z} \leq [\vec{\mathsf{X}} \mapsto \vec{\mathsf{T}}]\mathsf{T}) \Vdash (\mathsf{Z} \leq [\vec{\mathsf{X}} \mapsto \vec{\mathsf{T}}]\mathsf{T})$ **(11)**. Combining (10) and (11) yields $\vec{\mathsf{X}} = \vec{\mathsf{T}} \Vdash \exists \mathsf{Z}.(\mathsf{T} \leq \mathsf{Z} \wedge \mathsf{Z} \leq [\vec{\mathsf{X}} \mapsto \vec{\mathsf{T}}]\mathsf{T})$, which by C-EXTRANS may be read $\vec{\mathsf{X}} = \vec{\mathsf{T}} \Vdash \mathsf{T} \leq [\vec{\mathsf{X}} \mapsto \vec{\mathsf{T}}]\mathsf{T}$.

10.3.3 SOLUTION: The simplest possible derivation of $\mathsf{true}, \emptyset \vdash \lambda \mathtt{z}.\mathtt{z} : \mathsf{int} \to \mathsf{int}$ is syntax-directed. It closely resembles the Damas-Milner derivation given in Exercise 10.1.23.

$$\cfrac{\cfrac{}{\mathsf{true}, \mathtt{z} : \mathsf{int} \vdash \mathtt{z} : \mathsf{int}}\ \text{HMX-VAR}}{\mathsf{true}, \emptyset \vdash \lambda \mathtt{z}.\mathtt{z} : \mathsf{int} \to \mathsf{int}}\ \text{HMX-ABS}$$

As in Exercise 10.1.23, we may use a type variable X instead of the type int, then employ HMX-GEN to quantify universally over X.

$$\dfrac{\dfrac{\dfrac{}{\text{true}, z : X \vdash z : X}\ \text{HMX-VAR}}{\text{true}, \emptyset \vdash \lambda z.z : X \to X}\ \text{HMX-ABS} \qquad X \# \mathit{ftv}(\text{true}, \emptyset)}{\text{true}, \emptyset \vdash \lambda z.z : \forall X[\text{true}].X \to X}\ \text{HMX-GEN}$$

The validity of this instance of HMX-GEN relies on the equivalence true∧true ≡ true and on the fact that judgments are identified up to equivalence of their constraint assumptions.

If we now wish to instantiate X with int, we may use HMX-INST' as follows:

$$\dfrac{\text{true}, \emptyset \vdash \lambda z.z : \forall X[\text{true}].X \to X \qquad \text{true} \Vdash [X \mapsto \text{int}]\text{true}}{\text{true}, \emptyset \vdash \lambda z.z : \text{int} \to \text{int}}\ \text{HMX-INST'}$$

This is not, strictly speaking, an HM(X) derivation, since HMX-INST' is not part of the rules of Figure 10-7. However, since the proof of Lemma 10.3.1 and the solution of Exercise 10.3.2 are constructive, it is possible to exhibit the HM(X) derivation that underlies it. We find:

$$\dfrac{\dfrac{\dfrac{\dfrac{\dfrac{\dfrac{}{Y = \text{int}, z : X \vdash z : X}\ \text{HMX-VAR}}{Y = \text{int}, \emptyset \vdash \lambda z.z : X \to X}\ \text{HMX-ABS}}{Y = \text{int}, \emptyset \vdash \lambda z.z : \forall X.X \to X}\ \text{HMX-GEN}}{Y = \text{int}, \emptyset \vdash \lambda z.z : Y \to Y}\ \text{HMX-INST} \qquad Y = \text{int} \Vdash Y \to Y \leq \text{int} \to \text{int}}{Y = \text{int}, \emptyset \vdash \lambda z.z : \text{int} \to \text{int}}\ \text{HMX-SUB}}{\exists Y.(Y = \text{int}), \emptyset \vdash \lambda z.z : \text{int} \to \text{int}}\ \text{HMX-EXISTS}$$

Since ∃Y.(Y = int) is equivalent to true, the conclusion is indeed the desired judgment.

10.4.1 SOLUTION: Let $X \notin \mathit{ftv}(\Gamma)$ **(1)**. Assume that there exist a satisfiable constraint C and a type T such that $C, \Gamma \vdash t : T$ **(2)** holds. Thanks to (1), we find that, up to a renaming of C and T, we may further assume $X \notin \mathit{ftv}(C, T)$ **(3)**. Then, applying Lemma 10.3.1 to (2), we obtain $C \wedge T = X, \Gamma \vdash t : T$, which by HMX-SUB yields $C \wedge T = X, \Gamma \vdash t : X$ **(4)**. Furthermore, by (3) and C-NAMEEQ, we have $\exists X.(C \wedge T = X) \equiv C$. Because C is satisfiable, this implies that $C \wedge T = X$ is satisfiable as well. As a result, we have found a satisfiable constraint C' such that $C', \Gamma \vdash t : X$ holds.

Now, assume Γ is closed and X is arbitrary. Then, (1) holds, so the previous paragraph proves that, if t is well-typed within Γ, then there exists a satisfiable constraint C' such that $C', \Gamma \vdash t : X$ holds. By the completeness property, we must then have $C' \Vdash [\![\Gamma \vdash \mathsf{t} : \mathsf{X}]\!]$. Since C' is satisfiable, this implies that $[\![\Gamma \vdash \mathsf{t} : \mathsf{X}]\!]$ is satisfiable as well. Conversely, if $[\![\Gamma \vdash \mathsf{t} : \mathsf{X}]\!]$ is satisfiable, then, by the soundness property, t is well-typed within Γ.

10.7.1 SOLUTION: We have

$$\begin{array}{lll} & \mathsf{let}\ \Gamma_0\ \mathsf{in}\ [\![\mathsf{c}\ \mathsf{t}_1 \ldots \mathsf{t}_n : \mathsf{T}']\!] & \\ \equiv & \mathsf{let}\ \Gamma_0\ \mathsf{in}\ \exists \mathsf{Z}_1 \ldots \mathsf{Z}_n.(\bigwedge_{i=1}^{n} [\![\mathsf{t}_i : \mathsf{Z}_i]\!] \wedge \mathsf{c} \preceq \mathsf{Z}_1 \to \ldots \to \mathsf{Z}_n \to \mathsf{T}') & (1) \\ \equiv & \mathsf{let}\ \Gamma_0\ \mathsf{in}\ \exists \mathsf{Z}_1 \ldots \mathsf{Z}_n \bar{\mathsf{X}}.(\bigwedge_{i=1}^{n} [\![\mathsf{t}_i : \mathsf{Z}_i]\!] & (2) \\ & \qquad \wedge\ \mathsf{T}_1 \to \ldots \to \mathsf{T}_n \to \mathsf{T} \leq \mathsf{Z}_1 \to \ldots \to \mathsf{Z}_n \to \mathsf{T}') & \\ \equiv & \mathsf{let}\ \Gamma_0\ \mathsf{in}\ \exists \bar{\mathsf{X}}.(\bigwedge_{i=1}^{n} [\![\mathsf{t}_i : \mathsf{T}_i]\!] \wedge \mathsf{T} \leq \mathsf{T}') & (3) \end{array}$$

where (1) is by definition of constraint generation; (2) is by C-INID; (3) is by C-ARROW, C-EXAND, and by Lemma 10.4.6.

10.7.2 SOLUTION: We must first ensure that R-ADD respects $\sqsubseteq$ (Definition 10.5.4). Since the rule is pure, it is sufficient to establish that $\mathsf{let}\ \Gamma_0\ \mathsf{in}\ [\![\hat{n}_1 \mathbin{\hat{+}} \hat{n}_2 : \mathsf{T}]\!]$ entails $\mathsf{let}\ \Gamma_0\ \mathsf{in}\ [\![\widehat{n_1 + n_2} : \mathsf{T}]\!]$. In fact, we have

$$\begin{array}{lll} & \mathsf{let}\ \Gamma_0\ \mathsf{in}\ [\![\hat{n}_1 \mathbin{\hat{+}} \hat{n}_2 : \mathsf{T}]\!] & \\ \equiv & \mathsf{let}\ \Gamma_0\ \mathsf{in}\ ([\![\hat{n}_1 : \mathsf{int}]\!] \wedge [\![\hat{n}_2 : \mathsf{int}]\!] \wedge \mathsf{int} \leq \mathsf{T}) & (1) \\ \equiv & \mathsf{let}\ \Gamma_0\ \mathsf{in}\ (\mathsf{int} \leq \mathsf{int} \wedge \mathsf{int} \leq \mathsf{int} \wedge \mathsf{int} \leq \mathsf{T}) & (2) \\ \equiv & \mathsf{int} \leq \mathsf{T} & (3) \\ \equiv & \mathsf{let}\ \Gamma_0\ \mathsf{in}\ [\![\widehat{n_1 + n_2} : \mathsf{T}]\!] & (4) \end{array}$$

where (1) and (2) are by Exercise 10.7.1; (3) is by C-IN* and by reflexivity of subtyping; (4) is by Exercise 10.7.1 again.

Second, we must check that if the configuration $\mathsf{c}\ \mathsf{v}_1\ \ldots\ \mathsf{v}_k/\mu$ (where $k \geq 0$) is well-typed, then either it is reducible, or $\mathsf{c}\ \mathsf{v}_1\ \ldots\ \mathsf{v}_k$ is a value.

We begin by checking that every value that is well-typed with type int is of the form $\hat{n}$. Indeed, suppose that $\mathsf{let}\ \Gamma_0; \mathsf{ref}\ M\ \mathsf{in}\ [\![\mathsf{v} : \mathsf{int}]\!]$ is satisfiable. Then, v cannot be a program variable, for a well-typed value must be closed. v cannot be a memory location m, for otherwise $\mathsf{ref}\ M(m) \leq \mathsf{int}$ would be satisfiable—but the type constructors ref and int are incompatible. v cannot be $\hat{+}$ or $\hat{+}\ \mathsf{v}'$, for otherwise $\mathsf{int} \to \mathsf{int} \to \mathsf{int} \leq \mathsf{int}$ or $\mathsf{int} \to \mathsf{int} \leq \mathsf{int}$ would be satisfiable—but the type constructors $\to$ and int are incompatible. Similarly, v cannot be a λ-abstraction. Thus, v must be of the form $\hat{n}$, for it is the only case left.

Next, we note that, according to the constraint generation rules, if the configuration $\mathsf{c}\ \mathsf{v}_1\ \ldots\ \mathsf{v}_k/\mu$ is well-typed, then a constraint of the form $\mathsf{let}\ \Gamma_0; \mathsf{ref}\ M\ \mathsf{in}\ (\mathsf{c} \preceq \mathsf{X}_1 \to \ldots \to \mathsf{X}_k \to \mathsf{T} \wedge [\![\mathsf{v}_1 : \mathsf{X}_1]\!] \wedge \ldots \wedge [\![\mathsf{v}_k : \mathsf{X}_k]\!])$ is satisfiable. We now reason by cases on c.

∘ *Case* c is $\hat{n}$. Then, $\Gamma_0(\mathsf{c})$ is int. Because the type constructors int and $\to$ are incompatible with each other, this implies $k = 0$. Since $\hat{n}$ is a constructor, the expression is a value.

∘ *Case* c is $\hat{+}$. We may assume $k \geq 2$, because otherwise the expression is a value. Then, $\Gamma_0(\mathsf{c})$ is $\mathsf{int} \to \mathsf{int} \to \mathsf{int}$, so, by C-ARROW, the above constraint entails $\mathsf{let}\ \Gamma_0; \mathsf{ref}\ M\ \mathsf{in}\ (\mathsf{X}_1 \leq \mathsf{int} \wedge \mathsf{X}_2 \leq \mathsf{int} \wedge [\![\mathsf{v}_1 : \mathsf{X}_1]\!] \wedge [\![\mathsf{v}_2 : \mathsf{X}_2]\!])$, which, by Lemma 10.4.5, entails $\mathsf{let}\ \Gamma_0; \mathsf{ref}\ M\ \mathsf{in}\ ([\![\mathsf{v}_1 : \mathsf{int}]\!] \wedge [\![\mathsf{v}_2 : \mathsf{int}]\!])$. Thus, v_1 and v_2 are well-typed with type int. By the remark above, they must be integer literals $\hat{n}_1$ and $\hat{n}_2$. As a result, the configuration is reducible by R-ADD.

10.7.5 SOLUTION: We must first ensure that R-REF, R-DEREF and R-ASSIGN respect $\sqsubseteq$ (Definition 10.5.4).

∘ *Case* R-REF. The reduction is $\mathtt{ref}\ \mathsf{v}/\emptyset \longrightarrow m/(m \mapsto \mathsf{v})$, where $m \notin fpi(\mathsf{v})$ **(1)**. Let T be an arbitrary type. According to Definition 10.5.4, the goal is to show that there exist a set of type variables $\bar{\mathsf{Y}}$ and a store type M' such that $\bar{\mathsf{Y}} \# ftv(\mathsf{T})$ and $ftv(M') \subseteq \bar{\mathsf{Y}}$ and $dom(M') = \{m\}$ and $\mathsf{let}\ \Gamma_0\ \mathsf{in}\ [\![\mathtt{ref}\ \mathsf{v} : \mathsf{T}]\!]$ entails $\exists\bar{\mathsf{Y}}.\mathsf{let}\ \Gamma_0; \mathsf{ref}\ M'\ \mathsf{in}\ [\![m/(m \mapsto \mathsf{v}) : \mathsf{T}/M']\!]$. Now, we have

$$
\begin{array}{rll}
& \mathsf{let}\ \Gamma_0\ \mathsf{in}\ [\![\mathtt{ref}\ \mathsf{v} : \mathsf{T}]\!] & \\
\equiv & \exists \mathsf{Y}.\mathsf{let}\ \Gamma_0\ \mathsf{in}\ (\mathsf{ref}\ \mathsf{Y} \leq \mathsf{T} \wedge [\![\mathsf{v} : \mathsf{Y}]\!]) & \textbf{(2)} \\
\equiv & \exists \mathsf{Y}.\mathsf{let}\ \Gamma_0; \mathsf{ref}\ M'\ \mathsf{in}\ (m \preceq \mathsf{T} \wedge [\![\mathsf{v} : M'(m)]\!]) & \textbf{(3)} \\
\equiv & \exists \mathsf{Y}.\mathsf{let}\ \Gamma_0; \mathsf{ref}\ M'\ \mathsf{in}\ [\![m/(m \mapsto \mathsf{v}) : \mathsf{T}/M']\!] & \textbf{(4)}
\end{array}
$$

where (2) is by Exercise 10.7.1 and by C-INEX; (3) assumes M' is defined as $m \mapsto \mathsf{Y}$, and follows from (1), C-INID and C-IN*; and (4) is by definition of constraint generation.

∘ *Case* R-DEREF. The reduction is $!m/(m \mapsto \mathsf{v}) \longrightarrow \mathsf{v}/(m \mapsto \mathsf{v})$. Let T be an arbitrary type and let M be a store type of domain $\{m\}$. We have

$$
\begin{array}{rll}
& \mathsf{let}\ \Gamma_0; \mathsf{ref}\ M\ \mathsf{in}\ [\![!m/(m \mapsto \mathsf{v}) : \mathsf{T}/M]\!] & \\
\equiv & \mathsf{let}\ \Gamma_0; \mathsf{ref}\ M\ \mathsf{in}\ \exists \mathsf{Y}.(\mathsf{ref}\ M(m) \leq \mathsf{ref}\ \mathsf{Y} \wedge \mathsf{Y} \leq \mathsf{T} \wedge [\![\mathsf{v} : M(m)]\!]) & \textbf{(1)} \\
\equiv & \mathsf{let}\ \Gamma_0; \mathsf{ref}\ M\ \mathsf{in}\ \exists \mathsf{Y}.(M(m) = \mathsf{Y} \wedge \mathsf{Y} \leq \mathsf{T} \wedge [\![\mathsf{v} : M(m)]\!]) & \textbf{(2)} \\
\equiv & \mathsf{let}\ \Gamma_0; \mathsf{ref}\ M\ \mathsf{in}\ (M(m) \leq \mathsf{T} \wedge [\![\mathsf{v} : M(m)]\!]) & \textbf{(3)} \\
\Vdash & \mathsf{let}\ \Gamma_0; \mathsf{ref}\ M\ \mathsf{in}\ ([\![\mathsf{v} : \mathsf{T}]\!] \wedge [\![\mathsf{v} : M(m)]\!]) & \textbf{(4)} \\
\equiv & \mathsf{let}\ \Gamma_0; \mathsf{ref}\ M\ \mathsf{in}\ [\![\mathsf{v}/(m \mapsto \mathsf{v}) : \mathsf{T}/M]\!] & \textbf{(5)}
\end{array}
$$

where (1) is by Exercise 10.7.1 and by C-INID; (2) follows from C-EXTRANS and from the fact that ref is an invariant type constructor; (3) is by C-NAMEEQ; (4) is by Lemma 10.4.5 and C-DUP; and (5) is again by definition of constraint generation.

∘ *Case* R-ASSIGN. The reduction is $m := \mathsf{v}/(m \mapsto \mathsf{v}_0) \longrightarrow \mathsf{v}/(m \mapsto \mathsf{v})$. Let T be an arbitrary type and let M be a store type of domain $\{m\}$. We have

$$\begin{array}{lll}
 & \text{let } \Gamma_0; \text{ref } M \text{ in } [\![m := \mathsf{v}/(m \mapsto \mathsf{v}_0) : \mathsf{T}/M]\!] & \\
\Vdash & \text{let } \Gamma_0; \text{ref } M \text{ in } [\![m := \mathsf{v} : \mathsf{T}]\!] & (1)\\
\equiv & \text{let } \Gamma_0; \text{ref } M \text{ in } \exists \mathsf{Z}.(\text{ref } M(m) \leq \text{ref } \mathsf{Z} \wedge [\![\mathsf{v} : \mathsf{Z}]\!] \wedge \mathsf{Z} \leq \mathsf{T}) & (2)\\
\equiv & \text{let } \Gamma_0; \text{ref } M \text{ in } \exists \mathsf{Z}.(M(m) = \mathsf{Z} \wedge \mathsf{Z} \leq \mathsf{T} \wedge [\![\mathsf{v} : \mathsf{Z}]\!]) & (3)\\
\equiv & \text{let } \Gamma_0; \text{ref } M \text{ in } (M(m) \leq \mathsf{T} \wedge [\![\mathsf{v} : M(m)]\!]) & (4)\\
\Vdash & \text{let } \Gamma_0; \text{ref } M \text{ in } [\![\mathsf{v}/(m \mapsto \mathsf{v}) : \mathsf{T}/M]\!] & (5)
\end{array}$$

where (1) is by definition of constraint generation; (2) is by Exercise 10.7.1 and C-INID; (3) follows from the fact that ref is an invariant type constructor; (4) is by C-NAMEEQ; and (5) is obtained as in the previous case.

Second, we must check that if the configuration $\mathsf{c}\ \mathsf{v}_1 \ \ldots\ \mathsf{v}_k/\mu$ (where $k \geq 0$) is well-typed, then either it is reducible, or $\mathsf{c}\ \mathsf{v}_1\ \ldots\ \mathsf{v}_k$ is a value. We only give a sketch of this proof; see the solution to Exercise 10.7.2 for details of a similar proof.

We begin by checking that every value that is well-typed with a type of the form ref T is a memory location. This assertion relies on the fact that the type constructor ref is isolated.

Next, we note that, according to the constraint generation rules, if the configuration $\mathsf{c}\ \mathsf{v}_1\ \ldots\ \mathsf{v}_k/\mu$ is well-typed, then a constraint of the form let Γ_0; ref M in $(\mathsf{c} \preceq \mathsf{X}_1 \to \ldots \to \mathsf{X}_k \to \mathsf{T} \wedge [\![\mathsf{v}_1 : \mathsf{X}_1]\!] \wedge \ldots \wedge [\![\mathsf{v}_k : \mathsf{X}_k]\!])$ is satisfiable. We now reason by cases on c.

∘ *Case* c is `ref`. If $k = 0$, then the expression is a value; otherwise, it is reducible by R-REF.

∘ *Case* c is !. We may assume $k \geq 1$; otherwise the expression is a value. By definition of $\Gamma_0(!)$, the above constraint entails let Γ_0; ref M in $\exists \mathsf{Y}.(\text{ref } \mathsf{Y} \to \mathsf{Y} \leq \mathsf{X}_1 \to \ldots \to \mathsf{X}_k \to \mathsf{T} \wedge [\![\mathsf{v}_1 : \mathsf{X}_1]\!])$, which, by C-ARROW, Lemma 10.4.5, and C-INEX, entails $\exists \mathsf{Y}$.let Γ_0; ref M in $[\![\mathsf{v}_1 : \text{ref } \mathsf{Y}]\!]$. Thus, v_1 is well-typed with a type of the form ref Y. By the remark above, v_1 must be a memory location m. Furthermore, because every well-typed configuration is closed, m must be a member of $dom(\mu)$. As a result, the configuration `ref` $\mathsf{v}_1\ \ldots\ \mathsf{v}_k/\mu$ is reducible by R-DEREF.

∘ *Case* c is :=. We may assume $k \geq 2$, because otherwise the expression is a value. As above, we check that v_1 must be a memory location and a member of $dom(\mu)$. Thus, the configuration is reducible by R-ASSIGN.

10.8.2 SOLUTION: The record access operation $\cdot.\langle \ell_b \rangle$ may be given the type scheme $\forall \mathsf{X}_b.\{\ell_b : \mathsf{X}_b\} \to \mathsf{X}_b$. However, this type scheme isn't satisfactory, because it allows accessing ℓ_b *only* in records where ℓ_a and ℓ_c are undefined. The type scheme $\forall \mathsf{X}_a\mathsf{X}_b.\{\ell_a : \mathsf{X}_a; \ell_b : \mathsf{X}_b\} \to \mathsf{X}_b$ is also a valid type scheme for $\cdot.\langle \ell_b \rangle$, but allows accessing ℓ_b only in records where ℓ_a is defined and ℓ_c is not. To sum up, a satisfactory description of $\cdot.\langle\ell_b\rangle$ requires a whole *family* of type schemes, none of which is principal (more general than the others). A similar problem arises with record extension $\langle\cdot \text{ with } \ell_b = \cdot\rangle$.

A potential solution is to equip record types with a subtyping relationship, so that (say) both $\{\ell_a : \mathsf{T}_a; \ell_b : \mathsf{T}_b\}$ and $\{\ell_a : \mathsf{T}_a; \ell_b : \mathsf{T}_b; \ell_c : \mathsf{T}_c\}$ are subtypes of $\{\ell_b : \mathsf{T}_b\}$. Then, $\forall \mathsf{X}_b.\{\ell_b : \mathsf{X}_b\} \to \mathsf{X}_b$ becomes a satisfactory type scheme for the record access operation $\cdot.\langle\ell_b\rangle$. Indeed, the operation is now applicable to any record that admits a type of the form $\{\ell_b : \mathsf{T}_b\}$, that is, thanks to subtyping, to any record where ℓ_b is defined, regardless of which other fields are defined.

However, this is only half a solution, because there still is a problem with record extension. The type scheme $\forall \mathsf{X}_b.\{\ell_b : \mathsf{X}_b\} \to \{\ell_b : \mathsf{X}_b\}$ is valid, and makes record extension applicable to any record where ℓ_b is defined, which is good. The trouble is with its return type: it states that only ℓ_b may be safely assumed to be defined in the new record. In other words, it causes static information about *all fields other than* ℓ_b to be lost. Addressing this dramatic loss of precision is one of the key motivations for introducing rows.

10.8.5 SOLUTION: We let the reader check that X must have kind $\star.Type$ and Y must have kind $\star.Row(\{\ell\})$. The type with all superscripts made explicit is

$$\mathsf{X} \to^{Type} \Pi\ (\ell^{\star,Row(\emptyset)} : \mathsf{int}^{Type}\ ;\ (\mathsf{Y} \to^{Row(\{\ell\})} \partial^{\star,Row(\{\ell\})}\mathsf{X})).$$

In this case, because the type constructor Π occurs on the right-hand side of the toplevel arrow, it is possible to guess that the type must have kind $\star.Type$. There are cases where it is not possible to guess the kind of a type, because it may have several kinds; consider, for instance, $\partial\mathsf{int}$.

10.8.27 SOLUTION: For the sake of generality, we perform the proof in the presence of subtyping, that is, we do not assume that subtyping is interpreted as equality. We formulate some hypotheses about the interpretation of subtyping: the type constructors $(\ell : \cdot\ ;\ \cdot)$, ∂, and Π must be covariant; the type constructors $\to$ and Π must be isolated.

We begin with a preliminary fact: *if the domain of* V *is* $\{\ell_1, \ldots, \ell_n\}$, *where* $\ell_1 < \ldots < \ell_n$, *then the constraint* let Γ_0 *in* $[\![\{\mathsf{V};\mathsf{v}\} : \mathsf{T}]\!]$ *is equivalent to* let Γ_0 *in* $\exists \mathsf{Z}_1 \ldots \mathsf{Z}_n\mathsf{Z}.(\bigwedge_{i=1}^{n} [\![\mathsf{V}(\ell_i) : \mathsf{Z}_i]\!] \wedge [\![\mathsf{v} : \mathsf{Z}]\!] \wedge \Pi\ (\ell_1 : \mathsf{Z}_1; \ldots; \ell_n : \mathsf{Z}_n; \partial\mathsf{Z}) \leq \mathsf{T})$. We let the reader check this fact using the constraint generation rules, the definition of Γ_0 and rule C-INID, and the above covariance hypotheses. We note that, by C-ROW-LL, the above constraint is invariant under a permutation of the labels $\ell_1, \ldots, \ell_n$, so the above fact still holds when the hypothesis $\ell_1 < \ldots < \ell_n$ is removed.

We now prove that rules R-UPDATE, R-ACCESS-1, and R-ACCESS-2 enjoy subject reduction (Definition 10.5.4). Because the store is not involved, the goal is to establish that let Γ_0 in $[\![\mathsf{t} : \mathsf{T}]\!]$ entails let Γ_0 in $[\![\mathsf{t}' : \mathsf{T}]\!]$, where t is the redex and t′ is the reduct.

- *Case* R-UPDATE. We have:

$$\begin{array}{ll} & \text{let } \Gamma_0 \text{ in } [\![\{\{V; v\} \text{ with } \ell = v'\} : T]\!] \\ \equiv & \text{let } \Gamma_0 \text{ in } \exists XX'Y.([\![\{V; v\} : \Pi\ (\ell : X ; Y)]\!] \wedge [\![v' : X']\!] \wedge \Pi\ (\ell : X' ; Y) \leq T) \quad (1) \\ \equiv & \text{let } \Gamma_0 \text{ in } \exists XX'YZ_1 \dots Z_nZ.(\bigwedge_{i=1}^n [\![V(\ell_i) : Z_i]\!] \wedge [\![v : Z]\!] \quad (2) \\ & \qquad \wedge \Pi\ (\ell_1 : Z_1; \dots; \ell_n : Z_n; \partial Z) \leq \Pi\ (\ell : X ; Y) \\ & \qquad \wedge [\![v' : X']\!] \wedge \Pi\ (\ell : X' ; Y) \leq T) \end{array}$$

where (1) is by Exercise 10.7.1, and (2) follows from the preliminary fact and from C-EXAND, provided $\{\ell_1, \dots, \ell_n\}$ is the domain of V. We now distinguish two subcases:

Subcase $\ell \in dom(V)$. We may assume, *w.l.o.g.*, that ℓ is ℓ_1. Then, by our covariance hypotheses, the subconstraint in the second line of (2) entails $(\ell_2 : Z_2; \dots; \ell_n : Z_n; \partial Z) \leq Y$, which in turn entails $\Pi\ (\ell_1 : X'; \ell_2 : Z_2; \dots; \ell_n : Z_n; \partial Z) \leq \Pi\ (\ell : X' ; Y)$. By transitivity of subtyping, the subconstraint in the second and third lines of (2) entails $\Pi\ (\ell_1 : X'; \ell_2 : Z_2; \dots; \ell_n : Z_n; \partial Z) \leq T$. By this remark and by C-Ex*, (2) entails

$$\begin{array}{l} \text{let } \Gamma_0 \text{ in } \exists X'Z_2 \dots Z_nZ.([\![v' : X']\!] \wedge \bigwedge_{i=2}^n [\![V(\ell_i) : Z_i]\!] \wedge [\![v : Z]\!] \quad (3) \\ \qquad \wedge \Pi\ (\ell_1 : X'; \ell_2 : Z_2; \dots; \ell_n : Z_n; \partial Z) \leq T) \end{array}$$

which by our preliminary fact is precisely let Γ_0 in $[\![\{V[\ell \mapsto v']; v\} : T]\!]$.

Subcase $\ell \notin dom(V)$. By C-ROW-DL and C-ROW-LL, the term $(\ell_1 : Z_1; \dots; \ell_n : Z_n; \partial Z)$ may be replaced with $(\ell : Z; \ell_1 : Z_1; \dots; \ell_n : Z_n; \partial Z)$. Thus, reasoning as in the previous subcase, we find that (2) entails

$$\begin{array}{l} \text{let } \Gamma_0 \text{ in } \exists X'Z_1 \dots Z_nZ.([\![v' : X']\!] \wedge \bigwedge_{i=1}^n [\![V(\ell_i) : Z_i]\!] \wedge [\![v : Z]\!] \quad (4) \\ \qquad \wedge \Pi\ (\ell_1 : X'; \ell_1 : Z_1; \dots; \ell_n : Z_n; \partial Z) \leq T) \end{array}$$

which by our preliminary fact is precisely let Γ_0 in $[\![\{V[\ell \mapsto v']; v\} : T]\!]$.

- *Cases* R-ACCESS-1, R-ACCESS-2. We have:

$$\begin{array}{ll} & \text{let } \Gamma_0 \text{ in } [\![\{V; v\}.\{\ell\} : T]\!] \\ \equiv & \text{let } \Gamma_0 \text{ in } \exists XY.([\![\{V; v\} : \Pi\ (\ell : X ; Y)]\!] \wedge X \leq T) \quad (1) \\ \equiv & \text{let } \Gamma_0 \text{ in } \exists XYZ_1 \dots Z_nZ.(\bigwedge_{i=1}^n [\![V(\ell_i) : Z_i]\!] \wedge [\![v : Z]\!] \quad (2) \\ & \qquad \wedge \Pi\ (\ell_1 : Z_1; \dots; \ell_n : Z_n; \partial Z) \leq \Pi\ (\ell : X ; Y) \\ & \qquad \wedge X \leq T) \end{array}$$

where (1) is by Exercise 10.7.1, and (2) follows from the preliminary fact and from C-EXAND, provided $\{\ell_1, \dots, \ell_n\}$ is the domain of V. We now distinguish two subcases:

Subcase $\ell \in dom(\mathsf{V})$, *i.e.*, (R-ACCESS-1). We may assume, *w.l.o.g.*, that ℓ is ℓ_1. Then, by our covariance hypotheses, the subconstraint in the second line of (2) entails $\mathsf{Z}_1 \leq \mathsf{X}$. By transitivity of subtyping, by Lemma 10.4.5, and by C-Ex*, we find that (2) entails $\mathsf{let}\ \Gamma_0\ \mathsf{in}\ [\![\mathsf{V}(\ell) : \mathsf{T}]\!]$.

Subcase $\ell \notin dom(\mathsf{V})$, *i.e.*, (R-ACCESS-2). By C-ROW-DL and C-ROW-LL, the term $(\ell_1 : \mathsf{Z}_1; \ldots; \ell_n : \mathsf{Z}_n; \partial\mathsf{Z})$ may be replaced with $(\ell : \mathsf{Z}; \ell_1 : \mathsf{Z}_1; \ldots; \ell_n : \mathsf{Z}_n; \partial\mathsf{Z})$. Thus, reasoning as in the previous subcase, we find that (2) entails $\mathsf{let}\ \Gamma_0\ \mathsf{in}\ [\![\mathsf{v} : \mathsf{T}]\!]$.

Before attacking the proof of the progress property, let us briefly check that every value v that is well-typed with type $\Pi\ \mathsf{T}$ must be a record value, that is, must be of the form $\{\mathsf{V}; \mathsf{w}\}$. Indeed, assume that $\mathsf{let}\ \Gamma_0; \mathsf{ref}\ M\ \mathsf{in}\ [\![\mathsf{v} : \Pi\ \mathsf{T}]\!]$ is satisfiable. Then, v cannot be a program variable, for a well-typed value must be closed. Furthermore, v cannot be a memory location m, because $\mathsf{ref}\ M(m) \leq \Pi\ \mathsf{T}$ is unsatisfiable: indeed, the type constructors ref and Π are incompatible (recall that Π is isolated). Similarly, v cannot be a partially applied constant or a λ-abstraction, because $\mathsf{T}' \rightarrow \mathsf{T}'' \leq \Pi\ \mathsf{T}$ is unsatisfiable. Thus, v must be a fully applied constructor. Since the only constructors in the language are the record constructors $\{\}_L$, v must be a record value. (If there were other constructors in the language, they could be ruled out as well, provided their return types are incompatible with Π.)

We must now prove that if the configuration $\mathsf{c}\ \mathsf{v}_1\ \ldots\ \mathsf{v}_k/\mu$ is is well-typed, then either it is reducible, or $\mathsf{c}\ \mathsf{v}_1\ \ldots\ \mathsf{v}_k$ is a value. By the well-typedness hypothesis, a constraint of the form $\mathsf{let}\ \Gamma_0; \mathsf{ref}\ M\ \mathsf{in}\ [\![\mathsf{c}\ \mathsf{v}_1\ \ldots\ \mathsf{v}_k : \mathsf{T}]\!]$ is satisfiable.

∘ *Case* c is $\{\}_L$. If k is less than or equal to $n+1$, where n is the cardinal of L, then $\mathsf{c}\ \mathsf{v}_1\ \ldots\ \mathsf{v}_k$ is a value. Otherwise, unfolding the above constraint, we find that it cannot be satisfiable, because Π and $\rightarrow$ are incompatible; this yields a contradiction.

∘ *Case* c is $\{\cdot\ \mathsf{with}\ \ell = \cdot\}$. Analogous to the next case.

∘ *Case* c is $\cdot.\{\ell\}$. If $k = 0$, then $\mathsf{c}\ \mathsf{v}_1\ \ldots\ \mathsf{v}_k$ is a value. Assume $k \geq 1$. Then, the constraint $\mathsf{let}\ \Gamma_0; \mathsf{ref}\ M\ \mathsf{in}\ [\![\mathsf{c}\ \mathsf{v}_1 : \mathsf{T}]\!]$ is satisfiable. By Exercise 10.7.1, this implies that $\mathsf{let}\ \Gamma_0; \mathsf{ref}\ M\ \mathsf{in}\ [\![\mathsf{v}_1 : \Pi\ (\ell : \mathsf{X}\ ; \mathsf{Y})]\!]$ is satisfiable. Thus, v_1 must be a record value, and the configuration is reducible by R-ACCESS-1 or R-ACCESS-2.

10.8.33 SOLUTION: To make extension strict, it suffices to restrict its binding in the initial environment Γ_0, as follows:

$$\langle\cdot\ \mathsf{with}\ \ell = \cdot\rangle : \forall \mathsf{XY}.\Pi\ (\ell : \mathsf{abs}\ ; \mathsf{Y}) \rightarrow \mathsf{X} \rightarrow \Pi\ (\ell : \mathsf{pre}\ \mathsf{X}\ ; \mathsf{Y}).$$

The new binding, which is less general than the former, requires the field ℓ to be absent in the input record. The operational semantics need not be modified, since strict extension coincides with free extension when it is defined.

Defining the operational semantics of (free) restriction is left to the reader. Its binding in the initial environment should be:

$$\cdot \setminus \langle \ell \rangle : \forall \mathsf{XY}.\Pi\ (\ell : \mathsf{X} ; \mathsf{Y}) \rightarrow \Pi\ (\ell : \mathsf{abs} ; \mathsf{Y})$$

In principle, there is no need to guess this binding: it may be discovered through the encoding of finite records in terms of full records (10.8.32). Strict restriction, which requires the field to be present in the input record, may be assigned the following type scheme:

$$\cdot \setminus \langle \ell \rangle : \forall \mathsf{XY}.\Pi\ (\ell : \mathsf{pre}\ \mathsf{X} ; \mathsf{Y}) \rightarrow \Pi\ (\ell : \mathsf{abs} ; \mathsf{Y})$$

10.8.34 SOLUTION: The informal sentence "supplying a record with more fields in a context where a record with fewer fields is expected" may be understood as "providing an argument of type $\Pi\ (\ell : \mathsf{pre}\ \mathsf{T} ; \mathsf{T}')$ to a function whose domain type is $\Pi\ (\ell : \mathsf{abs} ; \mathsf{T}')$," or, more generally, as "writing a program whose well-typedness requires some constraint of the form $\Pi\ (\ell : \mathsf{pre}\ \mathsf{T} ; \mathsf{T}') \leq \Pi\ (\ell : \mathsf{abs} ; \mathsf{T}')$ to be satisfiable." Now, in a nonstructural subtyping order where $\mathsf{pre} \leqslant \mathsf{abs}$ holds, such a constraint is equivalent to true. On the opposite, if subtyping is interpreted as equality, then such a constraint is equivalent to false. In other words, it is the law $\mathsf{pre}\ \mathsf{T} \leq \mathsf{abs} \equiv \mathsf{true}$ that gives rise to width subtyping.

It is worth drawing a comparison with the way width subtyping is defined in type systems that do not have rows. In such type systems, a record type is of the form $\{\ell_1 : \mathsf{T}_1; \ldots; \ell_n : \mathsf{T}_n\}$. Let us forget about the types $\mathsf{T}_1, \ldots, \mathsf{T}_n$, because they describe the contents of fields, not their presence, and are thus orthogonal to the issue at hand. Then, a record type is a set $\{\ell_1, \ldots, \ell_n\}$, and width subtyping is obtained by letting subtyping coincide with (the reverse of) set containment. In a type system that exploits rows, on the other hand, a record type is a total mapping from row labels to either pre or abs. (Because we are ignoring $\mathsf{T}_1, \ldots, \mathsf{T}_n$, let us temporarily imagine that pre is a nullary type constructor.) The above record type is then written $\{\ell_1 : \mathsf{pre}; \ldots; \ell_n : \mathsf{pre}; \partial \mathsf{abs}\}$. In other words, a set is now encoded as its characteristic function. Width subtyping is obtained by letting $\mathsf{pre} \leqslant \mathsf{abs}$ and by lifting this ordering, pointwise, to rows (which corresponds to our convention that rows are covariant).

[illegible] the operational semantics of record restriction [illegible] the meaning [illegible] constraint should [illegible]

[illegible] abs(Y) [illegible]

[illegible] need to guess [illegible] may be [illegible] through the [illegible] of this record [illegible] the [illegible] may be [illegible] the following [illegible]

[illegible]

[illegible] the integral [illegible] equipped with [illegible] fields [illegible] [illegible] must be [illegible] [illegible] of type [illegible] more generally [illegible] some constraint of the form [illegible] such a constraint is equivalent to true. On the opposite [illegible] then such a constraint is equivalent to false [illegible] gives rise to [illegible]

It is worth [illegible] comparison with [illegible] subtyping [illegible] type systems that [illegible] In such type systems, a record type [illegible] the [illegible] because the [illegible] record type [illegible] with [illegible] the reverse [illegible] containment in a type system [illegible] On the other hand, a record type is a total mapping from row labels to [illegible] because we are [illegible] that the above record type [illegible] [illegible] is now encoded as its characteristic function [illegible] is obtained by [illegible] to rows [illegible] corresponds to our description [illegible]

References

Abadi, Martín, Luca Cardelli, Pierre-Louis Curien, and Jean-Jacques Lévy. Explicit substitutions. *Journal of Functional Programming*, 1(4):375–416, 1991. Summary in *ACM Symposium on Principles of Programming Languages (POPL), San Francisco, California*, 1990.

Adams, Rolf, Walter Tichy, and Annette Weinert. The cost of selective recompilation and environment processing. *ACM Transactions on Software Engineering and Methodology*, 3(1):3–28, January 1994.

Ahmed, Amal, Limin Jia, and David Walker. Reasoning about hierarchical storage. In *IEEE Symposium on Logic in Computer Science (LICS), Ottawa, Canada*, pages 33–44, June 2003.

Ahmed, Amal and David Walker. The logical approach to stack typing. In *ACM SIGPLAN Workshop on Types in Language Design and Implementation (TLDI), New Orleans, Louisiana*, pages 74–85, January 2003.

Aho, Alfred V., Ravi Sethi, and Jeffrey D. Ullman. *Compilers: Principles, Techniques, and Tools.* Addison-Wesley, Reading, Massachusetts, 1986.

Aiken, Alexander, Manuel Fähndrich, and Raph Levien. Better static memory management: Improving region-based analysis of higher-order languages. In *ACM SIGPLAN Conference on Programming Language Design and Implementation (PLDI), La Jolla, California*, pages 174–185, June 1995.

Aiken, Alexander, Jeffrey S. Foster, John Kodumal, and Tachio Terauchi. Checking and inferring local non-aliasing. In *ACM SIGPLAN Conference on Programming Language Design and Implementation (PLDI), San Diego, California*, pages 129–140, June 2003.

Aiken, Alexander and Edward L. Wimmers. Solving systems of set constraints. In *IEEE Symposium on Logic in Computer Science (LICS), Santa Cruz, California*, pages 329–340, June 1992.

Aiken, Alexander and Edward L. Wimmers. Type inclusion constraints and type inference. In *ACM Symposium on Functional Programming Languages and Computer Architecture (FPCA), Copenhagen, Denmark*, pages 31–41, June 1993.

Altenkirch, Thorsten. *Constructions, Inductive Types and Strong Normalization.* PhD thesis, Laboratory for Foundations of Computer Science, University of Edinburgh, Edinburgh, Scotland, 1993.

Amadio, Roberto M. and Luca Cardelli. Subtyping recursive types. *ACM Transactions on Programming Languages and Systems*, 15(4):575–631, 1993. Summary in *ACM Symposium on Principles of Programming Languages (POPL), Orlando, Florida*, pp. 104–118; also DEC/Compaq Systems Research Center Research Report number 62, August 1990.

Amtoft, Torben, Flemming Nielson, and Hanne Riis Nielson. *Type and Effect Systems: Behaviours for Concurrency.* Imperial College Press, 1999.

Ancona, Davide and Elena Zucca. A theory of mixin modules: Basic and derived operators. *Mathematical Structures in Computer Science*, 8(4):401–446, August 1998.

Ancona, Davide and Elena Zucca. A calculus of module systems. *Journal of Functional Programming*, 12(2):91–132, March 2002.

Appel, Andrew W. Foundational proof-carrying code. In *IEEE Symposium on Logic in Computer Science (LICS), Boston, Massachusetts*, pages 247–258, June 2001.

Appel, Andrew W. and Amy P. Felty. A semantic model of types and machine instructions for proof-carrying code. In *ACM SIGPLAN–SIGACT Symposium on Principles of Programming Languages (POPL), Boston, Massachusetts*, pages 243–253, January 2000.

Aspinall, David. Subtyping with singleton types. In *International Workshop on Computer Science Logic (CSL), Kazimierz, Poland*, volume 933 of *Lecture Notes in Computer Science*, pages 1–15. Springer-Verlag, September 1994.

Aspinall, David and Martin Hofmann. Another type system for in-place update. In *European Symposium on Programming (ESOP), Grenoble, France*, volume 2305 of *Lecture Notes in Computer Science*, pages 36–52. Springer-Verlag, April 2002.

Augustsson, Lennart. Cayenne—A language with dependent types. In *ACM SIGPLAN International Conference on Functional Programming (ICFP), Baltimore, Maryland*, pages 239–250, 1998.

Baader, Franz and Jörg Siekmann. Unification theory. In D. M. Gabbay, C. J. Hogger, and J. A. Robinson, editors, *Handbook of Logic in Artificial Intelligence and Logic Programming*, volume 2, *Deduction Methodologies*, pages 41–125. Oxford University Press, 1994.

Baker, Henry G. Lively linear Lisp—look ma, no garbage! *ACM SIGPLAN Notices*, 27 (8):89–98, 1992.

Barendregt, Henk P. *The Lambda Calculus.* North Holland, revised edition, 1984.

Barendregt, Henk P. Introduction to generalized type systems. *Journal of Functional Programming*, 1(2):125–154, 1991.

Barendregt, Henk P. Lambda calculi with types. In S. Abramsky, D. M. Gabbay, and T. Maibaum, editors, *Handbook of Logic in Computer Science*, volume 2, *Computational Structures.* Oxford University Press, 1992.

Barendsen, Erik and Sjaak Smetsers. Conventional and uniqueness typing in graph rewrite systems. In *Foundations of Software Technology and Theoretical Computer Science (FSTTCS), Bombay, India*, volume 761 of *Lecture Notes in Computer Science*, pages 41–51. Springer-Verlag, December 1993.

Barras, Bruno, Samuel Boutin, Cristina Cornes, Judicael Courant, Jean-Christophe Filliatre, Eduardo Gimenez, Hugo Herbelin, Gerard Huet, Cesar Munoz, Chetan Murthy, Catherine Parent, Christine Paulin-Mohring, Amokrane Saibi, and Benjamin Werner. The Coq proof assistant reference manual: Version 6.1. Technical Report RT-0203, INRIA, 1997.

Bauer, Lujo, Andrew W. Appel, and Edward W. Felten. Mechanisms for secure modular programming in Java. Technical Report TR-603-99, Princeton University, 1999.

Bellantoni, Stephan and Stephan Cook. A new recursion-theoretic characterization of polytime functions. *Computational Complexity*, 2(2):97–110, 1992.

Bellantoni, Stephan, K.-H. Niggl, and H. Schwichtenberg. Higher type recursion, ramification and polynomial time. *Annals of Pure and Applied Logic*, 104:17–30, 2000.

Berardi, Stefano. Towards a mathematical analysis of the Coquand-Huet calculus of constructions and the other systems in Barendregt's cube. Technical report, Department of Computer Science, CMU, and Dipartimento Matematica, Universita di Torino, 1988.

Berthomieu, Bernard. Tagged types: A theory of order sorted types for tagged expressions. Research Report 93083, LAAS, 7, avenue du Colonel Roche, 31077 Toulouse, France, March 1993.

Berthomieu, Bernard and Camille le Moniès de Sagazan. A calculus of tagged types, with applications to process languages. In *Workshop on Types for Program Analysis (TPA)*, informal proceedings, pages 1–15, May 1995.

Biagioni, Edoardo, Nicholas Haines, Robert Harper, Peter Lee, Brian G. Milnes, and Eliot B. Moss. Signatures for a protocol stack: A systems application of Standard ML. In *ACM Symposium on Lisp and Functional Programming (LFP), Orlando, Florida*, pages 55–64, June 1994.

Bierman, G. M., A. M. Pitts, and C. V. Russo. Operational properties of Lily, a polymorphic linear lambda calculus with recursion. In *Workshop on Higher Order Operational Techniques in Semantics (HOOTS), Montréal, Québec*, volume 41 of *Electronic Notes in Theoretical Computer Science.* Elsevier, September 2000.

Birkedal, Lars and Robert W. Harper. Constructing interpretations of recursive types in an operational setting. *Information and Computation*, 155:3–63, 1999.

Birkedal, Lars and Mads Tofte. A constraint-based region inference algorithm. *Theoretical Computer Science*, 258:299–392, 2001.

Birkedal, Lars, Mads Tofte, and Magnus Vejlstrup. From region inference to von Neumann machines via region representation inference. In *ACM SIGPLAN-SIGACT Symposium on Principles of Programming Languages (POPL), St. Petersburg Beach, Florida*, pages 171-183, 1996.

Blume, Matthias. *The SML/NJ Compilation and Library Manager*, May 2002. Available from `http://www.smlnj.org/doc/CM/index.html`.

Blume, Matthias and Andrew W. Appel. Hierarchical modularity. *ACM Transactions on Programming Languages and Systems*, 21(4):813–847, 1999.

Bonniot, Daniel. Type-checking multi-methods in ML (a modular approach). In *International Workshop on Foundations of Object-Oriented Languages (FOOL)*, informal proceedings, January 2002.

Bourdoncle, François and Stephan Merz. Type-checking higher-order polymorphic multi-methods. In *ACM SIGPLAN-SIGACT Symposium on Principles of Programming Languages (POPL), Paris, France*, pages 302–315, January 1997.

Bracha, Gilad and William R. Cook. Mixin-based inheritance. In *ACM SIGPLAN Conference on Object Oriented Programming: Systems, Languages, and Applications (OOPSLA)/European Conference on Object-Oriented Programming (ECOOP), Ottawa, Ontario*, pages 303–311, October 1990.

Brandt, Michael and Fritz Henglein. Coinductive axiomatization of recursive type equality and subtyping. In *International Conference on Typed Lambda Calculi and Applications (TLCA), Nancy, France*, volume 1210 of *Lecture Notes in Computer Science*, pages 63–81. Springer-Verlag, April 1997. Full version in *Fundamenta Informaticae*, 33:309–338, 1998.

Breazu-Tannen, Val, Thierry Coquand, Carl Gunter, and Andre Scedrov. Inheritance as implicit coercion. *Information and Computation*, 93(1):172–221, July 1991. Also in C. A. Gunter and J. C. Mitchell, editors, *Theoretical Aspects of Object-Oriented Programming: Types, Semantics, and Language Design*, MIT Press, 1994.

Bruce, Kim B. Typing in object-oriented languages: Achieving expressibility and safety, 1995. Available through `http://www.cs.williams.edu/~kim`.

Bruce, Kim B. *Foundations of Object-Oriented Languages: Types and Semantics*. MIT Press, 2002.

Bruce, Kim B., Luca Cardelli, Giuseppe Castagna, the Hopkins Objects Group (Jonathan Eifrig, Scott Smith, Valery Trifonov), Gary T. Leavens, and Benjamin Pierce. On binary methods. *Theory and Practice of Object Systems*, 1(3):221–242, 1996.

Bruce, Kim B., Luca Cardelli, and Benjamin C. Pierce. Comparing object encodings. In *International Symposium on Theoretical Aspects of Computer Software (TACS)*, September 1997. An earlier version was presented as an invited lecture at the Third International Workshop on Foundations of Object Oriented Languages (FOOL 3), July 1996; full version in *Information and Computation*, 155(1–2):108-133, 1999.

de Bruijn, Nicolas G. A survey of the project AUTOMATH. In J. P. Seldin and J. R. Hindley, editors, *To H. B. Curry: Essays in Combinatory Logic, Lambda Calculus, and Formalism*, pages 589–606. Academic Press, 1980.

Brus, Tom, Marko van Eekelen, Maarten van Leer, and Marinus Plasmeijer. Clean: A language for functional graph rewriting. In *ACM Symposium on Functional Programming Languages and Computer Architecture (FPCA), Portland, Oregon*, volume 274 of *Lecture Notes in Computer Science*, pages 364–384. Springer-Verlag, September 1987.

Burstall, Rod and Butler Lampson. A kernel language for abstract data types and modules. In *International Symposium on Semantics of Data Types, Sophia-Antipolis, France*, volume 173 of *Lecture Notes in Computer Science*, pages 1–50. Springer-Verlag, June 1984.

Burstall, Rod, David MacQueen, and Donald Sannella. HOPE: an experimental applicative language. In *ACM Symposium on Lisp and Functional Programming (LFP), Stanford, California*, pages 136–143, August 1980.

Calcagno, Cristiano. Stratified operational semantics for safety and correctness of region calculus. In *ACM SIGPLAN–SIGACT Symposium on Principles of Programming Languages (POPL), London, England*, pages 155–165, 2001.

Calcagno, Cristiano, Simon Helsen, and Peter Thiemann. Syntactic type soundness results for the region calculus. *Information and Computation*, 173(2):199–221, 2002.

Cardelli, Luca. A polymorphic λ-calculus with Type:Type. Research report 10, DEC/Compaq Systems Research Center, May 1986.

Cardelli, Luca. Phase distinctions in type theory, 1988a. Manuscript, available from `http://www.luca.demon.co.uk`.

Cardelli, Luca. Typechecking dependent types and subtypes. In *Foundations of Logic and Functional Programming, Trento, Italy, (*December, 1986*)*, volume 306 of *Lecture Notes in Computer Science*, pages 45–57. Springer-Verlag, 1988b.

Cardelli, Luca. Program fragments, linking, and modularization. In *ACM SIGPLAN–SIGACT Symposium on Principles of Programming Languages (POPL), Paris, France*, pages 266–277, January 1997.

Cardelli, Luca, James Donahue, Mick Jordan, Bill Kalsow, and Greg Nelson. The Modula-3 type system. In *Proceedings of the Sixteenth Annual ACM Symposium on Principles of Programming Languages*, pages 202–212, January 1989.

Cardelli, Luca and Xavier Leroy. Abstract types and the dot notation. In *IFIP TC2 Working Conference on Programming Concepts and Methods*. North Holland, 1990. Also appeared as DEC/Compaq SRC technical report 56.

Cardelli, Luca and Giuseppe Longo. A semantic basis for Quest. *Journal of Functional Programming*, 1(4):417–458, October 1991. Summary in *ACM Conference on Lisp and Functional Programming*, pp. 30-43, 1990. Also available as DEC/Compaq SRC Research Report 55, Feb. 1990.

Cardelli, Luca and John Mitchell. Operations on records. *Mathematical Structures in Computer Science*, 1:3-48, 1991. Also in C. A. Gunter and J. C. Mitchell, editors, *Theoretical Aspects of Object-Oriented Programming: Types, Semantics, and Language Design*, MIT Press, 1994; available as DEC/Compaq Systems Research Center Research Report #48, August, 1989; and in the *Proceedings of Workshop on the Mathematical Foundations of Programming Semantics (MFPS), New Orleans, Louisiana*, Springer LNCS, volume 442, pp. 22-52, 1989.

Cartmell, John. Generalised algebraic theories and contextual categories. *Annals of Pure and Applied Logic*, 32:209–243, 1986.

Cartwright, Robert and Mike Fagan. Soft typing. In *ACM SIGPLAN Conference on Programming Language Design and Implementation (PLDI), Toronto, Ontario*, pages 278–292, June 1991.

Cervesato, Iliano, Joshua S. Hodas, and Frank Pfenning. Efficient resource management for linear logic proof search. *Theoretical Computer Science*, 232(1–2):133–163, February 2000.

Cervesato, Iliano and Frank Pfenning. A linear logical framework. *Information and Computation*, 179(1):19–75, November 2002.

Chaki, Sagar, Sriram K. Rajamani, and Jakob Rehof. Types as models: Model checking message-passing programs. In *ACM SIGPLAN-SIGACT Symposium on Principles of Programming Languages (POPL), Portland, Oregon*, pages 45–57, 2002.

Chirimar, Jawahar, Carl A. Gunter, and Jon G. Riecke. Reference counting as a computational interpretation of linear logic. *Journal of Functional Programming*, 6(2): 195–244, March 1996.

Christiansen, Morten Voetmann and Per Velschow. Region-based memory management in Java. Master's thesis, University of Copenhagen, Department of Computer Science, 1998.

Church, Alonzo. *The Calculi of Lambda Conversion*. Princeton University Press, 1941.

Church, Alonzo. The weak theory of implication. *Kontroliertes Denken: Untersuchungen zum Logikkalk ul und zur Logik der Einzelwissenschaften*, pages 22–37, 1951.

Clement, Dominique, Joelle Despeyroux, Thierry Despeyroux, and Gilles Kahn. A simple applicative language: Mini-ML. In *ACM Symposium on Lisp and Functional Programming (LFP), Cambridge, Massachusetts*, pages 13–27, August 1986.

Colby, Christopher, Peter Lee, George C. Necula, Fred Blau, Mark Plesko, and Kenneth Cline. A certifying compiler for Java. *ACM SIGPLAN Notices*, 35(5):95–107, May 2000.

Comon, Hubert. Constraints in term algebras (short survey). In *Conference on Algebraic Methodology and Software Technology (AMAST)*, June, 1993, Workshops in Computing, pages 97-108. Springer-Verlag, 1994.

Constable, Robert L., Stuart F. Allen, Mark Bromley, Rance Cleaveland, James F. Cremer, Robert W. Harper, Douglas J. Howe, Todd B. Knoblock, Paul Mendler, Prakash Panangaden, James T. Sasaki, and Scott F. Smith. *Implementing Mathematics with the NuPRL Proof Development System*. Prentice-Hall, Englewood Cliffs, NJ, 1986.

Coquand, Catarina. The AGDA proof system homepage, 1998. `http://www.cs.chalmers.se/~catarina/agda/`.

Coquand, Thierry. An analysis of Girard's paradox. In *IEEE Symposium on Logic in Computer Science (LICS), Cambridge, Massachusetts*, pages 227–236, June 1986.

Coquand, Thierry. An algorithm for testing conversion in type theory. In G. Huet and G. Plotkin, editors, *Logical Frameworks*, pages 255–279. Cambridge University Press, 1991.

Coquand, Thierry. Pattern matching with dependent types. In *Workshop on Types for Proofs and Programs (TYPES), Båstad, Sweden*, informal proceedings. Available from `ftp://ftp.cs.chalmers.se/pub/cs-reports/baastad.92/proc.ps.Z`, June 1992.

Coquand, Thierry and Gérard Huet. The calculus of constructions. *Information and Computation*, 76(2–3):95–120, February/March 1988.

Coquand, Thierry, Randy Pollack, and Makoto Takeyama. A logical framework with dependently typed records. In *International Conference on Typed Lambda Calculi and Applications (TLCA), Valencia, Spain*, volume 2701 of *Lecture Notes in Computer Science*, pages 105–119. Springer-Verlag, June 2003.

Courant, Judicaël. Strong normalization with singleton types. In *Workshop on Intersection Types and Related Systems (ITRS), Copenhagen, Denmark*, volume 70 of *Electronic Notes in Theoretical Computer Science*. Elsevier, July 2002.

Crank, Erik and Matthias Felleisen. Parameter-passing and the lambda calculus. In *ACM Symposium on Principles of Programming Languages (POPL), Orlando, Florida*, pages 233–244, January 1991.

Crary, Karl. A simple proof technique for certain parametricity results. In *ACM SIGPLAN International Conference on Functional Programming (ICFP), Paris, France*, pages 82–89, September 1999.

Crary, Karl. Toward a foundational typed assembly language. In *ACM SIGPLAN-SIGACT Symposium on Principles of Programming Languages (POPL), New Orleans, Louisiana*, pages 198–212, January 2003.

Crary, Karl, Robert Harper, and Sidd Puri. What is a recursive module? In *ACM SIGPLAN Conference on Programming Language Design and Implementation (PLDI)*, pages 50–63, May 1999.

Crary, Karl, Stephanie Weirich, and Greg Morrisett. Intensional polymorphism in type-erasure semantics. In *ACM SIGPLAN International Conference on Functional Programming (ICFP), Baltimore, Maryland*, pages 301-312, 1998. Full version in *Journal of Functional Programming*, 12(6), Nov. 2002, pp. 567–600.

Curtis, Pavel. *Constrained Quantification in Polymorphic Type Analysis*. PhD thesis, Cornell University, Ithaca, New York, February 1990.

van Daalen, Diederik T. *The Language Theory of Automath*. PhD thesis, Technische Hogeschool Eindhoven, Eindhoven, The Netherlands, 1980.

Damas, Luis and Robin Milner. Principal type schemes for functional programs. In *ACM Symposium on Principles of Programming Languages (POPL), Albuquerque, New Mexico*, pages 207–212, 1982.

Danvy, Olivier. Functional unparsing. *Journal of Functional Programming*, 8(6):621–625, 1998.

DeLine, Rob and Manuel Fähndrich. Enforcing high-level protocols in low-level software. In *ACM SIGPLAN Conference on Programming Language Design and Implementation (PLDI), Snowbird, Utah*, pages 59–69, June 2001.

Donahue, James and Alan Demers. Data types are values. *ACM Transactions on Programming Languages and Systems*, 7(3):426–445, July 1985.

Došen, Kosta. A historical introduction to substructural logics. In K. Došen and P. Schroeder-Heister, editors, *Substructural Logics*, pages 1–30. Oxford University Press, 1993.

Dreyer, Derek, Karl Crary, and Robert Harper. A type system for higher-order modules. In *ACM SIGPLAN-SIGACT Symposium on Principles of Programming Languages (POPL), New Orleans, Louisiana*, pages 236–249, New Orleans, January 2003.

Dussart, Dirk, Fritz Henglein, and Christian Mossin. Polymorphic recursion and subtype qualifications: Polymorphic binding-time analysis in polynomial time. In *International Symposium on Static Analysis (SAS) , Paris, France*, volume 983 of *Lecture Notes in Computer Science*, pages 118–135. Springer-Verlag, July 1995.

Emms, Martin and Hans LeiSS. Extending the type checker for SML by polymorphic recursion—A correctness proof. Technical Report 96-101, Centrum für Informations- und Sprachverarbeitung, Universität München, 1996.

Erhard, Thomas. A categorical semantics of constructions. In *IEEE Symposium on Logic in Computer Science (LICS), Edinburgh, Scotland*, pages 264–273, July 1988.

Fähndrich, Manuel. BANE*: A Library for Scalable Constraint-Based Program Analysis.* PhD thesis, University of California at Berkeley, Berkeley, California, 1999.

Fähndrich, Manuel and Rob DeLine. Adoption and focus: Practical linear types for imperative programming. In *ACM SIGPLAN Conference on Programming Language Design and Implementation (PLDI), Berlin, Germany*, pages 13–24, June 2002.

Fähndrich, Manuel, Jakob Rehof, and Manuvir Das. Scalable context-sensitive flow analysis using instantiation constraints. In *ACM SIGPLAN Conference on Programming Language Design and Implementation (PLDI), Vancouver, British Columbia, Canada*, pages 253–263, June 2000.

Felleisen, Matthias and Robert Hieb. A revised report on the syntactic theories of sequential control and state. *Theoretical Computer Science*, 103(2):235–271, 1992.

Fisher, Kathleen and John H. Reppy. The design of a class mechanism for Moby. In *ACM SIGPLAN Conference on Programming Language Design and Implementation (PLDI), Atlanta, Georgia*, pages 37–49, May 1999.

Flanagan, Cormac and Shaz Qadeer. A type and effect system for atomicity. In *ACM SIGPLAN Conference on Programming Language Design and Implementation (PLDI), San Diego, California*, pages 338–349, June 2003.

Flatt, Matthew and Matthias Felleisen. Units: Cool modules for HOT languages. In *ACM SIGPLAN Conference on Programming Language Design and Implementation (PLDI), Montréal, Québec*, pages 236–248, 1998.

Fluet, Matthew. Monadic regions. In *Workshop on Semantics, Program Analysis and Computing Environments for Memory Management (SPACE)*, informal proceedings, January 2004.

Fluet, Matthew and Riccardo Pucella. Phantom types and subtyping. In *IFIP International Conference on Theoretical Computer Science (TCS)*, pages 448–460, August 2002.

Foster, Jeffrey S., Tachio Terauchi, and Alex Aiken. Flow-sensitive type qualifiers. In *ACM SIGPLAN Conference on Programming Language Design and Implementation (PLDI), Berlin, Germany*, pages 1–12, June 2002.

Frey, Alexandre. Satisfying subtype inequalities in polynomial space. In *International Symposium on Static Analysis (SAS) , Paris, France*, volume 1302 of *Lecture Notes in Computer Science*, pages 265–277. Springer-Verlag, September 1997.

Fuh, You-Chin and Prateek Mishra. Type inference with subtypes. In *European Symposium on Programming (ESOP), Nancy, France*, volume 300 of *Lecture Notes in Computer Science*, pages 94–114. Springer-Verlag, March 1988.

Furuse, Jun P. and Jacques Garrigue. A label-selective lambda-calculus with optional arguments and its compilation method. RIMS Preprint 1041, Kyoto University, October 1995.

Garcia, Ronald, Jaakko Jarvi, Andrew Lumsdaine, Jeremy Siek, and Jeremia h Willcock. A comparative study of language support for generic programming. In *ACM SIGPLAN Conference on Object Oriented Programming: Systems, Languages, and Applications (OOPSLA), Anaheim, California*, pages 115–134, October 2003.

Garrigue, Jacques. Programming with polymorphic variants. In *ACM SIGPLAN Workshop on ML*, informal proceedings, September 1998.

Garrigue, Jacques. Code reuse through polymorphic variants. In *Workshop on Foundations of Software Engineering (FOSE)*, November 2000.

Garrigue, Jacques. Simple type inference for structural polymorphism. In *International Workshop on Foundations of Object-Oriented Languages (FOOL)*, informal proceedings, January 2002.

Garrigue, Jacques. Relaxing the value restriction. In *International Symposium on Functional and Logic Programming (FLOPS), Nara, Japan*, volume 2998 of *Lecture Notes in Computer Science*, pages 196–213. Springer-Verlag, April 2004.

Garrigue, Jacques and Hassan Aït-Kaci. The typed polymorphic label-selective lambda-calculus. In *ACM SIGPLAN-SIGACT Symposium on Principles of Programming Languages (POPL), Portland, Oregon*, pages 35–47, 1994.

Garrigue, Jacques and Didier Rémy. Extending ML with semi-explicit higher-order polymorphism. *Information and Computation*, 155(1):134–169, 1999.

Gaster, Benedict R. *Records, variants and qualified types.* PhD thesis, University of Nottingham, Nottingham, England, July 1998.

Gaster, Benedict R. and Mark P. Jones. A polymorphic type system for extensible records and variants. Technical Report NOTTCS-TR-96-3, Department of Computer Science, University of Nottingham, November 1996.

Gay, David and Alexander Aiken. Language support for regions. In *ACM SIGPLAN Conference on Programming Language Design and Implementation (PLDI), Snowbird, Utah*, pages 70–80, June 2001.

Ghelli, Giorgio and Benjamin Pierce. Bounded existentials and minimal typing, 1992. Circulated in manuscript form. Full version in *Theoretical Computer Science*, 193(1–2):75–96, February 1998.

Gifford, David K. and John M. Lucassen. Integrating functional and imperative programming. In *ACM Symposium on Lisp and Functional Programming (LFP), Cambridge, Massachusetts*, pages 28–38, August 1986.

Girard, Jean-Yves. *Interprétation fonctionnelle et élimination des coupures de l'arithmétique d'ordre supérieur.* Thèse d'état, University of Paris VII, 1972. Summary in J. E. Fenstad, editor, *Scandinavian Logic Symposium*, pp. 63–92, North-Holland, 1971.

Girard, Jean-Yves. Linear logic. *Theoretical Computer Science*, 50:1–102, 1987.

Girard, Jean-Yves. Light linear logic. *Information and Computation*, 143:175–204, 1998.

Girard, Jean-Yves, Yves Lafont, and Paul Taylor. *Proofs and Types*, volume 7 of *Cambridge Tracts in Theoretical Computer Science*. Cambridge University Press, 1989.

Glew, Neal. Type dispatch for named hierarchical types. In *ACM SIGPLAN International Conference on Functional Programming (ICFP), Paris, France*, pages 172–182, 1999.

GNU. GNU C library, version 2.2.5, 2001. Available from `http://www.gnu.org/manual/glibc-2.2.5/html_mono/libc.html`.

Goguen, Healfdene. *A Typed Operational Semantics for Type Theory.* PhD thesis, LFCS, University of Edinburgh, Edinburgh, Scotland, 1994. Report ESC-LFCS-94-304.

Gordon, Andrew D. Bisimilarity as a theory of functional programming. In *Workshop on the Mathematical Foundations of Programming Semantics (MFPS), New Orleans, Louisiana*, volume 1 of *Electronic Notes in Theoretical Computer Science*. Elsevier, April 1995.

Gordon, Andrew D. Operational equivalences for untyped and polymorphic object calculi. In A. D. Gordon and A. M. Pitts, editors, *Higher-Order Operational Techniques in Semantics*, Publications of the Newton Institute, pages 9–54. Cambridge University Press, 1998.

Gordon, Andrew D. and Alan Jeffrey. Authenticity by typing for security protocols. In *IEEE Computer Security Foundations Workshop (CSFW), Cape Breton, Nova Scotia*, pages 145–159, 2001a.

Gordon, Andrew D. and Alan Jeffrey. Typing correspondence assertions for communiation protocols. In *Workshop on the Mathematical Foundations of Programming Semantics (MFPS), Aarhus, Denmark*, volume 45 of *Electronic Notes in Theoretical Computer Science*, pages 379–409. Elsevier, May 2001b.

Gordon, Andrew D. and Alan Jeffrey. Types and effects for asymmetric cryptographic protocols. In *IEE Computer Security Foundations Workshop (CSFW) , Cape Breton, Nova Scotia*, pages 77–91, 2002.

Gordon, Andrew D. and Don Syme. Typing a multi-language intermediate code. In *ACM SIGPLAN–SIGACT Symposium on Principles of Programming Languages (POPL), London, England*, pages 248–260, January 2001.

Gordon, Michael J., Robin Milner, and Christopher P. Wadsworth. *Edinburgh LCF*, volume 78 of *Lecture Notes in Computer Science*. Springer-Verlag, 1979.

Gough, John. *Compiling for the .NET Common Language Runtime*. .NET series. Prentice Hall, 2002.

Grossman, Dan, Greg Morrisett, Trevor Jim, Michael Hicks, Yanling Wang, and James Cheney. Region-based memory management in Cyclone. In *ACM SIGPLAN Conference on Programming Language Design and Implementation (PLDI), Berlin, Germany*, pages 282–293, 2002.

Gustavsson, Jörgen and Josef Svenningsson. Constraint abstractions. In *Symposium on Programs as Data Objects (PADO), Aarhus, Denmark*, volume 2053 of *Lecture Notes in Computer Science*, pages 63–83. Springer-Verlag, May 2001.

Hallenberg, Niels, Martin Elsman, and Mads Tofte. Combining region inference and garbage collection. In *ACM SIGPLAN Conference on Programming Language Design and Implementation (PLDI), Berlin, Germany*, pages 141–152, June 2002.

Hallgren, Thomas and Aarne Ranta. An extensible proof text editor (abstract). In *International Conference on Logic for Programming and Automated Reasoning (LPAR), Reunion Island*, volume 1955 of *Lecture Notes in Computer Science*, pages 70–84. Springer-Verlag, 2000.

Hamid, Nadeem, Zhong Shao, Valery Trifonov, Stefan Monnier, and Zhaozhong Ni. A syntactic approach to foundational proof-carrying code. In *IEEE Symposium on Logic in Computer Science (LICS)*, pages 89–100, July 2002.

Hanson, David R. Fast allocation and deallocation of memory based on object lifetimes. *Software—Practice and Experience*, 20(1):5–12, 1990.

Hardin, Thérèse, Luc Maranget, and Bruno Pagano. Functional runtimes within the lambda-sigma calculus. *Journal of Functional Programming*, 8(2):131–172, March 1998.

Harper, Robert, Furio Honsell, and Gordon Plotkin. A framework for defining logics. *Journal of the ACM*, 40(1):143–184, 1993. Summary in *IEEE Symposium on Logic in Computer Science (LICS), Ithaca, New York*, 1987.

Harper, Robert and Mark Lillibridge. A type-theoretic approach to higher-order modules with sharing. In *ACM SIGPLAN–SIGACT Symposium on Principles of Programming Languages (POPL), Portland, Oregon*, pages 123–137, January 1994.

Harper, Robert and John C. Mitchell. On the type structure of Standard ML. *ACM Transactions on Programming Languages and Systems*, 15(2):211–252, April 1993. An earlier version appeared in *ACM Symposium on Principles of Programming Languages (POPL), San Diego, California*, under the title "The Essence of ML" (Mitchell and Harper), 1988.

Harper, Robert, John C. Mitchell, and Eugenio Moggi. Higher-order modules and the phase distinction. In *ACM Symposium on Principles of Programming Languages (POPL), San Francisco, California*, pages 341–354, January 1990.

Harper, Robert and Frank Pfenning. On equivalence and canonical forms in the LF type theory. *ACM Transactions on Computational Logic*, 2004. To appear. An earlier version is available as Technical Report CMU-CS-00-148, School of Computer Science, Carnegie Mellon University.

Harper, Robert and Robert Pollack. Type checking with universes. *Theoretical Computer Science*, 89:107–136, 1991.

Harper, Robert and Christopher Stone. A type-theoretic interpretation of Standard ML. In G. Plotkin, C. Stirling, and M. Tofte, editors, *Proof, Language and Interaction: Essays in Honour of Robin Milner*. MIT Press, 2000.

Heintze, Nevin. Set based analysis of ML programs. In *ACM Symposium on Lisp and Functional Programming (LFP), Orlando, Florida*, pages 306–317, June 1994.

Heintze, Nevin. Control-flow analysis and type systems. In *International Symposium on Static Analysis (SAS) , Glasgow, Scotland*, volume 983 of *Lecture Notes in Computer Science*, pages 189–206. Springer-Verlag, 1995.

Helsen, Simon and Peter Thiemann. Syntactic type soundness for the region calculus. In *Workshop on Higher Order Operational Techniques in Semantics (HOOTS), Montréal, Québec*, volume 41(3) of *Electronic Notes in Theoretical Computer Science*, pages 1–20. Elsevier, September 2000.

Helsen, Simon and Peter Thiemann. Polymorphic specialization for ML. *ACM Transactions on Programming Languages and Systems*, 26(4):652–701, July 2004.

Henglein, Fritz. *Polymorphic Type Inference and Semi-Unification*. PhD thesis, Rutgers University, April 1989. Available as NYU Technical Report 443, May 1989, from New York University, Courant Institute of Mathematical Sciences, Department of Computer Science, 251 Mercer St., New York, NY 10012, USA.

Henglein, Fritz. Type inference with polymorphic recursion. *ACM Transactions on Programming Languages and Systems*, 15(2):253–289, 1993.

Henglein, Fritz, Henning Makholm, and Henning Niss. A direct approach to control-flow sensitive region-based memory management. In *ACM SIGPLAN International Conference on Principles and Practice of Declarative Programming (PPDP), Firenze, Italy*, pages 175–186, September 2001.

Henglein, Fritz and Christian Mossin. Polymorphic binding-time analysis. In *European Symposium on Programming (ESOP), Edinburgh, Scotland,* volume 788 of *Lecture Notes in Computer Science,* pages 287–301. Springer-Verlag, April 1994.

Hirschowitz, Tom and Xavier Leroy. Mixin modules in a call-by-value setting. In *European Symposium on Programming (ESOP), Grenoble, France,* pages 6–20, April 2002.

Hoare, C. A. R. Proof of correctness of data representation. *Acta Informatica,* 1: 271–281, 1972.

Hofmann, Martin. A mixed modal/linear lambda calculus with applications to bellantoni-cook safe recursion. In *International Workshop on Computer Science Logic (CSL), Aarhus, Denmark,* pages 275–294, August 1997a.

Hofmann, Martin. Syntax and semantics of dependent types. In A. M. Pitts and P. Dybjer, editors, *Semantics and Logic of Computation,* pages 79–130. Cambridge University Press, 1997b.

Hofmann, Martin. Linear types and non-size-increasing polynomial time computation. In *IEEE Symposium on Logic in Computer Science (LICS), Trento, Italy,* pages 464–473, June 1999.

Hofmann, Martin. Safe recursion with higher types and BCK-algebra. *Annals of Pure and Applied Logic,* 104(1–3):113–166, 2000.

Honsell, Furio, Ian A. Mason, Scott F. Smith, and Carolyn L. Talcott. A variable typed logic of effects. *Information and Computation,* 119(1):55–90, 1995.

Howard, William A. Hereditarily majorizable functionals of finite type. In A. S. Troelstra, editor, *Metamathematical Investigation of Intuitionistic Arithmetic and Analysis,* volume 344 of *Lecture Notes in Mathematics,* pages 454–461. Springer-Verlag, Berlin, 1973.

Howard, William A. The formulas-as-types notion of construction. In J. P. Seldin and J. R. Hindley, editors, *To H. B. Curry: Essays on Combinatory Logic, Lambda Calculus, and Formalism,* pages 479–490. Academic Press, 1980. Reprint of 1969 article.

Howe, Douglas J. Proving congruence of bisimulation in functional programming languages. *Information and Computation,* 124(2):103–112, 1996.

Huet, Gérard. *Résolution d'equations dans les langages d'ordre 1,2, ...,ω.* Thèse de Doctorat d'Etat, Université de Paris 7, Paris, France, 1976.

Igarashi, Atsushi and Naoki Kobayashi. A generic type system for the Pi-calculus. In *ACM SIGPLAN–SIGACT Symposium on Principles of Programming Languages (POPL), London, England,* pages 128–141, January 2001.

Igarashi, Atsushi and Naoki Kobayashi. Resource usage analysis. In *ACM SIGPLAN–SIGACT Symposium on Principles of Programming Languages (POPL), Portland, Oregon,* pages 331–342, January 2002.

Igarashi, Atsushi and Benjamin C. Pierce. Foundations for virtual types. In *European Conference on Object-Oriented Programming (ECOOP), Lisbon, Portugal,* June 1999. Also in informal proceedings of the *Workshop on Foundations of Object-Oriented Languages (FOOL),* January 1999. Full version in *Information and Computation,* 175(1): 34–49, May 2002.

Ishtiaq, Samin and Peter O'Hearn. BI as an assertion language for mutable data structures. In *ACM SIGPLAN-SIGACT Symposium on Principles of Programming Languages (POPL), London, England,* pages 14–26, January 2001.

Jacobs, Bart. *Categorical Logic and Type Theory.* Studies in Logic and the Foundations of Mathematics 141. Elsevier, 1999.

Jategaonkar, Lalita A. ML with extended pattern matching and subtypes. Master's thesis, Massachusetts Institute of Technology, August 1989.

Jategaonkar, Lalita A. and John C. Mitchell. ML with extended pattern matching and subtypes (preliminary version). In *ACM Symposium on Lisp and Functional Programming (LFP), Snowbird, Utah,* pages 198–211, Snowbird, Utah, July 1988.

Jensen, Kathleen and Niklaus Wirth. *Pascal User Manual and Report.* Springer-Verlag, second edition, 1975.

Jim, Trevor. What are principal typings and what are they good for? In *ACM SIGPLAN-SIGACT Symposium on Principles of Programming Languages (POPL), St. Petersburg Beach, Florida,* pages 42–53, 1996.

Jim, Trevor, J. Greg Morrisett, Dan Grossman, Michael W. Hicks, James Cheney, and Yanling Wang. Cyclone: A safe dialect of C. In *General Track: USENIX Annual Technical Conference,* pages 275–288, June 2002.

Jim, Trevor and Jens Palsberg. Type inference in systems of recursive types with subtyping, 1999. Manuscript, available from `http://www.cs.purdue.edu/homes/palsberg/draft/jim-palsberg99.pdf`.

Johann, Patricia. A generalization of short-cut fusion and its correctness proof. *Higher-Order and Symbolic Computation,* 15(4):273–300, 2002.

Jones, Mark P. *Qualified Types: Theory and Practice.* Cambridge University Press, 1994.

Jones, Mark P. Using parameterized signatures to express modular structure. In *ACM SIGPLAN-SIGACT Symposium on Principles of Programming Languages (POPL), St. Petersburg Beach, Florida,* January 21–24, 1996.

Jones, Mark P. Typing Haskell in Haskell. In *ACM Haskell Workshop,* informal proceedings, October 1999.

Jones, Mark P. and John C. Peterson. The Hugs 98 user manual, 1999. Available from `http://www.haskell.org/hugs/`.

Jones, Mark P. and Simon Peyton Jones. Lightweight extensible records for Haskell. In *ACM Haskell Workshop,* informal proceedings, October 1999.

Jouannaud, Jean-Pierre and Claude Kirchner. Solving equations in abstract algebras: a rule-based survey of unification. In J.-L. Lassez and G. Plotkin, editors, *Computational Logic: Essays in honor of Alan Robinson*, pages 257–321. MIT Press, 1991.

Jouvelot, Pierre and David Gifford. Algebraic reconstruction of types and effects. In *ACM Symposium on Principles of Programming Languages (POPL), Orlando, Florida*, pages 303–310, January 1991.

Jouvelot, Pierre and David K. Gifford. Reasoning about continuations with control effects. In *ACM SIGPLAN Conference on Programming Language Design and Implementation (PLDI), Portland, Oregon*, pages 218–226, June 1989.

Jung, Achim and Allen Stoughton. Studying the fully abstract model of PCF within its continuous function model. In *International Conference on Typed Lambda Calculi and Applications (TLCA), Utrecht, The Netherlands*, volume 664 of *Lecture Notes in Computer Science*, pages 230–244. Springer-Verlag, March 1993.

Jutting, L.S. van Benthem, James McKinna, and Robert Pollack. Checking algorithms for Pure Type Systems. In *International Workshop on Types for Proofs and Programs (TYPES), Nijmegen, The Netherlands*, May 1993, volume 806 of *Lecture Notes in Computer Science*, pages 19–61. Springer-Verlag, 1994.

Kfoury, Assaf J., Jerzy Tiuryn, and Pawel Urzyczyn. ML typability is DEXPTIME-complete. In *Colloquium on Trees in Algebra and Programming (CAAP), Copenhagen, Denmark*, volume 431 of *Lecture Notes in Computer Science*, pages 206–220. Springer-Verlag, May 1990.

Kfoury, Assaf J., Jerzy Tiuryn, and Pawel Urzyczyn. The undecidability of the semi-unification problem. *Information and Computation*, 102(1):83–101, January 1993.

Kfoury, Assaf J., Jerzy Tiuryn, and Pawel Urzyczyn. An analysis of ML typability. *Journal of the ACM*, 41(2):368–398, March 1994.

Kirchner, Claude and Francis Klay. Syntactic theories and unification. In *IEEE Symposium on Logic in Computer Science (LICS), Philadelphia, Pennsylvania*, pages 270–277, June 1990.

Knight, Kevin. Unification: a multidisciplinary survey. *ACM Computing Surveys*, 21 (1):93–124, March 1989.

Kobayashi, Naoki. Quasi-linear types. In *ACM SIGPLAN–SIGACT Symposium on Principles of Programming Languages (POPL), San Antonio, Texas*, pages 29–42, January 1999.

Kozen, Dexter, Jens Palsberg, and Michael I. Schwartzbach. Efficient recursive subtyping. *Mathematical Structures in Computer Science*, 5(1):113–125, 1995.

Kuncak, Viktor and Martin Rinard. Structural subtyping of non-recursive types is decidable. In *IEEE Symposium on Logic in Computer Science (LICS), Ottawa, Canada*, pages 96–107, June 2003.

Lafont, Yves. The linear abstract machine. *Theoretical Computer Science*, 59:157–180, 1988.

Lambek, Joachim. The mathematics of sentence structure. *American Mathematical Monthly*, 65:154–170, 1958.

Lampson, Butler and Rod Burstall. Pebble, a kernel language for modules and abstract data types. *Information and Computation*, 76:278–346, February/March 1988.

Lassen, Søren Bøgh. *Relational Reasoning about Functions and Nondeterminism.* PhD thesis, Department of Computer Science, University of Aarhus, Aarhus, Denmark, 1998.

Lassez, Jean-Louis, Michael J. Maher, and Kim G. Marriott. Unification revisited. In J. Minker, editor, *Foundations of Deductive Databases and Logic Programming*, pages 587–625. Morgan Kaufmann, 1988.

Lee, Oukseh and Kwangkeun Yi. Proofs about a folklore let-polymorphic type inference algorithm. *ACM Transactions on Programming Languages and Systems*, 20 (4):707–723, July 1998.

Leivant, Daniel. Stratified functional programs and computational complexity. In *ACM SIGPLAN–SIGACT Symposium on Principles of Programming Languages (POPL), Charleston, South Carolina*, pages 325–333, January 1993.

Leroy, Xavier. Polymorphic typing of an algorithmic language. Research Report 1778, INRIA, October 1992.

Leroy, Xavier. Manifest types, modules and separate compilation. In *ACM SIGPLAN–SIGACT Symposium on Principles of Programming Languages (POPL), Portland, Oregon*, pages 109–122, January 1994.

Leroy, Xavier. Applicative functors and fully transparent higher-order modules. In *ACM SIGPLAN–SIGACT Symposium on Principles of Programming Languages (POPL), San Francisco, California*, pages 142–153, January 1995.

Leroy, Xavier. A syntactic theory of type generativity and sharing. *Journal of Functional Programming*, 6(5):667–698, September 1996.

Leroy, Xavier. The Objective Caml system: Documentation and user's manual, 2000. With Damien Doligez, Jacques Garrigue, Didier Rémy, and Jérôme Vouillon. Available from `http://caml.inria.fr`.

Leroy, Xavier and François Pessaux. Type-based analysis of uncaught exceptions. *ACM Transactions on Programming Languages and Systems*, 22(2):340–377, March 2000. Summary in *ACM SIGPLAN–SIGACT Symposium on Principles of Programming Languages (POPL), San Antonio, Texas*, 1999.

Lillibridge, Mark. *Translucent Sums: A Foundation for Higher-Order Module Systems.* PhD thesis, School of Computer Science, Carnegie Mellon University, Pittsburgh, Pennsylvania, May 1997.

Lindholm, Tim and Frank Yellin. *The Java Virtual Machine Specification.* The Java Series. Addison-Wesley, Reading, MA, January 1997.

Liskov, Barbara. A history of CLU. *ACM SIGPLAN Notices*, 28(3):133–147, 1993.

Loader, Ralph. Finitary PCF is not decidable. *Theoretical Computer Science*, 266(1–2): 341–364, September 2001.

Lucassen, John M. *Types and Effects towards the Integration of Functional and Imperative Programming.* PhD thesis, Massachusetts Institute of Technology, Cambridge, Massachusetts, August 1987. Technical Report MIT-LCS-TR-408.

Lucassen, John M. and David K. Gifford. Polymorphic effect systems. In *ACM Symposium on Principles of Programming Languages (POPL), San Diego, California*, pages 47–57, 1988.

Luo, Zhaohui. *Computation and Reasoning: A Type Theory for Computer Science.* Number 11 in International Series of Monographs on Computer Science. Oxford University Press, 1994.

Luo, Zhaohui and Robert Pollack. The LEGO proof development system: A user's manual. Technical Report ECS-LFCS-92-211, University of Edinburgh, May 1992.

MacQueen, David. Modules for Standard ML. In *ACM Symposium on Lisp and Functional Programming (LFP), Austin, Texas*, pages 198–207, 1984.

MacQueen, David. Using dependent types to express modular structure. In *ACM Symposium on Principles of Programming Languages (POPL), St. Petersburg Beach, Florida*, pages 277–286, January 1986.

MacQueen, David B. and Mads Tofte. A semantics for higher-order functors. In *European Symposium on Programming (ESOP), Edinburgh, Scotland*, volume 788 of *Lecture Notes in Computer Science*, pages 409–423. Springer-Verlag, April 1994.

Magnusson, Lena and Bengt Nordström. The ALF proof editor and its proof engine. In *International Workshop on Types for Proofs and Programs (TYPES), Nijmegen, The Netherlands*, May, 1993, volume 806 of *Lecture Notes in Computer Science*, pages 213–237. Springer-Verlag, 1994.

Mairson, Harry G., Paris C. Kanellakis, and John C. Mitchell. Unification and ML type reconstruction. In J.-L. Lassez and G. Plotkin, editors, *Computational Logic: Essays in Honor of Alan Robinson*, pages 444–478. MIT Press, 1991.

Makholm, Henning. Region-based memory management in Prolog. Master's thesis, University of Copenhagen, Department of Computer Science, March 2000. Technical Report DIKU-TR-00/09.

Makholm, Henning. *A Language-Independend Framework for Region Inference.* PhD thesis, University of Copenhagen, Department of Computer Science, Copenhagen, Denmark, 2003.

Makholm, Henning and Kostis Sagonas. On enabling the WAM with region support. In *International Conference on Logic Programming (ICLP)*, volume 2401 of *Lecture Notes in Computer Science*, pages 163–178. Springer-Verlag, July 2002.

Martelli, Alberto and Ugo Montanari. Unification in linear time and space: A structured presentation. Internal Report B76-16, Istituto di Elaborazione delle Informazione, Consiglio Nazionale delle Ricerche, Pisa, July 1976.

Martelli, Alberto and Ugo Montanari. An efficient unification algorithm. *ACM Transactions on Programming Languages and Systems*, 4(2):258–282, 1982.

Martin-Löf, Per. *Intuitionistic Type Theory.* Bibliopolis, 1984.

Mason, Ian A., Scott F. Smith, and Carolyn L. Talcott. From operational semantics to domain theory. *Information and Computation*, 128(1):26–47, 1996.

Mason, Ian A. and Carolyn L. Talcott. Equivalence in functional languages with effects. *Journal of Functional Programming*, 1:287–327, 1991.

McAllester, David. On the complexity analysis of static analyses. *Journal of the ACM*, 49(4):512–537, July 2002.

McAllester, David. A logical algorithm for ML type inference. In *International Conference on Rewriting Techniques and Applications (RTA), Valencia, Spain*, volume 2706 of *Lecture Notes in Computer Science*, pages 436–451. Springer-Verlag, June 2003.

McBride, Conor. *Dependently Typed Functional Programs and their Proofs.* PhD thesis, LFCS, University of Edinburgh, Edinburgh, Scotland, 2000.

McBride, Conor and James McKinna. The view from the left. *Journal of Functional Programming*, 14(1):69–111, 2004.

McKinna, James and Robert Pollack. Pure Type Sytems formalized. In *International Conference on Typed Lambda Calculi and Applications (TLCA), Utrecht, The Netherlands*, volume 664 of *Lecture Notes in Computer Science*, pages 289–305. Springer-Verlag, March 1993.

Melski, David and Thomas Reps. Interconvertibility of a class of set constraints and context-free language reachability. *Theoretical Computer Science*, 248(1-2), November 2000.

Milner, Robin. A theory of type polymorphism in programming. *Journal of Computer and System Sciences*, 17:348–375, August 1978.

Milner, Robin, Mads Tofte, and Robert Harper. *The Definition of Standard ML.* MIT Press, 1990.

Milner, Robin, Mads Tofte, Robert Harper, and David MacQueen. *The Definition of Standard ML*, Revised edition. MIT Press, 1997.

Minamide, Yasuhiko. A functional representation of data structures with a hole. In *ACM SIGPLAN-SIGACT Symposium on Principles of Programming Languages (POPL), San Diego, California*, pages 75–84, January 1998.

Minamide, Yasuhiko, Greg Morrisett, and Robert Harper. Typed closure conversion. In *ACM SIGPLAN-SIGACT Symposium on Principles of Programming Languages (POPL), St. Petersburg Beach, Florida*, pages 271–283, January 1996.

Miquel, Alexandre. *Le calcul des constructions implicite: syntaxe et sémantique.* PhD thesis, University Paris 7, Paris, France, 2001.

Mitchell, John C. Coercion and type inference. In *ACM Symposium on Principles of Programming Languages (POPL), Salt Lake City, Utah*, pages 175–185, January 1984.

Mitchell, John C. Representation independence and data abstraction. In *ACM Symposium on Principles of Programming Languages (POPL), St. Petersburg Beach, Florida*, pages 263–276, January 1986.

Mitchell, John C. On the equivalence of data representations. In V. Lifschitz, editor, *Artificial Intelligence and Mathematical Theory of Computation: Papers in Honor of John McCarthy*, pages 305–330. Academic Press, 1991a.

Mitchell, John C. Type inference with simple subtypes. *Journal of Functional Programming*, 1(3):245–286, July 1991b.

Mitchell, John C. *Foundations for Programming Languages.* MIT Press, 1996.

Mitchell, John C. and Gordon D. Plotkin. Abstract types have existential types. *ACM Transactions on Programming Languages and Systems*, 10(3):470–502, 1988. Summary in *ACM Symposium on Principles of Programming Languages (POPL), New Orleans, Louisiana*, 1985.

Moggi, Eugenio. Computational lambda-calculus and monads. In *IEEE Symposium on Logic in Computer Science (LICS), Asilomar, California*, pages 14–23, June 1989. Full version, titled *Notions of Computation and Monads*, in Information and Computation, 93(1), pp. 55–92, 1991.

Moh, Shaw-Kwei. The deduction theorems and two new logical systems. *Methodos*, 2: 56–75, 1950.

Mohring, Christine. Algorithm development in the calculus of constructions. In *IEEE Symposium on Logic in Computer Science (LICS), Cambridge, Massachusetts*, pages 84–91, June 1986.

Monnier, Stefan, Bratin Saha, and Zhong Shao. Principled scavenging. In *ACM SIGPLAN Conference on Programming Language Design and Implementation (PLDI), Snowbird, Utah*, pages 81–91, June 2001.

Morrisett, Greg, Karl Crary, Neal Glew, and David Walker. Stack-based typed assembly language. *Journal of Functional Programming*, 12(1):43–88, January 2002.

Morrisett, Greg, David Walker, Karl Crary, and Neal Glew. From System-F to typed assembly language. *ACM Transactions on Programming Languages and Systems*, 21(3):527–568, May 1999.

Mossin, Christian. *Flow Analysis of Typed Higher-Order Programs.* PhD thesis, University of Copenhagen, Department of Computer Science, Copenhagen, Denmark, 1997. Also available as Technical Report DIKU-TR-97/1.

Müller, Martin. A constraint-based recast of ML-polymorphism. In *International Workshop on Unification*, June 1994. Also available as Technical Report 94-R-243, CRIN, Nancy, France.

Müller, Martin. Notes on HM(X), August 1998. Available from `http://www.ps.uni-sb.de/~mmueller/papers/HMX.ps.gz`.

Müller, Martin, Joachim Niehren, and Ralf Treinen. The first-order theory of ordering constraints over feature trees. *Discrete Mathematics and Theoretical Computer Science*, 4(2):193–234, 2001.

Müller, Martin and Susumu Nishimura. Type inference for first-class messages with feature constraints. In *Asian Computer Science Conference (ASIAN), Manila, The Philippines*, volume 1538 of *Lecture Notes in Computer Science*, pages 169–187. Springer-Verlag, December 1998.

Mycroft, Alan. Polymorphic type schemes and recursive definitions. In *International Symposium on Programming, Toulouse, France*, volume 167 of *Lecture Notes in Computer Science*, pages 217–228, Toulouse, France, April 1984. Springer-Verlag.

Necula, George C. Proof-carrying code. In *ACM SIGPLAN–SIGACT Symposium on Principles of Programming Languages (POPL), Paris, France*, pages 106–119, January 1997.

Necula, George C. *Compiling with Proofs*. PhD thesis, Carnegie Mellon University, Pittsburgh, Pennsylvania, September 1998. Technical report CMU-CS-98-154.

Necula, George C. Translation validation for an optimizing compiler. In *ACM SIGPLAN Conference on Programming Language Design and Implementation (PLDI), Vancouver, British Columbia, Canada*, pages 83–94, June 2000.

Necula, George C. and Peter Lee. Safe kernel extensions without run-time checking. In *USENIX Symposium on Operating Systems Design and Implementation (OSDI), Seattle, Washington*, pages 229–243, October 1996.

Necula, George C. and Peter Lee. The design and implementation of a certifying compiler. In *ACM SIGPLAN Conference on Programming Language Design and Implementation (PLDI), Montréal, Québec*, pages 333–344, June 1998a.

Necula, George C. and Peter Lee. Efficient representation and validation of logical proofs. In *IEEE Symposium on Logic in Computer Science (LICS), Indianapolis, Indiana*, pages 93–104, June 1998b.

Niehren, Joachim, Martin Müller, and Andreas Podelski. Inclusion constraints over non-empty sets of trees. In *Theory and Practice of Software Development (TAPSOFT), Lille, France*, volume 1214 of *Lecture Notes in Computer Science*, pages 217–231. Springer-Verlag, April 1997.

Niehren, Joachim and Tim Priesnitz. Non-structural subtype entailment in automata theory. *Information and Computation*, 186(2):319–354, November 2003.

Nielson, Flemming and Hanne Riis Nielson. From CML to its process algebra. *Theoretical Computer Science*, 155:179–219, 1996.

Nielson, Flemming, Hanne Riis Nielson, and Christopher L. Hankin. *Principles of Program Analysis*. Springer-Verlag, 1999.

Nielson, Flemming, Hanne Riis Nielson, and Helmut Seidl. A succinct solver for ALFP. *Nordic Journal of Computing*, 9(4):335–372, 2002.

Nielson, Hanne Riis and Flemming Nielson. Higher-order concurrent programs with finite communication topology. In *ACM SIGPLAN–SIGACT Symposium on Principles of Programming Languages (POPL), Portland, Oregon*, pages 84–97, January 1994.

Nishimura, Susumu. Static typing for dynamic messages. In *ACM SIGPLAN-SIGACT Symposium on Principles of Programming Languages (POPL), San Diego, California*, pages 266–278, 1998.

Niss, Henning. *Regions are Imperative: Unscoped Regions and Control-Flow Sensitive Memory Management.* PhD thesis, University of Copenhagen, Department of Computer Science, Copenhagen, Denmark, 2002.

Nöcker, Erick and Sjaak Smetsers. Partially strict non-recursive data types. *Journal of Functional Programming*, 3(2):191–215, 1993.

Nöcker, Erick G. M. H., Sjaak E. W. Smetsers, Marko C. J. D. van Eekelen, and Marinus J. Plasmeijer. Concurrent clean. In *Symposium on Parallel Architectures and Languages Europe, Volume I: Parallel Architectures and Algorithms (PARLE), Eindhoven, The Netherlands*, volume 505 of *Lecture Notes in Computer Science*, pages 202–219. Springer-Verlag, June 1991.

Odersky, Martin. Observers for linear types. In *European Symposium on Programming (ESOP), Rennes, France*, volume 582 of *Lecture Notes in Computer Science*, pages 390–407. Springer-Verlag, February 1992.

Odersky, Martin, Vincent Cremet, Christine Rockl, and Matthias Zenger. A nominal theory of objects with dependent types. In *International Workshop on Foundations of Object-Oriented Languages (FOOL)*, informal proceedings, 2003.

Odersky, Martin, Martin Sulzmann, and Martin Wehr. Type inference with constrained types. *Theory and Practice of Object Systems*, 5(1):35–55, 1999. Summary in *International Workshop on Foundations of Object-Oriented Languages (FOOL)*, informal proceedings, 1997.

O'Hearn, Peter. On bunched typing. *Journal of Functional Programming*, 13(4):747–796, 2003.

O'Hearn, Peter and David Pym. The logic of bunched implications. *Bulletin of Symbolic Logic*, 5(2):215–244, 1999.

Ohori, Atsushi. A polymorphic record calculus and its compilation. *ACM Transactions on Programming Languages and Systems*, 17(6):844–895, November 1995.

Ohori, Atsushi and Peter Buneman. Type inference in a database programming language. In *ACM Symposium on Lisp and Functional Programming (LFP), Snowbird, Utah*, pages 174–183, July 1988.

Ohori, Atsushi and Peter Buneman. Static type inference for parametric classes. In *Conference on Object Oriented Programming: Systems, Languages, and Applications (OOPSLA), New Orleans, Louisiana*, pages 445–456, October 1989. Also in C. A. Gunter and J. C. Mitchell, editors, *Theoretical Aspects of Object-Oriented Programming: Types, Semantics, and Language Design*, MIT Press, 1994.

Orlov, Ivan E. The calculus of compatibility of propositions (in Russian). *Matematicheskii Sbornik*, 35:263–286, 1928.

Owre, Sam, Sreeranga Rajan, John M. Rushby, Natarajan Shankar, and Mandayam K. Srivas. PVS: Combining specification, proof checking, and model checking. In *International Conference on Computer Aided Verification (CAV), New Brunswick, New Jersey*, volume 1102 of *Lecture Notes in Computer Science*, pages 411–414. Springer-Verlag, July 1996.

Palsberg, Jens. Efficient inference of object types. *Information and Computation*, 123 (2):198–209, 1995.

Palsberg, Jens. Type-based analysis and applications. In *ACM SIGPLAN-SIGSOFT Workshop on Program Analysis for Software Tools and Engineering (PASTE), Snowbird, Utah*, pages 20–27, June 2001.

Palsberg, Jens and Patrick O'Keefe. A type system equivalent to flow analysis. In *ACM SIGPLAN-SIGACT Symposium on Principles of Programming Languages (POPL), San Francisco, California*, pages 367–378, 1995.

Palsberg, Jens and Michael Schwartzbach. Type substitution for object-oriented programming. In *ACM SIGPLAN Conference on Object Oriented Programming: Systems, Languages, and Applications (OOPSLA)/European Conference on Object-Oriented Programming (ECOOP), Ottawa, Ontario*, volume 25(10) of *ACM SIGPLAN Notices*, pages 151–160, October 1990.

Palsberg, Jens and Michael I. Schwartzbach. *Object-Oriented Type Systems.* Wiley, 1994.

Palsberg, Jens, Mitchell Wand, and Patrick M. O'Keefe. Type inference with non-structural subtyping. *Formal Aspects of Computing*, 9:49–67, 1997.

Parnas, David. The criteria to be used in decomposing systems into modules. *Communications of the ACM*, 14(1):221–227, 1972.

Paterson, Michael S. and Mark N. Wegman. Linear unification. *Journal of Computer and System Sciences*, 16:158–167, 1978.

Paulin-Mohring, Christine. Extracting F_ω's programs from proofs in the calculus of constructions. In *ACM Symposium on Principles of Programming Languages (POPL), Austin, Texas*, pages 89–104, January 1989.

Petersen, Leaf, Perry Cheng, Robert Harper, and Chris Stone. Implementing the TILT internal language. Technical Report CMU-CS-00-180, Department of Computer Science, Carnegie Mellon University, 2000.

Petersen, Leaf, Robert Harper, Karl Crary, and Frank Pfenning. A type theory for memory allocation and data layout. In *ACM SIGPLAN-SIGACT Symposium on Principles of Programming Languages (POPL), New Orleans, Louisiana*, pages 172–184, January 2003.

Peyton Jones, Simon. Special issue: Haskell 98 language and libraries. *Journal of Functional Programming*, 13, January 2003.

Pfenning, Frank and Rowan Davies. A judgmental reconstruction of modal logic. *Mathematical Structures in Computer Science*, 11(4):511–540, 2001.

Pfenning, Frank and Carsten Schürmann. Algorithms for equality and unification in the presence of notational definitions. In T. Altenkirch, W. Naraschewski, and B. Reus, editors, *International Workshop on Types for Proofs and Programs (TYPES), Kloster Irsee, Germany*, volume 1657 of *Lecture Notes in Computer Science*. Springer-Verlag, 1998.

Pierce, Benjamin C. *Types and Programming Languages.* MIT Press, 2002.

Pierce, Benjamin C. and David N. Turner. Object-oriented programming without recursive types. In *ACM SIGPLAN-SIGACT Symposium on Principles of Programming Languages (POPL), Charleston, South Carolina*, pages 299–312, January 1993.

Pitts, Andrew M. Relational properties of domains. *Information and Computation*, 127:66–90, 1996.

Pitts, Andrew M. Existential types: Logical relations and operational equivalence. In *International Colloquium on Automata, Languages and Programming (ICALP), Aalborg, Denmark*, volume 1443 of *Lecture Notes in Computer Science*, pages 309–326. Springer-Verlag, 1998.

Pitts, Andrew M. Parametric polymorphism and operational equivalence. *Mathematical Structures in Computer Science*, 10:321–359, 2000.

Pitts, Andrew M. Operational semantics and program equivalence. In G. Barthe, P. Dybjer, and J. Saraiva, editors, *Applied Semantics, Advanced Lectures*, volume 2395 of *Lecture Notes in Computer Science, Tutorial*, pages 378–412. Springer-Verlag, 2002.

Pitts, Andrew M. and Ian D. B. Stark. Observable properties of higher order functions that dynamically create local names, or: What's new? In *International Symposium on Mathematical Foundations of Computer Science, Gdańsk, Poland*, volume 711 of *Lecture Notes in Computer Science*, pages 122–141. Springer-Verlag, 1993.

Pitts, Andrew M. and Ian D. B. Stark. Operational reasoning for functions with local state. In A. D. Gordon and A. M. Pitts, editors, *Higher-Order Operational Techniques in Semantics*, Publications of the Newton Institute, pages 227–273. Cambridge University Press, 1998.

Plotkin, Gordon D. Lambda-definability and logical relations. Memorandum SAI-RM-4, University of Edinburgh, Edinburgh, Scotland, October 1973.

Plotkin, Gordon D. LCF considered as a programming language. *Theoretical Computer Science*, 5:223–255, 1977.

Plotkin, Gordon D. Lambda-definability in the full type hierarchy. In J. P. Seldin and J. R. Hindley, editors, *To H. B. Curry: Essays on Combinatory Logic, Lambda Calculus and Formalism*, pages 363–373. Academic Press, 1980.

Plotkin, Gordon D. and Martín Abadi. A logic for parametric polymorphism. In *International Conference on Typed Lambda Calculi and Applications (TLCA), Utrecht, The Netherlands*, volume 664 of *Lecture Notes in Computer Science*, pages 361–375. Springer-Verlag, March 1993.

Polakow, Jeff and Frank Pfenning. Natural deduction for intuitionistic non-commutative linear logic. In *International Conference on Typed Lambda Calculi and Applications (TLCA), L'Aquila, Italy*, volume 1581 of *Lecture Notes in Computer Science*, pages 295–309. Springer-Verlag, April 1999.

Poll, Erik. Expansion Postponement for Normalising Pure Type Systems. *Journal of Functional Programming*, 8(1):89–96, 1998.

Pollack, Robert. *The Theory of LEGO: A Proof Checker for the Extended Calculus of Constructions*. PhD thesis, University of Edinburgh, Edinburgh, Scotland, 1994.

Popkorn, Sally. *First Steps in Modal Logic*. Cambridge University Press, 1994.

Pottier, François. A versatile constraint-based type inference system. *Nordic Journal of Computing*, 7(4):312–347, November 2000.

Pottier, François. A semi-syntactic soundness proof for HM(X). Research Report 4150, INRIA, March 2001a.

Pottier, François. Simplifying subtyping constraints: a theory. *Information and Computation*, 170(2):153–183, November 2001b.

Pottier, François. A constraint-based presentation and generalization of rows. In *IEEE Symposium on Logic in Computer Science (LICS), Ottawa, Canada*, pages 331–340, June 2003.

Pottier, François and Vincent Simonet. Information flow inference for ML. *ACM Transactions on Programming Languages and Systems*, 25(1):117–158, January 2003.

Pottier, François, Christian Skalka, and Scott Smith. A systematic approach to static access control. In *European Symposium on Programming (ESOP), Genova, Italy*, volume 2028 of *Lecture Notes in Computer Science*, pages 30–45. Springer-Verlag, April 2001.

Pratt, Vaughan and Jerzy Tiuryn. Satisfiability of inequalities in a poset. *Fundamenta Informaticae*, 28(1–2):165–182, 1996.

Pugh, William and Grant Weddell. Two-directional record layout for multiple inheritance. In *ACM SIGPLAN Conference on Programming Language Design and Implementation (PLDI), White Plains, New York*, pages 85–91, June 1990.

Rajamani, Sriram K. and Jakob Rehof. A behavioral module system for the pi-calculus. In *International Symposium on Static Analysis (SAS) , Paris, France*, volume 2126 of *Lecture Notes in Computer Science*, pages 375–394. Springer-Verlag, July 2001.

Rajamani, Sriram K. and Jakob Rehof. Conformance checking for models of asynchronous message passing software. In *International Conference on Computer Aided Verification (CAV), Copenhagen, Denmark*, pages 166–179, July 2002.

Rehof, Jakob. Minimal typings in atomic subtyping. In *ACM SIGPLAN-SIGACT Symposium on Principles of Programming Languages (POPL), Paris, France*, pages 278–291, January 1997.

Rehof, Jakob and Manuel Fähndrich. Type-based flow analysis: From polymorphic subtyping to CFL reachability. In *ACM SIGPLAN-SIGACT Symposium on Principles of Programming Languages (POPL), London, England*, pages 54–66, 2001.

Reid, Alastair, Matthew Flatt, Leigh Stoller, Jay Lepreau, and Eric Eide. Knit: Component composition for systems software. In *USENIX Symposium on Operating Systems Design and Implementation (OSDI), San Diego, California*, pages 347–360, October 2000.

Rémy, Didier. Typechecking records and variants in a natural extension of ML. In *ACM Symposium on Principles of Programming Languages (POPL), Austin, Texas*, pages 242–249, January 1989. Long version in C. A. Gunter and J. C. Mitchell, editors, *Theoretical Aspects of Object-Oriented Programming: Types, Semantics, and Language Design*, MIT Press, 1994.

Rémy, Didier. *Algèbres Touffues. Application au Typage Polymorphe des Objets Enregistrements dans les Langages Fonctionnels*. PhD thesis, Université Paris VII, 1990.

Rémy, Didier. Extending ML type system with a sorted equational theory. Research Report 1766, Institut National de Recherche en Informatique et Automatisme, Rocquencourt, BP 105, 78 153 Le Chesnay Cedex, France, 1992a.

Rémy, Didier. Projective ML. In *ACM Symposium on Lisp and Functional Programming (LFP), San Francisco, California*, pages 66–75, June 1992b.

Rémy, Didier. Syntactic theories and the algebra of record terms. Research Report 1869, Institut National de Recherche en Informatique et Automatisme, Rocquencourt, BP 105, 78 153 Le Chesnay Cedex, France, 1993.

Rémy, Didier. Programming objects with ML-ART: An extension to ML with abstract and record types. In *International Symposium on Theoretical Aspects of Computer Software (TACS), Sendai, Japan*, volume 789 of *Lecture Notes in Computer Science*, pages 321–346. Springer-Verlag, April 1994.

Rémy, Didier and Jérôme Vouillon. Objective ML: An effective object-oriented extension to ML. *Theory And Practice of Object Systems*, 4(1):27–50, 1998. Summary in *ACM SIGPLAN–SIGACT Symposium on Principles of Programming Languages (POPL), Paris, France*, 1997.

van Renesse, Robbert, Kenneth P. Birman, Mark Hayden, Alexey Vaysburd, and David Karr. Building adaptive systems using Ensemble. *Software: Practice and Experience*, 28(9):963–979, August 1998.

Restall, Greg. *An Introduction to Substructural Logics*. Routledge, February 2000.

Restall, Greg. Relevant and substructural logics. In D. Gabbay and J. Woods, editors, *Handbook of the History and Philosophy of Logic*, volume 6, *Logic and the Modalities in the Twentieth Century*. Elsevier, 2005. To appear.

Reynolds, John C. Automatic computation of data set definitions. In *Information Processing 68, Edinburgh, Scotland*, volume 1, pages 456–461. North Holland, 1969.

Reynolds, John C. Towards a theory of type structure. In *Colloque sur la Programmation, Paris, France*, volume 19 of *Lecture Notes in Computer Science*, pages 408–425. Springer-Verlag, 1974.

Reynolds, John C. Syntactic control of interference. In *ACM Symposium on Principles of Programming Languages (POPL), Tucson, Arizona*, pages 39–46, January 1978. Reprinted in O'Hearn and Tennent, *ALGOL-like Languages*, vol. 1, pages 273–286, Birkhäuser, 1997.

Reynolds, John C. Types, abstraction, and parametric polymorphism. In R. E. A. Mason, editor, *Information Processing 83, Paris, France*, pages 513–523. Elsevier, 1983.

Reynolds, John C. Syntactic control of interference, part 2. Report CMU-CS-89-130, Carnegie Mellon University, April 1989.

Reynolds, John C. Intuitionistic reasoning about shared mutable data structure. In J. Davies, A. W. Roscoe, and J. Woodcock, editors, *Millennial Perspectives in Computer Science: Proceedings of the 1999 Oxford-Microsoft Symposium in honour of Sir Tony Hoare*. Palgrave Macmillan, 2000.

Robinson, J. Alan. Computational logic: The unification computation. *Machine Intelligence*, 6:63–72, 1971.

Ross, Douglas T. The AED free storage package. *Communications of the ACM*, 10(8): 481–492, 1967.

Russo, Claudio V. *Types for Modules.* PhD thesis, Edinburgh University, Edinburgh, Scotland, 1998. LFCS Thesis ECS–LFCS–98–389.

Russo, Claudio V. Non-dependent types for standard ML modules. In *ACM SIGPLAN International Conference on Principles and Practice of Declarative Programming (PPDP), Paris France*, pages 80–97, September 1999.

Russo, Claudio V. Recursive structures for Standard ML. In *ACM SIGPLAN International Conference on Functional Programming (ICFP), Firenze, Italy*, pages 50–61, September 2001.

Sabry, Amr. What is a purely functional language? *Journal of Functional Programming*, 8(1):1–22, January 1998.

Saha, Bratin, Nevin Heintze, and Dino Oliva. Subtransitive CFA using types. Technical Report YALEU/DCS/TR-1166, Yale University, Department of Computer Science, October 1998.

Sangiorgi, Davide and David. *The π-Calculus: a Theory of Mobile Processes.* Cambridge University Press, 2001.

Sannella, Donald, Stefan Sokolowski, and Andrzej Tarlecki. Toward formal development of programs from algebraic specifications: Parameterisation revisited. *Acta Informatica*, 29(8):689–736, 1992.

Schneider, Fred B. Enforceable security policies. *ACM Transactions on Information and System Security*, 3(1):30–50, February 2000.

Schwartz, Jacob T. Optimization of very high level languages (parts I and II). *Computer Languages*, 1(2-3):161–194, 197–218, 1975.

Seldin, Jonathan. Curry's anticipation of the types used in programming languages. In *Proceedings of the Annual Meeting of the Canadian Society for History and Philosophy of Mathematics, Toronto, Ontario,* pages 143–163, May 2002.

Semmelroth, Miley and Amr Sabry. Monadic encapsulation in ML. In *ACM SIGPLAN International Conference on Functional Programming (ICFP), Paris, France,* pages 8–17, September 1999.

Sestoft, Peter. Replacing function parameters by global variables. In *ACM Symposium on Functional Programming Languages and Computer Architecture (FPCA), London, England,* pages 39–53, September 1989. Also available as University of Copenhagen, Department of Computer Science Technical Report 88-7-2.

Sestoft, Peter. Moscow ML homepage, 2003. `http://www.dina.dk/~sestoft/mosml.html`.

Severi, Paula and Erik Poll. Pure type systems with definitions. In *International Symposium on Logical Foundations of Computer Science (LFCS), St. Petersburg, Russia,* volume 813 of *Lecture Notes in Computer Science,* pages 316–328. Springer-Verlag, September 1994.

Shao, Zhong. An overview of the FLINT/ML compiler. In *ACM SIGPLAN Workshop on Types in Compilation (TIC), Amsterdam, The Netherlands,* June 1997.

Shao, Zhong. Typed cross-module compilation. In *ACM SIGPLAN International Conference on Functional Programming (ICFP), Baltimore, Maryland,* pages 141–152, September 1998.

Shao, Zhong. Transparent modules with fully syntactic signatures. In *ACM SIGPLAN International Conference on Functional Programming (ICFP), Paris, France,* pages 220–232, September 1999.

Shao, Zhong, Christopher League, and Stefan Monnier. Implementing typed intermediate languages. In *ACM SIGPLAN International Conference on Functional Programming (ICFP), Baltimore, Maryland,* pages 313–323, September 1998.

Shivers, Olin. Control flow analysis in Scheme. In *ACM SIGPLAN Conference on Programming Language Design and Implementation (PLDI), Atlanta, Georgia,* pages 164–174, June 1988.

Shivers, Olin. *Control-Flow Analysis of Higher-Order Languages or Taming Lambda.* PhD thesis, Carnegie Mellon University, Pittsburgh, Pennsylvania, May 1991.

Simonet, Vincent. Type inference with structural subtyping: a faithful formalization of an efficient constraint solver. In *Asian Symposium on Programming Languages and Systems (APLAS), Beijing, China,* pages 283–302, November 2003.

Skalka, Christian and François Pottier. Syntactic type soundness for $HM(X)$. In *Workshop on Types in Programming (TIP), Dagstuhl, Germany,* volume 75 of *Electronic Notes in Theoretical Computer Science.* Elsevier, July 2002.

Smith, Frederick, David Walker, and Greg Morrisett. Alias types. In *European Symposium on Programming (ESOP), Berlin, Germany,* volume 1782 of *Lecture Notes in Computer Science,* pages 366–381. Springer-Verlag, April 2000.

Smith, Geoffrey S. Principal type schemes for functional programs with overloading and subtyping. *Science of Computer Programming*, 23(2-3):197-226, December 1994.

Smith, Jan, Bengt Nordström, and Kent Petersson. *Programming in Martin-Löf's Type Theory: An Introduction.* Oxford University Press, 1990.

Statman, Richard. Logical relations and the typed λ-calculus. *Information and Control*, 65(2-3):85-97, May-June 1985.

Steele, Guy L., Jr. *Common Lisp: The Language.* Digital Press, 1990.

Stone, Christopher A. *Singleton Kinds and Singleton Types.* PhD thesis, Carnegie Mellon University, Pittsburgh, Pennsylvania, August 2000.

Stone, Christopher A. and Robert Harper. Deciding type equivalence in a language with singleton kinds. In *ACM SIGPLAN-SIGACT Symposium on Principles of Programming Languages (POPL), Boston, Massachusetts*, pages 214-227, January 2000.

Stone, Christopher A. and Robert Harper. Extensional equivalence and singleton types. 2005. To appear.

Streicher, Thomas. *Semantics of Type Theory.* Springer-Verlag, 1991.

Su, Zhendong, Alexander Aiken, Joachim Niehren, Tim Priesnitz, and Ralf Treinen. The first-order theory of subtyping constraints. In *ACM SIGPLAN-SIGACT Symposium on Principles of Programming Languages (POPL), Portland, Oregon*, pages 203-216, January 2002.

Sulzmann, Martin. *A General Framework for Hindley/Milner Type Systems with Constraints.* PhD thesis, Yale University, Department of Computer Science, New Haven, Connecticut, May 2000.

Sulzmann, Martin, Martin Müller, and Christoph Zenger. Hindley/Milner style type systems in constraint form. Research Report ACRC-99-009, University of South Australia, School of Computer and Information Science, July 1999.

Sumii, Eijiro and Benjamin C. Pierce. A bisimulation for type abstraction and recursion. In *ACM SIGPLAN-SIGACT Symposium on Principles of Programming Languages (POPL), Long Beach, California*, 2005.

Sun. *Java^{TM} 2 Platform Micro Edition (J2ME^{TM}) Technology for Creating Mobile Devices—White Paper.* Sun Microsystems, May 2000. Available from `http://java.sun.com/products/kvm/wp/KVMwp.pdf`.

Tait, William W. Intensional interpretations of functionals of finite type I. *Journal of Symbolic Logic*, 32(2):198-212, June 1967.

Talcott, C. Reasoning about functions with effects. In A. D. Gordon and A. M. Pitts, editors, *Higher Order Operational Techniques in Semantics*, Publications of the Newton Institute, pages 347-390. Cambridge University Press, 1998.

Talpin, Jean-Pierre and Pierre Jouvelot. Polymorphic type, region and effect inference. *Journal of Functional Programming*, 2(2):245-271, 1992.

Talpin, Jean-Pierre and Pierre Jouvelot. The type and effect discipline. *Information and Computation*, 111:245–296, 1994.

Tarditi, David, Greg Morrisett, Perry Cheng, Christopher Stone, Robert Harper, and Peter Lee. TIL: A type-directed optimizing compiler for ML. In *ACM SIGPLAN Conference on Programming Language Design and Implementation (PLDI), Philadephia, Pennsylvania*, pages 181–192, May 1996.

Tarjan, Robert Endre. Efficiency of a good but not linear set union algorithm. *Journal of the ACM*, 22(2):215–225, April 1975.

Tarjan, Robert Endre. Applications of path compression on balanced trees. *Journal of the ACM*, 26(4):690–715, October 1979.

Terlouw, J. Een nadere bewijstheoretische analyse van GSTTs. Manuscript, University of Nijmegen, Netherlands, 1989.

Thorup, Kresten Krab. Genericity in Java with virtual types. In *European Conference on Object-Oriented Programming (ECOOP), Jyväskylä, Finland*, volume 1241 of *Lecture Notes in Computer Science*, pages 444–471. Springer-Verlag, June 1997.

Tiuryn, Jerzy. Subtype inequalities. In *IEEE Symposium on Logic in Computer Science (LICS), Santa Cruz, California*, pages 308–317, June 1992.

Tiuryn, Jerzy and Mitchell Wand. Type reconstruction with recursive types and atomic subtyping. In *Theory and Practice of Software Development (TAPSOFT), Orsay, France*, volume 668 of *Lecture Notes in Computer Science*, pages 686–701. Springer-Verlag, April 1993.

Tofte, Mads. *Operational Semantics and Polymorphic Type Inference.* PhD thesis, Computer Science Department, Edinburgh University, Edinburgh, Scotland, 1988.

Tofte, Mads and Lars Birkedal. A region inference algorithm. *ACM Transactions on Programming Languages and Systems*, 20(4):724–767, 1998.

Tofte, Mads, Lars Birkedal, Martin Elsman, and Niels Hallenberg. Region-based memory management in perspective. In *ACM SIGPLAN International Conference on Principles and Practice of Declarative Programming (PPDP), Firenze, Italy*, pages 175–186, September 2001a.

Tofte, Mads, Lars Birkedal, Martin Elsman, Niels Hallenberg, Tommy Højfeld Olesen, and Peter Sestoft. Programming with regions in the ML Kit (for version 4). Technical report, IT University of Copenhagen, October 2001b.

Tofte, Mads and Jean-Pierre Talpin. Implementing the call-by-value lambda-calculus using a stack of regions. In *ACM SIGPLAN–SIGACT Symposium on Principles of Programming Languages (POPL), Portland, Oregon*, January 1994.

Tofte, Mads and Jean-Pierre Talpin. Region-based memory management. *Information and Computation*, 132(2):109–176, February 1997.

Torgersen, Mads. Virtual types are statically safe. In *International Workshop on Foundations of Object-Oriented Languages (FOOL)*, informal proceedings, January 1998.

Trifonov, Valery and Scott Smith. Subtyping constrained types. In *International Symposium on Static Analysis (SAS) , Aachen, Germany*, volume 1145 of *Lecture Notes in Computer Science*, pages 349–365. Springer-Verlag, September 1996.

Turner, David N. and Philip Wadler. Operational interpretations of linear logic. *Theoretical Computer Science*, 227:231–248, 1999. Special issue on linear logic.

Turner, David N., Philip Wadler, and Christian Mossin. Once upon a type. In *ACM Symposium on Functional Programming Languages and Computer Architecture (FPCA)San Diego, California*, pages 1–11, June 1995.

Vouillon, Jerome and Paul-André Melliès. Semantic types: A fresh look at the ideal model for types. In *ACM SIGPLAN–SIGACT Symposium on Principles of Programming Languages (POPL), Venice, Italy*, pages 52–63, 2004.

Wadler, Philip. Theorems for free! In *ACM Symposium on Functional Programming Languages and Computer Architecture (FPCA), London, England*, pages 347–359, September 1989.

Wadler, Philip. Linear types can change the world. In *IFIP TC 2 Working Conference on Programming Concepts and Methods, Sea of Galilee, Israel*, pages 546–566, April 1990.

Wadler, Philip. The marriage of effects and monads. *ACM Transactions on Computational Logic*, 4(1):1–32, 2003.

Wahbe, Robert, Steven Lucco, Thomas E. Anderson, and Susan L. Graham. Efficient software-based fault isolation. In *ACM Symposium on Operating Systems Principles (SOSP), Asheville, North Carolina*, pages 203–216, December 1993.

Walker, David, Karl Crary, and Greg Morrisett. Typed memory management via static capabilities. *ACM Transactions on Programming Languages and Systems*, 22(4): 701–771, July 2000.

Walker, David and Greg Morrisett. Alias types for recursive data structures. In *ACM SIGPLAN Workshop on Types in Compilation (TIC), Montréal, Québec*, September, 2000, volume 2071, pages 177–206. Springer-Verlag, 2001.

Walker, David and Kevin Watkins. On regions and linear types. In *ACM SIGPLAN International Conference on Functional Programming (ICFP), Firenze, Italy*, pages 181–192, September 2001.

Wand, Mitchell. Complete type inference for simple objects. In *IEEE Symposium on Logic in Computer Science (LICS), Ithaca, New York*, pages 37–44, June 1987a.

Wand, Mitchell. A simple algorithm and proof for type inference. *Fundamenta Informaticae*, 10:115–122, 1987b.

Wand, Mitchell. Corrigendum: Complete type inference for simple objects. In *IEEE Symposium on Logic in Computer Science (LICS), Edinburgh, Scotland*, page 132, 1988.

Wand, Mitchell. Type inference for objects with instance variables and inheritance. In C. A. Gunter and J. C. Mitchell, editors, *Theoretical Aspects of Object-Oriented*

Programming: Types, Semantics, and Language Design, pages 97–120. MIT Press, 1994.

Wang, Daniel C. and Andrew W. Appel. Type-preserving garbage collectors. In *ACM SIGPLAN-SIGACT Symposium on Principles of Programming Languages (POPL), London, England*, pages 166–178, January 2001.

Wansbrough, Keith and Simon Peyton Jones. Once upon a polymorphic type. In *ACM SIGPLAN-SIGACT Symposium on Principles of Programming Languages (POPL), San Antonio, Texas*, pages 15–28, January 1999.

Wells, Joe B. Typability and type checking in system F are equivalent and undecidable. *Annals of Pure and Applied Logic*, 98(1-3):111–156, 1999.

Wells, Joe B. The essence of principal typings. In *International Colloquium on Automata, Languages and Programming (ICALP)*, volume 2380 of *Lecture Notes in Computer Science*, pages 913–925. Springer-Verlag, 2002.

Werner, Benjamin. *Une Théorie des Constructions Inductives.* PhD thesis, Université Paris 7, Paris, France, May 1994.

Wirth, Niklaus. *Systematic Programming: An Introduction.* Prentice Hall, 1973.

Wirth, Niklaus. *Programming in Modula-2.* Texts and Monographs in Computer Science. Springer-Verlag, 1983.

Wright, Andrew K. Simple imperative polymorphism. *Lisp and Symbolic Computation*, 8(4):343–355, 1995.

Wright, Andrew K. and Robert Cartwright. A practical soft type system for Scheme. In *ACM Symposium on Lisp and Functional Programming (LFP), Orlando, Florida*, pages 250–262, June 1994. Full version available in *ACM Transactions on Programming Languages and Systems*, 19(1):87–52, January 1997.

Wright, Andrew K. and Matthias Felleisen. A syntactic approach to type soundness. *Information and Computation*, 115(1):38–94, November 1994.

Xi, Hongwei. *Dependent Types in Practical Programming.* PhD thesis, Carnegie Mellon University, Pittsburgh, Pennsylvania, 1998.

Xi, Hongwei and Robert Harper. A dependently typed assembly language. In *ACM SIGPLAN International Conference on Functional Programming (ICFP), Firenze, Italy*, pages 169–180, September 2001.

Xi, Hongwei and Frank Pfenning. Dependent types in practical programming. In *ACM SIGPLAN-SIGACT Symposium on Principles of Programming Languages (POPL), San Antonio, Texas*, pages 214–227, January 1999.

Zenger, Christoph. Indexed types. *Theoretical Computer Science*, 187:147–165, 1997.

Zwanenburg, Jan. Pure type systems with subtyping. In *International Conference on Typed Lambda Calculi and Applications (TLCA), L'Aquila, Italy*, volume 1581 of *Lecture Notes in Computer Science*, pages 381–396. Springer-Verlag, April 1999.

Index